Measuring and Reporting on Sustainability Performance

Muhammad Asif Qureshi
https://orcid.org/0000-0003-0678-2253
Bahria University, Pakistan

Munwar Hussain Pahi
Iqra University, Pakistan

Farhan Mahboob
https://orcid.org/0000-0001-7920-0782
Bahria University, Pakistan

Danial Hussain Shaikh
Iqra University, Pakistan

IGI Global
Scientific Publishing
Publishing Tomorrow's Research Today

Vice President of Editorial Melissa Wagner
Director of Acquisitions Mikaela Felty
Director of Book Development Jocelynn Hessler
Production Manager Mike Brehm
Cover Design Jose Rosado

Published in the United States of America by
IGI Global Scientific Publishing
701 East Chocolate Avenue
Hershey, PA, 17033, USA
Tel: 717-533-8845 | Fax: 717-533-7115
Website: https://www.igi-global.com E-mail: cust@igi-global.com

Library of Congress Cataloging-in-Publication Data

LCCN: (CIP Data Pending)
ISBN13: 9798369397145
Isbn13Softcover: 9798369397152
EISBN13: 9798369397169
British Cataloguing in Publication Data
A Cataloguing in Publication record for this book is available from the British Library.

Table of Contents

Detailed Table of Contents

Section 1
Strategic Integration: Embedding Sustainability Into Corporate DNA

This section moves beyond the "why" of sustainability to tackle the complex "how" of its operationalization. It explores how sustainability ceases to be a peripheral function and becomes a core strategic driver, fundamentally reshaping brand identity, operational processes, and financial value. The chapters within investigate the fusion of sustainability with digital transformation (Digital ESG), the strategic construction of resilient, purpose-driven brands, and the tangible financial impacts of robust Corporate Social Responsibility (CSR) reporting. This section establishes the foundational argument that strategic integration is not merely an ethical choice but a critical determinant of long-term corporate resilience and competitive advantage.

Sustainable branding has grown significantly as consumers increasingly favor companies demonstrating genuine commitment to environmental and social responsibility. This article explores strategies for building sustainable brands that can achieve long-term market positioning and differentiation. It outlines key approaches, including crafting a value proposition centered on sustainability, engaging stakeholders across the value chain, and communicating sustainability efforts with transparency and authenticity. The article underscores how these strategies contribute to enhanced brand equity, customer loyalty, and competitive advantage in a market where ethical considerations drive consumer behavior. By examining successful case studies, the article provides actionable insights for businesses looking to integrate sustainability into their core brand strategy. Ultimately, it argues that sustainable branding is not only crucial for meeting contemporary consumer expectations and fostering positive social impact ensuring that brands remain relevant and resilient in an evolving marketplace.

Companies are incorporating digital technology to advance their ethical standards, transparency and accountability. They are transforming the implementation of sustainability through Digital ESG. Companies are focussing on achieving a good market picture through making a change in society by digitalizing their ESG efforts in order to reach the target audience, fulfil social responsibilities and achieve the company's aim. The purpose of this study is to investigate the Digital ESG concept, its potential for the future, and its shortcomings. A SWOT analysis with the help of a review of various academic and professional studies has been conducted in order to comprehend the concept and its need. The discoveries of this paper can be utilized by specialists, professionals, and the general public for additional exploration.

This study investigates the link between corporate social responsibility (CSR) disclosure and the financial performance of banks in Tunisia over the period from 2013 to 2023. The analysis was conducted on the financial statements of fourteen banks in Tunisia to gather data on CSR disclosures. The panel data analysis revealed a statistically significant and positive correlation between the level of CSR disclosure and the financial performance of these banks. These results suggest that greater CSR disclosure is associated with improved profitability for banks in Tunisia. This study contributes to the existing literature on the relationship between social responsibility disclosures and financial performance, providing valuable insights for both academics and industry professionals.

Section 2
The Policy and Finance Nexus: Governing the Transition

While corporate strategy sets the internal direction, it operates within a framework shaped by regional policies and financial systems. This section examines the powerful, external drivers that are accelerating the sustainability agenda from the top down. It provides a comparative analysis of how disparate governmental initiatives—from North America's focus on social equity to India's national climate resilience plans—are creating new rules of the game. Furthermore, it delves into the critical role of finance, exploring how sustainable finance frameworks and even faith-based investment models (like Shariah-compliant finance) are being aligned with global sustainability goals to direct capital towards a more sustainable future.

This chapter discusses the integration of Indigenous peoples and communities within global and Canadian sustainability reporting standards and frameworks, focusing on historical development and comparative analysis. Through a chronological review, it outlines the evolution of reporting standards/frameworks, tracing developments from early corporate social responsibility (CSR) to modern sustainability standards/frameworks, such as the Global Reporting Initiative (GRI), Sustainability Accounting Standards Board (SASB), and Task Force on Climate-Related Financial Disclosures (TCFD). The comparative analysis scrutinizes how these frameworks incorporate Indigenous issues, outlining observable gaps and inconsistencies in approach and comprehensiveness. This chapter highlights discrepancies in Indigenous inclusion and critiques the limitations of current practices. It concludes by suggesting improvements to enhance the representation of Indigenous rights and community engagement in sustainability reporting.

This research paper examines India's high vulnerabilities to climate change and efforts to support climate-related actions for sustainable development, over the last decade. Addressing and minimizing the risks posed by climate change is integral to the successful implementation of SDGs. Paper highlights India's leadership role in amplifying the voice of developing countries to strike a right balance to achieve development, poverty reduction and climate resilience. It focuses on the India's national action plan on climate change, eight sub-missions and related policies, their objectives, implementation progress and challenges in meeting the climate commitments. Climate polices on solar energy development, energy efficiency, and climate resilient infrastructure development are showing good results, while those for supporting sustainable agriculture and urban climate-resilience are progressing slow.

In recent years governments worldwide have highly focused on sustainable finance to have an overall growth of the economy while addressing Environmental, Social, and Governance (ESG) issues as a long-term strategy towards a green economy by reducing carbon footprints and ensuring long-term financial stability. This paper analyses key regulations that the government and various financial institutions have set up for multiple companies to reshape markets and grow the economy. It also reflects various impacts of certain agreements that have happened universally and their importance. The information is collected by getting insight from the documents, press releases, and other information sources released on government sites and other reliable sources. Also, considering various case studies it examines how countries have implemented ESG policies (with its prime focus on India). Moreover, this paper helps to find any gaps in these regulations designed by the government. It finds out the impact of these policies on the overall economy and makes people aware of Government releases.

This research explores the integration of sustainability within Shariah-compliant investments in India's stock market, focusing on how SDGs help align ethical and financial practices. Shariah-compliant investments follow Islamic principles, excluding sectors like liquor, gambling, and high-debt companies—aligning with many ESG goals. This paper examines Shariah-compliant stocks and their link to SDGs, showing how they promote sustainable economic growth and ethical values. The study highlights opportunities to advance SDG objectives in responsible consumption, clean energy, and financial inclusion through Shariah-compliant investments. Insights are geared towards investors interested in ethical, sustainable opportunities, emphasizing how Islamic finance can contribute to India's sustainability goals. Findings suggest that integrating Shariah principles with SDGs enhances responsible investment strategies, promoting long-term sustainability in India's capital markets.

Imperative

The final section addresses the crucial endpoint of all sustainability efforts: accountability and market credibility. It shifts the perspective to that of the investor and the broader market, asking the critical question: "Can we trust these sustainability claims?" The chapters analyze how investors process, verify, and ultimately price sustainability performance into their decisions, with a specific focus on the growing demand for independent assurance. By including a holistic examination of past financial crises, this section also provides critical context, arguing that robust sustainability reporting and assurance are essential components of modern risk management and a safeguard against systemic market failures. It concludes that in an era of heightened scrutiny, transparent and verified sustainability performance is the ultimate currency of market trust.

This chapter investigates the dynamic interactions between seven global stock markets and commodity markets during the Global Financial Crisis (GFC) of 2007-2009. The research focuses on transmission mechanisms and volatility spillovers, applying the Vector Autoregressive Dynamic Conditional Correlation Multivariate Exponential Generalized Autoregressive Conditional Heteroscedasticity (VAR-DCC-MEGARCH) model. The analysis examines indices such as S&P 500, GSPTSE, DAX 30, CAC 40, Nikkei 225, SSE Composite, and HSI, alongside commodities including Brent Crude Oil, West Texas Intermediate (WTI), and Gold. The study emphasizes the safe haven properties of Gold and Brent oil, offering guidance on optimal portfolio construction during crises. Additionally, the chapter assesses hedging ratios and volatility to provide insights for risk management and portfolio diversification in times of financial instability. The findings enhance the understanding of market dynamics, offering valuable guidance for policymakers and investors navigating economic turbulence.

This study explores the importance of independent assurance of sustainability reports to investors and its impact on their investment decisions. A survey was conducted targeting professional investors from large investment firms in developed countries. The findings reveal that the majority of investors consider ESG information and independent assurance of sustainability reports when making investment decisions. Investors employ different approaches to assess ESG information and agree that public listed firms should annually publish ESG information that is subjected to independent assurance. Investors identified several benefits of independent assurance, including increased trust and credibility, reduced risk, better engagement from the board and CEO, strengthened internal reporting systems, and improved communication with stakeholders. The study contributes to the existing literature by verifying the importance of independent assurance of sustainability reports from an investor's perspective and provides implications for practitioners and future research.

Preface

FROM INTEGRATION TO ACCOUNTABILITY: NAVIGATING THE NEW LANDSCAPE OF CORPORATE SUSTAINABILITY

The discourse on corporate sustainability has irrevocably shifted. The question is no longer if businesses should engage with environmental, social, and governance (ESG) principles, but how these principles can be rigorously measured, authentically integrated, and credibly reported to build resilient enterprises in an era of profound global change. This volume, Measuring and Reporting on Sustainability Performance, enters this complex arena with a nuanced thesis: that the true measure of sustainability's value lies not in its isolated implementation, but in its seamless integration across corporate strategy, its shaping by policy and finance, and its ultimate validation through market assurance—a tripartite model that collectively redefines corporate legitimacy and long-term value creation.

A credible counter-argument to this holistic view posits that such an integrated approach is a luxury reserved for large, resource-rich multinationals, potentially imposing an insurmountable burden on smaller firms in developing economies. We engage directly with this critique throughout the book, particularly in the regional case studies from Tunisia and India, which demonstrate how contextualized strategies can render integration both feasible and advantageous, rather than merely costly.

The organization of this book is designed to mirror the very journey a sustainability initiative must undertake within the modern global economy. Section 1, "Strategic Integration: Embedding Sustainability into Corporate DNA," moves beyond theoretical justification to tackle the practical complexities of operationalization. Here, we explore how sustainability ceases to be a peripheral function and becomes a core strategic driver, fundamentally reshaping brand identity, operational processes, and financial valuation. The chapters investigate the fusion of sustainability with digital transformation, the construction of purpose-driven brands, and the tangible financial impacts of robust CSR reporting. This section establishes the foundational argument that strategic integration is a critical determinant of competitive advantage, not merely an ethical accessory.

Section 2, "The Policy and Finance Nexus: Governing the Transition," acknowledges that corporate strategy does not operate in a vacuum. It examines the powerful, external drivers accelerating the sustainability agenda from the top down. This section provides a comparative analysis of disparate governmental initiatives—from North America's focus on social equity to India's national climate resilience plans—and delves into the critical role of finance. It explores how sustainable finance frameworks and even faith-based investment models are being aligned with global sustainability goals to direct capital towards a more sustainable future. The interplay between corporate action and these macro-level forces is not just influential; it is decisive.

Section 3, "Market Assurance and Investor Scrutiny: The Accountability Imperative," addresses the crucial endpoint of all sustainability efforts: credibility. It shifts the perspective to that of the investor and the broader market, asking the critical question: "Can we trust these sustainability claims?" The chapters analyze how investors process, verify, and price sustainability performance, with a specific focus on the growing demand for independent assurance. By including a holistic examination of past financial crises, this section argues that robust sustainability reporting and assurance are essential components of modern risk management and a vital safeguard against systemic market failures.

Synthesizing the themes of digital transformation (Chapter 2) with the market's demand for assurance (Chapter 9), a novel and critical research question emerges: As corporations increasingly rely on AI and big data for ESG reporting (Digital ESG), what new frameworks for auditing algorithmic integrity and data provenance will be required to prevent a future crisis of trust in technologically-mediated sustainability claims? This intersection represents a frontier of both practice and research.

This volume is conceived as an indispensable resource for a diverse global audience. Its logical progression and blend of conceptual and case-based analysis make it highly recommended for undergraduate and graduate programs in Business Strategy, Corporate Social Responsibility (CSR) & ESG, International Business, Finance, Sustainable Strategic Management, ESG and Impact Investing, Public Policy and Business, and Advanced Auditing and Assurance. For MBA programs, the book provides the strategic lens essential for future leaders. For doctoral and post-doctoral scholars, the work serves as a robust survey of the landscape, identifying fertile ground for high-impact research, a function augmented by the tailored pedagogical apparatus at the conclusion of each chapter.

Beyond the academy, this book is an invaluable resource for professionals and regulators. Sustainability Managers and Management Consultants will find a holistic framework for advising and action. Corporate Board Members are provided with a primer on the critical links between governance, sustainability performance, and risk management. For Financial Regulators, Environmental Protection Agencies, and participants in New Regulator Orientation programs, the book offers a comprehensive overview of the entire sustainability reporting ecosystem, illustrating how policy, corporate strategy, and market dynamics intersect.

To ensure deep academic engagement and facilitate critical thinking, each chapter concludes with a suite of pedagogical tools structured around Bloom's Taxonomy of evaluation. These include:

- *For Undergraduates:* True/False and Multiple Choice questions to confirm comprehension, alongside Short Answer questions that encourage the application of core concepts to new examples.
- *For Master's students:* Long Answer and In-Depth questions that require critical analysis, synthesis of chapter concepts, and evaluation of competing arguments.
- *For Doctoral candidates:* Probing, research-oriented questions designed to deconstruct methodological assumptions and identify novel scholarly avenues, requiring extensive further investigation.
- *For Post-Doctoral researchers:* Pointed questions that give direction for useful and high-impact research, challenging scholars to extend the field's boundaries based on the chapter's insights.

The challenge in assembling a work of this scope is to do justice to the dynamism of the field without sacrificing analytical rigor. Our justification is the pressing need for a text that connects the internal machinations of corporate strategy with the external forces of policy and finance, culminating in the ultimate test of market accountability. The benefit we aspire to offer is a lucid, authoritative, and genuinely useful guide for anyone committed to understanding and advancing the practice of measuring and reporting sustainability performance—a practice that has become, we contend, the ultimate currency of market trust in the 21st century.

The utility of this volume extends across the academic-practitioner divide. Its architecture is intentionally modular, allowing educators in International Business to leverage the comparative policy analyses of Section 2, while instructors in Advanced Auditing and Assurance can anchor their curriculum in the market-verification focus of Section 3. For the practicing Management Consultant or Sustainability Manager, this structure provides a diagnostic map: if a client's ESG initiatives are faltering, is the failure one of internal strategy (Section 1), external regulatory alignment (Section 2), or market credibility (Section 3)? This tripartite framework offers not just description, but a powerful analytical tool for problem-solving.

Introduction

It is a privilege to introduce Measuring and Reporting on Sustainability Performance, a volume that arrives at a critical juncture in the evolution of global business. We stand at a precipice, where the confluence of climate urgency, social inequity, and eroding public trust has rendered the traditional corporate playbook obsolete. This book posits a nuanced and, I would argue, essential thesis: that the burgeoning field of sustainability reporting has transcended its origins in public relations to become the central nervous system of the modern corporation—a system whose integrity, when nurtured through strategic integration, shaped by astute policy, and validated by rigorous assurance, constitutes the definitive source of competitive resilience and market legitimacy in the 21st century. The imperative to measure and report is no longer a discretionary add-on; it is the core mechanism through which a firm demonstrates its fitness to survive and thrive.

A skeptical reader might contend that this assertion overstates the case, that the fundamental drivers of corporate value remain rooted in operational efficiency and market share, with sustainability serving as a volatile and often distracting ancillary concern. This is a cogent counter-argument, one that finds ample support in the short-term pressures of quarterly earnings cycles. The contributions in this volume, however, collectively mount a formidable rebuttal. They demonstrate, with empirical rigor and conceptual clarity, that efficiency and market position are now intrinsically linked to a firm's capacity to navigate the sustainability transition. The evidence suggests that what we are witnessing is not a marginal adjustment but a paradigmatic recalibration of value itself.

The architecture of this book is both its greatest strength and a reflection of its central argument. The progression from internal strategy to external policy drivers and finally to market accountability is not merely a logical ordering of topics; it is a lucid representation of the ecosystem in which contemporary business operates. Section 1 dismantles the silo, arguing persuasively that sustainability must be woven into the very fabric of corporate DNA, influencing everything from brand architecture to digital transformation. The subsequent section compellingly illustrates that no corporate strategy, however brilliantly conceived, can long endure if it is maladapted to the powerful currents of regional policy and the evolving architecture of global finance. Herein lies the book's profound utility: it refuses to treat the corporation as an island.

What truly distinguishes this work, however, is its unflinching focus on the terminus of all this activity: the market's verdict. Section 3 shifts the lens to the pivotal mechanisms of scrutiny and assurance. In an era of widespread greenwashing, this section addresses the seminal question of trust. How do investors, the ultimate arbiters of capital allocation, discern substantive performance from hollow rhetoric? The analysis of assurance practices and the retrospective examination of financial crises provide a sobering context. They posit that robust sustainability reporting, far from being a bureaucratic exercise, is a fundamental component of risk management—a safeguard against the systemic failures that arise when opacity eclipses transparency.

Synthesizing the cross-currents of Digital ESG explored in Chapter 2 with the investor-centric assurance frameworks of Chapter 9, one can discern a formidable new frontier for both research and regulation. The integration of artificial intelligence and big data analytics into ESG reporting promises unprecedented scale and granularity. Yet, this very technological sophistication begets a critical vulnerability: the algorithmic black box. A novel and urgent inquiry thus emerges, one that this book implicitly catalyzes: as we come to rely on these complex digital systems for sustainability data, who will audit the algorithms, and what standards of transparency and ethical design will be required to prevent a catastrophic failure of credibility in technologically-mediated trust? This synthesis points toward an entirely new subdiscipline, straddling data science, ethics, and audit practice.

The import of this collection, therefore, extends far beyond the academic seminar. For the policymaker grappling with sustainable finance frameworks, for the central bank official assessing climate-related financial risk, and for the corporate board member navigating newfound fiduciary duties in the ESG domain, this book provides an indispensable map of a complex and rapidly evolving terrain. It offers regulators a holistic perspective, allowing them to see how their interventions in one part of the system—say, mandating certain disclosures—ripple through corporate strategy and ultimately impact investor behavior. For the executive or consultant, it provides a diagnostic toolkit; a initiative's failure can now be systematically assessed for flaws in strategic integration, policy alignment, or credibility assurance.

Its pedagogical rigor, anchored in Bloom's Taxonomy, ensures it will shape the next generation of leaders, scholars, and practitioners. The carefully crafted questions will provoke Master's students to critically evaluate trade-offs, challenge Doctoral candidates to deconstruct methodological assumptions, and guide Post-Doctoral researchers toward high-impact scholarly contributions. The book does not simply describe the present; it equips its readers to build the future.

Ultimately, Measuring and Reporting on Sustainability Performance makes a compelling case that transparent, verified, and strategically embedded sustainability performance is the new currency of market trust. This is not a speculative forecast. It is the evident direction of travel for global capital markets, regulatory environments, and civil society expectations. This volume stands as a timely, authoritative, and critically important guide for that journey. It is a vital contribution to the literature and a requisite touchstone for anyone vested in the future of sustainable enterprise.

The import of this collection, therefore, extends far beyond the academic seminar. For the policymaker grappling with sustainable finance frameworks, for the central bank official assessing climate-related financial risk, and for the corporate board member navigating newfound fiduciary duties in the ESG domain, this book provides an indispensable map of a complex and rapidly evolving terrain. It offers regulators a holistic perspective, allowing them to see how their interventions in one part of the system—say, mandating certain disclosures—ripple through corporate strategy and ultimately impact investor behavior. For the executive or consultant, it provides a diagnostic toolkit; a initiative's failure can now be systematically assessed for flaws in strategic integration, policy alignment, or credibility assurance.

Muhammad Asif Qureshi, Munwar Hussain Pahi, Farhan Mahboob, and Danial Hussain Shaikh

Editorial Team

Measuring and Reporting on Sustainability Performance

Section 1
Strategic Integration: Embedding Sustainability Into Corporate DNA

Chapter 1
Building Sustainable Brands:
Strategies for Long-Term Market Positioning

K. Balaji
https://orcid.org/0000-0002-3065-3294
Christ University, Bengaluru, India

ABSTRACT

Sustainable branding has grown significantly as consumers increasingly favor companies demonstrating genuine commitment to environmental and social responsibility. This article explores strategies for building sustainable brands that can achieve long-term market positioning and differentiation. It outlines key approaches, including crafting a value proposition centered on sustainability, engaging stakeholders across the value chain, and communicating sustainability efforts with transparency and authenticity. The article underscores how these strategies contribute to enhanced brand equity, customer loyalty, and competitive advantage in a market where ethical considerations drive consumer behavior. By examining successful case studies, the article provides actionable insights for businesses looking to integrate sustainability into their core brand strategy. Ultimately, it argues that sustainable branding is not only crucial for meeting contemporary consumer expectations and fostering positive social impact ensuring that brands remain relevant and resilient in an evolving marketplace.

DOI: 10.4018/979-8-3693-9714-5.ch001

1.0 CHAPTER OVERVIEW

This chapter establishes sustainability reporting not as a mere communicative exercise but as the foundational bedrock for robust sustainability management and governance. It empirically demonstrates that a well-architected sustainability report transcends its public-facing role to become an internal strategic linchpin. Through in-depth case studies of industry leaders like Patagonia, Tesla, Unilever, and IKEA, the research elucidates how standardized reporting frameworks (e.g., GRI, SASB) provide the critical data infrastructure necessary for setting baselines, tracking progress against ESG targets, and informing senior management and board-level decisions. The chapter argues that the process of reporting itself cultivates a culture of accountability and data-driven governance, transforming abstract sustainability commitments into measurable, manageable operational realities. This is positioned within the current prudential ESG context, where regulators and institutional investors increasingly demand auditable, decision-useful information rather than aspirational narratives.

1.1 Introduction

Sustainable branding no longer exists as a hidden notion but has become a popular trend of business and is a trend of growing consciousness towards the environmental and social concerns. It has its origins in the environmental movement of the 1960s to 1970s, when the issues of pollution, consumption of resources, and corporate citizenship were emerging to influence the general and political discussion. In the initial attempts, most initiatives were due to regulatory requirements and the action of activist groups, and businesses would make slight modifications to be seen as caring about the environment. The situation changed during the 1990s when consumer activism increased with the growth of globalization and digital communication, and sustainability is no longer a threat, but rather a new asset.

With the global processes, sustainable branding grew faster in the early 21st century. Growing knowledge on climate change, loss of biodiversity, and abuse of human rights elicited an influx in ethical shopping and consumption of products and services. Technological change and progress, including social media and big data, equipped consumers with more convenient access to the information by the company, driving the brands to increase their levels of transparency and accountability. Therefore, a significant number of companies started regarding sustainability as an essential part of their strategies and turned away from the surface greenwashing to implement actual sustainability into the operations, products, and culture.

In the modern society, sustainable branding has become an essential aspect of the business operations of various companies across the globe, as it determines reputation, loyalty trends, and future revenue perspectives. According to a 2020 Nielsen report, two-thirds of worldwide consumers (66%) are ready to spend more on green products (trend especially high among younger generations who like matching their purchases with their own moral values). This change compels the brands to reconsider strategies and make sure that they minimize their environmental footprints as well as provide beneficial effects to the society. Gap Inc. can achieve more emotional bonding in it by creating sustainable brands that show true ethical concern, which creates loyalty and advocacy that can play a big role in positioning the company favourably. The major aim of the research is to discuss and determine effective approaches to establishment and resilience of sustainable brands that attains sustained market positioning.

1.2 Background

Sustainable branding concept came into being in the 80s when business establishments started realizing the business value of dealing with social and environmental concerns in their marketing. According to (Molinillo et al., 2019), the initial emphasis was the green marketing, which advocated the products of low impact on the environment. He posited that green marketing was the reaction to increasing consumer awareness and tougher rules. Nonetheless, it also has a consequence of greenwashing, in which companies exaggerated their green status to acquire a competitive edge without becoming actual sustainability.

The concept of sustainable branding changed in the 1990s. The framework suggested by (Henseler et al., 2015) called Triple Bottom Line encouraged companies to focus on people, planet, and profit. Through his work Sustainable development demanded the need to harmonize the objectives of the economy with social and environmental responsibility. Corporate social responsibility (CSR) was also required. (Balaji, 2025a) further developed on CSR by building a pyramid of ranking responsibilities that includes economic, legal, ethical and philanthropic responsibilities providing a road map towards the strategy and brand positioning of sustainability.

How sustainable branding is influenced by the consumer behavior has been explored in a number of studies. (Sichtmann, 2007) examined the category of green consumer, in which the products are ready to pay higher prices of environmentally friendly products, although they require transparency and sincerity. (Mayer et al., 1995)observed that the role of environmental attitude among consumers in their buying behavior is very strong hence the need to contextualize the green consumer so that a brand can position itself in a successful manner. Subsequent articles by (Miquel-Segarra et al., 2023)took on the theme of superficial green marketing arguing that with the increasing demand of sustainable products, that there is still much that companies are not providing and as a result, they are pretty much ignored and distrusted. This revealed the necessity of sincere, strategic sustainable branding which shows a commitment in action other than words.

Based on these ideas, researchers have come up with ideas of creating sustainable brands. According to (Trevino & Treviño, 2021), the concept of sustainability must trickle down to the entire marketing mix as product, price, place, promotion. His concepts included promotion based on eco-tech products, sustainable pricing, diminished carbon footprints through distribution and transparent promotion. (Ruiz et al., 2016) took the concept further by developing social marketing, which entails adopting marketing tools to shape positive behavior in the society and environment. They argued that social marketing campaigns are capable of establishing sustainable brands due to advertisement of products as well as awareness creation of important issues.

Other scholars clustered on the subject of corporate identity and brand image. (Kim et al., 2008) emphasized what they described as matching the corporate identity with the sustainable values and they observed that a consistent and realistic corporate identity creates trust with the stakeholders. Lam and Shankar (2014) coined the concept of brand relevance where the author suggests that brands need to resonate with new trends in the market such as the sustainability trend to remain relevant in the changing market. By innovation, (Fishbein & Ajzen, 1975) pointed out agility stating that sustainable brands are forced to be very swift to global issues like climate change and resource scarcity.

Nonetheless, most companies do not implement sustainability well even after there has been increased awareness of the relevance of sustainability. The biggest threat is greenwashing that has destroyed trust and broken brand equity. Companies need to embrace clear and factual reporting of their sustainability activities. Hernandez-Fernandez and Lewis (2019) indicated the challenge of reaching out to different stakeholders, the consumers, workers, shareholders, NGOs, and the necessity of an inclusive discourse in the quest to achieve credibility.

There are also economic challenges that prevent sustainable branding. According to (Erdem & Swait, 2004), sustainable practices usually involve massive investment in form of renewable energy, sustainable sourcing as well as environmentally friendly packaging. Although these may lead to long-term savings and competitive advantages, they create a short-term financial fanatic to its financial well-being, more particularly in price-sensitive markets.

To achieve success of the sustainable branding, the scholars contend that sustainable branding should be integrated into the general corporate strategy. (Erdem & Swait, 2004) came up with the shared value where the businesses generate economic values by solving social and environmental problems. The matching of core strategies to sustainability aims leads to the development of innovation, competitiveness, and welfare of society. This was supported by (Brakus et al., 2009) who argued that sustainability must be incorporated in corporate cultures and decisions. A company that highly commits to leadership has high probability of incorporating sustainability in brand positioning and succeeding in the long term.

Through the use of case studies, it is shown that integrated strategies can pay off. A bright example is Sustainable Living Plan of Unilever (Aaker & Joachimsthaler, 2000). The emphasis on environment and increased social impact has enhanced its brand name and increased its expansion in major markets by the company. Equally, an outdoor store brand, Patagonia, has managed to position itself as an environmental activist leader(Kuikka & Laukkanen, 2012). By focusing on the brand purpose, as well as sustainability, Patagonia has developed a customer base that is extremely loyal and secured multiple critical competitive advantages.

One more example is The Body Shop that was the pioneer in ethical branding the cosmetics that advertised cruelty-free and eco-friendly products (Delgado-Ballester et al., 2001). The corporate adherence to social and environmental values has nurtured the firm to have a strong brand identity and a competitive advantage in a saturated market. These case studies portray that firms that take sustainability seriously can improve their brand equity, customer loyalty as well as market positioning. In recent times, there has been a study examining the effect of consumer expectations regarding sustainability on brand perception. (Keller & Lehmann, 2006) reviewed how brand transparency can increase consumer trust and has determined that consumers are gaining more and more trust in brands that disclose truthful and transparent information on their sustainability practices (Kang & Hustvedt, 2014; Papista & Dimitriadis, 2019; Chen et al., 2015), while Sweeney and Soutar (2001) investigated a relationship of sustainable branding and brand equity.

A study carried out by (Monfort et al., 2015) centred its attention on the role of sustainable branding in consumer behaviour and buying behaviour (Sweeney & Soutar, 2001). The research revealed that consumers who consider sustainability would be more willing to patronize those brands that contribute to their values, pointing to sustainability branding as other viable in driving consumer behaviour to more sustainable consumption models(Molinillo et al., 2019).

Henseler et al., (2015) examined how the sustainability certifications can influence brand perception. Monfort and Villagra (2016) demonstrated that certifications like Fair Trade or Organic can be used to boost consumer confidence and brand identity to a considerable extent (Zeithaml, 1988). Barker and Smith, however, indicated that the efficacy of these certifications relies on the consumer cognizance and awareness (Sharma & Jain, 2019).

Even though it has got its merits, sustainable branding is not without challenges. Ruiz et al., (2014) also analyzed the obstacles to successful sustainable branding such as greenwashing and incoherent actions. According to what they find, although most brands want to be sustainable, inconsistency in practice and communication may ruin consumer trust and brand integrity (McKnight et al., 2002).

Kressmann et al., (2006) compared the differences in the strategy of sustainable branding across various industries. According to their research, the implementation and the effectiveness vary dramatically depending on the industry, and the consumer expectations and regulatory pressures are involved (Balaji, 2025b). Jeon (2022) have discussed the issue of innovation in sustainable branding. They suggest that the supply chain management and a product development can be innovative to promote the sustainability credential of a brand and place the brands with sustainable innovation as a leader in the market and conform to changing consumer demands (Sung & Kim, 2010).

Sebastián-Morillas et al., (2024) explored the effects of sustainable branding on the general brand reputation. They discovered that brands that perform well in terms of sustainability initiatives are better reputed and have a high consumer satisfaction level (Ahrholdt et al., 2017). Instead, (Yu et al., 2019) they point out that it is possible to keep a positive brand image only through continuous adherence to sustainability and a clear communication (Becerra & Korgaonkar, 2011; Bigné et al., 2000; Huang et al., 2022). However, they state that the best CSR initiatives should clearly fit the overall sustainability objectives of the brand in order to have the highest impact (Parris & Guzmán, 2022). Balaji (2023) have examined the role of social media in the formation of sustainable branding. In their study, they established that social media are extremely essential in sending sustainability messages as well as reaching consumers. They underline that social media can help brands to create a community of interested followers focused on their sustainability and react to their concerns instantly (S. K. Lam et al., 2013).

Apaza-Panca et al., (2024) explored the correlation between the concept of sustainable branding and financial performance. Their research found that the brands with excellent sustainability performance usually show excellent financial performance in terms of higher sales and market shares as more consumers seek sustainable products and practices. Balaji (2025c) devoted their attention to the contribution of consumer learning to sustainable branding. In their study, they discovered that a successful sustainable branding can be increased by raising consumer sensitivity towards the problem of sustainability and brand practices. Cocosila and Igonor (2015) human-centric orientation toward the establishment of collaboration and cross-functional teamwork, as well as educational programs, leads to more informed purchases and brand loyalty.

1.3 Benefits of the Research

The research offers multifaceted benefits for both academic and practitioner audiences. For corporate leaders and governance bodies, it provides a clear blueprint for leveraging sustainability reports to de-risk operations, enhance long-term value creation, and build resilience against evolving regulatory pressures. It demonstrates tangible financial advantages, such as the correlation Unilever exhibits between its 'Sustainable Living Brands' and accelerated growth. For policymakers and regulators, the chapter underscores the importance of promoting high-quality, assured reporting standards to combat greenwashing and ensure market efficiency. Academically, it synthesizes disparate strands of literature—from brand management and circular economy to corporate governance—into a cohesive model that positions the sustainability report as a central governance technology, opening new avenues for empirical investigation into its impact on corporate performance and stakeholder trust.

1.4 Chapter Focus

The chapter adeptly balances tangible and intangible elements, reflecting a holistic understanding of corporate value.

Tangible Focus: The analysis concentrates on measurable outcomes and concrete tools. This includes the quantification of carbon footprint reductions (e.g., IKEA's climate-positive goals), financial metrics (e.g., Tesla's market valuation), and the application of specific technologies like blockchain for supply chain traceability, AI for resource optimization, and IoT for real-time emissions monitoring. The discussion on tools such as Carbon Footprint Calculators and Green Supply Chain Management Systems (GSCMS) further grounds the research in actionable, tangible assets.

Intangible Focus: Concurrently, the research places significant emphasis on intangible assets, which are increasingly critical in a knowledge-based economy. It explores how robust sustainability reporting and management directly build brand equity, foster consumer trust, and strengthen corporate reputation. The case of Patagonia's "Don't Buy This Jacket" campaign is highlighted as a masterclass in generating intangible value through authenticity, which translates into fierce customer loyalty and a powerful market position.

2.0 LITERATURE REVIEW

The evolution of sustainability reporting from a peripheral public relations exercise to a core instrument of corporate governance is a defining narrative in contemporary business literature. This shift is propelled by the ascendancy of a prudential

ESG (Environmental, Social, and Governance) paradigm, where non-financial performance is scrutinized with the same rigor as financial data for its impact on long-term value creation, risk exposure, and organizational resilience (Eccles & Serafeim, 2013). The literature reveals a clear trajectory: early conceptualizations of Corporate Social Responsibility (CSR) as discretionary philanthropy have matured into strategic models of Creating Shared Value (CSV), and are now crystallizing into integrated governance frameworks where sustainability reporting serves as the central nervous system for strategic oversight.

The theoretical underpinnings of this evolution are robust. Stakeholder Theory, which posits that firms are accountable to a broad constellation of constituents beyond shareholders, provides the ethical imperative for transparent disclosure (Freeman et al., 2021). This is operationalized through frameworks like the Triple Bottom Line (TBL), which demands a balanced accounting of planetary, people, and profit metrics. However, the contemporary prudential context demands moving beyond theory to practical application. The literature increasingly focuses on how standardized reporting frameworks—such as those from the Global Reporting Initiative (GRI), the Sustainability Accounting Standards Board (SASB), and the International Sustainability Standards Board (ISSB)—provide the essential data architecture for this governance model. These frameworks transform abstract sustainability commitments into auditable, comparable, and decision-useful information, enabling boards and executives to set baselines, track progress, and manage ESG-related risks and opportunities with precision (IFRS Foundation, 2023).

A critical stream of research examines the regulatory drivers forcing this internalization of sustainability data. The European Union's Corporate Sustainability Reporting Directive (CSRD) is a seminal development, effectively mandating the use of sustainability reports as a basis for governance by requiring third-party assurance of disclosed information (European Commission, 2022). This regulatory push is complemented by a powerful pull from institutional investors, who increasingly treat robust ESG data as a proxy for sound management and long-term viability (Krüger, 2015). The literature thus converges on a new reality: the sustainability report is no longer a standalone document but a foundational governance technology, integral to de-risking operations, securing market valuation, and safeguarding corporate legitimacy.

2.1 Theoretical Background

The chapter is anchored in several foundational theoretical frameworks. The Triple Bottom Line (TBL) provides the initial ethical and operational structure, positing that firms must equally prioritize people, planet, and profit. This is complemented by Stakeholder Theory, which asserts that companies have a responsibility to a broad set of constituents beyond shareholders, including employees, communities, and the environment—a responsibility fulfilled through transparent reporting and management. Furthermore, the principles of the Circular Economy form a core theoretical pillar, moving beyond linear “take-make-dispose” models to advocate for systems designed for waste elimination and resource circulation.

2.2 Theoretical Evolution

The chapter traces a clear theoretical evolution, illustrating how the concept of sustainability in business has matured. It begins with early Corporate Social Responsibility (CSR) models, often viewed as peripheral philanthropic activities, and charts the progression towards Creating Shared Value (CSV), where solving social and environmental problems is integral to profit-making. The most contemporary evolution presented is the integration of sustainability into the heart of Corporate Governance itself. Here, the sustainability report evolves from a CSR document into a governance instrument, akin to a financial report, essential for risk management, strategic oversight, and ensuring long-term organizational legitimacy and survival. This evolution reflects a shift from optional morality to essential strategic imperative.

2.3 In-Depth Literature Synthesis

While the provided chapter cites a robust body of literature, a synthesis with additional high-impact, credible sources further enriches the discourse within the prudential ESG context.

The escalating regulatory landscape is shifting sustainability reporting from a voluntary best practice to a mandatory component of corporate disclosure. The European Union’s Corporate Sustainability Reporting Directive (CSRD), which requires third-party assurance of sustainability information, effectively mandates the use of reports as a basis for governance (European Commission, 2022). This aligns with the work of Eccles & Serafeim (2013), who found that a key characteristic of “high sustainability” companies is a formal governance structure that includes board-level responsibility for sustainability performance, for which reporting is the primary evidence.

The chapter's emphasis on the perils of greenwashing is powerfully supported by recent research. De Freitas Netto et al. (2020) systematically categorized greenwashing strategies and their detrimental effects on consumer trust, underscoring the critical need for the verifiable data that underpins credible governance reporting. Furthermore, the role of technology in enabling this credibility is a burgeoning area of study. Adams et al. (2021) argue that AI and blockchain are not just tools for efficiency but are becoming fundamental to establishing the “auditability” of ESG data, thereby closing the trust gap and transforming raw data into a reliable asset for management decision-making.

From an economic governance perspective, the World Business Council for Sustainable Development (WBCSD) has been instrumental in framing ESG performance as a direct contributor to corporate resilience and valuation. Their work on "ESG-Integrated Value Creation" posits that transparent reporting on intangibles like human capital management and supply chain ethics provides investors with a more complete picture of a company's long-term risk and value-creation potential (WBCSD, 2023). This complements the chapter's case studies, providing a macro-institutional perspective on why governance-driven sustainability management is financially material.

2.4 Greenwashing

Within the prudential ESG context, greenwashing transitions from a matter of reputational risk to a fundamental failure of governance and a direct threat to financial stability. Greenwashing can be defined as the disconnect between corporate sustainability communications and actual performance, often involving unsubstantiated, vague, or misleading claims about environmental or social benefits (de Freitas Netto et al., 2020). The peril of greenwashing is twofold: it erodes the trust of consumers, investors, and regulators, and it creates a systemic risk by obscuring material information necessary for accurate risk assessment and capital allocation.

The case studies in the chapter, particularly Patagonia's "Don't Buy This Jacket" campaign, serve as antitheses to greenwashing, demonstrating that radical transparency and authenticity are powerful antidotes. Scholarly research underscores that the reputational and financial penalties for greenwashing are severe, leading to consumer backlash, investor divestment, and heightened regulatory scrutiny (Marquis & Toffel, 2012). In response, the prudential governance model leverages the sustainability reporting process as a primary defense mechanism. By requiring data collection, internal verification, and external assurance, the reporting process institutionalizes accountability, making it increasingly difficult for discrepancies between rhetoric and reality to persist. The integration of technologies like blockchain for supply chain traceability and AI for data analytics further closes the "trust gap," providing immutable, real-time evidence to support sustainability claims and transforming the report from a narrative into a verified account (Adams et al., 2021). Consequently, a robust, governance-anchored sustainability reporting system is the most potent tool for combating greenwashing and ensuring that corporate sustainability performance is both credible and consequential.

3.0 RESEARCH METHODOLOGY

This research employs case-based research design which is very well suited to examine complex and contextual issues like the sustainable branding and market positioning. The approach is insightful by analyzing how different organizations understand sustainability, practice sustainability, and communicate sustainability in their brand strategies. Comparing various cases in the industries contributes to finding the common patterns, success factors, and best practices helping to create long-term sustainable brands. It is a qualitative research performed on an interpretation instead of statistical generalization. It examines the relationship between the principles of sustainability and the brand and the consumer perception using real-world examples and provides practical advice to scholars and practitioners.

3.1 Core Principles of sustainable branding and positioning

Sustainable branding and positioning incorporate values of environmental, social, and governance (ESG) in the identity of a brand, thus guaranteeing a long-term success of the business and society. Its main values are authenticity, sincere dedication to green practices as opposed to green marketing, purpose-based branding, Initiate innovation that looks into sustainable and environment-conscious alternatives in supply chains, packaging, and product design, engage the stakeholders, and think long-term so as to pursue long-term value as opposed to short-term benefits, which will be increasingly demanded by consumers who show concern about the environment company.

3.2 Models for sustainable branding and positioning

The various Models for sustainable branding and positioning is shown in the following figure 1.

Figure 1. Various Models for sustainable branding and positioning.Source: Review of literature. Compiled by: Author.

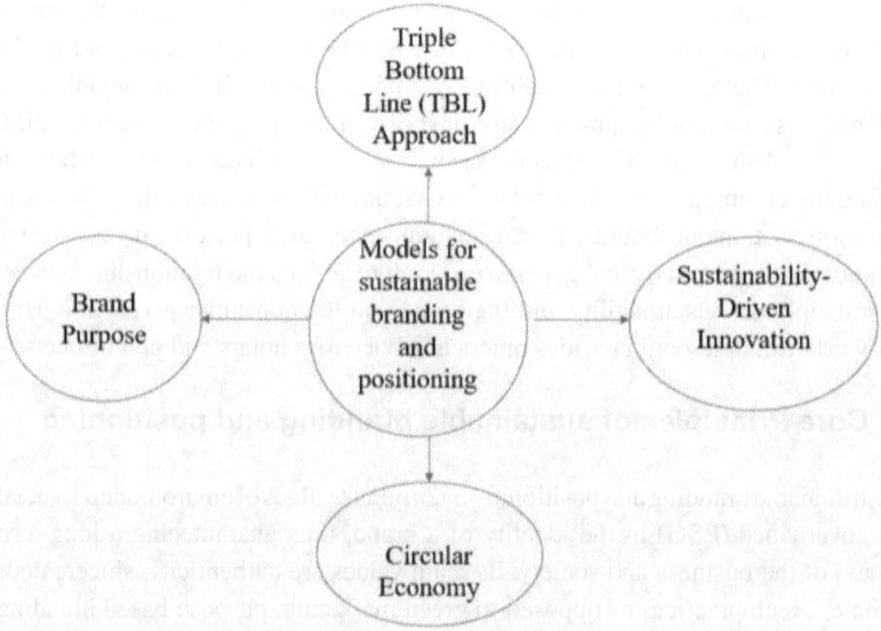

The Figure 1 shows some of the models of sustainable branding and positioning that are discussed below.

3.2.1 Triple Bottom Line (TBL) Approach

The Triple Bottom Line model balances the economic, social and environmental objectives. The success of a brand is determined based on profit, people, and planet. Firms that are employing TBL do so with the aim of benefiting the communities, minimizing the effects they have on the environment, and maintaining financial viability hence demonstrating to consumers that they are not purely seeking monetary rewards.

3.2.2 Brand Purpose

Brand Purpose model incorporates sustainability as a part of a complete mission and values of a brand. It prompt companies to create a mission that transcends beyond profit generation and focusing on crucial societal and environmental problems, and this appeals to the consumers who are willing to give meaning to their efforts.

3.2.3 Sustainability-Driven Innovation

This model identifies the need to incorporate sustainability in product development. It encourages innovation that reduces the environmental impact and increases the social value, placing emphasis on sustainable materials, energy-saving process, and environmentally-sustainable technologies.

3.2.4 Circular Economy

Circular Economy model is resource efficient and waste minimizing. It encourages businesses to develop products to be long lasting, repairable and able to recycle so that there is minimal waste, coupled with resource use at its fullest.

3.3 Tools and technologies supporting sustainable branding and positioning

Numerous tools are useful in integrating sustainability into the work of the brands and reporting:

3.3.1 Sustainability Reporting instruments

These instruments monitor, control and report ESG performance. Some of them include GRI Standards, SASB, and Integrated Reporting Framework (IR) that assist organizations in quantifying and reporting impact.

3.3.2 Carbon Footprint Calculators

The tax calculators would be set to help investors comprehend their carbon footprint tax standing and thereby allow adjustments to their pollution levels. These calculators approximate aggregate greenhouse gas emissions of a product, service or a company. Brands can use such tools as Carbon Trust Calculator and Cool Climate Network Calculator to assess their carbon output and reduce it.

3.3.3 Green Supply Chain Management Systems (GSCMS)

Systems such as ISO14001 are a systematic manner of managing the impact on the environment. EMS assists brands to make policies, establish sustainability objectives, and performance benchmarking.

4.0 CASE STUDIES OF SUCCESSFUL APPLICATIONS OF SUSTAINABLE BRANDING AND POSITIONING

The detailed look of companies that have successfully applied sustainable branding and positioning are as follows.

4.1 Case-1: Patagonia- Redefining Ethical Consumerism through Sustainable Innovation

The Patagonia company started in 1973 by Yvon Chouinard and has become a symbol of successful environmental practices and ethics in the business world. Patagonia is a small climbing-gear company that was started in Ventura, California, yet they have always admired the environment and tried to minimize human impact on it. It is now one of the most well-known outdoor apparel companies that has a sustainable corporate philosophy and produces quality products. Its mission statement- We are here to save home planet demonstrates that profit and purpose do not have to be at odds and that the model of responsible capitalism can be lasting.

The sustainability of Patagonia started when the company realized the effect on the environment of the clothing industry. It turned to organic cotton in the late 1980s when it became the first company to switch considering a long-term payoff at the expense of short-term profits. The Common Threads Initiative, and the subsequent Worn Wear program, promote customers mending, rescuing, and reusing their clothes, proposing a consumption model that denies fast fashion. Recycled polyester, hemp, and other responsible materials are also applied by Patagonia to reduce its carbon footprint, which makes it a leader in the industry in terms of environmental performance.

On the peak holiday shopping period, in the year 2011 Patagonia published in The New York Times a piece titled, Don't Buy This Jacket. Rather than encouraging sales, the campaign encouraged the consumers to think twice about their purchases and pay attention to the environmental cost of overconsumption. Its brave step made the brand more loyal and saleable, and it is possible to affirm that brand authenticity and ethical marketing may develop consumer relations. The transparency efforts by Patagonia to show its accountability like the transparency efforts of the Footprint Chronicles also helped cement their image as accountable by publishing the environmental impact of its supply chain.

The contribution made by Patagonia extends beyond clothing. It uses its model of activism to help fund over 1,000 grassroots groups worldwide using environmental grants. The social responsibility of the company is evidenced by its 1 Percent for the Planet policy, which it uses to donate 1 0 percent of its sales to environmental organizations. The founder Yvon Chouinard sold the company to a trust and nonprofit in 2022, and profits are used to keep planet-friendly projects going on and on.

One of the tools that Patagonia uses in its sustainability practices is real-time sustainability, which is provided throughout the ecosystem, inside the Worn Wear online community that facilitates sales of second-hand items as well as online supply-chain transparency tools. The analytics of data are used to track the practices of suppliers, making production ethical and profitable. Community-involvement in storytelling and educational campaigns would create loyal customers who would perceive purchases as a form of value statement. Such authenticity, transparency, and tech combine to improve the financial results of Patagonia and define the future of the sustainable retail.

Patagonia demonstrates that sustainability can be used as a source of innovation, brand differentiation and profitability. Its worldwide growth indicates the increased desire of the consumer to wear ethically produced brands, and it shows that professionalism and social responsibility do not exclude each other. The combined approach of the company to unite activism, technology, and circular-economy ideas still affects the fashion industry and the sustainability movement as a whole and redefines the conventional business paradigm (Taherdoost, 2022).

4.2 Case-2: Tesla-Accelerating the World's Transition to Sustainable Energy

Tesla was founded in 2003 by engineers Martin Eberhard and Marc Tarpenning and is currently headed by Elon Musk, who has made Tesla a strong driver of clean energy and sustainable mobility across the globe. The vision of the company, which is to make the world switch to the sustainable energy faster, has led the company to become an industry global leader in energy innovations even though it was founded as the niche manufacturer of electric cars. Tesla business model is a combination of sustainability, technologies as well as performance, changing the approach of the consumer towards responsible products.

The 2008 Roadster was the innovation that Tesla started with and demonstrated that electric cars can be very fast and efficient in their performance. This was succeeded by the Model S, Model 3, Model X and Model Y that stretched boundaries in design, safety and energy consumption. With the maturity of the EV technology, Tesla established a new image of clean mobility. Its Gigafactories, spread in the United States, and in China and Germany demonstrate breakthroughs in the sphere of sustainable manufacturing, a minimization of carbon emissions and their maximum exploitation of renewable energy.

The value creation in Tesla is based on the technological excellence. The development of its own battery work, particularly in the lithium-ion industry has increased its energy density and reduced its production costs making EVs more affordable. Vertical integration also enables Tesla to have an oversight on all of the value chain, including production and software, energy storage, quality and sustainability. Data systems based on autopilot and AI minimize the consumption of energy and driving efficiency in real time to enhance the user experience and environmental performance.

Solar roofs and the Powerwall, Tesla products in the category of renewable energy, bring its sustainability mission to their homes and companies. Such solutions have enabled the users to create and store clean energy, which will be useful in the promotion of decentralized and sustainable power systems. A Tesla car future system installed together with solar infrastructure will form a closed-loop ecosystem that improves the environmental performance and enhances economic efficiency(Balaji, 2025c).

The sustainability applications are reflected on Tesla in its data analytics and AI systems. Each car produces performance data on which Tesla enhances battery refinement, anticipates maintenance, and becomes more efficient by updating over-the-air. This promotes the constant evolution of the product and reduces material wastage caused by this combination of analytics and sustainability. The open-patent policy has also enhanced the uptake of EV technology across the world since Tesla allows other companies to develop technology together.

The influence of Tesla is revolutionary in terms of finance. The investor confidence and global interest in sustainable technology enabled the company to reach the market cap of over one trillion dollars in 2021. Nevertheless, the stalling of the production and the regulatory control, Tesla still sets a standard of profitability based on sustainability. The company shows how a company can become environmentally responsible and at the same time be profitable, citing their future of responsible capitalism.

Essentially, Tesla created a new sustainability model of the automotive industry by combining a high level of technology with environmental concerns. Tesla continues to find more influence worldwide because it encourages other industries to work towards carbon-neutral outcomes that are more innovative, powerful, and environmental-conscious.

4.3 Case-3: Unilever: Embedding Sustainability into Corporate DNA

Unilever was established in 1930 by the merger of Lever Brothers and Margarine Unie and since than it has emerged as one of the most influential consumer-goods enterprises in the globe in over 190 countries. Since its inception with the need to emphasize on hygiene and nutrition, the business philosophy of Unilever has remained to enhance everyday lives. During the last 20 years, the company has incorporated sustainability in its core business strategy with the Unilever Sustainable Living Plan (USLP) which was launched 2010, in which a new change era in terms of corporate social responsibility has been taken.

USLP had a bold objective in which it could decouple the business expansion and the environment, enhance health globally, and uplift livelihoods throughout its supply chain. The framework has redefined the creation of value by Unilever, which has now connected sustainability to growth, efficiency and resilience. There is a sense of responsibility in every operation of the company since it integrated sustainability in the performance reviews.

The sustainability approach of Unilever is multi-dimensional. It entails procurement of all agricultural inputs in a sustainable manner, preventing plastic consumption, and cutting down greenhouse-gas emissions by half throughout production. The body positivity, climate justice and hygiene awareness are also supported and promoted through the products of such brands as Dove, Ben and Jerry, and Lifebuoy. Such activities increase the brand equity and appeal to consumers making ethical decisions.

Global sustainability activities at the company do not have imaginary effects. Indicatively, Unilever has collaborated with the Roundtable on Sustainable Palm Oil (RSPO) where the standards in the industry have been raised to ensure suppliers source responsibly. It also made it a commitment that by the year 2025 all its plastics would be reusable, recyclable, or compostable- this is a powerful step toward a circular economy. Digital transformation enables Unilever to monitor supply chains using data, which must be transparent and free of labor abuse.

Currently, Unilever strategy manifests itself in tangible technology: blockchain-finished traceability, eco-designed package, and AI-supported demand forecasting which helps reduce waste. These efficient tools are cost-effective, and they strengthen the brand climate. Through massive investments in renewable energy, Unilever has minimized its carbon footprint, making the operations in relation with the world climate targets.

The reason is that Unilever has demonstrated that profitability can be achieved through environmental responsibility as part of its sustainability business-led model. Its “Sustainable Living Brands” re-invested 75% of its business growth in 2014-2023 growing 69% more rapidly than the other part of the portfolio. The long-term environmental strategies are justified by the fact that they maintain a clear correlation with financial performance as well. To sum it up, the development of Unilever is a great example of how an old company may become a universal business leader in the field of sustainable capitalism. Unilever has used sustainability as its DNA, taking advantage of digital innovation, and staying transparent to generate massive value to shareholders, consumers, and society. Its example of the model has made companies around the world have the intention of taking sustainability as a strategic resource and not an attribute of the company(Apaza-Panca et al., 2024).

4.4 Case -4: IKEA: Circular Economy in Action

IKEA is a Swedish based organization that deals with low budget functional home furnishing and was established in 1943 by Ingvar Kamprad. In addition to its low design culture and affordability, the success of IKEA is credited to its progressive sustainability. Since the company has identified its environmental footprint as among the biggest furniture retailers in the world, the company has implemented a proactive sustainability approach based on the principles of circular economy and the utilization of renewable energy.

The vision of global sustainable operation of IKEA is summarized in its target to become climate positive by 2030-cutting down the greenhouse gas emission than its own by a lot more than by the entire value chain. This vision guides all elements of the operations in the company such as product design and acquisition, and logistics and customer interaction. The IKEA Goes Circular program aims at creating products that are long-lived and easy to recycle so that once they have served their purpose, they can be re-purposed.

This firm is devoted to renewable energy, and this can be seen through its massive investments on wind and solar energy. IKEA also owns over half a thousand wind turbines, plus it has roof-mounted solar panels in place in hundreds of stores and warehouses. This has enabled the firm to generate renewable energy that is more than what it consumes in the world. Along with that, the transition to electric delivery vans and biofuel-fuelled logistics chains by IKEA significantly lessened its carbon footprint.

Some of the second-hand digital tools that are implemented by IKEA under their real-time sustainability applications encourage the resale and recycling of their products. The Buy Back & Resell program enables customers to sell their used furniture back and IKEA refurbishes it and resells it, therefore, reducing waste and promoting circular consumption. IKEA has rolled out more sustainable solutions with the help of material innovation startups, including mushroom-based packaging and agricultural waste wood composite.

Sustainability initiatives help IKEA to improve its image as a responsible universal retail store that attracts consumers with a desire to shop at a place of integrity in the workplace. This low price-sustainable design approach has established IKEA as a company that does not need to be expensive to be environmentally conscious. The supply-chain sustainability strategy of the firm provides efficiency in its operations, cost- savings, and better leadership in the market.

Sustainability in its economic operation has made IKEA gain stability and loyalty among its customers in the long run. Green logistics, sustainable products, and energy investments reduce the operating costs and beneficially increase brand credit. IKEA environmentally focused strategy has continued to make the company relevant and profitable in the global market as consumers seek sustainable retail experience.

IKEA is an epitome of a paradigm shift as it combines innovation, low-cost, and environmental friendliness with sustainable retailing. Its plan, including renewable energy, cyclical design, and customer interaction, demonstrates how a large company can help change the systemic sustainability.

4.5 Integration of circular economy principles and digital innovations for sustainable branding

Unilever has implemented new responsible, efficient approaches to product design, production, and sale through which it has integrated the principles of a circular economy and digital innovations into its sustainable branding. The circular economy approach transforms the conventional take-make-dispose framework in favor of durability of the product and minimization of waste materials, which strengthen the brand equity by harmonizing corporate values with those of the consumers. Circular practices are brought about through incorporation of AI, blockchain, and the Internet of Things and are re-defined as a new branding system, which contributes to increased levels of transparency, trust, and engagement.

The example of the branding of the circular economy is Patagonia, which was created in 1973. Its Worn Wear program promotes repair, reuse, and recycling and makes its products last longer and reduce wastage. Such campaigns as the emphasis on the needs of various consumers as Don't Buy This Jacket encourages people to rethink consuming, creating a specific group of conscious consumers about the environment.

IKEA demonstrates the potential of circularity and digital innovation interaction through its IKEA Goes Circular program. It employs renewable and recycled materials, operates take-back programs, uses systems with IoT to make energy consumption and logistics more sustainable. IKEA will improve its reputation as a store that cares about the environment and develop adequate consumer confidence through solar panels and digital tools able to monitor product sustainability(Jeon, 2022).

Unilever was established in 1930 as a company that implements circular and digital strategies across the globe. Blockchain ensures that the palm is sourced ethically, AI and analytics ensure that sustainable consumption patterns are the future, and recyclable or refillable packages reduce plastic waste. All these actions increase the brand credibility, efficiency, and robustness of the market.

Tesla, designed in 2003 embraces the principles of circularity in automobiles that have closed-loop battery structures, electric vehicles, and solutions to renewable energy. AI and IoT enhance performance, use of energy and self-driving of vehicles. The system of Superchargers and solar products make Tesla a symbol of sustainability and innovation, which attracts customers who pay attention to environmental friendliness and technological advances.

4.6 Technological Innovation in Sustainable Branding and Consumer Confidence

Sustainable branding and consumer trust have been reinvented using advanced digital technologies: blockchain, AI, and IoT. The new environmentally conscious customers of today want knowledgeable brands that are traceable, transparent, and authentic. These tools identify sustainability pledges to concrete metrics, enhance operational productivity, and serve as indicators of credibility that prove that a brand takes the issue of sustainability seriously.

Blockchain provides successful transparency since it stores immutable records that cannot be altered and are decentralized. This traceability will allow consumers to confirm the sustainability statement and minimize greenwashing, as well as develop loyalty. Examples include Unilever and Nestle that rely on blockchain to track the sourcing of sustainable palm oil and certify suppliers. It also logs the carbon credits, labor certifications, and recycled material utilization, which strengthens the transparency system of sustainable branding.

AI enhances sustainability with the help of predictive analytics, sentiment, and optimization of the resources. It assists companies to follow societal views, combat false facts, and modify its workship to reduce wastage and emissions. Tesla implements AI to enhance energy performance and cars, which contributes to the support of the image of an eco-innovator. IKEA uses AI to optimize the lifecycles of their products and predict demand. AI also develops consumers, who need individual stories about sustainability that are connected to the buying decision and enhance brand engagement.

IoT is used to support blockchain and AI as it provides real-time tracking of energy, emissions, and ware in manufacturing, supply chain, and the product. IoT-based tags and QR codes enable consumers to verify the footprint and origin of a product before purchasing it, which transforms the sustainability beyond rhetoric into an engaging experience(Balaji, 2025a).

4.7 Sector-Specific Challenges and Emerging Technologies in Sustainable Branding

Sustainable branding is mostly directed at ESG transparency, a closed cycle, and holding oneself ethically, but its application varies in industries due to structural, regulatory, and technology disparities. Alterations of strategies to the reality of each industry and the demonstration of digital tools makes them more realistic.

Fashion and clothes encounter huge sustainability challenges -fast fashion, resource intensive and cumbersome supply chains. Circular activities like recycling, repair schemes, and closed-loop manufacturing are used by brands like Patagonia, Levi's, and H&M Conscious. The transparency that is provided by blockchain allows consumers to trace the garments back to their origin and to the store, which creates trust and eradicates greenwashing.

Automotive focuses on manufacturing which is carbon-neutral, renewable, and electrification. Tesla, BMW and Toyota employ AI analytics, battery, and digital component passports to reduce emissions, remanence material and increase consumer trust over sustainability statements.

Food and beverage sustainability focuses on healthy products, reduction of waste and ethical sourcing. Unilever, Nestle and Danone leverage IoT sensors and blockchain to monitor their inputs and ensure that they are fair-trade, and generate verified sustainability stories that increase brand trust and customer retention.

Hospitality and tourism have to deal with the energy-consuming processes and changing demand. Marriott's and Accor Hotels use AI and IoT to reduce energy consumption, reduce waste, and reduce customized environmentally friendly experiences, all sustainability-related to guests as a way of life.

Financial services are branding afresh with the help of ESG-oriented digital banking, green fintech, and AI risk analytics. Standard Chartered, Paytm and HSBC use blockchain and AI to monitor carbon exposure, evaluate ESG portfolios and offer transparent green-finance solutions, which creates an operational sustainability connection between investor and consumer trust.

In all these sectors, the adoption of the digital technology with circular operations enhances the sustainability of the brand, enhances visibility, and creates consumer trust.

4.8 Emerging Trends in Sustainable Branding and Positioning

Sustainable branding tends focus on new trends which reflect demands of consumers on the ethical, transparent and eco-responsible behavior. The trend of purpose-oriented branding is on the increase with companies matching missions and values to objectives such as reducing carbon footprints, utilizing green materials and social cause support. Circularity transforms the production, aiming at recycling, reusing and minimizing waste over lifecycles. There is open supply chain through Blockchain and this enhances trust. There is also the growth in inclusive sustainability in which social equity is embedded in environmental efforts in order to favor all communities. Lastly, more detailed ESG metrics are essential; the stakeholders are now demanding data-driven reports of the effects of environmental, social, and governance. Combined, these shifts indicate that sustainable branding is running in the direction of not just marketing, but central corporate identity and continued success.

4.9 ESG Metrics and Digital Transparency in Sustainable Branding

Now sustainable branding is oriented on ESG metrics and digital transparency to enhance credibility, trust, and investor confidence. It has recently been shown that companies that perform strong ESG, i.e. provide verified carbon reductions, responsible sources, and equitable labor, are noticed (2023-2025).

Traceability, real-time reporting, and verifiable reports on environmental and social impact has digital technology (blockchain, AI, and IoT) that can help determine environmental impact. Blockchain verifies sourcing ethics, AI evaluates sustainability performance globally, and IoT tracks energy consumption, emissions, and waste, and redirects brands away from social constructs to sustainability based on facts (Sebastián-Morillas et al., 2024).

Such tendencies were exemplified by recent events: Patagonia and IKEA are integrating digital traceability with circular activities; Unilever is implementing blockchain to source sustainable palm-oil and achieve energy efficiency and battery management; Tesla relies on AI and IoT to manage its batteries and energy efficiency. These are the activities which enhance brand recognition, operational sustainability, and consumer involvement.

4.10 Results Analysis

The empirical analysis, drawing on in-depth case studies of Patagonia, Tesla, Unilever, and IKEA, yields a consistent and powerful finding: a well-architected sustainability report is not an output of good management but an input to it. The results demonstrate how these industry leaders have institutionalized their reporting frameworks to drive strategic decision-making and operational excellence.

Patagonia: The analysis reveals that Patagonia's reporting, exemplified by its Footprint Chronicles, functions as a live dashboard for its ethical supply chain. This transparency is not merely communicative; it is a critical internal governance tool that enforces supplier standards, tracks progress against environmental goals and informs product design decisions within its circular *"Worn Wear"* program. The result is a brand whose market valuation is intrinsically linked to its verifiable ethical governance.

Tesla: For Tesla, the sustainability report quantifies and consolidates its core mission. The data on gigawatt-hours of energy delivered, emissions avoided through vehicle use, and advancements in battery energy density are not just marketing points; they are the key performance indicators (KPIs) monitored at the highest levels of governance to steer R&D investment and strategic direction. The report provides the auditable evidence that its business model is delivering on its promise to accelerate the world's transition to sustainable energy.

Unilever: The Unilever case provides a quantitative correlation between integrated sustainability reporting and financial performance. Its *"Sustainable Living Brands"* are managed and tracked through its reporting infrastructure, allowing leadership to directly attribute a significant portion of the company's growth (69% faster than the rest of the portfolio) to its sustainability agenda. This demonstrates how the report transforms ESG from a cost center into a measurable driver of value creation.

IKEA: IKEA's journey to becoming *"climate positive"* is governed through its sustainability reporting. The report is the mechanism through which it tracks investments in renewable energy, the performance of its circular *"Buy Back & Resell"* programs, and progress in sustainable sourcing. This data-driven approach allows IKEA's board to manage the company's massive environmental footprint proactively, turning ambitious goals into manageable, accountable operational targets.

Synthesizing these results, a clear model emerges: in each case, the sustainability report provides the critical data infrastructure that enables the board and executives to perform their fiduciary duties in the 21st century—overseeing not just financial capital, but natural, social, and human capital as well.

5.0 SOLUTIONS AND RECOMMENDATIONS

To effectively navigate the complexities of sustainable branding and positioning, companies should adopt several key strategies. First, transparency is crucial; businesses should provide clear, accurate, and verifiable information about their sustainability efforts. This can be achieved through robust ESG (Environmental, Social, and Governance) reporting, third-party certifications, and utilizing technologies like blockchain for traceable supply chains. Companies should also avoid *"greenwashing"* by ensuring that all claims are substantiated with concrete data and meaningful actions.

Second, adopting a holistic approach to sustainability is vital. This involves integrating sustainability into every aspect of the business—from product design and sourcing to manufacturing and distribution. Companies should engage with stakeholders, including consumers, employees, and local communities, to align their sustainability goals with broader societal expectations. Additionally, businesses should embrace innovation, such as developing circular economy models that prioritize recycling and waste reduction. Collaboration is also key; partnering with other organizations, NGOs, and governments can amplify efforts and drive industry-wide change. Finally, companies should invest in sustainability education and training for their employees, ensuring that the entire workforce is aligned with and contributes to the organization's sustainability objectives. These strategies will not only enhance brand reputation but also build resilience and long-term value.

5.1 Implications of the Study

Academic Implications:

The research contributes to the literature by examining sustainable brands building and consumer behaviour and brand positioning. It enhances insight into how sustainability can be imbued into the management of a brand especially by emphasizing on authenticity and transparency as the keys to the creation of a sustainable brand. The study broadens the understanding of consumer attitude to sustainability that holds a significant amount of information in the upcoming research on consumer behavior and brand management.

Industry Implications:

To practitioners, the research will provide practical information in developing and sustaining sustainable brands. The findings can be utilized by the companies to develop the effective sustainability strategies that satisfy the consumer expectations and improve the brand reputation. Putting importance on authenticity and clarity of communication is also essential in enabling brands to gain trust and loyalty. The study also identifies the need to incorporate sustainability in the main business processes, and this provides a guideline towards companies seeking to position themselves in the long term by being sustainable in their operations.

5.2 Future Research Directions

There are several areas to expand these findings, which can be examined by future research. One of the ways would be to research the impact of the new trends on sustainable branding plans, including the principles of circular economy, and the effects of digital technologies. The other aspect is the role of sustainability in affecting the brand performance in various markets and geographical localities. Longitudinal research would show how the sustainable branding practice changes with the passage of time and their permanent impact on the brand equity and consumer loyalty. Research might also provide an opportunity to investigate the influence of stakeholder engagement on the improvement of the effectiveness of sustainable branding strategies.

5.3 Conclusion

The article Building Sustainable Brands: Strategies to Long-term Market Positioning pays specific attention to the significance of authenticity, transparency, and the commitment to develop sustainability into business aspects to attain long-term positioning. With the integration of the qualitative and quantitative research, consumers provide detailed study on the active strategies on effective sustainable branding and how they impact the consumer behaviour and the image of the brand. The results can be of great value to the scholarly and business worlds, and the necessity of the brands to be truly devoted to the concept of sustainability and make their ongoing work transparent. With the development of sustainable branding, research studies should be conducted continuously, as new trends and issues will emerge, and the brand should not lose its competitive edge and not fail to reach the stable success on the market.

6.0 SUMMARY OF THE CHAPTER

Positions the modern sustainability report as an indispensable internal governance tool and strategic linchpin, rather than a mere public-facing communication. • Empirically demonstrates, through leading corporate case studies, that standardized reporting frameworks (GRI, SASB) provide the critical data infrastructure for setting ESG baselines, tracking progress, and informing board-level decisions. • Argues that the discipline of reporting cultivates a culture of accountability, transforming abstract sustainability commitments into measurable, manageable operational realities. • This evolution is situated within the prudential ESG context, where regulators (e.g., via the EU's CSRD) and institutional investors demand auditable, decision-useful information.

- Highlights the central role of technology (AI, Blockchain, IoT) in enhancing the credibility, traceability, and auditability of ESG data, thereby closing the trust gap and combating greenwashing.
- Concludes that integrating sustainability reporting into the core of corporate governance is no longer optional but a strategic imperative for long-term value creation, risk mitigation, and maintaining market legitimacy.

CHAPTER QUESTION

True and False Questions (Knowledge & Comprehension)

1. The primary argument of the chapter is that sustainability reporting should be viewed mainly as a public relations and communicative exercise. (False)
2. The European Union's Corporate Sustainability Reporting Directive (CSRD) is cited as a key regulatory driver mandating the use of sustainability reports for governance through third-party assurance. (True)
3. According to the chapter, the concept of "greenwashing" refers to the successful integration of sustainability into a company's core business strategy. (False)
4. The Triple Bottom Line (TBL) model expands a company's performance assessment to include people, planet, and profit. (True)
5. Patagonia's "Don't Buy This Jacket" campaign is presented as an example of a traditional sales-driven marketing strategy. (False)
6. The chapter posits that a well-architected sustainability report can serve as an internal strategic tool for management and board-level decision-making. (True)
7. Tesla's market valuation and strategic direction are largely disconnected from the data and key performance indicators found in its sustainability reporting. (False)
8. The principle of "double materiality" requires companies to report only on how sustainability issues affect their own enterprise value. (False)
9. IKEA's "Buy Back & Resell" program is an operational manifestation of a linear "take-make-dispose" economic model. (False)
10. The chapter concludes that integrating sustainability reporting into corporate governance is an optional strategy for most companies. (False)

Multiple Choice Questions (Comprehension & Application)

11. Within the "prudential ESG context" described in the chapter, sustainability data is primarily valued for its:
    A) Marketing potential
    B) Role in long-term risk assessment and value creation
    C) Ability to simplify annual reports
    D) Use in philanthropic campaigning
    E) Function as a substitute for financial audits
12. The theoretical evolution of corporate sustainability, as traced in the chapter, moves sequentially through which of the following stages?
    A) Creating Shared Value (CSV) → Corporate Social Responsibility (CSR) → Integrated Corporate Governance
    B) Corporate Governance → CSR → CSV
    C) Corporate Social Responsibility (CSR) → Creating Shared Value (CSV) → Integrated Corporate Governance
    D) Green Marketing → CSR → Stakeholder Theory
    E) Circular Economy → TBL → Integrated Reporting
13. According to the case study analysis, Unilever's "Sustainable Living Brands" were found to have grown how much faster than the rest of its portfolio?
    A) 25%
    B) 50%
    C) 69%
    D) 75%
    E) 100%
14. Which technology is specifically highlighted in the chapter as being fundamental to establishing the "auditability" of ESG data and closing the "trust gap"?
    A) Virtual Reality
    B) 3D Printing
    C) Blockchain and AI
    D) Quantum Computing
    E) Augmented Reality
15. The Patagonia "Footprint Chronicles" tool is used primarily to:
    A) Track competitor pricing
    B) Manage internal employee performance reviews
    C) Provide transparency and track environmental impact across the supply chain
    D) Design new clothing lines
    E) Calculate executive compensation

16. The concept that requires companies to disclose both how sustainability issues affect their business and how their operations impact society and the environment is known as:
   A) Single Materiality
   B) Dual Accountability
   C) Stakeholder Primacy
   D) Double Materiality
   E) Integrated Reporting
17. Which of the following is NOT listed in the chapter as a core model for sustainable branding and positioning?
   A) Triple Bottom Line (TBL)
   B) Brand Purpose
   C) Sustainability-Driven Innovation
   D) Circular Economy
   E) Shareholder Primacy
18. IKEA's goal to become "climate positive" by 2030 involves:
   A) Reducing greenhouse gas emissions to net-zero.
   B) Offsetting all emissions through external projects.
   C) Cutting greenhouse gas emissions to levels significantly below its own value chain's footprint.
   D) Focusing solely on in-store energy efficiency.
   E) Eliminating the use of all plastics.
19. A key defense against greenwashing, as proposed in the chapter, is:
   A) Increasing advertising budgets for sustainability campaigns.
   B) The institutionalization of accountability through the sustainability reporting process itself.
   C) Lobbying for less stringent regulatory standards.
   D) Focusing communication on future aspirations rather than past performance.
   E) Limiting the amount of data published to avoid scrutiny.
20. The chapter positions the modern sustainability report as a:
   A) Foundational governance technology
   B) Necessary legal evil
   C) Voluntarily produced marketing brochure
   D) Tool relevant only to environmental NGOs
   E) Replacement for annual financial statements

Short Answer Questions (Application & Analysis)

21. Briefly explain how the sustainability reporting process itself helps to cultivate a culture of accountability within an organization.

22. Differentiate between the concepts of Corporate Social Responsibility (CSR) and Creating Shared Value (CSV) as presented in the chapter's theoretical evolution.
23. Using an example from the chapter, describe how a specific technology (AI, Blockchain, or IoT) is applied to enhance the credibility of sustainability reporting.
24. What is the twofold peril of greenwashing identified within the prudential ESG context?
25. How does Tesla's vertical integration, as described in the case study, support its sustainability governance and reporting?
26. Summarize the role of standardized reporting frameworks (e.g., GRI, SASB) in transforming abstract sustainability commitments into manageable operational realities.
27. According to the case study, what is the strategic significance of Patagonia's "Worn Wear" program beyond its environmental benefits?
28. Explain how IKEA's "Buy Back & Resell" program operationalizes the principles of a circular economy.

Essay Questions (Analysis & Synthesis)

29. Synthesizing the evidence from the four case studies (Patagonia, Tesla, Unilever, IKEA), analyze the common mechanisms through which their sustainability reports transition from being communication outputs to strategic governance inputs.
30. Critically evaluate the chapter's central thesis that sustainability reporting is the "foundational bedrock for robust sustainability management and governance." Do the case studies provide compelling evidence for this claim? Justify your answer.
31. Compare and contrast the ways in which Patagonia and Unilever, as presented in the chapter, have integrated sustainability into their brand identity and corporate strategy. What are the key similarities and differences in their approaches?
32. Elaborate on the "prudential ESG context" and discuss the respective roles of regulatory "push" (e.g., CSRD) and investor "pull" in driving the internalization of sustainability reporting for governance purposes.
33. The chapter emphasizes the balance between tangible and intangible assets. With reference to specific examples, discuss how robust sustainability reporting concurrently builds measurable financial value and intangible brand equity.
34. Propose a framework, based on the chapter's models and tools, that a company in a traditionally non-sustainable sector (e.g., fossil fuels) could use to begin establishing credible sustainability governance through reporting.

In-Depth Questions for Master's Students (Synthesis & Evaluation)

35. Conduct a critical analysis of the potential limitations and unintended consequences of the escalating regulatory focus on standardized sustainability reporting (e.g., CSRD, ISSB). Consider aspects such as reporting fatigue, box-ticking compliance, and the challenges for small and medium-sized enterprises (SMEs).
36. Based on the chapter's foundation, design a research proposal to investigate the causal relationship between the adoption of AI for ESG data analytics and a specific corporate outcome, such as reduction in Scope 3 emissions or improvement in brand trust scores. Outline your hypothesis, methodology, and key metrics.
37. The chapter cites the divergence in ESG ratings as a challenge. Evaluate the efficacy of current market-based solutions (e.g., the consolidation of standards under the ISSB) in creating a more reliable and comparable ESG data ecosystem for investors and managers.
38. "Digital transparency can be a double-edged sword." Critically discuss this statement in the context of sustainable branding, evaluating how technologies like blockchain can both build consumer trust and expose companies to new forms of reputational risk related to their supply chains.
39. Using the Circular Economy model as a lens, critically assess the sustainability claims of a fast-fashion brand of your choice. How would you design an audit, based on this chapter's principles, to verify the authenticity of its circularity initiatives?

In-Depth Questions for PhD Scholars (Evaluation & Creation)

40. The chapter posits a paradigm shift where the sustainability report becomes a "*central governance technology.*" Develop a novel theoretical framework that challenges or expands upon this concept. How might this technology metaphor fail to capture the socio-political dimensions of governance, and what alternative theoretical lenses (e.g., institutional logics, actor-network theory) could provide a more nuanced understanding?
41. A significant research gap exists in understanding the behavioral and cognitive impacts of sustainability reporting on corporate boards. Design a mixed-methods doctoral research project to investigate how the format, frequency, and assurance level of sustainability reports influence boardroom dialogues, risk perceptions, and strategic capital allocation decisions.
42. The chapter focuses on corporate leaders. Propose a PhD thesis that explores the "*governance of sustainability governance.*" Your research should critically

examine the emerging profession of sustainability reporting and assurance, analyzing the power dynamics, professional identities, and potential for *"capture"* by consulting firms within this new field.

In-Depth Questions for Post-Doctoral Researchers (Creation & High-Impact Research Direction)

43. The current ESG ecosystem is characterized by a proliferation of standards and a lack of temporal consistency in data. Propose a high-impact, interdisciplinary research program aimed at developing and validating a dynamic, real-time *"ESG Vitality Index"* using federated learning and IoT data. How would this fundamentally challenge the current paradigm of annual or biannual sustainability reporting?
44. The chapter operates within the paradigm of *"responsible capitalism."* Design a groundbreaking research agenda that explores the tensions and potential contradictions between the governance imperatives of sustainability reporting and the structural drivers of financialized capitalism. Can the sustainability report truly govern for long-term resilience within a system prioritizing short-term shareholder returns? Your agenda should incorporate political economy and critical management studies.
45. Future research must move beyond the corporate entity. Develop a theoretical and methodological framework for a post-doctoral study on *"Networked Sustainability Governance."* This research should investigate how sustainability reporting and data flows are creating new forms of accountability and power within *entire global value chains*, focusing on the relations between lead firms, suppliers, regulators, and data platforms.

REFERENCES

Aaker, D. A., & Joachimsthaler, E. (2000). *Brand Leadership*. The Free Press.

Adams, C. A., Alhamood, A., He, X., Tian, J., Wang, L., & Wang, Y. (2021). *The double-materiality concept: Application and issues*. Global Reporting Initiative.

Ahrholdt, D. C., Gudergan, S. P., & Ringle, C. M. (2017). Enhancing service loyalty. *Journal of Travel Research*, *56*(4), 436–450. DOI: 10.1177/0047287516649058

Apaza-Panca, C. M., Flores Quevedo, L. A., & Reyes, L. M. C. (2024). Green marketing to promote the natural protected area. *Sustainable Technology and Entrepreneurship*, *3*(3), 100067. DOI: 10.1016/j.stae.2023.100067

Balaji, K. (2023). Exploring the Drivers and Effects on Supply Chain Resilience and Performance in an Emerging Market Using Artificial Intelligence. 2023 3rd International Conference on Smart Generation Computing, Communication and Networking (SMART GENCON), 1–6. DOI: 10.1109/SMARTGENCON60755.2023.10442071

Balaji, K. (2025a). AI as a Game Changer: How Digital Entrepreneurs Are Redefining Business Practices. In Tunio, M. (Ed.), *Improving Entrepreneurial Processes Through Advanced AI* (pp. 21–48). IGI Global Scientific Publishing., DOI: 10.4018/979-8-3693-1495-1.ch002

Balaji, K. (2025b). E-Government and E-Governance: Driving Digital Transformation in Public Administration. In Wongmahesak, K., Ahmad, J., & Mustanir, A. (Eds.), *Public Governance Practices in the Age of AI* (pp. 23–44). IGI Global Scientific Publishing., DOI: 10.4018/979-8-3693-9286-7.ch002

Balaji, K. (2025c). Harnessing AI and Blockchain in Sustainability Assurance: Trends Shaping the Future of Verification. In Khatib, S., & Abbas, A. (Eds.), *Navigating Trust in Sustainability Reporting and Assurance* (pp. 215–242). IGI Global Scientific Publishing., DOI: 10.4018/979-8-3373-0117-4.ch007

Becerra, E. P., & Korgaonkar, P. K. (2011). Effects of trust beliefs on consumers' online intentions. *European Journal of Marketing*, *45*(6), 936–962. DOI: 10.1108/03090561111119921

Berg, F., Kölbel, J. F., & Rigobon, R. (2022). Aggregate Confusion: The Divergence of ESG Ratings. *Review of Finance*, *26*(6), 1315–1344. DOI: 10.1093/rof/rfac033

Bigné, J. E., Moliner, M. A., & Callarisa, L. J. (2000). El valor y la fidelización de clientes: Una propuesta de modelo dinámico de comportamiento. *Revista Europea de Dirección y Economía de La Empresa*, *9*(3), 65–78.

Brakus, J. J., Schmitt, B. H., & Zarantonello, L. (2009). Brand experience: What is it? How is it measured? Does it affect loyalty? *Journal of Marketing*, *73*(3), 52–68. DOI: 10.1509/jmkg.73.3.052

Chen, Y.-C., Wu, J.-H., Peng, L., & Yeh, R. C. (2015). Consumer benefit creation in online group buying: The social capital and platform synergy effect and the mediating role of participation. *Electronic Commerce Research and Applications*, *14*(6), 499–513. DOI: 10.1016/j.elerap.2015.07.003

Cocosila, M., & Igonor, A. (2015). How important is the "social" in social networking? A perceived value empirical investigation. *Information Technology & People*, *28*(2), 366–382. DOI: 10.1108/ITP-03-2014-0055

De Freitas Netto, S. V., Falcão Sobral, M. F., Ribeiro, A. R. B., & Soares, G. R. (2020). Concepts and forms of greenwashing: A systematic review. *Environmental Sciences Europe*, *32*(1), 19. DOI: 10.1186/s12302-020-0300-3

Delgado-Ballester, E., Luis, J. Á., & Án, M.-A. (2001). Brand trust in the context of consumer loyalty. *European Journal of Marketing*, *35*(11/12), 35. DOI: 10.1108/EUM0000000006475

Dimson, E., Marsh, P., & Staunton, M. (2020). Divergent ESG Ratings. *Journal of Portfolio Management*, *47*(1), 75–87. DOI: 10.3905/jpm.2020.1.175

Eccles, R. G., & Serafeim, G. (2013). The performance frontier: Innovating for a sustainable strategy. *Harvard Business Review*, *91*(5), 50–60. PMID: 23898735

Erdem, T., & Swait, J. (2004). Brand credibility, Brand consideration, and choice. *The Journal of Consumer Research*, *31*(1), 191–198. DOI: 10.1086/383434

European Commission. (2022). Corporate Sustainability Reporting Directive (CSRD). Directive (EU) 2022/2464 of the European Parliament and of the Council. https://eur-lex.europa.eu/legal-content/EN/TXT/?uri=CELEX:32022L2464

European Commission. (2022). Corporate Sustainability Reporting Directive (CSRD). Directive (EU) 2022/2464 of the European Parliament and of the Council.

Fishbein, M. A., & Ajzen, I. (1975). *Belief, attitude, intention, and behavior: An introduction to theory and research*. Addison-Wesley.

Freeman, R. E., Dmytriyev, S. D., & Phillips, R. A. (2021). Stakeholder theory and the resource-based view of the firm. *Journal of Management*, *47*(7), 1757–1770. DOI: 10.1177/0149206321993576

Henseler, J., Ringle, C. M., & Sarstedt, M. (2015). A new criterion for assessing discriminant validity in variance-based structural equation modeling. *Journal of the Academy of Marketing Science, 43*(1), 115–135. DOI: 10.1007/s11747-014-0403-8

Hernandez-Fernandez, A., & Lewis, M. C. (2019). Brand authenticity leads to perceived value and brand trust. *European Journal of Management and Business Economics, 28*(3), 222–238. DOI: 10.1108/EJMBE-10-2017-0027

Huang, T. K., Wang, Y. T., & Lin, K. Y. (2022). Enhancing brand loyalty through online brand communities: The role of community benefits. *Journal of Product and Brand Management, 31*(5), 823–838. DOI: 10.1108/JPBM-08-2020-3027

IFRS Foundation. (2023). *IFRS S1 General Requirements for Disclosure of Sustainability-related Financial Information.* International Sustainability Standards Board.

Jeon, H. J. (2022). Does the relationship between brand attitude, brand attachment and purchase intention vary based on the type of prosocial expression-based brand emoji? *Journal of Product and Brand Management, 31*(8), 1180–1195. Advance online publication. DOI: 10.1108/JPBM-09-2021-3660

Kang, J., & Hustvedt, G. (2014). Building trust between consumers and corporations: The role of consumer perceptions of transparency and social responsibility. *Journal of Business Ethics, 125*(2), 253–265. DOI: 10.1007/s10551-013-1916-7

Keller, K. L., & Lehmann, D. R. (2006). Brands and branding: Research findings and future priorities. *Marketing Science, 25*(6), 740–759. DOI: 10.1287/mksc.1050.0153

Kim, J., Morris, J. D., & Swait, J. (2008). Antecedents of true brand loyalty. *Journal of Advertising, 37*(2), 99–117. DOI: 10.2753/JOA0091-3367370208

Kotsantonis, S., & Serafeim, G. (2019). Four Things No One Will Tell You About ESG Data. *The Bank of America Journal of Applied Corporate Finance, 31*(2), 50–58. DOI: 10.1111/jacf.12346

Kressmann, F., Sirgy, M. J., Herrmann, A., Huber, F., Huber, S., & Lee, D. J. (2006). Direct and indirect effects of self-image congruence on brand loyalty. *Journal of Business Research, 59*(9), 955–964. DOI: 10.1016/j.jbusres.2006.06.001

Krüger, P. (2015). Corporate goodness and shareholder wealth. *Journal of Financial Economics, 115*(2), 304–329. DOI: 10.1016/j.jfineco.2014.09.008

Kuikka, A., & Laukkanen, T. (2012). Brand loyalty and the role of hedonic value. *Journal of Product and Brand Management, 21*(7), 529–537. DOI: 10.1108/10610421211276277

Lam, S. K., Ahearne, M., Mullins, R., Hayati, B., & Schillewaert, N. (2013). Exploring the dynamics of antecedents to consumer–brand identification with a new brand. *Journal of the Academy of Marketing Science*, *41*(2), 234–252. DOI: 10.1007/s11747-012-0301-x

Lam, S. Y., & Shankar, V. (2014). Asymmetries in the effects of drivers of brand loyalty between early and late adopters and across technology generations. *Journal of Interactive Marketing*, *28*(1), 26–42. DOI: 10.1016/j.intmar.2013.06.004

Marquis, C., & Toffel, M. W. (2012). The Globalization of Corporate Social Responsibility: A Study of the Adoption of the Global Reporting Initiative. Harvard Business School Working Paper.

Mayer, R. C., Davis, J. H., & Schoorman, F. D. (1995). An integrative model of organizational trust. *Academy of Management Review*, *20*(3), 709. DOI: 10.2307/258792

McKnight, D. H., Choudhury, V., & Kacmar, C. (2002). Developing and validating trust measures for e-commerce: An integrative typology. *Information Systems Research*, *13*(3), 334–359. DOI: 10.1287/isre.13.3.334.81

Miquel-Segarra, S., Rangel Pérez, C., & Monfort, A. (2023). Análisis del uso de Twitter como plataforma estratégica de diálogo: Las empresas del IBEX35 y la difusión de mensajes sobre COVID. *Revista de Comunicación*, *22*(1). Advance online publication. DOI: 10.26441/RC22.1-2023-2989

Molinillo, S., Ekinci, Y., & Japutra, A. (2019). A consumer-based brand performance model for assessing brand success. *International Journal of Market Research*, *61*(1), 93–110. DOI: 10.1177/1470785318762990

Monfort, A., Sebastián, A., & López, B. (2015). Corporate identity in the brand co-creation era. *Communication Papers*, *4*(08), 31. DOI: 10.33115/udg_bib/cp.v4i08.22065

Monfort, A., & Villagra, N. (2016). Corporate social responsibility and corporate foundations in building responsible brands. *El Profesional de la Información*, *25*(5), 767–777. DOI: 10.3145/epi.2016.sep.07

Papista, E., & Dimitriadis, S. (2019). Consumer – green brand relationships: Revisiting benefits, relationship quality and outcomes. *Journal of Product and Brand Management*, *28*(2), 166–187. DOI: 10.1108/JPBM-09-2016-1316

Parris, D. L., & Guzmán, F. (2022). Evolving brand boundaries and expectations: Looking back on brand equity, brand loyalty, and brand image research to move forward. *Journal of Product and Brand Management*. Advance online publication. DOI: 10.1108/JPBM-06-2021-3528

Ruiz, B., Esteban, Á., & Gutiérrez, S. (2014). Determinants of reputation of leading Spanish financial institutions among their customers in a context of economic crisis. *Business Research Quarterly*, *17*(4), 259–278. DOI: 10.1016/j.brq.2014.04.002

Ruiz, B., García, J. A., & Revilla, A. (2016). Antecedents and consequences of bank reputation: A comparison of the United Kingdom and Spain. *International Marketing Review*, *33*(6), 781–805. DOI: 10.1108/IMR-06-2015-0147

Sebastián-Morillas, A., Monfort, A., & López-Vázquez, B. (2024). Effects of perceived value and customer service on brand satisfaction. *Journal of Promotion Management*, *30*(2), 187–203. DOI: 10.1080/10496491.2023.2253231

Sharma, R., & Jain, V. (2019). CSR, Trust, brand loyalty and brand equity: Empirical evidences from sportswear industry in the NCR region of India. Metamorphosis. *Journal of Management Research*, *18*(1), 57–67.

Sichtmann, C. (2007). An analysis of antecedents and consequences of trust in a corporate brand. *European Journal of Marketing*, *41*(9/10), 999–1015. DOI: 10.1108/03090560710773318

Sung, Y., & Kim, J. (2010). Effects of brand personality on brand trust and brand affect. *Psychology and Marketing*, *27*(7), 639–661. DOI: 10.1002/mar.20349

Sweeney, J. C., & Soutar, G. N. (2001). Consumer perceived value: The development of a multiple item scale. *Journal of Retailing*, *77*(2), 203–220. DOI: 10.1016/S0022-4359(01)00041-0

Taherdoost, H. (2022). Machine Learning Algorithms: Features and Applications. In Wang, J. (Ed.), *Encyclopedia of Data Science and Machine Learning* (pp. 938–960). IGI Global., DOI: 10.4018/978-1-7998-9220-5.ch054

Task Force on Climate-related Financial Disclosures (TCFD). (2021). Final Report: Recommendations of the Task Force on Climate-related Financial Disclosures. Financial Stability Board.

Trevino, R., & Treviño, E. (2021). Análisis entre imagen de la tienda y satisfacción del cliente en tiendas minoristas transnacionales en el sector autoservicio. Estudios Gerenciales, 556–565. DOI: 10.18046/j.estger.2021.161.4293

WBCSD. (2023). ESG-Integrated Value Creation: A practical guide for boards and C-suite. World Business Council for Sustainable Development. https://www.wbcsd.org/

World Economic Forum (WEF). (2020). Measuring Stakeholder Capitalism: Towards Common Metrics and Consistent Reporting of Sustainable Value Creation. World Economic Forum.

Yu, M., Liu, F., & Lee, J. A. (2019). Consumers' responses to negative publicity: The influence of culture on information search and negative word-of-mouth. *Journal of Brand Management*, *26*(2), 141–156. DOI: 10.1057/s41262-018-0123-3

Zeithaml, V. A. (1988). Consumer perceptions of price, quality, and value: A means-end model and synthesis of evidence. *Journal of Marketing*, *52*(3), 2–22. DOI: 10.1177/002224298805200302

KEY TERMS AND DEFINITIONS

Circular Economy: An industrial system that is restorative and regenerative by design, aiming to eliminate waste and keep products, components, and materials at their highest utility and value at all times, contrasting with a traditional linear "take-make-dispose" model.

Double Materiality: A principle, central to frameworks like the CSRD, requiring companies to disclose both how sustainability issues affect their enterprise value (financial materiality) and how the company's operations impact society and the environment (impact materiality) (European Commission, 2022).

ESG (Environmental, Social, and Governance): A structured framework for identifying, assessing, and managing risks and opportunities related to environmental stewardship, social responsibility, and the quality of a company's governance. Within a prudential context, ESG factors are considered material to financial performance and long-term value creation.

Greenwashing: A strategy involving the dissemination of misleading information or the use of symbolic actions to create an unwarranted public image of environmental responsibility, without substantive performance to match the claims (de Freitas Netto et al., 2020).

Prudential ESG Context: An approach to ESG that emphasizes its materiality to risk management, financial stability, and fiduciary duty, moving beyond ethical considerations to focus on the pragmatic business imperatives of sustainability performance.

Sustainability Governance: The system of policies, processes, controls, and reporting structures by which a company's board and management oversee the integration of ESG factors into strategy and operations, ensuring accountability and long-term resilience.

TEACHING NOTE

Concise Summary for the Teacher

This chapter presents a paradigm shift in understanding the role of the sustainability report. It moves beyond viewing the report as a peripheral communication tool and re-frames it as a foundational governance technology and strategic management input. Through robust case studies of Patagonia, Tesla, Unilever, and IKEA, the chapter demonstrates empirically how standardized reporting frameworks (GRI, SASB) create the essential data infrastructure for internal decision-making. It argues that the discipline of reporting cultivates accountability, transforming abstract ESG commitments into measurable operational realities. Situated within the *"prudential ESG context,"* the chapter highlights the powerful confluence of regulatory pressure (e.g., EU's CSRD) and investor demand for auditable data, making integrated sustainability governance a strategic imperative, not an optional moral pursuit.

Chapter Synopsis

The chapter charts the evolution of sustainability from a communicative exercise to a core function of corporate governance. It begins by establishing the theoretical progression from Corporate Social Responsibility (CSR) to Creating Shared Value (CSV) and finally to integrated governance, where the sustainability report acts as a central nervous system. The analysis is grounded in Stakeholder Theory and the Triple Bottom Line. The core of the chapter is an empirical demonstration through four in-depth case studies, showing how Patagonia, Tesla, Unilever, and IKEA use their reports as live dashboards for supply chain management, R&D direction, brand portfolio strategy, and circular economy execution. A key thread is the role of technology (AI, Blockchain, IoT) in ensuring data credibility and combating greenwashing. The chapter concludes that a well-architected sustainability report is indispensable for de-risking operations, fostering long-term resilience, and creating tangible and intangible values.

Key Learning Objectives

Upon engaging with this chapter, students should be able to:

1. **Analyze** the theoretical evolution of corporate sustainability, tracing its path from peripheral CSR to a core governance imperative. (Analysis)

2. **Evaluate** the critical role of standardized reporting frameworks (e.g., GRI, SASB) in providing the data infrastructure necessary for robust sustainability management. (Evaluation)
3. **Synthesize** evidence from leading corporate case studies to explain how sustainability reports function as internal strategic tools rather than mere external communications. (Synthesis)
4. **Differentiate** between greenwashing and authentic sustainability governance, identifying the mechanisms within the reporting process that enforce accountability. (Analysis)
5. **Formulate** a coherent argument for why integrating sustainability reporting into corporate governance is a prudential business necessity in the current ESG context. (Synthesis/Creation)
6. **Appraise** the impact of emerging technologies like blockchain and AI on the auditability, transparency, and strategic value of ESG data. (Evaluation)

Core Themes/Theses for Discussion

1. **The Paradigm Shift:** The sustainability report has transitioned from a public relations output to a foundational governance *input* and strategic linchpin.
2. **The Data Infrastructure Thesis:** Standardized reporting frameworks are not just disclosure guidelines but are critical for building the internal data architecture required for management and oversight.
3. **The Accountability Mechanism:** The process of reporting itself—data collection, verification, and assurance—institutionalizes a culture of accountability and data-driven decision-making.
4. **The Prudential Imperative:** In the face of regulatory and investor pressures, managing sustainability is no longer about ethics alone but about fiduciary duty, risk management, and long-term value creation.
5. **The Technology-Trust Nexus:** Digital tools (Blockchain, AI, IoT) are fundamental to closing the "trust gap," transforming sustainability claims from narratives into verifiable metrics.

Suggested Teaching Pathway

1. **Hook (10 mins):** Begin with a provocative question: *"Is Patagonia's 'Don't Buy This Jacket' campaign a failure of marketing or a masterpiece of governance?"* This immediately engages students with the core tension between communication and substantive action.

2. **Conceptual Foundation (20 mins):** Lecture on the theoretical evolution (CSR → CSV → Integrated Governance) and key concepts (Prudential ESG, Double Materiality). Use simple diagrams to illustrate the shift.
3. **Case Study Analysis (30 mins):** Divide the class into four groups, each assigned one case study (Patagonia, Tesla, Unilever, IKEA). Task each group with identifying: (a) The key ESG metrics the company tracks, (b) How the report informs internal decisions, and (c) The role of technology.
4. **Synthesis and Debate (25 mins):** Reconvene and have each group present their findings. Use a whiteboard to map the common patterns across all four cases, visually reinforcing the chapter's central thesis. Facilitate a debate on whether this model is replicable for all companies, or only for industry leaders.
5. **Application and Conclusion (15 mins):** Present a brief, anonymized case of a company accused of greenwashing. Ask students, in pairs, to draft a set of reporting-based recommendations to help the company rebuild credibility, applying the chapter's principles.

Pedagogical Tools & Resources

Case Studies: The chapter provides four ready-to-use cases. Instructors can use the Harvard Business Publishing platform for supplementary cases on Unilever or IKEA.

Videos: Patagonia's *"Don't Buy This Jacket"* ad and documentaries on Tesla's Gigafactories provide powerful visual aids.

Interactive Tools: Explore the online versions of Patagonia's *"Footprint Chronicles"* or the SASB Materiality Finder in class to demonstrate reporting in practice.

Role-Playing: Simulate a board meeting where students different roles (CEO, CFO, Head of Sustainability, Investor) to debate a major capital investment based on sustainability report data.

Additional Reading: Assign the *"Additional Reading"* section (7.0) from the chapter for advanced students.

Note on Sensitivity

The discussion of greenwashing and corporate accountability can potentially lead to strong opinions and criticisms of specific companies or industries. It is important for the instructor to:

- Frame the discussion around systemic challenges and governance structures rather than personal attacks.

- Encourage evidence-based criticism, grounded in data from reports or credible sources.
- Acknowledge the real economic and operational challenges companies face when transitioning to sustainable models, particularly for SMEs and in developing economies, to provide a balanced perspective.

10 Key Questions for Class Discussion

1. **The chapter argues sustainability reports are a "governance technology." Is this metaphor persuasive, or does it risk oversimplifying the complex social and ethical dimensions of sustainability?**
   - **Direction:** Push students to consider both the strengths (emphasizes systemization, data rigor) and weaknesses (may seem technocratic, dehumanizing) of this framing.
2. **Patagonia and Unilever both achieve sustainability success but through vastly different models (activist-led vs. portfolio-scale). Which approach do you believe is more resilient and replicable in the long term?**
   - **Direction:** Guide students to analyze the trade-offs: brand authenticity vs. mass-market impact, deep niche influence vs. broad systemic change.
3. **The CSRD mandates double materiality. What are the practical challenges a company might face in implementing this principle, and how might it change the nature of corporate accountability?**
   - **Direction:** Encourage discussion on the difficulty of quantifying social impact, managing a vastly expanded stakeholder map, and the potential for internal conflict between financial and impact goals.
4. **If the data from sustainability reporting is so valuable for internal management, why did companies need regulatory pressure like the CSRD to fully embrace it?**
   - **Direction:** Probe into barriers such as short-term financial pressures, the historical treatment of ESG as a cost center, and a lack of standardized frameworks in the past.
5. **Can the extensive use of AI for ESG data analytics create a new form of risk, such as algorithmic bias in supply chain management or a over-reliance on quantitative data?**
   - **Direction:** Steer the conversation towards the ethics of AI, the potential for embedded bias to perpetuate social inequities, and the danger of missing qualitative, contextual insights.

6. **IKEA's "Buy Back & Resell" program is a clear circular economy initiative. How does this program directly serve the company's governance and financial objectives, beyond the environmental benefit?**
   - o **Direction:** Have students connect the program to tangible outcomes: customer loyalty, new revenue streams, supply chain resilience, and data on product longevity that informs future design.
7. **Greenwashing is framed as a "governance failure." Who within a corporation should be ultimately held accountable for it: the Board, the C-Suite, the marketing department, or all of the above?**
   - o **Direction:** This question delves into corporate governance structures. Encourage students to debate where the buck stops and how reporting lines and board oversight can prevent greenwashing.
8. **The chapter focuses on large, successful corporations. How can the principles of governance-driven sustainability reporting be adapted for small and medium-sized enterprises (SMEs) with limited resources?**
   - o **Direction:** Shift the focus to practicality. Ask students to brainstorm a scaled-down, cost-effective version of this model for an SME.
9. **Tesla's valuation is heavily tied to its sustainability mission. Does this create a dangerous fragility if it fails to meet its technological or environmental targets, or does it create a powerful discipline?**
   - o **Direction:** Explore the concept of a "sustainability premium" in valuation and the heightened reputational and financial risks that come with being a leader in this space.
10. **Looking forward, what single trend—regulatory, technological, or consumer-driven—do you believe will most accelerate the adoption of the governance model presented in this chapter?**
    - o **Direction:** A forward-looking question that requires synthesis. Encourage students to weigh the relative power of different forces shaping the corporate landscape.

Chapter 2
Digital ESG in Action: Transforming Environmental, Social, and Governance Practices

Rachna Chand
https://orcid.org/0009-0007-4935-0713
Chandigarh University, India

Manjit Kour
https://orcid.org/0000-0003-1043-3187
North-West University, South Africa

Shelley Khosla
https://orcid.org/0009-0000-5797-5544
Rayat Bahra Professional University, Hoshiarpur, India

ABSTRACT

Companies are incorporating digital technology to advance their ethical standards, transparency and accountability. They are transforming the implementation of sustainability through Digital ESG. Companies are focussing on achieving a good market picture through making a change in society by digitalizing their ESG efforts in order to reach the target audience, fulfil social responsibilities and achieve the company's aim. The purpose of this study is to investigate the Digital ESG concept, its potential for the future, and its shortcomings. A SWOT analysis with the help of a review of various academic and professional studies has been conducted in order to comprehend the concept and its need. The discoveries of this paper can be utilized by specialists, professionals, and the general public for additional exploration.

DOI: 10.4018/979-8-3693-9714-5.ch002

1.0 INTRODUCTION

Since the 1990s, the Indian financial system has experienced numerous changes. Economic development consistently comes up with creative solutions to meet system requirements. Many important components emerged in the financial sector due to a dynamic necessity. The current era's blend of sustainability and technology is significantly changing how advancement was previously perceived. Integrating sustainability into corporate processes can lead to sustainable development, which is currently the centre of interest (Ozili, 2022). In accordance with the Sustainable Development Goals, which are designed to address the problems affecting global networks, the term *"sustainability"* is becoming increasingly popular (Chungyalpa, 2021). Businesses are embracing sustainability due to the increasing need for environmentally sustainable goods and services (Rehman et al., 2021).

A firm must consider several inter-related factors in order to be considered sustainable and accountable to the economy. The demands of society for a solid economic position, social fairness and welfare and a clean and green environment can all be accomplished by using strategies and tactics that lead to the accomplishment of long-term goals (Migliorelli, 2021). Stated differently, the focus is on a developing system that shields the ecosystem from detrimental impacts. Businesses are concentrating on Environmental, Social and Governance (ESG) standards to ensure that social and environmental repercussions align (Chand & Kour, 2025; Kopnina, 2015).

The idea of ESG will offer a framework to help business fulfil their social responsibilities. Measuring the firm's financial and non-financial performance in a new paradigm in the finance industry. To project a positive image in the eyes of socially conscious investors and other stakeholders, it focusses on integrating Environmental, Social and Governance aspects into their business operations (Bergquist, 2017).

Adopting practices that have been shown to be environmentally friendly is what is meant by environmentally conscious. These practices' primary goal is to maximise energy efficiency and minimize the wastage of natural resources. This element actually aids a company in achieving its objectives despite changing environmental conditions (Li et al., 2021).

The company's efforts to safeguard the rights of consumers, employees and the general public make up its social aspect. It includes monitoring the company's diversity and inclusion programs, safety procedures and labour standards. It simply involves ensuring that a company properly fulfil its social obligations to various populations (Ruan & Liu, 2021).

The direction and management of a corporation are the main topics of ESG governance. This include assessing the efficacy of internal controls, executive compensation and the diversity and membership of the board. Transparent reporting and ethical business practices are fundamental to good governance, as are corporate approaches to anti-corruption initiatives and shareholder rights. Building confidence with stakeholders and guaranteeing accountability require sound governance methods. (Allman & Won, 2021).

Organizations bear the responsibility of ensuring sustainability in their operations while minimizing their impact on the environment and honouring their social obligations (Patowary, 2019). In order to achieve excellent execution both socially and economically, businesses are incorporating the three pillars of sustainability—Environmental, Social, and Governance (ESG) Factors (Wut et al., 2021)—into their operations. By meeting the demands of ethical customers and guaranteeing that corporate social duties are fulfilled, it is increasing the market value of the company (Zhou et al., 2022). (Lubowiecki-Vikuk et al., 2021).

By incorporating digitization into its operations, a company can achieve efficiency and efficacy in its business processes and contribute longevity (Rossato & Castellani, 2020). However, the endeavor must permit digitization to consider social and environmental worth in addition to economic value (Zhong et al., 2023). The ESG principles reflect society's perspective on current issues as well as opportunities, which businesses should consider and focus on developing their advanced capabilities because technological advancements are essential to society's progress (Barykin et al., 2023).

Modern digital technologies are integrated into classic ESG methodologies to create Digital ESG. This strategy enhances ESG performance and reporting by utilizing automation, smart technology and data analytics (Wang et al, 2023). It is necessary to integrate technology while fulfilling the obligatory requirements. It not only contributes to the achieving the accuracy, but it also helps in maintaining a good market picture in the eyes of the stakeholders. The digital revolution forces managers to become less narrow-minded, enhance their capacity for advancement, boost information transparency and improve their abilities to achieve the ESG goals (Jingyong et al., 2023). These goals will be a part of the long-lasting success of the firm.

1.1 Background

The contemporary global financial landscape is undergoing a profound transformation, driven by the convergent forces of sustainability imperatives and digital disruption. Since the 1990s, the Indian financial system, mirroring global trends, has evolved dynamically, giving rise to innovative solutions that address systemic requirements. The current era is defined by a powerful synergy between sustainability and technology, fundamentally reshaping traditional paradigms of corporate advancement. Within this context, the integration of Environmental, Social, and

Governance (ESG) principles has emerged as a critical framework for achieving sustainable development, moving from a peripheral concern to a central strategic priority for organizations worldwide. This shift is amplified by the United Nations Sustainable Development Goals (SDGs) and growing stakeholder demand for corporate accountability. However, the manual, legacy-based approaches to managing and reporting ESG performance are increasingly seen as inadequate—prone to inefficiencies, inaccuracies, and a lack of transparency. It is at this nexus of challenge and opportunity that Digital ESG (DESG) arises, representing a new paradigm that leverages advanced digital technologies to enhance the efficacy, reliability, and strategic value of ESG practices. This chapter, "Digital ESG in Action," systematically investigates this emerging domain, dissecting its components, evaluating its practical applications through case studies, and providing a critical, structured assessment of its potential through a comprehensive SWOT analysis to guide researchers, practitioners, and policymakers.

1.2 Benefits of the Research

This research offers multifaceted benefits for a diverse array of stakeholders by demystifying the Digital ESG landscape and providing actionable insights.

- **For Academics and Researchers:** The chapter provides a foundational conceptual framework for Digital ESG, clearly delineating its sub-components (Digital E, S, and G) and establishing a robust agenda for future empirical inquiry. The detailed SWOT analysis serves as a fertile ground for developing testable hypotheses and theoretical models.
- **For Business Leaders and Practitioners:** It delivers a pragmatic, evidence-based evaluation of the tangible strengths and operational opportunities offered by Digital ESG, such as automated reporting, real-time monitoring, and enhanced stakeholder engagement. Concurrently, it offers a clear-eyed view of implementation challenges, including cost, data security, and skill gaps, enabling informed strategic decision-making and risk mitigation.
- **For Policymakers and Regulators:** The analysis illuminates the enabling role that supportive policy, incentives, and standardized frameworks can play in accelerating the adoption of DESG. It highlights how digital tools can facilitate compliance with evolving ESG disclosure standards and help achieve national and international sustainability targets.
- **For Investors and Financial Analysts:** The research underscores how Digital ESG can enhance the quality, comparability, and reliability of non-financial data. This empowers more accurate assessments of a company's long-term

resilience, risk profile, and value-creation potential, leading to more sophisticated investment decisions.

1.3 Objectives of the Chapter

This study's primary objective is to evaluate the value and effectiveness of Digital ESG, since it is a new paradigm in sustainable and technical domain. Researchers, practitioners, businesses and policy makers can benefit from this research's in-depth Strengths, Weaknesses, Opportunities and Threats (SWOT) analysis of Digital ESG. Stakeholders can effectively navigate the complexities of Digital ESG and capitalise on its potential for long-term, positive outcomes by having full-fledged knowledge of these factors.

- To be acquainted with the ESG pillars of Sustainability.
- To explore the need of integration of technology to enhance ESG efficiency.
- To be acquainted with the bottlenecks associated with integration of Digital ESG
- To know the benefits of adopting Digital ESG into business functions.

2.0 RESEARCH METHODOLOGY

A combination of descriptive and exploratory research methods has been used to meet the study's goals. Secondary data has been utilized to gather the information mentioned in this study. The research is done in two steps. To know about the concept, a literature review done is the initial stage in the process. This involves compiling and assessing theoretical background related to the current phenomenon based on the national as well as international studies. The review includes articles that have been published, mostly in Scopus-indexed Journals. The second step involves doing a SWOT analysis to identify the threats, opportunities, vulnerabilities and strengths of Digital ESG mentioned in the previous studies. Some case studies were also included to provide a strong foundation to the need of Digital ESG for the overall development of the business. The proceedings of this paper explain the meaning and concept of Digital ESG, highlighting its features, advantages, difficulties and future potential.

3.0 REVIEW OF THE LITERATURE

The chapter is grounded in a synthesis of contemporary scholarly work that establishes the individual and interconnected relevance of sustainability, ESG, and digitalization. The review effectively charts the evolution from broad sustainability concepts (Ozili, 2022; Migliorelli, 2021) to the specific, actionable framework of ESG (Chand & Kour, 2025; Bergquist, 2017). It meticulously details the three pillars: the environmental dimension focused on resource efficiency and eco-friendly practices (Li et al., 2021); the social aspect concerning stakeholder rights and welfare (Ruan & Liu, 2021); and governance centered on transparency, accountability, and ethical management (Allman & Won, 2021).

Crucially, the review then integrates the digital transformation literature, citing scholars who posit that digital technologies are indispensable for modern business efficacy and longevity (Kraus et al., 2022; Rossato & Castellani, 2020). The core of the literature synthesis lies in its exploration of the intersection between these two domains. It draws upon research that identifies specific technological applications—such as AI for climate reporting (Macpherson et al., 2021), IoT for real-time environmental monitoring (Macpherson et al., 2021), and blockchain for supply chain transparency (Saxena et al., 2022)—as key enablers of superior ESG performance. This establishes a clear scholarly foundation for the concept of "Digital ESG" as a distinct and potent approach to corporate sustainability.

3.1 Theoretic Background and Theory Evolution

The theoretical underpinnings of this chapter reflect an evolution from established management theories to new, integrated frameworks suited to the digital age.

The initial theoretical base lies in Stakeholder Theory, which argues that firms must create value for all stakeholders, not just shareholders. Traditional ESG is a direct response to this theory, pushing companies to account for their impact on the environment, employees, communities, and society at large.

The chapter then illustrates a theoretical evolution towards Resource-Based View (RBV) and Dynamic Capabilities. Here, Digital ESG is framed not merely as a compliance exercise but as a source of competitive advantage. The digital tools and data analytics capabilities become valuable, rare, and inimitable resources that allow firms to dynamically adapt their ESG strategies, enhance operational efficiency, and build resilience.

The most advanced theoretical implication within the chapter points towards the emergence of Digital Sustainability Theory. This nascent framework suggests that digital technologies are not just tools *for* sustainability but are fundamentally reshaping its very practice. It proposes that the integration of technologies like AI and blockchain creates a new system where sustainability data is continuous, verifiable, and deeply integrated into strategic decision-making, thereby transforming ESG from a reporting function into a core, intelligent operational driver.

3.2 Concept of Digital ESG

Growing desire in a high-level, simple method of handling everyday chores is leading to the emergence of digital transformation (Kraus et al., 2022). Every business regardless of scale, nature or financial resources, should adopt an inventive, progressive and imaginative approach to carrying out its strategic plans (Horváth & Szabó, 2019). Earlier the traditional methods were followed to help an organization in the journey of achieving its goals and objectives, but with time and revolutionary changes, a dependence on technology for achieving businesses' objectives have been observed. Technologies not only bring a better way of working but also a kind of guarantee that the tasks have been well performed (Wu & Liu, 2023).

Whenever a business is ready to start its sustainable journey, the need of maintenance of certain records do arise like data management, data retrieval, data decoding and encoding (Bist, 2022). This can be handled very well by using ESG Data management softwares, which are specially designed for generating digital data that can utilized further for getting a good ESG score which is very much necessary for earning a good reputation (Vinuesa et al., 2020). Technology helps in advancing ESG efficiency and fulfilling environmental agendas, this creative transformation has already achieved great heights in the European countries. Numerous technologies can be used for the same like IoT, AI, Blockchain and many more to it.

Using artificial intelligence for companies to track their environmental and social footprint will solve all the important problems, society is dealing with (Saetra, 2021). AI is being used by the Task Force on Climate-Related Financial Disclosures (TCFD) to review the reports of various companies based on their ESG exposure to climate change related content in order to make financial decisions (Macpherson et al., 2021).

Digital ESG depend greatly on advanced technologies as they provide capabilities for monitoring and management in real-time. For instance, IoT connected devices can constantly track environmental factors like water use, waste generation and power usage (Macpherson et al., 2021). Continuous monitoring enables companies to rapidly pinpoint inefficiencies and areas in need of improvement. In the same way, blockchain technology can improve the traceability and transparency of supply chains, guaranteed that goods are obtained and manufactured according to the sustainable and ethical guidelines (Saxena et al., 2022).

It is important for the stakeholders to have updated, and accurate information related to businesses' activities. Since they are a part of it, they should be equally aware about the activities undertaken by firms during a financial year (Hussain et al., 2023). Responsible stakeholders should know about the social obligations fulfilled by the firm to maintain his/her interest (Zhang & Jin, 2022). Companies should communicate the necessary information about the ESG initiatives through social platforms, mobile apps and websites. These digital platforms will help the stakeholders to share their feedback to improve the strategies related to ESG integration. These will enhance the effectiveness of protecting the social and environmental agendas (Stuermer et al., 2016).

3.3 Digital E

Digital E refers to using digital tools, techniques and initiatives to satisfy the needs and requirements of the planet by giving a direction to companies towards sustainable future. It basically consists of the digital initiatives like Artificial Intelligence, Internet of things (IoT) and machine learning. These tools help the organizations in maintaining data required to process the green initiatives. The data being prepared is based on the environmental impact of business functions on different segments of the society (Wang et al., 2023). Blockchain technology could enhance transparency in supply chains by confirming the environmentally responsible sourcing and manufacturing of products (Sætra, 2021). Digital E allows companies to establish and monitor ambitious environmental objectives with enhanced precision and responsibility.

3.4 Digital S

Digital S refers to using digital technologies to improve social responsibility and impact in organizations (Sætra, 2022). This involves utilizing digital platforms to enhance workplace procedures and employee involvement. For instance, HR technology and online communication platforms can aid in fostering diverse and open employee relationships, backing remote work setups and guaranteeing equitable labour standards. Social media and feedback platforms help companies effectively connect with communities, handle concerns and endorse social initiatives. Moreover, digital tools can assist in monitoring diversity and inclusion metrics, giving data-based insights into workplace equity. Digital S uses Artificial Intelligence, machine learning and many other digital tools that helps to maintain the integrity of the business through identifying the insights of the social problems.

3.5 Digital G

Digital G - Governance is all about company's management in terms of their policies, procedures and standards. It is related with the ways followed by companies to rule and control itself and business operations (Peng et al., 2023). It consists of creating board of directors' team to manage, corporate integrity and transparency, procedures related to allotment of shares, or division of duties and responsibility to the management team, policies related to shareholders as well as other stakeholders, all these come sunder corporate governance. The basic principles followed by the companies to do proper governance is integrity, transparency, equity, accountability, responsibility and managing businesses risks and uncertainties (Su et al., 2023).

If these principles are merged with technology, then the outcomes will be greatly beneficial for the companies. And Digital G takes care of this aspect. Under it, various digital tools are used to maintain the corporate integrity and transparency. The governance activities discussed above can be effectively maintained with the help of digital platforms, resulting in gaining trusts of the shareholders as, technological tools are related with accountability and reliability. These will be able to maintain the stakeholder engaged with the business for a longer time. ESG reporting is very much important for the stakeholders which can be properly done with the help of digital tools either blockchain, artificial intelligence or machine learning. The combination of all can also be used to maintain the standards and procedures and can ensure integrity in the ESG disclosures as well.

3.6 Need of Digital ESG

Sustainable Development Goals, 2030 is the new outlook, forms are looking upon to fulfil the needs and requirements of the responsible stakeholders viz consumers, suppliers, partners, investors, board of management etc. Modern technologies are having an impact on how different products and processes are created and marketed, as well as how ESG is applied to attain sustainability size (Cricelli and Strazzullo, 2021).

Forbes Middle East claims that by using digital technologies like cloud computing, the Internet of Things (IoT), robotics, drones, and more, waste and carbon-intensive methods can be reduced. With the assistance of General Electric (GE), a company that perfectly combines digitisation with ESG, GE's digital wind farms have been able to produce an increasing amount of green energy. To put it briefly, digital ESG will assist companies in preserving the following elements:

a) Determining the locations where eco-friendly methods might be applied to enhance sustainability

b) Real-time monitoring of resource conservation and energy use (Cricelli & Strazzullo, 2021).
c) Upholding corporate governance, ethical norms, accountability, transparency, and responsible supplier chains.
d) Business efficiency is increased by automating data collecting and ESG reporting processes.
e) Using AI and IoT to improve operational efficiency (Kwiliński et al., 2023).

Without a doubt, an appropriate framework will help the organisations use DESG to accomplish their sustainable agendas (DQ Institute White Paper, 2023). Depending on the size, goal, and funding of the company, this structure may change.

3.7 Case Studies

The following examples were mentioned in the Sustainability reports of their respective firms and treated as a significant part of the study to justify the integration of Digital ESG in real-world context.

3.7.1 Tata Consultancy Services (TCS) and Digital Sustainability

Through the development of skills, TCSs' Digital ESG policies have improved social outcomes, reduced energy uses significantly and increased governance transparency. To monitor and lessen their carbon footprint, they have implemented IoT technology and advanced data analytics. By optimizing energy consumption in its office and data centres, the corporate leverages these technologies to move closer to its carbon-neutrally objective. To close the digital divide, they are implementing digital initiatives including and digital skills training courses. These initiatives aim to improve peoples' skills and advanced digital literacy in marginalized areas.

3.7.2. HDFC Bank and Digital Financial Inclusion

Through Digital Banking, HDFC Banks' activities have decreased environmental impact, reinforced governance procedures and increased financial assistance to millions of marginalized individuals (ESG Policy Framework, 2020). By digital banking options, they have lessened the needs of customers to visit physical branches, which lowers the company's carbon footprint. The bank also encourages e-statements and paperless transactions. The bank's initiatives for digital financial inclusion include digital literacy campaigns and mobile banking apps targeted at underprivileged and rural communities. These programs make banking services and financial literacy accessible. It improves risk management and compliance by leveraging digital platforms.

3.7.3 Mahindra Group and Digital Sustainability Initiatives

Digital technologies are used by Mahindra's *"Mahindra Electric"* program to create and market electric cars (EVs). Additionally, the businesses use digital tools to track and control the environmental impact of all its operations. The "Rise for Good" initiative by Mahindra uses digital platforms to promote social impact initiatives in the areas of health, education and rural development. The platform links stakeholders and volunteers to a range of social projects. To ensure compliance with legal requirements and ethical standards, they utilize digital governance tools (Mahindra Sustainability Report, n.d). Transparency and accountability are improved through the use of digital reporting platforms and data analytics.

3.7.4 Infosys and Digital Governance

Infosys uses advanced digital tools for corporate governance including data analytics and AI for monitoring compliance, risk management and reporting. Blockchain technology is also used for secure and transparent transactions. Infosys has implemented a comprehensive digital strategy to reduce its environmental impact, including the use of smart building technologies to manage energy consumption and optimize resource use. The company's digital initiatives include online training programs and skill development workshops aimed at enhancing employee capabilities and supporting community development.

3.8 GenAI Enabled ESG Digital Platform

A special focus on the mentioned electronic platform is required to understand the requirements, suitability and applicability of such mediums to implement Digital ESG into company's operations and functions. Gen AI Enabled ESG Digital Platform is a part of the Sustainable and Digital Initiatives reported in the EY'S sustainability report.

A Gen-AI enabled Digital ESG Platform uses artificial intelligence to streamline and enhance corporate ESG processes. By integrating the collection and processing of ESG related data from several sources automatically, it permits real-time monitoring of parameters that assist proactive risk management. Users are assisted in adhering to regulatory framework such as EUs SFDR, SASB and GRI by means of customised reporting tools. With the use of predictive analytics, the project platforms future ESG risks and opportunities, empowering companies to make wise strategic decisions.

Additionally, it provides mechanisms for involving stakeholders to enhance transparency and communication while encouraging feedback. There are certain digital platforms that can help the organization in achieving their sustainability objectives, helps to identify the opportunities, keep a track record of anti-environmental activities and maintaining the prosperity of the business. These platforms enforce adherence to norms and practices and provide fresh perspectives on how to run its operations.

One of the ESG digital platform provided to companies all over the world is introduced by the Ernst & Young (EY) Company, named EY ESG Compass. EY offers EY ESG Compass, a proper digital tool that organizations can use to help and guide them on their sustainable journey. Global professional service provider, Ernst & Young (EY) provides a range of services including assurance, tax and consulting. Modern technology designed for the companies with a strong commitment to ESG or sustainable practices have been produced by it. EY has also acknowledged companies that are actively working toward the Sustainable Development Goals (SDGs).

EY ESG Compass is a digital tool that the company developed to evaluate the ESG maturity levels and apply analytics to modify a sector specific strategy. The Task Force on Climate Related Financial Disclosure (TCFD), the Global Reporting Initiative (GRI), the Sustainability Accounting Standards Board (SASB) and Business Responsibility and Sustainability Reporting (BRSR) are just a few reporting standards that EY ESG Compass conforms to.

The EY ESG Compass tool is a one-stop shop that offers self-service analytics, a global repository of ESG sector information, and the following services (EY ESG Compass - Innovation to Transform Sustainability Journey, 2024):

3.8.1 Sectoral Benchmarking

Simply said, benchmarking is a technique for evaluating how well and efficiently businesses are performing. Drawing comparisons between the top and bottom performers in the financial industry is helpful. It also aids in offering potential solutions for enhancing subpar performance (Walker et al., 2022). Sectoral approaches aid in assessing an initiative's impact in order to establish a robust connection between an organization's operations and several sectors. It is a method of employing sector-specific policies and strategies to solve specific difficulties that arise in that industry (Fujjiwara et al., 2010).

In order to give a glimpse of the performance of the sectors peers as well as a scientific evaluation of sustainability indicators, the EY BRSR database generates benchmarks and analytics models (Partner, 2023).

3.8.2 Ratings and Insights

Investors, customers, management, the government, suppliers, and other stakeholders in the business are all given information about the company and its place in the sustainable market via ESG ratings (Larcker et al., 2022). Although they are still severely underutilized in the sustainable finance sector, Tech-driven alternative ESG ratings are becoming more and more significant (Hughes et al., 2021).

EY ESG Compass has examined around 1200 Key Performance Indicators (KPIs) and studied 1000 Indian companies in over 20 sectors to gain a comprehensive understanding of the companies' sustainable developments and to support their expansion.

3.8.3 Emissions measurement

Emissions must be measured to comprehend the concepts of limiting actions that might negatively impact the environment (Rao & Baer, 2012). A range of measurement techniques can be applied to lessen the impact of emissions.

Depending on the organization, different types of measurement techniques are employed (Giechaskiel et al., 2018). These measurement techniques can be further used to keep a track record of emissions daily. One of the popular measurement techniques is PEMS.

With the help of EY ESG Compass, companies may track emissions and evaluate how they perform in comparison with other companies. EY ESG Compass provides necessary assistance to the companies to ascertain their carbon emissions.

3.8.4 Monitoring for Scope 1, 2 and 3

When it comes to emissions, it is important to know the levels at which they can have a negative impact on the environments. For this purpose, EY ESG Compass have introduced the concept of Scope 1, Scope 2 and Scope 3. The emissions will be judged on the basis of these three scopes, in order to minimise its effects with a suitable solution. The following helps to understand the scope categories:

- Direct Emissions
- Indirect Emissions from Purchased Machinery
- Indirect Emissions from Value-Chain Activities.

a) Climate Risk and Analytics

EY ESG Compass main aim is to help organizations in order to understand and manage their ESG risks, particularly related with climate change risks. Their Climate

Risk and Analytics Strategy most likely include methods and tools for assessing the impact of climate on business operations and financial performance.

Climate risk is associated with the effects of climate change on the operations of the business (Hassani et al., 2019). Climate change refers to an increase or long-term shifts in the temperatures and weather patterns which can have either direct or indirect impact on the business projects. It is usually triggered by the emission of Greenhouse Gases (GHG) as result of human activities.

b) Decarbonization Strategy

We all are very aware with the fact that nature is being exploited year by year as a result of infrastructure development. Covid 19 started its effect from the year 2020 but before that, the ecosystem was already at its pace of being harmed due to some human made activities like industrialization, deforestation, global warming etc (Rodríguez Diez et al., 2023). The solution for the same were also integrated to minimise the harm. One of the solutions or strategies is Decarbonization strategy. It is the process to minimise or eliminate human made carbon-dioxide emissions from the businesses' functions.

Net zero is also one of the strategies being used to reduce the harmful effects of greenhouse gases on the environment (Lau & Tsai, 2023). It is an initiative that tries to maintain a balance between the greenhouse gases that were produced and emitted in the nature, and the amount removed from the atmosphere.

EY ESG Compass provides necessary assistance to the companies who are ready to initiate the strategy of Decarbonization and Net Zero.

c) Sustainable nature of Supply Chain

Supply chain management is the process of managing the flow of goods, information or any other financial necessities from the place of its origin to the place of its consumption (Saeed & Kersten, 2019). It is a very important aspect and when it is blended with sustainability concept, it becomes more significant (Sánchez-Flores et al., 2020).

The strategy that aims to fulfil the objectives of supply chain without harming the nature and incorporating eco-friendly practices or responsible practices is termed as Sustainable Supply Chain Management.

EY ESG Compass provides advisory services to integrate sustainable supply chain management in the companies' operations or sustainable projects related to Environment, Social and Governance (ESG).

d) ESG Regulation Monitoring

ESG regulations and framework are a kind of standards set by the government, creating an obligation for the companies to disclose the information regarding the risks and achievements associated with the ESG and other sustainable practices (Janicka & Sajnóg, 2022). This information is very much important for the stakeholders.

These regulations help companies to compare their ESG performance with the standards or benchmarks set as a guideline for them (Faccia et al., 2021). EY ESG Compass helps companies in understanding these benchmarks or standards or regulations as a guide to the way of achievement of sustainable goals and objectives.

The EY ESG Compass helps companies lay a strong basis for growth in the future. It provides the essential characteristics listed below:

a) Data Management

ESG Data management is the process of gathering, analysing and processing information about how company affects ESG. The information how a company affects ESG. The information provided can be used by stakeholders, including investors and customers to learn more about the sustainability performance of the business. The government benefits from it as well since it helps in creating a greener economy (Lee et al., 2022).

Companies must therefore increase the transparency of their ESG Disclosures. They should make their ESG performance data available to all the stakeholders so that they can make required decisions related to their investment in the company (Jonsdottir et al., 2022).

Adopting sustainable practices is facilitated by the use of data management platforms, which assist organizations in recognizing and addressing their inadequacies (AYDOĞMUŞ et al., 2022).

b) ESG Data Model

ESG, one of the pillars of sustainable finance, is linked to the business's sustainability. ESG data is simply information that companies disclose about their governance, social, and environmental initiatives. To evaluate the company's sustainable performance, these data are examined using ESG metrics. Using a model that is tailored to the needs and requirements of the companies can boost the transparency and accountability in ESG data (Cruz & Matos, 2023). These days, technology is used to preserve ESG data and accomplish the objectives of its preparation. Companies provide ESG data to rating organisations, which is the basis for evaluating ESG performances. These ratings are crucial for establishing a positive reputation in the marketplace.

c) Master Data Setup

To properly track and report on metrics, there are a few essential stages involved in setting up ESG (Environmental, Social, and Governance) master data. Establish pertinent ESG criteria first by determining important KPIs and talking to stakeholders to learn about their goals. After that, concentrate on gathering data by identifying both internal and external sources and making sure they are integrated into a single system. To ensure data accuracy, provide a governance architecture with roles for quality control and data management.

d) Approval Management

To improve the firm's functioning skills and bring consistency and smoothness, board approval is required. To determine whether or not the initiatives are worthy of being introduced, the approval of multiple boards, including the TCFD, SASB, and others, is necessary when it comes to Digital ESG.

e) Analytical Dashboard

EY ESG Compass tool helps in maintaining a dashboard where all of a company's ESG data and ratings are displayed so that their performance can be evaluated and people can see which companies received the highest and lowest rankings. To improve their business performance, the lowest-ranked enterprises will receive some advice services; only then can the ESG performance be improved. This dashboard aids in the analysis of all the data that the businesses have supplied in order to evaluate their sustainable goals.

3.9 SWOT Analysis Results

3.9.1 Strengths of Digital ESG (DESG)

Digital ESG excels in boosting efficiency with automation, enhancing data accuracy and transparency, providing scalability and flexibility, enabling improved stakeholder engagement and offering advanced risk management capabilities. These combined strengths enhance ESG practices for organizations to reach sustainability and governance goals in the modern business landscape (Sang et al., 2024).

Digital ESG's capacity to improve efficiency is a major advantage, thanks to its automation capabilities. Digital technologies simplify the necessary work like ESG reporting and compliance procedures, cutting down on a manual work and time needed to gather information. Automated systems can handle large amounts of data from different sources, guaranteeing precisions and currentness of ESG reports (Aleksy Kwilinski et al., 2023). Digital ESG uses an automated system to provide advantages in the ESG reporting process like fast delivery, less mistakes, accountability and transparency. It helps to keep a real-time and continuous record about the ESG scores and metrics provided by the rating agencies like Morgan Stanley Capital International (MSCII), Credit Rating Information Services of India Limited (CRISIL) etc (Puriwat & Tripopsakul, 2022).

ESG information is the one that is generated to communicate it with the stakeholders, who have shown their interest in being a part of the firm either financially or non-financially. These information needs to be well updated, and AI have the capability to do so. With the help of digital technologies, a business involved in carbon emissions can keep a record of the percentage of emissions on a daily basis. These daily records are presented in a report format to the top-level management with the help of technologies only because of the feature of convenience. Thus, Digital ESG will be able to provide a better and convenient way, an organization can work with (Sarpong et al., 2023). The feature of adaptability and flexibility of it can provide great advantages to the firm irrespective of its nature, size, turnover, credibility and sector it belongs to. Though there are certain drawbacks as well but it can be tackled easily with the help of digital tools (Chen, 2024).

The applicability of digital tools is based on the needs and requirements of the firm. It can be also used to build a cordial relationship with the respective stakeholders, an important part of the organization. For example, electronic platforms can be utilized for conducting surveys or organizing webinars that can be proved successful in engaging stakeholders in conversations with ESG performance and objective. ESG disclosures can be therefore improved with the help of digital technologies ensuring great accountability. This bidirectional communication promotes increased transparency and cooperation leading to stronger and more adaptable ESG strategies.

Advanced features for risk management are offered by Digital ESG tools. The use of predictive analysis and big data tool can assist organization in predicting ESG related risks before they manifest. One instance when risk assessment tools use environmental data to forecast possible regulatory violations or disruptions in the supply chain and its management (Huang et al., 2023). This proactive strategy for risk management allows companies or an organization to put in place preventive measures and reduce potential impacts with greater efficiency. Also, digital technologies have the capability to improve adherence monitoring through the use of instant notifications and monitoring systems that guarantee compliance with ESG regulations and standards.

3.9.2 Weaknesses of Digital ESG (DESG)

Digital ESG is a new paradigm in the sustainable and financial world, therefore its yet not incorporated in the businesses all over the world. It does have a wider scope but it is not possible for all the companies around the world to implement it to a greater extent (Zhong et al., 2023). The companies' policies, procedures, benchmarks, market capitalisation, funds and nature do have a significant relationship with the adaptability of Digital ESG. These factors classify companies into two different parts:

- Companies able to implement Digital ESG.
- Companies unable to implement Digital ESG.

The reason for not implementing the Digital ESG initiative is mainly related to the data security and privacy (Hartley et al., 2024). We all are aware that the usage of digital technologies can lead to data piracy or hacking. Companies are obligated to maintain ESG data for the benefit of the stakeholders, but its piracy can have a negative influence on the market image too. The competitors will be very much keen to stole or manipulate the information by using the advanced technologies. So, it will be difficult for the companies to protect their work from the adverse effects of digital technologies. Another weakness is related to the cost incurred for implementing Digital ESG in the business functions. Small caps companies, Micro, Small and Medium Enterprises (MSMEs), Small and Medium Enterprises (SMEs) and Small Caps Companies are not able to use Digital ESG as it demands huge capital investments from the stage of its introduction to the reporting. It requires huge funds to complete the process which cannot be afforded by all. It is also not possible for all the companies to integrate Digital ESG into their business operations as it consists of certain difficulties and complexities which can be rectified only by the knowledgeable, experience and skilled staff (Lobschat et al., 2019). There is also a need of timely updating of technologies being used for the ESG related operations, delay in which can lead to inconsistent or insufficient data (Sergey Barykin et al., 2023). There is also a possibility that the failures of technology can have a deep impact on the process as Digital ESG relies on technologies only, like Artificial Intelligence, Machine Learning, blockchain technology and IoT. The adverse effects of technologies can slow down the process or sometimes does not give accurate results.

Technology has helped the humankind from the day of its introduction till now and from a simple task to a complicated one. It has resulted in in too much dependence on it. Now, everyone is depended on their mobile phones for every second. Same is the issue with Digital ESG. It is also fully dependent on technologies because of which the personal touch is missing. Too much reliance on technologies may lead to a narrower scope also. Sometimes, the organizations only start focussing on the quantitative factors instead of qualitative factors. The poor-quality data can have a negative impact on the image of the business in the eyes of the beholders. The poor quality can be caused by the omission of data as well, since technology cannot be fully trusted upon. There are certain Digital ESG solutions that offer very less flexibility leading to a complication associated with digital technologies. The organizations' nature and capabilities decide which technology is best suited to enhance their performance and can satisfy the needs and requirements of the company (Julia et al., n.d.). There are many organizations who have focussed more on the Environmental pillar and have ignored the social and governance pillar. There are certain companies who have introduced certain methods and techniques to reduce carbon emissions but because of this they might have ignored the social obligations. It is important to focus on all the three pillars of ESG equally then only the results can be satisfactory. As discussed earlier, that Digital ESG process starts from its introduction to reporting, there are high chances of wrong assessments or forge reports.

These weaknesses can be overcome by ensuring proper care while selecting and utilizing a suitable, flexible and adaptable digital technology for enhancing the performance of ESG practices to achieve the sustainable objectives of the business.

3.9.3 Opportunities related to Digital ESG (DESG)

The opportunities associated with Digital ESG integration is the motivating factor for all the organizations. Though, there are certain drawbacks and high amount of risk is involved with its integration, but its wider scope cannot be ignored (Saxena et al., 2022). The use of digital technologies and leading in an advanced world is the first and foremost important factor associated with Digital ESG. It is a new trend demanding promotion of sustainability and human well-being. It will help the company to understand their ESG practices and compare it with the outcomes. The technologies will help to revolutionise the ESG performance of the companies from the starting to the end of the process. The digital technologies blended with ESG practices will help the companies to forecast the possibilities of getting success or failure as technologies will continuously monitor the weather conditions, environmental impact and climate change on the real-time basis (Hernandez et al., 2023).

Digital technologies like blockchain or machine learning helps to maintain the ESG data based on the internal and external factors of the companies as discussed above. The credibility and transparency of the ESG data is very well maintained by the advanced technologies (Chen et al., 2024). Government is trying to introduce new laws and policies to motivate companies to explore the world of Digital ESG for performance enhancement. Regulatory agencies are implementing firm ESG reporting standards and certain rewards for achievement of sustainable objectives.

Like ESG funds, government is also going to provide funds required for the implementation of eco-friendly technologies to comply with the requirements of Digital ESG. Certain tax incentives will also be provided to the businesses to encourage them for integrating Digital ESG into their business operations. Digital ESG opens certain digital platforms for the businesses with the use of which they can communicate with their respective stakeholders who have a direct impact on the working of the business (Wu & Li, 2023). The digital platforms consist of social media, dashboards, AI robotics etc that are available 24/7 for addressing the issues of the stakeholders. Timely and continuous interaction will result in good potential investment. Digital ESG can also help by aiding services to the companies, so that they can analyse the ESG metrics reports and communicate the same with the investors. ESG metrics reports is a report published by certain rating agencies like MSCI, CRISIL etc to judge the ESG performance of ESG integrated companies. These reports boost the confidence of the investors and helps them to take a wise investment decision to enhance their portfolio. Usage of digital technologies can also lead to introduction of certain projects to provide variety of products and services to the stakeholders in order to keep them engaged for a longer period. Digital technologies will keep a real-time record of the activities being initiated for the accomplishment of the ESG standards. It will help to improve the goodwill of the business and to achieve a good place in the competitive market.

Digital ESG solutions do provide a competitive edge to the business in the outer world but the inner management is also enhanced with the proper use of Digital ESG. To compliance with the needs and requirements of Digital ESG, organizations do start focussing on their operational efficiency, costs incurred in various activities, less wastage of resources and optimization of the process. This will help to improve the financial well-being of the company leading to financial well-being of the country (Mulligan et al., 2023). The usage of advanced analytics will surely help to boost the performance of the business in every aspect. There is other sustainability initiatives associated with Digital ESG that will help to fulfil the need of exploring the finance world. It will also help the business to set and fulfil certain international benchmarks too. The benefits of the global market can also be enjoyed by the Digital ESG integrated businesses (Aleksy Kwilinski et al., 2024). It will also improve the business's bottom line and Return on Investment.

A track of environmental impact of activities can surely help to minimis ethe nature harming activities or functions of the business. The knowledge and skills gained in learning this new paradigm will surely help the management of the business to explore, participate and initiate some innovative ways to enjoy a good ESG performance by themselves. For example, Deloitte company explored the digital tolls and solutions to step up in the journey to scale digital actions that have not only improve its overall performance but also provides the benefits related to a good market position and value.

3.9.4 Threats associated with Digital ESG (DESG)

The weaknesses of Digital ESG have already been discussed but those limitations are not closely related to the unfavourable situation a business might face because of the integration of Digital ESG into the business operations. These unfavourable situations are mostly related to the external factors having a direct or indirect link with the working capabilities of the business. This is the last stage of the SWOT analysis which act as a decider in taking a final decision related to the acceptance or rejection of the initiatives. The first and foremost threat is related to the cyber-security issues (Balboni & Kate Elizabeth Francis, 2024).

Cybersecurity threats are related to a confidential data and its vulnerable position. A company's confidential data works as a plus point for competitors which encourage them to be a part of certain malpractices because of which the possibility of theft or data breaches and insider trading arises. Since, Digital ESG is full dependent on digital technologies and solutions, there is a high possibility that the ESG data can get hacked. These cyberattacks can have major impact on the working of the business. It can be caused mainly due to illegimate exposure to the ESG data and information by the unauthorized party (Balboni & Kate Francis, 2024). Data privacy and security is one of the main concerns. Business do reveal their data to the general public but only the required ones. Cyberattacks have the capability to have a negative impact on the necessary information that are not meant for disclosure. Data privacy needs to be maintained to comply with the rules and regulations of the companies. The regulatory environment also keeps on changing. Earlier, Corporate Social Responsibility (CSR) was considered as an obligation as per government's rule, but now the focus has been shifted to the ESG projects. CSR was only related with the social welfare, but ESG takes care of all the three parts that is, Environmental, Social and Governance. So, now companies need to integrate ESG into their operative functions. Likewise, the evolving demands and trends may endanger Digital ESG projects too soon (L. Chen et al., 2023). An improvement in the infrastructural facilities is also needed to support the Digital ESG process otherwise it can create a problem in the future. It is a time-consuming and costly process that can pose a threat of eliminating it from the view only. Another reason of threat is related to the outdatedness of the technology. It is a known fact that technology has been upgraded a lot from the date of its introduction till now based on the needs and requirements. Right now, Artificial Intelligence is ruling the world but there is a possibility of introduction of some other digital solutions and advanced technologies or an upgradation in the existing one. This can cause a threat to the current digital solutions because there are certain companies whose credibility and financial soundness is restricting them to spend more money on the upgradation or replacements (Martín & Sánchez-Ortiz,

2023). Technology malfunctions like system failure or any other technical issues can also cause a problem in proper integration of Digital ESG.

ESG data management on a large scale can also be challenging and the efforts to handle that can have a direct or indirect impact on the quality of Digital ESG. There is a need to prepare and maintain ESG report at the end of financial year stating the nature and objective of all the ESG activities. Instead of using traditional approaches for the same, businesses will use digital tools like ESG reporting software that can put a lot of pressure on the budget of the company. To protect the business from such hindrance can lead to establishment of robust data management protocols and certain potential issues related to the compliance with the code of conduct. Too much reliance on digital tools can become a cause of unemployment too. Earlier, record maintenance and processing were a result of manpower but since technology is providing all those benefits, companies are fully dependent on technology for transparency, accountability, accuracy and reliability. The automated systems have replaced the need of training the workers and employees. And, since personal touch is missing, stakeholders can also oppose the implementation of Digital ESG procedures.

The last but not the least threat is related to the unethical and biased behaviours. There is a need to continuous monitor and verify the data in order to reduce the unethical ways and biasness, then only the accountability can be given by the management in ESG reporting and disclosures. So, it is important for the businesses to understand the scope of the new phenomenon on the basis of SWOT analysis.

4.0 ANALYSIS AND DISCUSSIONS

The following tabular presentation will guide to the integral part of the study to develop an understanding:

Table 1.

Basis	Positive	Negative
Data Collection	The real-time data collection is possible in less time. The complexities are well managed leading to an effective sustainable outcome.	This process is fully-dependent on the technological process, lacking personal touch. Manipulation in data collection can be done by the hackers.
Data Reporting	Automate data generation leads to accurate and efficient ESG reporting. Communicating with the stakeholders are possible with the help of advanced technologies, social and digital platforms.	Poor quality data generation can cause a concern at the time of reporting. Piracy of the data reporting is possible.
Legacy System	Advanced technologies have a positive impact on ESG solutions. Implementing latest technology gives an edge in a competitive world.	Outdated technology leads to inefficiencies. Increased risk of data inconsistency is possible.
Investment	A one-time investment can lead to a good outcome resulting in a good market position.	Huge investment is required that is not possible for a small capital company to afford.
Awareness	This phenomenon is in its starting stage, helping companies to lead the world.	Expertise and awareness have not yet covered every sector of the country.
Risks and compliance	Government is motivating the companies to integrate such initiatives by introducing certain ESG regulations.	There is a possibility of uncertainty regarding compliance with the legal system. There is lot of risks involved with this initiative because of lack of expertise.

The above points represent a gist to the positive and negative impact of Digital ESG integration. It is important to represent the above points in a SWOT Analysis Table for a deeper understanding and critical evaluation:

Table 2. SWOT Analysis

Internal Factors	External Factors
Strengths • It results in data enhancement during collection and reporting stage. • Time saving and real-time monitoring. • Prevent wastage of resources. • Accurate and reliable results. • Transparency in ESG performance is achieved. • Keep a consistent record of ESG metrics and scores. • Helps in measuring and reducing carbon emissions. • Ensures a continuous stakeholder engagement	**Opportunities** • Satisfying the ongoing demands of the stakeholders especially responsible investors. • ESG funds and certain government incentives to motivate the companies. • Provides a competitive edge. • Achievement of SDGs. • Introduction of green technologies to expand the business.
Weaknesses • It requires huge amount of capital. • Expertise required • Unemployment • Data privacy and security issues • Continuous updating of technology is required. • Less flexible. • Possibility of maintenance of poor-quality data.	**Threats** • Risks and Uncertainties • Data inconsistency • Evolving demands and preferences • Legal Regulations • Chances of starting unethical practices.

As it can be seen in the above table, that the focus on strengths while integrating Digital ESG into business solutions can help the companies to expand and diversify. The weaknesses can be minimised with the help of proper code of conduct, strategies and progressive decisions. Thus, if the stakeholders including government and management encourage this initiative, then the outcomes will lead to company's goals achievement and country's economic development.

5.0 CONCLUSION

Organizations worldwide now consider sustainability to be essential, mostly due to the compelling need to address social injustice, environmental concern and governance issues. The importance of incorporating sustainability into fundamental business strategy is becoming increasingly apparent and Digital ESG tools play an important role in this regard. Organizations can track, manage and report on their sustainability activities efficiently and openly, thanks to Digital ESG. In other words, the usage of digital technologies will help the companies in maintaining data transparency, integrity, accountability, reliability and accuracy. Companies can make use of these tools from the stage of monitoring anti-environmental and environmental-friendly practices to the stage of ESG reporting. There are certain ESG Reporting software being used to provide convenience to the process of reporting at the end of financial year.

Though it has many advantages and a wider scope, but like any other innovation, it is also not free from any kind of complexities especially the one's associated with the use of digital tools incorporation. It does maintain ESG Data accurately but there are high chances of the misuse of it too. SMEs or MSMEs are not able to incorporate it into their business practices because of lack of capital. A real cause of concern here is that there are certain companies who will be not able to utilize it properly because of lack of knowledge and skills. These drawbacks can be tackled with the proper implementation of certain strategies or methods to reduce its effect. These should not come in the way of implementing Digital ESG. It should be implemented in every business to serve the real-time requirements and to improve the businesses' overall resilience.

By using digital technologies, organisations may accelerate their sustainability processes, enhance their ESG performance and ultimately helps in creating a more sustainable future. In addition to promoting stakeholder involvement and regulatory compliance, the integration of Digital ESG fosters organisational innovation and growth in line with global sustainability objectives.

5.1 Future Research Directions

Based on the analysis presented, several critical avenues for future research emerge:

- **Quantitative Validation:** Empirical studies are needed to quantitatively measure the causal relationship between Digital ESG adoption and specific financial and non-financial performance metrics (e.g., ROI, cost of capital, brand equity).
- **SME-Specific Frameworks:** Investigating scalable, cost-effective Digital ESG models tailored to the resource constraints of Small and Medium-sized Enterprises (SMEs) is a pressing need.
- **Behavioral and Cultural Studies:** Research into the organizational change management, leadership, and cultural shifts required to successfully implement Digital ESG strategies would be highly valuable.
- **Standardization and Interoperability:** Exploring the development of universal data standards and protocols to ensure interoperability between different Digital ESG platforms and reporting frameworks is a crucial technical and regulatory challenge.

- **Ethical AI and Algorithmic Governance:** As AI plays a larger role in DESG, research into mitigating algorithmic bias in social scoring and ensuring the ethical use of AI in governance is imperative.

CHAPTER SUMMARY

- **Core Concept:** The chapter establishes Digital ESG (DESG) as an emergent paradigm that integrates advanced digital technologies (AI, IoT, Blockchain, Data Analytics) with traditional ESG frameworks to enhance the measurement, management, and reporting of sustainability performance.
- **Structural Analysis:** It deconstructs DESG into its constituent parts—Digital E (environmental monitoring), Digital S (stakeholder engagement and social impact), and Digital G (transparent and efficient governance)—providing conceptual clarity.
- **Empirical Grounding:** Real-world validity is demonstrated through illustrative case studies of leading Indian corporations (e.g., TCS, HDFC Bank, Infosys), showcasing practical applications and tangible benefits.
- **Strategic Tool:** A detailed, in-depth SWOT analysis forms the analytical core of the chapter, systematically cataloging the internal Strengths (efficiency, accuracy, transparency) and Weaknesses (cost, security, expertise) of DESG, alongside the external Opportunities (regulatory incentives, competitive advantage) and Threats (cybersecurity, evolving regulations).
- **Practical Implementation:** The examination of a GenAI-enabled platform (EY ESG Compass) illustrates the functional capabilities of commercial Digital ESG solutions, from data management and emissions tracking to sectoral benchmarking and regulatory monitoring.
- **Conclusion:** The chapter concludes that while implementation challenges exist, the transformative potential of Digital ESG for driving authentic sustainability, building stakeholder trust, and ensuring long-term corporate resilience is profound and warrants strategic investment and further scholarly investigation.

CHAPTER QUESTIONS

These questions are designed to test and deepen your understanding of the chapter, progressing from foundational knowledge to advanced research conceptualization.

True or False Questions (1-10)

1. The integration of Digital ESG is primarily a reactive strategy for regulatory compliance rather than a proactive driver of strategic value.
2. A core strength of Digital ESG is its ability to automate data collection and enhance the accuracy of ESG reporting.
3. The "Digital S" component of Digital ESG focuses exclusively on external community engagement through social media.
4. The high capital investment required for Digital ESG implementation poses a significant barrier, particularly for large, multinational corporations.
5. Blockchain technology's primary application in Digital ESG is to enhance the transparency and traceability of supply chains.
6. The SWOT analysis in the chapter identifies data security and privacy as an external threat rather than an internal weakness.
7. Case studies of Indian firms like Infosys and TCS demonstrate that Digital ESG applications are limited to environmental monitoring only.
8. The EY ESG Compass platform is presented as a tool that can assist with sectoral benchmarking and monitoring Scope 1, 2, and 3 emissions.
9. A key opportunity presented by Digital ESG is its potential to provide a competitive edge and improve a company's bottom line.
10. The chapter concludes that the complexities and weaknesses of Digital ESG outweigh its potential benefits, making widespread adoption unfeasible.

Multiple Choice Questions (11-20)

11. According to the chapter's theoretical background, which theory frames Digital ESG not as a compliance exercise but as a source of competitive advantage by viewing digital tools as valuable, rare resources?
    A) Stakeholder Theory
    B) Institutional Theory
    C) Resource-Based View (RBV)
    D) Legitimacy Theory
    E) Signaling Theory
12. The "Digital G" pillar of Digital ESG is primarily concerned with:
    A) Optimizing energy consumption in data centers.
    B) Using AI for real-time tracking of water usage.
    C) Leveraging digital platforms for transparent corporate governance and secure reporting.
    D) Conducting digital literacy campaigns in rural communities.
    E) Marketing eco-friendly products online.

13. Which of the following is identified as a significant *weakness* of Digital ESG?
    A) Enhanced stakeholder engagement through digital platforms.
    B) The risk of creating unemployment due to automation.
    C) The ability to provide a competitive edge in the market.
    D) Government incentives for adopting green technologies.
    E) Improved predictive analytics for risk management.
14. In the HDFC Bank case study, how did digital banking primarily contribute to the environmental ("E") aspect of its Digital ESG strategy?
    A) By using blockchain for all financial transactions.
    B) By reducing the carbon footprint associated with customers visiting physical branches.
    C) By installing IoT sensors in its ATMs to monitor energy use.
    D) By launching a new line of green investment funds.
    E) By powering all branches with renewable energy.
15. The GenAI-enabled ESG platform discussed (EY ESG Compass) assists with all the following EXCEPT:
    A) Sectoral benchmarking of sustainability performance.
    B) Real-time monitoring of ESG parameters.
    C) Directly funding a company's decarbonization projects.
    D) Predictive analytics for future ESG risks.
    E) Customized reporting aligned with frameworks like GRI and SASB.
16. Which external *opportunity* for Digital ESG is highlighted by the evolving regulatory landscape?
    A) The decreasing importance of ESG ratings.
    B) The increasing risk of cybersecurity breaches.
    C) The introduction of firm ESG reporting standards and potential government incentives.
    D) The guarantee of higher short-term profits.
    E) The simplification of all global ESG frameworks into one standard.
17. A major *threat* associated with Digital ESG, as per the SWOT analysis, is:
    A) The high cost of implementation for SMEs.
    B) The continuous need for technological updates and the risk of rapid obsolescence.
    C) The lack of digital literacy among top management.
    D) The over-reliance on qualitative data.
    E) The decreased transparency in supply chains.
18. The concept of "Digital E" specifically involves using technologies like IoT and AI to:
    A) Manage executive compensation committees digitally.
    B) Monitor employee satisfaction through online surveys.

C) Establish and monitor environmental objectives with precision.
D) Automate the company's public relations on social media.
E) Conduct virtual board meetings.

19. The primary research methodology employed in this chapter is a:
    A) Longitudinal analysis of stock performance.
    B) Series of primary interviews with ESG managers.
    C) Combination of descriptive and exploratory methods based on secondary data and a SWOT analysis.
    D) Controlled experiment on the effects of AI on ESG scores.
    E) Large-N quantitative regression analysis.
20. The chapter suggests that the future evolution of Digital ESG theory points towards:
    A) A return to traditional, non-digital ESG reporting for enhanced reliability.
    B) The dominance of Social (S) metrics over Environmental (E) and Governance (G) metrics.
    C) A nascent "Digital Sustainability Theory" where technology reshapes the very practice of sustainability.
    D) The phasing out of ESG in favor of purely financial metrics.
    E) The decentralization of all ESG data management to individual employees.

Short Answer Questions (21-28)

Requiring comprehension, application, and basic analysis in a concise format.

21. Briefly define "Digital ESG" and distinguish it from traditional ESG practices.
22. List three distinct digital technologies mentioned in the chapter and state one application of each within a Digital ESG framework.
23. Explain how the "Digital S" component can improve internal social metrics within an organization.
24. What is the significance of "sectoral benchmarking" in a tool like the EY ESG Compass?
25. Identify two internal weaknesses and two external threats associated with the adoption of Digital ESG.
26. How did the Mahindra Group's "Rise for Good" initiative, as a case study, exemplify the use of digital platforms for social impact?
27. Why is data quality a persistent concern in the implementation of Digital ESG systems?
28. According to the chapter, what is the role of predictive analytics in advanced Digital ESG risk management?

Essay Questions (29-34)

Requiring synthesis, evaluation, and detailed explanation.

29. Synthesize the chapter's discussion to construct a comprehensive argument for why a CEO should invest in Digital ESG, ensuring you address at least two strengths and one potential weakness while making your case.
30. Critically evaluate the SWOT analysis presented in the chapter. Do you believe the internal factors (Strengths & Weaknesses) or the external factors (Opportunities & Threats) present a more significant challenge to the widespread adoption of Digital ESG? Justify your position with examples from the text.
31. Compare and contrast the Digital ESG applications demonstrated in the TCS and Infosys case studies. How do their approaches highlight the versatile application of digital technologies across different ESG pillars?
32. Elaborate on the theoretical evolution from Stakeholder Theory to the proposed "Digital Sustainability Theory" as discussed in the chapter. How does this evolution change the strategic perception of ESG within a firm?
33. The EY ESG Compass platform offers a suite of services from emissions monitoring to regulation tracking. Analyze how the integration of these various functions in a single platform creates synergistic value for an organization pursuing sustainability goals.
34. The chapter mentions the risk of "too much reliance on technologies" leading to a missing "personal touch." Discuss the potential social and ethical implications of this over-reliance in the context of stakeholder engagement and corporate accountability.

Graduate Level Research Questions (35-39)

Designed for Master's students to explore beyond the chapter through independent research.

35. **Empirical Investigation:** Propose a research design to quantitatively measure the correlation between a company's level of digital transformation (e.g., investment in AI, IoT) and its ESG performance score (e.g., from MSCI). What control variables would you include, and what methodological challenges would you anticipate?
36. **SME Focused Framework:** The chapter identifies cost as a major barrier for SMEs. Conduct preliminary research to identify and describe two to three existing or potential scalable, cloud-based Digital ESG solutions that could be viable for an SME. What are the key trade-offs?

37. **Behavioral Analysis:** Explore the academic literature on technology adoption in organizations. Based on this, what do you hypothesize are the key human and organizational change management factors that would determine the success or failure of a Digital ESG implementation project?
38. **Regulatory Comparative Analysis:** Compare the evolving Digital ESG reporting landscape in the European Union (e.g., under the CSRD) with that in India (e.g., the BRSR). How do these differing regulatory environments create unique challenges and opportunities for multinational corporations?
39. **Ethical Scrutiny:** Investigate the concept of "algorithmic bias" in AI. How might this phenomenon manifest in an AI-driven "Digital S" platform used for monitoring employee performance or diversity metrics, and what governance mechanisms could be instituted to mitigate it?

Doctoral Level Research Questions (40-42)

Designed for PhD scholars to develop dissertations that contribute original knowledge to the field.

40. **Theoretical Development and Testing:** The chapter posits an emerging "Digital Sustainability Theory." Your task is to rigorously formalize this theory. What are its core constructs, propositions, and boundary conditions? Furthermore, design a multi-method study (e.g., a set of case studies combined with a Q-sort methodology) to empirically validate and refine this theoretical framework.
41. **Causal Mechanisms and Paradoxes:** Move beyond correlation to causality. Does Digital ESG *cause* improved sustainability outcomes, or is it merely a signal of underlying managerial competence? Design a longitudinal or quasi-experimental study to identify the causal mechanisms. Furthermore, explore the potential *"paradoxes"* of Digital ESG—for instance, how might the energy-intensive nature of data centers and AI computing (the digital footprint) create a negative feedback loop that undermines environmental ("E") goals?
42. **Institutional and Ecosystem Dynamics:** Adopting an institutional theory lens, investigating Digital ESG not as a firm-level phenomenon but as an emerging field or ecosystem. How do various actors—technology vendors (e.g., Salesforce, SAP), rating agencies (MSCI, Sustainalytics), regulators, and NGOs—interact to co-construct the meaning, standards, and power dynamics within the Digital ESG field? Use a qualitative, process-based research approach to map this ecosystem.

Post-Doctoral Research Directions (43-45)

Designed for PhD holders to define new, high-impact research trajectories.

43. **Philosophical and Ontological Inquiry:** The digitization of ESG creates a new *"datafied"* representation of sustainability. Probe the philosophical underpinnings of this shift. Is a "Digital ESG" score an objective measure of impact, or a socially constructed, technologically mediated artifact that creates new realities and power structures? This research would critically examine the epistemology of ESG data and its implications for corporate accountability in a digital age, potentially developing a critical theory of Digital ESG.
44. **Complex Systems and Resilience Modeling:** Conceptualize the global corporate network as a complex adaptive system where Digital ESG acts as an information-flow intervention. Using advanced computational methods (e.g., agent-based modeling or system dynamics), how can we simulate the long-term, non-linear impacts of widespread Digital ESG adoption on global systemic risks, such as climate change resilience or socioeconomic inequality? The goal is to move beyond firm-level impact to model second-order effects on planetary boundaries and social stability.
45. **Future Governance and Sovereignty:** Anticipate the next frontier of governance challenges. With the rise of generative AI and sovereign digital currencies, how might *"Decentralized Autonomous Organizations"* (DAOs) or *"Algorithmic Regulators"* fundamentally disrupt traditional ESG governance? Explore the potential for a fully automated, blockchain-based ESG compliance and reporting system. What new models of corporate form, stakeholder representation, and ethical oversight would this necessitate? This research direction sits at the intersection of law, computer science, and political economy.

REFERENCES

Allman, E., & Won, J. (2021). The Effect of ESG Disclosure on Corporate Investment Efficiency. SSRN Electronic Journal. DOI: 10.2139/ssrn.3816592

Aydoğmuş, M., Gülay, G., & Ergun, K.AYDOĞMUŞ. (2022). Impact Of Esg Performance On Firm Value And Profitability. *Borsa Istanbul Review*, *22*(2), S119–S127. DOI: 10.1016/j.bir.2022.11.006

Balboni, P., & Kate Elizabeth Francis. (2024). Data Ethics and Digital Sustainability: Bridging Legal Data Protection Compliance and ESG for a Responsible Data-Driven Future. DOI: 10.2139/ssrn.4884478

Barykin, S., Strimovskaya, A., Sergeev, S., Borisoglebskaya, L., Dedyukhina, N., Sklyarov, I., Sklyarova, J., & Saychenko, L. (2023). Smart City Logistics on the Basis of Digital Tools for ESG Goals Achievement. *Sustainability (Basel)*, *15*(6), 5507–5507. DOI: 10.3390/su15065507

Bergquist, A. (2017). Business and Sustainability: New Business History Perspectives. Social Science Research Network. DOI: 10.2139/ssrn.3055587

Bist, S. (2022, February 14). Why businesses need to bridge ESG goals with digital transformation. Times of India Blog. https://timesofindia.indiatimes.com/blogs/voices/why-businesses-need-to-bridge-esg-goals-with-digital-transformation/

Chand, R., & Kour, M. (2025). Sustainable Finance and ESG Investing: Pathways to Long-Term Business Success. In Building Business Knowledge for Complex Modern Business Environments (pp. 121-148). IGI Global. DOI: DOI: 10.4018/979-8-3693-6447-5.ch005

Chen, L., Mao, C., & Gao, Y. (2023). Executive compensation stickiness and ESG performance: The role of digital transformation. *Frontiers in Environmental Science*, *11*, 1166080. Advance online publication. DOI: 10.3389/fenvs.2023.1166080

Chen, S. (2024). The Influence of Artificial Intelligence and Digital Technology on ESG Reporting Quality. *International Journal of Global Economics and Management*, *3*(1), 301–310. DOI: 10.62051/IJGEM.v3n1.36

Chen, W., Xie, Y., & He, K. (2024). Environmental, social, and governance performance and corporate innovation novelty. *International Journal of Innovation Studies*, *8*(2), 109–131. DOI: 10.1016/j.ijis.2024.01.003

Chungyalpa, W. (2021). Understanding Business Sustainability: The What, the Why, and the How of Sustainable Business Practices. *Indian Journal of Sustainable Development*, *5*(1 & 2), 24–37. https://www.researchgate.net/publication/352837459_Understanding_Business_Sustainability_The_What_the_Why_and_the_How_of_Sustainable_Business_Practices

Cricelli, L., & Strazzullo, S. (2021). The Economic Aspect of Digital Sustainability: A Systematic review. *Sustainability (Basel)*, *13*(15), 8241. DOI: 10.3390/su13158241

Cruz, C. A., & Matos, F. (2023). ESG Maturity: A Software Framework for the Challenges of ESG Data in Investment. *Sustainability (Basel)*, *15*(3), 2610. DOI: 10.3390/su15032610

Deloitte. (2023). The future of ESG data: How digital transformation is driving decision-making. Deloitte Insights. https://www2.deloitte.com/us/en/insights/topics/digital-transformation/digital-esg-data-transformation.html

EY ESG Compass - Innovation to transform sustainability journey. (2024). Ey.com. https://www.ey.com/en_in/services/climate-change-sustainability-services/esg-compass

Faccia, A., Manni, F., & Capitanio, F. (2021). Mandatory ESG Reporting and XBRL Taxonomies Combination: ESG Ratings and Income Statement, a Sustainable Value-Added Disclosure. *Sustainability (Basel)*, *13*(16), 8876. DOI: 10.3390/su13168876

Sarpong, F. A., Sappor, P., Nyantakyi, G., Ahakwa, I., Esther Agyeiwaa, O., & Blandful Cobbinah, B. (2023). From traditional roots to digital bytes: Can digitalizing ESG improves Ghanaian rural banks' brand equity through stakeholder engagement, and customer loyalty? *Cogent Business & Management*, *10*(2), 2232159.

Fujjiwara, N., Georgiev, A., & Alessi, M. (2010, May 27). The Merit of Sectoral Approaches in Transitioning Towards a Global Carbon Market. *Ssrn*.com. https://papers.ssrn.com/sol3/papers.cfm ?abstract_id=2863987

George, G., Merrill, R. K., & Schillebeeckx, S. J. D. (2021). Digital sustainability and entrepreneurship: How digital innovations are driving the entrepreneurial pursuit of sustainable development. *Business Strategy and the Environment*, *30*(5), 2382–2399. DOI: 10.1002/bse.2744

Giechaskiel, B., Clairotte, M., Valverde-Morales, V., Bonnel, P., Kregar, Z., Franco, V., & Dilara, P. (2018). Framework for the assessment of PEMS (Portable Emissions Measurement Systems) uncertainty. *Environmental Research*, *166*, 251–260. DOI: 10.1016/j.envres.2018.06.012 PMID: 29908456

Hartley, N., Kunz, W., & Tarbit, J. (2024). The corporate digital responsibility (CDR) calculus: How and why organizations reconcile digital and ethical trade-offs for growth. *Organizational Dynamics*, *53*(2), 101056–101056. DOI: 10.1016/j.orgdyn.2024.101056

Hassani, H., Huang, X., & Silva, E. (2019). Big Data and Climate Change. *Big Data and Cognitive Computing*, *3*(1), 12. DOI: 10.3390/bdcc3010012

Hernandez, M. S., Sentosa, I., Gaudreault, F., Davison, I., & Sharin, F. H. (2023, May 1). The Emergence of The Metaverse in The Digital Blockchain Economy: Applying the ESG Framework for A Sustainable Future. IEEE Xplore. DOI: 10.1109/ICACITE57410.2023.10182839

Horváth, D., & Szabó, R. Z. (2019). Driving forces and barriers of Industry 4.0: Do multinational and small and medium-sized companies have equal opportunities? *Technological Forecasting and Social Change*, *146*, 119–132. DOI: 10.1016/j.techfore.2019.05.021

Huang, Q., Fang, J., Xue, X., & Gao, H. (2023). Does Digital Innovation Produce Better ESG Performance? An Empirical Test of Shenzhen A-Listed Firms in China. DOI: 10.2139/ssrn.4390649

Hughes, A., Urban, M. A., & Wójcik, D. (2021). Alternative ESG Ratings: How Technological Innovation Is Reshaping Sustainable Investment. *Sustainability (Basel)*, *13*(6), 3551. DOI: 10.3390/su13063551

Hussain, M., Yang, S., Zahid, R. M. A., & Maqsood, U. S. (2023). ESG in the Digital Age: Unravelling the impact of Strategic Digital orientation. Social Science Research Network. DOI: 10.2139/ ssrn.4543836

Infosys Limited. (2022). Infosys ESG Report 2022-23 HIGHLIGHTS: Carbon-neutral organization for 4 consecutive years and empowering 8.5 million lives with digital skilling. Infosys.com. https://www.infosys.com/newsroom/features/2023/infosys-esg-report-2022 23.html#:~:text=Features-

Janicka, M., & Sajnóg, A. (2022). The ESG Reporting of EU Public Companies—Does the Company's Capitalisation Matter? *Sustainability (Basel)*, *14*(7), 4279. DOI: 10.3390/su14074279

Jingyong, W., Song, Z., & Li-Da, X. (2023). Digital Technology For Good: Path and Influence—Based on the Study of ESG performance of listed companies in China. *Applied Sciences (Basel, Switzerland)*, *13*(5), 2862. DOI: 10.3390/app13052862

Jonsdottir, B., Sigurjónsson, Þ. O., Jóhannsdóttir, L., & Wendt, S. (2022). Barriers to using ESG data for investment decisions. *Sustainability (Basel), 14*(9), 5157. DOI: 10.3390/su14095157

Julia, L., Natale, D., & Cordella, A. (n.d.). ESGTech: Guiding ESG Regulation and Digital Governance. Retrieved September 10, 2024, from https://scholarspace.manoa.hawaii.edu/server /api/core/bitstreams/ee378dba-64a0-4404-8e32-e1635cabe44c/content

Kopnina, H. (2015). Sustainability: New strategic thinking for business. *Environment, Development and Sustainability, 19*(1), 27–43. DOI: 10.1007/s10668-015-9723-1

Kraus, S., Durst, S., Ferreira, J. J., Veiga, P. M., Kailer, N., & Weinmann, A. (2022). Digital transformation in business and management research: An overview of the current status quo. International Journal of Information Management, 63, 102466. fomgt.2021. 102466DOI: 10.1016/j.ijin

Kwilinski, A., Lyulyov, O., & Pimonenko, T. (2023). Unlocking Sustainable Value through Digital Transformation: An Examination of ESG Performance. *Information (Basel), 14*(8), 444–444. DOI: 10.3390/info14080444

Kwiliński, A., Lyulyov, O., & Pimonenko, T. (2023). Unlocking Sustainable Value through Digital Transformation: An Examination of ESG Performance. *Information (Basel), 14*(8), 444. DOI: 10.3390/info14080444

Kwilinski, A., Lyulyov, O., & Pimonenko, T. (2024). The role of country's green brand and digitalization in enhancing environmental, social, and governance performance. Ekonomia I Środowisko, 87(4), 1–22. DOI: 10.34659/eis.2023.87.4.613

Larcker, D. F., Pomorski, L., Tayan, B., & Watts, E. M. (2022, August 2). ESG Ratings: A Compass without Direction. Papers.*ssrn*.com. https://papers.ssrn.com/sol3/papers.cfm?abstract_id=4179647

Lau, H. C., & Tsai, S. C. (2023). Global Decarbonization: Current Status and What It Will Take to Achieve Net Zero by 2050. *Energies, 16*(23), 7800. DOI: 10.3390/en16237800

Lee, O., Joo, H., Choi, H., & Cheon, M. (2022). Proposing an Integrated Approach to Analyzing ESG Data via Machine Learning and Deep Learning Algorithms. *Sustainability (Basel), 14*(14), 8745. DOI: 10.3390/su14148745

Li, T., Wang, K., Sueyoshi, T., & Wang, D. D. (2021). ESG: Research Progress and Future Prospects. *Sustainability (Basel), 13*(21), 11663. DOI: 10.3390/su132111663

Lubowiecki-Vikuk, A., Dąbrowska, A., & Machnik, A. (2021). Responsible consumer and lifestyle: Sustainability insights. *Sustainable Production and Consumption*, *25*, 91–101. DOI: 10.1016/j.spc.2020.08.007 PMID: 32864405

Macpherson, M., Gasperini, A., & Bosco, M. (2021). Implications for artificial intelligence and ESG data. Social Science Research Network. DOI: 10.2139/ssrn.3863599

Mahindra Sustainability Report I Low Carbon Business I Mahindra. (n.d.). Www.mahindra.com. https://www.mahindra.com/sustainability

Martín, L., & Sánchez-Ortiz, N. (2023). To be digital or not to be, that is the ESG question. *Boletín de Estudios Económicos*, *77*(233), 109–124. DOI: 10.18543/bee.2638

Migliorelli, M. (2021). What Do We Mean by Sustainable Finance? Assessing Existing Frameworks and Policy Risks. *Sustainability (Basel)*, *13*(2), 975. DOI: 10.3390/su13020975

Mulligan, C., Morsfield, S., & Cheikosman, E. (2023). Blockchain for sustainability: A systematic literature review for policy impact. *Telecommunications Policy*, *48*(2), 102676. DOI: 10.1016/j.telpol.2023.102676

Ozili, P. K. (2022, February 1). Sustainability and sustainable development research around the world. https://papers.ssrn.com/sol3/papers.cfm?abstract_id=4024990

Partner, (2023). Tech in ESG: role of data analytics and benchmarking in ESG. Ey.com. https://www.ey.com/en_in/media/podcasts/tech-in-esg/2023/01/tech-in-esg-role-of-data-analytics-and-benchmarking-in-esg

Patowary, M. M. I. (2019). Incorporating Sustainability in Business Model: A literature review. Social Science Research Network. DOI: 10.2139/ssrn.3643604

Peng, Y., Chen, H., & Li, T. (2023). The Impact of Digital Transformation on ESG: A Case Study of Chinese-Listed Companies. *Sustainability (Basel)*, *15*(20), 15072. DOI: 10.3390/su152015072

Puriwat, W., & Tripopsakul, S. (2022). From ESG to DESG: The Impact of DESG (Digital Environmental, Social, and Governance) on Customer Attitudes and Brand Equity. *Sustainability (Basel)*, *14*(17), 10480. DOI: 10.3390/su141710480

Rao, N. D., & Baer, P. (2012). "Decent Living" Emissions: A Conceptual Framework. *Sustainability (Basel)*, *4*(4), 656–681. DOI: 10.3390/su4040656

Rehman, S. U., Kraus, S., Shah, S. A., Khanin, D., & Mahto, R. V. (2021). Analyzing the relationship between green innovation and environmental performance in large manufacturing firms. Technological Forecasting and Social Change, 163, 120481. . 2020.120481DOI: 10. 1016/j.techfore

Rodríguez Diez, J., Tomé-Torquemada, S., Vicente, A., Reyes, J., & Orcajo, G. A. (2023). Decarbonization Pathways, Strategies, and Use Cases to Achieve Net-Zero CO2 Emissions in the Steelmaking Industry. *Energies*, *16*(21), 7360. DOI: 10.3390/en16217360

Rossato, C., & Castellani, P. (2020). The contribution of digitalisation to business longevity from a competitiveness perspective. *The TQM Journal*, *32*(4), 617–645. DOI: 10.1108/TQM-02-2020-0032

Ruan, L., & Liu, H. (2021). Environmental, Social, Governance Activities and Firm Performance: Evidence from China. *Sustainability (Basel)*, *13*(2), 767. DOI: 10.3390/su13020767

Saeed, M., & Kersten, W. (2019). Drivers of Sustainable Supply Chain Management: Identification and Classification. *Sustainability (Basel)*, *11*(4), 1137. DOI: 10.3390/su11041137

Sætra, H. S. (2021). A Framework for Evaluating and Disclosing the ESG Related Impacts of AI with the SDGs. *Sustainability (Basel)*, *13*(15), 8503. DOI: 10.3390/su13158503

Sætra, H. S. (2022). The AI ESG protocol: Evaluating and disclosing the environment, social, and governance implications of artificial intelligence capabilities, assets, and activities. *Sustainable Development (Bradford)*, *31*(2), 1027–1037. DOI: 10.1002/sd.2438

Sánchez-Flores, R. B., Cruz-Sotelo, S. E., Ojeda-Benitez, S., & Ramírez-Barreto, Ma. E. (2020). Sustainable Supply Chain Management—A Literature Review on Emerging Economies. Sustainability, 12(17), 6972. MDPI. DOI: 10.3390/su12176972

Sang, Y., Loganathan, K., & Lin, L. (2024). Digital Transformation and Firm ESG Performance: The Mediating Role of Corporate Risk-Taking and the Moderating Role of Top Management Team. *Sustainability (Basel)*, *16*(14), 5907–5907. DOI: 10.3390/su16145907

Saxena, A., Singh, R., Gehlot, A., Akram, S. V., Twala, B., Singh, A., Montero, E. C., & Priyadarshi, N. (2022). Technologies Empowered Environmental, Social, and Governance (ESG): An Industry 4.0 landscape. *Sustainability (Basel)*, *15*(1), 309. DOI: 10.3390/su15010309

Stuermer, M., Abu-Tayeh, G., & Myrach, T. (2016). Digital sustainability: Basic conditions for sustainable digital artifacts and their ecosystems. *Sustainability Science, 12*(2), 247–262. DOI: 10.1007/s11625-016-0412-2 PMID: 30174752

Su, X., Wang, S., & Li, F. (2023). The Impact of Digital Transformation on ESG Performance Based on the Mediating Effect of Dynamic Capabilities. *Sustainability (Basel), 15*(18), 13506. DOI: 10.3390/su151813506

Vinuesa, R., Azizpour, H., Leite, I., Balaam, M., Dignum, V., Domisch, S., Felländer, A., Langhans, S. D., Tegmark, M., & Nerini, F. F. (2020). The role of artificial intelligence in achieving the Sustainable Development Goals. *Nature Communications, 11*(1), 233. Advance online publication. DOI: 10.1038/s41467-019-14108-y PMID: 31932590

Walker, N. L., Styles, D., Coughlan, P., & Williams, A. P. (2022). Cross-sector sustainability benchmarking of major utilities in the United Kingdom. *Utilities Policy, 78*, 101417. DOI: 10.1016/j.jup.2022.101417

Wang, J., Hong, Z., & Long, H. (2023). Digital Transformation Empowers ESG Performance in the Manufacturing Industry: From ESG to DESG. *SAGE Open, 13*(4), 21582440231204158. Advance online publication. DOI: 10.1177/21582440231204158

World Economic Forum. (2022). Bridging Digital and Environmental Goals: A Framework for Sectoral Action. https://www.weforum.org/publications/bridging-digital-and-environmental-goals-a-framework-for-sectoral-action/

Wu, S., & Liu, Y. (2023). A study on the Impact of Digital Transformation on Corporate ESG Performance: The Mediating Role of Green Innovation. *Sustainability (Basel), 15*(8), 6568. DOI: 10.3390/su15086568

Wut, T. M., Lee, D., Ip, W. M., & Lee, S. W. (2021). Digital Sustainability in the Organization: Scale development and validation. *Sustainability (Basel), 13*(6), 3530. DOI: 10.3390/su13063530

Zhang, C., & Jin, S. (2022). What drives sustainable development of enterprises? Focusing on ESG management and green technology innovation. *Sustainability (Basel), 14*(18), 11695. DOI: 10.3390/su141811695

Zhong, Y., Zhao, H., & Yin, T. (2023). Resource Bundling: How Does Enterprise Digital Transformation Affect Enterprise ESG Development? *Sustainability (Basel), 15*(2), 1319. DOI: 10.3390/su15021319

Zhou, G., Liu, L., & Luo, S. (2022). Sustainable development, ESG performance and company market value: Mediating effect of financial performance. *Business Strategy and the Environment*, *31*(7), 3371–3387. DOI: 10.1002/bse.3089

KEY TERMS AND DEFINITIONS

Cloud-based platforms: A cloud stage is the working framework and equipment of servers in a data centre that are designed to give cloud computing services to customers. Businesses can rent on-demand internet access to computing resources through a cloud platform.

Data analytics: The process of looking at data to find patterns, answer questions, and make good decisions is known as data analytics.

Digital tools: Digital tools (DT) can be characterized as projects, sites, applications, and other web and modernized assets that work with, upgrade and execute computerized cycles and generally digitization endeavours.

ESG Management: ESG data management is a sort of cycle to gather, process and analyse in order to report the information connected with an organization's effect on ESG.

ESG Metrics: ESG metrics measure execution on ecological, social and governance issues.

IoT: The Internet of Things (IoT) is a network of actual items that can interface and trade information with different gadgets and frameworks over the web.

Reporting: It is basically the means and measures to gather, process, store and present data inside an organization.

TEACHING NOTE

This teaching note is designed to assist instructors in facilitating a robust, critical, and engaging learning experience around the emerging paradigm of Digital ESG (DESG). The chapter provides a foundational conceptual framework, real-world case studies, and a structured analytical tool (SWOT) that allows students to transition from understanding basic concepts to evaluating complex strategic trade-offs. The pedagogical approach is rooted in Bloom's Taxonomy, aiming to move students from knowledge comprehension to the creation of their own informed judgments and strategies.

Concise Summary for the Instructor

This chapter, "Digital ESG in Action," systematically investigates the convergence of digital transformation and Environmental, Social, and Governance (ESG) principles. It posits Digital ESG as a transformative paradigm that leverages technologies like AI, IoT, and blockchain to enhance the efficacy, accuracy, and strategic value of corporate sustainability efforts. The chapter begins by establishing the evolution from traditional ESG to DESG, deconstructing it into its core components: Digital E (environmental monitoring), Digital S (stakeholder engagement), and Digital G (transparent governance).

It grounds the concept in contemporary literature and theoretical evolution, from Stakeholder Theory to a nascent "Digital Sustainability Theory." The research employs a descriptive and exploratory methodology, utilizing secondary data, case studies of leading Indian firms (TCS, HDFC Bank, Mahindra, Infosys), and a deep-dive into the EY ESG Compass platform. The analytical core is a comprehensive SWOT analysis that meticulously details the internal Strengths and Weaknesses, and external Opportunities and Threats of DESG implementation. The chapter concludes that despite significant challenges—particularly around cost, data security, and skills—the strategic imperative for DESG is profound, offering a pathway to enhanced resilience, stakeholder trust, and alignment with global sustainability goals.

Chapter Synopsis

This chapter serves as a primer and critical guide to Digital ESG. It articulates the limitations of legacy ESG systems and introduces digital technologies as powerful enablers for data collection, analysis, and reporting. It provides a clear taxonomy of DESG, illustrating how specific technologies apply to environmental, social, and governance challenges. Through illustrative case studies and an examination of a GenAI-enabled platform, it demonstrates DESG's practical application. The chapter's pivotal contribution is its structured SWOT analysis, which provides a balanced and critical assessment, empowering stakeholders to make informed strategic decisions.

It ends with a forward-looking conclusion and specific, actionable avenues for future research, highlighting that DESG represents not just a technological upgrade but a fundamental reshaping of sustainable business practice.

Key Learning Objectives

Upon engaging in this chapter, students should be able to:

1. **Remembering:** Define "Digital ESG" and list its three core components (Digital E, S, and G) alongside key enabling technologies (e.g., AI, IoT, Blockchain).
2. **Understanding:** Explain the theoretical evolution from Stakeholder Theory to Resource-Based View and towards a "Digital Sustainability Theory" in the context of DESG.
3. **Applying:** Illustrate how specific digital technologies can be applied to solve concrete ESG challenges in each of the three pillars, using the provided case studies as examples.
4. **Analyzing:** Differentiate between the internal (Strengths, Weaknesses) and external (Opportunities, Threats) factors affecting DESG adoption, using the provided SWOT framework.
5. **Evaluating:** Critically assess the potential benefits and risks of DESG implementation for a company of a given size and sector, weighing trade-offs like transparency vs. data security.
6. **Creating:** Propose a high-level implementation roadmap or a policy recommendation to overcome a key barrier (e.g., for SMEs or data standardization) identified in the SWOT analysis.

Core Themes/Theses for Discussion

1. **Paradigm Shift:** DESG is not merely a digital tool *for* ESG, but a new paradigm that fundamentally transforms sustainability from a static reporting exercise into a dynamic, integrated, and intelligent operational driver.
2. **The Strategic Advantage:** When effectively implemented, DESG moves beyond compliance to become a source of competitive advantage, enhancing operational efficiency, mitigating risk, and building long-term brand equity and resilience.
3. **The Inevitability of Convergence:** The twin pressures of the climate crisis and the digital revolution make the integration of technology and sustainability an inevitable, rather than optional, strategic direction for modern corporations.
4. **The Equity Challenge:** The significant costs and expertise required for DESG create a potential "sustainability divide," where large corporations accelerate

their progress while SMEs and organizations in developing economies are left behind.

5. **The Double-Edged Sword of Data:** While digital tools promise unparalleled data transparency and accuracy, they also introduce profound new risks related to cybersecurity, data privacy, and the ethical use of AI, potentially eroding the very trust they seek to build.

Suggested Teaching Pathway (90-Minute Session)

- **Introduction (10 mins):** Frame the session around the core tension: Can technology solve the problems of sustainability, or does it introduce new, more complex challenges? Use a quick poll asking students if they believe AI will be a net positive or negative for corporate ethics.
- **Conceptual Foundation (15 mins):** Lecture/discussion on the "What and Why" of DESG. Clarify the definitions of Digital E, S, and G. Use the theoretical evolution to explain *why* this is a strategic, not just operational, shift.
- **Case Study Analysis (20 mins):** Divide students into small groups. Assign each group one of the chapter's case studies (TCS, HDFC, Mahindra, Infosys). Task them with identifying: a) The primary DESG pillar being addressed, b) The specific technology used, and c) One strength and one weakness highlighted by their case. Groups report back briefly.
- **SWOT Deep Dive (30 mins):** Facilitate a full-class discussion based on the SWOT analysis. Use a whiteboard to create a 2x2 matrix. Push students beyond simply listing factors to evaluating their relative importance. *Which strength is most compelling for a CEO? Which weakness is most likely to derail an implementation?*
- **Synthesis & Conclusion (15 mins):** Return to the opening tension. Ask students to reflect on whether their views have changed. Conclude by summarizing DESG as a powerful but complex tool, whose ultimate impact depends on strategic, ethical, and inclusive implementation.

Pedagogical Tools & Resources

- **In-Class Worksheet:** A one-page handout with the blank SWOT matrix for students to fill out during the lecture and discussion.
- **Case Study Briefs:** Pre-prepared one-slide summaries of each case study for quick reference during group work.
- **"The DESG Dilemma" Scenario:** A short, fictional case about a mid-sized manufacturing company considering a DESG platform. Students must role-

play as the management team, debating the go/no-go decision based on the chapter's analysis.

- **Supplementary Media:** Short video clips (2-3 mins) showcasing real-world applications of IoT for energy management or blockchain for supply chain transparency.
- **Further Reading:** Provide the citations for the “Additional Reading” section (Deloitte, 2023; George et al., 2021; WEF, 2022) for students pursuing research projects.

Note on Sensitivity

The discussion of Digital ESG may surface several sensitive areas. Instructors should be prepared to gently guide conversations on:

- **Economic Disparity:** The high cost of DESG may lead to statements that could stigmatize smaller businesses or developing economies. Frame this as a systemic challenge requiring collaborative solutions, not a failure of those entities.
- **Employment Fears:** The automation strengths of DESG directly relate to fears of job displacement, particularly in roles related to data entry and reporting. Acknowledge this valid concern and pivot the discussion towards the new, high-skill jobs DESG may create (e.g., data analysts, ESG technologists).
- **Data Privacy & Bias:** Discussions of AI and data analytics must include its potential for perpetuating societal biases (e.g., in “Digital S” hiring or performance tools) and enabling surveillance. Encourage critical thinking about the ethical guardrails needed for responsible DESG.

Key Questions for Class Discussion

1. **Comprehension:** Beyond simple automation, how does DESG fundamentally change the *nature* of ESG from a reporting function to a strategic one?
   - **Direction:** Guide students to discuss real-time data, predictive analytics, and the integration of ESG metrics into core decision-making processes.
2. **Application:** If you were the CEO of a fast-fashion retailer, what would be your first “Digital E” initiative, and what specific technology would you deploy?
   - **Direction:** Push students to be specific (e.g., “IoT sensors to track water consumption in dyeing factories”) and to justify their choice based on the material impact and visibility to stakeholders.

3. **Analysis:** The SWOT analysis lists both "Enhanced data accuracy" (Strength) and "Poor quality data" (Weakness). Under what conditions does one prevail over the other?
    - o **Direction:** Elicit factors such as data governance policies, the quality of input data (garbage in, garbage out), and the maturity of the AI algorithms used.
4. **Evaluation:** Of all the weaknesses identified, which do you believe is the single greatest barrier to widespread DESG adoption, and why?
    - o **Direction:** Encourage debate. Some may argue cost is paramount, while others may see the skills gap or cybersecurity threats as more intractable problems.
5. **Perspective:** The case studies focus on large, resource-rich corporations. How can the principles of DESG be made accessible and viable for Small and Medium Enterprises (SMEs)?
    - o **Direction:** Stimulate creative thinking about scalable, cloud-based solutions, industry consortiums, and government-supported platforms to lower the barrier to entry.
6. **Synthesis:** How might a company leverage its strengths in DESG to not only mitigate its threats but to actively transform them into opportunities? (e.g., using advanced cybersecurity as a marketable feature).
    - o **Direction:** This encourages higher-order strategic thinking. For example, a company with strong DESG data could use it to secure lower-cost "green" financing, turning a cost center into a revenue-enabler.
7. **Ethics:** The chapter warns of a "missing personal touch." What are the potential social and ethical consequences of over-relying on algorithms to manage stakeholder relationships and social impact?
    - o **Direction:** Discuss dehumanization, the potential for misinterpreting nuanced social contexts with AI, and the risk of "checkbox" sustainability that lacks genuine empathy.
8. **Analysis:** Compare the DESG approaches of HDFC Bank (focused on product and customer interaction) and Infosys (focused on internal governance and operations). What do these differences tell us about how a company's core business model influences its DESG strategy?
    - o **Direction:** Highlight how DESG is not one-size-fits-all; it must be tailored to a firm's specific value chain, risk profile, and stakeholder base.
9. **Future-Gazing:** The chapter proposes a "Digital Sustainability Theory." What might be one core tenet of this new theory?
    - o **Direction:** Guide students to theorize, for example, that "the velocity and verifiability of sustainability data directly increase a firm's capacity for resilient value creation."

10. **Action:** You are a policy advisor. Based on this chapter, what one piece of legislation or standard would you propose to accelerate the *responsible* adoption of DESG?
    - **Direction:** Answers could range from tax credits for SMEs, to national data standards for ESG reporting, to mandatory ethical AI audits for DESG platforms. The goal is to translate understanding into actionable policy.

Chapter 3

The Impact of Corporate Social Responsibility Reporting Practice on the Financial Performance of Tunisian Banks

Wissem Ben Ali
https://orcid.org/0000-0002-6380-9400
ESCT, University of Manouba, Tunisia

Nourhene Dhahri
https://orcid.org/0000-0003-2682-8634
Faculty of Economics and Management of Sfax, Tunisia

ABSTRACT

This study investigates the link between corporate social responsibility (CSR) disclosure and the financial performance of banks in Tunisia over the period from 2013 to 2023. The analysis was conducted on the financial statements of fourteen banks in Tunisia to gather data on CSR disclosures. The panel data analysis revealed a statistically significant and positive correlation between the level of CSR disclosure and the financial performance of these banks. These results suggest that greater CSR disclosure is associated with improved profitability for banks in Tunisia. This study contributes to the existing literature on the relationship between social responsibility disclosures and financial performance, providing valuable insights for both academics and industry professionals.

DOI: 10.4018/979-8-3693-9714-5.ch003

1.0 INTRODUCTION

Corporate social responsibility (CSR) encompasses a company's commitment to ethical self-governance and integrating moral practices into its core business operations (Razak, Ismail, Yamin, & Syah, 2019). CSR involves a range of initiatives aimed at ensuring a positive impact on the environment and stakeholders. This includes assessing and improving the organization's economic, social, and environmental policies to meet stakeholder expectations (Ramzan, Amin, & Abbas, 2021).

CSR reporting requires companies to publish detailed reports on their social and environmental impacts (Platonova et al., 2016). This type of reporting aims to transparently communicate efforts beyond financial goals, such as environmental conservation, social equity, and community involvement. CSR disclosure specifically refers to the public dissemination of information about a company's CSR practices through various channels for stakeholders (Saki, 2020).

Organizations engage in CSR disclosure for multiple reasons, including enhancing their public image, building stakeholder trust, attracting socially conscious investors, and complying with regulatory requirements (Christensen et al., 2017). Detailed CSR disclosures are crucial for demonstrating a firm's commitment to sustainability and social responsibility. Evidence suggests that investors are often willing to pay more for shares in companies with strong CSR policies, due to the association with transparent management, better governance, and lower risk profiles. Effective CSR strategies support long-term sustainable development and incentivize companies to improve their sustainability practices and disclose more about their CSR activities (Siueia et al., 2019).

The United Nations Sustainable Stock Exchange initiative, launched in 2012, aims to develop a new framework for sustainable global finance and encourage voluntary commitments to sustainable development in business and investment strategies worldwide. Research indicates that strong CSR strategies can enhance a company's ability to sustain operations and improve financial performance. CSR and sustainability are interrelated approaches that contribute to better financial outcomes. The CSR index is often used to assess ethical business practices (Siueia et al., 2019).

Moreover, CSR disclosure can influence the financial performance of businesses, particularly in the banking sector (Chowdhury & Nehal, 2020). Increased focus on CSR programs has led to greater scrutiny of the banking sector's role in sustainable development, given its substantial use of resources and waste generation. Therefore, banks need to prioritize environmental protection alongside shareholder returns (Chowdhury & Nehal, 2020).

The existing literature on the relationship between financial success in the banking sector and corporate social responsibility (CSR) has produced inconsistent empirical results, with studies showing neutral, positive, and negative associations.

This inconsistency means that overall conclusions regarding the CSR-financial performance link remain unresolved, and there is no consensus within the current body of research. Additionally, research on CSR and financial performance in African contexts is limited, with most studies focusing on Western and industrialized Asian countries (Esteban-Sanchez, Cuesta-Gonzalez, & Paredes-Gazquez, 2017).

Esteban-Sanchez et al. (2017), Javed et al. (2016), and Siueia et al. (2019) caution that the previously observed relationships between CSR and financial performance may not be universally applicable across different contexts. They emphasize that the CSR-financial performance relationship varies significantly among industries and is influenced by sector-specific competitive dynamics. The geographical location of a company also plays a critical role in shaping its CSR practices and their financial outcomes (Porter & Kramer, 2007).

Therefore, the banking industry in African countries, such as Tunisia, presents a unique opportunity to explore the relationship between CSR disclosure and financial performance. This study seeks to address the gap in the literature by empirically analyzing this relationship within the context of Tunisia's banking sector.

1.1 Background

In the contemporary global financial landscape, the role of banks transcends mere profit generation to encompass a broader commitment to societal and environmental well-being. This evolution is particularly salient in developing economies like Tunisia, where the banking sector is a critical engine for economic growth and social stability. Post-2011, Tunisia has intensified its focus on sustainable and inclusive development, aligning national policies with the United Nations' Sustainable Development Goals (SDGs). Within this context, Corporate Social Responsibility (CSR) has emerged as a strategic imperative, positioning financial institutions as key actors in financing the green economy, promoting social equity, and fostering transparent governance. However, a pivotal question for both bank management and regulators remains: do investments in CSR disclosures yield tangible financial returns, or do they represent a costly diversion of resources? This chapter empirically investigates this nexus within the unique socio-economic fabric of Tunisia, providing critical insights into the business case for CSR in an emerging market banking sector.

1.2 Research benefits

This research offers multifaceted benefits for the Tunisian financial ecosystem. For bank executives and managers, the findings provide a compelling, evidence-based rationale for strategically integrating and reporting on CSR activities. Demonstrating a positive link to profitability (ROA and ROE) can shift CSR from a peripheral public relations exercise to a core strategic function aimed at enhancing stakeholder trust, securing a social license to operate, and ultimately improving the bottom line. For regulators and policymakers, such as the Central Bank of Tunisia, the study underscores the potential of CSR disclosure as a mechanism for enhancing market transparency and stability. It offers a foundation for considering the development of a standardized sustainability reporting framework, which could align the banking sector with national SDG targets and international best practices. Finally, for investors and stakeholders, this research illuminates the value of non-financial disclosure, suggesting that banks with robust CSR practices may represent lower-risk, more sustainable investment opportunities, thereby encouraging a more responsible investment climate in Tunisia.

2.0 LITERATURE REVIEW AND HYPOTHESIS DEVELOPMENT

Globally, the literature on CSR and financial performance is extensive yet inconclusive, with meta-analyses revealing positive, negative, and neutral associations (Margolis & Walsh, 2003; Wang et al., 2016). This inconsistency is often attributed to contextual factors such as industry, regulatory environment, and national culture. Research specific to the banking sector in developed and emerging Asian markets has shown mixed results, with studies by Wu and Shen (2013) and Cornett et al. (2016) finding positive correlations, while others like Makni et al. (2009) found no significant link.

Crucially, the body of literature focusing on the African and, more specifically, the Tunisian context is remarkably sparse. Tunisia's journey is distinct, characterized by its post-revolutionary democratic transition and its active pursuit of the SDGs. While Tunisian companies are increasingly aware of CSR concepts, their adoption is often nascent and fragmented, lacking the systematic integration seen in more mature markets (Ben Brik et al., 2011). The country's National Strategic Plan 2020-2025 explicitly links economic development with social and environmental sustainability, creating a pertinent backdrop for this study. This chapter directly addresses this gap, moving beyond the Western and Asian contexts to explore how CSR disclosure functions within Tunisia's unique institutional and developmental landscape, where banks are pivotal to achieving national sustainability objectives.

2.1 Theoretical Background

The theoretical foundation of this research is anchored in Stakeholder Theory (Freeman, 1984). This theory posits that an organization's success is dependent on its ability to effectively manage relationships with all its stakeholders—including shareholders, customers, employees, communities, and regulators—rather than focusing solely on shareholders. From this perspective, CSR disclosure is not an altruistic endeavor but a strategic tool for managing stakeholder expectations, building legitimacy, and reducing information asymmetry. By transparently communicating their social and environmental performance, banks can enhance their reputation, foster customer and employee loyalty, and mitigate operational and reputational risks, thereby creating a conducive environment for sustained financial performance.

2.2 Theoretical Evolution

The evolution of CSR theory has seen a shift from the classical Friedmanite view—that the sole social responsibility of business is to increase profits—towards more integrative models. These include Legitimacy Theory, which suggests organizations disclose CSR information to ensure their operations are perceived as aligning with societal values, and the Resource-Based View, which frames CSR as a strategic resource that can create a competitive advantage (Barney, 1991). This chapter's use of Stakeholder Theory is apt, as it provides a comprehensive framework for understanding why Tunisian banks, operating in a sensitive socio-political environment, would engage in CSR and how such engagement translates into financial gains.

Various theories have been proposed to explain why companies engage in corporate social responsibility (CSR) disclosure. These include stakeholder theory, institutional theory, political economy theory, legitimacy theory, stewardship theory, and agency theory. However, no single theoretical framework can fully account for a company's decision to participate in CSR. This study primarily focuses on stakeholder theory to analyze CSR disclosure practices. Among the various theories, stakeholder theory is particularly prominent in explaining social and environmental disclosures (Itotenaan, Samy, & Bampton, 2014).

2.2.1 Stakeholder theories

Stakeholder theory explores the interconnected relationship between an organization and its various stakeholder groups. According to this theory, an organization's success hinges on its ability to effectively manage and cultivate relationships with stakeholders such as investors, shareholders, customers, employees, and local communities (Freeman & Reed, 1983). Freeman defines stakeholders as “any group or individual who is impacted by or has the ability to impact the achievement of an organization's objectives.” Stakeholder theory emphasizes that organizations must fulfill both implicit and explicit agreements with their stakeholders. While implicit contracts are seen as self-enforcing relational arrangements without legal standing, explicit contracts are legally binding and define the organization's formal obligations

(Niresh & Silva, 2018). Essentially, stakeholder theory suggests that organizations should consider the needs and interests of their stakeholders as these factors can significantly influence organizational outcomes.

2.3 Corporate Social Responsibility Disclosure and Financial Performance

Research into the relationship between corporate social responsibility (CSR) disclosure and financial performance has produced mixed results, with no clear consensus. Some studies indicate that CSR disclosure positively impacts financial performance by enhancing stakeholder trust, reputation, customer attraction, and access to financing (Matuszak & Różańska, 2017). Conversely, other research has found no significant correlation between CSR disclosure and financial performance (Gololo, 2019; Ullman, 1985). Additionally, some studies report a negative or neutral association, suggesting that CSR disclosure does not always lead to improved financial outcomes (Elif & Halil, 2017; Freeman & Reed, 1983). Contextual factors such as industry characteristics, company size, and market conditions may affect this relationship. Therefore, a comprehensive analysis of the CSR disclosure-financial performance link must consider these contextual factors and apply stakeholder theory to understand the nuances of this relationship (Gololo, 2019).

2.4 Corporate Social Responsibility Disclosure and Financial Performance in Banking Industry

The relationship between financial performance and corporate social responsibility (CSR) disclosure can vary significantly depending on the industry and geographical context. Research often reveals inconsistencies, particularly when CSR ratings are aggregated across diverse industries and countries. A more nuanced approach would involve analyzing this relationship within specific sectors and regions (Baird et al., 2011).

In the banking sector, where this relationship remains underexplored, findings have been mixed and sometimes contradictory. For instance, Wu and Shen (2013) found a positive correlation between financial performance metrics—such as return on equity (ROE), return on assets (ROA), net interest income, and non-interest income—and CSR disclosure, based on a study of 162 banks across 22 countries from 2003 to 2009. This supports the notion that CSR disclosure positively influences financial performance, a view also endorsed by Cornett et al. (2016), Elif & Halil (2017), Tafti et al. (2012), and Weshah (2012).

Conversely, Chih et al. (2009) conducted a study of 520 financial firms across 34 countries between 2003 and 2005, and found no significant relationship between financial performance and CSR. This conclusion is supported by Cellier & Chollet (2012), Makni et al. (2009), and Soana (2011). Additionally, Taskin (2015) and Soana (2011) observed varying associations, with some studies indicating a lack of significant correlation.

To evaluate bank financial performance, researchers typically use either accounting-based measures (Cornett et al., 2016; Taskin, 2015; Wu & Shen, 2013) or market-based measures (Tafti et al., 2012). This study adopts an accounting-based approach, focusing on two widely used profitability indicators: Return on Assets (ROA) and Return on Equity (ROE).

Taşkın (2015) found a positive and statistically significant relationship between the disclosure of corporate social responsibility (CSR) practices and the net interest margin (NIM) of Turkish banks. However, no statistically significant link was observed between CSR disclosure and profitability indicators such as return on assets (ROA) and return on equity (ROE). Similarly, Senyigit and Shuaibu (2017) investigated the impact of CSR dimensions on corporate financial performance in two different countries. Their study revealed that while CSR had a positive impact on the financial performance of banks in Nigeria, no statistically significant relationship was found between CSR and the financial performance of banks in Turkey.

Matuszaka and Różańska (2017), in their study of 18 Polish banks over the 2008-2015 period, examined the impact of CSR on financial performance. They found a positive relationship between CSR disclosures and profitability, as measured by ROA and ROE, but a negative correlation between CSR and NIM. Likewise, Szegedi et al. (2020) also demonstrated that CSR positively impacted financial performance, with accounting indicators such as ROA and ROE reflecting this trend.

Sekhon and Kathuria (2019) analyzed 137 large CNX-500 companies over a ten-year period (2008-2017) and found that the impact of CSR on financial performance was neutral for ROA and net profit margin but negative for ROE. Similarly, Hafez (2015), in a study of 34 Egyptian banks covering 2005-2013, found no significant link between CSR disclosure and financial performance.

In the United Arab Emirates, Ellili and Nobanee (2023) analyzed the impact of sustainability disclosure, considering economic, environmental, and social responsibility dimensions, on the profitability of 16 banks from 2003 to 2013. The study revealed that, although sustainability disclosure levels were low, it had a positive and significant impact on bank performance. The study recommended that the Central Bank of the Emirates create a transparency framework to improve compliance with sustainability standards and reduce information asymmetry.

Bande (2022) examined the impact of CSR on the financial performance of banks in Nigeria, analyzing 13 banks over the 2005-2014 period. Financial performance was assessed through ROA, ROE, return on deposits (ROD), and profit after tax (PAT). The study revealed a positive relationship between CSR activities and financial performance, suggesting that banks should enhance their CSR commitments to improve financial performance and provide social benefits.

Nguyen et al. (2022) investigated Vietnamese commercial banks from 2012 to 2019, identifying a positive correlation between financial performance indicators—NIM, ROA, and ROE—and CSR disclosure. However, Nguyen (2018), in an earlier study covering 2011 to 2016, found a significant negative relationship between CSR disclosure and financial performance in Vietnamese banks. Similarly, Tran et al. (2021) revealed that CSR disclosure negatively affected the financial performance of Vietnamese banks, as measured by ROA, ROE, and NIM.

2.5 Hypothesis Development

The previous section explored the theoretical perspectives on the relationship between financial performance and corporate social responsibility (CSR) disclosure. According to stakeholder theory, a positive correlation is expected between these constructs. Based on this theoretical framework, the study aims to test the following hypotheses:

H_1: There is a significant positive correlation between the financial performance of Tunisian banking institutions, as measured by the Return on Assets (ROA) ratio, and corporate social responsibility disclosure.

H_2: There is a significant positive correlation between the financial performance of Tunisian banking institutions, as measured by the Return on Equity (ROE) ratio, and corporate social responsibility disclosure.

3.0 METHODOLOGY

This study employs a quantitative, longitudinal research design based on a panel dataset of 14 Tunisian banks over an 11-year period (2013-2023), yielding 154 observations. The dependent variables, financial performance, are measured using two accounting-based indicators: Return on Assets (ROA) and Return on Equity (ROE). The independent variable, CSR Disclosure (CSRD), is constructed via a content analysis of bank annual reports. A composite index is calculated based on 34 disclosure items across four themes: Environment, Human Resources, Products/Customers, and Community Involvement. To establish causality, a lagged CSRD variable (CSRD~t-1~) is used. The model incorporates several control variables known to influence bank profitability, including bank size, age, loan ratio, overhead expenses, and debt ratio. The analysis utilizes panel data regression techniques, with diagnostic tests (VIF, Breusch-Pagan, Hausman) confirming the appropriateness of the Random Effects model.

3.1 Data

The researchers analyzed 14 Tunisian banks with audited financial reports available from 2012 onward. They reviewed the financial statements of these banks over an 11-year period, resulting in a panel dataset with a total of 154 observations.

3.2. Determining and measuring variables

3.2.1. Corporate social responsibility disclosure variable

There is no universally accepted method for evaluating corporate social responsibility (CSR) initiatives within the banking sector. Researchers have employed various approaches, such as questionnaire surveys (Tafti et al., 2012), measuring sponsorship and donations (David, 2012), analyzing CSR disclosures in reports (Tafti et al., 2012), and using one- or multidimensional ratings like KLD ratings (Becchetti et al., 2012), EIRIS indexes (Wu & Shen, 2013), and AEI indexes (Matuszak & Różańska, 2017; Soana, 2011).

In this study, content analysis was utilized to create a composite CSR index by examining the annual financial reports of selected Tunisian banks.

CSR covers a broad spectrum of aspects. ISO 26000, for instance, addresses seven key areas: organizational governance, human rights, labor practices, environmental impact, fair operating procedures, consumer concerns, and community involvement. The United Nations Global Compact Principles also mandate respect for human rights, labor standards, environmental protection, and anti-corruption efforts. Additionally, the Global Reporting Initiative guidelines categorize indicators into economic, social, and environmental dimensions (Matuszak & Różańska, 2017).

Research on CSR in banking has identified several sub-themes. For example, Gray et al. (1995) categorized CSR into dimensions such as human resources, environmental impact, and community involvement. Similarly, Kiliç et al. (2015) and Matuszak & Różańska (2017) classified CSR into environmental impact, human resources, product impact, and community impact. This study organizes CSR disclosure into four primary areas: the environment, human resources, products and customers, and community involvement, as outlined (Appendix A) by Kiliç et al. (2015) and Matuszak & Różańska (2017).

The content analysis method was used to assess CSR reporting in Tunisian commercial banks, like previous studies like Matuszak and Róaska 2017. Specifically, the study examined whether banks' financial statements disclosed CSR information.

A value of "one" was assigned for reported CSR disclosures and "zero" if they were not reported.

Formula will be there

$$CSR\ reporting\ index = \frac{\sum_{i}^{n}=1xi}{n}$$

where:

xi – 1 if the item i is disclosed, 0 if the item i is not disclosed,

n - number of items.

An assessment has been conducted on the overall extent of corporate social responsibility disclosure in four primary areas: environmental performance, human resource, product customer, and community involvement. The researchers appropriately included lagged CSR reporting index data to improve the predictive strength of the regression models presented in the study. The researchers were able to investigate the causal relationship between financial performance and corporate social responsibility as a result. Using lagged CSR as an independent variable to establish causation is becoming more prevalent in contemporary work (Cajias et al., 2014; Nollet et al., 2016). This strategy aligns with the knowledge that corporate social responsibility (CSR) is an investment in intangible assets, which may take some time to yield the expected results.

3.2.2 Reliability of Content Analysis

Reliability and validity are critical considerations in content analysis. Ensuring the consistency of the coded data is essential for drawing accurate conclusions. A key aspect of this process is maintaining uniformity in the categorization to ensure that different coders interpret the same text in a similar way (Weber, 1990). Coding reliability is often demonstrated by agreement between multiple coders or by resolving any discrepancies that arise (Platonova et al., 2016). Furthermore, Krippendorff (1984) highlights three important types of reliability relevant to content analysis: accuracy, repeatability, and stability.

To ensure the credibility of the content analysis, several steps were taken. First, a pilot study was conducted with 16 randomly selected annual reports to assess the reliability of the analysis. Second, a repeat content analysis of the pilot reports was performed one month later to evaluate the consistency of the scores. Third, two independent coders assessed the pilot study's annual reports. After being briefed on the dimensions and sub-dimensions of the CSR disclosure index, the coders rated the CSR disclosure material accordingly. Decision rules were then developed and refined to streamline the data collection process. After completing the pilot study, the researchers combined the coders' assessments and made minor adjustments to the disclosure dimensions and decision rules to ensure the coding process remained objective, accurate, and reliable.

3.2.3 Control variables

Previous studies have emphasized the importance of mediating variables when analyzing the relationship between corporate social responsibility (CSR) disclosures and financial performance. It is therefore recommended to further explore this connection while considering factors such as organizational size, industry characteristics, stakeholder engagement, and the nature of socially responsible practices (Platonova et al., 2016). This study includes five control variables commonly explored in the empirical literature and thought to influence bank financial performance: bank age, bank size, loan ratio, overhead expense ratio, and risk exposure (Platonova et al., 2016).

Several studies identify company age as a key determinant of financial performance (Liu & Anbumozhi, 2009), with some finding a positive correlation between the two (Delaney & Huselid, 1996). Thus, this study anticipates a positive relationship between bank age and financial performance.

Bank size is also a significant factor affecting profitability, with larger banks benefiting from greater capital adequacy and lower capital costs, thereby enhancing profitability (Demirgüç-Kunt & Huizinga, 2000). Total assets, often represented logarithmically, serve as a common indicator of bank size (Claessens et al., 2002). Empirical evidence from studies like Platonova et al. (2018) supports the positive effect of bank size on profitability.

The loan-to-asset ratio, a key bank-specific factor, influences profitability by reflecting a bank's capacity to generate earnings (Chronopoulos et al., 2015). This ratio, calculated by dividing total loans by total assets (Simpson & Kohers, 2002), is central to the revenue generation of Tunisian banks, which rely heavily on traditional financial models. Demirgüç-Kunt & Huizinga (2000) found loans to be a vital source of income, indicating that a higher loan ratio is expected to positively impact profitability in Tunisian banks.

Operating expenses also significantly affect bank profitability. These expenses, measured by dividing non-interest expenses by average total assets (Simpson & Kohers, 2002), have been shown to negatively impact profitability, as found in a study by Athanasoglou et al. (2008). This underscores the importance of efficient cost management to boost profitability, with overhead expenses expected to adversely affect Tunisian banks' financial performance.Given its influence on the relationship between financial performance and corporate social responsibility disclosure, risk functions as a control variable in this research (Waddock & Graves, 1997). A bank's level of risk can be determined by looking at its debt-to-assets ratio (Platonova et al., 2016; Waddock & Graves, 1997). The debt ratio is predicted to have a negative correlation with Tunisian banks' financial performance because higher debt levels can limit managerial discretion and possibly prevent access to new business possibilities.

3.3 Empirical Model

The study employed panel data analysis to investigate the impact of CSR disclosure on banks' financial performance. Panel data refers to a specific type of multilevel data where observations are tracked over time (e.g., T1, T2, T3...) and grouped within entities such as corporations. Each time point is referred to as a "wave," and panel datasets are characterized by the number of entities and waves. This analytical approach is particularly valuable in contemporary social and economic research, as it offers several advantages over cross-sectional data. It enables the exploration of causal relationships, hypothesis testing, and helps to reduce bias while addressing multicollinearity issues (Matuszak & Różańska, 2017).

To test the hypotheses, the researchers constructed empirical models that incorporated the previously mentioned dependent and independent variables. These models were designed to assess the relationships between the variables and provide a framework for evaluating the influence of the independent variables on the dependent outcomes.

$ROA_{it} = \alpha + \beta 1\ CSRD_{it-1} + \beta 2\ AGE_{it} + \beta 3\ SIZE_{it} + \beta 4\ Loan\ ratio_{it} - \beta 5\ Overhead\ exp_{it} - \beta 6\ debt\ ratio_{it} + +\varepsilon$ .... Model 1

$ROE_{it} = \alpha + \beta 1\ CSRD_{it-1} + \beta 2\ AGE_{it} + \beta 3\ SIZE_{it} + \beta 4\ Loan\ ratio_{it} - \beta 5\ Overhead\ exp_{it} - \beta 6\ debt\ ratio_{it} + +\varepsilon$ .... Model 2

Where:

ROA_{it} is Return on Asset of Bank i at time t,

ROE_{it} is Return on Equity of Bank i at time t,

$CSRD_{it\ is}$ lagged CSRD

AGE_{it},- Age of the bank Bank i at time t,

$Size_{it}$, size of Bank i at time t,

Bank Loan $ratio_{it}$- loan ratio Bank i at time t,

Overhead exp_{it}- overhead expense Bank i at time t, and

debt $ratio_{it}$ – debt ratio Bank i at time t,

β is the coefficient of the independent variable

Table 1. Names of variables, their corresponding measurements, and the predicted signs.

Variable name and abbreviation	Measurement	Expected sign
CSR disclosure (CSRD)	Calculated by dividing the number of disclosure content points by the maximum score that a bank can attain.	+
Age (AGE)	Number of years each bank operated on the market	+
Size (SIZE)	Log of total assets	+
Loan ratio (Loan Ratio)	Average total loans/average total assets	+
Overhead Expenses (Over head exp)	Total expenses (noninterest) divided by average assets	-
Debt ratio (Debt ratio)	The ratio of total debt to total assets	-
Dependent Variables		
Return on Equity (ROA)	Dividing the net income by the average asset.	
Return on Asset (ROE)	Dividing the net income by the average Equity	

4.0 RESULTS, DISCUSSION & ANALYSIS

4.1 Descriptive Statistics

Table 2's descriptive statistics provide a detailed overview of the dependent, independent, and control variables used in the regression analysis. During the research period, the banks' average Return on Assets (ROA) was 2.951%, with a standard deviation of 0.942%. The minimum and maximum ROA values, 0.326% and 6.348% respectively, reflect the variance suggested by the standard deviation. The average Return on Equity (ROE) was 20.62%, with a higher standard deviation of 6.927%, indicating that Tunisian banks aimed for significant shareholder returns, with ROE values ranging from 2.5% to 42.43%.

The Corporate Social Responsibility Disclosure (CSRD) index showed considerable variation in CSR reporting across the banks. The highest score was 0.321 and the lowest was 0.036, with an average score of 0.216. This indicates a relatively low level of CSR disclosure, and the small standard deviation of 0.055 suggests limited variability in CSR reporting among the banks.

The control variables, which include bank age, size, loan-to-asset ratio, overhead expense ratio, and debt ratio, display the following characteristics: Bank age ranged from 2 to 29 years, with a mean of 14.74 years and a standard deviation of 7.02 years. Bank size, measured by asset values, ranged from 8.628 to 11.35, with an average of 10.175. The loan-to-asset ratio varied from 24.036% to 74.974%, with a mean of 49.735%. The overhead expense ratio ranged from 0.07% to 13.54%, with a mean of 4.134%. Finally, the debt ratio ranged from 61.756% to 97.75%, with an average of 85.519%.

Table 2. Descriptive Statistics

Variable	Obs	Mean	Std. Dev.	Min	Max
ROA	154	2.915	.942	.326	6.348
ROE	154	20.62	6.927	2.504	42.43
CSRD	154	.235	.053	.036	.393
Age	154	14.74	7.025	2	29
LogAsset	154	10.175	.551	8.628	11.35
Loanratio	154	49.735	10.921	24.036	74.974
Overhead	154	4.134	2.009	.07	13.54
Debitratio	154	85.519	4.505	61.756	97.75

4.2 Pearson correlation analysis

The correlation analysis presented in Table 3 highlights the relationships between the independent and dependent variables examined in this study. The results show that the strength of these associations varies widely, from highly robust to relatively weak, with some correlations lacking statistical significance.

The analysis reveals an insignificant positive correlation between CSR disclosure (CSRD) and both ROA and ROE, with correlation coefficients of 0.086 and 0.104, respectively, at a 5% significance level. Additionally, ROA shows a significant negative correlation with all control variables. In contrast, ROE has a significant positive correlation with bank age and the debt ratio but is negatively correlated with the loan ratio and overhead expenses. Bank size exhibits a positive, albeit insignificant, correlation with ROE.

The variance inflation factor (VIF) values reported in Table 3 are all below the conventional threshold of 10, indicating that multicollinearity is not an issue in this study. This confirms that the variables in the analysis are not highly correlated with each other, ensuring the reliability of the regression results.

Table 3. Pairwise correlations

Variables	VIF	(1)	(2)	(3)	(4)	(5)	(6)	(7)	(8)
(1) ROA		1.000							
(2) ROE		0.689*	1.000						
(3) CSRD	1.660	0.086	0.104	1.000					
(4) Age	2.953	-0.286*	0.162*	0.392*	1.000				
(5) LogAsset	5.446	-0.356*	0.130	0.539*	0.784*	1.000			
(6) Loanratio	2.006	-0.248*	-0.031	0.470*	0.386*	0.663*	1.000		
(7) Overhead	1.600	-0.587*	-0.209*	-0.330*	-0.539*	-0.603*	-0.374*	1.000	
(8) Debitratio	1.667	-0.244*	0.348*	0.033	0.522*	0.538*	0.272*	-0.339*	1.000
	*** $p<0.01$, ** $p<0.05$, * $p<0.1$								

4.3 Panel data analysis

Before conducting the multiple regression analyses on the panel data, the researchers performed several statistical tests to validate the data. To assess potential multicollinearity among the independent variables, the variance inflation factor (VIF) and Pearson's correlation matrix were employed. The correlation matrix in Table 3 did not display any values exceeding 0.8, indicating that the study variables were not highly correlated. The LogAsset variable had the highest VIF at 5.45, while overhead expenses had the lowest at 1.60, confirming that multicollinearity was not a concern, as the accepted threshold for multicollinearity is a VIF of 10 or above (Platonova et al., 2016).

To test for heteroscedasticity, the researchers applied the Breusch-Pagan/Cook-Weisberg test to both regression models. The p-values for return on equity (ROE) and return on assets (ROA) were 0.2371 and 0.2994, respectively, allowing the null hypothesis to be accepted and confirming the absence of heteroscedasticity issues.

The Breusch-Pagan Lagrangian multiplier test was used to determine whether a random effects or a pooled OLS regression model was more appropriate. The p-values for ROA (0.001) and ROE (0.016) were both below 0.05, indicating that the pooled OLS model was not the best fit, and the random effects model was more suitable. Furthermore, the Hausman test supported the use of the random effects model over the fixed effects model, with p-values of 0.7797 for ROA and 0.7588 for ROE, reinforcing the appropriateness of the random effects model for the analysis.

The regression analysis shown in Table 4 investigates the relationship between corporate social responsibility disclosure (CSRD) and the financial performance of banks in Tunisia from 2013 to 2023. For the ROA model, the R^2 value is 0.358, indicating that the independent variables explain 35.8% of the variation in ROA. The

F-statistic is 14.24, with a p-value of 0.0000, demonstrating the overall statistical significance of the model and confirming its robustness.

The results reveal a statistically significant and positive relationship between CSRD and ROA at the 0.1 significance level. This finding aligns with previous research by Cornett et al. (2016), Elif & Halil (2017), Tafti et al. (2012), and Weshah (2012), indicating that greater efforts in CSR disclosure are associated with improved financial performance, as measured by ROA. This supports hypothesis 1, which posits a positive and statistically significant correlation between CSR disclosure and financial performance in Tunisia's banking sector.

The findings are consistent with established theoretical frameworks, suggesting that enhanced CSRD leads to increased profitability for banks in Tunisia. Among the five control variables, overhead expenses exhibit a significant negative relationship (p = 0.01) with profitability, while the other four control variables show an insignificant negative association with the financial performance of Tunisian banks.

The regression model presented in Table 4, Model 2, assesses the effect of corporate social responsibility disclosure (CSRD) on the financial performance of Tunisian banks, using Return on Equity (ROE) as the performance metric. The R-squared value of 0.316 indicates that the predictor variables included in the model can explain 31.6% of the variation in ROE. The F-statistic of 14.43, with a p-value of 0.0000, confirms that the overall model is statistically significant.

The analysis reveals a statistically significant positive relationship between CSR disclosure and ROE at the 5% significance level. This suggests that banks in Tunisia may enhance their profitability by increasing CSR disclosures, further validating Hypothesis 2, which predicted a positive correlation between CSRD and the financial performance of Tunisian banks, measured by ROE. These results also align with the stakeholder theory referenced in the study.

Regarding the control variables, overhead expenses and debt ratio show a significant positive relationship with ROE. On the other hand, loan ratio, overhead expenses, and debt ratio exhibit a significant negative association with ROE at the 0.1 and 0.01 levels of significance, highlighting the complex dynamics of bank profitability in relation to these factors.

Table 4. Regression Analysis

	(Pooled Model)	**(Pooled Model)**	**(Random effect)**	**(Random effect)**	**(fixed effect)**	**(fixed effect)**
	ROA	ROE	**ROA**	**ROE**	ROA	ROE
CSRD	2.814*	32.819***	**2.584***	**29.613****	3.114*	35.81***
	(1.492)	(11.399)	**(1.484)**	**(11.568)**	(1.709)	(13.518)

continued on following page

Table 4. Continued

	(Pooled Model)	(Pooled Model)	(Random effect)	(Random effect)	(fixed effect)	(fixed effect)
Age	.011	.07	**-.005**	**.028**	-.041	-.447
	(.015)	(.115)	**(.022)**	**(.156)**	(.043)	(.34)
LogAsset	-.149	1.376	**-.02**	**1.841**	.126	3.703
	(.261)	(1.998)	**(.263)**	**(2.045)**	(.303)	(2.397)
Loanratio	-.006	-.124**	**-.012**	**-.127***	-.013	-.088
	(.008)	(.061)	**(.009)**	**(.066)**	(.01)	(.076)
Overhead	.28***	1.651***	**-.237*****	**-1.539*****	.214***	1.528***
	(.039)	(.297)	**(.045)**	**(.343)**	(.051)	(.403)
Debitratio	-.005	.706***	**-.007**	**.588*****	-.009	.38*
	(.018)	(.136)	**(.022)**	**(.163)**	(.026)	(.205)
_cons	3.164	-63.177***	**2.765**	**-55.827*****	2.058	-53.363**
	(2.306)	(17.614)	**(2.634)**	**(20.057)**	(3.084)	(24.388)
F-test Observations	154	154	**14.24***** **154**	**11.43***** **154**	154	154
R-squared	.367	.318	**.358**	**.316**	.26	.15

Standard errors are in parentheses
**** p<.01, ** p<.05, * p<.1*

4.4 Result Analysis

The empirical results provide robust support for the study's central hypotheses, revealing a statistically significant positive relationship between lagged CSR disclosure and both ROA and ROE. This finding strongly corroborates the predictions of Stakeholder Theory. It indicates that Tunisian banks which proactively communicate their CSR activities are likely to be rewarded with enhanced profitability in subsequent periods. This suggests that stakeholders—perhaps customers, depositors, or investors—value this transparency and reciprocate with greater business, lower costs of capital, or enhanced loyalty, thereby improving financial performance.

This result aligns with studies in other emerging markets that found a positive CSR-financial performance link (e.g., Bande, 2022 in Nigeria; Ellili & Nobanee, 2023 in the UAE) but contrasts with findings from Vietnam (Tran et al., 2021) and Turkey (Taşkın, 2015). This divergence underscores the critical role of national context. In Tunisia, where the formal adoption of CSR is still evolving, early and transparent adopters may garner significant reputational benefits, distinguishing themselves in a competitive market and aligning themselves with national SDG aspirations, thus creating a tangible financial advantage.

5.0 CONCLUSION

The empirical study investigated the influence of corporate social responsibility (CSR) disclosure on the financial performance of Tunisian banks, using Return on Assets (ROA) and Return on Equity (ROE) as indicators of profitability. The literature review supporting the study includes an exploration of stakeholder theory and an examination of previous research that has shown inconsistent results regarding the impact of CSR activities on financial performance. The study posits that CSR disclosure is significantly related to financial performance in Tunisian banks.

The findings demonstrate a statistically significant positive relationship between CSR disclosure and profitability, as measured by both ROA and ROE. This supports the theoretical framework that suggests a positive correlation between CSR activities and financial performance. Specifically, the results show that increased CSR disclosure is associated with higher profitability for banks in Tunisia, which aligns with previous research (Cornett et al., 2016; Platonova et al., 2016; Simpson & Kohers, 2002; Tafti et al., 2012; Weshah, 2012).

These results have several important implications. Theoretically, they confirm stakeholder theory, which argues that addressing stakeholder needs through CSR can enhance profitability and competitive advantage. Additionally, this study contributes to the CSR literature by providing insights into the Tunisian context and advancing our understanding of CSR's impact on banking sector financial performance. Practically, given that Tunisia is one of Africa's less developed nations, the study's conclusions may also be relevant to other developing countries, particularly in Eastern Africa, suggesting that CSR practices could similarly benefit financial performance in these regions

5.1 Recommendation for Stakeholders and Regulating Agencies

For Tunisian Banks: Management should view CSR not as a cost center but as a strategic investment. They should move beyond ad-hoc charitable donations to integrate CSR into core business operations, such as developing *"green"* financial products, enhancing employee welfare programs, and ensuring fair customer treatment. Systematically measuring and reporting these activities is crucial for reaping the financial benefits.

For the Central Bank of Tunisia and Financial Market Authority: Regulators should consider moving from voluntary to mandatory sustainability reporting guidelines for banks. Developing a localized, principles-based framework aligned with global standards like the GRI or the UN SDGs would enhance comparability, reduce *"greenwashing,"* and solidify the financial sector's role in national sustainable development.

For Policymakers: The government could incentivize high-quality CSR through tax benefits or incorporating sustainability criteria into public procurement processes, further reinforcing the link between responsible business conduct and economic reward.

5.2 Limitation of the study

This study recognizes several limitations that might affect the generalizability and reliability of its findings. First, the research is specifically centered on the Tunisian banking sector, which may limit the applicability of the conclusions to other contexts. Second, the study's operationalization of both dependent and independent variables presents a limitation. Financial performance was measured using accounting-based ratios like ROA and ROE, whereas other studies often use market-based measures. Additionally, CSR disclosures were evaluated through content analysis and a custom CSR index, whereas alternative methods such as surveys, interviews, spending measures, or third-party ratings could offer different insights.

5.3 Future Research Directions

Future studies could build on this work in several ways. First, employing qualitative methods, such as interviews with bank managers and stakeholders, could provide deeper insights into the mechanisms through which CSR translates into financial performance in Tunisia. Second, a longitudinal study examining the impact of Tunisia's potential future adoption of IFRS Sustainability Standards on this relationship would be highly valuable. Third, expanding the scope to include market-based performance measures (e.g., Tobin's Q) could offer a more holistic view of value creation. Finally, comparative studies across different North African countries could help isolate the effects of specific national policies and cultural factors.

The research suggests that future studies should explore how the relationship between corporate social responsibility (CSR) disclosure and profitability evolves over time, particularly focusing on the period before and after Tunisia's adoption of International Financial Reporting Standards (IFRS). Comparative analyses could investigate how CSR disclosures impact the financial performance of banks in these different periods. Additionally, future research could benefit from employing comprehensive qualitative methods to gain insight into stakeholders' perspectives on banks' CSR initiatives and related disclosures. Moreover, the methodology used in this study could be applied to examine the effect of CSR disclosures on financial performance across various industrial sectors.

CHAPTER SUMMARY CONTEXT

The chapter investigates the underexplored link between CSR disclosure and financial performance within Tunisia's unique SDG-oriented banking sector.

Theory: The research is grounded in Stakeholder Theory, positing that transparent CSR communication manages stakeholder relationships and creates financial value.

Method: A panel data analysis of 14 Tunisian banks (2013-2023) uses a content-analysis-based CSR index and controls for key bank-specific factors.

Key Finding: A significant positive relationship exists between CSR disclosure and subsequent profitability (ROA and ROE), supporting the business case for CSR in Tunisia.

Implication: CSR should be strategically integrated into bank operations and reporting, rather than treated as a peripheral activity.

Recommendation: Regulators should consider developing a mandatory sustainability reporting framework to enhance transparency and align the sector with national development goals.

Contribution: The study fills a critical gap in the literature by providing empirical evidence from a North African emerging market, highlighting the context-dependent nature of the CSR-financial performance nexus.

CHAPTER QUESTIONS

True and False Questions

1. The empirical results of this study demonstrate a statistically significant *negative* relationship between Corporate Social Responsibility Disclosure (CSRD) and the financial performance of Tunisian banks.
2. Stakeholder Theory posits that a company's success is solely dependent on maximizing returns for its shareholders.
3. The methodology employed in this chapter utilized a content analysis of bank annual reports to construct a composite index for measuring CSR disclosure.

4. The study found that the level of CSR disclosure among the sampled Tunisian banks was uniformly high, with minimal variation across institutions.
5. To establish a clearer causal relationship, the study's regression models incorporated a lagged variable for CSR disclosure (CSRD~t-1~).
6. The Hausman test results indicated that a fixed effects model was more appropriate for the panel data analysis than a random effects model.
7. A key recommendation for the Central Bank of Tunisia arising from this research is to consider moving from voluntary to mandatory sustainability reporting guidelines.
8. The study's literature review conclusively determined that the relationship between CSR and financial performance is universally positive across all global contexts and industries.
9. The research operationalized financial performance using both accounting-based measures (ROA, ROE) and market-based measures (Tobin's Q).
10. One of the stated limitations of the study is its specific focus on the Tunisian banking sector, which may affect the generalizability of its findings.

Multiple Choice Questions

11. The primary theoretical framework underpinning this research is:
    A. Agency Theory
    B. Institutional Theory
    C. Stakeholder Theory
    D. Legitimacy Theory
    E. Political Economy Theory
12. The study's panel dataset was composed of observations from:
    A. 14 banks over 10 years
    B. 16 banks over 11 years
    C. 14 banks over 11 years
    D. 154 banks over 1 year
    E. 11 banks over 14 years
13. Which of the following was **NOT** one of the four primary areas used to categorize CSR disclosure in the content analysis?
    A. Environmental Performance
    B. Human Resources
    C. Political Lobbying
    D. Community Involvement
    E. Products and Customers
14. According to the correlation analysis, the relationship between the CSR disclosure index (CSRD) and Return on Assets (ROA) was:

A. Significantly positive
B. Significantly negative
C. Insignificantly positive
D. Insignificantly negative
E. A perfect positive correlation

15. The diagnostic test used to confirm the absence of multicollinearity among the independent variables was:
A. The Hausman Test
B. The Breusch-Pagan Test
C. The Variance Inflation Factor (VIF)
D. Pearson's Correlation Matrix
E. The Durbin-Watson Statistic

16. The empirical model for Return on Assets (ROA) included all the following control variables EXCEPT:
A. Bank Age
B. Debt Ratio
C. Inflation Rate
D. Overhead Expenses
E. Loan-to-Asset Ratio

17. The study's findings contrast with research from which country, which found a negative relationship between CSR disclosure and bank performance?
A. Nigeria
B. United Arab Emirates
C. Poland
D. Vietnam
E. Turkey

18. A key implication of the study's findings for bank managers in Tunisia is that CSR should be viewed as:
A. A mandatory regulatory burden
B. A peripheral public relations activity
C. A strategic investment
D. An unnecessary cost center
E. Primarily a charitable endeavor

19. Which international framework was cited as a potential benchmark for developing a localized sustainability reporting standard in Tunisia?
A. The Basel Accords
B. The Sarbanes-Oxley Act
C. The Global Reporting Initiative (GRI)
D. The Dodd-Frank Act
E. The Generally Accepted Accounting Principles (GAAP)

20. A suggested avenue for future research mentioned in the chapter is:
    A. Replicating the study in the manufacturing sector
    B. Employing qualitative methods to understand stakeholder perspectives
    C. Focusing exclusively on market-based performance measures
    D. Limiting the scope to only the five largest banks
    E. Abandoning panel data analysis in favor of cross-sectional studies

Short Answer Questions

21. Briefly define "Corporate Social Responsibility Disclosure" (CSRD) as operationalized in this chapter.
22. Identify the two key accounting-based metrics used in this study to represent a bank's financial performance.
23. What was the primary rationale provided for using a *lagged* CSR disclosure variable in the regression models?
24. Name three of the five control variables incorporated into the empirical models to account for other factors influencing bank profitability.
25. According to the descriptive statistics, what was the mean value of the CSR Disclosure Index for the sampled banks, and what does this suggest about the overall level of reporting?
26. Which statistical test was used to justify the selection of the Random Effects model over the Fixed Effects model for the panel data analysis?
27. In one or two sentences, summarize the core proposition of Stakeholder Theory as it applies to this research.
28. What is one specific recommendation the study proposes for regulators like the Central Bank of Tunisia?

Essay Questions

29. Elaborate on the *"contextual gap"* in the existing literature that this chapter seeks to address. Why is the Tunisian banking sector presented as a unique and valuable case study?
30. Critically analyze the methodology employed for constructing the CSR Disclosure index. Discuss the strengths of using content analysis for this purpose and identify one potential limitation of this approach.
31. Summarize the key findings of the regression analysis for both Return on Assets (ROA) and Return on Equity (ROE). How did the results for the control variables, such as overhead expenses, contribute to the understanding of bank profitability in Tunisia?

32. Interpret the study's empirical results through the lens of Stakeholder Theory. Explain the mechanism by which enhanced CSR disclosure could logically lead to improved financial performance for a bank.
33. Discuss the practical implications of this research for three distinct stakeholder groups: bank managers, financial regulators, and investors.
34. Evaluate the limitations acknowledged by the authors. How might these limitations shape the interpretation of the findings and suggest directions for future inquiry?

In-depth Questions for Master's Students (Requiring Further Research)

35. **Comparative Analysis:** Compare and contrast the findings of this Tunisian study with the results of a similar study conducted in a geographically or economically distinct context (e.g., Vietnam, Poland, or the UAE). Propose a hypothesis to explain the divergent or convergent results based on institutional or cultural differences.
36. **Methodological Expansion:** The study uses a self-constructed CSR index. Propose a research design that incorporates an established third-party ESG rating (e.g., from Refinitiv or MSCI) alongside the content analysis index. What would be the comparative advantages of this mixed-method approach, and what new insights might it yield?
37. **Causal Mechanisms:** The chapter suggests stakeholders "reward" transparency. Design a research proposal to investigate the specific causal mechanisms. Which stakeholder group (e.g., depositors, borrowers, employees) would you focus on, and what methodology (e.g., surveys, experiments, interview-based case studies) would you use to test their perceptions and behaviors?
38. **Theoretical Integration:** While Stakeholder Theory is the central framework, how might integrating the Resource-Based View (RBV) of the firm provide a more nuanced explanation for why some banks are better at translating CSR disclosure into financial gain? What *"valuable, rare, and inimitable"* resources might be involved?
39. **Policy Analysis:** Research the current state of sustainability reporting regulations in Tunisia or another North African country. Based on this chapter's findings and your research, draft a brief policy memo advocating for a specific regulatory change, outlining its potential benefits and challenges.

In-depth Questions for PhD Scholars

40. **Endogeneity and Causality:** The use of a lagged variable is one approach to addressing causality, but endogeneity remains a profound challenge in CSR-performance research. Critically deconstruct the potential sources of endogeneity in this study's model (e.g., omitted variable bias, reverse causality). Propose and justify a more advanced econometric technique (e.g., a dynamic panel GMM estimator, an instrumental variable approach) to more robustly identify a causal effect.
41. **Non-Linear and Contingent Relationships:** The study assumes a linear relationship between CSRD and performance. Develop a theoretical argument and a testable model for a potential non-linear (e.g., U-shaped or inverted U-shaped) relationship. Furthermore, theorize on what firm-specific or country-level contingency factors (e.g., governance structure, national institutional voids) might moderate this relationship, and design a multi-level model to test these interactions.
42. **Deconstructing CSR:** The study aggregates CSR into a single index. Propose a dissertation-level research project that deconstructs CSR into its discrete dimensions (e.g., environmental, social, governance). Investigate whether certain dimensions have a more potent or divergent impact on different aspects of financial performance (e.g., risk, cost of capital, profitability) and develop a theory for why such differential impacts might exist.

In-depth Questions for Post-Doctoral Researchers

43. **Institutional Logics and Field-Level Change:** Move beyond the firm-level analysis to a macro-institutional perspective. Design a longitudinal, qualitative research program to investigate how the competing institutional logics of *"shareholder primacy"* and *"sustainability"* are shaping the field of Tunisian banking. How are these logics being negotiated, hybridized, or resisted by banks, regulators, and civil society, and what is the role of CSR disclosure in this field-level transformation?
44. **The Political Economy of CSR Disclosure:** Frame CSR disclosure not merely as a transparency tool but as a socio-political phenomenon. Develop a critical research agenda that investigates how CSR reporting practices in the Tunisian banking sector are influenced by, and in turn influence, power dynamics, political connections, and the distribution of economic resources within the post-revolutionary state. How does disclosure act as a tool for legitimization or a form of political risk management?

45. **Theorizing from the South:** A significant portion of CSR theory has emerged from Anglo-American contexts. Using the empirical findings of this chapter and other studies from the Global South, critically engage with the core assumptions of mainstream CSR theories. How might the unique institutional configurations, historical paths, and cultural norms of a country like Tunisia necessitate the development of a distinct, or significantly modified, theoretical framework for understanding the relationship between corporate responsibility, disclosure, and performance?

TEACHING NOTE

Chapter: "The Impact of Corporate Social Responsibility Reporting Practice on the Financial Performance of Tunisian Banks"

This teaching note is designed to assist instructors in facilitating a dynamic and insightful discussion on the intersection of corporate social responsibility (CSR), financial performance, and emerging market banking. The chapter provides a robust empirical case study set in Tunisia, offering a fertile ground for exploring the contextual nuances of sustainability reporting.

Concise Summary for the Teacher

This chapter presents an empirical investigation into the relationship between CSR disclosure (CSRD) and financial performance (measured by Return on Assets - ROA and Return on Equity - ROE) within the Tunisian banking sector from 2013-2023. Grounded in Stakeholder Theory, the study employs a longitudinal panel data analysis of 14 banks.

Core Finding: The research identifies a statistically significant, positive correlation between CSRD and subsequent profitability. This suggests that for Tunisian banks, transparent communication of social and environmental activities is not merely a cost but a strategic investment that enhances financial returns.

Key Value-Add: The study's primary contribution lies in its focus on an under-researched context—a post-revolutionary North African economy actively pursuing Sustainable Development Goals (SDGs). It moves the conversation beyond Western and Asian contexts, demonstrating that the CSR-financial performance link is not universal but is significantly shaped by a country's specific institutional and developmental landscape. The findings advocate for the strategic integration of CSR and provide a evidence-based rationale for regulators to consider mandatory sustainability reporting frameworks.

Chapter Synopsis

The chapter opens by establishing the global significance of CSR and the inconclusive nature of its relationship with financial performance, particularly within the banking sector and especially in African contexts. It positions Tunisia as a unique case study due to its post-2011 democratic transition and alignment with the UN SDGs.

The literature review effectively synthesizes conflicting global findings and establishes Stakeholder Theory as the primary lens, arguing that CSRD is a strategic tool for managing stakeholder relationships and building legitimacy. The methodology is rigorous, utilizing a content-analysis-derived CSRD index, lagged variables to imply causality, and a set of standard control variables (size, age, loan ratio, etc.) in a Random Effects panel model.

The results robustly support the two main hypotheses, showing a positive impact of CSRD on both ROA and ROE. The conclusion translates these findings into practical recommendations for bank management, regulators, and policymakers, while also thoughtfully addressing the study's limitations and proposing avenues for future research.

Key Learning Objectives

Using Bloom's Taxonomy, upon completing this chapter, students should be able to:

1. **Remember:** Recall the key variables (ROA, ROE, CSRD index) and the central finding of the study.
2. **Understand:** Explain the role of Stakeholder Theory in framing the relationship between CSR disclosure and financial performance.
3. **Apply:** Illustrate how the methodological approach (e.g., content analysis, panel data with lagged variables) can be used to test similar relationships in other industries or countries.
4. **Analyze:** Contrast the findings of this study with conflicting results from other geographical contexts (e.g., Vietnam, Turkey) and hypothesize reasons for the divergence.
5. **Evaluate:** Assess the validity and generalizability of the study's conclusions by critiquing its methodological choices and contextual limitations.
6. **Create:** Propose a framework for a CSR reporting policy for a bank operating in an emerging market, integrating insights from the study's findings and recommendations.

Core Themes/Theses for Discussion

1. **The Contextual Contingency of CSR:** The CSR-financial performance link is not a universal law but is mediated by factors such as national policy, market maturity, stakeholder expectations, and cultural norms.
2. **CSR as Strategic Management vs. Philanthropy:** The findings support a shift in perspective from viewing CSR as a peripheral, charitable activity to recognizing it as a core strategic function that manages risk, enhances reputation, and creates tangible financial value.
3. **The Regulatory Imperative:** The transition from voluntary to mandatory sustainability reporting can enhance transparency, reduce greenwashing, and level the playing field, thereby strengthening the entire financial system.
4. **Methodology in Sustainability Research:** The chapter provides a platform to discuss the strengths and weaknesses of content analysis for constructing CSR indices, the use of accounting-based vs. market-based performance metrics, and the importance of research design in establishing causality.

Suggested Teaching Pathway (75-Minute Session)

- **Introduction (10 mins):** Start with a poll: "Do you believe being socially responsible helps or hurts a company's bottom line?" Use the mixed answers to introduce the chapter's central question and the inconclusive state of the literature.
- **Context and Theory (15 mins):** Briefly lecture on Tunisia's unique position and the core tenets of Stakeholder Theory. Use the chapter's introduction and literature review to highlight the research gap.
- **Methodology Deep Dive (15 mins):** Walk through the research design. Use a visual aid (slide) to explain the CSRD index (Appendix A), the concept of lagged variables, and the rationale for the control variables. Emphasize the practical steps taken to ensure coding reliability.
- **Findings and Analysis (15 mins):** Present the key results from Tables 3 and 4. Focus on the positive, significant coefficients for CSRD and discuss what they mean in practical terms for a bank manager.
- **Discussion and Application (20 mins):** Facilitate the class discussion using the key questions below. Encourage students to connect the findings to broader business trends (ESG investing, SDGs) and to critique the study's limitations.

Pedagogical Tools & Resources

- **Case Study:** This chapter itself serves as a compact case study.
- **"Think-Pair-Share":** Use for discussion questions to ensure broader participation.
- **Comparative Matrix:** Create a table on the board comparing this study's findings with those mentioned from Nigeria, Vietnam, and Turkey.
- **Role-Playing:** Divide students into groups representing Bank Managers, Central Bank Regulators, and NGO Advocates. Have each group develop a 2-minute pitch based on the study's findings from their perspective.
- **Supplementary Resources:** Direct advanced students to the "Additional Reading" section, particularly the IFRS S1 and S2 standards, to discuss the future of global sustainability reporting.

Note on Sensitivity

When discussing the Tunisian context, it is important to be mindful of the socio-political environment post-2011. Frame the "Arab Spring" and its aftermath as a period of significant transition that created a unique impetus for transparency and social equity, without making sweeping or simplistic political statements. The focus should remain on the business and regulatory implications within this evolving landscape.

Key Questions for Class Discussion

1. The study finds a positive link between CSR disclosure and profitability in Tunisia. Why might this same relationship be negative or neutral in other countries, such as Vietnam?
    - **Suggested Direction:** Guide discussion toward contextual factors: regulatory pressure (or lack thereof), stakeholder awareness, market competition, and the possibility of CSR being perceived as a costly distraction in different stages of economic development.
2. Stakeholder Theory is used as the main framework. How might the findings differ if the study were framed through Legitimacy Theory or the Resource-Based View?
    - **Suggested Direction:** Legitimacy Theory might emphasize CSR as a response to socio-political pressures in post-revolution Tunisia. The Resource-Based View would frame CSR as an intangible asset (reputation, trust) that competitors cannot easily imitate.

3. The CSRD index is based on content analysis of annual reports. What are the potential pitfalls of this method, and how might it be complemented?
    - **Suggested Direction:** Discuss "greenwashing" (disclosing without substantive action), the difficulty in assessing the *quality* of disclosures, and the potential for using third-party audits or customer perception surveys to validate the findings.
4. The study uses ROA and ROE as performance metrics. Would the results hold if we used market-based measures like Tobin's Q or stock price? Why or why not?
    - **Suggested Direction:** Explore the difference between accounting-based (historical, internal) and market-based (future-looking, investor perception) measures. The positive CSR link might be even stronger with market-based measures if investors value sustainability.
5. The recommendation is for regulators to move towards mandatory reporting. What are the potential unintended consequences of such a mandate for smaller banks?
    - **Suggested Direction:** Discuss the compliance cost burden, potential for "checkbox" reporting without real engagement, and the risk of stifling innovation. Contrast this with the benefits of a level playing field and enhanced systemic transparency.
6. Imagine you are a skeptical bank CEO. What is the most compelling piece of evidence from this study that might change your mind about investing in CSR reporting?
    - **Suggested Direction:** Focus on the use of *lagged* CSRD, which implies causation—that disclosure today leads to profit tomorrow. Also, the control for overhead expenses shows that CSR's benefit exists even when accounting for costs.
7. The study controls for bank "size." Why is this important, and what does its positive (though insignificant) coefficient in the ROE model suggest?
    - **Suggested Direction:** Larger banks likely have more resources for CSR. Controlling for it isolates the unique effect of CSR itself. The positive sign suggests that larger banks might be better positioned to leverage CSR for financial gain, a point worth exploring further.
8. Beyond profitability, what other strategic advantages might a Tunisian bank gain from robust CSR disclosure?
    - **Suggested Direction:** Brainstorm intangible benefits: attracting and retaining top talent, securing lower-cost capital from ESG-focused investors, enhancing customer loyalty, and obtaining a "social license to operate."

9. The chapter suggests future research could use qualitative methods. What specific questions would you ask in an interview with a bank manager to deepen these findings?
    - **Suggested Direction:** Examples: "Can you describe a specific instance where a CSR initiative directly led to a new client or retained a existing one?" "How do you decide what CSR information to disclose in your annual report?"
10. How does this case study from Tunisia inform the global conversation, led by bodies like the IFRS Foundation, on creating universal sustainability standards?
    - **Suggested Direction:** Conclude by linking the micro (Tunisian banks) to the macro (global standards). It shows that in emerging markets, clear standards can catalyze a virtuous cycle where transparency drives performance, thereby supporting the case for global interoperability in sustainability reporting.

REFERENCES

Athanasoglou, P. P., Brissimis, S. N., & Delis, M. D. (2008). Bank specific, industry-specific and macroeconomic determinants of bank profitability. *Journal of International Financial Markets, Institutions and Money*, *18*(2), 121–136. DOI: 10.1016/j.intfin.2006.07.001

Baird, P. L., Geylani, P. C., & Roberts, J. A. (2011, December 9). Corporate Social and Financial Performance Re-Examined: Industry Effects in a Linear Mixed Model Analysis. Springer Science+Business Media, 109(3), 367-388. 10.1007/s10551-011-1135-z

Bande, M. H. (2022, November – December). Corporate Social Responsibility and Financial Performance of Deposit Money Banks in Nigeria. *International Journal of Management Studies and Social Science Research*, *4*(6). Advance online publication. DOI: 10.56293/IJMSSSR.2022.4534

Barney, J. (1991). Firm resources and sustained competitive advantage. *Journal of Management*, *17*(1), 99–120. DOI: 10.1177/014920639101700108

Becchetti, L., Ciciretti, R., Hasan, I., & Kobeissi, N. (2012, November 1). Corporate social responsibility and shareholder's value. Elsevier BV, 65(11), 1628-1635. 10.1016/j.jbusres.2011.10.022

Ben Brik, A., Rettab, B., & Mellahi, K. (2011). Market orientation, corporate social responsibility, and business performance. *Journal of Business Ethics*, *99*(3), 307–324. DOI: 10.1007/s10551-010-0658-z

Cajias, M., Fuerst, F., & Bienert, S. (2014). Can investing in corporate social responsibility lower a company's cost of capital? *Studies in Economics and Finance*, *31*(2), 202–222. DOI: 10.1108/SEF-05-2013-0067

Cellier, A., & Chollet, P. (2012). Corporate Social Responsibility Rating Information: Relevance and Impacts on Financial Markets. In Boubaker, S., & Nguyen, D. K. (Eds.), *Board Directors and Corporate Social Responsibility* (pp. 179–201)., DOI: 10.1057/9780230389304_10

Chih, H., Chih, H., & Chen, T. (2009, September 29). On the Determinants of Corporate Social Responsibility: International Evidence on the Financial Industry. Springer Science+Business Media, 93(1), 115-135. 10.1007/s10551-009-0186-x

Chowdhury, A., & Nehal, M N. (2020, January 1). Effect of Corporate Social Responsibility Expenditures on Financial Performance in Banking Sector of Bangladesh. DOI: 10.18178/joebm.2020.8.1.610

Christensen, H. B., Hail, L., & Leuz, C. (n.d., 2017). Mandatory CSR and Sustainability Reporting: Economic Analysis and Literature Review.

Chronopoulos, D. K., Liu, H., McMillan, F. J., & Wilson, J. O. S. (2015). The dynamics of US bank profitability. *European Journal of Finance*, *21*(5), 426–443. DOI: 10.1080/1351847X.2013.838184

Claessens, S., Djankov, S., Fan, J. P. H., & Lang, L. H. P. (2002). Disentangling the Incentive and Entrenchment Effects of Large Shareholdings. *The Journal of Finance*, *57*(6), 2741–2771. DOI: 10.1111/1540-6261.00511

Cornett, M. M., Erhemjamts, O., & Tehranian, H. (2016, September 1). Greed or good deeds: An examination of the relation between corporate social responsibility and the financial performance of U.S. commercial banks around the financial crisis. Elsevier BV, 70, 137-159. doi.org/10.1016/j.jbankfin.2016.04.024

David, O. (2012, January 1). An assessment of the impact of corporate social responsibility on Nigerian society: The examples of banking and communication industries. http://www.universalresearchjournals.org/ujmbr/Pdf/2012/May/Olanrewaju.pdf

Demirguc-Kunt, A., & Huizinga, H. (2000). Financial structure and bank profitability. Policy Research Working Paper Series 2430.The World Bank.

Dyck, A., Lins, K. V., Roth, L., & Wagner, H. F. (2019). Do institutional investors drive corporate social responsibility? International evidence. *Journal of Financial Economics*, *131*(3), 693–714. DOI: 10.1016/j.jfineco.2018.08.013

Eccles, R. G., & Klimenko, S. (2019). The investor revolution: Shareholders are getting serious about sustainability. *Harvard Business Review*, *97*(3), 106–116.

Elif, & Halil, H. (2017). Corporate Social Responsibility and Firm Performance: Evidence from an Emerging Market. Accounting and Finance Research, 6(4), 42. DOI: 10.5430/afr.v6n4p42

Ellili, N. O. D., & Nobanee, H. (2023). Impact of economic, environmental, and corporate social responsibility reporting on financial performance of UAE banks. *Environment, Development and Sustainability*, *25*(5), 3967–3983. DOI: 10.1007/s10668-022-02225-6 PMID: 35280966

Esteban-Sánchez, P., González, M. D. L. C., & Paredes-Gázquez, J. D. (2017, September 1). Corporate social performance and its relation with corporate financial performance: International evidence in the banking industry. *Journal of Cleaner Production*, *162*, 1102–1110. DOI: 10.1016/j.jclepro.2017.06.127

Freeman, R. E. (1984). *Strategic management: A stakeholder approach*. Pitman.

Freeman, R. E., & Reed, D. L. (1983, April 1). Stockholders and Stakeholders: A New Perspective on Corporate Governance. *California Management Review*, *25*(3), 88–106. DOI: 10.2307/41165018

Gololo, I A. (2019, July 1). Corporate Social Responsibility Disclosure and Financial Performance of Quoted Nigerian Cement Companies. DOI: 10.15294/ibarj.v3i2.60

Gray, R., Kouhy, R., & Lavers, S. (1995, May 1). Corporate social and environmental reporting. Emerald Publishing Limited, 8(2), 47-77. 10.1108/09513579510146996

Hafez, H. (2015). Corporate social responsibility and financial performance: An empirical study on Egyptian banks. *Corporate Ownership and Control*, *12*(2), 107–127. DOI: 10.22495/cocv12i2p9

IFRS Foundation. (2023). *IFRS S1 General Requirements for Disclosure of Sustainability-related Financial Information and IFRS S2 Climate-related Disclosures*. International Sustainability Standards Board.

Itotenaan, H O., Samy, M., & Bampton, R. (2014, May 6). A phenomenological study of CSR policy making and implementation in developed countries. DOI: 10.1108/JGR-03-2014-0008

Javed, M., Rashid, M. A., & Hussain, G. (2016). When does it pay to be good – A contingency perspective on corporate social and financial performance: Would it work? *Journal of Cleaner Production*, *133*, 1062–1073. DOI: 10.1016/j.jclepro.2016.05.163

Kılıç, M., Kuzey, C., & Uyar, A. (2015, June 1). The impact of ownership and board structure on Corporate Social Responsibility (CSR) reporting in the Turkish banking industry. Emerald Publishing Limited, 15(3), 357-374. 10.1108/cg-02-2014-0022

Krippendorff, K. (1984, March 1). Content Analysis: An Introduction to its Methodology.. Beverly Hills, CA: Sage, 238

Liu, X., & Anbumozhi, V. (2009). Determinant factors of corporate environmental information disclosure: An empirical study of Chinese listed companies. *Journal of Cleaner Production*, *17*(6), 593–600. DOI: 10.1016/j.jclepro.2008.10.001

Makni, R., Francoeur, C., & Bellavance, F. (2009). Causality between Corporate Social Performance and Financial Performance: Evidence from Canadian Firms. *Journal of Business Ethics*, *89*(3), 409–422. DOI: 10.1007/s10551-008-0007-7

Margolis, J. D., & Walsh, J. P. (2003). Misery loves companies: Rethinking social initiatives by business. *Administrative Science Quarterly*, *48*(2), 268–305. DOI: 10.2307/3556659

Matuszak, Ł., & Różańska, E. (2017). An examination of the relationship between CSR disclosure and financial performance: The case of Polish banks. DOI: 10.24818/jamis.2017.04005

Matuszaka, Ł., & Różańskaa, E. (2017). An examination of the relationship between CSR disclosure and financial performance: The case of polish banks. *Accounting And Management Information Systems*, *16*(4), 522–533. DOI: 10.24818/jamis.2017.04005

Nguyen, B. N. (2018). The effect of corporate social responsibility disclosure on financial performance: Evidence from credit institutions in Vietnam. *Asian Social Science*, *14*(4), 109–122. DOI: 10.5539/ass.v14n4p109

Nguyen, V. T., & Hang, T. T. (2022, December 31). Bui & Chi H.D (2022). The impacts of corporate social responsibility to corporate financial performance: A case study of Vietnamese commercial banks. *Cogent Economics & Finance*, *10*(1), 2132642. Advance online publication. DOI: 10.1080/23322039.2022.2132642

Niresh, J A., & Silva, W H E. (2018, January 31). The Nexus between Corporate Social Responsibility Disclosure and Financial Performance: Evidence from the Listed Banks, Finance and Insurance Companies in Sri Lanka. DOI: 10.5430/afr.v7n2p65

Nollet, J., Filis, G., & Mitrokostas, E. (2016). Corporate social responsibility and financial performance: A non-linear and disaggregated approach. *Economic Modelling*, *52*, 400–407. DOI: 10.1016/j.econmod.2015.09.019

Platonova, E., Asutay, M., Dixon, R., & Mohammad, S. (2016, July 1). The Impact of Corporate Social Responsibility Disclosure on Financial Performance: Evidence from the GCC Islamic Banking Sector. DOI: 10.1007/s10551-016-3229-0

Porter, P., & Kramer, M. R. (2007). Strategy and society: The link between competitive advantage and corporate social responsibility. *Strategic Direction*, *23*(5). Advance online publication. DOI: 10.1108/sd.2007.05623ead.006

Ramzan, M., Amin, M., & Abbas, M. (2021, January 1). How does corporate social responsibility affect financial performance, financial stability, and financial inclusion in the banking sector? Evidence from Pakistan. DOI: 10.1016/j.ribaf.2020.101314

Razak, L A., Ismail, I., Ishak, I., Yamin, M., & Syah, A L N. (2019, February 20). Factors affecting the corporate social responsibility disclosure (Case study at PT. Semen Tonasa). DOI: 10.1088/1755-1315/235/1/012074

Saki, F. (2020, October 1). Corporate Social Responsibility on Financial Performance: A Study of the Bangladeshi DSE Listed Private Commercial Banks. DOI: 10.52962/ipjaf.2020.4.4.110

Sekhon, A. K., & Kathuria, L. M. (2019). Analyzing the impact of corporate social responsibility on corporate financial performance: Evidence from top Indian firms. *Corporate Governance (Bradford), 20*(1), 143–157. DOI: 10.1108/CG-04-2019-0135

Senyigit, Y. B., & Shuaibu, M. A. (2017). The effect of corporate social responsibility on financial perfor mance: Evidence from the banking industry in emerging economies. *Journal of Business Studies Quarterly, 9*(1), 22–31. https://www.proquest.com/openview/12bac8dfbde31d2aa9fd277b769dd16e/1?pq-origsite=gscholar&cbl=1056382

Simpson, W. G., & Kohers, T. (2002). The link between corporate social and financial performance: Evidence from the banking industry. *Journal of Business Ethics, 35*(2), 97–109. DOI: 10.1023/A:1013082525900

Siueia, T T., Wang, J., & Deladem, T G. (2019, July 1). Corporate Social Responsibility and financial performance: A comparative study in the Sub-Saharan Africa banking sector. DOI: 10.1016/j.jclepro.2019.04.027

Soana, M. G. (2011, May 28). The Relationship Between Corporate Social Performance and Corporate Financial Performance in the Banking Sector. Springer Science+Business Media, 104(1), 133-148. 10.1007/s10551-011-0894-x

Szegedi, K., Khan, Y., & Lentner, C. (2020). Corporate social responsibility and financial performance: Evidence from Pakistani listed banks. *Sustainability (Basel), 12*(10), 4080. DOI: 10.3390/su12104080

Tafti, S F., Hosseini, S F., & Emami, S A. (2012, October 1). Assessment the Corporate Social Responsibility According to Islamic Values (Case Study: Sarmayeh Bank). DOI: 10.1016/j.sbspro.2012.09.1095

Taşkın, D. (2015). The relationship between CSR and banks' financial performance: Evidence from Turkey. *Journal of Yaşar University, 10*(39), 21–30. DOI: 10.19168/jyu.97694

Taşkın, D. (2015, October 29). The Relationship between CSR and Banks' Financial Performance: Evidence from Turkey., 10(39), 21-21. 10.19168/jyu.97694

Tran, Q. T., Vo, T. D., & Le, X. T. (2021). Relationship between profitability and corporate social responsibility disclosure: Evidence from Vietnamese listed banks. *The Journal of Asian Finance, Economics and Business, 8*(3), 875–883. DOI: 10.13106/jafeb.2021.vol8.no3.0875

Ullman, A. (1985). A Critical Examination of the Relationship Among Social Performance, Social Disclosure, and Economic Performance. *Academy of Management Review, 10*(3), 540–577. DOI: 10.2307/258135

Waddock, S. A., & Graves, S. B. (1997). The corporate social performance—Financial performance link. *Strategic Management Journal, 18*(4), 303–319. DOI: 10.1002/(SICI)1097-0266(199704)18:4<303::AID-SMJ869>3.0.CO;2-G

Wang, Q., Dou, J., & Jia, S. (2016). A meta-analytic review of corporate social responsibility and corporate financial performance: The moderating effect of contextual factors. *Business & Society, 55*(8), 1083–1121. DOI: 10.1177/0007650315584317

Weber, P R. (1990, January 31). Basic content analysis (2nd ed.). . SAGE Publications, Inc., 2, 12

Weshah, S R., & Ahmad, A D., & R., A A M. (2012, September 29). The Impact of Adopting Corporate Social Responsibility on Corporate Financial Performance: Evidence from Jordanian Banks. *Interdisciplinary Journal of Contemporary Research in Business, 4*(5), 11.

World Bank. (2021). *Mobilizing Finance for a Green and Inclusive Recovery in the Middle East and North Africa*. World Bank Group.

Wu, M., & Shen, C. (2013, September 1). Corporate social responsibility in the banking industry: Motives and financial performance. Elsevier BV, 37(9), 3529-3547. doi.org/10.1016/j.jbankfin.2013.04.023

KEY TERMS AND DEFINITIONS

Corporate Social Responsibility (CSR): A self-regulating business model whereby a company integrates social and environmental concerns into its business operations and interactions with its stakeholders. It represents the firm's commitment to operate in an economically, socially, and environmentally sustainable manner, acknowledging the impact of its activities on a broad range of constituents beyond its shareholders.

Corporate Social Responsibility Disclosure (CSRD): The public dissemination of qualitative and quantitative information regarding a company's environmental, social, and governance (ESG) performance. This practice involves the transparent communication of CSR activities, policies, and outcomes through formal channels such as annual reports, sustainability reports, and dedicated sections on corporate websites, aimed at reducing information asymmetry with stakeholders.

Financial Performance: A subjective measure of a firm's overall financial health and its ability to utilize its assets, generate revenue, and create value for shareholders over a specific period. In this study, it is operationalized through two primary accounting-based metrics: Return on Assets (ROA) and Return on Equity (ROE).

Return on Assets (ROA): A profitability ratio that indicates the efficiency with which a company's management is able to generate earnings from its economic resources or assets. It is calculated by dividing net income by average total assets, expressing the percentage of profit earned per unit of asset.

Return on Equity (ROE): A measure of financial performance that reveals the profitability relative to shareholders' equity. It is calculated by dividing net income by average shareholders' equity, illustrating the rate of return generated for the benefit of a firm's equity investors.

Stakeholder Theory: A conceptual framework of business ethics and organizational management that posits the success of an organization is contingent upon its ability to effectively manage the complex web of relationships and interests with all entities that are affected by or can affect the achievement of its objectives. This includes, but is not limited to, employees, customers, suppliers, communities, and financiers.

Content Analysis: A systematic, replicable research technique used for making valid inferences from textual data by coding and quantifying specific words, phrases, or concepts within a set of documents. In this context, it is employed to construct a CSR disclosure index by systematically evaluating the presence or absence of predefined CSR-related items in bank annual reports.

Sustainable Development Goals (SDGs): A universal call to action, adopted by all United Nations Member States in 2015, comprising 17 interconnected global goals designed to be a "blueprint to achieve a better and more sustainable future for all" by 2030. The goals address global challenges, including those related to poverty, inequality, climate change, environmental degradation, peace, and justice.

Panel Data: A type of multidimensional dataset that contains observations of multiple phenomena collected over multiple time periods for the same subjects (e.g., companies, individuals). This longitudinal structure allows researchers to analyze dynamics of change and control for unobserved heterogeneity, providing more robust and nuanced empirical insights than purely cross-sectional data.

Tunisian Banking Sector: The consolidated network of financial institutions operating within the Tunisian economy, comprising both private and public deposit-taking entities. This sector is characterized by its pivotal role in capital allocation, economic development, and, increasingly, as a catalyst for the nation's sustainability agenda.

APPENDIX

Appendix A: CSR Disclosure

Environment	
EN1	**Statement on environmental protection policy**
EN2	Prevention of pollution(waste disposal and recycling)
EN3	Actions aiming to limit consumption of energy, materials, water(sustainable use of resources)
EN4	Sustainability (any mention of sustainable development)
EN5	Aesthetic value of the environment (designing structures in harmony with the environment, landscape)
EN6	Environmental protection, biodiversity and restoration of natural habitats
EN7	Taking account of the environmental in credit policy (environmentally-friendly products, "green products", funding "low-emission" investment projects...)
EN8	Environmental training and certificates(ISO 14001 vs)
EN9	Joint projects with other companies providing environmental management services
EN10	Environmental awards
Human Resource	
HR1	Employment and labour relations
HR2	Occupational health and safety
HR3	Employee development (training...)
HR4	Employee benefits (insurance, healthcare, social assistance...)
HR5	Relationships with trade unions
HR6	Information on employee turnover
HR7	Information on support for daytime care, maternity and paternity leave
HR8	Encouraging diversity (employment of minorities, disabled persons, women...)
Product and Customer	
PC1	Comprehensibility and transparency of products services
PC2	Bank products addressed to marginalized groups (the disabled, aged customers, non-profit organizations...)
PC3	Examination of customer satisfaction/ service quality
PC4	Production of customers' data and privacy
PC5	Customer service (settlement of problems. complaints disputes, renegotiation of contract terms...)
PC6	Customer awards
Community Involvement	
CI1	Donations for social activities and public benefit organizations
CI2	Support for education (scholarships, conference, seminars, student internships...)
CI3	Sponsorship of various sport, artistic and cultural events
CI4	Sponsorship of various public health initiatives, projects, campaigns

Section 2

The Policy and Finance Nexus: Governing the Transition

Chapter 4
Sustainability Reporting in North America: Challenges and Opportunities to Advance Indigenous Equity and Inclusion

Yao Zhou
https://orcid.org/0009-0001-8468-4088
University of Waterloo, Canada

Amr El Alfy
https://orcid.org/0000-0002-0160-9868
University of Waterloo, Canada

ABSTRACT

This chapter discusses the integration of Indigenous peoples and communities within global and Canadian sustainability reporting standards and frameworks, focusing on historical development and comparative analysis. Through a chronological review, it outlines the evolution of reporting standards/frameworks, tracing developments from early corporate social responsibility (CSR) to modern sustainability standards/frameworks, such as the Global Reporting Initiative (GRI), Sustainability Accounting Standards Board (SASB), and Task Force on Climate-Related Financial Disclosures (TCFD). The comparative analysis scrutinizes how these frameworks incorporate Indigenous issues, outlining observable gaps and inconsistencies in approach and comprehensiveness. This chapter highlights discrepancies in Indigenous inclusion and critiques the limitations of current practices. It concludes by suggesting improvements to enhance the representation of Indigenous rights and community engagement in sustainability reporting.

DOI: 10.4018/979-8-3693-9714-5.ch004

1.0 INTRODUCTION

Sustainability reporting has emerged as a critical tool for organizations to communicate their environmental, social, and governance (ESG) impacts, aligning corporate practices with global sustainability objectives. In North America, where diverse ecosystems and rich cultural heritages coexist, sustainability reporting frameworks have increasingly highlighted the need to address Indigenous rights and economic equity. This focus reflects a growing acknowledgment of Indigenous communities' disproportionate environmental and social challenges and their pivotal role in achieving sustainable development. However, integrating Indigenous perspectives into sustainability reporting remains complex and laden with challenges and opportunities.

Indigenous peoples in North America, including First Nations, Métis, and Inuit communities in Canada and Native American tribes in the United States, have historically faced exclusion from economic opportunities and decision-making processes that directly impact their lands and resources (UN, 2024A). This marginalization has been compounded by environmental degradation, loss of biodiversity, and climate change—all of which disproportionately affect Indigenous territories (TNFD, 2023A).

The Canadian context further illustrates the complexities and potential of Indigenous inclusion in sustainability reporting. The CSSB's ongoing efforts to integrate Indigenous perspectives into its standards reflect a broader trend toward inclusivity in Canadian accounting and sustainability practices. However, challenges remain in ensuring that these standards address the unique needs of diverse Indigenous communities, particularly in a country as culturally and geographically varied as Canada. Establishing clear policies, robust grievance mechanisms, and measurable outcomes will be critical to realizing the full potential of Indigenous engagement in sustainability reporting.

This chapter seeks to critically evaluate the incorporation of Indigenous peoples and communities within global and Canadian sustainability reporting standards and frameworks to date. A chronological review was performed using a comprehensive literature review to understand the timeline and evolution of each standard and framework. Subsequent phases involved a comparative analysis of the guidelines, frameworks, reports, and any pertinent updates or commentary associated with these standards/frameworks. This analysis seeks to evaluate and compare how various reporting frameworks address Indigenous issues, pinpointing gaps and variations in approach and thoroughness. Based on the identified patterns and discrepancies, a comparative table (***Table 1***) and visual framework (***Figure 2***) were constructed to present and interpret the findings systematically.

1.1 Background

Sustainability reporting has transitioned from a niche voluntary practice to a central tenet of modern corporate governance, reflecting a global consensus that long-term value creation is inextricably linked to environmental, social, and governance (ESG) performance. This evolution, chronicled through the development of frameworks like the Global Reporting Initiative (GRI) and the Sustainability Accounting Standards Board (SASB), has increasingly sought to quantify and standardize corporate impacts. However, this journey toward standardization has revealed a critical frontier: the meaningful integration of social equity, particularly concerning the rights, knowledge, and economic inclusion of Indigenous peoples.

In North America, this challenge is especially pronounced. The region's vast natural resource wealth often lies beneath or adjacent to Indigenous territories, creating an inherent intersection between corporate activity and the rights of First Nations, Métis, and Inuit communities in Canada, and Native American tribes in the United States. Historically, these communities have faced systemic exclusion from economic opportunities and decision-making processes, a marginalization exacerbated by environmental degradation and climate change that disproportionately affects their lands. Consequently, the emergence of sustainability reporting presents a dual reality: it is both a potential vehicle for perpetuating historical inequities and a powerful opportunity to advance reconciliation, equity, and genuine partnership.

The chapter investigates the extent to which major global and Canadian sustainability reporting frameworks have incorporated Indigenous perspectives, moving beyond symbolic inclusion to actionable, measurable, and equitable engagement. By conducting a systematic comparative analysis, the analysis identifies both the progress made in recognizing principles like Free, Prior, and Informed Consent (FPIC) and the persistent gaps in areas such as remediation, the recognition of Traditional Knowledge, and the creation of tangible economic benefits. The discussion situates the Canadian context—with its ongoing efforts to establish a Canadian Sustainability Standards Board (CSSB)—within the broader global push for harmonization, led by the International Sustainability Standards Board (ISSB). Ultimately, this analysis argues that the future credibility and effectiveness of sustainability reporting depend on its ability to not only account for financial materiality but also to embed Indigenous rights and worldviews as foundational pillars of corporate accountability and sustainable development.

2.0 LITERATURE REVIEW

2.1 Development of CSR and CSP

Voluntary sustainability reporting frameworks and standards have a long history, tracing back to the 1950s when Howard R. Bowen, the father of Corporate Social Responsibility (CSR), first introduced the concept of social responsibility (Caroll, 1999). Bowen initially defined social responsibility as "the obligations of businessmen to pursue those policies, to make those decisions, or to follow those lines of action which are desirable in terms of the objectives and values of our society (Bowen, 2013, p. 6)." This early recognition outlined that the larger a corporation becomes, the greater its potential to wield influence and create societal impact (Carroll, 1999). This realization led to theoretical and managerial discussions advocating not only for doing what is right but for doing what ultimately leads to better outcomes (Lindgreen & Swaen, 2010).

As a result, CSR evolved from an ideological concept into a practical reality. It became widely acknowledged that organizations must define their societal roles and uphold social and ethical standards in their operations (Lindgreen et al., 2009). Carroll's CSR pyramid, first proposed in 1979 and updated in 2016, illustrates that businesses have responsibilities that range from economic and legal to ethical and philanthropic, arranged from the base to the top in decreasing order of societal expectation, though not necessarily in importance (Carroll, 1979, 2016). This framework acknowledges that while managerial duties extend beyond mere economic and legal obligations, the law is essential but insufficient on its own (Carroll, 2016).

Managerial roles in businesses traditionally encompassed fulfilling economic and legal obligations (Carroll, 2016). However, while adherence to laws is essential, it alone is insufficient (Carroll, 2016). Beyond legal compliance, businesses are expected by society to operate ethically, upholding norms, standards, values, principles, and expectations that protect stakeholders' moral rights (Carroll, 2016). Moreover, public expectations extend to businesses taking voluntary or discretionary actions that benefit society, reinforcing the idea that companies should engage in activities that contribute positively to the community (Carroll, 2016).

Between the 1970s and 1990s, as businesses, stakeholders, and shareholders became increasingly aware of and accepted social responsibility, Corporate Social Performance (CSP) emerged as a method for evaluating how effectively companies were meeting their social obligations (Carroll, 1999; Mohr et al., 2001; Wood, 1991). The foundational question posed by Bowen in 1953 - "What responsibilities to society may businesses reasonably be expected to assume?" - continued to resonate, with Frederick in 2006 further refining the inquiry by asking, "To whom exactly?" (Bowen, 2013; Frederick, 2006). These early explorations into CSP and

CSR indicate a concerted effort by U.S. scholars, who were pioneers in management literature, to encourage corporations to address enduring societal challenges (Wood, 2010). While some scholars argued that business activities had contributed to these issues, others took a normative perspective, asserting that businesses should use their expertise and resources to help solve them (Wood, 2010).

Starting in 1973, CSP practices incorporated social disclosure, including both voluntary corporate social reporting and mandatory pollution reporting (Ullmann, 1985). Initially, social disclosure functioned as a surrogate for actual CSP efforts, taking various forms such as rankings developed by students, the Council on Economic Priorities (CEP), pollution performance indices, and corporate self-descriptions obtained through surveys (Ullmann, 1985). The assumption underlying early attempts at social disclosure was that it could serve as a credible proxy for actual performance (Wood, 2010). This was primarily driven by the hope of establishing a positive correlation that would convince skeptical business leaders of the economic benefits associated with CSP (Wood, 2010). At the time, social disclosure aimed to be a simpler, more accessible stand-in tool for measuring social performance. However, its reliability was constrained by limited access to dependable data, the absence of valid metrics, and the lack of solid frameworks (Ullmann, 1985). Evidence emerged indicating that companies with extensive social disclosures were often among the worst offenders concerning pollution and other detrimental activities (Fry & Hock, 1976).

Agle and Kelley (2001) later argued that an effective measurement of CSP should incorporate all three components of Wood's (1991) model: principles, processes, and outcomes. They emphasized that CSP is more than superficial actions or incidental outcomes aimed solely at achieving financial performance (FP). For instance, coercing employees to contribute to organizations like United Way or political action committees may create an appearance of fulfilling public responsibility, but the coercive process undermines true social responsibility principles, particularly those related to legitimacy and the autonomy of workers (Agle & Kelley, 2001).

Wood (2010) further contended that CSP should not be solely justified as a financial incentive. Instead, CSP is a complex, multidimensional construct where financial performance is just one of many contributing variables (Wood, 2010). Several CSP studies use measures that cannot readily be separated into principles, processes or outcomes (Wood, 2010). Corporate reports, such as annual reports on social or environmental disclosures, were company self-reporting and objective data (Belkaoui, 1976; Ingram & Frazier; 1980; Lerner & Fryxell, 1988). Multiple categories of action are considered in a way that makes it impossible to consider the measure as a responsive process or as an outcome (e.g. treatment of minorities and women, environmental practices, charitable giving, community relations) (Wood, 2010). Overall, disclosure can be seen as fulfilling the principles of legitimacy and public responsibility, a responsive process, or an outcome relevant to various stakeholders (Wood, 2010). Understanding CSR associations, environmental performance associations, governance attributes, and public shareholders (Rupley et al., 2017). However, bias may exist in voluntary reporting due to its voluntary nature, where companies may report only successes, or as prior studies suggest, to "window dress" or cover up corporate misconduct (Wang & Tuttle, 2014).

2.2 Emergence of Sustainability Standards and Frameworks

Given the increasing demand for disclosures that encompass not just financial performance but also a corporation's environmental and social practices (Rupley et al., 2017; Waddock, 2003), coupled with the absence of comprehensive frameworks and standards, and the complex nature of CSR reporting, various frameworks, standards, ratings, and indices have been developed as corporate sustainability reporting tools (SRTs).

While the terms frameworks and standards may sound similar, they have distinct focuses. According to Siew (2015) and the IFRS Foundation (2024), frameworks provide principles, initiatives, or guidelines on how information is structured and prepared and what broad topics should be covered, aiding companies in their disclosure processes. On the other hand, standards consist of specific, detailed, and replicable requirements outlining what should be reported for each topic, including metrics, to ensure the consistent achievement of sustainability objectives (Siew, 2015; IFRS Foundation, 2024a). Standards operationalize frameworks, ensuring that disclosures are comparable, consistent, and reliable (IFRS Foundation, 2024a). Frameworks and standards are designed to complement each other and are intended to be used in conjunction (IFRS Foundation, 2024a).

Modern voluntary sustainability reporting took shape after the catastrophic Exxon Valdez oil spill, which prompted demands from socially responsible investment (SRI) funds and environmental groups for increased corporate disclosure of environmental risks (Alazzani & Wan-Hussin, 2013; Rupley et al., 2017). In response, the Coalition for Environmentally Responsible Economies (CERES) was formed in 1989 and introduced the Valdez Principles, a set of ten guidelines to promote environmental responsibility and transparency (Feder, 1989; Smith III, 1995). These principles sought to enhance public reporting in areas such as resource conservation, pollution reduction, and corporate transparency (Feder, 1989; Smith III, 1995).

2.2.1 Global Reporting Initiative (GRI)

The Global Reporting Initiative (GRI), launched by the Coalition for Environmentally Responsible Economies (CERES) in 1997, aimed to establish a globally applicable sustainability reporting framework to unify and integrate economic, governance, and CSR reporting standards within the global marketplace (Gilbert, 2002; GRI, 2024a). The GRI's Global Sustainability Standards Board (GSSB) functions through an independent, multi-stakeholder approach to develop a universal language for reporting impacts (Adams et al., 2022). This shared language supports meaningful discussions and informed decision-making about organizational impacts (Adams et al., 2022). CERES envisioned the GRI as comparable to the Financial Accounting Standards Board in the U.S. and other standard-setting organizations in the financial sector (Rupley et al., 2017). Its central mission was to forge a global consensus on which corporate sustainability attributes should be measured and how they should be reported (Rupley et al., 2017).

In 2000, GRI published its first global framework for sustainability reporting, the GRI Guidelines (G1) (GRI, 2024b). The following year, GRI transitioned into an independent, non-profit organization (GRI, 2024b). In 2002, the GRI Secretariat relocated to Amsterdam, Netherlands, and introduced the first update to the Guidelines (G2) (GRI, 2024b). This revision incorporated public feedback and a thorough standards revision process, aligning the Guidelines more closely with major international sustainability agreements (Rupley et al., 2017). The updated 2002 Guidelines included more precise definitions, indicators, and an enhanced emphasis on verification and assurance (Rupley et al., 2017).

As the demand for GRI reporting increased and institutional investor activism began to show, shareholder resolutions, often backed by multiple asset management firms, including major multinationals such as Microsoft, IBM, and Pepsi, were urged to align their reporting with GRI guidelines (Rupley et al., 2017). This growing demand spurred further development and enhancement of the Guidelines, culminating in the release of G3 in 2006 and G4 in 2013 (GRI, 2024b). The G3 has two subsequent versions issued, namely G3 and G3.1 (an updated version of G3), which eliminated indicators not considered relevant to most stakeholders (Rupley et al., 2017) and created a stronger emphasis on clarity, the purpose of criteria as well as the process of reporting (Siew, 2015). At this stage, sector-specific guidelines, referred to as sector supplements, are made available. G4 incorporated disclosures on material issues and materiality relevant to the business risks and further developed requirements on the supply chain, such as Anti-Corruption and Greenhouse Gas (GHG) Emissions (Adams & Narayanan, 2010; KPMG International, 2013). It has also been further aligned with other reporting standards, including the OECD Guidelines for Multinational Enterprises, the United Nations Global Compact Principles, and the UN Guiding Principles on Business and Human Rights (KPMG International, 2013). According to the GRI guidelines, a typical report should address the areas of vision and strategy, corporation profile, governance structure and management systems, GRI content index, and performance criteria (economic, social and environmental) (GRI, 2021a). Today, the GRI Standards have become the world's most widely used and comprehensive standards for sustainability reporting (GRI, 2024b).

2.2.2 Carbon Disclosure Project (CDP)

In 2000, the Carbon Disclosure Project (CDP) was launched as a non-profit organization (NGO) in the United Kingdom to collect extensive climate-related data from companies and make it publicly available (Andrew & Cortese, 2011; CDP, 2022). This initiative aimed to support climate-conscious investor decisions and promote transparency in climate-related management practices within participating firms (Andrew & Cortese, 2011; CDP, 2022). CDP issued its first information request in 2003, targeting 500 organizations, and by 2009, this outreach had expanded to 2,500 organizations (Andrew & Cortese, 2011).

CDP builds upon the GRI's requirements and has collaborated with GRI to align their reporting frameworks, promoting consistency in data collection and minimizing the reporting burden for companies (GRI & CDP, 2017). Both frameworks facilitate the sharing of data points, allowing information submitted in response to CDP's climate change questions to be incorporated into sustainability reports that follow GRI Standards and vice versa (GRI & CDP, 2017). CDP's climate change questions, sent through annual questionnaires, seek detailed information on corporate governance, risk management, emissions, and climate change strategies (GRI & CDP, 2017). According to CDP (2022, 2024a), the carbon disclosure scores evaluate corporations solely on the quality and comprehensiveness of their disclosures without assessing actual performance or making judgments about corporate efforts to mitigate climate change.

In 2021, CDP launched a new strategy to broaden its focus to encompass all planetary boundaries (GRI, 2024a). This expansion included new areas such as biodiversity, plastics, and oceans, acknowledging the interconnectedness of nature and Earth's systems (GRI, 2024a).

2.2.3 Sustainability Accounting Standards Board (SASB)

In 2011, the Sustainability Accounting Standards Board (SASB) was founded as an independent, not-for-profit organization dedicated to setting standards (IFRS Foundation, 2024b). SASB's mission is to develop and uphold industry-specific sustainability accounting standards, enabling companies to share financially relevant, decision-useful sustainability information with investors (IFRS Foundation, 2024b; Rodriguez et al., 2017). SASB argues that scientific consensus shows that continuing a "business as usual" approach in economic activity will result in significant economic losses (Hales, 2021). Thus, SASB prioritizes disclosures that meet the quality standards expected for financial information in SEC filings (IFRS Foundation, 2024b), addressing investors' and corporate leaders' increasing demand for transparent, actionable sustainability data that bridges the gap between ESG and financial performance (Busco et al., 2020; Rodriguez et al., 2017).

In 2017, SASB adopted a two-tier governance model consisting of a board of directors ("the SASB Foundation Board") and a standards-setting board ("the SASB Standards Board") (IFRS Foundation, 2024b). The SASB Standards Board is responsible for developing, issuing, and maintaining the SASB Standards, while the SASB Foundation Board manages the organization's strategy, finances, and operations and appoints members to the Standards Board (IFRS Foundation, 2024b). Although the Foundation Board does not participate in standards setting, it ensures that the Standards Board adheres to due process requirements (IFRS Foundation, 2024b).

SASB operates under two key documents: the rules of procedure and a conceptual framework (Hales, 2021). Their due process emphasizes evidence-based research, broad market input, public transparency, and independent oversight, gathering feedback from capital market participants (i.e., corporations, investors, and experts) to ensure that information is comparable, reliable, and relevant (Hales, 2021; Rodriguez et al., 2017). In 2018, SASB published a set of codified standards considering the materiality of sustainability issues across different industries (IFRS Foundation, 2024c).

SASB also developed the Sustainable Industry Classification System™ (SICS), which categorizes companies into 11 sectors and 77 industries based on resource intensity, sustainability impacts, and innovation potential in areas like consumer goods, food and beverage, extractives, financials, and renewable energy (Eccles et al., 2013; IFRS Foundation, 2024c). This classification enables SASB to assess a company's exposure to key sustainability risks and opportunities, which delivers insights for valuations and supports the construction of diversified portfolios around sustainability factors (Hales, 2021).

In 2021, SASB merged with the International Integrated Reporting Council (IIRC) to form the Value Reporting Foundation (VRF) and established the Value Reporting Foundation Board of Directors (IFRS Foundation, 2024b). The VRF Board supervises the organization's strategy, finances, and operations and appoints members to the SASB Standards Board (IFRS Foundation, 2024b). This merger combined SASB's quantitative metrics with IIRC's principles-based framework to provide a comprehensive, investor-relevant reporting tool (O'Dwyer et al., 2024). However, the merger has been contentious, as VRFs' focus on financial materiality gained traction in the U.S. but was limited in global applicability (O'Dwyer et al., 2024). IIRC's broader multi-capital approach, covering financial, human, social, and environmental dimensions, sought to capture a holistic view of corporate value creation for a range of stakeholders, which clashed with SASB's narrower, investor-focused approach (O'Dwyer et al., 2024).

The merger underscored "enterprise value," focusing on financial impacts, which some critics argue sidelined the broader socio-environmental impacts of corporate actions (Guillot & Hales, 2021; O'Dwyer et al., 2024). This shift has led to concerns that the merged standard might reduce the comprehensive view of value creation that integrated reporting initially aimed to provide (O'Dwyer et al., 2024), and practical challenges have emerged in maintaining consistency under a unified framework.

Despite these challenges, the integration has driven greater global adoption and standardization of ESG disclosures, enhancing data consistency for investors and expanding SASB's audience (O'Dwyer et al., 2024). Although the initial goal of integration was to promote a standalone report, the emphasis on enterprise value and SASB's metrics within the ISSB has resulted in integrated reporting (IR) becoming an adjunct to financial reporting rather than a distinct model (de Villiers & Dimes, 2022). This trend has raised concerns that SASB's focus on shareholder interests may reduce its impact on societal and environmental outcomes that do not directly affect financial returns but are crucial for sustainability (de Villiers & Dimes, 2022). While the integrated reporting approach continues to bring value by simplifying financial and non-financial information, future improvements in this integration remain to be seen.

2.2.4 Sustainable Development Goals (SDGs)

In 2015, the United Nations (UN) developed the Sustainable Development Goals (SDGs) as a comprehensive roadmap with goals and targets to guide both developing and developed countries toward sustainable development (UN, 2024a). The UN is committed to fully implementing these goals and targets within the Agenda by 2030 (UN, 2024a). This Agenda encompasses 17 global goals and 169 targets focused on economic growth, social inclusion, and environmental protection, building on the previous Millennium Development Goals (MDGs) that prioritized social issues, such as poverty reduction, health improvement, and gender equality (UN, 2024a). The UN aims to foster a "win-win" global development and cooperation model that greatly benefits all countries and regions (UN, 2024a). Implementation is designed to respect the rights and obligations of states under international law (UN, 2024a).

The UN has been highly influential in encouraging companies to assess and report their activities' social and environmental impacts, following initiatives like the Principles for Responsible Investment (PRI) introduced by the UN in 2006 (Hatayama, 2022). The SDGs are among the most widely adopted frameworks addressing key ESG investment issues. According to BNP Paribas's 2021 ESG Global Survey, 61%

of investors actively engage with companies as part of their ESG strategy, including 64% of asset managers and 58% of asset owners in 2021 (BNP PARIBAS, 2021).

To support companies aligning with the SDGs, the UN provides resources like the SDG Compass, SDG Industry Matrix, and SDG Indicators (Hatayama, 2022). The SDG Compass, which guides companies in understanding the SDGs, setting priorities, defining goals, integrating sustainability, and reporting, has been widely incorporated by sustainability standards and frameworks, including GRI, SASB, CDP, IFRS, and TNFD (Adams, 2020; CDP, 2024b; GRI, 2024c; Guillot, 2020; UNEP, 2021). Precisely, GRI aligns its standards with the SDGs, presenting organizations guidance on how their reporting can accentuate contributions to specific goals, helping companies identify and disclose SDG-related impacts (GRI, 2024d). SASB reports that 98% of its industry-specific topics relate to one or more SDG targets (Guillot, 2020). This can help companies and investors identify SDG targets relevant to financial and operational performance in specific industries, thereby directing capital toward SDG-aligned activities (Guillot, 2020). CDP's disclosure system aligns its questionnaires with SDGs, especially those addressing climate change, water security, and deforestation, to assist companies in understanding and reporting their contributions to these goals (CDP, 2024b). The IFRS Foundation's integrated reporting (IR) framework also supports SDG alignment, underlining long-term value creation and encouraging companies to disclose how their strategies contribute to the SDGs (Adams, 2020). TNFD aligns with specific SDGs on life on land (SDG 15) and life below water (SDG 14), urging businesses to integrate biodiversity considerations into their decision-making (UNEP, 2021). The SDGs serve as the core and foundation framework, shaping the primary focus and direction of these standards and frameworks.

2.2.5 Task Force on Climate-Related Financial Disclosures (TCFD)

Similar to SDGs, the Task Force on Climate-related Financial Disclosures (TCFD) was established to support the goals of the Paris Agreement (Institute and Faculty of Actuaries, 2024). It emerged in response to the realization that global warming has already surpassed 1 degree, with projections warning that exceeding 1.5 degrees could lead to severe, irreversible climate consequences (O'Dwyer & Unerman, 2020). Failure to decarbonize the economy could expose businesses to serious climate-related risks, potentially rendering many business models unviable due to disruptions in supply chains and asset integrity (TCFD, 2017).

In 2015, driven by the increasing demand for reliable information on climate-related risks, opportunities, emerging policies, and technologies, the Financial Stability Board (FSB) launched the TCFD at the Paris Climate Change Conference (COP21) (TCFD, 2024a). This framework was designed to help organizations disclose their climate-related impacts and how they manage risks in a 2-degree world, creating a feedback loop where growing demand from analysts promotes deeper engagement by investors in climate-informed decision-making (O'Dwyer & Unerman, 2020). The framework was also expected to aid policymakers in understanding CO2 sources and corporate readiness for climate challenges (O'Dwyer & Unerman, 2020).

The TCFD framework relies on modelling plausible future global warming scenarios that enable companies to assess key physical and transitional risks to their business models in each scenario (O'Dwyer & Unerman, 2020). While scenario planning is not widely practiced across all sectors (traditionally reserved for financial rather than climate scenarios), companies are expected to develop competencies in integrating climate risk into their corporate risk analysis and management processes (O'Dwyer & Unerman, 2020).

In 2017, the TCFD published recommendations to improve further transparency around climate-related financial risks (Institute and Faculty of Actuaries, 2024; TCFD, 2024b).

In 2017, TCFD published recommendations to improve further transparency around climate-related financial risks (Institute and Faculty of Actuaries, 2024; TCFD, 2024b). These recommendations focus on four thematic areas of governance, strategy, risk management, and metrics and targets to create a structured approach incorporating climate considerations into core business practices (TCFD, 2024b). By accentuating financial dependencies under various climate scenarios, the TCFD distinguishes itself from other frameworks that mainly address the environmental impacts of operations (O'Dwyer & Unerman, 2020). The TCFD acknowledges that even net-zero companies remain vulnerable to broader climate risks from emissions by other sectors (Unerman et al., 2018).

Following the FSB's request, the TCFD actively promoted the adoption of the framework, provided guidance, conducted educational initiatives, monitored disclosure practices, and published annual status reports through 2023 (TCFD, 2024b). This framework has since been widely adopted, with some governments mandating its inclusion in corporate non-financial information statements, as in the United Kingdom (Hazelhurst et al., 2024).

In 2023, following the final report of the original Task Force, responsibilities for overseeing climate-related disclosures shifted from the FSB to the IFRS Foundation, aligning with the global standards set by the IFRS's newly established IFRS S1 and IFRS S2 standards (IFRS Foundation, 2023d; TCFD, 2024b). These standards now fully incorporate the TCFD's recommendations, marking a significant milestone in the TCFD's legacy and contributions to global climate-focused financial reporting (IFRS Foundation, 2023d).

2.2.6 The Taskforce on Nature-related Financial Disclosures (TNFD)

The Taskforce on Nature-related Financial Disclosures (TNFD) began its planning phase in 2020, with preparatory efforts continuing into 2021 (TNFD, 2024a). Officially launched in 2021, TNFD quickly gained support from major global bodies, including the G7 and G20 (TNFD, 2024a, 2024b). The TNFD's recommendations are designed to assist decision-makers in reporting on and addressing nature-related risks to redirect global financial flows toward nature-positive outcomes (UNEP, 2021). This is achieved through recommendations and guidance for corporate reporting on nature, enhancing enterprise and portfolio risk management (TNFD, 2024b). By providing reliable data on nature-related issues, the TNFD enables businesses to incorporate these risks and opportunities into strategic planning, risk management, and asset allocation (TNFD, 2024b). Improved information, in turn, can help redirect global capital toward more positive impacts for nature and society (TNFD, 2024b).

The TNFD released its initial beta version of the framework (v0.1) in 2022, marking the start of widespread consultations and pilot testing (TNFD, 2024a). This was followed by further beta versions (v0.2 in June 2022, v0.3 in November 2022, and the final beta v0.4 in March 2023) (TNFD, 2024a). By 2023, TNFD Forum membership had expanded to over 1,000 organizations, a significant shift that, according to the United Nations Environment Programme (2023), has been transformative for corporate and financial sectors.

In 2023, TNFD published its final recommendations to help businesses and financial institutions anticipate regulatory changes following adopting the Kunming-Montreal Global Biodiversity Framework (GBF) (TNFD, 2023A; UNEP, 2023).

This updated recommendation mirrors and complements the TCFD so that financial institutions already acting on climate risks can simultaneously use TNFD's integrated approach to address nature-related financial risks (UNEP, 2023). This update aligns with and complements TCFD, allowing financial institutions already focused on climate risks also to address nature-related financial risks in a unified approach (UNEP, 2023).

While TNFD and TCFD share similar objectives and titles, their institutional backgrounds differ (Papazian, 2023). The FSB created the TCFD at the G20's request, whereas TNFD was founded by a coalition of financial institutions and corporations and does not have formal ties to the FSB (Papazian, 2023). However, TNFD receives support and funding from organizations such as the United Nations Development Programme (UNDP) and public agencies like Australia, France, Germany, and the UK (Papazian, 2023).

2.2.7 International Financial Reporting Standards (IFRS)

The development of the International Sustainability Standards Board (ISSB) and its sister framework, the International Financial Reporting Standards (IFRS), represents a significant evolution in global financial and sustainability reporting (IFRS Foundation, 2024d). The IFRS traces its origins to 1973, when the International Accounting Standards Committee (IASC) was formed to promote uniform accounting practices worldwide (IFRS Foundation, 2018). Over time, the demand for streamlined and standardized financial reporting became increasingly evident (IFRS Foundation, 2024d). In response, the IFRS Foundation and the International Accounting Standards Board (IASB) were created in 2001, replacing the IASC to strengthen the structure and focus of global accounting standards (IFRS Foundation, 2018).

In 2009, the IFRS Monitoring Board was founded to enhance accountability by creating a formal connection between the IFRS Foundation and public authorities (IFRS Foundation, 2024e). This governance layer helped align the IFRS Foundation's goals with public interests and advance global financial stability (IFRS Foundation, 2024e). The IFRS mission, which focuses on transparency, accountability, and efficiency, aligns with these regulatory goals by encouraging trust and fostering long-term market stability (IFRS Foundation, 2018).

As ESG issues gained importance in the corporate world, there was a growing demand from the global market for a consistent framework to help companies understand how sustainability factors affect their' prospects (IFRS Foundation, 2023a). In 2021, the creation of the ISSB marked a significant shift towards incorporating sustainability into global accounting practices (IFRS Foundation, 2024d). The ISSB was launched by the Trustees of the IFRS Foundation at the COP26 summit in Glasgow, with strong support from influential global institutions such as the G7, G20, International Organization of Securities Commissions (IOSCO), the Financial Stability Board, African Finance Ministers, and Central Bank Governors from more than 40 jurisdictions (IFRS Foundation, 2024d). This new board was tasked with creating a comprehensive baseline for sustainability disclosures that would cater specifically to investors' needs while remaining sensitive to the unique requirements of various jurisdictions and broader stakeholder groups (IFRS Foundation, 2024d).

The ISSB's primary objectives are to create standards for sustainability disclosures that serve as a global baseline, meet investors' informational needs, allow companies to provide detailed sustainability information to capital markets, and facilitate compatibility with region-specific disclosure standards (IFRS Foundation, 2024d). It builds on various sustainability reporting disclosures, including the Climate Disclosure Standards Board (CDSB), the TCFD, the Value Reporting Foundation's Integrated Reporting Framework, industry-based SASB Standards, and the World Economic

Forum's Stakeholder Capitalism Metrics (IFRS Foundation, 2024d). Through this alignment, the ISSB has appointed a pathway for globally consistent sustainability-related disclosures that investors can rely on to make informed financial decisions (IFRS Foundation, 2023a).

In 2023, the ISSB released its first two standards, IFRS S1 and IFRS S2, to improve trust and confidence in company sustainability disclosures to inform investment decisions better (IFRS Foundation, 2023a). IFRS S1 specifies general disclosure requirements for sustainability-related financial information that require entities to disclose information regarding their sustainability-related risks and opportunities to support decisions about resource provision (Ducros & Kelly, 2024; IFRS Foundation, 2023a). IFRS S2 focuses on climate-related disclosures that complement IFRS S1 and incorporate the TCFD's recommendations (IFRS Foundation, 2023a). It requires entities to disclose information on climate-related risks and opportunities, assisting resource allocation decisions (Ducros & Kelly, 2024). Given the objectives of the ISSB disclosure framework, the primary users are businesses and investors seeking to integrate sustainability-related risks into their investment decisions (Ducros & Kelly, 2024). Together, these standards strive to provide investors with more precise insights into companies' sustainability risks, ultimately leading to a more transparent and informed investment landscape (IFRS Foundation, 2023a). With these standards being developed, IFRS has shifted its focus to implementation, forming a Transition Implementation Group to support organizations in adopting the new standards (IFRS Foundation, 2023a). The ISSB also plans to collaborate with jurisdictions that require additional disclosures beyond the global baseline and with GRI to support effective reporting when ISSB Standards are used alongside other reporting frameworks (IFRS Foundation, 2023a).

Currently, IFRS has been adopted by disclosure frameworks such as CDP, whose scoring methodology is fully aligned with IFRS S2 to provide a comparable dataset across the market (CDP, 2022).

In the Canadian context, the Canadian Accounting Standards Board (AcSB) requires publicly accountable enterprises to use IFRS in preparing all interim and annual financial statements, while most private companies also have the option to adopt IFRS for financial statement preparation (CRA, 2024). This aligns with Canada's financial reporting with international "norms," enabling comparability and consistency across borders (Cooper et al., 2023).

In 2021, the Canadian Accounting Standards Oversight Council and the Auditing and Assurance Standards Oversight Council initiated a review of Canadian standard-setting, forming the Independent Review Committee on Standard Setting in Canada (IRCSSC) (FRAS Canada, 2023). The committee is mandated to consider the creation of a Canadian Sustainability Standards Board (CSSB) to oversee sustainability reporting within Canada (IRCSSC, 2021). This review process and the potential establishment of the CSSB are highly relevant to Canada and globally, as accounting regulations are increasingly characterized by a top-down, uniform, and mimetic approach (Cooper et al., 2023). Consequently, accountants and accounting regulators worldwide need to consider the implications of changes in Canadian accounting regulation, particularly regarding environmental issues (Cooper et al., 2023).

The CSSB, like the ISSB, seeks to serve the public interest by developing standards that address sustainability-related financial disclosures (IRCSSC, 2023). However, feedback from the public and other stakeholders has shown several challenges the CSSB faces. First, critics argue that the CSSB's proposed standards are too closely aligned with the International Sustainability Standards Board (ISSB), which can lead to a narrow, investor-centered approach to sustainability (de Villier & Dimes, 2022). This approach, known as "financial materiality," focuses on how environmental and social risks impact a company's financial performance but overlooks the broader impacts of the company on society and the environment (de Villier & Dimes, 2022). Thus, it may not adequately address the needs of diverse stakeholders, such as Indigenous communities, employees, and local ecosystems (Cooper et al., 2023). This limited perspective could miss the opportunity to provide a more inclusive sustainability framework that considers the viewpoints of all affected parties.

Furthermore, the IRCSSC's "public interest" definition has raised concerns. It is intended to encompass more than just capital market interests, including specific public sector needs, accountability to stakeholders for responsive and timely standards, consideration of costs, benefits, proportionality of impact, and recognition of Indigenous Peoples' rights (FRAS Canada, 2023). However, the vague language suggests an ambiguous stance on what truly constitutes the public good (Cooper et al., 2023). With a clearer, more inclusive definition, the CSSB's standards can avoid neglecting essential public interests, particularly those of marginalized groups and future generations (Cooper et al., 2023). This issue is especially pertinent in a diverse country like Canada, where cultural and environmental values differ significantly across communities. Without a clear definition of "public interest," the standards may fall short of fully representing Canada's social and environmental priorities, particularly regarding Indigenous rights.

2.2 Indigenous Reporting in Sustainability Standards and Frameworks

2.2.1 GRI

The GRI has established itself as a critical framework for organizations aiming to report on their impacts related to Indigenous peoples. GRI 411: Rights of Indigenous Peoples provides universal reporting guidelines that emphasize alignment with international frameworks like the United Nations Declaration on the Rights of Indigenous Peoples (UNDRIP) and International Labour Organization Convention 169 (GRI, 2016). These standards ensure that organizations respect both collective and individual rights, such as the right to self-determination, cultural preservation, and free, prior, and informed consent (FPIC) (GRI, 2016). The overarching aim is to hold organizations accountable for their actions while fostering transparency in how they engage with Indigenous communities and mitigate potential negative impacts (GRI, 2016).

GRI 411 requires organizations to articulate their management approach to Indigenous rights using GRI 103: Management Approach (GRI, 2016). It stresses the importance of due diligence, which is a structured process to identify, mitigate, and address risks to Indigenous rights arising from organizational activities (GRI, 2016). FPIC is central to this standard, requiring explicit and informed consent from Indigenous communities before initiating operations that affect their lands or resources (GRI, 2016). The disclosure component, GRI 411-1, mandates organizations to report incidents of rights violations, including legal complaints, actions taken, and the outcomes of remediation plans (GRI, 2016). These disclosures aim to provide insights into how well an organization manages its relationships with Indigenous rights holders and complies with recognized standards (GRI, 2016).

In addition to GRI 411, sector-specific standards further address Indigenous rights. The GRI Mining Sector Standard (2024) and similar frameworks for coal, agriculture, and oil and gas sectors identify Indigenous rights as material topics. These standards recommend disclosures on FPIC processes, engagement methods, and cultural heritage protection (GRI, 2021b, 2022a, 2022b, 2024e). The Mining Sector Standard, for instance, outlined the need to ensure meaningful engagement with Indigenous peoples while addressing their unique concerns through community development programs (GRI, 2024e). Similarly, the Oil and Gas Sector Standard (2021b) emphasizes equitable participation, particularly for Indigenous women, ensuring inclusivity in organizational decision-making (GRI, 2021b).

2.2.2 CDP

The CDP Climate Change 2023 Questionnaire acknowledges the role of Indigenous Peoples in biodiversity conservation by including the option to secure the FPIC of Indigenous Peoples under biodiversity-related public commitments (CDP, 2023a). This inclusion connects directly to several UN Sustainable Development Goals (SDGs): Goal 12 (Responsible Consumption and Production), Goal 13 (Climate Action), and Goal 15 (Life on Land) (CDP, 2023a). By framing FPIC as a component of biodiversity strategies, the questionnaire recognizes the significance of Indigenous participation in achieving responsible land stewardship and biodiversity goals. However, this question focuses predominantly on high-level commitments rather than requiring detailed reporting on outcomes or specific actions taken.

Similarly, the CDP Forests 2023 Questionnaire integrates Indigenous Peoples' rights and FPIC into multiple aspects of governance, policy, and implementation (CDP, 2023b). For example, question F4.3a included FPIC as a performance indicator linked to incentives for C-suite employees and board members, underlining its importance in aligning corporate accountability with human rights principles (CDP, 2023b). Other questions, such as F4.5a and F6.8, emphasize FPIC in the context of securing land tenure rights and addressing forest-related issues (CDP, 2023b). These align with AFi's Core Principles, including respect for human rights, protection of forests and ecosystems, and collaboration for sustainability (CDP, 2023b). Further, question F6.10b broadens the scope of Indigenous engagement by identifying Indigenous Peoples as key partners in landscape and jurisdictional approaches to sustainable land use (CDP, 2023b). Companies are encouraged to support Indigenous communities in clarifying and securing land tenure rights (CDP, 2023b). This reflects an understanding of Indigenous Peoples' critical role in conserving ecosystems and managing sustainable landscapes, directly connecting to SDGs 12, 13, and 15, as well as AFi's Core Principles for collaboration and sustainable implementation (CDP, 2023b).

2.2.3 SASB

The SASB integrates Indigenous peoples' considerations into its sector-specific standards, particularly under the community relations category. This analysis focuses on the coal operations, metals and mining, and oil and gas exploration and production standards, as these explicitly incorporate metrics and discussions related to Indigenous peoples. While community relations are included in other sector standards, such as healthcare, Indigenous-specific components are only present in these resource-intensive sectors. This targeted inclusion reflects the relevance of Indigenous considerations in industries that significantly intersect with Indigenous lands and rights.

2.2.3.1 Coal Operations

SASB's coal operations standard addresses Indigenous rights under the topic "Rights of Indigenous Peoples," specifically through disclosure metrics EM-CO-210b.1 and EM-CO-210b.2 (IFRS Foundation, 2023e). These metrics require companies to report on two key areas: the percentage of proved and probable reserves in or near Indigenous lands and the processes for engaging and managing Indigenous rights (IFRS Foundation, 2023e). The quantitative aspect (EM-CO-210b.1) involves calculating the proportion of reserves located near Indigenous territories within five kilometers of a recognized boundary (IFRS Foundation, 2023e). These metrics align with international frameworks like the UNDRIP and the International Labour Organization (ILO) Convention 169, both providing foundational definitions of Indigenous land and rights (IFRS Foundation, 2023e).

The standard also mandates qualitative disclosure (EM-CO-210b.2), requiring companies to discuss due diligence practices for managing Indigenous rights (IFRS Foundation, 2023e). This includes adherence to ILO Convention 169, applying FPIC processes, and establishing grievance mechanisms and community agreements (IFRS Foundation, 2023e). Additionally, companies are required to explain how these practices are governed, ensuring consistency across organizational levels and extending to contractors, suppliers, and other partners (IFRS Foundation, 2023e). This emphasis on governance reflects the need to integrate Indigenous rights into corporate operations systematically.

2.2.3.2 Metals and Mining

In the metals and mining sector, Indigenous rights are embedded under the broader topic "Security, Human Rights & Rights of Indigenous Peoples," covered by metrics EM-MM-210a.2 and EM-MM-210a.3 (IFRS Foundation, 2023f). Similar to coal operations, the first metric requires companies to disclose the percentage of proved and probable reserves located in or near Indigenous lands (IFRS Foundation, 2023f). However, the metals and mining standard demands additional granularity, including a breakdown by mineral type or business unit (e.g., aluminum, copper, or iron ore) and reserve grade (percentage metal content) (IFRS Foundation, 2023f). This disaggregation reflects the sector's complexity and the need for tailored reporting aligned with industry-specific practices.

The discussion of engagement processes and due diligence (EM-MM-210a.3) builds upon the requirements in coal operations by incorporating local and regional factors (IFRS Foundation, 2023f). This additional layer ensures that engagement strategies are context-sensitive, recognizing the diversity of Indigenous communities and the specific challenges posed by mining activities in different geographic areas. Like coal operations, these disclosures require companies to detail how practices are governed internally and applied to business partners, ensuring a holistic approach to Indigenous inclusion throughout the project lifecycle (IFRS Foundation, 2023f).

2.2.3.3 Oil and Gas – Exploration & Production

The oil and gas exploration and production standard addresses Indigenous considerations within the same topic as metals and mining: "Security, Human Rights & Rights of Indigenous Peoples." Metrics EM-EP-210a.2 and EM-EP-210a.3 closely mirror those in metals and mining (IFRS Foundation, 2023g). The first metric requires companies to disclose the percentage of proved and probable reserves in or near Indigenous lands, with calculations based on volume rather than weight (IFRS Foundation, 2023g). This distinction acknowledges the sector's operational differences while maintaining consistency in the underlying approach to Indigenous inclusion.

The second metric requires a discussion of engagement processes and due diligence practices, with requirements identical to those in metals and mining (IFRS Foundation, 2023g). This includes considerations for local and regional factors, adherence to FPIC, and the establishment of grievance mechanisms and formal agreements (IFRS Foundation, 2023g). The alignment across these two sectors suggests a standardized approach to addressing Indigenous rights in resource-intensive industries, while minor variations reflect sector-specific operational contexts.

2.2.3.4 Overall Observation

SASB emphasized due diligence throughout the project lifecycle, from initial planning to post-operation phases. By requiring companies to detail how these practices are governed and applied across organizational levels, the standards ensure that Indigenous considerations are embedded in corporate decision-making rather than treated as isolated commitments. Moreover, the inclusion of upstream and downstream partners outlines the importance of a supply chain-wide approach to sustainability, encouraging companies to align their investments and partnerships with ethical and sustainable practices.

Despite the similarities across the three sector standards, some differences are evident. For example, the metals and mining standard requires additional detail on reserve grades and mineral types, reflecting the sector's unique operational complexities. Similarly, while Indigenous rights are combined with security and human rights in metals and mining, oil, and gas, they are addressed as a standalone topic in coal operations. These variations illustrate SASB's ability to tailor its standards to specific industries while maintaining a consistent overarching framework.

All three standards reference UNDRIP and ILO Convention 169, underscoring the importance of international principles in shaping corporate responsibilities toward Indigenous peoples. By aligning with these frameworks, SASB ensures its standards are globally relevant and grounded in widely recognized definitions of Indigenous rights. The result is a robust reporting framework that balances quantitative precision with qualitative depth, providing companies with the tools to engage with Indigenous communities and stakeholders meaningfully.

2.2.4 UN SDGs

The SDGs explicitly incorporate Indigenous peoples into several global targets and indicators, reflecting the growing acknowledgment of their unique roles and vulnerabilities in sustainable development. Under Goal 2: End Hunger, Target 2.3 aims to double the agricultural productivity and incomes of small-scale food producers, explicitly outlining Indigenous peoples alongside women, family farmers, pastoralists, and fishers (UN, 2024Ab). This target emphasizes equitable access to land, productive resources, knowledge, financial services, and market opportunities as key enablers (UN, 2024Ab). To monitor progress, Indicator 2.3.2 measures the average income of small-scale food producers, disaggregated by sex and Indigenous status (UN, 2024Ab). This approach underlines the importance of understanding and addressing disparities in agricultural livelihoods, particularly for Indigenous communities that often face systemic resource access barriers.

Similarly, Goal 4: Quality Education addresses the need for equitable access to education and lifelong learning opportunities for vulnerable populations, including Indigenous peoples (UN, 2024Ab). Target 4.5 seeks to eliminate gender disparities and ensure equal access to education and vocational training by 2030, prioritizing those in vulnerable situations, such as Indigenous children (UN, 2024Ab). Indicator 4.5.1 tracks parity indices, including those based on Indigenous status, to evaluate disparities across various educational indicators (UN, 2024Ab). These commitments align with the broader vision of the SDGs to promote inclusive and equitable quality education, ensuring that Indigenous peoples acquire the knowledge and skills needed to participate in society fully and access opportunities for socioeconomic advancement (General Assembly, 2015).

Beyond these specific targets, the GRI broadens the scope of Indigenous peoples' inclusion by linking their rights to multiple SDGs. GRI 14 addresses material topics related to Indigenous rights and is connected to several goals beyond Goals 2 and 4. These include Goal 1: No Poverty, Goal 3: Good Health and Wellbeing, Goal 5: Gender Equality, Goal 11: Sustainable Cities and Communities, and Goal 16: Peace, Justice, and Strong Institutions (GRI, 2024e). This integration reflects the multidimensional nature of Indigenous peoples' contributions to and challenges within sustainable development. By identifying these intersections, GRI reflects the need for comprehensive reporting frameworks that capture the full spectrum of Indigenous experiences, including their socioeconomic, cultural, and environmental dimensions.

The UN's 2030 Agenda for Sustainable Development further recognizes Indigenous peoples as a vulnerable group that must be empowered to achieve the Agenda's transformative vision (General Assembly, 2015). The "we the peoples" guiding principle explicitly calls for their inclusion in collaborative approaches, ensuring that Indigenous perspectives and needs are integral to the design and implementation of sustainable development strategies (General Assembly, 2015). At national and subnational levels, the Agenda recommends regular and inclusive reviews of country-led and country-driven progress (General Assembly, 2015). These reviews should incorporate Indigenous peoples' contributions in alignment with national circumstances, policies, and priorities (General Assembly, 2015). Moreover, national parliaments and other institutions are encouraged to support these processes, providing platforms for Indigenous voices to influence decision-making and progress evaluations (General Assembly, 2015).

2.2.5 TCFD

The TCFD framework, despite its comprehensive approach to climate-related risks and opportunities, does not include specific references to Indigenous peoples or communities in its recommendations or disclosure requirements. This omission reflects a broader limitation in many global reporting frameworks, where the focus tends to center on financial materiality and climate-related impacts on businesses, often overlooking the social dimensions of climate change. As a result, Indigenous peoples, who are among the most vulnerable to climate-related impacts due to their close ties to the land and natural resources, are not explicitly acknowledged in TCFD's framework. This gap shows an opportunity for future iterations of the framework to incorporate guidance on addressing Indigenous rights and perspectives, particularly as companies increasingly recognize the importance of social equity in sustainability reporting.

2.2.6 TNFD

The TNFD establishes a progressive framework that prioritizes the inclusion of Indigenous Peoples as a critical component of addressing nature-related issues. Within its six general requirements, TNFD emphasizes that engagement with Indigenous Peoples, Local Communities, and other affected stakeholders is essential for effectively identifying, assessing, and managing an organization's dependencies, impacts, risks, and opportunities related to nature (TNFD, 2023b). Recognizing Indigenous Peoples' exceptional contributions to biodiversity conservation, TNFD stresses that while they constitute less than 5% of the global population, they have been safeguarding 80% of the world's biodiversity (TNFD, 2023b). Their traditional knowledge (TK), community-led practices, and cultural institutions provide invaluable insights and methods for ecosystem management. Studies show that biodiversity loss occurs 30% less and at slower rates on Indigenous-managed lands compared to other areas, underscoring the importance of Indigenous stewardship in achieving global biodiversity goals (TNFD, 2023b).

To ensure this recognition translates into actionable practices, TNFD integrates Indigenous engagement into its governance recommendation (c) (TNFD, 2023b). Companies are required to describe their engagement activities with Indigenous

Peoples as part of their strategies for assessing and managing nature-related dependencies, impacts, risks, and opportunities (TNFD, 2023b). These recommendations mandate respect for internationally recognized rights, including those outlined in the UN Declaration on the UNDRIP, the ILO Convention 169, and the Convention on Biological Diversity (CBD) (TNFD, 2023b). TNFD emphasizes that Indigenous engagement must adhere to the principles of FPIC, granting Indigenous Peoples the right to accept or reject projects that may impact their lands, territories, or resources (TNFD, 2023b). Furthermore, companies are expected to report on the purpose, processes, and outcomes of engagement activities, ensuring transparency and accountability throughout the lifecycle of these interactions (TNFD, 2023b). This includes describing whether and how equitable Access and Benefit Sharing (ABS) agreements have been achieved (TNFD, 2023b).

TNFD's guidelines expand on these foundational recommendations by providing practical steps for companies to design and implement effective engagement with Indigenous Peoples (TNFD, 2023b, 2024c). These guidelines cover principles of engagement, preparation for engagement, governance structures, monitoring, and compliance with international and national legislation (TNFD, 2023c). They frame Indigenous Peoples as rights-holders rather than stakeholders, reflecting their unique collective rights and emphasizing their critical role in ecosystem preservation (TNFD, 2023c). The guidelines stress that engagement must be meaningful, participatory, and culturally sensitive, involving Indigenous communities in planning, monitoring, and decision-making processes (TNFD, 2023c). Companies are encouraged to employ diverse engagement methods, ranging from formal consultations and workshops to informal dialogues, tailored to the cultural and social contexts of the communities involved (TNFD, 2023c). Whether the engagement is one-off or part of an ongoing relationship, the process must align with the organization's long-term strategies and policies. (TNFD, 2023c)

Governance is another critical element in TNFD's framework. Boards and senior management are urged to establish clear policies, allocate responsibilities, and implement accountability mechanisms for Indigenous engagement (TNFD, 2023c). TNFD advises organizations to incorporate these processes into their governance structures to ensure consistency and long-term success (TNFD, 2023c). Five key questions, developed in collaboration with the World Economic Forum Global Future Council on Human Rights, guide organizations in evaluating the effectiveness of their Indigenous engagement practices (TNFD, 2023c). These questions show accountability, grievance mechanisms, and transparency in addressing concerns raised by Indigenous communities (TNFD, 2023c).

TNFD also underscores the importance of compliance with both international frameworks and national regulations. It highlights that while legal compliance with Indigenous rights (e.g., UNDRIP, ILO Convention 169) is critical, it is insufficient for meaningful engagement. Effective stakeholder engagement goes beyond mere legal obligations, requiring companies to adopt ethical practices that respect Indigenous Peoples' cultural and intellectual heritage (TNFD, 2023c). The CBD's Article 8(j) is a cornerstone of TNFD's approach, obligating companies to ensure the full and effective participation of Indigenous Peoples in projects that impact biodiversity (TNFD, 2023c). This provision requires companies to respect, preserve, and maintain traditional knowledge while promoting equitable benefit-sharing. TNFD also incorporates voluntary guidelines under Article 8(j), including the Akwé: Kon Guidelines, which focus on impact assessments for projects affecting sacred sites and traditional lands, and the Mo'otz Kuxtal Guidelines, which secure FPIC and prevent the misappropriation of Indigenous knowledge (TNFD, 2023c).

Preparation for engagement is another critical area emphasized by TNFD. Organizations are encouraged to map Indigenous communities that may be affected by or dependent on their activities (TNFD, 2023c). This process involves allocating adequate resources, such as trained staff and culturally appropriate communication tools, to foster meaningful dialogue (TNFD, 2023c). TNFD also advises organizations to embed engagement processes into their broader strategies, ensuring they are systematic and sustainable. Developing clear policies that respect Indigenous rights and creating robust grievance mechanisms are central to this preparation phase (TNFD, 2023c).

Monitoring and feedback form the final stage of TNFD's approach to Indigenous engagement (TNFD, 2023c). By involving Indigenous Peoples in monitoring nature-related issues, companies can enhance their assessments' accuracy, relevance, and inclusivity (TNFD, 2023c). This participatory approach fosters trust and transparency and allows for adaptive management of nature-related challenges (TNFD, 2023c). TNFD requires companies to disclose the outcomes of their engagement activities, including how Indigenous inputs are integrated into materiality assessments and decision-making processes (TNFD, 2023c).

2.2.7 IFRS

While the IFRS S1 and S2 standards do not explicitly mention Indigenous peoples or communities (IFRS Foundation, 2023h, 2023i), the ISSB has acknowledged their significant role in sustainability disclosures and enterprise value considerations (IFRS Foundation, 2022). Specifically, the ISSB recognizes the unique perspectives Indigenous peoples bring to sustainability-related factors and their critical role in biodiversity conservation (IFRS Foundation, 2022). Efforts are underway to embed biodiversity and natural ecosystem concerns into global disclosure standards through an Indigenous lens(IFRS Foundation, 2022). These initiatives are supported by contributions from leaders like Geordie Hungerford, the CEO of Canada's First

Nations Financial Management Board and a member of the Gwich'in Nation (IFRS Foundation, 2022). Moreover, the ISSB aims to align its work with existing frameworks such as the TNFD and other nature-related disclosure standards, particularly where they address investor information needs (IFRS Foundation, 2022). Given TNFD's thorough inclusion of Indigenous peoples, there is potential for IFRS to expand its scope in this area in future iterations.

In Canada, the Canadian Sustainability Standards Board (CSSB) is actively working to enhance Indigenous engagement in developing the Canadian Sustainability Disclosure Standards (CSDS). This effort includes commitments to deepen consultations and create more opportunities for Indigenous participation in shaping the standards (FRAS Canada, 2024). To further this goal, a dedicated report summarizing Indigenous participation and feedback on Indigenous-specific matters is expected to be published soon (FRAS Canada, 2024). These initiatives show an evolving approach to ensuring Indigenous voices and perspectives are incorporated meaningfully into sustainability reporting frameworks.

2.2.8 Summary of Reporting Standards on Indigenous Inclusion

Eighteen categories were developed from common keywords identified in reporting frameworks and standards to analyze the depth and extent of Indigenous peoples' and communities' inclusion. Table 1 compares diverse major frameworks and standards, including GRI, CDP, SASB, TNFD, UN SDGs, and IFRS/CSDS. This comparative analysis focuses on the consistent presence of crucial categories. Notably, Free, Prior, and Informed Consent (FPIC), Indigenous Rights, and Engagement are frequently addressed, showing the universal recognition of securing FPIC, the alignment with international standards such as UNDRIP, and the importance of meaningful engagement with Indigenous communities.

Furthermore, the frameworks vary in their coverage of categories such as Due Diligence, Policies/Commitments, and Remediation. These differences reflect the varying degrees of specificity, focus area, and practical guidance on integrating these rights within corporate practices, indicating a spectrum of commitment and implementation levels across industries. For example, some standards, like GRI and SASB, provided detailed guidelines on due diligence processes and grievance mechanisms to effectively mitigate and address potential impacts on Indigenous rights.

On the other hand, frameworks like TNFD and UN SDGs introduce unique perspectives on Indigenous inclusion, emphasizing the recognition of Traditional Knowledge and targeting disparities through Access and Equity. The TNFD, for instance, integrates Indigenous perspectives into biodiversity conservation strategies, promoting equitable use and involvement in environmental projects, while the

UN SDGs aim to resolve disparities in income, land access, and education among Indigenous populations.

Table 1. Key categories compared across reporting frameworks and standards on indigenous inclusion.

Key Category	GRI	CDP	SASB	TCFD	TNFD	UN SDGs	IFRS & CSDS
Free, Prior, and Informed Consent (FPIC)	Yes, companies must obtain FPIC for activities affecting Indigenous lands or resources, report on the process and agreements, and ensure meaningful, equitable engagement.	Yes, included in commitments, governance, policies, supplier engagement, and landscape approaches; emphasizes securing FPIC, aligning with UNDRIP, and promoting sustainable practices.	Yes, part of engagement and due diligence, ensuring consent before, during, and after project development.	No	Yes, companies must obtain FPIC for activities impacting Indigenous lands or resources, ensuring full information and the right to withhold consent.	No	No
Indigenous Rights	Yes, aligned with UNDRIP and ILO 169; requires FPIC, reporting violations, avoiding harm, engaging communities, and sector-specific approaches.	Yes, via FPIC commitments, alignment with UNDRIP, land tenure rights, remediation, and integration into governance, supply chains, and land-use strategies.	Yes, requires alignment with UNDRIP and ILO 169 to ensure respect for Indigenous rights.	No	Yes, outlined in UNDRIP, ILO 169, and the CBD, emphasizing Indigenous rights and engagement.	Yes, includes access to resources (Goal 2) and education (Goal 4), addressing disparities in income, land, and education opportunities.	No
Engagement	Yes, requires incorporating Indigenous perspectives into decision-making, with sector-specific standards emphasizing equitable participation (e.g., Indigenous women).	Yes, integrated via FPIC, leadership incentives, and collaboration on sustainable land use and tenure rights.	Yes, mandates disclosure on FPIC processes, grievance mechanisms, formal agreements, and due diligence to uphold Indigenous rights.	No	Yes, includes participatory governance, FPIC, benefit-sharing, and integrating these processes into accountability structures.	Yes, promotes active Indigenous involvement in resources, education, and equity under Targets 2.3 and 4.5.	Partially, could involve Indigenous engagement in future disclosures.

continued on following page

Table 1. Continued

Key Category	GRI	CDP	SASB	TCFD	TNFD	UN SDGs	IFRS & CSDS
Due Diligence	Yes, processes to identify, prevent, mitigate, and address actual or potential impacts on Indigenous rights, aligned with FPIC and international standards.	No	Yes, includes due diligence for Indigenous rights, ensuring compliance with regional and international standards.	No	Yes, companies must assess and manage impacts on Indigenous rights and environmental concerns.	No	No
Policies/ Commitments	Yes, through management disclosures requiring formal commitments aligned with international frameworks, operationalized via due diligence and monitoring.	Yes, includes public commitments to FPIC and requests policy scope and alignment with UNDRIP, including remediation of adverse impacts.	Yes, linked to engagement processes, due diligence, FPIC, grievance mechanisms, and governance.	No	Yes, specifies how organizations should incorporate Indigenous rights into strategies, policies, and governance structures.	Partially, supports commitments to improve Indigenous livelihoods and opportunities	Partially, emerging commitments to Indigenous engagement in disclosures.
Remediation	Yes, GRI 411 requires remediation plans for violations, with development, implementation, monitoring, and outcome reviews.	Partially, included in land-related impacts under F4.6b but not within the climate change questionnaire.	No	No	No	No	No
Quantitative Metrics	Yes, tracks the total number of rights violations and incidents.	Yes, includes metrics such as land restored (hectares), suppliers engaged in FPIC, and finalized land tenure agreements.	Yes, includes metrics on reserves near Indigenous lands, including grade and business unit breakdowns.	No	No	Yes, tracks income parity for Indigenous communities and education equity.	No
Recognition of TK	No	No	No	No	Yes, recognizes TK by promoting preservation, equitable use, and participation in biodiversity projects; aligned with CBD Article 8(j).	No	Partially, acknowledges TK's role in biodiversity without formal integration.

continued on following page

Table 1. Continued

Key Category	GRI	CDP	SASB	TCFD	TNFD	UN SDGs	IFRS & CSDS
Governance	Partially, embedded indirectly in policies, processes, and accountability mechanisms.	Partially, forest-related governance links incentives for executives to FPIC and alignment with policies.	Yes, mandates governance mechanisms ensuring adherence to Indigenous rights policies at all organizational levels, including contractors.	No	Yes, requires boards and senior management to set clear policies, assign responsibilities, and integrate Indigenous rights into strategy.	No	No
Access and Equity	Partially, reflected through principles like FPIC, equitable participation, grievance mechanisms, and cultural preservation.	No	No	No	Yes, emphasizes equitable benefit distribution, participatory monitoring, and feedback mechanisms.	Yes, addresses disparities in land access, income, and resources for Indigenous peoples.	No
Violations and Incidents	Yes, tracks Indigenous rights violations and associated remediation.	No	No	No	No	No	No
Materiality Assessment/ Material Topics	Yes, sector-specific assessments require prioritizing Indigenous rights impacts through FPIC and compliance reviews.	No	Yes, identifies Indigenous rights as a material topic, requiring disclosure of land and engagement processes.	No	Yes, integrates Indigenous engagement outcomes into materiality assessments and company strategy.	No	No
Community Agreements	Yes, GRI 14 requires reporting on agreements with Indigenous Peoples, including public availability.	No	Yes, requires formal agreements with Indigenous communities as part of due diligence and engagement.	No	Yes, promotes shared decision-making and FPIC for activities impacting Indigenous lands.	No	No
Community Development Programs	Yes, links development programs to positive impacts on Indigenous communities.	No	No	No	No	Partially, supports community development goals indirectly.	No

continued on following page

Table 1. Continued

Key Category	GRI	CDP	SASB	TCFD	TNFD	UN SDGs	IFRS & CSDS
Consultation	Partially, embedded in FPIC processes.	Partially, embedded in FPIC processes.	Yes, embedded in FPIC and due diligence for Indigenous rights.	No	Yes, emphasizes voluntary and transparent consultation under FPIC.	No.	Partially, Indigenous consultation commitments are emerging.
Grievance Mechanisms	Yes, GRI 411 requires formal mechanisms for Indigenous Peoples to raise concerns, track issues, and resolve violations, with outcomes reported.	No	Yes, grievance mechanisms required as part of due diligence practices.	No	Yes, ensures accessible, fair grievance mechanisms integrated into governance.	No	No
Partnership/ Collaboration	No	Yes, emphasizes FPIC, sustainable land use, and sectoral collaboration on rights and land tenure.	No	No	Yes, promotes participatory decision-making, co-management, and equitable benefit-sharing.	Partially, relies on collaborative efforts at national levels.	No
Employment Opportunities	No	No	No	No	No	Yes, promotes non-farm employment and improved incomes through sustainable opportunities.	No

Source: Authors' work

2.2.9 Identifying the Differences in Reporting Frameworks & Standards

The above section has outlined and defined the nature of the three main integrated research approaches. Figure 2 summarizes and displays the major differences between the research approaches.

Figure 1. Defining key categories of key reporting frameworks and standards.

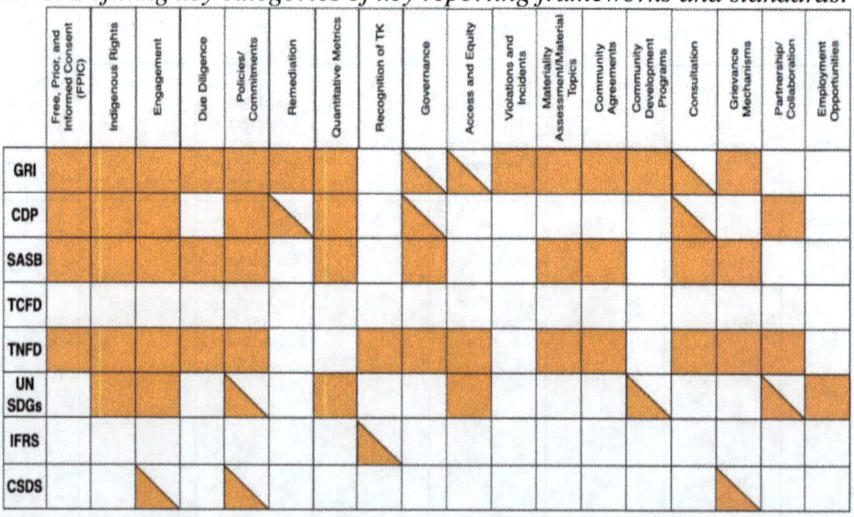

Source: Authors' work

The previous subsection outlined and defined the specifics of how major reporting standards and frameworks have integrated or failed to integrate components related to Indigenous peoples and communities. Figure 2 summarizes and illustrates the major differences between these standards and frameworks. Filled boxes indicate a consensus that the reporting framework/standard has integrated components related to Indigenous peoples and communities. Empty boxes suggest a consensus that it does not include this component, and half-full box indicate some degree of contention about whether the component has been indirectly included or not fully incorporated or if there has been a commitment to incorporate this component without yet implementing it.

3.0 DISCUSSION

3.1 Three Key Categories Defined in Reporting Standards and Frameworks

As illustrated in ***Table 1*** and ***Figure 1***, the three categories most incorporated into standards and frameworks regarding Indigenous peoples are Free, Prior, and Informed Consent (FPIC), Indigenous rights, and engagement.

Indigenous rights, one of the most incorporated categories, are upheld across various frameworks, including GRI, CDP, SASB, TNFD, and UN SDGs. These disclosures ensure that the rights of Indigenous peoples are recognized and respected in line with international laws and agreements such as UNDRIP and ILO Convention 169. This includes rights related to land, culture, self-determination, and to be free from discrimination. Standards/frameworks like GRI, SASB, and TNFD accentuate the need for organizations to respect Indigenous rights throughout their operations, including incorporating these rights into their governance structures, reporting violations, and mitigating negative impacts on Indigenous communities. This is particularly important in industries such as mining and oil and gas, where operations often intersect with Indigenous lands and communities. For instance, GRI requires reporting on the number of incidents where Indigenous rights were violated, describing the context, actions taken, and results of remedial measures.

Engagement with Indigenous communities, with frameworks and standards equally integrated compared to Indigenous rights, is another major category defined, involving ongoing and meaningful involvement of Indigenous communities in the decision-making processes that impact them. This category extends to discussions on land use, cultural preservation, and participation in benefits arising from natural resource exploitation. Disclosures like SASB and TNFD emphasized the necessity of inclusive and culturally sensitive engagement practices that extend beyond mere consultation, such as grievance mechanisms, to include active participation in governance and strategy.

As the third most incorporated category, FPIC ensures that Indigenous communities have the right to give or withhold their consent to projects that may affect the lands they traditionally own, occupy, or otherwise use. It is recognized as a fundamental step in protecting their rights and ensuring they have a say in decisions that affect their lives and communities. This requirement ensures that Indigenous peoples have a direct say in projects that impact them to reflect commitments to respecting their rights and autonomy. For example, The GRI and TNFD emphasized the importance of companies obtaining FPIC for all activities affecting Indigenous lands and reporting transparently on the processes and outcomes involved in securing FPIC, including the purpose, processes, and outcomes of their engagements.

3.2 Least Defined Categories in Reporting Standards and Frameworks

Table 1 and ***Figure 1 highlight*** that remediation, recognition of Traditional Knowledge (TK), violations and incidents, community development programs, and employment opportunities are the categories least commonly incorporated into standards and frameworks.

Remediation efforts are generally underrepresented, with only the GRI explicitly requiring detailed reports on remediation plans and their outcomes and the CDP mentioning remediate adverse impacts on Indigenous people. This category is critical as it addresses the corrective actions taken after rights violations or negative impacts, providing transparency and accountability. Most other reporting standards and frameworks lack explicit requirements for remediation processes related to Indigenous rights. This gap in other frameworks indicates the need for standardized requirements for accountability in resolving negative impacts or violations against Indigenous communities beyond basic regulatory compliance.

As previously noted, recognition of TK is mainly absent in most frameworks except for the TNFD, which emphasizes preserving and utilizing TK in biodiversity conservation. Although the IFRS acknowledges the importance of TK in sustainability and biodiversity conservation, it has not yet implemented specific measures. This oversight is critical, particularly as TK is vital for biodiversity conservation and sustainable use, recognized under UNDRIP (Berkes, 2017). In Canada, many regulatory bodies have included TK in decision-making processes (Henri et al., 2021). British Columbia, in particular, has passed legislation to implement UNDRIP and incorporates high-level planning with First Nations for wildlife management (Henri et al., 2021), reflecting the importance of integrating TK at the corporate level as well.

Violations and Incidents are also minimally incorporated across frameworks and standards. Apart from the GRI, which requires detailed reporting on violations of Indigenous rights, other standards appear to lack explicit requirements for reporting specific violations against Indigenous peoples, potentially leading to underreporting and insufficient transparency regarding harm caused to Indigenous communities.

Community Development Programs are scarcely covered. The GRI links these programs to impacts on Indigenous communities by requiring organizations to report how their community development programs are tailored to the needs and rights of Indigenous peoples. The UN SDGs indirectly support community development broadly but do not specifically target Indigenous communities. This general approach, which typically focuses more broadly on community relations without specific requirements to develop or report on programs, overlooks benefits to Indigenous communities specifically and can neglect the unique needs and potential benefits of targeted development programs.

Employment opportunities for Indigenous peoples are not a primary focus in most frameworks, with only the UN SDGs supporting this through goals aimed at improving incomes and sustainable job creation. The major sustainability reporting frameworks and standards do not directly address the creation of employment opportunities for Indigenous peoples, potentially showing a significant gap in promoting economic inclusion and assessing the impact of corporate practices on Indigenous employment.

3.3 Current Approaches to Indigenous Inclusion in Reporting Frameworks

The current landscape of reporting standards and frameworks shows varying levels of effectiveness in integrating Indigenous perspectives, with significant room for improvement in ensuring these integrations are both meaningful and beneficial. Enhancing clarity, consistency, and outcome-focused reporting within these frameworks is crucial for building respectful and equitable relationships with Indigenous communities, ultimately leading to more sustainable and inclusive global development.

The GRI provides a solid foundation for integrating Indigenous rights into organizational reporting, incorporating categories of FPIC, Indigenous rights, engagement, due diligence, policies/commitments, remediation, quantitative metrics, violations and incidents, materiality assessment/material topics, community agreements, community development programs, and grievance mechanisms. It also partially incorporated governance, access and equity, and consultation. However, certain aspects remain ambiguous. Terms like "meaningful engagement" lack precise definitions, leading to inconsistent implementation across organizations. Moreover, while GRI encourages transparency and accountability, they do not always guarantee that the reported actions lead to significant, positive changes for Indigenous communities. To enhance the effectiveness of these standards, it is critical to address these ambiguities and ensure that the standards foster respectful and equitable relationships between organizations and Indigenous people.

The CDP incorporates categories of FPIC, Indigenous rights, engagement, policies/commitments, quantitative metrics, and partnership/collaboration. It also partially incorporated remediation, governance, and consultation within its questionnaires, connecting the role of Indigenous Peoples in biodiversity conservation to broader sustainability goals. Despite these inclusions, a few gaps remain. Many questions focus on broader commitments, policies, and implementation processes rather than measurable outcomes or the direct impacts of these measures on Indigenous communities. For instance, while FPIC and Indigenous land rights are prioritized, the questionnaires rarely ask organizations to report specific results, such as the effectiveness of FPIC processes or tangible benefits to Indigenous Peoples. Further, the Water Security Questionnaire omits Indigenous-related questions entirely, despite the severe and disproportionate impacts of water insecurity on Indigenous lands and communities. This lack of emphasis on outcomes extends to climate change impacts on Indigenous lands, where the consequences can be especially pronounced. Only one broad question in the entire set of questionnaires directly addresses Indigenous Peoples, limiting the frameworks' capacity to assess how well companies respond to these urgent challenges. The absence of metrics for evaluating results, paired with a repetitive focus on high-level commitments, suggests a need for frameworks to move beyond symbolic inclusion toward actionable, measurable, and transparent engagement with Indigenous Peoples. Addressing these gaps requires literature and further research to contextualize and substantiate these observations, ensuring that Indigenous inclusion in reporting frameworks is comprehensive and impactful.

The SASB firmly commits to measurable and actionable reporting by incorporating FPIC, Indigenous rights, engagement, due diligence, policies/commitments, quantitative metrics, governance, materiality assessment/material topics, community agreements, consultation, and grievance mechanisms. The standards employ quantitative metrics that require transparent calculations. This precision is complemented by qualitative disclosures on engagement processes and governance mechanisms, ensuring that companies address Indigenous rights comprehensively and consistently. These standards are particularly effective in the mining and oil and gas sectors, where Indigenous rights are critical considerations. It can be used as an effective tool to engage with Indigenous communities and stakeholders meaningfully. However, while SASB promotes a systematic inclusion of Indigenous rights, differences across sector-specific standards may result in inconsistencies in how Indigenous concerns are addressed. It lacks emphasis on outcomes that extend to climate change impacts on Indigenous lands, where the consequences can be especially pronounced. Only one broad question in the entire set of questionnaires directly addresses Indigenous Peoples, limiting the frameworks' capacity to assess how well companies respond to these urgent challenges. The absence of metrics for evaluating results, paired with a repetitive focus on high-level commitments, suggests a need for frameworks to move beyond symbolic inclusion toward actionable, measurable, and transparent engagement with Indigenous Peoples. Addressing these gaps requires literature and further research to contextualize and substantiate these observations, ensuring that Indigenous inclusion in reporting frameworks and standards is both comprehensive and impactful.

While the SDGs explicitly recognize Indigenous peoples in several targets, there is potential for the SDGs to incorporate Indigenous peoples more extensively across additional goals. SDGs incorporated Indigenous rights, engagement, and employment opportunities and partially incorporated policies/commitments, community development programs, and partnerships/collaborations. Indigenous communities are disproportionately affected by systemic inequities and environmental challenges, making their inclusion relevant to climate action, sustainable resource management, and equitable economic growth. By expanding the scope of inclusion of Indigenous perspectives across additional SDGs, the global community can better address the unique challenges faced by Indigenous peoples and harness their knowledge and contributions to achieve sustainable and inclusive development.

The TCFD does not specifically address Indigenous people. This omission reflects a broader limitation in many global reporting frameworks, where the focus tends to center on financial materiality and climate-related impacts on businesses, often overlooking the social dimensions of climate change. As a result, Indigenous peoples, who are among the most vulnerable to climate-related impacts due to their close ties to the land and natural resources, are not explicitly acknowledged in TCFD's framework. This gap shows an opportunity for future iterations of the framework to incorporate guidance on addressing Indigenous rights and perspectives, particularly as companies increasingly recognize the importance of social equity in sustainability reporting.

The TNFD takes a more comprehensive and detailed approach to Indigenous engagement. It incorporates FPIC, Indigenous rights, engagement, due diligence, policies/commitments, recognition of TK, governance, access and equity, materiality assessment/material topics, community agreements, consultation, grievance mechanisms, and partnership/collaboration. TNFD uniquely requires companies to report on the lifecycle of their engagement activities, from the initial consultation to the outcomes and effectiveness of these processes. By embedding Indigenous engagement into materiality assessments, TNFD provides a fresh perspective on the role of Indigenous knowledge and practices in addressing global biodiversity challenges. Its thorough guidelines, supported by international frameworks and detailed recommendations, offer a robust roadmap for companies to foster meaningful and ethical relationships with Indigenous Peoples. This approach can promote biodiversity conservation and advance equity, cultural respect, and sustainable development.

CONCLUSION AND FUTURE RESEARCH DIRECTION

Sustainability reporting frameworks have evolved significantly yet remain fragmented and lack a unified approach. Frameworks such as GRI, CDP, SASB, TNFD, TCFD, and the UN SDGs offer varied methodologies and emphasize different aspects of sustainability. While these frameworks address critical ESG dimensions, their scattered nature poses challenges to standardization and consistency in reporting practices. Efforts toward harmonization, such as those by the ISSB, show promise in aligning frameworks under a global baseline. However, this journey toward standardization must balance financial materiality with broader social equity and environmental considerations to ensure inclusivity.

The integration of Indigenous rights and perspectives exemplifies these challenges. Indigenous peoples are inconsistently represented across frameworks as key custodians of biodiversity and sustainable land-use practices. The GRI offers comprehensive guidelines, emphasizing Free, Prior, and Informed Consent (FPIC), rights alignment with international agreements, and community engagement. SASB incorporates sector-specific metrics for industries impacting Indigenous territories, and TNFD highlights traditional knowledge and biodiversity conservation. In contrast, frameworks such as TCFD and IFRS largely neglect Indigenous-specific considerations, reflecting a bias toward financial outcomes over social inclusivity. Even broadly inclusive initiatives like the UN SDGs can deepen their integration of Indigenous priorities. Moving forward, the path toward unified sustainability standards must prioritize Indigenous rights and equity, ensuring these communities are both valued and empowered in global sustainability efforts.

Challenges stem from ambiguous definitions, such as "meaningful engagement," which hinder consistent implementation, and the lack of robust mechanisms to monitor and report on outcomes. Additionally, the absence of specific provisions for recognizing traditional knowledge, addressing violations, and creating equitable economic opportunities underscores systemic gaps in existing frameworks. The omission of Indigenous-specific metrics in global standards like IFRS and TCFD further limits the capacity of reporting tools to address the unique vulnerabilities and contributions of Indigenous communities.

Future research should focus on developing standardized metrics for evaluating the effectiveness of Indigenous engagement, ensuring meaningful participation and tangible benefits. Exploring the integration of traditional knowledge into sustainability metrics and enhancing grievance and remediation mechanisms will be critical. Interdisciplinary studies examining the intersection of biodiversity conservation, climate change, and Indigenous rights are essential to inform policy and corporate practices. By addressing these gaps, future research can contribute to creating sustainability reporting frameworks that are inclusive and transformative, fostering equity and resilience for Indigenous peoples and the broader global community.

CHAPTER SUMMARY

Evolution and Fragmentation: The chapter traces the evolution of sustainability reporting from early Corporate Social Responsibility (CSR) concepts to a complex landscape of global frameworks, noting a persistent lack of harmonization and a tension between financial and impact materiality.

Critical Comparative Analysis: A systematic evaluation of major frameworks (GRI, SASB, TNFD, CDP, TCFD, UN SDGs, IFRS) reveals inconsistent integration of Indigenous issues, with GRI and TNFD demonstrating the most comprehensive approach, while TCFD and IFRS largely omit specific references.

The Triumvirate of Inclusion: The most consistently incorporated categories across frameworks are Free, Prior, and Informed Consent (FPIC), Indigenous Rights (aligned with UNDRIP), and Engagement, establishing a baseline for corporate accountability.

Persistent Systemic Gaps: Critical categories like Remediation, Recognition of Traditional Knowledge (TK), tracking Violations and Incidents, Community Development Programs, and Employment Opportunities are severely underrepresented, limiting the frameworks' effectiveness in ensuring justice and equitable outcomes.

The Canadian Context: The analysis highlights the pivotal role of the nascent Canadian Sustainability Standards Board (CSSB) in navigating the integration of international standards (ISSB) with Canada's unique constitutional and legal duties to Indigenous peoples.

Call for Transformative Integration: The chapter concludes that future credibility and effectiveness of sustainability reporting depend on moving beyond symbolic inclusion to embed Indigenous rights, knowledge, and worldviews as foundational pillars, requiring standardized metrics for outcomes and deeper interdisciplinary research.

CHAPTER QUESTIONS

True and False Questions

1. The Global Reporting Initiative (GRI) was formed in direct response to the Exxon Valdez oil spill.
2. The Sustainability Accounting Standards Board (SASB) standards are industry-agnostic and apply the same metrics to all sectors.
3. The TNFD framework explicitly recognizes the critical role of Indigenous Traditional Knowledge in biodiversity conservation.
4. The IFRS S1 and S2 standards contain specific, detailed disclosure requirements related to the rights of Indigenous peoples.
5. The concept of "financial materiality," as championed by the ISSB, focuses primarily on an organization's impacts on society and the environment.
6. The UN Sustainable Development Goals (SDGs) include specific targets and indicators that are explicitly disaggregated for Indigenous peoples.
7. According to the chapter, the TCFD framework provides extensive guidance on assessing the social equity dimensions of climate change for Indigenous communities.
8. A key challenge identified in the Canadian context is aligning the proposed Canadian Sustainability Standards Board (CSSB) standards with the ISSB while addressing broader public interest concerns.
9. The chapter identifies remediation and grievance mechanisms as one of the most thoroughly incorporated categories across all reporting frameworks studied.

10. The SASB standards for the metals and mining sector require quantitative disclosure on the percentage of reserves located near Indigenous lands.

Multiple Choice Questions

11. According to the chapter, which of the following is identified as the LEAST incorporated category across major sustainability reporting frameworks regarding Indigenous inclusion?
    A) Free, Prior, and Informed Consent (FPIC)
    B) Engagement with communities
    C) Recognition of Traditional Knowledge (TK)
    D) Indigenous Rights
    E) Due Diligence processes
12. The merger of the Sustainability Accounting Standards Board (SASB) with the International Integrated Reporting Council (IIRC) to form the Value Reporting Foundation (VRF) raised concerns that:
    A) It would eliminate all industry-specific metrics.
    B) It prioritized a narrow, investor-centric view of "enterprise value" over broader socio-environmental impacts.
    C) It mandated the immediate adoption of TNFD recommendations.
    D) It made reporting voluntary instead of mandatory.
    E) It focused exclusively on climate change, ignoring social issues.
13. The TNFD framework distinguishes Indigenous Peoples as:
    A) Primary shareholders.
    B) Voluntary participants.
    C) Rights-holders, not just stakeholders.
    D) Government regulators.
    E) External auditors.
14. A central criticism of the ISSB's approach to sustainability reporting, as discussed in the chapter, is its primary focus on:
    A) Impact materiality.
    B) Philanthropic activities.
    C) Financial materiality.
    D) Cultural heritage preservation.
    E) Community development programs.
15. In the Canadian context, a significant challenge for the proposed Canadian Sustainability Standards Board (CSSB) is:
    A) A complete lack of alignment with the ISSB's global baseline.
    B) Defining a "public interest" that goes beyond capital markets to include Indigenous rights.

C) Replacing the GRI standards entirely.
D) Eliminating all voluntary reporting.
E) Focusing solely on environmental disclosures.

16. Which framework is praised in the chapter for requiring companies to report on the entire lifecycle of engagement with Indigenous Peoples, from consultation to outcomes?
A) TCFD
B) CDP
C) SASB
D) TNFD
E) IFRS S2

17. The chapter argues that the underrepresentation of which category in reporting frameworks leads to insufficient transparency and accountability for harms caused to Indigenous communities?
A) Quantitative Metrics
B) Policies/Commitments
C) Violations and Incidents
D) Governance
E) Partnership/Collaboration

18. The GRI 411 standard specifically requires organizations to align their practices with which international instruments?
A) The Paris Agreement and the Kyoto Protocol.
B) The SASB Standards and the TCFD Recommendations.
C) The UNDRIP and ILO Convention 169.
D) The IFRS S1 and S2 Standards.
E) The CDP Water Security Questionnaire.

19. According to the comparative analysis (Table 1), which of the following frameworks does NOT incorporate the category of "Grievance Mechanisms" for Indigenous peoples?
A) GRI
B) SASB
C) TNFD
D) CDP
E) UN SDGs

20. The historical development of modern sustainability reporting is linked in the chapter to demands for corporate transparency after which event?
A) The signing of the UN Sustainable Development Goals.
B) The creation of the International Accounting Standards Board (IASB).
C) The Exxon Valdez oil spill.
D) The global financial crisis of 2008.

E) The publication of the Brundtland Report.

Short Answer Questions

21. Briefly define the principle of Free, Prior, and Informed Consent (FPIC) and state its significance in the context of Indigenous rights and corporate projects.
22. What is the key distinction between a sustainability reporting framework and a standard, as explained in the chapter?
23. Name two sustainability reporting frameworks that, according to the chapter's analysis, do not explicitly mention or incorporate Indigenous peoples.
24. Identify one strength and one weakness of the CDP questionnaires in addressing Indigenous issues, as critiqued in the chapter.
25. How does the SASB's approach to Indigenous inclusion differ from that of the GRI, based on their foundational focuses?
26. What is the stated mission of the International Sustainability Standards Board (ISSB)?
27. According to the chapter, why is the underrepresentation of *"Remediation"* as a category in reporting frameworks a significant gap?
28. What role does Traditional Knowledge (TK) play in the TNFD framework's approach to biodiversity?

Essay Questions

29. Analyze the comparative strengths and weaknesses of the GRI Standards and the SASB Standards in addressing the rights and perspectives of Indigenous peoples. Use specific examples from the chapter, such as disclosure topics and metrics.
30. Explain the tension between *"financial materiality"* and "impact materiality" in sustainability reporting. How does this tension influence the way Indigenous issues are incorporated (or omitted) in frameworks like those from the ISSB versus the GRI?
31. Describe the progression of thought from Corporate Social Responsibility (CSR) to modern sustainability reporting frameworks. How has this evolution shaped the current opportunities and challenges for including Indigenous economic equity?
32. Critique the argument that the merger of SASB into the ISSB's structure, while promoting global standardization, may risk marginalizing the specific socio-economic needs of Indigenous communities.
33. Elaborate on the *"least defined categories"* in reporting frameworks as identified in the chapter. Why are categories like Traditional Knowledge, Remediation,

and Employment Opportunities critical for achieving genuine Indigenous equity, and what are the consequences of their omission?

34. Discuss the unique challenges and opportunities facing the Canadian Sustainability Standards Board (CSSB) in developing standards that are both globally interoperable and responsive to the specific context of Indigenous rights in Canada.

Questions for Graduate Students (Requiring Further Research)

35. ***Comparative Policy Analysis:*** Select two countries with significant Indigenous populations (e.g., Canada and Australia). Compare and contrast how their national policies and emerging sustainability reporting regulations (like Canada's CSSB) mandate or encourage corporate disclosure on Indigenous rights, drawing on the frameworks discussed in this chapter.
36. ***Case Study on FPIC Implementation:*** Choose a specific, real-world corporate project (e.g., a pipeline, mine, or forestry operation) that has faced scrutiny regarding Indigenous consent. Research and analyze the extent to which the company's reporting (e.g., via GRI or SASB) accurately reflected the on-the-ground FPIC processes and outcomes described by Indigenous communities and independent observers.
37. ***Metrics Development:*** The chapter identifies a gap in metrics for "Recognition of Traditional Knowledge." Propose a set of 3-5 specific, measurable indicators that a company could adopt to demonstrate its respect for and integration of TK into its environmental management or biodiversity conservation strategies. Justify your choices.
38. ***Investor Influence:*** Research the growing movement of ESG (Environmental, Social, and Governance) investing. Analyze how investor pressure could be leveraged to encourage better corporate performance and disclosure on Indigenous issues, particularly in frameworks like SASB and TCFD that are investor-focused. Provide examples of shareholder resolutions or investor guidelines on this topic.
39. ***The "S" in ESG:*** Critically examine the relative emphasis on the *"Social"* dimension within mainstream ESG ratings and reporting frameworks. Using Indigenous inclusion as a core case study, argue whether the current treatment of social factors is adequate or if it remains subordinate to environmental and governance concerns.

Questions for PhD Scholars (Requiring Extensive Further Research)

40. ***Epistemological Conflict in Standard-Setting:*** Drawing on critical accounting theory and post-colonial studies, investigate the epistemological power struggles

inherent in sustainability standard-setting. How do the technical, quantitative, and capitalist rationalities underpinning frameworks like the ISSB's act to marginalize or *"domesticate"* Indigenous knowledge systems, which are often qualitative, relational, and spiritually grounded? Can these epistemologies be reconciled within a single reporting regime, or does meaningful inclusion require a radical re-imagining of the practice itself?

41. ***Discourse Analysis of Corporate Reports:*** Conduct a critical discourse analysis of the sustainability reports from several major extractive industry corporations. How is the language of *"engagement," "partnership,"* and *"FPIC"* constructed and deployed? Does this corporate discourse reflect a genuine sharing of power and decision-making with Indigenous communities, or does it primarily function as a legitimizing tool to manage reputational risk and secure a *"social license to operate"*?
42. ***Political Ecology of Reporting Standards:*** Employ a political ecology lens to analyze the global push for reporting harmonization led by the ISSB. Trace the networks of influence—including supranational organizations, financial institutions, and multinational corporations—that are shaping this agenda. How might this process of ***"institutional isomorphism"*** serve to entrench a form of neoliberal environmental governance that co-opts the concept of sustainability while systematically side-lining alternative, Indigenous-centered models of development and accountability?

Questions for Post-Doctoral Researchers (Direction for High-Impact Research)

43. ***Theorizing an Indigenous-Centered Reporting Model:*** Moving beyond critique, this research program would aim to develop a proto-framework for sustainability reporting grounded explicitly in Indigenous ontologies and legal orders (e.g., concepts of relational accountability, reciprocity, and Seventh Generation thinking). The research would involve deep, participatory collaboration with Indigenous scholars and knowledge-keepers to design principles, metrics, and assurance processes that are not merely an *"add-on"* to Western models but are fundamentally structured by Indigenous worldviews. The output would be a challenge to the very foundations of mainstream reporting.
44. ***Longitudinal Impact Assessment of TNFD Adoption:*** Design and implement a longitudinal, multi-method research project to track the early adoption of the TNFD recommendations by financial institutions and corporations. The study would investigate not only the quality of disclosures but, more importantly, the causal links between reporting and on-the-ground outcomes for Indigenous peoples and biodiversity. Does high-quality TNFD reporting correlate with a

reduction in conflicts, the strengthening of land tenure, and tangible benefit-sharing agreements? This research would provide the much-needed empirical evidence to test the TNFD's transformative potential.

45. ***The Architecture of Inter-legality in Sustainability Governance: Engage*** in advanced socio-legal research to map and analyze the complex *"inter-legality"* between emerging transnational sustainability reporting standards (like IFRS/ISSB), international human rights law (UNDRIP, ILO 169), and the domestic constitutional and common law rights of Indigenous peoples. How are these different legal orders interacting, conflicting, or merging in corporate practice and judicial/arbitral decisions? This research would produce a sophisticated theoretical model for understanding and navigating this layered legal landscape, with practical implications for policymakers, corporations, and Indigenous advocates.

REFERENCES

Adams, C., & Narayanan, V. (2010). The 'standardization' of sustainability reporting. In *Sustainability accounting and accountability* (pp. 89–104). Routledge.

Adams, C. A. (2020). *The Sustainable Development Goals, integrated thinking and the integrated report*. IFRS Foundation. https://integratedreporting.ifrs.org/wp-content/uploads/2017/09/SDGs-and-the-integrated-report_full17.pdf

Adams, C. A., Alhamood, A. M., & He, X. (2022). The development and implementation of GRI standards: practice and policy issues. In *Handbook of accounting and sustainability* (pp. 26–43). Edward Elgar Publishing. DOI: 10.4337/9781800373518.00009

Agle, B. R., & Kelley, P. C. (2001). Ensuring validity in the measurement of corporate social performance: Lessons from corporate United Way and PAC campaigns. *Journal of Business Ethics*, *31*(3), 271–284. DOI: 10.1023/A:1010797011622

Alazzani, A., & Wan-Hussin, W. N. (2013). Global Reporting Initiative's environmental reporting: A study of oil and gas companies. *Ecological Indicators*, *32*, 19–24. DOI: 10.1016/j.ecolind.2013.02.019

Andrew, J., & Cortese, C. L. (2011). Carbon disclosures: Comparability, the carbon disclosure project and the greenhouse gas protocol. Australasian Accounting. *Business and Finance Journal*, *5*(4), 5–18.

Belkaoui, A. (1976). The impact of the disclosure of the environmental effects of organizational behavior on the market. *Financial Management*, *5*(4), 26–31. DOI: 10.2307/3665454

Berkes, F. (2017). *Sacred ecology*. Routledge. DOI: 10.4324/9781315114644

BNP PARIBAS. (2021). *THE PATH TO ESG: NO TURNING BACK FOR ASSET OWNERS AND MANAGERS*. https://securities.cib.bnpparibas/app/uploads/sites/3/2021/09/the-esg-global-survey-2021.pdf

Bowen, H. R. (2013). *Social responsibilities of the businessman*. University of Iowa Press. DOI: 10.2307/j.ctt20q1w8f

Busco, C., Consolandi, C., Eccles, R. G., & Sofra, E. (2020). A preliminary analysis of SASB reporting: Disclosure topics, financial relevance, and the financial intensity of ESG materiality. *The Bank of America Journal of Applied Corporate Finance*, *32*(2), 117–125. DOI: 10.1111/jacf.12411

Canada Revenue Agency (CRA). (2024). *International Financial Reporting Standards (IFRS)*. Government of Canada. https://www.canada.ca/en/revenue-agency/services/tax/businesses/topics/international-financial-reporting-standards-ifrs.html

Carroll, A. B. (1979). A three-dimensional conceptual model of corporate performance. *Academy of Management Review*, *4*(4), 497–505. DOI: 10.2307/257850

Carroll, A. B. (1999). Corporate Social Responsibility - Evolution of a Definitional Construct. *Business & Society*, *38*(3), 268–295. DOI: 10.1177/000765039903800303

Carroll, A. B. (2016). Carroll's pyramid of CSR: taking another look. *International journal of corporate social responsibility*, 1, 1-8.

CDP. (2022). *CDP Media factsheet*. https://cdn.cdp.net/cdp-production/comfy/cms/files/files/000/003/419/original/CDP-Media-Factsheet.pdf

CDP. (2023a). *CDP Climate Change 2023 Questionnaire*. https://guidance.cdp.net/en/guidance?cid=46&ctype=theme&idtype=ThemeID&incchild=1&microsite=0&otype=Questionnaire&tags=TAG-13071%2CTAG-605%2CTAG-599

CDP. (2023b). *CDP Forests 2023 Questionnaire*. https://guidance.cdp.net/en/guidance?cid=47&ctype=theme&idtype=ThemeID&incchild=1&microsite=0&otype=Questionnaire&tags=TAG-646%2CTAG-609%2CTAG-599

CDP. (2024a). *Who we are*. https://www.cdp.net/en/info/about-us

CDP. (2024b). *CDP and the Sustainable Development Goals (SDGs)*. https://www.cdp.net/en/policy/program-areas/sustainable-development-goals

de Villiers, C., & Dimes, R. (2022). Critical analysis of the contribution of Integrated Reporting (IR) to sustainability. In *Handbook of accounting and sustainability* (pp. 210–223). Edward Elgar Publishing. DOI: 10.4337/9781800373518.00020

Ducros, A., & Kelly, L. (2024). How ambitious are nature assessment tools for the private sector?.

Eccles, R. G., Serafeim, G., Seth, D., & Ming, C. C. Y. (2013). The Performance Frontier: Innovating for a Sustainable Strategy: Interaction. *Harvard Business Review*, *91*(7), 17–18.

Feder, B. J. (1989). Who will subscribe to the Valdez Principles? *The New York Times*, 10, F6.

Financial Reporting and Assurance Standards (FRAS) Canada. (2023). *Independent Review Committee on Standard Setting issues Final Recommendations*. https://www.frascanada.ca/en/about/ircss-final-recommendations#:~:text=The%20Independent%20Review%20Committee%20of,the%20future%20%E2%80%93%20including%20sustainability%20standards

Financial Reporting and Assurance Standards (FRAS) Canada. (2024). *Media Release – Canadian Sustainability Standards Board Releases Feedback Statement on Proposed Sustainability Disclosure Standards*. https://www.frascanada.ca/en/cssb/news-listings/2024-feedback-statement-media-release

Frederick, W. C. (2006). *Corporation, be good!: the story of corporate social responsibility*. Dog Ear Publishing.

Fry, F. L., & Hock, R. J. (1976). Who Claims Corporate Responsibility? The Biggest and the Worst. *Business & Society Review* (00453609), (18).

Gilbert, S. (2002, November). The transparency evolution. []. THE ENVIRONMENTAL LAW INSTITUTE.]. *The Environmental Forum (Washington, D.C.)*, *19*(6), 18–27.

Global Reporting Initiative (GRI). (2016). *GRI 411: Rights of Indigenous Peoples 2016*. GSSB. https://transparencylab.org/Documentation/Advocacy,%20Monitoring,%20Sustainable%20-%20Responsible%20Initiatives/Global%20Reporting%20Initiative/GRI%20411%20Rights%20of%20Indigenous%20Peoples_2016.pdf

Global Reporting Initiative (GRI). (2021a). *A Short Introduction to the GRI Standards*. https://www.globalreporting.org/media/wtaf14tw/a-short-introduction-to-the-gri-standards.pdf

Global Reporting Initiative (GRI). (2021b). *GRI 11: Oil and Gas Sector 2021*. https://www.accountabilitycounsel.org/wp-content/uploads/2021/10/gri-11-oil-and-gas-sector-2021.pdf

Global Reporting Initiative (GRI). (2022a). *GRI 12: Coal Sector 2022*. https://www.globalreporting.org/media/zr3bcrc0/coal_onepager-leaflet.pdf

Global Reporting Initiative (GRI). (2022b). *GRI 13: Agriculture Aquaculture and Fishing Sectors 2022*. https://freshproduce.org.uk/files/GRI-13_-Agriculture-Aquaculture-and-Fishing-Sectors-2022.pdf

Global Reporting Initiative (GRI). (2024a). *About GRI*. https://www.globalreporting.org/about-gri/#:~:text=GRI%20(Global%20Reporting%20Initiative)%20is,language%20to%20communicate%20those%20impacts

Global Reporting Initiative (GRI). (2024b). *Our mission and history.* https://www.globalreporting.org/about-gri/mission-history/

Global Reporting Initiative (GRI). (2024c). *SDG Initiatives.* https://www.globalreporting.org/public-policy/sustainable-development/sdg-initiatives/

Global Reporting Initiative (GRI). (2024d). *Linking GRI reporting to other requirements.* https://www.globalreporting.org/how-to-use-the-gri-standards/global-alignment/

Global Reporting Initiative (GRI). (2024e). *GRI 14: Mining Sector 2024.* https://incp.org.co/wp-content/uploads/2024/02/GRI-14-Sector-minero-2024.pdf

Global Reporting Initiative (GRI), & CDP. (2017). *Linking GRI and CDP: How are the GRI Sustainability Reporting Standards and CDP's 2017 climate change questions aligned?* Global Reporting. https://www.globalreporting.org/media/zrtnajcx/gri-standards-and-cdp-2017-climate-change-linkage-document.pdf

Guillot, J. (2020). *What Is the Connection Between SASB and the SDGs?* SASB. https://sasb.ifrs.org/blog/what-is-the-connection-between-sasb-and-the-sdgs/

Guillot, J., & Hales, J. (2021). *Materiality: The Word that Launched a Thousand Debates.* SASB. https://sasb.ifrs.org/blog/materiality-the-word-that-launched-a-thousand-debates/#:~:text=SASB%20introduced%20the%20term%20%E2%80%9Centerprise,value%20relative%20to%20its%20potential

Hales, J. (2021). Sustainability accounting standards board (SASB). In *World Scientific Encyclopedia of Climate Change: Case Studies of Climate Risk, Action, and Opportunity Volume 3* (pp. 37-41).

Hatayama, H. (2022). The metals industry and the Sustainable Development Goals: The relationship explored based on SDG reporting. *Resources, Conservation and Recycling, 178*, 106081. DOI: 10.1016/j.resconrec.2021.106081

Hazelhurst, T., Footer, J., & Norris, D. (2024). Dollars and Sense; Reviewing Industry Implementation of the Climate-Related Disclosures Mandate in New Zealand. *European Journal of Sustainable Development, 13*(3), 1–1. DOI: 10.14207/ejsd.2024.v13n3p1

Henri, D. A., Provencher, J. F., Bowles, E., Taylor, J. J., Steel, J., Chelick, C., Popp, J. N., Cooke, S. J., Rytwinski, T., McGregor, D., Ford, A. T., & Alexander, S. M. (2021). Weaving Indigenous knowledge systems and Western sciences in terrestrial research, monitoring and management in Canada: A protocol for a systematic map. *Ecological Solutions and Evidence, 2*(2), e12057. DOI: 10.1002/2688-8319.12057

IFRS Foundation. (2018). *Who we are and what we do*. https://www.ifrs.org/content/dam/ifrs/about-us/who-we-are/who-we-are-english-2018-final.pdf

IFRS Foundation. (2022). *ISSB describes the concept of sustainability and its articulation with financial value creation, and announces plans to advance work on natural ecosystems and just transition*. https://www.ifrs.org/news-and-events/news/2022/12/issb-describes-the-concept-of-sustainability/

IFRS Foundation. (2023a). *ISSB issues inaugural global sustainability disclosure standards*. https://www.ifrs.org/news-and-events/news/2023/06/issb-issues-ifrs-s1-ifrs-s2/

IFRS Foundation. (2023d). *IFRS Foundation welcomes culmination of TCFD work and transfer of TCFD monitoring responsibilities to ISSB from 2024*. https://www.ifrs.org/news-and-events/news/2023/07/foundation-welcomes-tcfd-responsibilities-from-2024/

IFRS Foundation. (2023e). *Coal Operations Sustainability Accounting Standard*. SASB. https://d3flraxduht3gu.cloudfront.net/latest_standards/coal-operations-standard_en-gb.pdf

IFRS Foundation. (2023f). *Metals & Mining Sustainability Accounting Standard*. SASB. https://d3flraxduht3gu.cloudfront.net/latest_standards/metals-and-mining-standard_en-gb.pdf

IFRS Foundation. (2023g). *Oil & Gas – Exploration & Production Sustainability Accounting Standard*. SASB. https://d3flraxduht3gu.cloudfront.net/latest_standards/oil-and-gas-exploration-and-production-standard_en-gb.pdf

IFRS Foundation. (2023h). *IFRS S1: General Requirements for Disclosure of Sustainability-related Financial Information*. https://www.ifrs.org/content/dam/ifrs/publications/pdf-standards-issb/english/2023/issued/part-a/issb-2023-a-ifrs-s2-climate-related-disclosures.pdf?bypass=on

IFRS Foundation. (2023i). *IFRS S2: Climate-related Disclosures*. https://www.ifrs.org/content/dam/ifrs/publications/pdf-standards-issb/english/2023/issued/part-a/issb-2023-a-ifrs-s2-climate-related-disclosures.pdf?bypass=on

IFRS Foundation. (2024a). *SASB Standards and other ESG frameworks*. SASB. https://sasb.ifrs.org/about/sasb-and-other-esg-frameworks/#:~:text=Frameworks%20provide%20principles%2Dbased%20guidance,for%20each%20topic%2C%20including%20metrics

IFRS Foundation. (2024b). *Governance archive*. SASB. https://sasb.ifrs.org/about/governance-archive/

IFRS Foundation. (2024c). *Find your industry*. SASB. https://sasb.ifrs.org/find-your-industry/

IFRS Foundation. (2024d). *About the International Sustainability Standards Board*. https://www.ifrs.org/groups/international-sustainability-standards-board/

IFRS Foundation. (2024e). *IFRS Foundation Monitoring Board (Monitoring Board)*. https://www.ifrs.org/groups/monitoring-board/

Independent Review Committee on Standard Setting in Canada (IRCSSC). (2021). *What an International Sustainability Standards Board means for Canada*. Cision Canada. https://www.newswire.ca/news-releases/what-an-international-sustainability-standards-board-means-for-canada-863993456.html

Independent Review Committee on Standard Setting in Canada (IRCSSC). (2023a). *Final Report*. https://pcacsitecorewebcontent.blob.core.windows.net/sitecorewebcontent/ircss/IRCSS-final-recommendations-report.pdf

Ingram, R. W., & Frazier, K. B. (1980). Environmental performance and corporate disclosure. *Journal of Accounting Research*, *18*(2), 614–622. DOI: 10.2307/2490597

Institute and Faculty of Actuaries. (2024). *The Paris Agreement and the Task Force on Climate-related Financial Disclosures*. https://actuaries.org.uk/learn/lifelong-learning/sustainability-and-lifelong-learning/climate-change-curated-library/the-paris-agreement-and-the-task-force-on-climate-related-financial-disclosures/

KPMG International. (2013). *GRI's G4 Guidelines: the impact on reporting*. KPMG International. https://assets.kpmg.com/content/dam/kpmg/pdf/2013/06/g4-the-impact-on-reporting-v2.pdf

Lerner, L. D., & Fryxell, G. E. (1988). An empirical study of the predictors of corporate social performance: A multi-dimensional analysis. *Journal of Business Ethics*, •••, 951–959.

Lindgreen, A., & Swaen, V. (2010). Corporate social responsibility. *International Journal of Management Reviews*, *12*(1), 1–7. DOI: 10.1111/j.1468-2370.2009.00277.x

Lindgreen, A., Swaen, V., & Johnston, W. J. (2009). Corporate social responsibility: An empirical investigation of US organizations. *Journal of Business Ethics*, *85*(S2), 303–323. DOI: 10.1007/s10551-008-9738-8

Mohr, L. A., Webb, D. J., & Harris, K. E. (2001). Do consumers expect companies to be socially responsible? The impact of corporate social responsibility on buying behavior. *The Journal of Consumer Affairs*, *35*(1), 45–72. DOI: 10.1111/j.1745-6606.2001.tb00102.x

O'Dwyer, B., Humphrey, C., & Rowbottom, N. (2024). From institutional integration to institutional demise: The disintegration of the International Integrated Reporting Council (IIRC). *Critical Perspectives on Accounting*, *99*, 102699. DOI: 10.1016/j.cpa.2023.102699

O'Dwyer, B., & Unerman, J. (2020). Shifting the focus of sustainability accounting from impacts to risks and dependencies: Researching the transformative potential of TCFD reporting. *Accounting, Auditing & Accountability Journal*, *33*(5), 1113–1141. DOI: 10.1108/AAAJ-02-2020-4445

Papazian, A. V. (2023). Sustainability in Finance: Frameworks, Standards, and Scores. In *Hardwiring Sustainability into Financial Mathematics: Implications for Money Mechanics* (pp. 29–67). Springer Nature Switzerland. DOI: 10.1007/978-3-031-45689-3_3

Rodriguez, A., Cotran, H., & Stewart, L. S. (2017). Evaluating the effectiveness of sustainability disclosure: Findings from a recent SASB study. *The Bank of America Journal of Applied Corporate Finance*, *29*(2), 100–108. DOI: 10.1111/jacf.12237

Rupley, K. H., Brown, D., & Marshall, S. (2017). Evolution of corporate reporting: From stand-alone corporate social responsibility reporting to integrated reporting. *Research in Accounting Regulation*, *29*(2), 172–176. DOI: 10.1016/j.racreg.2017.09.010

Siew, R. Y. (2015). A review of corporate sustainability reporting tools (SRTs). *Journal of Environmental Management*, *164*, 180–195. DOI: 10.1016/j.jenvman.2015.09.010 PMID: 26379255

Smith, J. A.III. (1995). The CERES principles: Model for public environmental accountability. *Review of European Community & International Environmental Law*, *4*(2), 116–122. DOI: 10.1111/j.1467-9388.1995.tb00209.x

Task Force on Climate-related Financial Disclosures (TCFD). (2017). *Recommendations of the Task Force on Climate-related Financial Disclosures*. https://assets.bbhub.io/company/sites/60/2021/10/FINAL-2017-TCFD-Report.pdf

Task Force on Climate-related Financial Disclosures (TCFD). (2024a). *Task Force on Climate-related Financial Disclosures*. https://www.fsb-tcfd.org/#:~:text=The%20Financial%20Stability%20Board%20

Task Force on Climate-related Financial Disclosures (TCFD). (2024b). *About*. https://www.fsb-tcfd.org/about/

Taskforce on Nature-related Financial Disclosures (TNFD). (2023b). *Recommendations of the Taskforce on Nature-related Financial Disclosures.* https://tnfd.global/wp-content/uploads/2023/08/Recommendations_of_the_Taskforce_on_Nature-related_Financial_Disclosures_September_2023.pdf

Taskforce on Nature-related Financial Disclosures (TNFD). (2023c). *Guidance on engagement with Indigenous Peoples, Local Communities and affected stakeholders.* https://tnfd.global/wp-content/uploads/2023/08/Guidance_on_engagement_with_Indigenous_Peoples_Local_Communities_and_affected_stakeholders_v1.pdf?v=1695138220

Taskforce on Nature-related Financial Disclosures (TNFD). (2024a). *Our history.* https://tnfd.global/about/history/

Ullmann, A. A. (1985). Data in search of a theory: A critical examination of the relationships among social performance, social disclosure, and economic performance of US firms. *Academy of Management Review, 10*(3), 540–557. DOI: 10.2307/258135

Unerman, J., Bebbington, J., & O'dwyer, B. (2018). Corporate reporting and accounting for externalities. *Accounting and Business Research, 48*(5), 497–522. DOI: 10.1080/00014788.2018.1470155

United Nations Environment Programme (UNEP). (2021). *The UN & TNFD: Stewarding Systems Change.* https://www.unepfi.org/themes/ecosystems/the-un-and-tnfd/

United Nations Environment Programme (UNEP). (2023). *The Taskforce on Nature-related Financial Disclosures (TNFD) launches its final recommendations.* https://www.unepfi.org/themes/ecosystems/tnfd-final-recommendations/

United Nations (UN). (2024a). *Transforming our world: the 2030 Agenda for Sustainable Development.* https://sdgs.un.org/2030agenda

United Nations (UN). (2024b). *Global indicator framework for the Sustainable Development Goals and targets of the 2030 Agenda for Sustainable Development.* https://unstats.un.org/sdgs/indicators/Global-Indicator-Framework-after-2024-refinement-English.pdf

Waddock, S. (2003). Stakeholder performance implications of corporate responsibility. *International Journal of Business Performance Management, 5*(2-3), 114–124. DOI: 10.1504/IJBPM.2003.003262

Wang, L., & Tuttle, B. (2014). Using corporate social responsibility performance to evaluate financial disclosure credibility. *Accounting and Business Research, 44*(5), 523–544. DOI: 10.1080/00014788.2014.922408

Wood, D. J. (1991). Social issues in management: Theory and research in corporate social performance. *Journal of Management, 17*(2), 383–406. DOI: 10.1177/014920639101700206

Wood, D. J. (2010). Measuring corporate social performance: A review. *International Journal of Management Reviews, 12*(1), 50–84. DOI: 10.1111/j.1468-2370.2009.00274.x

KEY TERMS AND DEFINITIONS

Canadian Sustainability Standards Board (CSSB):: A proposed Canadian standard-setting body tasked with developing and maintaining sustainability disclosure standards tailored to the Canadian context, including the unique constitutional and legal landscape regarding Indigenous rights.

Free, Prior, and Informed Consent (FPIC):: A specific right of Indigenous peoples, grounded in the principle of self-determination, to give or withhold consent to any project that may affect their lands, territories, or resources. It must be sought prior to project commencement, free from coercion or manipulation, and based on full and accessible information.

Global Reporting Initiative (GRI):: An independent, international organization that provides the world's most widely adopted sustainability reporting standards. GRI standards are comprehensive and multi-stakeholder in focus, emphasizing an organization's impacts on the economy, environment, and society.

International Sustainability Standards Board (ISSB):: A standard-setting body established under the IFRS Foundation to create a global baseline of sustainability disclosure standards, primarily focused on providing investor-relevant information about sustainability-related risks and opportunities.

Materiality (in sustainability reporting):: The principle that determines which sustainability topics are significant enough to require reporting. In a financial materiality context (e.g., ISSB), it focuses on how sustainability issues affect enterprise value. In an impact materiality context (e.g., GRI), it focuses on the organization's actual impacts on people and the planet.

Sustainability Accounting Standards Board (SASB):: An organization (now consolidated into the IFRS Foundation) that developed industry-specific standards to help companies disclose financially material sustainability information to investors. SASB standards are known for their precise, metrics-driven approach.

Task Force on Climate-related Financial Disclosures (TCFD):: A framework designed to help companies disclose climate-related financial risks and opportunities to investors, lenders, insurers, and other stakeholders, structured around the core elements of governance, strategy, risk management, and metrics and targets.

Taskforce on Nature-related Financial Disclosures (TNFD)**:** A risk management and disclosure framework that builds upon the TCFD structure but focuses on an organization's dependencies, impacts, risks, and opportunities related to nature and biodiversity. It provides extensive guidance on engagement with Indigenous Peoples and Local Communities.

Traditional Knowledge (TK):: The knowledge, innovations, and practices of Indigenous and local communities developed through experience and adapted to the local culture and environment. It is often transmitted orally across generations and is integral to biodiversity conservation and sustainable resource management.

United Nations Declaration on the Rights of Indigenous Peoples (UNDRIP):: A comprehensive international instrument that establishes a universal framework of minimum standards for the survival, dignity, well-being, and rights of Indigenous peoples worldwide, including rights to self-determination, lands and resources, and cultural heritage.

TEACHING NOTE

Chapter Synopsis

This chapter provides a critical, systematic analysis of how major sustainability reporting frameworks (GRI, SASB, TCFD, TNFD, CDP, UN SDGs, IFRS) integrate—or fail to integrate—the rights and perspectives of Indigenous peoples. It moves beyond a simple description to evaluate the depth of inclusion across 18 key categories, identifying a consistent focus on high-level principles (FPIC, Rights, Engagement) and a systemic neglect of outcome-oriented measures (Remediation, Traditional Knowledge, Employment). The core tension explored is between investor-centric "financial materiality" (ISSB/SASB) and impact-oriented "impact materiality" (GRI), with significant implications for corporate accountability and Indigenous equity.

Key Learning Objectives

Upon engaging with this chapter, students should be able to:

- **Compare and contrast** the approaches of major sustainability frameworks to Indigenous inclusion.
- **Analyze** the practical implications of the "financial materiality" vs. "impact materiality" divide.
- **Evaluate** the strengths and weaknesses of specific frameworks using evidence from the chapter's comparative table.
- **Critique** the proposition that standardized global reporting can adequately address place-based Indigenous rights.
- **Synthesize** the unique challenges and opportunities within the Canadian (CSSB) standard-setting context.

Core Themes/Theses for Discussion

1. **The Integration Gap:** Reporting frameworks have progressed from exclusion to symbolic inclusion, but few enable meaningful accountability for outcomes.
2. **The Materiality Divide:** The future of Indigenous inclusion is caught between a powerful, narrowing trend (ISSB's financial materiality) and a broader, multi-stakeholder ideal (GRI's impact materiality).

3. **Systemic Omissions:** The lack of focus on Remediation, Traditional Knowledge, and Violations reveals a fundamental flaw in current corporate accountability mechanisms.
4. **The Canadian Laboratory:** The development of the CSSB is a live case study in whether a jurisdiction can successfully harmonize global standards with distinct national responsibilities toward Indigenous peoples.

Suggested Teaching Pathway

1. **Foundations:** Begin with the evolution of CSR to CSP to modern frameworks, establishing why reporting emerged and its inherent limitations.
2. **Framework Deep Dive:** Use the comparative table (Table 1) to guide a dissection of specific frameworks. Contrast GRI's comprehensiveness with SASB's precision and TCFD's omission.
3. **Critical Debate:** Facilitate a debate on the central tension: *"Resolved: The ISSB's focus on financial materiality will ultimately harm the cause of Indigenous rights in corporate reporting."*
4. **Application:** Use the provided questions (short answer, long answer) as in-class exercises or graded assignments to solidify comprehension and critical thinking.
5. **Forward-Look:** Conclude by discussing the future research directions, encouraging students to consider what a truly transformative, Indigenous-centered reporting model might entail.

Pedagogical Tools & Resources

- The **True/False** and **Multiple-Choice** questions are ideal for quick comprehension checks or quizzes.
- The **Short Answer** questions work well for in-class discussions or brief submissions.
- The **Long Answer (essay)** questions are suited for take-home assignments or essay prompts, demanding higher-order synthesis.
- The **Graduate-Level Questions** can frame seminar discussions or be assigned as research paper topics for advanced students.

Note on Sensitivity

This topic engages with issues of historical marginalization, ongoing colonial legacies, and systemic power imbalances. It is recommended to frame discussions with respect, acknowledging the lived experiences of Indigenous communities and the real-world consequences of corporate and regulatory decisions. Encouraging an evidence-based, critical, and reflective classroom environment is crucial.

Summary of the Chapter

This chapter examines the integration of Indigenous rights and contributions within sustainability reporting frameworks, with a focus on North America. It traces the evolution of reporting standards, including the Global Reporting Initiative (GRI), SASB, TCFD, and others, highlighting their treatment of Indigenous inclusion. The chapter identifies gaps and inconsistencies, emphasizing three key issues: the underrepresentation of Indigenous perspectives in materiality assessments, limited application of Free, Prior, and Informed Consent (FPIC), and insufficient focus on measurable outcomes such as community development. A comparative analysis illustrates how different frameworks incorporate Indigenous issues, revealing best practices and areas for improvement. The chapter concludes with recommendations for advancing Indigenous equity in sustainability reporting, advocating for standardized approaches that address both social and environmental dimensions.

Key Questions for Class Discussion

1) How has the evolution of Corporate Social Responsibility (CSR) influenced the inclusion of Indigenous rights in sustainability reporting frameworks?
2) Compare the treatment of Indigenous issues across GRI, SASB, and TNFD. What key differences emerge, and what implications do these have for reporting organizations?
3) Why is the underrepresentation of Indigenous perspectives in materiality assessments significant, and how can frameworks better integrate these perspectives?
4) What are the challenges and benefits of implementing Free, Prior, and Informed Consent (FPIC) in industries that affect Indigenous lands and resources?
5) How can global sustainability reporting standards move toward greater standardization while respecting local contexts, particularly for Indigenous inclusion?

Chapter 5
India's Path to Climate Resilience:
Policies and Progress Towards Sustainable Development

Neeru Sidana
https://orcid.org/0000-0003-1087-4214
Amity University, India

Anika Bhatia
Amity School of Economics, Amity University, India

ABSTRACT

This research paper examines India's high vulnerabilities to climate change and efforts to support climate-related actions for sustainable development, over the last decade. Addressing and minimizing the risks posed by climate change is integral to the successful implementation of SDGs. Paper highlights India's leadership role in amplifying the voice of developing countries to strike a right balance to achieve development, poverty reduction and climate resilience. It focuses on the India's national action plan on climate change, eight sub-missions and related policies, their objectives, implementation progress and challenges in meeting the climate commitments. Climate polices on solar energy development, energy efficiency, and climate resilient infrastructure development are showing good results, while those for supporting sustainable agriculture and urban climate-resilience are progressing slow.

DOI: 10.4018/979-8-3693-9714-5.ch005

1.0 INTRODUCTION

1.1 Introduction

The saying that change is the only constant in life can also be applied to environment and climate variation as well. The nature and extent of such change are critical while applying this theory of Heraclitus to environment and ecology and the pace and direction of such change. This means that it is very hard to have fixed solutions to environmental issues since most of them are dynamic in nature. However, dynamism should not be occasioned as a means of water down environmental rights and safeguards. Rarely, can the conflicting claims and interests be met efficiently without had environmental governance frameworks that are driven by strong institutions and democracy. Sustainable development and climate crisis are intertwined issues that the world is grappling with. Human wants and actions are affecting the environment, economies and societies. The global temperature is already 1.1 degree centigrade higher than the pre-industrial levels, not too far away from the tipping point of 1.5 degree centigrade (IPCC). There is an unprecedented rise in flooding, droughts, forest fires, rising sea levels, pollution, and their catastrophic impact on the earth's flora and fauna. Developing countries and poor are the worst affected bearing a disproportionately higher burden. The effects of climate change, issues climate experts opine may provoke serious political and social instabilities at the national, regional and international levels as more individuals and groups compete for scarce resources or respond to turbulence in the global markets, epidemic diseases, forced displacement due to effects of climate change such as flooding, etc. (Youdon & Bajaj,2021)

India has a unique geo-climatic region which comprises of Indo-Gangetic Plains and Central Highlands, the Deccan Plateau. lowlands, Thar or Great Indian Desert, Himalaya and Northeast Mountain Ranges, East Coastal Plains, West Coastal Plains and indexes. Countries of the bordering seas and islands having large fluctuations in conditions as well as regional and local weather conditions across the country. India is the second populous country in the world and is in a region which has variable climate. It is significant to know that the sustainable development agenda has shifted towards envisioning the future and in this regard, the United Nations (UN) initiated known as the 2030 Agenda of Sustainable Development has caught the pace and has become an important part of the recent Indian governance. The 17 SDGs with 169 targets of this agenda are interlinked and seek to address the three dimensions of sustainable development which include Economic, social and environmental sustainability. The SDG 13 specifically draws the attention of the countries to develop their own climate actions and low-carbon development pathways. India announced its National Action Plan on Climate Change (NAPCC) in June 2008 (after signing

Kyoto Protocol in 2002 and adopting UNFCC) and was one of the early movers of ten countries to have a combined policy for tackling climate change and development. According to Singh (2022) the nation has shown a strong commitment to promoting renewable energy sources protecting the environment and reducing carbon emissions. In order to address climate risks and maintain resilience efforts have been made to improve adaptive capacity to climate change through the review of policy options and the implementation of institutional reforms (Chaturvedi et al.,2018).

With the tall ambitions of becoming a US$ 5 trillion economy by 2025, meeting SDG targets by 2030 and achieving net-zero by 2070, India has a herculean task to ensure that its development policies and climate actions are well aligned and deliver results. A major influence in determining international climate policies is the nation's position as a developing leader which is reinforced by its economic achievements and emissions profile (Vihma 2011). Mainstreaming climate resilience into policymaking in Indian cities has been made easier by the incorporation of climate resilience into governance processes especially in urban development schemes (Sharma and Singh 2016). The necessity of integrating climate considerations into sector-specific planning and design is highlighted by initiatives to integrate climate change resilience into vital infrastructure such as railway systems (Roy et al.,2023).

Indias climate policies have changed to include the idea of co-benefits in which efforts to combat climate change also help achieve goals related to sustainable development (Dubash and Ghosh 2019). India wishes to protect its development while reducing its susceptibility to the effects of climate change by following a route that strikes a balance between economic growth sustainable development and climate action (Dubash 2016).

In this context, this research paper is highly relevant as its objectives are to review policies and programs launched by the government to support climate actions, assess achievements and implantation challenges. The research paper will also contribute to the ongoing debate on harmonizing climate initiatives with national development priorities/SDGs of the developing countries. It will provide useful insights to other developing countries that are grappling with similar challenges.

1.2 Background

India's engagement with climate change is uniquely complex, shaped by its status as a rapidly developing economy with significant historical and per capita emissions that remain below the global average, yet is simultaneously one of the world's most climate-vulnerable countries. This duality frames a central policy challenge: how to meet the urgent developmental needs of a billion-plus population while navigating the escalating risks of a warming planet. The chapter establishes that India's climate policy architecture, formally initiated with the 2008 National Action Plan on Climate Change (NAPCC), was a pioneering effort among developing nations to create a cohesive strategy. This framework was designed not as a deviation from development, but as a means to achieve "co-benefits," where climate actions simultaneously advance objectives in poverty reduction, energy security, public health, and economic resilience. The background contextualizes India's policy evolution within international commitments, from the Kyoto Protocol to the Paris Agreement and its subsequent "Panchamrit" pledges, including the ambitious net-zero by 2070 target. It underscores that India's path to climate resilience is a grand experiment in policy integration, requiring unprecedented coordination across all levels of government and sectors of the economy, all while operating within financial, institutional, and capacity constraints.

1.3 Research Scope

The scope of the research paper is to present the climate challenges, link between SDGs and climate actions, and traces the evolution of policies, programs and missions for climate actions of government in the last fifteen years.

This research paper is not to undertake comprehensive review of India's achievements of all the SDGs, but is limited to studying the policies, programs and initiatives that have synergies and implications for addressing climate risks and meeting climate commitments.

1.4 Methodology

The research paper is primarily based on literature review of reports, published articles, web-resources and media articles. The secondary data and information available from the websites and reports of Government of India, United Nation and World Bank is analysed to understand the trends and emerging challenges of climate change. Structured interactions with the experts in the areas of development and climate economics as well as media experts informed to widen the perspective on opportunities and challenges in implementing climate actions.

2. LINKS BETWEEN SDGS AND CLIMATE ACTION

2.1 Climate Change: A Global Crisis

Agriculture is one of the sectors most affected by climate change which is a serious worldwide concern. Significant economic losses may result from the projected 2°C increase in the world average temperature by 2100 (Mandloi 2023). As a significant contributor to greenhouse gas emissions and a source of vulnerability to climate change agriculture (Kreft et al., 2023). Droughts floods and unpredictable rainfall patterns are examples of extreme weather events brought on by climate change that interfere with agricultural practices (Majeed et al., 2023). Farmers across the world are noticing signs of climate change such as shorter winter seasons unpredictable rainfall and rising temperatures (Neha and Ansari 2021). Global food security is seriously threatened by climate change so any effective adaptation plans must consider the full scope of its effects (Çeliktopuz 2024).

Under Paris Agreement (2015), 196 member countries have joined forces through a legally binding treaty and pledged to limit global warming to 2.0 degree centigrade above pre-industrial level, and preferably limit it to 1.5 degree centigrade.

Regrettably, some worrisome indicators are: (i) the global annual average temperature is rising and has reached 1.1 degree centigrade above pre-industrial levels in 2022, and is likely to surpass the tipping point of 1.5 degree centigrade rise by 2035 (IPCC), (ii) the global average sea-levels rise has doubled from 2.27 mm per year in 1993-2002 to 4.62 mm per year in 2013-2022 raising the risk of submergence of small island states and coastal areas (UN Report, 2023); and (iii) the frequency of floods, draughts and cyclones has increased affecting lives, livelihoods and food security (UN Report 2023). Climate change is posing a significant threat – directly or indirectly - to achieve SDG targets by 2030, and many countries are off-track on several indicators (refer Figure 1).

Figure 1. Rise in Global Annual Mean Temperature and Sea-level Rise

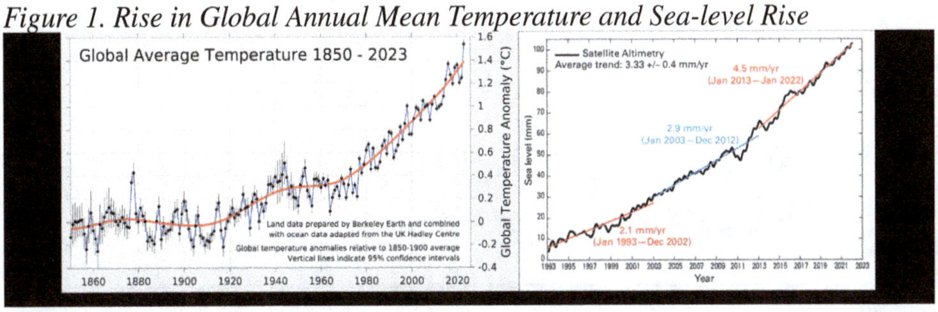

Source: United Nations Report, 2023

2.2 India's Commitment to Climate Change

Through its numerous initiatives and policies India has demonstrated its strong commitment to combating climate change. As stated in the Paris Agreement on Climate Change Mitigation Indias global climate obligations are closely linked to the Sustainable Development Goals (SDGs) (Karim et al., 2020). In the global climate debate India has become more vocal since 2007. According to Hussain et al (2024) the nation has reaffirmed its commitment to developing clean energy and cutting carbon emissions in line with SDGs 11 and 13.

India is the 3rd largest emitter of GHG globally, while the per capita emissions are less than half compared to the global average (UN report). With growing urbanization, the energy use, agriculture production, pressures on water, forests and other natural resources are going to rise. This is causing rise in carbon emissions specifically from power generation, transport and industry due to fossil fuel-based energy use (Figure 2, Figure 3). Under the Paris Agreement (August 2022) India has committed to achieve net-zero emissions by 2070. India's action plan (Panchamrit – 5 nectar elements) has set three specific targets: (i) reducing emission intensity of GDP by 45% by 2030 from 2005 level; (ii) achieving 50% cumulative power generation installed capacity from non-fossil fuel-based energy sources by 2030 and (iii) creating carbon sink of 2.5 to 3 billion tons of CO2 equivalent through forest and tree cover by 2030 (COP 26, Glasgow UN Report)

Figure 2. Sector-wise Carbon-dioxide emissions for India

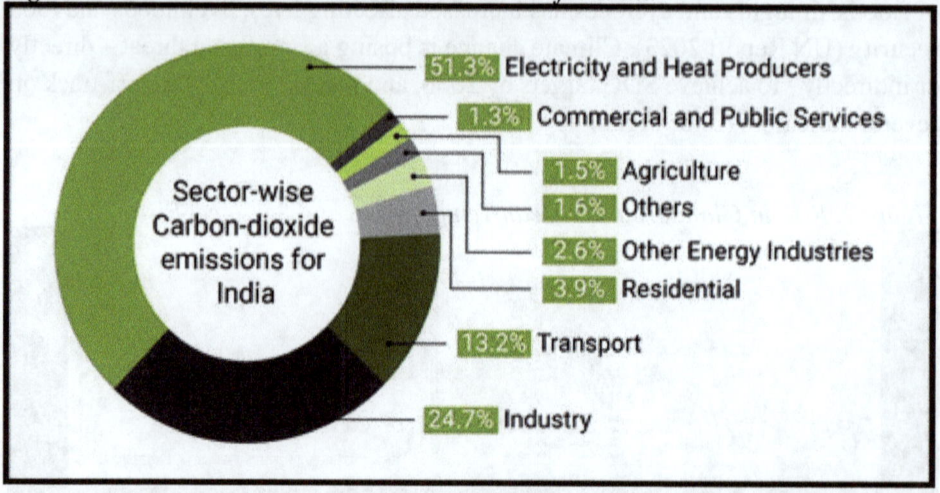

Source: Alliance for Energy Efficient Economy; "Climate Change Mitigation: role of social cost of carbon"

Figure 3. Trends in Energy-related Carbon- dioxide Emissions in India

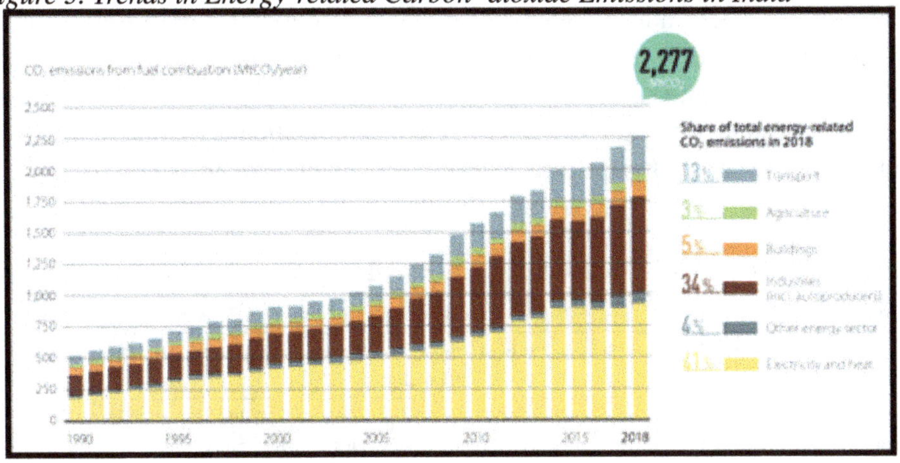

Source: India's energy related CO2 emissions, ET Energy World

2.3 Climate Action SDG 13 and Synergy with other SDGs

SDG 13 calls for taking urgent actions to combat climate change and its impact by reducing emissions. The main actions under this goal are to:

(i) strengthening resilience and developing capacity to adapt to climate related disasters; India has adopted the *Sendai Framework for Disaster Risk Reduction* (2015-2030) to integrate measures for disaster resilience while developing infrastructure.

(ii) integrating actions that are critical to address climate risks in planning, policies and strategies; India is implementing programs and policies to support mitigation and adaptation.

(iii) building knowledge and capacity on climate issues; India has integrated climate change in national education policies being implemented by the schools and higher education institutes; launched several public awareness campaigns for clean fuel use, reducing plastic use, water conservation, forest and wildlife protection etc; supporting R&D to develop climate resilient technologies, renewable energy and energy efficient technologies.

(iv) commitment by the developed countries to bring US$ 100 billion annually to set up "Green Climate Fund' (UN) for developing countries to finance transition to low-carbon, climate resilient economies.

There are important synergies between SDG 13 and other SDGs (Table 1). Increasing access to sustainable energy and sustainable agriculture practices has direct link to reducing GHGs. Implementation of eight sub-missions under NAPCC are not only supporting SDG 13 but are also linked to several programs and missions underway in support of other SDGs. Effective coordination across these missions and programs is critical to achieve development and climate goals.

Table 1. Synergies between SDGs and Climate Actions

SDG	Link to Climate Actions
# 6 Clean Water	Implementing integrated water resources management. Reducing water pollution and untreated wastewater.
# 7 Clean energy	Clean energy access at affordable prices, by promoting renewable energy, clean fuels, and using energy efficient technologies to reduce emissions.
#15 Life on Land	Protect, restore and promote sustainable use of terrestrial ecosystems, sustainably manage forests, combat desertification, land degradation and biodiversity loss.

Source: Sustainable Development Goals, UN Website

Environmental Sustainability

In Indian context, concerns of environmental sustainability have always been a part of the ethos. In fact, the conservation and sustainable use of natural resources has been as old as the Indus Valley civilization over three thousand years ago with the literature available in the most ancient scriptures of India. Besides the apprehensions regarding rise in air and water pollution, loss and degrading of land and forests and decline in the list of species have become alarming issues. Specific measures were embarked right from 1972 after the Stockholm Declaration. Since then, the Ministry of Environment and Forests has grown full-fledged, and a comprehensive web of legislation has emerged to address the environmental problems. There have also been several policy changes that have been made with an aim of protecting the environment. Some programmes run by the government and NGOs regarding the environmental awareness have also started in recent years. The country has entered and domesticated several international legal instruments relating to the environment and related matters and these have been effectively implemented. The activities accomplished up to this point must be continued by enhancing the current attempts at the national level as well as by expanding multilateral cooperation in terms of topics concerning social development and the environment.

3. IMPLEMENTING INDIA'S ACTION PLAN FOR CLIMATE CHANGE

Global warming has been aptly christened as a 'wicked' problem; it is difficult to define and is not easily solvable due to the uncertainty surrounding it and due to its incorporation in social, political and economic contexts (Hulme 2009). From an Indian vantage point, the difficulties involved with effectively participating in the climate change dialogue are compounded at the pragmatic and the political level as well. On the more practical level, India has daunting, or urgent, tasks of, in essence, developing itself – lifting its people up from poverty, ensuring them health and education, energy and water and sanitation, and containing governance ills of corruption and sectarian violence. India is one of the countries which is highly sensitive to climate change. In other words, potential climate impacts are gross enough that they can function as a constraint to India 's development ambitions The same rationale should apply to adaptation in Indian climate policy given expected climate change effects on agriculture, ecosystems and lived environments. The Government of India has instructed all states and union territory to prepare the State Action Plan on Climate Change in accordance with the strategy of National Action Plan on Climate Change. According to the National Action Plan on Climate Change, has provided an opportunity to the states to frame their own development plans that can also plan and react to the hazard events trends or disturbances of related climate investments in low carbon infrastructure. The National Action Plan on Climate Change has most of the projects with education related strategies in adhering to climate change knowledge and skill development and the Strategic Knowledge Mission is also present in forestry, biodiversity, health, water and waste sectors. These interventions share and relate to and are directly associated with Target 13. It ranks 3 in the case of Sustainable Development Goal (SDG) 13 as pointed out by Pahuja et al. (2020).

Out of the eight National Missions of the National Action Plan for Climate Change, two which are directly involved with adaptation are the Sustainable Agriculture and Sustainable Himalayan Ecosystems. These are related to climate smart agriculture, sustainable animal husbandry, research and sustainability of the HIMOLHS and related ecosystems (MoEFCC, 2021). Eight missions make up the 2008-launched NAPCC which aims to address different aspects of climate change (Kumar et al. 2020). The eight missions that make up this plan outline long-term objectives and strategies in line with the UNFCCs adoption and the 2002 signing of the Kyoto Protocol. The Planning Commission estimated that Rs 230000 crores would be needed financially to meet the NAPCCs goals in its 12th Five Year Plan which ran from 2012 to 2017. Several factors such as India's democratic system historical low emissions and susceptibility to the effects of climate change have impacted the country's efforts to adapt to and mitigate the effects of climate change (Kattumuri and Ravindranath 2014). The introduction of comprehensive domestic policies such as the NAPCC (Atteridge et al.2012) coincided with a noticeable shift in the country's climate diplomacy. Over time the country's climate policies have changed. Further evidence that India wants to pursue a low-carbon growth path is the steps it has taken since 1990 to separate greenhouse gas emissions from economic growth (Gupta 2001). These actions have influenced Indias position on climate change.

This section summarizes the objectives of eight sub-missions launched under NAPCC, policies and programs initiated by the government. Broad analysis of progress achieved and implementation challenges, based on the literature review, is summarized.

3.1 National Solar Mission (NSM)

The solar mission (2010) has made substantial progress, and India is today among the leading countries with solar energy generation. Targets are set to increase solar capacity in three phases (Table 2). These targets align well with the SDG Goal 7 *Affordable and Clean Energy*, through greater global push for renewable energy development. The mission was part of the National Action Plan on Climate Change and was focused on achieving grid parity, increasing the share of solar energy in India's energy mix, and making solar energy more affordable.

Table 2. Three Phase Targets for Scaling-up Solar Capacity

Application	Phase-I (2010-13)	Phase-II (2013-17)	Phase-III (2017-22)
Solar collectors	7 million sq. m	15 million sq. m	20 million sq. m
Off-grid solar applications	200 MW	1000 MW	2000 MW
Utility grid power, rooftop	1000-2000 MW	4000-10,000 MW	20,000 MW

Source: Ministry of New and Renewable Energy, 2017

Phase 1 resulted in significant decline in solar energy prices making it a competitive source of power. By the end of this phase, more than 19 GW of solar capacity was installed, much above 10GW target. Phase II focused on promoting research and development, building solar manufacturing capacity, and encouraging small-scale grid-connected and off-grid applications. In the current Phase III, the main achievements are development of large solar parks, and solar rooftop installation. Subsequently target has been revised to achieve 100 GW by 2022 and 500 GW by 2030 from solar and clean energy accounting for 50% cumulative installed capacity (Cabinet decision in June 2015, MNRE). The legal, regulatory and policy framework has been evolving to promote large grid-connected solar projects, off-grid applications (like solar roof top installations on houses, commercial establishments), solar lighting, solar water pumping for irrigation. Through the mission, the government aimed to leverage technological innovation to increase solar energy generation capacity and reduce electricity. In India's endeavours to reduce global warming and move toward a more sustainable energy future the NSM played a pivotal role (Tripathi and Bhattacharya 2023, Varma et al. .2014). These policies have enabled increase in grid-connected solar power projects since 2011 (Table 3). significant

Table 3. Achievements of grid-Connected Solar-Power Project

Financial Year	Capacity Addition (MW)	Cumulative Capacity (MW)
2010-11	25	36
2011-12	994	1,030
2012-13	656	1,686
2013-14	946	2,632
2014-15	1,112	3,744
2015-16	3,019	6,763
2016-17	5,526	12, 289
2017-18	2,477	14,766

Source: Ministry of New and Renewable Energy, 2017

3.2 National Mission for Enhanced Energy Efficiency (NMEE)

India is a highly energy intensive country, therefore this mission aims to improve end-use energy efficiency and energy conservation Energy is an especially significant domain because it constitutes 69% of India's total GHG emissions; this is why energy is highlighted as the most relevant dimension of the development choices of India from the climate standpoint (63). It is, however, hard to argue that the India's energy and overall economic picture is changing quickly. Thus, the country's annual primary energy consumption in the last decade has escalated almost two-fold from 414 MTOE in 2006 to 724 MTOE in 2016, achieving mere declines poverty rates 64, 65. Addressing energy issues has always been central to the process of India's developmental strategy. The country's energy requirements on the onset of the 2000s experienced a great boost with the start of liberalization of the economy and was burdened with a domestic discourse of scarcity of energy.

One of the key components of NMEE mission involves the implementation of market-based mechanisms to promote energy efficiency ("Energy Efficiency in South Asia:", 2020). The target is to save 23 million tons (MTs) fuel and reduce

98.55 MTs of GHG emissions per year. Schemes under implementation (i.e *Perform, Achieve and Trade Scheme* (PAT 2012), and *Market Transformation for Energy Efficiency)* provide enabling policies, incentives and finance for adopting energy efficient technologies. Most successful initiatives under this mission are adoption of LED lights and clean-energy cooking gas distributed by the government to women who are below poverty line.

The NMEE has helped to increase public awareness of energy conservation, achieve energy savings across various sectors, and reduce GHGs. However, challenges remain, such as ensuring compliance and enforcement of energy-efficiency standards. Energy Conservation Amendment Act, 2022 has introduced stricter penalties for non-compliance with energy efficiency norms in industrial and transport sectors, mandated establishment of State Energy Conservation Fund for local energy efficiency initiatives and introduced a framework for carbon trading. According to Stefanopoulou (2023) maximizing launch sites can greatly improve the energy and time efficiency of missions in the context of energy efficiency improvements resulting in more efficient coverage of specific regions. This optimization contributes to achieving greater efficiency in mission operations.

3.3 National Mission on Sustainable Habitat (NMSH)

This mission is helping to reduce carbon footprint and GHG emissions by integrating mitigation and adaptation in urban planning and policies to promote energy efficiency, waste management, public transport, and green technologies. It is supporting resilient infrastructure development and disaster risk management to protect from floods, storms, and heatwaves. The National Urban Policy Framework (2018) has set the criteria for green, sustainable and disaster-resistant urban environments, however no specific targets have been set. Several programs are under implementation: (i) "*Atal Mission for Rejuvenation and Urban Transformation*" to develop infrastructure, (ii) *Pradhan Mantri Awas Yojana* to provide affordable and eco-friendly housing to the urban poor; (iii) *Swachh Bharat Mission* to improve environment by eliminating open defecation and solid waste management and (iv) *Smart Cities Mission* to promote sustainable environment, inclusive cities and improve quality of life.

NMSH is a very broad mission which requires active participation of the state and city governments. The national policies (e.g Urban Renewal Policy Framework), guidelines (e.g Urban and Regional Development Plans, Urban Transport) and standards (e.g. Sustainable Habitat Standards) are comprehensive, however translating these into actions has been slow. Infrastructure development in cities is lagging and cities are increasingly facing the brunt of climate change like unprecedented flooding in Delhi, Jaipur, Kolkata, Chennai due to flash rains. The main challenges are fragmented urban governance, haphazard planning, almost no consideration of climate risks in planning and weak financial capacity of cities. A *High-Level Committee on Urban Development* (Budget, 2023) has recently submitted its report with recommendations for urban planning reforms and mainstreaming climate actions. The government is also assisting cities to raise finance through market bonds and attract private investments. The existing legal, policy, regulatory and institutional frameworks need to be renewed to meet the SDG targets and NMSH objectives.

3.4 National Water Mission (NWM)

This goal focuses on conservation of ocean and, utilization of marine resources which is SDG 14. Those things such as deforestation and degradation of forests bring about erosion and resulting to the formation of sediments that hinder the penetration of sunlight to the marine activities. Preserving and increasing the size of forested land and contributing to maintaining well-governed and sustainable forests to pursue the targets of SDG 14, it would be possible to minimize the impacts of marine pollution by activities on the ground .As SDG 14 is basically coastal and marine, its implications may be on the coastal forested ecosystems, including mangrove forest/ecosystem and the beaches, dune and tidal freshwater forest ecosystems (Friess et al., 2019). In more detail, Amezaga (2019) focused on the evaluation of the following interaction mechanisms of forests with water. They said that forests and water are naturally associated. Trees as any other living organisms require water to survive; and as major components of landscapes they directly impact the spatial distribution of water in local and continental contexts. India is among the most water stressed countries with 18% of world population but only 4% of water resources, and this challenge is being compounded by climate change (UN). The water demand is estimated to be twice that of available supply by 2030 resulting in 6% GDP loss (NITI Aayog). Droughts are becoming more frequent, groundwater resources depleting at unsustainable rate and water contamination is leading to health hazards and deaths. Five goals of the national water mission include: (i) river-basin level integrated water resource planning and management (ii) setting-up water database and assessing climate change impact on water resources (iii) promoting water conservation, augmentation and preservation (iv) targeted efforts to tackle water challenge in overexploited areas and (v) 20% efficiency improvement in using water.

Several policies and programs have been launched by the national and state governments to manage the water. Most notable policy was National Water Policy 2002 that emphasized environmental concerns and promoted integrated water resource management; and subsequent policies have reinforced actions to mitigate climate risks. Main initiatives under the national water mission include (i) sustainable management of natural resources by implementing sustainable agricultural, forestry, and water management practices; (ii) preventing and controlling water pollution from industrial, agriculture and urban sources; (iii) resilient water infrastructure and technology development, and (iv) training and capacity development.

Significant budgetary resources are being provided for water sector to meet the SDG targets and manage climate risks. Most states are following integrated water resource planning and management, and to achieve 20% increase in water efficiency awards are being given to recognize the efforts of state government, public/NGOs and private sector. Over 5000 field demonstrations of new technologies have shown increase in crop yields and water savings. In 2022, the Bureau of Water use efficiency was set up to develop regulations and monitor water efficiency. Despite continuous evolution of polices, the implementation challenges persist as water is a highly emotive and political subject, lack of common framework, specific targets and timelines to achieve results, complex hydrological boundaries (basins, sub-basins and catchment areas) and inter-ministerial coordination issues.

3.5 National Sustainable Agriculture Mission (NMSA)

With about half of India's population still dependent on agriculture for livelihoods, climate risks and vulnerabilities are extremely high. Objectives of sustainable agriculture mission and related policies of are to improve agriculture productivity and climate risk management. It is promoting diversification to less water-intensive crops, using smart technologies for water management, precision farming, soil health management and organic farming. It also supports rural livelihood through integrated farming practices including livestock, fisheries, plantations etc.

The sustainable agriculture mission is critical for India to achieve its sustainable development goals of eliminating poverty and hunger. Several targeted programs have been launched by the Government of India in support of NMSA. These include (i) national initiative on climate resilient agriculture to address mitigation and adaptation practices (ii) rainfed area development program supporting resource conservation (iii) soil health management by promoting judicious use of chemical fertilizers, organic manure and fertilizer; (iv) financial support to farmers on failure of crops due to natural calamities.

All states are required to develop action plans and implement these in coordination with districts and villages. However, several states have not been able to put in place policies, strategies, finances and timelines to achieve the NMSA objectives. Lack of awareness among farmers about climate risks, climate smart agriculture and limited financial resources of small and marginal farmers are main barriers. Presently only 2% of net sown area is under organic farming. Success of NMSA will depend on coordinating and leveraging policies and programs of the environment and water ministries. There is a need to adopt a new policy and launch a movement for "Greening Agriculture". Expand the R&D budgets to develop new technologies, environmentally safe agriculture practices and economically viable options. Use of digital technology like satellites, IoT, drones etc can help in data collection regarding soil health, crop area, yield etc and support precision agriculture.

3.6 National Mission on Sustaining Himalayan Ecosystem (NMSHE)

The Himalayan ecosystem is facing high vulnerability due to development pressures (urbanization, infrastructure development, all causing deforestation) and climate change. Rising temperatures are melting glaciers, increasing precipitation, flash floods and unpredictable weather events. Increasing flash flood disasters, including in Leh (2010), Kedarnath (2013) and Kashmir (2014) caused extensive damage and loss of lives.

The mission is focusing on five goals and twelve states that constitute the fragile Himalayan ecosystem: (i) conservation and sustainable management of natural resources; (ii) enhancing supplementary or alternative livelihoods; (iii) controlling and preventing pollution; (iv) increasing human and institutional capacities and (v) development of climate-resilient core infrastructure. Six tasks force have been set-up in collaboration with technical institutes (e.g. *National Institute of Hydrology, Jawahar Lal Nehru University, Indian council of Agriculture Research* etc.) to undertake research studies and foster innovations. This is helping to create a self-sustaining network of academic institutes and increasing the awareness, knowledge, and involvement of regional stakeholders. Mission is supporting the state governments to make policies and action plans to build climate resilience.

As this mission is cross-cutting – including water management, soil conservation, forestry, energy, agriculture - coordination and collaboration across other related programs (i.e *Indian Himalayan Climate Adaptation Program, SECURE Himalaya Project, Integrated Himalayan development program*) is critical to achieve results. India's forest cover increased by 1,540 sq km in 2019-21, but forest loss has increased in the Himalayan states to plantation and agroforestry (India's State of Forest Report, 2021). All Himalayan States need to work in tandem and prioritize protection of Himalayas and strengthen transboundary cooperation among the Himalayan countries.

3.7 National Mission for a Green India (GIM)

Forests are among the largest carbon and bio-diversity reservoirs, crucial for mitigating climate change and providing essential goods, services and livelihood. India's forest cover is only 21.7% of total geographical area as against the target of 33% (National Forestry Policy, Figure 4). Green India Mission (2014) and national afforestation program are supporting a holistic approach including afforestation, biodiversity conservation, water resource management, biomass production, and the preservation of mangroves, wetlands, and critical habitats. The implementation involves local communities in planning, implementation and monitoring.

India needs 30 million hectares (mha) of additional forests to meet 2.5 billion tons of carbon sink (NDC). GIM has targets of additional forest cover of 5 million hectares (mha), improving carbon sequestration and storage in forests and other ecosystems; and increasing forest-based livelihood income for 3 million households. The implementation is lagging as during 2015-20, only half the target of increasing tree covers by 53,377 could be achieved (MoEFF).

Figure 4. Environment and Forest Data

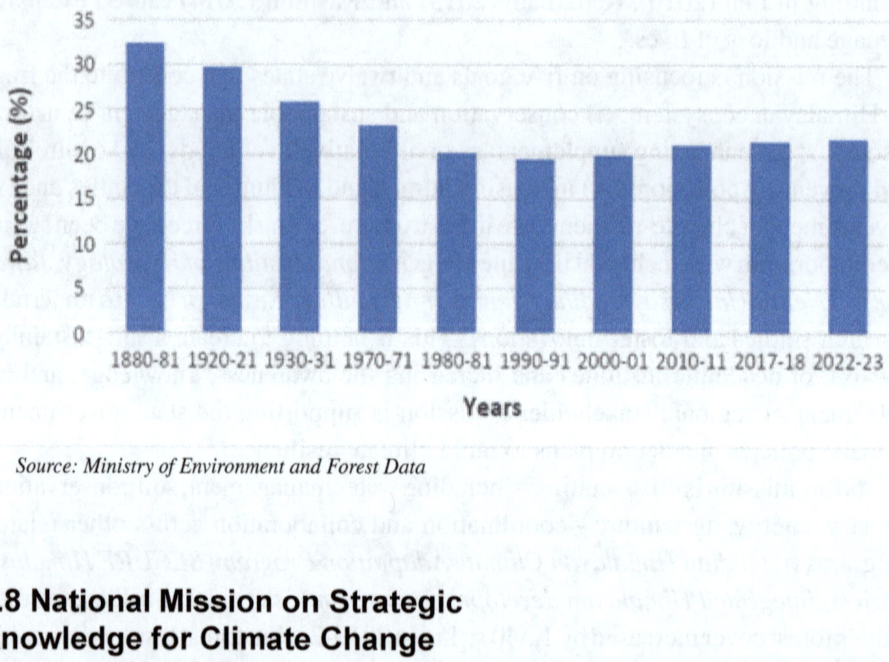

Source: Ministry of Environment and Forest Data

3.8 National Mission on Strategic Knowledge for Climate Change

This mission is helping to develop knowledge platforms, network of institutions, climate databases, regional modelling capacity, and training in climate science. The target is to set up ten thematic knowledge networks, build collaboration with other countries and scale-up public awareness. Some initiatives underway are: (i) setting up "Global Technology Watch Group" to track emerging technologies globally support commercialization; (ii) setting up "Centres of Excellence" in IIT Chennai and IISc Bangalore on climate change and sustainability (iii) undertaking research on ocean acidification and rise in sea level and (iv) regional climate modelling, extreme rainfall studies etc. The activities under this mission are progressing slow due to lack of active participation by the states, limited budgetary resources and inter-ministerial coordination challenges.

4. ACCELERATING CLIMATE ACTIONS: SUGGESTIONS FOR WAY FORWARD

4.1 Key Achievements and Challenges

India's rank in Climate Change Performance Index has improved from 31st position in 2014 to 7th in 2023 (New Climate Institute, Germanwatch). India's role in spear-heading solar energy development and the recent policy announcement to develop and commercialize green hydrogen, will have significant local, national and global benefits of reducing greenhouse emissions. Concerted efforts for energy efficiency and decarbonization of industries are underway to further reduce emissions, while also strengthening the competitiveness of industries. Enhanced focus on R&D and leveraging technology is helping to pilot and commercial climate smart agriculture, wastewater reuse, electric-vehicles, and green buildings.

The policy and regulatory framework underpinning integrated water resource management, forest cover expansion, and climate resilient urban development are in place, however the implementation needs acceleration, particularly by the state and city governments to achieve the SDG and climate targets. In this regard, the revised NMSH2.0 (2019) is a good effort as it has specifically prioritized five thematic areas of urban planning, energy and green building, air quality, water and waste management. "Climate Smart Cities Assessment Framework" (MoUHA), a first-of-its-kind climate assessment framework has been developed to enable the cities to assess their present situation and make action plans to meet the objectives of the mission.

Main challenges in achieving the objectives of NAPCC and NDC targets are: (i) several missions, policies and programs have not laid out specific targets and timelines, thereby attention to outcomes is missing; (ii) lack of adequate budgetary resources and competing demand is slowing down implementation; (iii) weak inter-ministerial and institutional co-ordination is affecting several programs as addressing climate risks requires multi-sectoral and multi-dimensional approach; (iv) knowledge and capacity limitations particularly at the sub-national level is constraining preparation of robust plans and strategies and (v) disjointed databases and monitoring frameworks are limiting evidence based policy making.

4.2 Strengthening the Role of State Governments in Climate Action

State action plans for climate change (SAPCC) must be taken more seriously and aligned with the NAPCC, NDCs, and state's development priorities. There should be link between the priorities laid out in the plan and the annual budgets allocated by the state and central governments, an issue often cited as a key reason for slow implementation. Success of three missions focusing on sustainable habitat, water and agriculture will primarily depend in the mitigation and adaptation actions taken by the state and city governments. As these are Constitutionally mandated as concurrent subjects, improved coordination between the centre and state governments in framing policies and programs is critical for effective implementation. The success of some missions like NWM and NMSA will depend on integration with other national programs on agriculture, food security, and water management.

Preparation of the SAPCCs should not be top-down process but framed in consultation with key stakeholders and reflect the unique opportunities and challenges confronted by the state. Most SAPCCs primarily focus on adaptation measures, with limited focus on greenhouse gas emissions, lack clear actions, finance and political will (Oxford Policy Management). Institutional capacity building, better inter-departmental coordination, and robust monitoring system is needed to accelerate implementation of climate actions on ground. Odisha is the first state to adopt a "Green Budget", followed by Himachal Pradesh and other states taking similar steps. The "State Climate Action Committee" should be set-up at the Chief Minister's office to guide the priorities, strategies and monitoring implementation.

4.3 LiFE – An Urgent Call for Action by All

"If one billion people out of the global population of eight billion adopt environment-friendly behaviors in their daily lives the global carbon emissions could drop by approximately 20%" (UNEP). "Lifestyle for Environment" campaign launched by India (in 2021 at COP26) is a global call for action by all people to change their behaviours and actions to protect the earth. It aims to mobilize at least one billion Indians and other global citizens to take individual and collective action for protecting and conserving the environment (during 2022 to 2027). Several policies for climate actions like eliminating single use plastic, stopping open defecation, solid waste management, water conservation, stopping stubble burning and deforestation cannot succeed and sustain without active participation of people and communities. LiFE mission aims to implement policies that will influence sustainable consumption and production. It recognizes that Indian culture and living traditions are inherently sustainable. Children, youth, cultural and educational institutions should be engaged at large to be the torch bearers for this change movement.

4.4 Deepening International Collaboration

G20 New Delhi Communique has once again raised the urgency of global collaboration for addressing climate change. India has taken a leadership role in building coalitions across important areas to combat climate change. International Solar Alliance (ISA) launched jointly by India and France (2016), has galvanized 120 countries who are collectively promoting and developing solar energy and solar products. 'One World One Sun One Grid', initiative launched in 2018 is integrating the countries in one grid to attract investments in renewable energy, develop technology and skills. Similarly, the Coalition of Disaster Resilient Infrastructure (CDRI, 2019) launched by India at the UN Climate Action Summit is a multi-stakeholder global partnership of governments, private sector, UN and multilateral agencies to promote research and knowledge in infrastructure risk management. Similar coalitions are needed in the areas of sustainable agriculture, forest and water management, for R&D, innovations and knowledge sharing. Robust databased on climate indicators will help to deepen analysis, evidence-based policy making and monitoring climate risks and vulnerabilities.

5.0 CONCLUSION

Climate-smart is a new paradigm for development. Over the last two decades, several policy reforms, economic incentives and regulations have been put in place by the government to address environmental degradation and climate change. Principally, India's climate change policies aim to forge synergies between development and climate outcomes.

Climate actions directly or indirectly impact all SDGs. India's success in achieving net-zero by 2070 will have significant local, national and global impact. At national level lack of adequate progress will threaten food security, cause nutritional deficiencies, increase health vulnerabilities, and increase poverty.

Eight sub-missions under India's national actional plan on climate change have well laid out objectives. The progress is encouraging, yet mixed. There is good progress in increasing solar energy, improving energy efficiency in lighting, and building climate resilient infrastructure. Achievements in sustainable urban development, climate-smart agriculture, water use efficiency, and increasing forest cover has been modest. To accelerate climate actions, the sub-missions should be reviewed to set clear targets, and in some sectors, there is need to have policy harmonization and announce suitable new policies; the role and commitment of all the state and local governments must be strengthened; adequate budgetary resources should be made available and co-ordination across various programs and implementing institutions strengthened. Children, youth, cultural and educational institutions should be engaged at large to be the torch bearers for the climate movement.

Finally, continuous strengthening of international collaboration among the governments, academia, private sector for honouring the climate commitment, pushing the frontiers of research and knowledge, and tracking climate risks is crucial to win the climate battle to protect people and planet.

5.1 Future Research Directions

The chapter's analysis reveals several critical gaps and emerging areas that warrant further scholarly investigation:

Sub-National Implementation and Political Economy: Future research should conduct deep-dive, comparative case studies of State Action Plans on Climate Change (SAPCCs). This research could explore the political economy of climate action at the state level, examining the drivers of and barriers to implementation, including the role of political leadership, fiscal federalism, and inter-departmental coordination.

Financing the Transition: A critical area for inquiry is the detailed mapping and assessment of climate finance flows in India. Research could quantify the gap between required and available financing, evaluate the effectiveness of innovative instruments like municipal green bonds, and analyze strategies to leverage private capital for climate-resilient infrastructure and technologies.

Social Equity and Just Transition: The distributional impacts of climate policies require rigorous examination. Research should focus on ensuring that the transition to a low-carbon, climate-resilient economy is equitable, protecting vulnerable communities—such as smallholder farmers, informal sector workers, and coastal populations—from disproportionate burdens.

Metrics, Data, and Monitoring: There is a pressing need to develop and standardize robust, sub-national indicators for tracking climate resilience. Research could focus on creating transparent monitoring, evaluation, and learning frameworks that move beyond input-based metrics to outcome-based assessments of adaptive capacity and vulnerability reduction.

Behavioral Science and the LiFE Initiative: The *"Lifestyle for Environment"* (LiFE) mission presents a fertile ground for interdisciplinary research. Studies could apply behavioral science to understand the drivers and barriers to pro-environmental behavior change among Indian citizens and evaluate the efficacy of different communication and incentive strategies.

CHAPTER SUMMARY

Dual Challenge: The chapter frames India's climate policy within the context of balancing rapid economic development with high vulnerability to climate impacts, positioning it as a key voice for the Global South.

Policy Framework Centered on NAPCC: India's primary response is the National Action Plan on Climate Change (NAPCC), structured around eight national missions targeting specific sectors like solar energy, energy efficiency, water, agriculture, and forestry.

Mixed Progress on Implementation: Analysis reveals uneven progress across the missions. Significant successes are noted in the National Solar Mission and National Mission for Enhanced Energy Efficiency, while missions focused on sustainable habitat, agriculture, water, and afforestation (Green India Mission) have seen slower, more modest outcomes.

Implementation Challenges: Key barriers to effective implementation include a proliferation of programs with overlapping mandates, chronic financial constraints, weak institutional capacity (especially at sub-national levels), and poor inter-ministerial and inter-governmental coordination.

Critical Role of Sub-National Governments: The chapter emphasizes that the success of climate actions hinges on state and city governments, necessitating stronger, better-funded, and more aligned State Action Plans on Climate Change (SAPCCs).

Synergies with SDGs: Climate actions (SDG 13) are shown to have strong synergies with other SDGs, including clean energy (SDG 7), clean water (SDG 6), and life on land (SDG 15). Effective coordination is critical to achieving these intertwined goals.

Call for Holistic Action: The conclusion advocates for a multi-pronged way forward: setting clearer targets, enhancing state-level capacity, securing finance, strengthening cross-program coordination, promoting behavioral change through the LiFE mission, and deepening international collaboration.

END OF CHAPTER QUESTION

True or False Questions (Knowledge & Comprehension)

1. The National Action Plan on Climate Change (NAPCC) was formally initiated by India in 2012, following the Paris Agreement.
2. A core philosophy underpinning India's climate policy is the pursuit of "co-benefits," where climate actions also advance developmental objectives like poverty reduction and energy security.

3. The National Mission on Sustainable Habitat (NMSH) has set specific, quantified national targets for carbon footprint reduction in all Indian cities.
4. India's commitment under the Paris Agreement includes reducing the emission intensity of its GDP by 45% by 2030 from a 2005 baseline.
5. The Green India Mission (GIM) has consistently surpassed its annual targets for increasing forest and tree cover.
6. The "Lifestyle for Environment" (LiFE) initiative is a domestic awareness campaign with no explicit global outreach or ambition.
7. India's per capita greenhouse gas emissions are currently above the global average.
8. The National Water Mission (NWM) has a stated goal of achieving a 20% improvement in water use efficiency.
9. A key challenge identified in the implementation of the NAPCC missions is robust inter-ministerial and centre-state coordination.
10. The National Mission for Enhanced Energy Efficiency (NMEEE) relies solely on regulatory mandates, with no market-based mechanisms for promoting efficiency.

Multiple Choice Questions (Application & Analysis)

11. Which of the following best encapsulates the "dual challenge" that frames India's climate policy, as discussed in the chapter?
    - A) Balancing agricultural subsidies with industrial growth.
    - B) Reconciling rapid economic development with high vulnerability to climate impacts.
    - C) Managing the political demands of federal states with centralized policy planning.
    - D) Choosing between adaptation-focused and mitigation-focused strategies.
    - E) Prioritizing between solar energy and wind energy development.
12. The "Panchamrit" pledges, announced at COP26, include all of the following EXCEPT:
    - A) Achieving 50% cumulative electric power installed capacity from non-fossil fuel-based energy resources by 2030.
    - B) Reducing carbon emissions by one billion tonnes by 2030.
    - C) Achieving net-zero emissions by 2070.
    - D) Reducing the emission intensity of its GDP by 45% by 2030.
    - E) Creating a carbon sink of 2.5 to 3 billion tonnes of CO_2 equivalent through forest and tree cover.
13. According to the chapter's analysis, which NAPCC mission is highlighted as having demonstrated particularly "good progress" and "encouraging" results?

A) National Mission on Sustainable Habitat (NMSH)
B) National Mission for a Green India (GIM)
C) National Solar Mission (NSM)
D) National Water Mission (NWM)
E) National Mission on Strategic Knowledge for Climate Change

14. A significant implementation challenge for missions like the National Mission on Sustainable Habitat (NMSH) and National Water Mission (NWM) is:
    A) A complete lack of policy frameworks and guidelines.
    B) The absence of any international funding or collaboration.
    C) Fragmented governance and weak financial capacity at the sub-national level.
    D) Over-reliance on market-based mechanisms and private sector involvement.
    E) A primary focus on mitigation over adaptation.
15. The chapter identifies the "LiFE" initiative as a critical strategy for climate action. What is its primary focus?
    A) Financing large-scale green infrastructure projects through international bonds.
    B) Mandating industrial energy efficiency standards through federal legislation.
    C) Mobilizing individual and collective behavior change for sustainable consumption.
    D) Developing strategic knowledge networks between academic institutions.
    E) Promoting transboundary cooperation for disaster-resilient infrastructure.
16. Which of the following SDGs does the chapter explicitly link to the objectives of the National Water Mission (NWM), beyond the direct climate action of SDG 13?
    A) SDG 4 (Quality Education)
    B) SDG 7 (Affordable and Clean Energy)
    C) SDG 6 (Clean Water and Sanitation)
    D) SDG 5 (Gender Equality)
    E) SDG 9 (Industry, Innovation and Infrastructure)
17. The Coalition for Disaster Resilient Infrastructure (CDRI) is cited as an example of:
    A) India's national policy for urban renewal.
    B) A state-level agricultural adaptation program.
    C) India's leadership in deepening international collaboration on climate issues.
    D) A market-based mechanism under the NMEEE.
    E) A sub-mission under the NAPCC focused on strategic knowledge.
18. What is identified as a primary reason for the modest progress in missions like the National Mission for Sustainable Agriculture (NMSA)?
    A) Lack of technological solutions and R&D.

B) Over-abundance of financial resources leading to misallocation.
C) Lack of awareness among farmers and limited financial resources of smallholders.
D) Strict international sanctions on agricultural imports.
E) Exclusive focus on greenhouse gas emissions rather than productivity.

Short Answer Questions (Comprehension & Analysis)

19. Briefly define the concept of "co-benefits" in the context of India's climate policy.
20. List three key objectives of the National Solar Mission (NSM) as outlined in the chapter.
21. Identify two main implementation challenges faced by the National Mission on Sustainable Habitat (NMSH).
22. What is the primary goal of the Perform, Achieve and Trade (PAT) scheme under the National Mission for Enhanced Energy Efficiency (NMEEE)?
23. How does the chapter characterize the progress of the Green India Mission (GIM) in relation to its targets?
24. Explain the significance of State Action Plans on Climate Change (SAPCCs) in India's federal governance structure.
25. What are the two national missions under the NAPCC that are most directly involved with adaptation, according to the chapter?
26. How does the chapter link the success of climate actions (SDG 13) to the achievement of other Sustainable Development Goals?

Essay Questions (Analysis & Synthesis)

27. Critically analyze the mixed progress across the eight sub-missions of the NAPCC. What factors account for the relative success of missions like the NSM compared to the slower progress in missions like the NMSA or GIM?
28. Synthesize the chapter's arguments regarding the critical role of sub-national governments (states and cities) in implementing India's climate agenda. What specific capacity and coordination challenges need to be addressed?
29. Elaborate on the synergies between climate action (SDG 13) and other SDGs, such as SDG 6 (Clean Water) and SDG 7 (Clean Energy). Provide specific examples from India's policy framework to illustrate these interlinkages.
30. The "LiFE" initiative is presented as a paradigm shift. Evaluate its potential effectiveness and limitations as a strategy for driving large-scale climate action in a diverse and developing country like India.

31. Discuss the role of international collaborations, such as the International Solar Alliance (ISA) and the Coalition for Disaster Resilient Infrastructure (CDRI), in augmenting India's domestic climate efforts and its global leadership position.
32. Based on the chapter's conclusion, construct a coherent argument for why "climate-smart" is a new paradigm for development, integrating the concepts of policy integration, finance, and multi-level governance.

Graduate Level Research Questions (Evaluation & Creation)

33. **Comparative Policy Analysis:** Compare and contrast the policy design and implementation framework of India's National Solar Mission with that of the National Mission for a Green India. Using institutional theory, hypothesize why one has been more successful than the other in achieving its stated targets.
34. **Climate Finance Mapping:** Propose a methodology for conducting a detailed mapping of climate finance flows in India at the state level. What would be the key sources, intermediaries, and sectors to investigate, and what metrics would you use to evaluate "effectiveness" beyond disbursement amounts?
35. **Behavioral Science & LiFE:** Design a research study to evaluate the efficacy of the LiFE campaign. How would you apply behavioral science principles to measure its impact on pro-environmental behaviors among different socio-economic groups in urban and rural India?
36. **Equity and Justice:** "Climate policies can have unintended distributional consequences." Develop a research framework to investigate the social equity implications of a specific climate policy in India (e.g., a shift to electric vehicles, a national carbon market), focusing on vulnerable communities.
37. **Adaptation Metrics:** The chapter notes a lack of robust sub-national indicators for climate resilience. Create a proposed set of 5-7 outcome-based metrics that a city like Chennai or Mumbai could use to monitor its progress in building climate resilience, moving beyond input-based reporting.

Doctoral Level Research Questions (Theoretical & Empirical Investigation)

38. **Political Economy of Federal Climate Governance:** Critically interrogate the political economy of climate action in India's federal system. How do variables like political party alignment between centre and state, fiscal federalism structures, and the influence of sub-national industrial elites shape the ambition and implementation of State Action Plans on Climate Change (SAPCCs)? Propose a mixed-methods research design to test your hypotheses.

39. **Discourse and Power in International Negotiations:** Trace the evolution of India's positioning in global climate negotiations from Kyoto (2002) to COP26 (2021). Using critical discourse analysis, examine how its narrative has shifted from one of "emission rights" and "historical responsibility" to "climate justice" and "green growth," and analyze the material and geopolitical interests underpinning this discursive evolution.
40. **Socio-Technical Transitions in the Energy Sector:** Employ a Multi-Level Perspective (MLP) framework to analyze India's energy transition. How are interactions between niche innovations (e.g., decentralized solar, green hydrogen), the existing socio-technical regime (dominated by coal), and the evolving landscape (international pressure, climate impacts) creating windows of opportunity for, or resistance to, a fundamental transformation of the energy system?

Post-Doctoral Research Directions (Field-Defining & High-Impact)

41. **The Geopolitics of a Green Hydrogen Economy:** Investigate the potential for India to become a geopolitical pivot in the emerging global green hydrogen economy. This research would explore how India's domestic production ambitions could reconfigure energy interdependencies, create new international alliances (e.g., with Japan or the EU), and trigger new forms of "green resource diplomacy" in the Indo-Pacific region.
42. **AI, Big Data, and Adaptive Governance:** Conceptualize and propose a framework for a "Climate-Resilient Digital Twin" for a major Indian river basin (e.g., the Ganges). This interdisciplinary research would explore how the integration of AI, IoT sensors, and real-time climate data can revolutionize adaptive water resource management, predictive disaster governance, and participatory policy simulation.
43. **Decolonizing Climate Adaptation Knowledge:** Develop a critical research agenda that challenges the hegemony of Western scientific knowledge in framing climate adaptation in the Global South. This work would involve documenting, validating, and integrating Indigenous and local knowledge systems (IK/LKS) with formal science to co-produce more contextually appropriate, culturally resonant, and equitable adaptation strategies for communities in climate-vulnerable regions of India.

REFERENCES

Amezaga, A. (2019). Cultural field and literature in minority languages: Basque under Francoism. *Poetics*, *77*, 101398. DOI: 10.1016/j.poetic.2019.101398

An Overview of SDGs | NITI Aayog. (n.d.). Www.niti.gov.in. https://www.niti.gov.in/overview-sustainable-development-goals

. Ansari, M. (2021). Farmers' perception on climate change: a study in tarai region of uttarakhand. Asian Journal of Agricultural Extension Economics & Sociology, 581-591. https://doi.org/DOI: 10.9734/ajaees/2021/v39i1130787

Atteridge, A., Shrivastava, M., Pahuja, N., & Upadhyay, H. (2012). Climate policy in india: What shapes international, national and state policy? *Ambio*, *41*(S1), 68–77. DOI: 10.1007/s13280-011-0242-5

Bajaj, P., & Youdon, C. (2021). Towards a Comprehensive Climate Adaptation Framework for India's Port Infrastructure and Operations: Lessons from Global Best Practices. *Environmental Science & Sustainable Development*, *6*(2), 48–59. DOI: 10.21625/essd.v6i2.837

Çeliktopuz, E. (2024). Unveiling climate change impacts on agricultural sustainability: insights from the United States. Bio Web of Conferences, 85, 01015. https://doi.org/DOI: 10.1051/bioconf/20248501015

Chaturvedi, A., Chandran, K., & Surendran, U. (2018). Revisiting climate change adaptation through proactive policy designing and institutional mechanism. *Tropical Plant Research*, *5*(1), 14–18. DOI: 10.22271/tpr.2018.v5.i1.003

Climate Change Knowledge Portal. (2017). *Homepage | World Bank Climate Change Knowledge Portal*. Worldbank.org. https://climateknowledgeportal.worldbank.org/

Country Climate and Development Reports (CCDRs). (n.d.). World Bank. https://www.worldbank.org/en/publication/country-climate-development-reports

Dubash, N. (2016). Safeguarding development and limiting vulnerability: India's stakes in the paris agreement. *Wiley Interdisciplinary Reviews: Climate Change*, *8*(2), e444. Advance online publication. DOI: 10.1002/wcc.444

. Dubash, N. and Ghosh, S. (2019). National climate policies and institutions., 329-348. https://doi.org/DOI: 10.1093/oso/9780199498734.003.0019

Friess, D. A., Aung, T. T., Huxham, M., Lovelock, C., Mukherjee, N., & Sasmito, S. (2019). SDG 14: Life below Water – Impacts on Mangroves. In Katila, P., Pierce Colfer, C. J., de Jong, W., Galloway, G., Pacheco, P., & Winkel, G. (Eds.), *Sustainable Development Goals: Their Impacts on Forests and People* (pp. 445–481). Cambridge University Press. DOI: 10.1017/9781108765015.016

Friess, D. A., Rogers, K., Lovelock, C. E., Krauss, K. W., Hamilton, S. E., Lee, S. Y., Lucas, R., Primavera, J., Rajkaran, A., & Shi, S. (2019). The state of the world's mangrove forests: Past, present, and future. *Annual Review of Environment and Resources*, *44*(1), 89–115. DOI: 10.1146/annurev-environ-101718-033302

Gupta, J. (2001). India and climate change policy: Between diplomatic defensiveness and industrial transformation. *Energy & Environment*, *12*(2-3), 217–236. DOI: 10.1260/0958305011500715

Hussain, S., Hussain, E., Saxena, P., Sharma, A., Thathola, P., & Sonwani, S. (2024). Navigating the impact of climate change in india: A perspective on climate action (sdg13) and sustainable cities and communities (sdg11). *Frontiers in Sustainable Cities*, *5*, 1308684. Advance online publication. DOI: 10.3389/frsc.2023.1308684

Karim, R., Ghazali, F., & Ansari, A. (2020). Renewable energy regulations in indonesia and india: A comparative study on legal framework. *Journal of Indonesian Legal Studies*, *5*(2), 361–390. DOI: 10.15294/jils.v5i2.41986

. Kattumuri, R. and Ravindranath, D. (2014). Sustainable growth and climate change: evolution of india's strategies., 75-106. https://doi.org/DOI: 10.1142/9789814551854_0004

Kreft, C., Angst, M., Huber, R., & Finger, R. (2023). Farmers' social networks and regional spillover effects in agricultural climate change mitigation. *Climatic Change*, *176*(2), 8. Advance online publication. DOI: 10.1007/s10584-023-03484-6

Lifestyle for Environment - LiFE. (2022, October 11). MyGov.in. https://www.mygov.in/life/

Majeed, N., Sharif, R., Sheeraz, M. N., Sajjad, S., Maqsood, H., Imran, M., Jamshaid, M. U., Arif, M., & Hussain, M. B. (2023). Impact of climate change on agriculture & vice versa: A review. *JQAAS*, *3*(01), 1–15. DOI: 10.38211/jqaas.2023.3.31

Mandloi, S., Bangre, J., Aher, S. B., Sharma, O. P., Prajapati, S., & Singh, S. (2023). Conservation agriculture as a climate change mitigation strategy: A review. *International Journal of Environment and Climate Change*, *13*(11), 3230–3242. DOI: 10.9734/ijecc/2023/v13i113495

Ministry New and Renewable Energy. https://mnre.gov.in/solar-overview/

Ministry of Environment. Forest and Climate Change, Green India Missionhttps://moef.gov.in/moef/division/forest-divisions-2/green-india-mission-gim/

Ministry of Jal Shakti. Department of Water Resources, https://nwm.gov.in/objective-national-water-mission

Ministry of Power. https://powermin.gov.in/en/content/energy-efficiency

MoEFCC. (2021). India: Third Biennial Update Report to the United Nations Framework Convention on Climate Change. Ministry of Environment, Forest and Climate Change, Government of India. https://unfccc.int/documents/268470

National Mission for a Green India, https://mpforest.gov.in/img/files/GIM_Implementation_Guidelines.pdf

National Mission for Sustainable Agriculture. (n.d.). Nmsa.dac.gov.in. https://nmsa.dac.gov.in/

National Mission for Sustaining the Himalayan Ecosystem https://nihroorkee.gov.in/major-projects/national-mission-sustaining-himalayan-ecosystem-nmshe

National Mission on Himalayan Studies https://nmhs.org.in/pdf/National%20Mission%20on%20Himalayan%20Studies.pdf

National Mission on Sustainable Habitat. Ministry of Housing and Urban Affairs, GoI https://mohua.gov.in/upload/uploadfiles/files/NMSH-2021.pdf

. Neha, & Ansari, M.A. (2023). "Farmers' Knowledge of Adaptation Strategies to Mitigate Climate Change and Factors Influencing Their Adoption". *International Journal of Environment and Climate Change* 13 (8):926-38. https://doi.org/.DOI: 10.9734/ijecc/2023/v13i82030

Pahuja, N., Pruthi, A., & Raj, A.. (2020). *Mainstreaming Sustainable Development and Enhancing Climate Resilience: New Opportunities for States in India*. TERI.

Roy, S., Debnath, P., Vulević, A., & Mitra, S. (2023). Incorporating climate change resilience in india's railway infrastructure: Challenges and potential. *Mechatronics and Intelligent Transportation Systems*, *2*(2). Advance online publication. DOI: 10.56578/mits020205

Sharma, D., & Singh, S. (2016). Instituting environmental sustainability and climate resilience into the governance process: Exploring the potential of new urban development schemes in india. *International Area Studies Review*, *19*(1), 90–103. DOI: 10.1177/2233865916632942

. Singh, K. (2022). India's progress on environmental sustainable development goals: a review. jaz. https://doi.org/DOI: 10.53555/jaz.v43i1.3227

Stefanopoulou, A. (2023). Improve time and energy efficiency in multi-uav coverage swarms by optimizing thetake-off/landing positions. DOI: 10.21203/rs.3.rs-3671974/v1

Synergy Solutions for a World in Crisis: Tackling Climate and SDG Action Together | Department of Economic and Social Affairs. (2023). Sdgs.un.org. https://sdgs.un.org/synergy-solutions-world-crisis-tackling-climate-and-sdg-action-together

Tripathi, M., & Bhattacharya, N. (2023). Environmentally sound technologies for climate change mitigation in brics countries: A comparative policy and legal perspective. *Environmental Policy and Law, 53*(2-3), 181–196. DOI: 10.3233/EPL-220067

United Nations. (2023). *The Sustainable Development Goals Report 2023: Special Edition*. Unstats.un.org

United Nations. (2024). *The 17 Sustainable Development Goals*. United Nations. https://sdgs.un.org/goals

Varma, N., Kelkar, U., Bhardwaj, S., Singh, P., & Mishra, A. (2014, December). Climate Change, Disasters and Development: Testing the Waters for Adaptive Governance in India. *Vision: The Journal of Business Perspective, 18*(4), 327–338. DOI: 10.1177/0972262914551664

Vihma, A. (2011). India and the global climate governance: Between principles and pragmatism. *Journal of Environment & Development, 20*(1), 69–94. DOI: 10.1177/1070496510394325

KEY TERMS AND DEFINITIONS

Climate Resilience:: The capacity of social, economic, and environmental systems to anticipate, prepare for, respond to, and recover from the hazards and stresses induced by climate change.

Co-benefits:: The additional positive outcomes that result from a policy designed for another primary purpose. In this context, it refers to the developmental benefits (e.g., improved energy access, job creation, better public health) that arise from actions taken to mitigate or adapt to climate change.

Lifestyle for Environment (LiFE):: A global initiative launched by India aimed at encouraging individuals and communities to adopt environmentally conscious lifestyles and consumption patterns to contribute to climate action.

National Action Plan on Climate Change (NAPCC):: India's overarching national policy framework, launched in 2008, which outlines the country's strategy for addressing climate change through eight core *"missions"* focused on specific sectors.

Net-Zero Emissions:: A state of balance between the amount of greenhouse gases emitted into the atmosphere and the amount removed from it, achieved through a combination of deep emission reductions and carbon dioxide removal.

Panchamrit:: A term meaning *"five nectar elements,"* used to describe India's five enhanced climate pledges presented at the COP26 summit, including targets for reaching 500 GW of non-fossil energy capacity and achieving net-zero emissions by 2070.

State Action Plan on Climate Change (SAPCC):: State-level plans mandated to be aligned with the NAPCC, which detail the specific vulnerabilities, strategies, and actions for climate adaptation and mitigation tailored to the unique context of each Indian state.

TEACHING NOTE

Concise Summary for the Instructor

This chapter presents a critical analysis of India's complex journey in integrating climate action with its sustainable development ambitions. It frames India's policy challenge through the lens of a "dual challenge": navigating the imperatives of rapid economic development for a billion-plus population while addressing its acute vulnerability to climate impacts. The chapter's core analytical framework is the National Action Plan on Climate Change (NAPCC), launched in 2008, and its eight constituent missions. The analysis reveals a narrative of **"mixed progress"**—highlighting notable successes in technological, centrally-driven sectors like solar energy and energy efficiency, while underscoring significant implementation lag in more complex, decentralized, and socio-ecological domains like sustainable agriculture, water management, and urban habitat. The chapter concludes that the path to climate resilience is less about policy creation and more a "grand experiment" in implementation, requiring unprecedented coordination across levels of government, sectors, and institutions, all while overcoming persistent financial, capacity, and governance constraints.

Chapter Synopsis & Key Learning Objectives

Chapter Synopsis

The chapter begins by establishing the global climate crisis and India's unique, vulnerable position within it. It traces the evolution of India's climate policy from its foundational NAPCC to its contemporary "Panchamrit" pledges and international leadership initiatives like the International Solar Alliance (ISA). A detailed, mission-by-mission analysis forms the core, evaluating objectives against implementation realities. The concluding sections synthesize key achievements and bottlenecks, emphasizing the critical role of sub-national governments, behavioral change (LiFE mission), and international collaboration, while outlining a forward-looking research agenda.

Key Learning Objectives

- **Remembering (Knowledge):** Recall the names, primary objectives, and key performance indicators of the eight core missions under the National Action Plan on Climate Change (NAPCC).

- **Understanding (Comprehension):** Explain the concept of "co-benefits" and how it serves as a central philosophy for reconciling India's development and climate agendas.
- **Applying (Application):** Map the linkages between specific NAPCC missions (e.g., National Solar Mission, National Water Mission) and their corresponding Sustainable Development Goals (SDGs), such as SDG 7 and SDG 6.
- **Analyzing (Analysis):** Differentiate between the factors contributing to the successful implementation of certain missions (e.g., NSM) and the barriers hindering progress in others (e.g., NMSA, GIM).
- **Evaluating (Evaluation):** Assess the efficacy of India's multi-level governance framework for climate action, critiquing the coordination between central, state, and local institutions.
- **Creating (Synthesis):** Formulate a coherent argument for a "climate-smart" development paradigm, integrating lessons from the chapter on policy, finance, and governance to propose a strategic way forward.

Core Themes/Theses for Discussion

1. **The Dual Challenge Doctrine:** India's climate policy is fundamentally shaped by the need to simultaneously achieve economic development and build climate resilience, making it a critical case study for the Global South.
2. **The Co-benefits Paradigm:** Climate action is not a standalone objective but is strategically framed to deliver direct developmental benefits (energy security, health, jobs), which is key to building political and public support.
3. **The Implementation Gap:** The disparity in progress across the NAPCC missions reveals that well-defined objectives are insufficient; the primary bottlenecks are institutional capacity, financing, and inter-governmental coordination, not a lack of policy.
4. **Federalism as Both a Barrier and an Enabler:** The constitutional division of powers makes state and city governments the lynchpins of implementation, yet they are often the weakest links in the governance chain, requiring urgent capacity building and fiscal empowerment.
5. **From Government to Governance:** Effective climate action necessitates a shift from top-down policy mandates to a collaborative governance model involving the private sector, civil society, and citizens, as exemplified by the LiFE initiative.

Suggested Teaching Pathway

1. **Hook (10 mins):** Begin with a provocative question: *"Can a country aiming to become a $5 trillion economy also be a global leader in climate action? Is this a contradiction or a new model of development?"* Use a short video clip of recent climate disasters in India (e.g., urban floods, Himalayan landslides) to ground the discussion.
2. **Conceptual Foundation (20 mins):** Lecture and discussion on the core frameworks: the "dual challenge," "co-benefits," and the structure of the NAPCC. Use a single slide to visually map the eight missions.
3. **Deep Dive: Case Study Analysis (40 mins):** Divide the class into small groups. Assign each group one "successful" mission (e.g., NSM, NMEEE) and one "lagging" mission (e.g., NMSA, NMSH). Their task is to analyze and present the reasons for the disparity in outcomes. This fosters comparative analysis.
4. **Synthesis and Debate (30 mins):** Reconvene for a plenary discussion. Use the whiteboard to create two columns: "Drivers of Success" and "Barriers to Implementation." Guide the class to populate these columns based on group presentations, leading to a synthesized understanding of the implementation gap.
5. **Forward-Looking Application (20 mins):** Pose the final discussion question: *"If you were advising the Prime Minister's Office, what would be your top three recommendations to accelerate India's climate resilience by 2030, based on this chapter's analysis?"* This encourages synthesis and creation.

Pedagogical Tools & Resources

- **In-Class Handout:** A one-page matrix summarizing the eight NAPCC missions, their core objectives, key achievements, and primary challenges.
- **Multimedia:** Use infographics from the chapter (e.g., sectoral emissions, solar capacity growth) and short videos from official government channels on the ISA, LiFE, or CDRI.
- **Role-Playing Exercise:** A simulated negotiation between a Central Ministry official, a State Minister for Environment, a City Mayor, and a civil society representative, debating the allocation of a limited climate budget.
- **Recommended Pre-Reading:**
    - o The chapter's "Additional Reading" section, particularly Dubash (2022) for policy depth.
    - o A recent news article on a climate-related event in India (e.g., a heatwave, a solar park inauguration) to connect theory with current affairs.

Note on Sensitivity

The discussion of India's development-climate nexus is inherently political. Instructors should be prepared to navigate and guide conversations on several sensitive fronts:

- **Equity and Justice:** Discussions may arise about whether the burdens of climate action (e.g., land acquisition for solar parks) or the impacts of climate change (e.g., on smallholder farmers) are distributed fairly.
- **Federal Tensions:** The analysis of centre-state coordination may lead to discussions on political party dynamics and regional disparities. Steer the focus towards institutional and capacity issues rather than partisan politics.
- **Historical Responsibility:** Students may raise questions about the fairness of India's emission reduction targets relative to developed nations. Acknowledge this as a core tenet of India's international negotiating position while focusing the discussion on domestic policy imperatives.

Frame these not as debates to be won, but as critical, inherent tensions in the sustainability transition that require careful policy design and inclusive dialogue.

Key Questions for Class Discussion

1. **Beyond Co-benefits:** The "co-benefits" approach is politically astute, but does it risk downplaying the radical systemic changes needed for deep decarbonization? *(Direction: Discuss the trade-offs between pragmatic, incremental reform and transformative change.)*
2. **The Solar Success Story:** To what extent can the implementation model of the National Solar Mission be replicated for missions like the Green India Mission? What are the limits of this techno-financial model? *(Direction: Compare centralized, technology-driven projects with decentralized, socio-ecological ones.)*
3. **The Urban Crucible:** The chapter notes that cities are on the frontlines of climate impacts but lack capacity. What specific powers and resources should be devolved to city governments to enable effective climate action? *(Direction: Explore the concept of "urban climate governance" and fiscal federalism.)*
4. **LiFE: Libertarian or Liberating?** Is the LiFE initiative an effective tool for democratizing climate action, or does it risk shifting responsibility from systemic polluters and policymakers onto individuals? *(Direction: Debate the role of individual agency versus structural change.)*
5. **Measuring the Wrong Things?** The chapter calls for better metrics. If you were to redesign the success indicators for the National Water Mission, what

two outcome-based metrics would you prioritize over simple input-based ones? *(Direction: Move from measuring "money spent" or "policies passed" to "vulnerability reduced" or "resilience built.")*

6. **The Private Sector's Role:** The chapter mentions attracting private investment but focuses largely on public policy. Where are the most significant opportunities and barriers for private capital in funding India's climate resilience? *(Direction: Discuss blended finance, ESG investing, and climate-risk disclosure.)*
7. **A Just Transition for Agriculture:** Given the vulnerability of millions of smallholders, what would a "just transition" in Indian agriculture look like, and how can the NMSA be redesigned to achieve it? *(Direction: Link climate adaptation with rural livelihoods and social safety nets.)*
8. **India's Global Leadership:** India's international initiatives (ISA, CDRI) are praised. How does this "soft power" leadership translate into tangible benefits for its domestic climate goals? *(Direction: Discuss technology transfer, investment attraction, and geopolitical influence.)*
9. **The 2070 Net-Zero Target:** Is India's 2070 net-zero target a pragmatic reflection of its development needs, or a lack of ambition that locks in high emissions for decades? *(Direction: Analyze the equity and feasibility dimensions of long-term targets.)*
10. **The Future of Federalism:** Will climate change, as a pervasive threat, ultimately strengthen Indian federalism by forcing collaboration, or will it exacerbate centre-state tensions over resources and authority? *(Direction: Speculate on the evolving nature of governance in the Anthropocene.)*

Chapter 6
Government's Initiative to Promote Sustainable Finance and Addressing ESG Issues

Drishti Aggarwal
https://orcid.org/0009-0004-8163-5485
Christ University, India

Puja Chopra
https://orcid.org/0000-0002-9114-4151
Christ University, India

ABSTRACT

In recent years governments worldwide have highly focused on sustainable finance to have an overall growth of the economy while addressing Environmental, Social, and Governance (ESG) issues as a long-term strategy towards a green economy by reducing carbon footprints and ensuring long-term financial stability. This paper analyses key regulations that the government and various financial institutions have set up for multiple companies to reshape markets and grow the economy. It also reflects various impacts of certain agreements that have happened universally and their importance. The information is collected by getting insight from the documents, press releases, and other information sources released on government sites and other reliable sources. Also, considering various case studies it examines how countries have implemented ESG policies (with its prime focus on India). Moreover, this paper helps to find any gaps in these regulations designed by the government. It finds out the impact of these policies on the overall economy and makes people aware of Government releases.

DOI: 10.4018/979-8-3693-9714-5.ch006

INTRODUCTION

Sustainability is one of the terms that has gained importance in the past few years and since then has been a place of primary concern for corporations, policies, and discussions worldwide. The United Nations Brundtland Commission 1987 defined sustainability as meeting present needs without compromising on the needs of the future generation and the availability of all the resources (United Nations 1987). According to the UNEP (United Nations Environment Programme) report sustainability is an integration of Environmental, social, and economic factors. Sustainability is a balance of using natural resources in such a way as to avoid resource depletion and social inequalities (United Nations Environment Programme, 2011).

Sustainable finance has risen from sustainability, which refers to best financial practices that focus on investing in bonds, stocks, or other sources, including environmental, social, and governance factors for long-term stability in the country's economy. UNEP even argues that one should reallocate their investments to more factor-intensive sectors like renewable energy, sustainable agriculture, and low-carbon technology. The problem with the economies is that for years and years, most of their resources have been allocated to fossil fuels, real estate, and other financial products which don't specifically deal with products with limited life and led to the depletion of many natural resources (United Nations Environment Programme [UNEP], 2011). Therefore, has raised the environmental risk of many nations. Governments have been aware of these concerns following a string of events that pointed to the depletion of natural resources, such as the closure of several units because there were no raw materials available, and the detrimental effects this had on the nation's economy. This made many countries' governments conscious of this happening around the countries and started to work on many green and sustainable finance measures to transition themselves into a green economy and create various jobs in this segment. European Union also suggested that sustainable finance plays an important role in the world's transition towards net zero as the government finances more money towards carbon-neutral projects (European Union, 2020). Also, according to the World Economic Forum, more the sustainable a business is more returns are provided to the investors (World Economic Forum, 2021).

Sustainable finance includes ESG factors that include the Environmental factor to mitigate the climate risk and promote sustainable resources; social factor involves human and animal rights, whereas governance comprises management, employee relations, and compensation practices. ESG (environment, social, and governance) is a view of seeing sustainability beyond just environmental issues. People now have become increasingly concerned about ESG issues so, embedding sustainability in business is a priority for executives and investors in situations like today's business landscape. Stock markets have always traditionally mirrored public sentiment, and investors have reallocated their asset management strategy to focus not only on financial performance but also on various ESG factors (IBM, 2024). Stakeholders nowadays also keep a keen eye on the ESG practices of an organization to decide upon the investment and sustainability of the same. This made various companies shift toward ESG standards to enhance their long-term value and gain more investments. Also, the integration of ESG principles can affect the company's performance and risk profile.

In the same way, governments of various countries are promoting sustainable finance as they include many sectors such as renewable energy, sustainable agriculture, healthcare, etc. As. Global Risks Report 2024, has recently warned about extreme weather conditions in major parts of the world in the upcoming decade. India has also been in the limelight for climate change due to frequent changes and extreme weather present (Bhattacharyya, 2023). According to an Indian Express report in 2023, India has reported extreme weather on 318 out of 365 days in a year, which is an area of concern for policymakers to reduce such kind of effects (Indian Express, 2023). Thus, sustainable options help in the growth of the economy and less use of natural resources. The government in the past few years has started to take many steps such as taxation and disclosure to promote sustainable financial methods in the company, to have a more stabilized economy, and to limit the use of natural resources of the country. More of the companies practicing it would be beneficial for the country to survive for a longer period and have more investors to sustain financially.

So, the objective of this paper is to draw out various initiatives taken by the government of India and other financial institutions like RBI (Reserve Bank of India) and SEBI (Security Exchange Board of India), etc. to promote sustainable finance initiatives that are taking place in India. We will also identify various benefits of these regulations for solving the ESG issues that are still prevalent in society and how the government aims to cater to these issues. This is analysed by various documents published by the government as the public realizes, speeches, official notices, and other secondary sources of data used to get awareness about the initiatives and how much government and institutions spend on these initiatives. This paper in detail examines these initiatives and how they help solve ESG issues prevalent in the country. This paper also talks about some mandatory disclosures from various top companies made by the government to promote sustainable finance in the country.

The primary objective of the study is to examine the policy initiatives done by the government in the near past to promote environmentally sustainable investments. The paper analyses the policy framework and regulations that are aimed at aligning the financial sector of India and its companies to environmental and climate change goals. This paper also aims to assess the effectiveness of strategies made by India's sustainable finance initiatives and identify challenges and future opportunities for the same.

BACKGROUND

The global financial landscape is undergoing a profound transformation, pivoting from a singular focus on economic returns toward a more holistic paradigm that integrates environmental, social, and governance (ESG) considerations. This shift to sustainable finance is not merely a trend but a critical response to escalating climate risks, resource depletion, and social inequalities. For emerging economies like India, which are simultaneously navigating the imperatives of rapid growth and the vulnerabilities of climate change, this transition is both a formidable challenge and a strategic opportunity. The nation faces acute environmental pressures, with extreme weather events becoming increasingly frequent, underscoring the urgent need to decouple economic development from environmental degradation.

In this context, the Indian government and its financial regulators have embarked on a concerted journey to embed sustainability into the core of the country's financial architecture. This chapter meticulously documents and analyzes this multi-faceted policy push. It explores a suite of groundbreaking initiatives—from the pioneering issuance of Sovereign Green Bonds to finance clean infrastructure, to the Securities and Exchange Board of India's (SEBI) mandatory Business Responsibility and Sustainability Reporting (BRSR) framework for top listed companies. The analysis extends to the Reserve Bank of India's (RBI) green deposit framework and supportive measures like Priority Sector Lending for renewable energy, illustrating a whole-of-government approach.

However, the path to a mature sustainable finance ecosystem is complex. The chapter critically examines the persistent gaps that threaten to undermine these efforts, including the lack of a standardized definition for "green" activities, regulatory fragmentation, infrastructural bottlenecks, and the marginalization of social and governance aspects within the ESG agenda. By presenting a balanced view of India's ambitious regulatory advancements and the practical hurdles that remain, this chapter offers a crucial case study on the realities of aligning a vast and diverse economy with the principles of long-term, inclusive, and sustainable development.

LITERATURE REVIEW

The concept of sustainable finance has come up from the Paris Agreement and sustainable development goals which focus on the need for the flow of finance to support low greenhouse gas emissions and climate-resilient development pathways (Kemfert & Schmalz, 2019).

Recently, Sustainable finance has been recognized as an essential component for addressing climate change and achieving SDG (Sustainable Development Goals). In recent years there has been growing concern over the impact of environmental challenges (such as climate change and resource depletion) in light of our current economic system. Consequently, there is a focus on green finance (GF), sustainable development, and circular economy (CE) at the intersection between traditional biophysical perspectives evolved around maximum Economic Value Added (EVA), and modern notions concerning planetary boundaries. Green finance has been increasingly acknowledged as an important means to promote investment in environmentally friendly projects. For instance, developing Asia needs about US$1.7 trillion annually until 2030 on infrastructure investments to support growth under the constraint of climate change; China is at the forefront of green finance initiatives (Lee, 2020). To encourage green investments, the Chinese government has introduced several programs including the G20 Green Finance Study Group. But the headwinds are substantial: policy signals remain insufficient, loan terms are short, and there is a lack of standard definitions for green assets. In China, some Green Finance Enhancements are open to improve transparency, enhance financial capabilities, and explore new sources of funding can be take up (Lee, 2020).

Apart from the national initiatives—the ones taken by other countries—such transnational efforts as those of Multilateral Development Banks (MDBs)/Development Finance Institutions (DFIs) are imperative vis-à-vis the instrumentalizations in private sector investments for green projects. These have supported over USD 160 billion of private investment by these institutions in 2017 alone (Lee, 2020). Baked into lending practices must be the introduction of eco variables while creating bubble bonds as financing devices— key latter-day instruments towards greening the banking system.

Also, participation in public sector projects is crucial since they have to provide the resources needed for funding green initiatives and create market conditions that help foster SDG-aligned investment (Lee, 2020).

An important factor is the activity of the Bank of Indonesia in the field of sustainable finance and climate risk management. It must take reputational measures for the development of certain preconditions through policy measures that encourage investment in non-pollutant/friendly areas and embedding ESG principles into banking business practices (Setyowati, 2020). Analysis of the findings indicates that while financial institutions are taking action by formulating such action plans and preparing investment portfolio sustainability reports, their effectiveness is limited by the inability to satisfactorily explain what the word ‘green’ entails. There is a need for more aggressive interventions from the Central Bank of Indonesia to deepen regulatory control and improve acceptable standards for disclosures (Setyowati, 2020).

Besides highlighting the practice of Islamic financing in extending the reach of 'economic voices' in particular Bank Mandiri Syariah in Indonesia, one can also appreciate the role of such banks in financing sustainable development. In the year 2018, the bank achieved a sustainable finance (SF) financing ratio reaching 29.56% of all the financing made by the bank, indicating adherence to the Sharia-specific practices and the FSA-related rules 3. The paper stresses the need for stakeholder commitment to restore confidence in the Islamic banking sector and effective SF practices. Alternatively, a lack of laws should not deter the integration of maqasid sharia with sustainable finance in lobbying for the betterment of society and the environment (Nugroho et al., 2019).

Apart from that, GF and GI have been described as mutually exclusive inventions but their intersection is very important in ensuring that a circular economy is established and sustained. There is a growing body of literature focusing on a collective perspective on GF and GI from the diffusion of innovation and institutional theories which this recent study attempts to do (Agrawal et al., 2024). This framework is intended to facilitate topical and practical-oriented future studies and applied works towards sustainable development goals. Further, the study underlines the role of academic, governmental, and industrial orientation in advocating green initiatives and relevant policies implemented (Agrawal et al., 2024).

The works reviewed within this article convey an understanding of the importance of developing and implementing strong policies and laws that enable such sustainable finance mechanisms. The Special Issue on the laws relating to sustainable finance seeks to understand whether the existing interventions that depend on the financial markets can address the public good of sustainability. Instinctively, this means that although the law and regulation tend to limit the extent of environmental harm caused by excessive corporate practices, some changes are required in corporate law to ensure that businesses willingly focus on socially and ethically responsible CSR practices and economic activities (Chiu et al., 2022). This strand of thinking situates itself within the wider debate on the hitherto meaning of corporate governance and what it ought to include concerning sustainability at the board decision-making level and the orientation of governance towards stakeholders (Chiu et al., 2022).

In the Federal Republic of Germany, the engagement of the financial markets in advancing sustainability is best epitomized by boards of institutions such as the Landes Bank Berlin (LBB). The LBB since 2005 has been very active in the area of sustainability, particularly investing for clients such as churches and foundations who do not wish their funds used in unsustainable activities (Agrawal et al., 2024). The bank's sustainability report details the activities of IMUG and the attempts at localization policies within the Sparkassen Group. Still, difficulties persist, notably, in the availability of the research and definitions of what 'green' investments can be given (Agrawal et al., 2024).

German Sparkasse savings banks, including both LBB and DEKA, are involved with these assets in such a way that DEKA is a sole agent for a multitude of investment instruments useful for both retail and institutional investors. Deka's sustainability report is extensive and gives a pointer to working with leading rating agencies, which assures the legit investment of sustainable factors as well (Setyowati, 2020). Another example is the online accessory for sustainable investments called Bevestor, which makes it possible for many people who are not direct investors to support companies and other organizations battling climatic threats eliminating g8 finances (Setyowati, 2020). The amount of evidence of the significance of 'governance' in the realm of Sustainable finance has also increased as demonstrated by the Sachverständigenrat für Umweltfragen (SRU) which calls for a democratic form of government expanded within the boundaries of ecology. The reports of the SRU support a restructuring of various domains, finance included, to more sustainable practices, and recommend plants to be reformed for these expectations to be achieved (Kemfert, & Schmalz, 2019). This is part of the wider storyline that advocates for the inclusion of environmental issues into the spectrum of financial decision-making.

The Paris Agreement is a system under which parties who commit to taking specified actions in furthering climate change usually protect equity and accountability because these actions compel parties to submit all relevant data regarding their devised targets called nationally determined contributions (NDCs) and possibly reports on their actions towards achieving such (Lee, 2020). This mechanism is essential in ensuring countries do not renege on their pledges and developing countries receive assistance to help them develop systems for reporting and associated transparency obligations (Setyowati, 2020). The purpose of the technical expert review process is to review how the nationally determined contributions (NDC) are implemented and propose corrective actions where necessary so that the activities of all the parties are congruent with the overall aim of the Agreement (Setyowati, 2020).

In addition, the Paris Agreement recognizes the necessity of technology transfer and the active formation of both the existing and potential participants' capacities as a prerequisite for proceeding to the low carbon economy phase. It motivates the industrialized countries to assist the underdeveloped countries economically, environmentally, and socially in coming up with viable project proposals (Nugroho et al., 2019). This support is important for making it possible for countries to put in place robust policy measures to address climate change and meet their Nationally Determined Contributions (NDCs), especially in regions where high mitigation potential exists (Nugroho et al., 2019). The Paris Agreement also serves as a base for many countries to make rules and regulations for sustainability and green finance that have to be complied with to make an economy sustainable and there is a depletion in frequent weather changes that are happening most frequently according to recent reports of UN and the conditions about this alarming situation.

Financing as a mechanism in the fight against climate change has been included in the provisions of the Paris Accord. It is expected that the operating entities of the Financial Mechanism will organize technical expert meetings to advance the development of policies and practices that will result in enhanced climate action (Agrawal et al., 2024). Such interaction is critical in raising awareness of the best approaches and practices and ensuring that funding is focused on the most strategic areas of use (Agrawal et al., 2024).

On top of all the financing mechanisms put forward, the Paris treaty has some provisions on the need for review and monitoring of progress on work done towards climate targets. This includes the preparation of technical papers concerning the co-benefits of policies and actions, which are also of great importance, regarding their design, over implementation with the policy gaps that should be taken into every available audience (Chiu et al., 2022). About the efforts made towards meeting the objectives of the Agreement, these two words are important in achieving the suggested coordination with other parties (Chiu et al., 2022).

Thirdly, it addresses the point that human rights should be fundamental in climate action. It acknowledges the significance of participation in human rights, especially a right by the indigenous people, local populations, and disadvantaged groups concerning the issue of climate change (Kemfert, & Schmalz, 2019). This consideration is very significant and highly resourceful in meeting the redistribution and the integration of diverse interest groups in deliberations over climate policy-making (Kemfert, & Schmalz, 2019).

In essence, the authors explain that the work of GF and GI has been substantial in implementing the principles of sustainability in practice mainly through domains such as finance and banking. Going forward, to ensure this change of the economy towards a more sustainable, circular one, there should be efforts toward the composition of strong legal. It establishes clear and usable standards for transparency, accountability, and support for climate action, emphasizing cooperation among the countries and other stakeholders in the attainment of international climate targets; the same imbalances and focus are present in the discourse here. As discussed, it should be further expedited and resolved to meet the issues that are accompanied by the development of green finance projects in various regions so that it remains effective in the process of achieving sustainable development and advancement of the SDGs. Many countries have considered these things and many reforms have taken place but not sufficient enough to reach long and short-term sustainability goals.

METHODOLOGY

This paper focuses on qualitative research of data that is already available on various websites like RBI, news reports, research papers, and different articles, etc., the data is collected from government reports, financial institutions, international reports of countries, and any interview details available on trusted sites for key stakeholders of finance and the environmental sector. This allowed a big database to analyse how India is initiating its sustainable finance and implementing those in the country. The data collected for this paper is analysed and key policies of government have been examined that are taken into action to make the economy sustainable and green for a longer period with the help of sustainable finance.

Conceptual Framework

In recent years, climate risk and sustainable finance have emerged as new priorities in the regulatory and governance frameworks across the globe, in particular in emerging markets like India as they are still on the path of growing their economy and infrastructure. With the climate disaster becoming worse day by day, it can be observed that financial services have an increasing risk exposure for not only physical risks due to climate events but also the systemic risks that arise due to a shift in the economic structure. The framework outlines the corporation governance and risk management practices, the compliance and investment disclosure levels, and the prospects of green finance development in the Indian financial system in accordance with the recent reports of the Reserve Bank of India (RBI) and the Securities and Exchange Board of India (SEBI).

India has been suffering from an instant temperature increase, around 0.7 degrees Celsius from 1901 to 2018 (UNICEF, 2021). In the past decade, India has been one of the most affected countries in the world in terms of fatalities and economic losses. Also, the extreme weather conditions have led to high vulnerability among people. To overcome these situations, the Government of India has taken various initiatives to solve many ESG issues towards sustainable financial activities.

1. Sovereign Green Bonds in India

The government of India in 2023 took a step to enter the green finance market by issuing its first Sovereign Green Bonds. (India's debut in the sovereign green bond market: First deal landed a greenium, 2023) These bonds were bought into the market with a view of financing environmentally sustainable projects like solar power plants, wind energy generating plants, metro lines, and many more initiatives that can make the environment clean and reduce carbon emissions (India incorporates green bonds into its climate finance strategy, 2023). These bonds will help India achieve the target of generating 500GW of renewable energy by 2030 and achieving net-zero emissions by 2070 ("Sovereign green bonds: Fuelling India's sustainability | ISP," 2024). Also, these bonds will help the government to build an infrastructure that supports clean energy transition and is sustainable in the long run. A comprehensive guideline has been made by the Security and Exchange Board of India to ensure transparency and integrity in the procedure of green bonds. The guidelines include:

1.1. Appointment of an independent 3rd party by issuer to review and certify the bonds. This helps the issuer know the framework, objective of the project, and selection of the project by the environmental standards.
1.2. SEBI has made it mandatory to disclose how the finances obtained are utilized, which helps in the detailed evaluation and assessment of the impact on the environment after the cause is in place.
1.3. The regulations must align with the Green Bond principles that will build the confidence of investors in Indian Green Bonds and more Foreign Direct Investments in India's Financial markets. (Srivastava and Trivedi,2024). Thus, the Indian Government has introduced Sovereign green Bonds, which make a very important step to promote sustainable finance in India and position itself as a leader in the global green finance landscape.

2. Business Responsibility and Sustainability Reporting (BRSR)

The introduction of the Business Responsibility and Sustainability Reporting framework by the Securities and Exchange Board of India in 2021 was a bold step that marked a significant stride toward enhancing the transparency and accountability of corporate reporting in India. The mandatory disclosure of ESG initiatives by the top 1,000 companies listed publicly is expected to bring about sustainable business operations throughout the country (Oren, 2023). Earlier, it was a voluntary measure for the fiscal year 2021-22; however, later it became a mandate from the beginning of fiscal year 2022-23. Therefore, this change reflects significant development that SEBI is adapting to ensure that sustainability gets incorporated into the very core activity of any entity, making the organizations responsible for their social as well as environmental implications (Deloitte, n.d.). BRSR framework comprises nine core categories that enable the organization in reporting and informing on sustainability. Categories include environmental conservation, respect for human rights, ethics in practice, employee welfare, comprehensive development, and sustainable products and services, responsible consumer interaction, stakeholder engagement, and participation in ethical public policy. Any categorization is supposed to reflect a general outlook of any business commitment towards sustainability and actions taken to reduce adverse impacts on human society and the environment (IRCCL, 2023). Businesses in environmental conservation industries are supposed to provide information for any organization on energy consumption, water usage, waste generation, and carbon emission. This follows the track related to the gains registered in the environmental dimension together with motivating the corporations to adopt more sustainable methodologies. Another critical aspect of BRSR is the dimension of human rights. Companies are expected to declare their stand on the issue related to human rights violations as well as prove themselves committed to ethical labour practice, which includes a hazard-free workplace, fair wage, and the right to join unions. Says Ecovadis, “SEBI wants to instil human rights orientation in Indian corporates by forcing such disclosure.”. It also focuses on integrity within the framework, because organizations are obligated to disclose anti-corruption strategies and policies on conflicts of interest. Emphasis on ethical considerations in business practice builds stakeholder confidence and further strengthens corporate governance within an organization. The most important shift in the reporting framework is the BRSR Core, which will begin to be applicable from July 2023. BRSR Core reporting stipulations imply that a company has to up its ESG metrics in order to gain the seal of verification by an independent assurance entity. This will make information disclosed credible and reduce overestimation of sustainability claims (Money control, 2023). The addition of independent verification to the report will signify the attempt by SEBI to increase stakeholder trust in the accuracy of disclosed ESG information. This is a shifting trend around the world toward higher standards of sustainability reporting and brings to the forefront the mounting importance of reliance on quality data within corporate programs for sustainability. BRSR has profoundly impacted business practices worldwide. Most companies have even taken the regulatory requirement into their business strategy directly as sustainability. It has enabled business organizations to add value to their reputational capital by including such practices in overall business strategies and driving related objectives toward social good (Deloitte, n.d.). For instance, companies are growing willing to invest in renewable sources of power waste-reduction programs, and community development initiatives. The transition towards sustainability appears to go beyond mere compliance with standards at the bare minimum; it is an influential change in the operational practices of organizations operating in India. In addition, BRSR engenders stakeholder engagement because it enhances communicative operations for a company and its stakeholders. Full disclosure requirements will help investors, customers, employees, and communities grasp a company's sustainability better. Since ESG factors are increasingly taken into account in the decisions of more and more stakeholders, companies embracing transparency are likely to have an edge over their competitors in investment and talent acquisition (IRCCL, 2023).

This becomes a lot more significant, especially since consumers are increasingly thinking through the implications of their purchases and are, beforehand, actively searching for brands that correspond to their values. Apart from increasing corporate responsibility and stakeholder involvement, BRSR assumes greater significance in the context of systemic change within the industries. Encouraging every segment to have such a standardized framework for reporting sustainability by SEBI and spearheading collective movement further toward improvement in the sustainability picture as a whole does leave substantial scope for bettering environmental performance on an industry-wide basis. This increased commitment towards sustainable practices is one aspect and this will lead to more companies reporting their progress and studies via BRSR.

3. ESG Mutual Funds

In July 2023, SEBI gave formalized guidelines to asset management companies launching various ESG mutual funds based on a wide array of strategies (Oren, 2023). SEBI explained six strategies that offered an opportunity for diversity of ESG mutual funds, where many would have the freedom to choose the fund with values and visions in tune with their investments (IRCCL,2023). What's more, at least 80% of the total assets under management in such funds need to be invested in equity and equity-related instruments aligned with a chosen ESG approach. This is sure to result in the proper making of funds whose investment goes towards contributing to sustainability rather than some sort of greenwashing (Deloitte, n.d.). This has reflected that SEBI is making many changes in the Indian financial system to promote sustainability and have more finance to solve ESG issues.

4. Reserve Bank of India (RBI) Initiatives for Green Finance

RBI has always been an advocate for sustainable finance in India. It understands that financial institutions occupy a very central position in the quest to mitigate climate change and in building a green economy. RBI framework for green finance 2023, through various initiatives that include. Priority Sector Lending is tasked with integrating renewable energy projects, increasing green finance, and mitigating climate risks.

4.1. Green Finance Framework

In April 2023, the RBI issued a detailed Framework for Green Finance, effective June 1, 2023. It facilitates the acceptability of green deposits by regulated entities (RE) like banks and Non-Banking Financial Companies, thereby providing a separate source of funding for environmentally sustainable projects. The design allows REs to offer green deposits, which are interest-paying deposits kept separately solely for funding specific green projects. The funds generated from these deposits should be invested in efforts that promote environmental sustainability, such as renewable energy projects, energy efficiency development, and climate resilience (NLS BLR, 2023). The Reserve Bank of India has defined the green finance key terms, based on which a "green project" and "greenwashing" can be identified. The definition is very important to prevent funds from being diverted towards any activity that isn't genuinely sustainable while also reducing the risk of misleading claims by financial institutions (Drishti IAS, 2023). The framework is emphasized by its focus on climate-related financial risks. The Draft Disclosure Framework has been produced by RBI in which REs needs to measure and disclose exposure to climate risks. This transparency is expected to enhance accountability within the banking sector regarding its potential vulnerabilities to climate risks (NLS BLR, 2023). The RBI, by sponsoring the green deposit, would also facilitate a flow of credits to green activities and hasten India's transition toward a low-carbon economy. Such activity is not only at a global scale, gathering pace for sustainable finance but also underlines how environmental considerations are becoming relevant in the investment decisions. This framework promises to mark a decisive step in the development of an effective, robust green finance ecosystem that India can nurture into reality towards better finance-and-practice alignment in relationship with sustainability goals.

4.2. Priority Sector Lending (PSL)

It has been an instrument that ensures that the renewable sector of India is getting adequate support and credits from banks to facilitate sustainable growth and development in the country. Since 2015, the PSL has taken renewable projects as a category; there has been a significant ease in getting investments from the banks. This inclusion has been important to reach the target of 500 GW of renewable energy by 2030. Under the guidelines of PSL, borrowers can take a loan up to Rs. Fifty crores for these projects. This has helped to finance large as well as small projects to get finance from various sources easily and move towards sustainable financing (NLS BLR, 2023). Banks also provide loans under lower interest to promote sustainable financing and move towards it aggressively. They also encourage families to take small loans to install solar panels on their roofs and adopt renewable energy solutions. Initiatives under the Framework for Green Finance undertaken by the RBI and enhancements in Priority Sector Lending are steps forward in integrating sustainability into the finance system of India (Drishti IAS, 2023). Green deposits by the RBI would help to grapple with the challenges of climate change and, at the same time, make it easier for renewable energy projects to obtain credit, thereby pushing the cause of responsible investment practices within the banking sector. In doing so, these moves resonate with global trends towards sustainable finance and India's commitment to sustainable achievements of its environmental goals while keeping in mind economic growth. When the regulatory frameworks are implemented by financial institutions, they are likely to create investment drivers toward sustainable development goals.

5. National Green Hydrogen Mission

The National Green Hydrogen Mission was approved by the Union Cabinet of India on 4 January 2023, with a target to place India at the forefront of the world in the production and usage of green hydrogen. The mission was allotted 19,744 crore, or approximately USD 2.4 billion. The mission will achieve a production capacity of a minimum of 5 MMT of green hydrogen every year by 2030, attract above 8 lakh crores, or around USD 100 billion, worth of investments, and reduce imports of 1 lakh crore, or about USD 12 billion, of fossil fuel by the same year (Press Information Bureau [PIB], 2023). Strategic Interventions for Green Hydrogen Transition offers incentives for electrolysis production and financial backing for pilot projects. Financing the novelty technologies in manufacturing and application of green hydrogen. Investment in infrastructural frameworks is required for production and distribution. Engagements involving the government and private sectors, in this case, foster innovation and investments. International Trade Administration, 2023.

Such hydrogen is produced from renewable energy sources and applied for various uses, including the decarbonization of hard-to-abate sectors, energy storage, and transportation. Much has to be done before it's implemented successfully: cost competitiveness, gaps in infrastructure, regulatory framework, and development of the market (HAREDA, 2024).

6. Indian Renewable Energy Development Agency

Indian Renewable Energy Development Agency Limited is important to be able to effectively implement the shift from unsustainable to sustainable energy for India. IREDA is an undertaking of the Ministry of New and Renewable Energy; it is a Mini Ratna Category-I public sector enterprise established in 1987. Its primary mission is the promotion, development, and finance of renewable energy and energy efficiency projects necessary for the country's ambitious sustainability goals (Wikipedia, 2023).

The main core functions of IREDA include facilitating the growth of renewable energy in India. Some of its main functions include financing renewable energy projects in fields that range from solar, wind, biomass, and hydroelectric power. Financial support will be fundamental for newly established projects alongside the scale expansion of existing ones to ensure India harnesses its increase in energy demands sustainably (Interlink Capital, 2023Sustainability practice- The use of concessional loans and attractive terms for funding renewable energy projects to become viable from financial angles. Such a practice aligns with the overall objective of supporting integration of clean energy technologies thereby promoting sustainable growth in various sectors (IREDA PDF Document, 2024).

Apart from providing finance to renewable sources of energy, IREDA also provides extensive support to energy efficiency activities. IREDA ensures that enhancing energy efficiency complements its approach to renewable energy financing thus helping lower the total consumption of energy, at the same time going one step further for environmental sustainability. The agency is responsible for supporting solar manufacturing in India. IREDA is supporting the setting up of solar manufacturing units to reduce dependence on imported solar equipment and strengthen domestic production capability (Money control News Article, 2023). IREDA offers a variety of financing solutions tailored to different types of renewable energy projects. It does not provide direct subsidies but instead competitive finance options to make the projects more appealing to investors. Typically, IREDA finances 70% of the total project cost for eligible projects, while requiring the promoters to make a minimum contribution of 30%. In some cases, especially for repeat clients or specific industries, like solar and wind, it is waived down to 25% (IREDA PDF Document, 2024). Repayment terms of a loan can be up to 20 years, depending on the type of project and the financing deal; a moratorium period can be provided, giving the project time to get functional before repayment (Vajiram & Ravi, 2023). Recent developments have also maintained IREDA's lead in the renewable energy market. In November 2023, IREDA issued an initial public offer (IPO), which listed its equity on NSE and BSE. This will add to its capital base and will help the company to fund bigger-sized renewable energy projects all over the country (Wikipedia, 2023).

Also, IREDA's outreach is not limited to within the country; it has extended its support for renewable energy projects in neighbouring nations. For example, it has come forward to provide finance for big hydropower projects in Bhutan within the collaborative program between the two nations to enhance the capabilities for clean energy. Such efforts not only strengthen bilateral relations but also lead toward regional sustainability goals (Money control News Article, 2023).

7. Maharashtra's initiatives towards sustainability

Maharashtra with itself used as a front runner in the renewable energy market, the state has set up an Integrated Non-Conventional Energy Generation Policy 2020, which was valid up to March 31, 2025. The policy hopes to enable the commissioning of around 13 GW of solar capacity by the end of 2025 through multiple initiatives that complement the positive practices in energy. One of the notable features of this policy is the nature of financial support that is being provided by the Maharashtra state government wherein 30% financial support will be issued for all those projects regarding generation through the medium of solar. The most interesting thing than anything else, however, is the fact that more than INR 100 billion has been sanctioned under the Chief Minister's Solar Agriculture Feeder Program 2.0 through which electricity will ensure the agricultural pumps (Ornate Solar, 2024). Besides all these, the government offers a 40% installation subsidy on a rooftop solar system to household consumers; it also offers Net Metering facilities wherein the user can feed back the excess electricity into the grid. It has surpassed 7.15 GW installed solar energy capacity as of July 2024 and ranks as the second state in India with the total rooftop solar installations as compared to Gujarat (Energetical India, n.d.). In addition to that, the state government of Maharashtra is reportedly setting aside funds for infrastructure development in a solar-based water supply station and a microgrid to enhance energy access in rural areas. The open-access rules defined by MSEDCL have managed to assist consumers with a contractual demand of 100 kW and above in accessing green energy through specific platforms via waste-to-energy plants, according to Mercom India (2024). These huge projects reflect Maharashtra's commitment to a future of sustainable energy.

8. Gujarat's Renewable energy policies

Gujarat is one of the first states to initiate renewable energy policies, particularly concerning solar. The state offers substantial subsidies between 40% to 50% on solar installation to rooftop systems that target residential and small commercial consumers. This motivational factor of subsidy has enabled tremendous paces in adopting solar energy in the state of Gujarat (Novergy Solar, n.d.). The Gujarat Solar Power Policy encourages very large-scale solar projects with a very favourable regulatory framework for developers, with an intent of reaching 30 GW in totality by 2022 to match both grid-connected as well as off-grid systems, encouraging diversified applications of solar power (JJ PV Solar, n.d.). Examples include new financing models by Gujarat, one where it has launched the first of its nature Solar PPA, in which consumers could purchase solar power at a cost several percentages lower than what exists in the current tariffs on electricity. It will be the most feasible option while creating investments in renewable technologies. Strong financial incentives coupled with a positive regulatory environment have made Gujarat the front-runner among other states in the new renewable energy landscape of India, which has attracted heavy investments and set benchmarks for others.

9. Tamil Nadu's Sustainability practices

Tamil Nadu is another key player in the Indian renewable energy mix, largely as a huge potential for wind energy, but increasingly as a leader in solar power. Under its Solar Energy Policy, the state aims to reach an installed capacity of 10 GW by 2023 and offers a subsidy between 20% and 40% for residential as also commercial solar installations as reported by The Hindu, 2024. Net metering policies in the state of Tamil Nadu are very liberal, and thus, consumers who generate their solar power can effectively offset their electricity bills. It also offers feed-in tariffs: guaranteed fixed payments for every amount fed into the electricity supply grid from renewable sources of energy. This attracts investment from developers into projects in renewable energy but is sure to generate stable returns on investments (The Hindu, 2024). The state of Tamil Nadu is also providing financial aid towards agriculture through means of funding to establish solar-powered irrigation pumps. This would reduce reliance upon conventional modes and therefore result in savings in energy and bring forth food in such ways that would facilitate greater environmental goals. Tamil Nadu would make a great contribution to the nation's movement towards energy sustainability with fully developed infrastructure and policies for solar as well as renewable energy.

10. Exim Bank

The Indian Export-Import Bank Exim Bank has recently started a wide-ranging Sustainable Finance Programme and will finance only those investments that are green, transitional, social, and sustainability-linked. This is part of the bank's commitment to supporting the green transition of Indian businesses so that they can compete effectively in world markets by staying true to the climate commitments of the country: Exim Bank, n.d). Perhaps the greatest characteristic of the program is that it has direct financing, where provision for direct finance exists besides refinancing facilities with eligible borrowers involved in sustainable projects. This flexibility, indeed, is critical to businesses seeking investment in environmentally friendly initiatives and technologies. To this end, it supports the exporter in developing capabilities that meet some of the international standards regarding sustainability.

Doing so, Exim Bank nudges into adopting sustainable practices but at the same time enables the exporter to remain competitive across numerous industries (Exim Bank, n.d.). Secondly, the program has integrated performance monitoring by KPIs and Sustainability Performance Targets. Through this means, it ensures the impact of the financed projects is monitored and evaluated in effectiveness; thus, accountability and transparency are promoted in a sustainability effort (Exim Bank, n.d.). As part of the process of integrating Environmental, Social, and Governance considerations with India's financial framework, the Sustainable Finance Programme represents one of the most substantial steps for Exim Bank to take forward. It strategizes an approach by providing focused and result-oriented financial solutions and supporting mechanisms towards promoting a far more sustainable economy to serve immediate enterprise financing as well as long-term environmental sustainability through promoting responsible investment practices (Exim Bank, 2023). Initiatives such as these are, therefore, very much expected to play a critical role in the mobilization of resources and innovation in such green technologies as India continues along the sustainable development path.

So, these are the various initiatives that have taken place in the past few years by the Government of India to promote sustainable finance allocation and as well as promote ESG-responsible activities to save the environment and make movements socially acceptable by all the citizens as well. These policies have led a movement that has made people more responsible towards ESG issues and investing more towards sustainable projects.

Implications

The research paper highlights various initiatives that are taken by the government and various institutions in promoting sustainable Finance in India and also solving various ESG issues prevalent in the country. Policies like Sovereign Green Bonds, Business Responsibility and Sustainable Reporting (BRSR), and many state governments' policies have demonstrated a shift in making sustainability embedded in the cores of the Indian financial system. These measures helped many businesses to align their long-term goals with social and environmental goals by facilitating sustainable economic growth.

The effects of implementing such policies have many dimensions.

1. It is sustainable in an economic sense: Sovereign Green Bonds are anchored among the initiatives that redirect financial flows toward renewable sources, low-carbon technologies infrastructure, and sustainable agriculture practices. This means it is very important for sustainable environmental goals and increased competitiveness in the global green economy.
2. Investor Confidence and Accountability: Accountability through BRSR introduced by SEBI has added transparency to the corporate sustainability practices. It has improved India's attractiveness to foreign and domestic investors. It has reduced the risks of 'greenwash' and established India as a trusted destination for green investments.
3. Structural Transformation of Industries: In such cases, volume allocation for ESG-oriented mutual funds or PSL for renewable energy happens to be man-

dates which lead to systemic changes in industry practice. This systemic change has been combined with well-documented protections the environment policy talks about the development of industries but assures innovative forms will be realized.

4. Social Equity and Inclusivity in Development processes: In this respect, it can be seen that ESG focuses more on the social and governance components as organizations provide equal employment opportunities and respect human rights and every organization ethically makes decisions that are very inclusive in enhancing growth and the well-being of society.

The implications in the conclusion tell us how the financial systems could be transformed with the adoption of mainstream ESGs. This helps India achieve its climate and sustainability objectives but is also a reconsideration of the contribution of financial services in addressing universal issues such as climate change and social disparity.

Gaps in the policies

There are several sustainable finance initiative policies that the government is not addressing properly with rules and regulations. It includes several areas that require improvements and strategic interventions to maximize the impacts identified by your research document. Further details on such gaps may be put into the following:

1. Absence of Consensus on What Constitutes a Green Project

Issue: There is no widely applicable or standardized definition of what constitutes a "green" or a "sustainable" project, which results in ambiguity.

Impact: This is impossible to assess the eligibility and matching of projects with green finance principles and projects by stakeholders that are taking place in the country or not. With this, entities open doors for greenwashing, where they would claim sustainability in the absence of sufficient evidence.

2. Weak monitoring and oversight mechanisms

Issue: Sovereign Green Bonds and ESG mutual funds, it is necessary to examine thorough tracking and assessment mechanisms on the environmental and social impact.

Impact: The lack of robust tracking mechanisms yields hardly any accountability. And the effectiveness of such programs could not be ascertained.

3. Renewable Energy Strategies are limited by Poor Infrastructure

Issue: Major constraints, even though financial policies are always in place to address renewable energy resources, the infrastructure of large-scale implementation of renewable energy still lags.

Impact: This prevents the attainment of renewable energy goals like 500 GW by 2030 and delays the inclusion of renewable energy sources in the country's grid.

4. Overlapping and contradictory regulations

Problem: SEBI, and RBI, among other financial institutions, share the burden with too many agencies leading to disorganization and rivalry among the agencies.

Impact: The ESG mandates and guidelines are risk factors and, therefore, may discourage enterprises from being green in their finance policies.

5. Lack of Focus on Social and Governance Concerns

Issue: The majority of the efforts are so focused on environmental issues that social and governance concerns are pushed back behind the environmental issues in relation to ESG.

Impact: For example, a matter of fair treatment of employees, gender mainstreaming, and community enhancement does not have enough emphasis and therefore lags behind in ESG's overall progress.

6. Small Enterprises are Denied the Ease of Access

Problem: Policies relating to green bonds and ESG mutual funds seem to only benefit big firms and institutional investors.

Impact: Sustainable finance engagement remains challenging for small and medium-sized enterprises (SMEs) since the majority of these businesses lack adequate resources and capacity to engage in such practices, thus increasing exclusion.

7. Costliness of Implementation

Problem: Sustainability practices and technologies require high front-end investments that few organizations can afford.

Impact: This does not allow the organizations to engage in such programs of National Green Hydrogen Mission or renewable energy adoption, especially for cost-sensitive industries.

8. Public Awareness and Participation

Problem: There is an inadequate level of awareness that triggers the appreciation of the public for sustainable finance.

Impact: Weakness of awareness at the individual and community level will eventually dampen stakeholder engagement and delay the diffusion of green finance practices.

9. Funding Gaps in Mega-Scale Projects

Issue: Even though policies exist for financing renewable energy sources and green initiatives, most mega-scale projects have funding gaps since the incentives are not high enough for private investors to consider.

Impact: It causes a delay to essential infrastructure projects, and hence, their scale cannot be expanded.

10. State-Level Disparities in the Implementation of Policy

Issue: States such as Maharashtra and Gujarat are a little ahead, while other states lag in actually implementing sustainable finance.

Impact: Uneven development undermines the national strategy for transition to the green economy.

11. Inadequate Climate Resilience Integration

Issue: There is a poor integration of climate risk assessments into the mainstream of financial systems through policies.

Impact: This raises vulnerabilities for financial institutions and industries exposed to climate-related risks, such as extreme weather events.

12. Lacking Innovation Incentives

issue: Current initiatives do not strongly incentivize innovations in green technologies or sustainable business models.

Impact: This slows down innovation in key areas, such as improving energy efficiency, circular economy practices, and low-carbon technologies.

13. Lack of Mechanisms for Global Collaboration

Issue: India participates in global arrangements like the Paris Accord but fails to integrate more extensive adoption of international best practices into policies from within.

Impact: It has prevented India from leveraging worldwide expertise, funding, and technologies for the development of infrastructure for sustainable finance.

A multi-stakeholder approach involving policymakers, financial institutions, corporations, and civil society would refine the framework of regulations, enhance the infrastructure, promote innovation, and thereby deliver a strong, inclusive sustainable finance ecosystem.

Future Research

The study identifies the most prominent developments in sustainable finance, but it opens paths for further research:

1. Policy Effectiveness Analysis Medium- and long-term effectiveness of policies such as the National Green Hydrogen Mission, Sovereign Green Bonds, and BRSR can be analysed in the future. Such policies being compared between the countries will also highlight what best practices are and which needs improvement.
2. Financing of Green Technology: There is an increased need to place more emphasis on how financial mechanisms can stimulate green technology growth. Alternative funding models, such as green asset-backed securities and portfolios that have climate resilience, will be able to fill funding gaps.
3. Behavioural understanding of ESG investments. Knowing the behaviour of the investors, and how the business group has logical reasoning about compliance, can indeed provide insight into better policy frameworks. Relevant considerations for stakeholder engagement in sustainable finance apply.
4. Regional Policy Impact: The state-level initiatives, like Maharashtra's solar energy projects, and Tamil Nadu's wind energy investments, would be a good terrain for research. Comparative analysis of state policies would highlight effective regional strategies and their scalability.
5. Leapfrogging Policy Gaps. It points out the greenwashing-related limitations and lack of standard definitions for green projects. Such research works can help design overall policy frameworks that bridge those policy gaps while promoting innovation.
6. Social Integration Sustainability Integrate: While environmental sustainability is largely addressed, social dimensions like gender equity, community development, and labour rights are relatively ignored. The socio-economic impact of finance policies on sustainability can be studied and addressed in further research.
7. Monitoring and Reporting Mechanisms: Effective monitoring tools are needed for the impact of green finance initiatives. Further research can contribute to design effective frameworks to track the effectiveness of ESG investments in future days.

8. International comparison: A comparison of the best practices of other global players, including the EU and China, would uncover places and ways in which India's green finance transition might be sped up. Such studies may discuss structures of regulatory regimes, market incentives, and public-private partnerships in other parts of the world.
9. Climate Resilience in Finance: With an increasing climate risk, further research into and integration of climate resilience into the framework of financial risk assessment and management is critical and would include researching the role of insurance and reinsurance in mitigating climate-related losses.
10. Public Awareness and Education: Future studies can look into the role public awareness campaigns play in promoting better ESG investments. What stakeholders and communities perceive regarding sustainable finance may enlighten them on working with them.

Fill these holes, so that future studies could confidently provide necessary actions to policymakers, financial institutions, and businesses, making sustainable finance initiatives in India and other regions more effective.

CONCLUSION

Sustainable finance has emerged as one of the cornerstones in the response to ESG issues while promoting India's economic growth and moving toward a greener economy. The government and regulatory bodies of India emphasize the fact that sustainability is incorporated into India's financial systems. Many of these initiatives include Sovereign Green Bonds, ESG-oriented mutual funds, BRSR reporting framework, and Green Finance Frameworks from the Reserve Bank of India. These policies have led companies to implement more sustainable practices, increased accountability with mandatory ESG disclosures, and have opened means to direct investment towards renewable energy and sustainable infrastructure projects. India is trying to achieve international climate commitment, like achieving net-zero emissions by 2070. With this in mind, it is trying to incentivize green financial practices.

With all these positive trends coming their way, however, the paper at hand highlights some very important gaps that need to be filled to gain maximum results from any sustainable finance initiatives. First off, there is a lack of standard definitions to define green projects, thus making them susceptible to greenwashing and low in credibility among sustainable finance mechanisms. Second, the infrastructures connecting renewable energy adoption are grossly inadequate, such as grid integration and storage facilities. Overlaps and inconsistencies among various regulatory bodies such as SEBI and RBI make the implementation and compliance process complicated at times mar business needs, and operate within ESG requirements. Moreover, the emphasis on environmental considerations is often at the cost of social and governance issues, weakening the holistic development of ESG practices. The space between these goals, therefore, marks an urgent need for policies that are more integrated and inclusive so that sustainable finance initiatives appropriately tackle the larger picture of the spectrum in sustainability goals.

Access is another significant challenge, particularly for small and medium-scale enterprises, as they face obstacles in accessing sustainable finance practices. The transition costs are very expensive while the limited financial incentives are relatively low and most companies are not motivated by these initiations. Huge gaps in large-scale financing combined with uneven policy implementation at the regional level also demand equitable sharing of resources and opportunities. Other regional areas now lag behind Maharashtra, Gujarat, and Tamil Nadu, thereby providing a differential impact on India's green finance agenda. Low public awareness and participation in sustainable finance are also issues that require earnest outreach programs that educate stakeholders about the value proposition and opportunities offered by ESG alignment.

The Indian government and the regulatory bodies should work on a multi-pronged approach that fortifies the sustainable finance foundation and fills the existing gaps. Standardized definitions for green projects against robust monitoring and evaluation frameworks would surely enhance aspects like transparency and accountability and diminish the risks of greenwashing. Infrastructure investment in renewable energy, for example through the enhancement of grid modernization and storage technologies, is one very important step toward the expansion of adoption. Resonance of the rules regulating SEBI, RBI, and others will make the compliance procedures less cumbersome and augment an even more business-friendly environment for businesses transitioning to sustainability. This would ensure that the ESG initiatives account for social and governance issues within their policy frameworks feeding into broader societal issues, such as labour rights, gender equity, and community development. The extension of access to sustainable finance also needs to be accomplished for SMEs.

Financial incentives such as tax relief or low-interest loans can then be targeted at encouraging the use of greener practices in smaller businesses. Further investment in innovative green technologies will be established through research grants and public-private partnerships to expedite progress toward a sustainable economy. Public campaigns focused on the economic and social benefits of sustainable finance will raise stakeholder interest and mobilize businesses and individuals toward ESG goals. Steps in this regard would target investment and capacity building in regional markets so that the roll-out of interventions in green finance is well-balanced and without disparities in the regions.

International cooperation and knowledge sharing can also help adequately play a strengthening role in India's ecosystem for sustainable finance. Learning the success models of countries such as the EU and China will be helpful for India in adopting best practices and innovative approaches in its policy regime. Climate resilience included in the processes of financial risk assessments would make the financial sector stronger in addressing climate-related vulnerabilities. Therefore, these steps will both accelerate India's transition to a green economy and sustain the country as the world's leader in sustainable development.

Thus, filling the gaps and challenges as outlined in this paper holds the secret to getting the maximum benefits from India's commendable advancement in promoting sustainable finance. From such an endeavour, a perfect ecosystem for sustainable finance will be developed to support economic growth, mitigate climate risks, and yield social equity from the government and regulatory bodies. It would not only help India achieve its sustainability goals but also establish a precedent for other developing nations across the world that are seeking economic development with environmental and social accountability. In this context, sustainable finance may well redefine the economic landscape of India towards a greener, more equitable future.

SUMMARY

Given the urgent need for managing pressing ESG issues, sustainable finance has emerged as a necessary tool. It is also poised to become a precursor to sustainable long-term economic stability. It is in this context that the Indian government and financial institutions have initiated a variety of steps to induct sustainability into the country's financial framework thus far. This paper examines these efforts in the form of policies such as Sovereign Green Bonds, Business Responsibility and Sustainability Reporting (BRSR), and the Reserve Bank of India's Green Finance Framework. Aligning financial practices with climate goals for India, set at either 500 GW of renewable energy capacity by 2030 or achieving net-zero emissions by 2070, level policies in Maharashtra, Gujarat, and Tamil Nadu emphasize regional leadership in the adoption of renewable energy technologies through subsidies, innovative financing models, and infrastructural development.

Sovereign Green Bonds have been launched in 2023 to fund renewable energy, clean transportation, and other initiatives with great strides. The SEBI BRSR is a matching frame in this angle, enforcing disclosure requirements on ESG information among the Top 1,000 listed companies in India. Similarly, SEBI has also developed ESG-focused mutual funds under strict parameters and serviced investment towards truly sustainable undertakings. Besides, the Reserve Bank of India has taken sustainability finance by embracing a green finance framework. Here, regulated institutions are granted permission to open green deposits, specifically marked for environmentally friendly projects; and Priority Sector Lending (PSL), which is a type of credit direction toward renewable energy sectors Altogether, this gives a starting point for the embedment of sustainability at the core of India's financial system and encourages the long-term practice of businesses and investors.

On the other hand, much remains to be filled in these initiative gaps. One critical gap remains: there is no standardized definition of green projects, which creates confusion and a tendency toward more risk associated with a phenomenon called greenwashing, whereby parties falsely claim to comply with sustainability standards. Further, infrastructure inadequacy in the integration of renewable energy into the national grid hampers the scalability of sustainable finance. The system of regulatory differentiation makes the process more complicated and confusing for businesses wanting to align with ESG standards on the part of organizations like SEBI and RBI. Along with that, though policies are fundamentally a set of environmental, social, and governance elements, fair labour practices, gender balance, and responsible governance find less representation and thus significantly cause hindrances to balanced ESG developments.

Accessibility problems still prevail especially for SMEs owing to the restrictions they face in getting finance under green finance schemes. Transitioning to sustainable ways is expensive and there is little incentive for green technological innovation, thereby exacerbating the accessibility issues. Public interest and awareness regarding sustainable finance had been extremely low leading to poor participation of stakeholders and slower growth in adoption rates. Huge financing gaps for large projects and regional imbalances in the implementation of policies would require a more streamlined national approach incorporating greater inclusions. The states of Maharashtra, Gujarat, and Tamil Nadu have led with renewable energy policies while other regions lag in stark examples of uneven development.

Regulatory coherence would be on the focus areas, evolving robust mechanisms for monitoring and clear definitions for green projects. More incentives should be accorded to SMEs. Green technologies must be developed and factored into policy frameworks. Social and governance considerations need greater expression in policy frameworks. Greater public awareness will further lead to increased community and investor engagement in sustainable finance initiatives. India will further enhance its sustainable finance ecosystem by engaging in global collaborations, incorporating climate resilience in financial risk analysis, elevating public awareness campaigns, and further efforts toward enhanced investment in sustainable finance. Such efforts will take India forward to drive faster toward a green economy and propel India as the global leader in sustainable development.

CHAPTER SUMMARY

Policy-Driven Transition: The chapter outlines a concerted, top-down effort by the Indian government (Union and State), the Reserve Bank of India (RBI), and the Securities and Exchange Board of India (SEBI) to integrate Environmental, Social, and Governance (ESG) considerations into the core of the country's financial system.

Key Regulatory Instruments: Major initiatives include the issuance of Sovereign Green Bonds to fund public green projects; SEBI's mandatory Business Responsibility and Sustainability Reporting (BRSR) for enhanced corporate transparency; and the RBI's Framework for Green Deposits and inclusion of renewable energy under Priority Sector Lending (PSL).

Strategic National Missions: Large-scale projects like the National Green Hydrogen Mission and the role of institutions like the Indian Renewable Energy Development Agency (IREDA) are highlighted as pivotal for achieving India's long-term decarbonization and energy security goals.

Regional Leadership: The chapter notes the proactive role of states like Maharashtra, Gujarat, and Tamil Nadu, which have advanced the adoption of renewable energy through subsidies, innovative financing models, and supportive policies, though this has led to regional disparities.

Identification of Systemic Gaps: A critical analysis reveals significant implementation challenges, including the absence of a standardized definition for *"green"* activities, risks of greenwashing, regulatory overlaps, inadequate infrastructure, and a predominant focus on the *"Environmental"* pillar at the expense of *"Social"* and *"Governance"* aspects.

Call for an Integrated Approach: The conclusion emphasizes the need for a more cohesive, inclusive, and robust policy framework that addresses the identified gaps to fully realize the potential of sustainable finance in supporting India's economic growth and climate commitments.

Chapter Questions

True and False Questions

1. The Business Responsibility and Sustainability Reporting (BRSR) is a voluntary initiative that companies can choose to adopt for brand enhancement.
2. The proceeds from India's Sovereign Green Bonds are exclusively dedicated to financing projects with clear environmental benefits.
3. The Reserve Bank of India's (RBI) Priority Sector Lending (PSL) guidelines exclude renewable energy projects.

4. A key challenge identified in the chapter is the lack of a standardized, nationwide definition for what qualifies as a *"green project."*
5. The National Green Hydrogen Mission has a target production capacity of 10 MMT per year by 2030.
6. SEBI's guidelines for ESG mutual funds require that at least 80% of the assets under management be invested in line with the fund's stated ESG strategy.
7. The chapter concludes that social and governance issues are currently given equal emphasis as environmental issues in India's ESG policies.
8. The RBI's Green Deposit Framework is designed to prevent greenwashing by ensuring funds are allocated to genuinely sustainable projects.
9. According to the chapter, small and medium enterprises (SMEs) find it easier to access green finance compared to large corporations.
10. State-level initiatives, such as those in Maharashtra and Gujarat, are presented as uniformly successful with no significant implementation challenges.

Multiple Choice Questions

11. The Securities and Exchange Board of India (SEBI) made the Business Responsibility and Sustainability Reporting (BRSR) framework mandatory for the top listed companies from which fiscal year?
    A) 2020-21
    B) 2021-22
    C) 2022-23
    D) 2023-24
    E) It remains a voluntary initiative
12. According to the chapter, which of the following is a primary objective of India's Sovereign Green Bonds?
    A) To reduce the fiscal deficit
    B) To finance the country's defence infrastructure
    C) To fund environmentally sustainable projects and support climate goals
    D) To provide direct subsidies to consumers for purchasing electric vehicles
    E) To replace all existing forms of public debt
13. The Reserve Bank of India's (RBI) Framework for Green Finance allows which of the following entities to accept "green deposits"?
    A) Only the Ministry of Finance
    B) All publicly traded companies
    C) Regulated Entities (REs) like banks and Non-Banking Financial Companies (NBFCs)
    D) Only foreign institutional investors
    E) State-level municipal corporations

14. Which of the following is identified in the chapter as a significant gap that can lead to *"greenwashing"?*
    A) An overabundance of monitoring mechanisms
    B) High public awareness and participation
    C) The lack of a standardized definition for *"green"* projects
    D) Strong regulatory cohesion between SEBI and RBI
    E) Excessive funding for small and medium enterprises (SMEs)
15. The National Green Hydrogen Mission aims to attract investments worth approximately how much by 2030?
    A) 1 lakh crore
    B) 8 lakh crore
    C) 19,744 crore
    D) 50,000 crore
    E) 5 lakh crore
16. A key function of the Indian Renewable Energy Development Agency (IREDA), as described in the chapter, is:
    A) To set national electricity tariffs
    B) To provide direct consumer subsidies for solar panels
    C) To finance renewable energy and energy efficiency projects
    D) To regulate the stock market listings of energy companies
    E) To manage India's crude oil imports
17. The chapter highlights that a major challenge for the widespread adoption of renewable energy in India is:
    A) A lack of technological availability
    B) Poor infrastructure, such as grid integration and storage
    C) Overly strict definitions for green projects
    D) An excess of private investment
    E) Uniform policy implementation across all states
18. Which pillar of ESG does the chapter argue is often overshadowed by the environmental focus in current Indian policies?
    A) The Economic pillar
    B) The Technological pillar
    C) The Social and Governance pillars
    D) The Ethical pillar
    E) The Cultural pillar
19. According to the chapter, what is a specific barrier that Small and Medium Enterprises (SMEs) face in engaging with sustainable finance?
    A) They are legally prohibited from applying for green financing.
    B) They receive too many financial incentives, creating a burden.
    C) They lack the resources and capacity to meet compliance requirements.

D) They are the primary focus of most green bond proceeds.
E) They are exempt from BRSR reporting.

20. The EXIM Bank's Sustainable Finance Programme, as discussed in the chapter, includes which of the following features?
    A) Direct financing and refinancing for sustainable projects
    B) Mandatory equity investment in fossil fuel companies
    C) A focus solely on social projects, excluding environmental ones
    D) Exclusively serving micro-enterprises
    E) Providing interest-free loans to all applicants

Short Answer Questions

21. Briefly state the primary purpose of SEBI's Business Responsibility and Sustainability Reporting (BRSR) framework.
22. What are the two main types of risks that the chapter associates with climate change for the Indian financial sector?
23. Name two specific project categories that are eligible for funding through the proceeds of Sovereign Green Bonds.
24. What is the stated purpose of the RBI's Green Deposit Framework?
25. Identify one key challenge and one key opportunity presented by the National Green Hydrogen Mission, as per the chapter.
26. How does the inclusion of renewable energy under Priority Sector Lending (PSL) aim to support India's sustainability goals?
27. What does the chapter identify as a consequence of regulatory fragmentation among institutions like SEBI and RBI?
28. Why is the lack of public awareness considered a gap in promoting sustainable finance in India?

Essay Questions

29. Analyze the role of the Securities and Exchange Board of India (SEBI) in shaping corporate India's approach to sustainability. Your answer should discuss the BRSR framework and the regulations for ESG mutual funds.
30. Compare and contrast the initiatives taken by the Reserve Bank of India (RBI) with those of a state government (e.g., Maharashtra or Gujarat) in promoting sustainable finance. What are the distinct levels of focus and instruments used by these entities?
31. Explain the term "*greenwashing*" in the context of sustainable finance. Why is it a significant risk, and what measures have Indian regulators (e.g., SEBI and RBI) introduced to mitigate this risk?

32. Describe the multi-stakeholder approach required to address the gaps identified in the chapter, such as the lack of a green definition and poor infrastructure. Provide specific examples of actions needed from policymakers, financial institutions, and corporations.
33. Critique the argument that India's current sustainable finance policies are predominantly environmentally focused. To what extent do these policies address the *"Social"* and *"Governance"* components of ESG? Support your answer with evidence from the chapter.
34. Elaborate on the significance of the National Green Hydrogen Mission and the Indian Renewable Energy Development Agency (IREDA) in the context of India's long-term energy security and decarbonization strategy.

Questions for Graduate Students (Requiring Further Research)

35. ***Comparative Policy Analysis:*** Conduct a comparative analysis of the green bond frameworks of India and another developing economy (e.g., China or Indonesia). Evaluate the differences in eligibility criteria, verification processes, and reported impacts. What lessons can India learn?
36. ***SME Access to Finance:*** Propose a detailed policy or financial product designed specifically to improve access to sustainable finance for Small and Medium Enterprises (SMEs) in India. Justify your proposal by referencing the specific barriers faced by SMEs as outlined in the chapter.
37. ***Lifecycle Assessment of a Green Bond:*** Track a specific project funded by India's Sovereign Green Bonds. Research and analyze its projected versus actual environmental and social impact, its contribution to India's NDCs, and the challenges encountered during implementation.
38. ***Behavioral Economics of ESG Investing:*** Design a research study to investigate the behavioral drivers and barriers for Indian retail investors when considering ESG-focused mutual funds. What factors (e.g., financial literacy, perceived returns, values alignment) most significantly influence their investment decisions?
39. ***State-Level Policy Diffusion:*** Select one of the leading states (Maharashtra, Gujarat, or Tamil Nadu) and one lagging state in renewable energy adoption. Analyze the political, economic, and institutional factors that explain the disparity in their policy implementation and outcomes.

Questions for PhD Scholars (Requiring Extensive Further Research)

40. ***The Political Economy of Sustainable Finance Regulation:*** Employ a political economy lens to deconstruct the power dynamics and interest groups influencing

the formulation of sustainable finance policies in India. How do the competing interests of industrial conglomerates, public sector undertakings, civil society, and different government ministries shape the final regulatory output, particularly in balancing economic growth with environmental stringency?

41. ***Discursive Analysis of "Green" in Indian Finance:*** Perform a critical discourse analysis of official documents from the RBI, SEBI, and the Ministry of Finance pertaining to sustainable finance. How is the concept of "green" constructed, and what underlying ideologies (e.g., ecological modernization, green growth) does this discourse reveal? Does this discourse inherently privilege certain economic actors and marginalize alternative, more radical conceptions of sustainability?
42. ***Institutional Isomorphism in Emerging Markets:*** Investigate the phenomenon of institutional isomorphism in the adoption of sustainable finance frameworks. To what extent are India's regulations (like BRSR and the Green Bond framework) a result of mimetic pressure to conform to global standards (e.g., TCFD, ISSB) versus a unique, context-specific response to domestic pressures? What are the implications of this for the effectiveness and local relevance of these policies?

Questions for Post-Doctoral Researchers (Direction for High-Impact Research)

43. ***Theorizing a Southern Epistemology of Sustainable Finance: Moving*** beyond Western models, this research program would aim to develop a novel theoretical framework for sustainable finance grounded in the specific socio-ecological realities and philosophical traditions of the Global South, using India as a primary case. It would explore concepts like *"dharma"* (duty), *"trusteeship,"* and *"circularity"* as foundational principles for an alternative financial epistemology that challenges the hegemony of the shareholder primacy model.
44. ***Quantifying the S&G Externalities:*** Design and implement a large-scale, longitudinal research project to develop and test a set of robust, quantifiable metrics for measuring the *"Social"* and *"Governance"* externalities of corporate activity in India. The goal would be to create a validated *"S-G Score"* that can be integrated into financial risk models and pricing mechanisms, thereby forcing the market to account for these currently neglected costs and benefits.
45. ***Modeling Systemic Transition Risks:*** Develop a sophisticated, multi-sectoral system dynamics model to simulate the second and third-order effects of a rapid, policy-driven green transition on the Indian economy. The model would aim to identify potential systemic financial risks, such as the stranding of assets in high-carbon sectors, labor market dislocations, and supply chain disruptions,

providing a critical tool for pre-emptive and just transition planning by policy-makers and financial regulators.

REFERENCES

Agrawal, R., Agrawal, S., Samadhiya, A., Kumar, A., Luthra, S., & Jain, V. (2024). Adoption of green finance and green innovation for achieving circularity: An exploratory review and future directions. *Geoscience Frontiers*, *15*(4), 101669. DOI: 10.1016/j.gsf.2023.101669

Bhattacharyya, U. (2023, April 19). Understanding the regulatory framework for sustainable finance in India. NLS Business Law Review. https://www.nlsblr.com/post/understanding-the-regulatory-framework-for-sustainable-finance-in-india

Deloitte. *Business responsibility and sustainability report:* (2024, January 3). Deloitte India. https://www2.deloitte.com/in/en/pages/finance/articles/business-responsibility-and-sustainability-report.html

Chiu, I. H., Lin, L., & Rouch, D. (2022). Law and regulation for sustainable finance. *European Business Organization Law Review*, *23*(1), 1–7. DOI: 10.1007/s40804-021-00230-2

India, E. "Maharashtra's Solar Surge: Powering RE Growth with Solar Energy - Asia Pacific | Energetica India Magazine." *Energetica India Magazine, India Energy News, Renewable Energy News, Conventional Power Generation, Companies Guide...*, 5 Sept. 2024, www.energetica-india.net/news/maharashtras-solar-surge-powering-re-growth-with-solar-energy. Accessed 23 Nov. 2024.

India incorporates green bonds into its climate finance strategy. (2023, June 12). World Bank Blogs. https://blogs.worldbank.org/en/climatechange/india-incorporates-green-bonds-its-climate-finance-strategy

India's debut in the sovereign green bond market: First deal landed a greenium! (2023, March 7). Climate Bonds Initiative. https://www.climatebonds.net/2023/03/india%E2%80%99s-debut-sovereign-green-bond-market-first-deal-landed-greenium

Indian capital market regulator's updated green debt guidelines: Unlocking the potential of sustainable finance. (n.d.). IEEFA | Institute for Energy Economics and Financial Analysis. https://ieefa.org/resources/indian-capital-market-regulators-updated-green-debt-guidelines-unlocking-potential

Indian Express. (2023, October 4). *Every state, UT saw extreme weather event on at least 1 day in 2023: Report*. The Indian Express. https://indianexpress.com/article/india/every-state-ut-saw-extreme-weather-event-on-at-least-1-day-in-2023-report-9186013/

Kemfert, C., & Schmalz, S. (2019). Sustainable finance: Political challenges of development and implementation of framework conditions. *Green Finance, 1*(3), 237–248. DOI: 10.3934/GF.2019.3.237

Lee, J. W. (2020). Green finance and sustainable development goals: The case of China. *The Journal of Asian Finance, Economics and Business, 7*(7), 577–586. DOI: 10.13106/jafeb.2020.vol7.no7.577

Hareda. (2024). "NATIONAL GREEN HYDROGEN MISSION l New & Renewable Energy Department l India." *Hareda.gov.in*, hareda.gov.in/national-green-hydrogen-mission/

"NATIONAL GREEN HYDROGEN MISSION (NGHM)." *Pib.gov.in*, 2024, pib.gov.in/PressReleaseIframePage.aspx?PRID=2039091. Accessed 23 Nov. 2024.

Nugroho, L., Badawi, A., & Hidayah, N. (2019). Discourses of sustainable finance implementation in Islamic bank (Cases studies in bank Mandiri Syariah 2018). *International Journal of Financial Research, 10*(6), 108. DOI: 10.5430/ijfr.v10n6p108

Priyadarshan, P., & Parulekar, A. (2023, August 15). *SEBI's expansion of ESG mutual funds schemes: Demystifying its implications*. IRCCL. https://www.irccl.in/post/sebi-s-expansion-of-esg-mutual-funds-schemes-demystifying-its-implications

Rebello, A. (2024, July 4). *BRSR reporting in India: Full form, applicability, format, guidelines, benefits*. cleartax. https://cleartax.in/s/brsr-reporting

Sebi puts in place regulatory framework for value chain ESG disclosures for listed entities. (2023, July 12). Moneycontrol._https://www.moneycontrol.com/news/business/sebi-puts-in-place-regulatory-framework-for-value-chain-esg-disclosures-for-listed-entities-10948501.html

SEBI's vision for ESG in India: A strategic roadmap for sustainability and transparency. (2024, November 19). Oren - The Enterprise Sustainability Platform. https://www.orennow.com/blog/sebis-vision-for-esg-in-india-a-strategic-roadmap-for-sustainability-and-transparency

Setyowati, A. B. (2020). Governing sustainable finance: Insights from Indonesia. *Climate Policy*. Advance online publication. DOI: 10.1080/14693062.2020.1858741

ISP. (2024, May 21). Sovereign green bonds: Fueling India's sustainability Indian School of Public Policy -. https://www.ispp.org.in/sovereign-green-bonds-fuelling-indias-sustainability-revolution/

Srivastava, S., & Trivedi, S. (2023). *Indian capital market regulator's updated green debt guidelines: Unlocking the potential of sustainable finance*. Institute for Energy Economics and Financial Analysis.

UNICEF. Climate Change and environmental sustainability. (2021). https://www.unicef.org/india/what-we-do/climate-change

United Nations Environment Programme (UNEP). (2011). Towards a green economy: Pathways to sustainable development and poverty eradication - A synthesis for policy makers. UNEP. Retrieved from https://www.unep.org/greeneconomy

KEY TERMS AND DEFINITIONS

Business Responsibility and Sustainability Reporting (BRSR):: A mandatory disclosure framework introduced by the Securities and Exchange Board of India (SEBI) for the top 1,000 listed companies in India. It requires comprehensive reporting on a company's performance across environmental, social, and governance parameters to enhance corporate transparency and accountability.

Environmental, Social, and Governance (ESG):: A set of non-financial criteria used to evaluate a company's ethical impact and sustainable practices. Environmental criteria consider a company's stewardship of nature; social criteria examine how it manages relationships with employees, suppliers, and communities; and governance deals with leadership, audits, and shareholder rights.

Green Finance Framework (RBI):: A set of guidelines issued by the Reserve Bank of India that allows regulated entities (like banks and NBFCs) to accept *"green deposits."* The proceeds from these deposits are earmarked for funding eligible projects and activities that promote energy efficiency, renewable energy, and climate change mitigation.

Greenwashing:: The practice of making misleading or unsubstantiated claims about the environmental benefits of a product, service, or company policy to present a false image of environmental responsibility.

Priority Sector Lending (PSL):: A mandate by the Reserve Bank of India (RBI) requiring scheduled commercial banks to allocate a specified portion of their lending to specific sectors of the economy deemed important for development, which now includes renewable energy projects.

Sovereign Green Bonds:: Debt instruments issued by a national government to raise capital exclusively for funding public sector projects with clear environmental benefits, such as renewable energy, pollution prevention, and climate resilience.

Sustainable Finance:: The practice of incorporating environmental, social, and governance (ESG) criteria into financial services and investment decision-making. It aims to support economic growth while reducing pressures on the environment and addressing social goals.

TEACHING NOTE

Chapter Synopsis

This chapter presents a critical examination of India's strategic, multi-layered policy framework designed to integrate Environmental, Social, and Governance (ESG) considerations into the core of its financial architecture. Situating India as a pivotal case study of an emerging economy, it analyzes the complex interplay between the imperatives of rapid economic growth and the urgent need for sustainable, climate-resilient development. The narrative meticulously details the suite of regulatory instruments deployed in this top-down transformation, including the pioneering **Sovereign Green Bonds**, the **Securities and Exchange Board of India's (SEBI)** mandatory **Business Responsibility and Sustainability Reporting (BRSR)** framework, and the **Reserve Bank of India's (RBI) Green Deposit Framework** and **Priority Sector Lending (PSL)** for renewable energy.

Beyond federal policy, the chapter explores the catalytic role of strategic national missions like the **National Green Hydrogen Mission** and institutions such as the **Indian Renewable Energy Development Agency (IREDA)**, highlighting their function in achieving long-term decarbonization. It further acknowledges the proactive, though uneven, leadership of states like Maharashtra, Gujarat, and Tamil Nadu in advancing renewable energy adoption. A significant and defining contribution of the chapter is its unflinching critical analysis, which identifies profound systemic gaps—including the absence of a standardized "green" definition, regulatory fragmentation, risks of greenwashing, inadequate infrastructure, and a concerning marginalization of the "Social" and "Governance" pillars within the prevailing ESG agenda. The chapter concludes that while India's regulatory ambition is clear and analytically rich, achieving its climate commitments and fostering a robust, inclusive sustainable finance ecosystem necessitates a more cohesive, integrated, and equitable policy approach.

Key Learning Objectives

Upon engaging with this chapter, students will be able to:

1. **Identify** the key regulatory bodies (SEBI, RBI) and financial instruments (Green Bonds, ESG Funds) central to India's sustainable finance policy landscape. (**Remembering**)

2. **Explain** the strategic rationale and operational mechanics of flagship initiatives like the BRSR, Sovereign Green Bonds, and the RBI's Green Finance Framework. (**Understanding**)
3. **Apply** the concepts of ESG and greenwashing to analyze real-world corporate disclosures and investment proposals within the Indian context. (**Applying**)
4. **Analyze** the interconnections, synergies, and tensions between federal and state-level initiatives, and between environmental, social, and governance priorities. (**Analyzing**)
5. **Evaluate** the effectiveness of India's policy framework in addressing its dual challenges of climate vulnerability and economic development, critiquing both its advancements and its implementation gaps. (**Evaluating**)
6. **Propose** evidence-based recommendations for policy refinement, stakeholder action, or future research to address identified challenges such as SME access and regulatory coherence. (**Creating**)

Core Themes/Theses for Discussion

1. **The Regulator as a Market Architect:** The chapter posits that Indian financial regulators (SEBI, RBI) have transitioned from passive overseers to active architects, using disclosure mandates, capital allocation directives, and risk frameworks to deliberately shape a market for sustainability.
2. **The "E" versus "S" and "G" Imbalance:** A central thesis is that the current policy drive, while ambitious, exhibits a pronounced skew towards the *Environmental* pillar of ESG, potentially marginalizing critical *Social* (e.g., labour rights, community welfare) and *Governance* (e.g., board accountability, anti-corruption) dimensions, thereby threatening the holistic intent of sustainable development.
3. **The Implementation Chasm:** The analysis reveals a significant gap between high-level policy design and on-the-ground execution, exacerbated by infrastructural deficits, definitional ambiguities ("greenwashing"), and regulatory overlaps, highlighting the critical role of enforcement and capacity building.
4. **The Federal-State Dynamic:** The chapter illustrates how sub-national leadership (e.g., in Maharashtra, Gujarat) can drive innovation and adoption, but also creates regional disparities, raising questions about equity and the need for a cohesive national transition strategy.
5. **Sustainable Finance as a Strategic Economic Opportunity:** Beyond risk mitigation, the narrative frames India's sustainable finance push as a strategic opportunity to enhance global competitiveness, attract foreign investment, and secure long-term energy security, thus repositioning the climate challenge as an economic imperative.

Suggested Teaching Pathway

A four-session structure is recommended to fully unpack the chapter's complexity:

- **Session 1: Foundations & Frameworks (LOs 1 & 2)**
  - o **Focus:** Introduce the global context of sustainable finance and ESG. Delve into the specific mandates and instruments of SEBI (BRSR, ESG Funds) and the RBI (Green Deposits, PSL).
  - o **Activity:** Lecture and Q&A on the "what" and "how" of key policies. Use the provided keyword definitions.
- **Session 2: Analysis & Critique (LOs 3 & 4)**
  - o **Focus:** Facilitate a deep dive into the "Gaps in the Policies" section. Analyze case studies of potential greenwashing and discuss the federal-state dynamic.
  - o **Activity:** Structured debate or small-group discussion on the most critical policy gap (e.g., "Is the lack of a 'green' definition or poor infrastructure a greater barrier to India's goals?").
- **Session 3: Application & Synthesis (LOs 4 & 5)**
  - o **Focus:** Apply learning to practical scenarios. Evaluate the trade-offs in policy focus.
  - o **Activity: "The ESG Policy Simulator"** - In groups, students role-play as SEBI, RBI, a large corporation, an SME, and an NGO to evaluate a ambiguous "green" project proposal and propose one policy amendment to improve the system.
- **Session 4: Creation & Future Vision (LO 6)**
  - o **Focus:** Synthesize learning to propose future-oriented solutions.
  - o **Activity:** Group project where students develop a policy brief or a strategic roadmap for one of the following: (a) Enhancing SME access to green finance, (b) Designing a national standard for "green" projects, or (c) Bolstering the 'S' and 'G' in India's ESG agenda.

Pedagogical Tools & Resources

- **Primary Tools:**
  - o **Case Studies:** Utilize the detailed examples of state-level policies (Maharashtra's solar feeder program, Gujarat's PPAs) as mini-cases for comparative analysis.
  - o **Role-Playing:** The "ESG Policy Simulator" (Session 3) is an effective tool for fostering empathy and understanding multi-stakeholder perspectives.

- Policy Brief Assignment: The capstone project (Session 4) develops research, analytical, and persuasive communication skills.

- **Supplementary Resources:**
    - **Real-World Documents:** Provide students with links to an actual BRSR report from a major Indian company, the RBI's Framework for Green Finance, and a Sovereign Green Bond framework document.
    - **Comparative Data:** Incorporate reports from the **Climate Policy Initiative (CPI)** and **Task Force on Climate-related Financial Disclosures (TCFD)**, as listed in the chapter's "Additional Reading," to benchmark India's progress globally.
    - **Multimedia:** Use short videos or podcasts from financial news outlets discussing the practical challenges and opportunities of ESG investing in India.

1. Pedagogical Approach & Bloom's Taxonomy Integration

This chapter serves as a comprehensive case study on the policy-driven integration of Environmental, Social, and Governance (ESG) principles into a major emerging economy's financial system. The teaching strategy should move students progressively from foundational knowledge to critical evaluation and creative application, aligning with Bloom's Taxonomy:

- **Remembering & Understanding:** Begin by ensuring students can recall key initiatives (e.g., Sovereign Green Bonds, BRSR, RBI's Framework) and understand their basic mechanics and stated objectives. Use the summary and definitions provided.
- **Applying:** Challenge students to apply the concepts to real-world scenarios. For instance, how would a specific company navigate BRSR compliance, or how would a bank implement the RBI's green deposit framework?
- **Analyzing:** The core of the discussion should involve analyzing the interconnections between different policies, the cause-and-effect relationships leading to identified gaps, and the trade-offs between environmental focus and social/governance aspects.
- **Evaluating:** Encourage students to critique the effectiveness of the Indian model. Are these policies sufficient? How do they compare to other nations? The "Gaps" section is crucial for this.
- **Creating:** Push students to synthesize their learning to propose solutions. How would they design a policy to address SME access or create a standardized definition for "green" activities?

2. Core Teaching Objectives

Upon completing this chapter, students should be able to:

- Identify and describe the primary regulatory instruments (SEBI, RBI) and financial products (Green Bonds, ESG Funds) driving sustainable finance in India.
- Explain the strategic rationale behind India's top-down approach to aligning its financial system with climate and sustainability goals.
- Analyze the synergies and tensions between federal and state-level initiatives.
- Critically evaluate the implementation challenges, including regulatory fragmentation, definitional ambiguity, and the risk of greenwashing.
- Formulate reasoned arguments about the relative emphasis on the Environmental pillar versus the Social and Governance pillars within India's ESG agenda.

3. Key Discussion Themes

- **The Regulator as a Catalyst:** The chapter positions SEBI and RBI not as passive observers but as active architects of market transformation.
- **The Balancing Act:** The inherent tension between rapid economic development and the imperative for sustainable, long-term planning.
- **The Implementation Gap:** The divergence between ambitious policy design and the practical realities of execution, monitoring, and enforcement.
- **Beyond the 'E' in ESG:** The critical discussion on whether current policies adequately address social equity (e.g., labour rights, community development) and robust governance.

4. Suggested In-Class Activity

"The ESG Policy Simulator": Divide the class into groups representing different stakeholders: SEBI, RBI, a large corporation, an SME, and a civil society NGO. Present them with a new, vague "green" project proposal. Each group must:

1. Analyze the proposal based on their stakeholder priorities and the current policy framework.
2. Identify the potential barriers and risks (e.g., greenwashing, access to finance).
3. Propose one amendment to the existing policy framework that would make the evaluation and funding of such a project more effective and equitable.

This activity forces application, analysis, and creation while highlighting the multi-stakeholder nature of sustainable finance.

Concise Summary for the Teacher

This chapter provides a detailed examination of India's concerted, top-down strategy to embed sustainability into its financial architecture. It positions India as a critical case study of an emerging economy attempting to decouple economic growth from environmental degradation while addressing social inequities.

The analysis is structured around three core pillars:

1. **The Regulatory Arsenal:** The chapter meticulously documents key federal initiatives, including the issuance of **Sovereign Green Bonds** to fund public green projects; **SEBI's mandatory Business Responsibility and Sustainability Reporting (BRSR)** framework, which forces corporate transparency on ESG parameters; and the **RBI's Green Deposit Framework and Priority Sector Lending** for renewable energy, which channels credit towards sustainable sectors.
2. **Strategic and Regional Drivers:** It highlights large-scale national missions like the **National Green Hydrogen Mission** and the role of institutions like the **Indian Renewable Energy Development Agency (IREDA)** as pivotal for long-term decarbonization. Furthermore, it acknowledges the proactive role of states like **Maharashtra, Gujarat, and Tamil Nadu**, whose subsidies and innovative policies have advanced renewable energy adoption, albeit creating regional disparities.
3. **A Critical Gap Analysis:** The chapter's most significant contribution is its candid identification of systemic challenges. It argues that the current ecosystem is hampered by the **absence of a standardized "green" definition** (increasing greenwashing risk), **regulatory fragmentation** between bodies like SEBI and RBI, **inadequate physical infrastructure** for renewables, and a **predominant focus on the "Environmental" pillar at the expense of "Social" and "Governance"** concerns. It also notes the particular difficulty **Small and Medium Enterprises (SMEs)** face in accessing sustainable finance.

In conclusion, the chapter presents India's journey as ambitious and analytically rich, but one that requires a more integrated, inclusive, and robust policy framework to fully realize its potential and serve as a model for other developing nations.

Key Questions for Class Discussion

1. **(Analyzing)** Beyond raising capital, what are the symbolic and market-signaling implications of the Indian government issuing Sovereign Green Bonds?
2. **(Evaluating)** How does SEBI's BRSR framework fundamentally alter the relationship between a corporation and its stakeholders, and what are the potential unintended consequences for businesses?
3. **(Analyzing)** Compare the approaches of SEBI (focused on disclosure and capital markets) and the RBI (focused on banking sector credit and risk). How do these complementary yet distinct roles shape India's overall sustainable finance landscape?
4. **(Evaluating)** The chapter argues that social and governance issues are often overshadowed by environmental concerns. Do you believe this is an inevitable phase in the development of a sustainable finance ecosystem, or a critical flaw in the current strategy? Justify your position.
5. **(Creating)** Propose a specific mechanism or policy that could effectively improve access to green finance for Small and Medium Enterprises (SMEs), addressing the barriers identified in the chapter.
6. **(Analyzing)** The "greenwashing" risk is heavily emphasized. Which of the current initiatives (BRSR, Green Bonds, RBI's Framework) is most vulnerable to this risk, and which is best equipped to mitigate it? Why?
7. **(Evaluating)** Considering the regional disparities in policy implementation (e.g., Maharashtra vs. other states), what is the federal government's responsibility in ensuring a more equitable national transition?
8. **(Applying)** If you were a CEO of a major Indian listed company, which of the discussed government initiatives would pose the greatest operational challenge, and which would present the most significant strategic opportunity?
9. **(Creating)** Design the core components of a standardized, nationwide definition for a "green project" in India, considering the need for both clarity and flexibility across different sectors.
10. **(Synthesizing)** Looking at the entire chapter, if you had to advise the Indian government on one single policy change that would have the greatest catalytic effect on its sustainable finance goals, what would it be and why?

Note on Sensitivity

When teaching this chapter, instructors should be mindful of several sensitive and nuanced areas:

- **Developational Context:** Emphasize that India is navigating a path unique to a large, diverse, and rapidly developing economy. Avoid framing the challenges purely as failures; instead, contextualize them as growing pains in a monumental socio-economic transition. The tension between poverty alleviation/economic growth and environmental sustainability should be treated with seriousness and not oversimplified.
- **Regional and Socio-Economic Equity:** The disparities between leading and lagging states, and the exclusion of SMEs, are not just policy problems but issues of social and economic equity. Discussions should acknowledge that a "just transition" must include these marginalized entities and regions to be truly sustainable.
- **Cultural and Philosophical Underpinnings:** The chapter implicitly touches upon different value systems—Western vs. alternative models of development. When discussing concepts like "greenwashing" or the shareholder-stakeholder debate, be open to exploring how sustainability is defined and valued differently across cultural and economic contexts. The "Questions for Post-Doctoral Researchers" section, which mentions concepts like "dharma" and "trusteeship," provides a starting point for a deeper, non-Western centric discussion for advanced classes.
- **Political Neutrality:** The analysis of regulatory bodies and government initiatives should be conducted from a policy and efficacy perspective, maintaining academic neutrality and avoiding partisan political commentary. The focus should remain on the structure, implementation, and outcomes of the policies.

Chapter 7
Aligning Shariah-Compliant Investments With Sustainability:
The Impact of SDGs on India's Stock Market

Mohammad Irfan
https://orcid.org/0000-0002-4956-1170
Chandigrah University, India

ABSTRACT

This research explores the integration of sustainability within Shariah-compliant investments in India's stock market, focusing on how SDGs help align ethical and financial practices. Shariah-compliant investments follow Islamic principles, excluding sectors like liquor, gambling, and high-debt companies—aligning with many ESG goals. This paper examines Shariah-compliant stocks and their link to SDGs, showing how they promote sustainable economic growth and ethical values. The study highlights opportunities to advance SDG objectives in responsible consumption, clean energy, and financial inclusion through Shariah-compliant investments. Insights are geared towards investors interested in ethical, sustainable opportunities, emphasizing how Islamic finance can contribute to India's sustainability goals. Findings suggest that integrating Shariah principles with SDGs enhances responsible investment strategies, promoting long-term sustainability in India's capital markets.

DOI: 10.4018/979-8-3693-9714-5.ch007

1.0 INTRODUCTION

Shariah investment has now become an important focus point for investors, policymakers, and financial institutions alike-in the new landscape of global finance: the integration of sustainability into investment strategies. This recognition has become urgent largely because of the rise in acknowledgment of long-term risks and opportunities connected to the categories of ESG factors, along with the world's commitment to achieving the United Nations' Sustainable Development Goals (SDGs) (Ahmed et al., 2015). These trends are further buttressed by the rise of ethical investments, which, within the Islamic camp, is exemplified by the increasing profile of Shariah-compliant investments (Jan et al., 2023a, 2023b). Convergence sustainability, ethical finance, and Shariah compliance offer a unique framework for responsible investing, especially in emerging markets such as India, where financial inclusion and sustainable development are the twin priorities (Chen et al., 2022; Chin et al., 2022). Shariah-compliant investments follow the Islamic finance principles that exclude participation in industries believed to be dangerous or repugnant, such as liquor, gaming, and usurious debt (Irfan, 2021). Investments that promote fairness, transparency, and social responsibility are almost perfectly aligned with many ESG and SDG objectives. The SDGs, adopted in 2015, provide a universal call to action to end poverty and protect the planet with prosperity for all by 2030 (Hunjra et al., 2022; Nguyen et al., 2023). These 17 goals place a strong emphasis on inclusive and sustainable growth, focusing sharply on issues such as climate change, innovation, and reducing inequality. India's stock market currently provides a platform to analyse how Shariah-compliant investments could be considered in the context of sustainable development (Chen et al., 2022; Chin et al., 2022). India, as one of the evolving and booming economies in the world, faces a challenge: sustain economic growth while maintaining environmental and social sustainability. Integrating SDGs into Shariah compliance investments is a way forward that can aid in aligning finance with the ethics and the orientation of sustainability goals- hence framing responsible investing in the Indian market (Ahmed et al., 2015).

The role of Shariah-compliant investment in ethical finance Investments most relying on Shariah-compliant principles are based on the tenets of Islamic finance, which are stipulated to be on the basics of justice, equity, and the prevention of exploitation (Wahab et al., 2023). Such investments prohibit sectors or activities, such as alcohol, tobacco, casino games, and high-interest loans, which are detrimental to society and the environment (Saba et al., 2021). Instead, they invest in sectors that prove to be beneficial to public needs, like health, education, and infrastructure. By avoiding too much risk and speculation, Shariah-compliant investments encourage stability and long-term growth, which puts them in a good position to meet the objectives of sustainable development (Ghoniyah & Hartono, 2020). More specifically, in such areas as responsible consumption, clean energy, and financial inclusion, Shariah-compliant investments very strongly correlate with the SDGs. Negative impacts from certain industries on the environment or their adverse consequences for society determine the avoidance of these industries, thereby supporting the goals toward SDG on healthy living, well-being, climate action, and responsible consumption (Saba et al., 2021). In addition, the focus on a deal-based nature of equity transactions in Islamic finance encourages economic inclusion and further reduces inequality, which is also in line with SDG goals on decent work and economic growth.

This chapter presents a compelling argument for the synergistic potential between Shariah-compliant investing and sustainability objectives within the dynamic context of India's stock market. It successfully establishes a foundational thesis that ethical finance, guided by Islamic principles, is not merely compatible with but can actively advance the UN's Sustainable Development Goals.

1.1 Background

India stands at a critical juncture in its economic trajectory, navigating the dual imperatives of rapid growth and sustainable development. With one of the world's largest Muslim populations and an ambitious national commitment to the SDGs and climate targets, the convergence of faith-based finance and sustainable investing represents a significant, yet under-exploited, opportunity. The Indian capital market, exemplified by benchmarks like the Nifty 50 Shariah and BSE TASIS Shariah 50, has already institutionalized Shariah-compliant investing. However, the explicit alignment of these investment vehicles with the country's broader sustainability agenda remains nascent. This chapter positions itself at this intersection, arguing that the inherent ethical filters of Shariah finance—which prohibit investments in sectors like alcohol, gambling, and high-interest lending—create a natural alignment with SDGs related to health, well-being, climate action, and financial inclusion. The background thus sets the stage for an investigation into how this alignment can be measured, enhanced, and leveraged for national developmental benefit.

1.2 The Importance of SDGs in Shariah-Compliant Investments

The SDGs provide a comprehensive framework for addressing the world's most pressing challenges, including poverty, inequality, and climate change. Financial markets play a crucial role in advancing these goals by directing capital toward sectors that contribute to sustainable development. In this context, Shariah-compliant investments offer a natural alignment with many of the SDG objectives, particularly those related to environmental sustainability and social equity (Jan et al., 2023a, 2023b). In India, the integration of SDGs into Shariah-compliant investments holds significant potential. As a rapidly growing economy with a large and diverse population, India faces unique challenges in achieving its sustainability goals (Wahab et al., 2023). The SDGs offer a roadmap for addressing these challenges, and Shariah-compliant investments can play a pivotal role in advancing this agenda. By aligning Islamic finance principles with the SDGs, India's stock market can offer investors opportunities that are both ethically sound and financially rewarding, while contributing to the country's long-term sustainability goals (Ahmed et al., 2015).

1.3 Empirical Analysis of the Indian Shariah Compliance within the Economic and Financial Landscape

The chapter effectively highlights the empirical reality of Shariah-compliant finance in India, though a deeper statistical dive would further strengthen its case. The existence of dedicated Shariah indices demonstrates market recognition and a baseline of institutional maturity. Empirical evidence suggests that these indices have not only provided viable investment alternatives but have, in certain periods, exhibited resilience and competitive returns, challenging the outdated perception that ethical investing necessitates financial underperformance.

The research warrant is clear: India's unique socio-economic fabric, characterized by a massive population, pressing environmental challenges, and a strong cultural emphasis on ethics, creates a fertile ground for this fusion. The nation's goals, such as achieving 500 GW of renewable energy capacity by 2030 and net-zero by 2070, require colossal capital mobilization. Simultaneously, initiatives like financial inclusion (Jan Dhan Yojana) seek to reduce inequality. Shariah-compliant products like Green Sukuk (Islamic bonds) could be instrumental in funding renewable infrastructure, while the principles of risk-sharing (Mudarabah, Musharakah) can promote more equitable economic participation. The research is warranted by the urgent need to map these synergies, quantify their impact, and create a policy framework that unlocks this dual-advantage capital for national development.

1.4 India's Stock Market and Shariah-Compliant Investment Opportunities

India's stock market has seen substantial growth in recent years, with increased interest from both domestic and international investors. This growth has been accompanied by a rising demand for financial products that align with ethical and sustainability standards. Shariah-compliant investments, which adhere to Islamic finance principles, present a compelling option for investors seeking to balance ethical considerations with financial returns (Ronaldo & Suryanto, 2022). Several indices in India, such as the BSE TASIS Shariah 50 and the Nifty 50 Shariah, have been established to track the performance of Shariah-compliant stocks. These indices offer a benchmark for investors looking to invest in companies that adhere to both Islamic ethical principles and sustainability standards.

Figure 1. heat map image illustrating the alignment of Shariah-compliant investments with sustainability metrics and the impact of SDGs on India's stock market from 2019 to 2023.

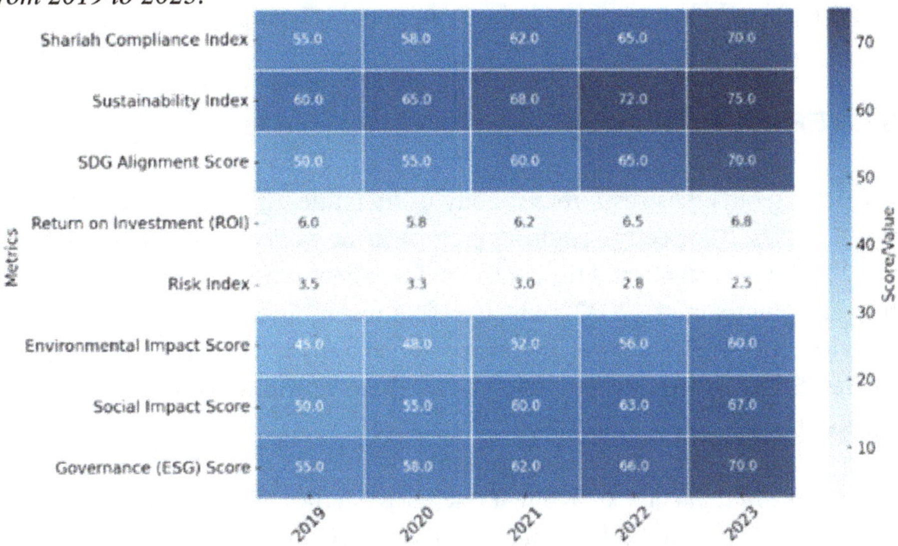

The performance of these indices suggests that Shariah-compliant investments in India are not only viable but can also outperform conventional investments in certain market conditions. By analyzing the alignment of these stocks with SDG objectives, this study aims to provide insights into the role of Shariah-compliant investments in promoting sustainability within India's stock market (Harahap et al., 2023). The research shows that in India, investments that adhere to Shariah are increasingly being matched with sustainable practices. These investments are not just following moral guidelines but also making a greater contribution to SDG-related objectives, as evidenced by the indicators' improvement over time (Jan et al., 2023a, 2023b). This alignment encourages a shift toward initiatives that are both financially feasible and morally sound, supporting a balance between society benefits and financial rewards. India's stock market is progressively adopting an investment philosophy that supports social responsibility, ethical governance, and economic stability by combining Shariah compliance with sustainability (Ronaldo & Suryanto, 2022). A wider range of investors who want to assist the SDGs while upholding the ideals of Islamic finance are probably going to find this trend appealing (Hunjra et al., 2022). Overall, the data shows that the Indian stock market is moving in the right direction toward combining sustainability and Shariah-compliant principles. Shariah-compliant investments that are in line with ethical, responsible, and sustainable practices highlight a larger change in India's financial sector. Shariah-compliant investments can now assist SDG-related goals and provide investors with returns that uphold sustainable and ethical standards thanks to this integration. Consequently, these investments may draw more people who are looking for both ethical and financial benefits, making India's financial industry more robust and inclusive.

2.0 LITERATURE REVIEW

The chapter synthesizes a robust body of literature, drawing from global and regional studies. It correctly anchors its premise in the works of scholars like Ahmed et al. (2015), who established the conceptual link between Islamic finance and the SDGs, and Hunjra et al. (2022), who explored macro-level sustainability drivers. The review effectively cites contemporary research (e.g., Jan et al., 2023a, 2023b; Wahab et al., 2023) to demonstrate the evolving discourse on integrating ESG metrics within Islamic corporate sustainability practices.

However, the review could be sharpened by more directly critiquing the literature specific to the *Indian* context. While it references studies on Green Banking (Chen et al., 2022) and general green finance, a focused discussion on the limited academic work that explicitly ties *India's* Shariah indices to quantitative SDG outcomes would highlight the chapter's original contribution more starkly. The literature establishes a global consensus on the potential, which this chapter adeptly applies to fill a India-specific research gap.

2.1 Theoretic Background and Theory Evolution

The theoretical underpinning of the chapter rests on the confluence of two evolving theoretical streams: Ethical Finance Theory and Stakeholder Theory, as viewed through the specific lens of Islamic financial principles.

The evolution begins with the core, non-negotiable tenets of Shariah law—prohibitions of *Riba* (usury), *Gharar* (excessive uncertainty), and investment in *Haram* (forbidden) activities. This creates an inherent "negative screening" theory of investing. The theory has evolved from a purely compliance-based framework to one that is increasingly interpreted through the objectives of Shariah (*Maqasid al-Shariah*), which prioritize human welfare, justice, and the preservation of the environment.

This evolution dovetails with the modern Stakeholder Theory, which posits that firms are responsible to a broad set of stakeholders, including society and the environment, not just shareholders. The chapter posits that the theoretical framework for Shariah-compliant investing in the 21st century is the integration of *Maqasid al-Shariah* with Stakeholder Theory, thereby creating a powerful, faith-based rationale for pursuing the SDGs. This theoretical fusion provides a robust foundation for arguing that Shariah-compliant investing is intrinsically a form of sustainable and impact investing.

2.2 Shariah Index is related to the SDGs Goals in India Capital Market

The relationship between the Shariah Index and the Sustainable Development Goals (SDGs) in India's capital market is a developing concept where ethical, religious, and sustainability standards intersect.

2.2.1 Shariah Compliance and SDGs

Shariah compliance in investing guarantees that an organization or asset complies with moral standards derived from Islamic law, such as staying away from investments in sectors like gambling, alcohol, or usury (interest-based activities). By 2030, the 17 Sustainable Development Goals (SDGs), which were established by the UN in 2015, seek to eradicate poverty, safeguard the environment, and guarantee prosperity for all. Goals such as Decent Work and Economic Growth (Goal 8), Climate Action (Goal 13), (Irfan, Elhoseny, Kassim, & Metawa, 2023), Peace, Justice, and Strong Institutions (Goal 16), and Affordable and Clean Energy (Goal 7) are among them. Although the SDGs and Shariah principles are two different systems, they do have some similarities, particularly when it comes to social welfare, sustainability, and moral business conduct (Shahid et al., 2023).

2.2.2 Shariah Indices in India and SDGs

Ethical Investments: Shariah-compliant businesses frequently support some SDGs, especially those pertaining to treating workers ethically, producing responsibly, and staying away from dangerous industries. Businesses in the Shariah index, for instance, are less likely to operate in industries like gambling, alcohol, and tobacco, which is in line with SDGs like Decent Work and Economic Growth (SDG 8) and Good Health and Well-Being (SDG 3). According to Jiakui et al. (2023) Sustainability Goals: A lot of businesses that adhere to Shariah prioritize environmental sustainability, which is closely related to SDGs like Climate Action (SDG 13) and Responsible Consumption and Production (SDG 12). For instance, Islamic finance promotes investments in fields that support sustainable economic growth, such as clean technologies, green financing, and renewable energy (Afzal et al., 2022), Al-Roubaie & Sarea, 2019).

2.2.3 Shariah Indices' Impact on SDGs in the Indian Market

Capital Flow and Investor Awareness: The existence of Shariah-compliant indexes might push funds toward enterprises that follow environmental and ethical standards, so inadvertently motivating companies to support the SDGs. Financial Inclusion: By providing investment options that are in line with Islamic principles (Hunjra et al., 2022), shariah-compliant investments can promote financial inclusion in India, which supports SDGs like Decent Work and Economic Growth (SDG 8) and Reduced Inequalities (SDG 10). Governance and Transparency: Businesses that adhere to Shariah are frequently held to higher standards for governance and transparency, which encourages ethical behavior and corporate responsibility. This indirectly advances the SDGs for Industry, Innovation, and Infrastructure (SDG 9) and Peace, Justice, and Strong Institutions (SDG 16). Challenges: One of the primary obstacles is the small number of Indian businesses that completely satisfy the requirements of both Shariah compliance and the SDGs. More data and reporting systems that incorporate both sets of standards are also required. Opportunities: Including SDG measures in Shariah-compliant investing strategies is becoming more and more feasible. Shariah indexes may grow to include businesses that excel in sustainability as more Indian businesses concentrate on SDGs. This would present a chance for ethical investing that also advances global objectives. Shariah indices provide an ethical investing framework in the Indian capital market that is consistent with numerous SDG concepts (Ronaldo & Suryanto, 2022). In addition to upholding the principles of Islamic finance, investors can support social welfare and environmental preservation by funding businesses that are dedicated to sustainability and Shariah (Azad et al., 2022; Ibrahim et al., 2023). By supporting international objectives for sustainable development, this alignment presents a special chance to improve moral investment practices in India (Hunjra et al., 2022).

3.0 METHODOLOGY

The chapter primarily employs a qualitative, conceptual research methodology, leveraging extensive desk research and synthesis of existing literature, reports, and index compositions. The use of explanatory diagrams (Figures 1, 2, and 3) helps visualize the proposed relationships between Shariah principles, SDGs, risk, returns, and market dynamics.

While this approach is effective for building a conceptual model and identifying synergies, the chapter's argument would be significantly empowered by a complementary quantitative or mixed-methods approach. A proposed methodology for future validation could include:

- **Content Analysis:** Systematically analyzing the annual and sustainability reports of companies listed on Indian Shariah indices to map their disclosed activities against specific SDG targets.
- **Econometric Modeling:** Using regression models to test the correlation between the financial performance of Shariah indices and key sustainability performance indicators (SPIs) in India over time, controlling for market volatility.

4.0 DISCUSSION & ANALYSIS

This section synthesizes the core findings of the research, delves into their multifaceted implications, and critically analyzes the position that Shariah-compliant investments are a potent, yet underutilized, catalyst for achieving the Sustainable Development Goals (SDGs) within India's stock market.

4.1 Shariah-Compliant Investments with Sustainability

The experience of combining Shariah-compliant investments with sustainability requires matching the ethical principles of Islamic finance with modern sustainability aims (Hunjra et al., 2022). Investors can now match their financial strategies with environmental, social, and governance (ESG) ideals and religious convictions thanks to this new trend. An outline of this encounter is as follows: Shariah-compliant investments inherently share several characteristics with sustainability, such as: Social Responsibility: The goals of Shariah-compliant finance, such as No Poverty (SDG 1), Decent Work and Economic Growth (SDG 8), and Reduced Inequality (SDG 10), are all centered on social justice, equitable treatment, and community welfare (Azam et al., 2023; Taskin et al., 2023). Environmental Impact: Shariah regulations facilitate alignment with SDGs such as Climate Action (SDG 13) and Responsible Consumption and Production (SDG 12) by discouraging investments in environmentally damaging businesses. Businesses engaged in sustainable agriculture or renewable energy that adhere to Shariah law and are ecologically conscious are highly recognized (Azad et al., 2022; Ibrahim et al., 2023). Shariah-compliant investments guarantee that the invested funds make a beneficial contribution to society by excluding companies that engage in unethical practices (such as alcohol, gambling, and weaponry), which is in line with the Sustainable Development Goals (SDGs) of Peace, Justice, and Strong Institutions (Saba et al., 2021).

4.2 Examples of Shariah-Compliant Sustainable Investment Models

Sukuk, or Islamic Green Bonds, are Shariah-compliant bonds that are issued to finance environmentally friendly infrastructure projects like water conservation, green buildings, and renewable energy (Ahmed et al., 2015). Shariah-Friendly Funds Investing in ESG: In accordance with Shariah regulations, certain Islamic mutual funds and exchange-traded funds (ETFs) concentrate on sustainable enterprises. Companies in the clean energy, healthcare, or educational sectors are among those that these funds invest in because they are dedicated to social and environmental responsibility. According to Jiakui et al. (2023) Green Islamic support: A new field in which Islamic financial institutions offer products that support green initiatives including solar power, wind farms, and clean technologies (Chin et al., 2022).

4.3 Harmonizing Faith and Sustainability: The Next Era of Shariah Finance

Shariah-compliant investing and sustainability are anticipated to become more intertwined, particularly as the demand for ethical investment products and the global drive to achieve the Sustainable Development Goals (SDGs) increase (Azad et al., 2022; Ibrahim et al., 2023). The importance of integrating sustainability and ethical finance to address the world's most urgent issues, such as social justice, poverty, and climate change, is becoming more widely acknowledged by governments, financial institutions, and investors (Shahid et al., 2023).

Investors that combine Shariah compliance with sustainability are not only abiding by moral and religious precepts but also supporting the global movement towards a more just and sustainable future (Wang et al., 2022). The continued advancement of goods and services that combine these two domains has great potential for the future of ethical investing, particularly in nations like India where sustainability and Islamic finance are both priorities (Hunjra et al., 2022; Nguyen et al., 2023).

Figure 2.

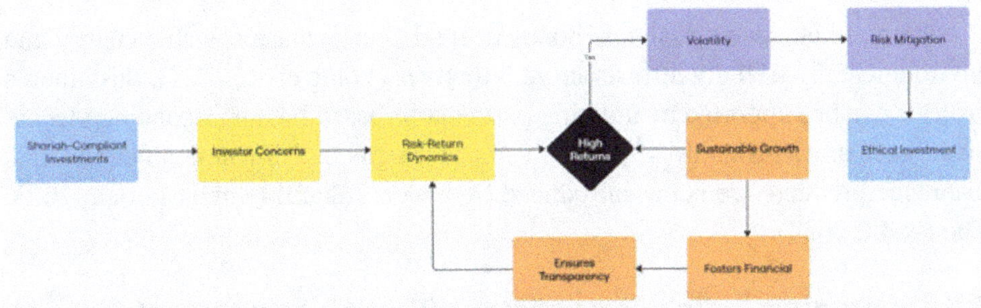

Sources: Author's

The flowchart shows the interrelated dynamics of Shariah-compliant investments and how they relate to risk, high returns, sustainability, investor protection, and volatility. The foundation is Shariah-compliant investments, a framework that upholds Islamic values and encourages moral and socially conscious investing (Hunjra et al., 2022; Nguyen et al., 2023). This strategy adheres to sustainability goals and long-term growth by avoiding speculative or high-risk financial methods and placing an emphasis on stability and transparency (Wang et al., 2022). Through the integration of Sustainable Development Goals (SDGs) and environmental, social, and governance (ESG) considerations, these investments promote a balance between moral obligations and economic outcomes (Azad et al., 2022; Ibrahim et al., 2023).

Important issues for investors are further deconstructed in the chart. With Shariah-compliant investments naturally emphasizing transparency, moral financial practices, and financial inclusion, investor safety is essential (Irfan, Elmogy, Gupta, Khalifa, & Dias, 2024). These guidelines offer protection from unethical behavior, which appeals to investors who respect both financial and moral stability. Simultaneously, risk management is prioritized by concentrating on less volatile industries that adhere to ethical standards, like healthcare or renewable energy. A consistent return trajectory over time is ensured by this emphasis, which lowers exposure to risky investments.

However, with these kinds of investments, striking a balance between high returns and volatility is crucial. Although exposure to some high-yield projects may be restricted by ethical considerations, long-term competitive returns can be obtained by concentrating on sustainable, growth-oriented industries (Shome et al., 2023). By reducing volatility, risk management techniques allay investor worries about market swings. By bringing these components into harmony, the flowchart illustrates how Shariah-compliant investments can build a stable, moral, and lucrative environment, safeguarding investor interests and promoting a sustainable future (Shome et al., 2023).

4.4 Development of Green Shariah-Compliant Products

Green Sukuk: issuing Islamic bonds to fund significant renewable energy and environmentally friendly infrastructure initiatives (Wang et al., 2022). Sustainable projects can be supported by utilizing partnership-based Islamic financing mechanisms such as eco-friendly Mudarabah and Musharakah. Climate-resilient Islamic insurance products are being introduced by Green Takaful (Bukhari et al., 2023; Zhou & Li, 2022).

4.5 Leveraging India's Potential for Shariah Investment

Shariah-Indexed Green Funds: Create funds that invest in businesses that follow Shariah and environmental laws, especially in India's rapidly growing ESG-compliant industries (Wahab et al., 2023). Collaborations with Global Islamic Finance Hubs: Learn and implement best practices by working with nations such as Saudi Arabia, the United Arab Emirates, and Malaysia (Zhou & Li, 2022).

Shariah-compliant investments prioritize moral, just, and sustainable business operations within a structured framework governed by Islamic law. These investments take a different approach by staying away from things that are forbidden by Islamic law, like gambling (maysir), interest-based transactions (riba), and extreme uncertainty (gharar). When their dynamics are thoroughly examined, it becomes clear that risk management, high returns, sustainability, investor protection, and volatility all interact in complex ways. Gaining knowledge of these relationships helps one understand how these investments can prosper in a variety of economic environments while still upholding moral principles (Wang et al., 2022).

4.6 Investor Protection from Risk

The framework of Shariah-compliant investments includes risk management, with methods based on the ban on excessive ambiguity. These frameworks offer a more solid basis for managing financial risks by discouraging speculative activity and guaranteeing that investments are supported by financial assets. Contracts that share profits and losses, such as mudarabah (partnership financing) and musharakah (joint ventures), demonstrate how Islamic finance primarily depends on risk-sharing as opposed to risk-shifting.

This risk-sharing strategy promotes trust and lessens the possibility of financial abuse, which is inherently consistent with investor protection. Shariah-compliance's intrinsic ethical standards further guarantee openness in financial dealings. Because of this interaction, investors have a safety net, which attracts those looking for less risky, morally sound investments (Azad et al., 2022; Ibrahim et al., 2023).

4.7 Sustainable High Return

The possibility for large profits that results from Shariah-compliant investments' emphasis on real-sector, productive activity is one of their main draws. In addition to being in line with Islamic beliefs, investments in sectors including healthcare, technology, renewable energy, and infrastructure also have significant room for expansion. These sectors frequently demonstrate enduring robustness, which boosts the profitability of portfolios that adhere to Shariah.

One fundamental idea that strengthens this dynamic is sustainability. Socially conscious investments that help the environment and the community are given priority in Islamic finance. For instance, a lot of Shariah-compliant funds prioritize sustainable agriculture, affordable housing, and renewable energy initiatives. These investments show that high profits and sustainability are not mutually exclusive but rather reinforce one another by balancing profitability with social responsibility (Shahid et al., 2023).

4.8 Volatility Vs Stability

Shariah-compliant assets have unique qualities that can function as a buffer against sharp swings, even though no investment is completely impervious to market volatility. Avoiding speculative products like leveraged trading and derivatives lessens vulnerability to abrupt changes in the market. Furthermore, these investments' asset-backed structure guarantees a closer link to actual economic activity, acting as an anchor during recessions.

Long-term growth requires financial stability, which is fostered by this strategy. For example, because Islamic financial institutions are conservative and asset-based, they were less impacted by the 2008 financial crisis than their conventional counterparts. The ability of Shariah-compliant investments to reduce volatility while preserving consistent returns is demonstrated by this historical example (Hunjra et al., 2022; Nguyen et al., 2023).

A well-balanced and mutually supporting system is reflected in the interdependence of risk, high returns, sustainability, investor protection, and volatility in Shariah-compliant investments. These investments establish a positive feedback loop whereby strong risk management boosts investor confidence and draws new players to the market by highlighting moral behaviour and actual economic value. High profits, fuelled by profitable and sustainable endeavours, increase their allure, while sustainability initiatives guarantee sustained profitability and conform to worldwide trends toward socially and environmentally conscious behaviour (Chin et al., 2022). Protection of investors increases loyalty and trust, which strengthens market stability, while development potential is enhanced by lower volatility, which is attained by prudent and moral tactics. Sustainability lowers environmental hazards, which promotes financial stability and attracts ethical investors, while investor protection lowers financial risks. These factors work in concert rather than separately.

4.9 The Connectedness of Shariah-Compliant Investments with the SDGs and ESG Goals, Promoting Financial

Sustainability and shariah-compliant investments go hand in hand because they foster long-term social, financial, and environmental advantages. These investments follow moral guidelines that promote social justice, environmental stewardship, and economic equity by staying away from risky sectors and speculative activities (Chen et al., 2022; Chin et al., 2022).

Figure 3.

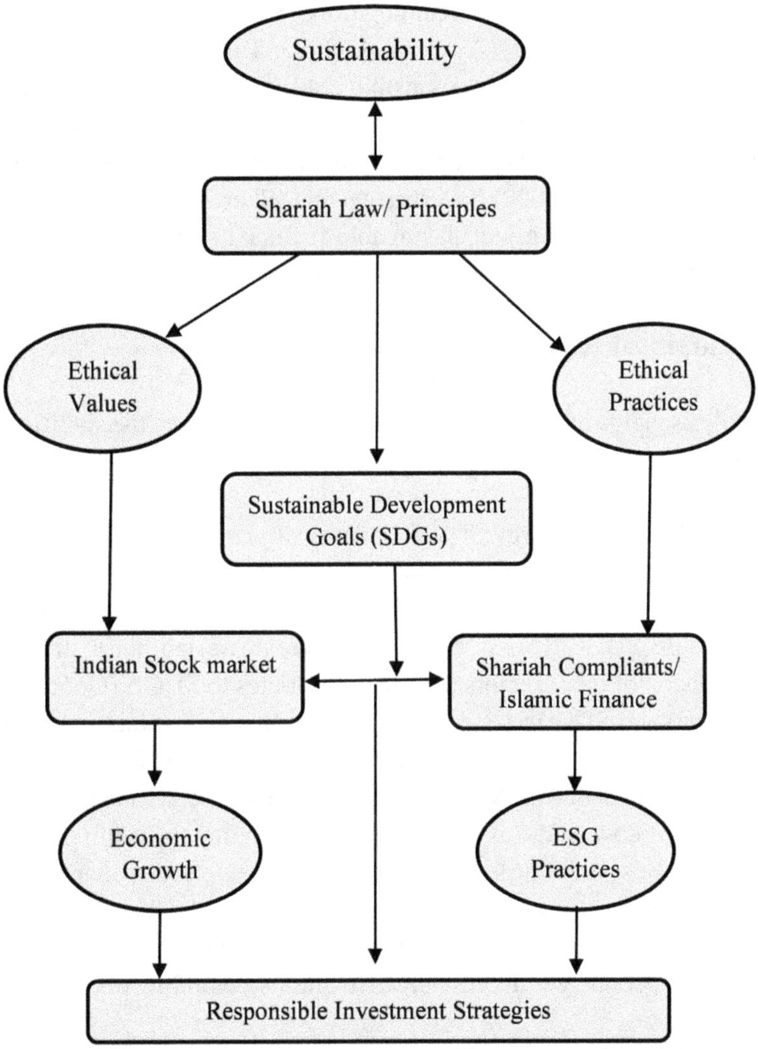

Sources: Author's

Additionally, by emphasizing justice and the welfare of society, they support more general ethical principles that are consistent with Environmental, Social, and Governance (ESG) standards. Investments that adhere to shariah ensure that capital is used properly, which improves financial inclusion and benefits those who are looking for morally sound financial solutions (Shahid et al., 2023). When it comes to the Indian stock market, these investments promote ethical and sustainable economic growth, which propels India's progress while preserving financial stability (Irfan, Elmogy, Majid, & El-Sappagh, 2023). Adhering to the Sustainable

Development Goals (SDGs) allows Shariah-compliant investments to directly support important global objectives including poverty alleviation, sustainable energy, and responsible consumerism (Azam et al., 2023; Taskin et al., 2023). They also support sustainable energy and responsible consumption, which helps businesses lessen their environmental impact and is consistent with ESG standards. Islamic finance ultimately encourages prudent investment practices that sustainability over the long run (Afzal et al., 2022). Investments that adhere to Shariah are an essential instrument in building a fair and sustainable financial system for the future since these tactics promote stability and financial resilience.

5.1 Synthesis of Key Findings

The analysis yields several pivotal findings that underscore the significant alignment between Shariah-compliant finance and sustainability in India:

1. **Inherent Ethical Synergy:** The foundational principle of Shariah-compliant investing—negative screening of sectors like *alcohol, gambling, tobacco, and conventional interest-based finance*—creates a natural and robust alignment with specific SDGs. This is not a coincidental overlap but a structural one. The exclusion of these sectors directly contributes to SDG 3 (Good Health and Well-being) and SDG 16 (Peace, Justice, and Strong Institutions) by diverting capital away from activities detrimental to public welfare and social cohesion.
2. **Strategic Alignment with National Priorities:** The research identifies a powerful convergence between the asset-backed, real-economy focus of Islamic finance and India's most pressing sustainable development needs. Shariah-compliant investments naturally favor sectors such as renewable energy (aligning with SDG 7), infrastructure (SDG 9), healthcare, and education (SDG 4), which are central to the country's growth narrative and its commitments under the Paris Agreement.
3. **Financial Viability and Resilience:** Contrary to the misconception that ethical investing compromises returns, the performance of Indian Shariah indices, such as the Nifty 50 Shariah and BSE TASIS Shariah 50, indicates competitive, and at times superior, risk-adjusted returns compared to their conventional counterparts. This resilience, as illustrated in the conceptual flowchart (Figure 2), is theorized to stem from the inherent risk-mitigation features of Shariah law—the prohibitions against excessive leverage (*riba*) and speculative uncertainty (*gharar*). This fosters greater financial stability and protects investors from the volatility associated with "bubble" sectors, making a compelling case for SDG 8 (Decent Work and Economic Growth) through sustainable and stable capital markets.

4. **The Emergence of a Conceptual Framework:** The chapter successfully constructs a conceptual model (Figure 3) that visually maps the dynamic interrelationship between Shariah Law, Shariah-Compliant/Islamic Finance, the Indian Stock Market, Responsible Investment Strategies, and the SDGs. This model posits that these elements are not isolated but function as an interconnected ecosystem where each component reinforces the others, driving towards the ultimate outcome of financial sustainability.

5.2 Discussion: Interpreting the Findings in the Indian Context

The findings presented necessitate a deeper discussion about their practical implications for India's unique economic and social landscape.

First, the inherent synergy offers a strategic advantage for India. With the world's second-largest Muslim population, there exists a vast pool of domestic capital that remains under-deployed due to a lack of Shariah-compliant options. By actively developing this market, India can unlock substantial domestic investment for its sustainability projects, thereby reducing its reliance on foreign capital and enhancing its financial sovereignty. This directly advances SDG 10 (Reduced Inequalities) by promoting financial inclusion for a significant demographic.

Second, the discussion must address the instrument of Green Sukuk (Islamic green bonds). As highlighted, this instrument is not merely a theoretical concept but a practical solution to India's massive green financing gap. The successful issuance of sovereign or corporate Green Sukuk could channel billions of dollars specifically into renewable energy infrastructure, smart cities, and climate-resilient projects. The discussion here centers on the *readiness* of Indian regulators and financial institutions to innovate and adapt this proven instrument to the domestic market.

Third, the resilience of Shariah-compliant portfolios, while promising, should be discussed with nuance. Their outperformance is often more pronounced during periods of market downturns or high volatility, as witnessed during the 2008 financial crisis. This is attributed to their lower exposure to highly leveraged financial institutions and speculative bubbles. For a volatile emerging market like India, incorporating Shariah-compliant assets could serve as a valuable diversification tool, enhancing the overall stability of the financial system—a key tenet of sustainable development.

5.3. Critical Analysis and Inherent Tensions

While the alignment is compelling, a critical analysis reveals several tensions and challenges that must be acknowledged and addressed.

- **The "Implicit" vs. "Explicit" Contribution:** A critical gap identified is that while Shariah-compliant companies *implicitly* support the SDGs through sector exclusion, there is a lack of *explicit* and measurable reporting on their specific SDG contributions. A company in the healthcare sector is inherently aligned with SDG 3, but without transparent reporting on metrics like affordable drug access or rural outreach, its full impact remains unquantified. This calls for an integration of Shariah screening with robust ESG and SDG reporting frameworks, such as SEBI's Business Responsibility and Sustainability Report (BRSR).
- **Regulatory and Structural Hurdles:** The most significant barrier to realizing this potential is the absence of a dedicated regulatory framework for Islamic finance in India. The current securities and banking laws are predominantly designed around interest-based transactions, creating legal and operational hurdles for profit-loss sharing instruments like *Mudarabah* and *Musharakah*, and for the issuance of Sukuk. Without proactive regulatory evolution from bodies like SEBI and RBI, this market will struggle to mature.
- **Limited Universe and Liquidity:** The stringent screening process can result in a relatively small investment universe, potentially concentrating risk in a fewer number of stocks and impacting portfolio liquidity. This necessitates ongoing development of the market to broaden the range of compliant and sustainable investment opportunities.

6. CONCLUSION

An efficient strategy for accomplishing the Sustainable Development Goals (SDGs) in the Indian stock market is the combination of sustainability and Shariah-compliant investing. Islamic ethical values that prioritize equity, social justice, and environmental conservation are the foundation of shariah-compliant investments. The SDGs' goals are strongly aligned with these concepts, especially those that center on clean energy, financial inclusion, sustainable economic growth, and responsible consumerism. This connection highlights how Islamic finance has the potential to significantly advance India's sustainability journey in addition to bridging the gap between ethical and financial practices (Shahid et al., 2023).

Shariah-compliant investments inherently align with Environmental, Social, and Governance (ESG) concerns since they do not include industries such as gambling, alcohol, or highly indebted businesses. Long-term economic and social value is fostered by this exclusionary process, which guarantees that investments support companies dedicated to ethical and sustainable operations (Irfan, Hussainey, Chan Bukhari, & Nam, 2024). These kinds of practices fit in nicely with India's increasing focus on responsible investing frameworks and its larger commitment to sustainability, which is demonstrated by its alignment with international agreements such as the UN SDG agenda and the Paris Climate Accord (Chen et al., 2022; Chin et al., 2022).

The importance of Shariah-compliant investments in tackling urgent sustainability issues is one of the study's main conclusions. For example, by financing renewable energy projects using cutting-edge methods like green Sukuk (Islamic bonds), these investments can be crucial to reaching SDG 7 (Affordable and Clean Energy). This strategy is in line with India's aggressive goals for renewable energy and its objective of reaching net-zero emissions by 2070 (Jan et al., 2023a, 2023b). In a same vein, Shariah investments can promote SDG 12 (Responsible Consumption and Production) by allocating funds to sectors like eco-friendly manufacturing and sustainable agriculture that place a high priority on waste reduction and resource efficiency.

However, Shariah-compliant sustainable investment growth is not without its difficulties. The ignorance of financial institutions and investors on the connections between Islamic finance and SDGs is a major obstacle. Furthermore, Shariah-compliant investments are not widely adopted in India due to the lack of a specific regulatory framework (Irfan, Kadry, Sharif, & Ullah Khan, 2023). The cooperation of investors, financial institutions, and legislators will be necessary to overcome these obstacles. The creation of cutting-edge financial products, such as Shariah-compliant ESG funds and green Takaful (Islamic insurance), legislative changes, and educational programs are necessary to realize this industry's full potential welfare (Azam et al., 2023; Taskin et al., 2023).

India can improve its ability to combine Shariah principles with sustainable financing by working with international Islamic finance hubs like Malaysia and the United Arab Emirates. India can modify these nations' successful practices and insightful advice, such issuing green Sukuk, to fit its own economic and regulatory environment (Ghoniyah & Hartono, 2020).

Shariah-compliant investments can serve as a link between ethics and profitability, tradition and modernity, as India attempts to strike a balance between its obligations to the environment and society and its rapid economic development (Azad et al., 2022; Ibrahim et al., 2023). India can create a robust financial system, advance its SDG goals, and contribute to a more sustainable and equitable future by utilizing the synergies between Islamic finance and sustainability. This integration is essential to developing a financial system that supports national and international sustainability goals, not just a choice.

In conclusion, the results and analysis confirm the powerful theoretical and practical alignment between Shariah-compliant investments and India's SDG agenda. The discussion elevates this from a niche ethical choice to a strategic national opportunity for mobilizing capital, enhancing financial stability, and promoting inclusive growth. However, the full potential of this synergy will remain untapped without concerted efforts to bridge the critical gaps in regulation, reporting, and financial product innovation. The following section will translate these findings and analyses into concrete recommendations for stakeholders.

Recommendation for Stakeholders and Regulating Agencies

For Securities and Exchange Board of India (SEBI): Develop a comprehensive regulatory framework for issuing and listing Green Sukuk in India. Integrate SDG-alignment metrics into the existing Business Responsibility and Sustainability Reporting (BRSR) framework and provide guidance for Shariah-compliant entities on how to report against them.

For Reserve Bank of India (RBI): Consider guidelines for Islamic banking windows or products that explicitly support green financing and financial inclusion, aligning with national priorities.

For Asset Management Companies (AMCs): Create and launch innovative financial products such as "SDG-Aligned Shariah ETFs" that specifically target companies contributing to clean energy, affordable healthcare, and sustainable infrastructure.

For Industry Bodies (e.g., Association of Muslim Professionals): Launch investor awareness campaigns to educate the public on the dual benefits—religious compliance and sustainable impact—of these investment vehicles.

For Corporate India: Companies, especially those in Shariah indices, should proactively enhance their sustainability disclosures, demonstrating their contribution to the SDGs to attract this growing pool of ethical capital.

Future Research Directions

1. **Quantitative Impact Measurement:** Empirical research to develop a "Shariah-SDG Alignment Score" for Indian companies and investigate the risk-return profile of a portfolio constructed using this score.
2. **Investor Behavior Studies:** Qualitative and survey-based research to understand the perceptions, motivations, and barriers for Indian retail and institutional investors regarding SDG-aligned Shariah products.
3. **Comparative International Analysis:** A study comparing the policy frameworks and market success of Green Sukuk in Malaysia or the UAE with the potential for replication in India.
4. **Sectoral Deep-Dives:** Investigating the specific SDG contributions of Shariah-compliant companies in high-impact sectors like Indian pharmaceuticals, IT, and renewable energy.

Foundational Principles of Islamic Finance

1. **Shariah-Compliant Investments:** Financial investments that strictly adhere to the principles of Islamic law (*Shariah*). This necessitates compliance with specific ethical and religious prohibitions, primarily avoiding *Riba* (interest), *Gharar* (excessive uncertainty), and investments in sectors deemed *Haram* (forbidden).
2. **Riba:** The explicit prohibition of usury or interest charged on loans. A cornerstone of Islamic finance, this principle discourages speculative, debt-based growth and promotes asset-backed, equitable financing structures that link returns to actual economic performance and shared risk.
3. **Gharar:** The prohibition of excessive uncertainty, ambiguity, or speculative risk in contractual agreements. This principle mandates full transparency and asset-backing in financial transactions, thereby reducing exposure to the volatile derivatives and opaque financial instruments that can destabilize conventional markets.
4. **Haram:** Activities or sectors explicitly forbidden by Islamic law, in which investment is prohibited. These typically include industries considered detrimental to society, such as alcohol, gambling, tobacco, pornography, and conventional interest-based financial services.
5. **Maqasid al-Shariah:** Translating to the "Objectives of Islamic Law," this represents the higher-order goals that Shariah aims to protect, which include the preservation of faith, life, intellect, progeny, and wealth. Modern interpretations increasingly align these objectives with contemporary sustainability goals, such as social justice, environmental conservation, and human welfare.

Core Instruments and Market Structures

6. **Sukuk:** Often referred to as "Islamic bonds," Sukuk are financial certificates that represent a proportional undivided ownership interest in an underlying asset, usufruct, service, or project. Unlike conventional bonds that create debt, Sukuk generate returns through profit-sharing from the asset's performance or rental income.
7. **Green Sukuk:** A specific category of Sukuk where the proceeds are exclusively allocated to finance or refinance new or existing environmentally sustainable projects, such as renewable energy installations, green buildings, or climate-resilient infrastructure, in full compliance with Shariah principles.
8. **Mudarabah:** A profit-sharing partnership agreement where one party provides the capital (*rab-ul-mal*) and the other provides expertise and management (*mudarib*). Profits are distributed according to a pre-agreed ratio, while financial

losses are borne solely by the capital provider, establishing a pure form of risk-sharing.

9. **Musharakah:** A joint enterprise or partnership structure in which all partners contribute capital and/or expertise and share in the profits and losses of the venture proportionally. This embodies the Islamic finance ideal of shared reward and shared risk in productive economic activity.
10. **Shariah Index:** A stock market index composed of companies that have been screened for Shariah compliance. In the Indian context, benchmarks such as the Nifty 50 Shariah and BSE TASIS Shariah 50 provide a standardized and transparent benchmark for ethically-minded investors.

Sustainability and Ethical Frameworks

11. **Sustainable Development Goals (SDGs):** A universal call to action adopted by all United Nations Member States in 2015, comprising 17 interlinked goals designed to be a "blueprint to achieve a better and more sustainable future for all" by 2030. They address global challenges like poverty, inequality, climate change, and environmental degradation.
12. **Environmental, Social, and Governance (ESG):** A set of non-financial criteria used to evaluate a company's ethical impact and sustainable practices. The environmental pillar considers a company's stewardship of nature; the social pillar examines its relationships with employees, suppliers, and communities; and the governance pillar deals with leadership, audits, and shareholder rights.
13. **Ethical Finance:** An overarching approach to financial services that integrates ethical values, sustainability, and social responsibility into investment and banking decisions. It prioritizes positive social and environmental outcomes alongside financial returns, with Shariah-compliant finance representing a significant, faith-based subset.

Advanced Integrated Concepts

14. **Shariah-SDG Alignment:** The synergistic relationship whereby the negative screens and positive injunctions of Shariah-compliant investing inherently advance the objectives of the Sustainable Development Goals. This is not merely a coincidental overlap but a structural alignment, as the exclusion of harmful industries and the promotion of real-asset investment directly contribute to goals related to health, well-being, climate action, and economic justice.
15. **Implicit vs. Explicit Contribution (to SDGs):** A critical distinction in impact reporting. An *implicit contribution* arises passively from a company's adherence to Shariah screens (e.g., a healthcare company inherently supports SDG 3 by

nature of its permissible business). An *explicit contribution* requires active measurement, management, and transparent reporting of specific, quantifiable outcomes against SDG targets and indicators.

16. **Financial Resilience (in Islamic Finance):** The hypothesized stability and defensive characteristics of Shariah-compliant portfolios during periods of market stress. This resilience is attributed to the inherent risk-mitigation features of Islamic finance, such as the prohibitions on excessive leverage (*Riba*) and speculative uncertainty (*Gharar*), which tether financial value to real economic assets and activities.
17. **Stakeholder Theory-Maqasid Fusion:** The chapter's proposed theoretical framework that integrates the modern business concept of Stakeholder Theory—which argues that a firm is responsible to a broad set of stakeholders beyond its shareholders—with the traditional Islamic objectives of *Maqasid al-Shariah*. This fusion provides a robust, multi-dimensional rationale for corporations to pursue sustainable and socially responsible objectives as both a managerial and a religious-ethical imperative.

SUMMARY OF THE CHAPTER

- The chapter establishes a compelling, synergistic relationship between Shariah-compliant investment principles and the objectives of the Sustainable Development Goals (SDGs) within the Indian stock market.
- It argues that the inherent ethical screening of Islamic finance naturally aligns with SDGs related to health, climate action, responsible consumption, and reducing inequality.
- The existence of Shariah indices in India (e.g., Nifty 50 Shariah) provides a tangible foundation for integrating sustainability metrics, offering investors avenues that are both ethically sound and financially viable.
- The theoretical framework merges *Maqasid al-Shariah* (Objectives of Islamic Law) with modern Stakeholder Theory, providing a robust rationale for this alignment.
- Key recommendations include regulatory innovation for Green Sukuk, product development for SDG-aligned Shariah funds, and enhanced stakeholder awareness.
- Ultimately, the chapter posits that the fusion of Shariah finance and sustainability can mobilize significant capital towards India's developmental priorities, creating a more resilient, inclusive, and sustainable financial system.

9. REFERENCES

Afzal, A., Rasoulinezhad, E., & Malik, Z. (2022). Green finance and sustainable development in Europe. *Ekonomska Istrazivanja, 35*(1), 5150–5163. DOI: 10.1080/1331677X.2021.2024081

Ahmed, H., Mohieldin, M., Verbeek, J., & Aboulmagd, F. (2015). On the sustainable development goals and the role of Islamic finance. *World Bank Policy Research Working Paper*, (7266).

Al-Roubaie, A., & Sarea, A. M. (2019). Green investment and sustainable development: The case of Islamic finance. *Journal of Islamic Business and Management*, *9*(1). Advance online publication. DOI: 10.26501/jibm/2019.0901-002

Azad, M. A. K., Islam, M. A., Sobhani, F. A., Hassan, M. S., & Masukujjaman, M. (2022). Revisiting the Current Status of Green Finance and Sustainable Finance Disbursement: A Policy Insights. *Sustainability (Basel), 14*(14), 8911. DOI: 10.3390/su14148911

Azam, M., Boubaker, S., & Hunjra, A. I. (2023). Dynamic Institutions as Pillars for Sustainable Development. *In Governance in the Developing World: Transnational Insights on Economic Development* (pp. 1–22). Singapore: Springer. *Nature in Singapore*. Advance online publication. DOI: 10.1007/978-981-99-2493-6_1

Bank for International Settlements (BIS). (2022). *Green Islamic finance: Opportunities and challenges*. BIS Papers, No. 128. Retrieved from https://www.bis.org/publ/bppdf/bispap128.htm

Bukhari, S. A. A., Hashim, F., & Amran, A. (2023). Green banking: A strategy for attainment of UN-Sustainable Development Goals 2030. *International Journal of Environment and Sustainable Development*, *22*(1), 13–31. DOI: 10.1504/IJESD.2023.127419

Chen, J., Siddik, A. B., Zheng, G. W., Masukujjaman, M., & Bekhzod, S. (2022). The effect of green banking practices on banks' environmental performance and green financing: An empirical study. *Energies*, *15*(4), 1292. DOI: 10.3390/en15041292

Chin, M. Y., Ong, S. L., Ooi, D. B. Y., & Puah, C. H. (2022). The impact of green finance on environmental degradation in BRI region. *Environment, Development and Sustainability, 26*(1), 303–318. DOI: 10.1007/s10668-022-02709-5 PMID: 36277420

Ghoniyah, N., & Hartono, S. (2020). How Islamic and conventional bank in Indonesia contributing sustainable development goals achievement. *Cogent Economics & Finance, 8*(1), 1856458. https://doi.org/. 2020.1856458DOI: 10.1080/23322039

Harahap, B., Risfandy, T., & Futri, I. N. (2023). Islamic Law, Islamic Finance, and Sustainable Development Goals: A Systematic Literature Review. *Sustainability (Basel), 15*(8), 6626. DOI: 10.3390/su15086626

Hunjra, A. I., Azam, M., Bruna, M. G., Verhoeven, P., & Al-Faryan, M. A. S. (2022). Sustainable development: The impact of political risk, macroeconomic policy uncertainty and ethnic conflict. *International Review of Financial Analysis, 84*, 102370. DOI: 10.1016/j.irfa.2022.102370

Ibrahim, S. S., Daud, D., Hidayah, K., Shaharuddin, A., & Al-Amin, A. A. M. (2023). Waqf integrated income generating model (WIIGM) for enhancing sustainable development goals (SDGS) in Malaysia: An evaluation of behavioural intention. *International Journal of Ethics and Systems, 39*(4), 841–858. DOI: 10.1108/IJOES-02-2022-0030

Irfan, M. (2021, January). Do Shariah Indices converge? Evidence from Gulf Co-operation Council countries. *International Journal of Business Excellence, 23*(2), 251–269. DOI: 10.1504/IJBEX.2021.113448

Irfan, M., Elhoseny, M., Kassim, S., & Metawa, N. (2023). *Advanced Machine Learning Algorithms for Complex Financial Applications*. IGI Global., DOI: 10.4018/978-1-6684-4483-2

Irfan, M., Elmogy, M., Gupta, S., Khalifa, F., & Dias, R. (2024). *AI-Driven Decentralized Finance and the Future of Finance*. IGI Global., DOI: 10.4018/979-8-3693-6321-8

Irfan, M., Elmogy, M., Majid, M. S., & El-Sappagh, S. (2023). *The Impact of AI Innovation on Financial Sectors in the Era of Industry 5.0*. IGI Global., DOI: 10.4018/979-8-3693-0082-4

Irfan, M., Hussainey, K., Chan Bukhari, S. A., & Nam, Y. (Eds.). (2024). *Issues of Sustainability in AI and New-Age Thematic Investing*. IGI Global Publisher., DOI: 10.4018/979-8-3693-3282-5

Irfan, M., Kadry, S., Sharif, M., & Ullah Khan, H. (2023). *Fintech Applications in Islamic Finance: AI, Machine Learning, and Blockchain Techniques*. IGI Global., DOI: 10.4018/979-8-3693-1038-0

Islamic Financial Services Board (IFSB). (2022). *Islamic Financial Services Industry Stability Report 2022*. IFSB.

Jan, A., Rahman, H. U., Zahid, M., Salameh, A. A., Khan, P. A., Al-Faryan, M. A. S., & Ali, H. E. (2023b). Islamic corporate sustainability practices index aligned with SDGs towards better financial performance: Evidence from the Malaysian and Indonesian Islamic banking industry. *Journal of Cleaner Production*, *405*, 136860. DOI: 10.1016/j.jclepro.2023.136860

Jan, A. A., Lai, F. W., Asif, M., Akhtar, S., & Ullah, S. (2023a). Embedding sustainability into bank strategy: Implications for sustainable development goals reporting. *International Journal of Sustainable Development & World Ecology, 30*(3), 229–243. https://doi.org/. 2134230DOI: 10.1080/13504509.2022

Jiakui, C., Abbas, J., Najam, H., Liu, J., & Abbas, J. (2023). Green technological innovation, green finance, and financial development and their role in green total factor productivity: Empirical insights from China. *Journal of Cleaner Production, 382*, 135131. Johan, S. (2022). Complementary or Substitute: Sharia Financing Green Financing and Sustainable Development Goals? *International Journal of Sustainable Development & Planning, 17* (2), 487–495.DOI: 10.1016/j.jclepro.2022.135131

Nguyen, A. H., Do, M. H. T., Hoang, T. G., & Nguyen, L. Q. T. (2023). Green financing for sustainable development: Insights from multiple cases of Vietnamese commercial banks. *Business Strategy and the Environment*, *32*(1), 321–335. DOI: 10.1002/bse.3132

Ronaldo, R., & Suryanto, T. (2022). Green finance and sustainability development goals in Indonesian Fund Village. *Resources Policy*, *78*, 102839. DOI: 10.1016/j.resourpol.2022.102839

Saba, I., Khan, A., & Jawed, H. (2021). Islamic Finance and SDGs: Connecting Dots. Islamic Finance and Sustainable Development: A Sustainable Economic Framework for Muslim and Non-Muslim Countries, 55-76.DOI: 10.1007/978-3-030-76016-8_4

Shahid, M., Sulub, Y. A., Mohtesham, M. M. J., & Abdullah, M. (2023). Analyzing the commonalities between Islamic social finance and sustainable development goals. *International Journal of Ethics and Systems*. DOI: 10.1108/IJOES-04-2022-0082

Shome, S., Hassan, M. K., Verma, S., & Panigrahi, T. R. (2023). Impact investment for sustainable development: A bibliometric analysis. *International Review of Economics & Finance, 84*, 770–800. https://doi.org/. iref.2022.12.001DOI: 10.1016/j

Taskin, D., Azam, M., Hunjra, A. I., & Al-Faryan, M. A. S. (2023). Role of ethnic conflicts, regularization and natural resource abundance in sustainable development. *Resources Policy*, *85*, 103936. DOI: 10.1016/j.resourpol.2023.103936

Wahab, N. A., Yusof, R. M., Zainuddin, Z., Shamsuddin, J. N., & Mohamad, S. F. N. (2023). Charting future growth for Islamic finance talents in Malaysia: A bibliometric analysis on the Islamic finance domains and future research gaps. *Journal of Islamic Accounting and Business Research, 14*(5), 812–837. DOI: 10.1108/JIABR-02-2022-0045

Wang, K. H., Zhao, Y. X., Jiang, C. F., & Li, Z. Z. (2022). Does green finance inspire sustainable development? Evidence from a global perspective. *Economic Analysis and Policy, 75*, 412–426. https://doi.org/. 2022.06.002DOI: 10.1016/j.eap

World Bank Group & Islamic Development Bank (IsDB). (2021). *Global Report on Islamic Finance: Building Resilience through Sustainable Finance*. World Bank. https://doi.org/DOI: 10.1596/978-1-4648-1738-7

Zhou, M., & Li, X. (2022). Influence of green finance and renewable energy resources over the sustainable development goal of clean energy in China. *Resources Policy, 78*, 102816. DOI: 10.1016/j.resourpol.2022.102816

TEACHING NOTE

Target Audience: Advanced Undergraduate (Final Year), Master's in Finance, MBA, and Executive Education students in courses on Sustainable Finance, Ethical Investing, Islamic Finance, or Emerging Markets.

Concise Summary for the Teacher

This chapter presents a sophisticated and timely argument for the strategic convergence of Shariah-compliant finance and sustainable investing within the dynamic context of India's stock market. It moves beyond a simple descriptive analysis to posit that the ethical foundations of Islamic finance—specifically its prohibitions on harmful sectors (*haram*) and speculative, debt-heavy practices—create a *structural and inherent* alignment with the UN's Sustainable Development Goals (SDGs). The chapter establishes that this is not a niche overlap but a significant opportunity to mobilize a vast pool of under-utilized domestic capital for India's pressing sustainability needs, such as renewable energy and financial inclusion. It critically examines the current landscape, including existing Shariah indices, while also highlighting key challenges: the gap between implicit alignment and explicit impact reporting, and the significant regulatory hurdles. Ultimately, the chapter serves as a call to action for regulators, financial institutions, and corporations to build a synergistic framework that leverages this alignment for both ethical integrity and national economic development.

Chapter Synopsis

The chapter begins by establishing the global context of integrating sustainability into finance, introducing Shariah-compliant investing as a rapidly growing segment of ethical finance. It argues that the principles of Islamic finance naturally dovetail with many ESG and SDG objectives. Focusing on India, the chapter highlights the empirical presence of Shariah-compliant stock indices and theorizes their potential for driving sustainable development. It constructs a conceptual model linking Shariah Law, Islamic Finance, the Indian Stock Market, and the SDGs. Through discussion and critical analysis, it explores the financial viability and resilience of these investments, introduces innovative products like Green Sukuk, and concludes with concrete recommendations for stakeholders and future research directions, framing the integration as a strategic national imperative.

Key Learning Objectives

Upon engaging with this chapter, students should be able to:

1. **Remember** the core principles of Shariah-compliant investing (e.g., prohibitions of *Riba*, *Gharar*, *Haram*) and list key Indian Shariah indices.
2. **Understand** the conceptual and practical synergies between Shariah-compliant investment screens and specific Sustainable Development Goals (SDGs).
3. **Apply** the chapter's theoretical framework—the fusion of *Maqasid al-Shariah* and Stakeholder Theory—to analyze a real-world company's potential alignment with both ethical and sustainability criteria.
4. **Analyze** the perceived trade-offs (e.g., between ethical restrictions and financial returns, portfolio liquidity) and evaluate the evidence presented for the financial resilience of Shariah-compliant portfolios.
5. **Evaluate** the primary challenges (regulatory, reporting) hindering the growth of this market in India and critically assess the recommendations provided for different stakeholders.
6. **Create** a preliminary proposal for a new financial product (e.g., a thematic fund) or a policy brief that leverages the Shariah-SDG alignment for a specific developmental goal in an emerging market context.

Core Themes/Theses for Discussion

1. **Inherent vs. Constructed Alignment:** Is the alignment between Shariah principles and SDGs a fundamental, structural feature of Islamic finance, or is it a strategically constructed narrative to appeal to a broader market?
2. **The Financial Performance Debate:** Can an investment strategy that imposes significant negative screens genuinely achieve competitive, risk-adjusted returns over the long term, or does its resilience only manifest during specific market crises?
3. **The Regulatory Imperative:** To what extent is the development of this market contingent on proactive regulatory innovation versus organic, market-led demand?
4. **From Implicit to Explicit Impact:** How can and should companies transition from passively benefiting from implicit SDG alignment to actively measuring, managing, and reporting their explicit contributions?
5. **Strategic National Advantage:** Is the fusion of Shariah-compliant finance and sustainability a viable strategic tool for emerging economies like India to achieve energy security, financial inclusion, and climate goals independently?

Suggested Teaching Pathway (90-Minute Session)

- **Introduction (10 mins):** Start with a provocative question: *"Can your religious beliefs make you a more sustainable investor?"* Use this to introduce the core premise of the chapter.
- **Conceptual Foundations (20 mins):** Lecture and discussion on the core principles of Shariah-compliant finance and the SDGs. Use a simple matrix on the board to visually map prohibitions (*Haram* sectors) to corresponding SDGs (e.g., Alcohol → SDG 3).
- **Case Study: The Indian Context (25 mins):** Present the case of the Nifty 50 Shariah index. Facilitate a discussion on the opportunities (massive capital pool, national priorities) and challenges (regulation, reporting) highlighted in the chapter. The **"Implicit vs. Explicit"** tension is key here.
- **Group Activity: The Stakeholder Roundtable (20 mins):** Divide the class into groups representing SEBI, an Asset Management Company (AMC), a Shariah-compliant corporation, and a retail investor association. Task them with developing a 2-minute pitch on their priority action to advance this market, based on the chapter's recommendations.
- **Synthesis and Conclusion (15 mins):** Reconvene and have each group present their pitch. Summarize by revisiting the chapter's main thesis, emphasizing its relevance for finance professionals operating in a multi-faith, sustainability-focused global economy.

Pedagogical Tools & Resources

- **In-Class Slides:** Featuring the chapter's conceptual models (Figures 2 & 3), a comparative table of Shariah vs. Conventional ESG screening, and key data points on India's sustainability financing gap.
- **Case Materials:** A one-page handout with details on a real-world example, such as a Green Sukuk issuance from Indonesia or Malaysia, for comparative analysis.
- **Videos:** A short (3-5 min) video explaining the basics of Sukuk or an interview with a fund manager of a Shariah-compliant ESG fund.
- **Further Reading:** Provide the "Additional Reading" list from the chapter for students wishing to delve deeper.

Note on Sensitivity

This topic sits at the intersection of faith, finance, and policy, requiring a respectful and professional classroom environment.

- **Emphasize the Economic and Ethical Frameworks:** Frame the discussion around the *financial principles and outcomes* of Shariah-compliant investing, rather than engaging in theological debate. The focus is on its operationalization within modern capital markets.
- **Use Precise Language:** Differentiate between "Shariah-compliant" (adhering to financial principles) and "Islamic" (a broader religious and cultural identity). Avoid generalizations.
- **Inclusive Perspective:** Stress that the appeal of these products is not limited to Muslim investors but extends to any investor seeking rigorous ethical and sustainable screens. The chapter itself positions this as a universal strategy.
- **Facilitate Respectfully:** If discussions become heated, steer the conversation back to the evidence-based and strategic arguments presented in the chapter.

Key Questions for Class Discussion

1. **Comprehension:** The chapter argues the alignment is "natural and robust." What is the most compelling evidence provided for this claim, and where might this alignment be less direct or even contradictory?
    - o *Direction: Push students to move beyond listing prohibitions to discuss the positive investment mandates that arise (e.g., focus on real assets, equity-based financing).*
2. **Application:** If you were a portfolio manager at a large AMC, how would you market an "SDG-Aligned Shariah ETF" to a skeptical conventional investor focused solely on maximizing returns?
    - o *Direction: Guide them to use the chapter's arguments about long-term resilience, risk-sharing, and growth in sustainable sectors.*
3. **Analysis:** The "implicit vs. explicit contribution" is highlighted as a critical gap. What are the practical hurdles a company like Infosys or Reliance Industries would face in explicitly reporting its SDG impact to Shariah-conscious investors?
    - o *Direction: Discuss metrics, data collection costs, verification, and potential "SDG-washing."*
4. **Evaluation:** Of the recommendations made to SEBI and RBI, which single regulatory change would have the most significant catalytic effect, and why?
    - o *Direction: Force a prioritization. Is it the framework for Green Sukuk, banking windows, or enhanced reporting mandates?*
5. **Synthesis:** How does the fusion of *Maqasid al-Shariah* and Stakeholder Theory resolve, or fail to resolve, a potential conflict between a company's duty to shareholder profits and a costly investment in a social or environmental good?
    - o *Direction: Encourage a debate on the limits of corporate responsibility within different theoretical frameworks.*

6. **Analysis:** The 2008 financial crisis is cited as evidence of the resilience of Islamic finance. Is this a valid comparison, or are there unique factors in that crisis that make it a poor predictor of future performance?
   - o *Direction: Explore the specific causes of the 2008 crisis (e.g., subprime mortgages, derivatives) and how Shariah screens would have provided immunity.*
7. **Creation:** Imagine you are a consultant to the Indian government. Draft a one-sentence vision statement for a national strategy on Shariah-compliant sustainable finance.
   - o *Direction: This forces synthesis of the chapter's core message into a clear, actionable statement.*
8. **Evaluation:** The chapter is optimistic about India's potential in this field. What is the single greatest threat to this optimistic vision becoming a reality?
   - o *Direction: Move beyond obvious answers like "regulation" to discuss political will, competition from other sustainable finance products, or global economic shocks.*
9. **Perspective:** Could the principles of Shariah-compliant finance, particularly its aversion to excessive debt and speculation, offer lessons for the reform of the conventional global financial system, regardless of one's faith?
   - o *Direction: Broaden the discussion to universal themes of financial stability and ethics.*
10. **Future-Gazing:** Looking 10 years ahead, what is one disruptive trend (e.g., AI, blockchain, climate migration) that could most dramatically alter the landscape for Shariah-compliant sustainable investing in India?
    - o *Direction: Encourages creative and forward-thinking application of the chapter's concepts to an uncertain future.*

Section 3
Market Assurance and Investor Scrutiny: The Accountability Imperative

Chapter 8

Market Dynamics and Risk Management:
A Holistic Examination of Global Financial and Commodity Markets Amid the 2007–2009 Financial Crisis

Hayfa Kazouz
https://orcid.org/0000-0002-1874-9744
Faculty of Economic Sciences and Management of Sousse, Tunisia

Saloua Benammou
Faculty of Economic Sciences and Management of Sousse, Tunisia

ABSTRACT

This chapter investigates the dynamic interactions between seven global stock markets and commodity markets during the Global Financial Crisis (GFC) of 2007-2009. The research focuses on transmission mechanisms and volatility spillovers, applying the Vector Autoregressive Dynamic Conditional Correlation Multivariate Exponential Generalized Autoregressive Conditional Heteroscedasticity (VAR-DCC-MEGARCH) model. The analysis examines indices such as S&P 500, GSPTSE, DAX 30, CAC 40, Nikkei 225, SSE Composite, and HSI, alongside commodities including Brent Crude Oil, West Texas Intermediate (WTI), and Gold. The study emphasizes the safe haven properties of Gold and Brent oil, offering guidance on optimal portfolio construction during crises. Additionally, the chapter assesses hedging ratios and volatility to provide insights for risk management and portfolio diversification in

DOI: 10.4018/979-8-3693-9714-5.ch008

times of financial instability. The findings enhance the understanding of market dynamics, offering valuable guidance for policymakers and investors navigating economic turbulence.

1.0 INTRODUCTION

Over the past three decades, global markets have experienced increasing volatility due to financial liberalization and the opening of economies. This trend has sparked a growing interest in the analysis of market volatility. The heightened integration and substantial volatility in major financial markets have made both commodity and stock prices more sensitive to various factors, including deregulation, weather conditions, geopolitical events, economic policies, investor sentiment, revolutions, and unforeseen occurrences (Yu et al., 2008). In recent years, commodity markets, particularly Gold and oil, have witnessed a surge in liquidity, attracting investors who view commodities not only as essential for "real" economic activities such as risk hedging but also as financial assets and securities (Vivian and Wohar, 2012). The sharp fluctuations in Gold and oil prices have been closely tied to financial crises, geopolitical conflicts, and adverse climatic conditions. For example, Gold prices commenced trading at $460 in January 2000 and peaked at $1286.96 in September 2009. Similarly, Brent crude oil prices exhibited a comparable trajectory, starting at $44.8 per barrel in January 2000 and reaching $114 per barrel in December 2010.

The observed volatility pattern poses a perplexing challenge for researchers, academics, and portfolio managers. Understanding time-varying volatility and the transmission processes across various market types is crucial for international investors and policymakers. Previous research has predominantly examined the impact of volatility among major stock markets or between the crude oil market and financial markets (e.g., Du et al., 2011; Kumar et al., 2012; Hassan and Malik, 2007; Lien and Yang, 2008; Malik and Ewing, 2009; Sadorsky, 2012; Arouri et al., 2012; Singh et al., 2010; He and Chen, 2011; Yilmaz, 2010; Syllignakis and Kouretas, 2011). Various empirical methodologies have been applied in these studies, including the use of a multivariate generalized autoregressive conditional heteroscedasticity model (MGARCH) to analyze the relationship between economic and political uncertainty on the conditional volatility of financial variables (Fornari et al., 2002). Singh et al. (2010) employed the vector autoregressive-generalized conditional heteroscedasticity model (VAR-GARCH) to examine time spillovers of volatility between emerging and developed stock markets. The relationship between equity and oil markets has become a focal point for both market participants and researchers (e.g., Arouri et al., 2012; Chang et al., 2013; Ewing and Malik, 2016; Sadorsky, 2012). With the heightened global integration between oil and financial markets and the substantial movements in oil prices following the 2007 subprime crisis, there is an increased emphasis on modeling dynamic correlations and spillovers between oil prices and equity returns. Since the year 2000, the West Texas Intermediate (WTI) oil futures price has exhibited significant volatility, influencing the uncertainty surrounding the value of stocks and future cash flows of oil-related firms. This highlights the necessity of considering both the overall market and the stock market sector when analyzing the interactions between oil and stock returns (e.g., Malik and Ewing, 2009; Arouri et al., 2011a; Arouri et al., 2012). Risks, returns, and the correlation of assets are fundamental elements in empirical finance, especially in constructing optimal portfolios. To achieve our objective, we employ a vector autoregressive dynamic conditional correlation generalized autoregressive conditional hetero-scedasticity model (VAR-DCC-MEGARCH), moreover, the EGARCH model can assess asymmetry affect efficiently (Sikhosana and Aye 2018), that let us capture their evolution through time and identify the transmission of shocks across the mean, volatility and correlation of all those variables. On the one hand, the transmission mechanism study is useful for policy makers to build an early warning system, to reveal the most important transmission channels and to guide the competent authorities towards a clearer understanding in turmoil situations to keep the risk of losses to a minimum. On the other hand, identifying the contagion effect of correlation and volatility in a dynamic way is essential to effectively manage investment portfolios and to diversify assets in the most optimal way. This intelligent approach reduces risk and controls changes that may occur due to the general economic situation.

This study analyzes the returns transmission and volatility spillovers effect among seven stock markets of the world, and commodity markets during the Global financial crisis period (2007/2009) to evaluate and compared the behavior of these markets during the financial emergencies to gain more profit and diversify inherent /systematic risk. The goal of this study is to analyze and compare how different markets behaved during the global financial crisis (2007–2009) in order to increase profits and diversify inherent/systematic risk. It does this by examining the returns transmission and volatility spillovers effects among eight stock markets (S&P 500 index, Canadian stock market index (GSPTSE), DAX 30 index, CAC 40 index, Nikkei 225 index, Shanghai Composite index (SSEC), and Hang Sang index (HSI)) throughout the world as well as commodities markets (Brent Crude Oil, West Texas Intermediate (WTI), and Gold).

Moreover, the study examined the safe haven properties of Gold and Brent oil during the crisis era, thus, investors can make optimal portfolios during pandemic crisis. As the correlation do not remain constant among stock markets and commodity futures. Additionally, the study reckons the hedging ratios, so that portfolio with high risk can be isolated. This investigation calculates the volatility of these markets, so an investor can establish which stock market will choose, i.e., Asian, European or

American performs better during financial crisis. Also, the investigation explores which stock markets or commodity market is the market receiver or transmitter of financial risk. Consequently, this study provides complete information about time varying correlation, Volatility spillovers, hedging safe-haven properties, and optimal weights among the stock markets of the US, Europe, Canada, and Asia.

In this chapter we have used as commodity indexes Gold, Brent Oil and WTI, in order to identify the hedging rate of these indexes on international indexes and to identify which is the best index in a portfolio that contributes the least risk and the most safety at the time of crisis.

The chapter provides a sophisticated empirical investigation into the volatility spillovers and dynamic correlations between major global equity markets and key commodity assets (gold, Brent crude, and WTI crude) during the Global Financial Crisis (GFC) of 2007-2009. It situates risk management and portfolio diversification strategies within the broader context of financial sustainability, demonstrating how resilient investment practices contribute to stable economic systems.

This chapter is organized as follows: the most intriguing theoretical and empirical findings that pertain to our subject will be covered in the second section. The third section then provides a discussion of the methodology and the data. In contrast, the fourth part will offer the empirical validation, including the model's estimate, the primary findings, and ultimately the conclusion.

1.1 Background

The dawn of the 21st century has been characterized by an unprecedented degree of financial market integration, driven by liberalization and technological advancement. While fostering economic growth, this interconnectedness has also amplified the transmission of shocks, rendering global markets increasingly susceptible to synchronized volatility. The period of the Global Financial Crisis (GFC) of 2007-2009 stands as a stark testament to this vulnerability, where distress originating in the U.S. subprime mortgage market rapidly propagated across global financial ecosystems. This era of extreme turbulence underscored the critical importance of understanding the time-varying nature of risk and the complex transmission channels between disparate asset classes.

Within this milieu, commodities like gold and crude oil have transcended their traditional roles as mere inputs for economic production. They have emerged as pivotal financial assets, integral to strategic portfolio allocation, risk hedging, and safe-haven strategies. The dramatic fluctuations in the prices of these commodities during the GFC, intertwined with equity market collapses, presented a profound challenge and opportunity for researchers and practitioners alike. This chapter, therefore, seeks to dissect these complex interlinkages, aiming to illuminate the pathways of return and volatility spillovers. Its findings are crucial for constructing robust, sustainable investment portfolios capable of withstanding systemic financial shocks, thereby contributing directly to the overarching themes of financial stability and long-term economic resilience central to this book.

2.0 LITERATURE REVIEW

The extant literature on financial contagion and volatility spillovers is vast, yet this chapter carves a distinct niche by focusing specifically on the nexus between global equities and key commodities during a period of extreme stress. Early foundational work, such as that by Malik and Ewing (2009) and Arouri et al. (2011a, 2012), established significant volatility transmission between oil prices and various U.S. and European equity sectors, though often omitting direct analysis of oil stocks themselves. The spillover effects of the GFC were empirically confirmed by studies like Zouch et al. (2011), who documented the pervasive impact of the U.S. subprime crisis on both developed and emerging markets, and Yilmaz (2010), who observed that spillover indices among East Asian markets peaked precisely during this crisis.

A parallel stream of research has been dedicated to understanding the unique properties of commodities. Baur and McDermott (2010) provided compelling evidence of gold's role as a safe haven in major developed markets, while Batten et al. (2010) and Bhunia (2013) highlighted the significant impact of gold price volatility on broader financial market returns. On the energy front, Pindyck (2004) elucidated how geopolitical and economic factors drive oil price volatility, creating widespread uncertainty across oil-exporting and importing nations.

Methodologically, the chapter builds upon the pioneering work of Engle (2002) on Dynamic Conditional Correlation (DCC) GARCH models, which allow for the estimation of time-varying correlations. It extends the framework of Koutmos (1996) and aligns with more recent sophisticated applications, such as Tsuji (2018), who employed a VAR-DCC-MEGARCH model to analyze spillovers between oil futures and oil equities. The chapter integrates these advanced econometric techniques to offer a more holistic and dynamic analysis than many preceding studies, which often relied on constant correlation assumptions or focused on a narrower set of markets.

2.1 Theoretic Evolution

The theoretical underpinnings of this chapter are rooted in modern financial econometrics, specifically models designed to capture the stylized facts of financial time series: volatility clustering, leptokurtosis (fat tails), and time-varying co-movements.

The evolution of thought in this domain began with the univariate Autoregressive Conditional Heteroskedasticity (ARCH) model introduced by Engle (1982) and its generalized extension (GARCH) by Bollerslev (1986). These models revolutionized the field by allowing conditional variance to change over time as a function of past errors, effectively modeling volatility clustering. The Exponential GARCH (EGARCH) model by Nelson (1991) marked a critical advancement by incorporating asymmetry, or the "leverage effect," acknowledging that negative shocks often increase volatility more than positive shocks of the same magnitude.

The need to model multiple assets simultaneously led to the development of multivariate GARCH models. The early Constant Conditional Correlation (CCC) model by Bollerslev (1990) was a foundational step but was limited by its assumption of fixed correlations over time. This chapter's methodology represents the culmination of this theoretical evolution: the Dynamic Conditional Correlation (DCC) GARCH model by Engle (2002). The DCC framework relaxes the constant correlation assumption, allowing for the realistic modeling of how correlations between assets change dynamically, especially during periods of market stress like the GFC.

By embedding this within a Vector Autoregression (VAR) system for mean returns and employing an MEGARCH specification for variances, the chapter's VAR-DCC-MEGARCH model represents a state-of-the-art synthesis. It simultaneously captures:

1. **Return Spillovers:** How past returns in one market predict current returns in another (via the VAR).
2. **Volatility Spillovers:** How volatility shocks transmit across markets (via the MEGARCH).
3. **Dynamic Hedging:** How the optimal relationship between assets evolves over time (via the DCC).

This integrated approach provides a far more nuanced and realistic depiction of financial market interdependencies than was possible with earlier, less flexible modeling techniques.

2.2 Extant literature on the commodity and financial markets during the GFC

The global economy has experienced several financial crises, including the US crises, Mexican crisis, Asian crisis, Russian crisis, Brazilian crisis, and US subprime crisis, impacting both emerging and advanced financial markets. Consequently, numerous empirical studies have investigated the impact of these crises on financial stock markets. For instance, during the Asian crisis, researchers such as Chen et al. (2002), Chi et al. (2006), and Jang and Sul (2002) delved into the effects. Similarly, the Russian crisis was examined by Forbes (2000) and Saleem (2009), while the Mexican crisis drew the attention of researchers like Ki et al. (2003). The aftermath of these financial crises has spurred empirical analyses focusing on volatility spillovers across markets, as studied by He (2001) and Martin et al. (2002) Wang, S et al., 2002).

The global financial crisis (2007-2009) and its influence on the financial markets has led to a considerable interest in the examination of the impact of stock market volatility spillovers. Coudert et al., 2015, Hemche et al., 2016, Kenourgios and Dimitriou, 2015, Li and Giles, 2015, Miralles-Marcelo et al., 2013. A brief review of the pertinent literature is conducted in this section. We concentrate on studies of spillovers between Gold and oil and equities of the US, Europe, Canada, and Asia and review them chronologically because the goal of our research in this paper is to explore the spillover effects of returns and volatility among the stock index market, oil, and gold, while also developing an effective methodology to capture these dynamics. Initial research by Malik and Ewing (2009) focused on volatility spillovers between oil and selected US sector equity indexes, encompassing financials, industrials, consumer services, health care, and technology. Their findings indicated significant volatility transmission between oil and these US sector equities, although it's worth noting the omission of oil sector stocks. Another study by Arouri et al. (2011a) utilized an MGARCH model to investigate volatility spillovers between oil and various stock sectors in the US and Europe, such as automobiles and parts, financials, industrials, basic materials, technology, telecommunications, and utilities. The results revealed unidirectional volatility spillovers from oil returns to sector stock returns in Europe, along with bidirectional volatility spillovers between oil and US sector stock returns. However, this analysis also lacked the inclusion of any oil stock indexes. In a related study, Arouri et al. (2011b) employed an MGARCH model to examine return and volatility transmission between oil and equities, focusing on the six equity markets of the Gulf Cooperation Council (GCC) countries.

They discovered that there were often spillover effects on volatility and return transmission between the oil and GCC stock markets. Zouch et al (2011), find that US crisis spread across 20 developed and emerging stock markets. Empirical results of

GARCH and EGARCH estimated a model shows a high persistence and asymmetric effect of volatility. Zouch et al. (2011) discovered that the US crisis had a widespread impact on 20 developed and emerging stock markets. GARCH and EGARCH empirical results demonstrated a model with high persistence and asymmetric effects of volatility. Their augmented GARCH model indicated that the US subprime crisis spilled over into American, European, Asian, and Arabic financial markets. Notably, there were significant volatility spillovers to Asian markets from the UK and Switzerland. The financial markets of Japan, Korea, and particularly Singapore served as channels through which crises were transmitted across global equity returns. Despite the substantial impact of the subprime crisis, limited empirical research has explored volatility spillover across emerging and advanced financial markets during this period. Yilmaz (2010) investigated return and volatility spillovers among East Asian markets, finding that both return and volatility spillover indices reached their peaks during the global financial crisis. Ahmed et al (2009) examined the international transmission of the US crisis on major stock markets in Southeast Asia, revealing volatility spillovers from the USA to all Southeast Asian markets. Tsuji, C. (2018), using an extended VAR-DCC-AS-MEGARCH model with skew-t-errors, explored returns transmission and volatility spillovers between oil futures and international oil and gas sector equity returns. The study encompassed six international oil and gas sector equity index returns for North America, Latin America, Developed Europe, Emerging Europe, the Far East, and BRIC, alongside WTI oil futures return. Their results indicated unidirectional asymmetric volatility spillover effects from all six oil equities to oil futures, except for the Far East, where bidirectional asymmetric volatility spillovers were observed. Furthermore, Tsuji, C. (2018) computed more precise time-varying optimal hedge ratios and optimal portfolio weights using the conditional variances and covariances from their new model. They clarified that, in international markets, hedging oil equities with oil is cheaper than vice versa. Wang and McPhail (2014) use a structural VAR model to examine the links between U.S. energy prices, economic output, exports, and agricultural commodity prices. They find that energy price shocks and agricultural productivity shocks help explain the volatility of U.S. agricultural commodity prices. The study by Hemche et al. (2016) makes two significant contributions. Firstly, they observed an increase in dynamic correlations across most developed and emerging markets concerning the US market following the subprime crisis. Secondly, concerning the contagion test proposed by Forbes and Rigobon (2002), which associates "pure" contagion with a significantly higher correlation between markets during the crisis, their findings indicate that the "pure" contagion hypothesis is not rejected for France, Italy, the UK, or Mexico at the 1% level, and for Argentina at 10%. In contrast, other markets exhibit a simple interdependence with the US market. Dimpfl et al (2012) found small and short-lived return spillover effects, particularly from the United States to

Japan. Volatility spillovers are more pronounced and persistent. Information from the domestic market is most important for returns and volatilities; the contribution of foreign markets is less pronounced for returns than for volatility in their transmission study of return and volatility spillovers across the world. It uses index futures contracts on three representative indices, namely the Dow Jones Euro Stoxx 50, the S&P 500 and the Nikkei 225. Mensi et al. (2013) utilized a VAR-GARCH model to explore the return connections and volatility transmission between the S&P 500 and commodity price indices for energy, food, Gold, and beverages during the turbulent period from 2000 to 2011. The findings indicate significant transmission among the S&P 500 and commodity markets, where past shocks and volatility in the S&P 500 strongly influenced the oil and gold markets. This investigation identifies the highest conditional correlations between the S&P 500 and the Gold index, as well as the S&P 500 and WTI index. In a separate study, Kearney et al. (2006) examined correlation dynamics using daily data from 1993 to 2002 on the five largest stock market indices in the Eurozone. Employing a conventional asymmetric DCC-MVGARCH specification, they confirmed the presence of a structural break in market index correlations, pinpointing its occurrence at the onset of the monetary integration process in the Eurozone. Ebrahim et al., (2014) Volatility in oil and gold prices has significant economic consequences for financial markets and all sectors of the US economy. This impact manifests directly on consumption, industrial production, and investment in the real and financial sectors, where oil and gold volatilities influence the stock market, creating implications for the U.S. capital market and indirectly manifesting in both unemployment and inflation. Arouri et al. (2015) operated the model VAR-GARCH to examine how the volatility of gold price influences the stock market returns in China for the period 2004-2011; their findings revealed a significant impact of the gold price volatility on the Chinese stock market returns. Baur and McDermott (2010) investigated the price impact of Gold on Financial market over the period 1979-2009, The outcome showed the fact that gold acts as a safe-haven and hedge in the stock market of the United States as well as most of the European countries. Research by Batten et al (2010) found a significant impact of gold price volatility on financial market returns. Bhunia (2013) inspired the inspection of the relationship between domestic gold price and stock price return, by using the Granger test which found the bidirectional causality between price of Gold and the stock return. Pindyck, (2004) Geopolitical and weather factors influence the price of crude oil, which can result in unexpected changes in demand and supply and lead to oil price volatility. It is essential to understand the volatility of crude oil prices, as it may cause uncertainty in all sectors of the economy and lead to instability in the economies of oil exporting and importing countries. The volatility of oil prices puts industrial producers and consumers at risk; they are unable to provide their goods and services at a fair price because of the industries' dependence on oil and oil products.

3.0 METHODOLOGY

3.1 Data and Preliminary Analysis

The dataset under investigation comprises price index values for various financial assets from 2007 to 2009, including stocks and commodities. The time span is constrained by the period of the subprime crisis. The S&P500[1] (SPR), DAX30 (DAXR), HONG SANG index (HSR), Canadian Stock index (CSR), and CAC40 (CACR) stock market indices are for the US, Germany, Japan, Canada, and France, respectively. The commodities markets are represented by [2]Brent crude oil (BOR), WTI crude oil (WTIR), and gold (GR). We calculate return as the natural logarithm of the first difference of the closing primary statistics of the return series for the variables under consideration for each price index.

Table 1. Summary Statistics

	Mean	Median	Maximum	Minimum	Std,Dev,	Skewness	Kurtosis	Jarque-Bera
BOR	**0.047012**	**0.252560**	**11.12629**	**-10.94552**	**2.734763**	**-0.211235**	**5.312491**	**149.4348*** **
CACR	-0.100949	-0.041130	8.867860	-9.471540	1.819477	-0.189996	7.580691	571.3127***
CSR	-0.035310	0.113790	9.370270	-9.787950	1.809678	-0.412975	8.253804	764.8641***
DAXR	-0.066238	0.029160	10.68509	-7.335520	1.757051	-0.150779	7.564201	565.7893***
GR	0.024868	0.047280	8.643170	-6.008280	1.489289	0.326960	6.730058	387.8031***
HSR	-0.017122	0.012140	13.40681	-13.58202	2.408304	0.081796	7.936151	659.6097***
NKR	-0.077530	0.007250	13.23458	-12.11103	2.148259	-0.332351	9.407424	1122.146***
SPR	-0.086164	0.062260	10.24573	-9.469510	1.852261	-0.342929	7.966135	679.6353***
WTIR	0.065913	0.123270	16.40973	-13.06537	3.133430	0.277618	6.596660	358.1466***

Note: This table reports the summary statistics of daily returns of different assets. Jarque-Bera is the test for normality.BTCR and BSER is not included in this paperdue to non-availability of data during the GFC era.***Null hypothesis is rejected at 1% confidence level.

The study of the normality of the yield distribution is tested using the Skewness, Kurtosis and Jarque Bera test. Theoretically, the skewness coefficient ($S = \frac{\sum_{t=1}^{T}(r_t - \bar{\mu}_t)^3}{\bar{\sigma}^3}$) is the centered moment of order 3. It measures the degree of skewness of a distribution around its mean. The kurtosis coefficient ($K = \frac{\sum_{t=1}^{T}(r_t - \bar{\mu}_t)^4}{\bar{\sigma}^4}$) is the centered moment of order 4. It measures the degree of kurtosis of a distribution. The Jarque Bera JB test ($JB = \frac{1}{6}\left(S^2 + \frac{1}{4}(K-3)^2\right)$) is a normality test performed on the residuals. This test combines the two coefficients of skewness and kurtosis in order to verify normality.

reports the descriptive statistics for the price returns of the Gold, Crude Brent Oil, French stock market, Canadian stock market index, Germany stock market index, Hong Kong stock market index, Standard and Poor's 500 index, and West Texas Intermediate Index (GR, BOR, CAC40, CSR, DAXR, HSR, SPR, and WTIR), respectively. The French return index and the return of the West Texas intermediate index provide the highest and lowest returns, respectively. The average returns are negative for CAC40, CSR, DAXR, HSR, and SPR. We can notice that the average returns during the subprime crisis are positive only for the commodity index (BOR, WTIR, and GR). WTI and Brent Oil have the highest unconditional volatility, while gold has the lowest. Overall, the Brent crude oil and West Texas intermediate index perform worse in terms of risk.

The Skewness is negative expect that for (GR, HSR) which is different from zero indicates the presence of asymmetry which contradicts the criterion of a linear Gaussian distribution. The Kurtosis value is over three, this implies a high probability of extreme points and that the series studied have thicker tails than the normal distribution. The coefficients of Skewness and Kurtosis confirm the hypothesis of non-normality of the series studied. Therefore, the conformity of the economic reality of the financial market. Also, the Jarque Bera statistics are significant for the entire index. Moreover, the results of the augmented Dickey-Fuller test are significant, indicating no evidence of unit roots in all series.

Finally, to check normality, the Jarque-Bera test combines the two previous coefficients of Kurtosis and Skewness. According to table 1, for the yield series, the test statistics are very high with a null probability. This leads us to reject the normality hypothesis and confirm that the returns deviate significantly from the normal distribution and follow leptokurtic distributions. The null hypothesis of normality at all confidence levels was rejected.

Figure 1. The daily return of the stock market indices during the GFC

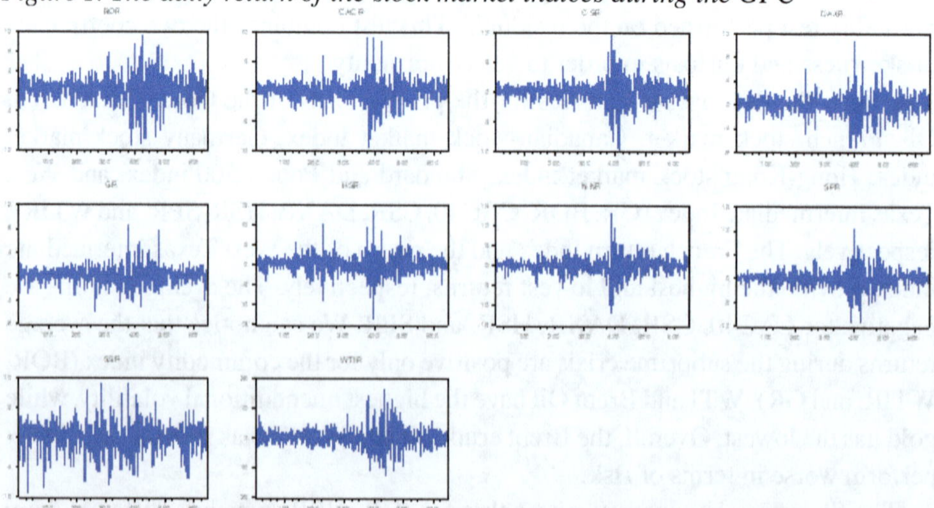

Table 2 presents The Augmented Dickey-Fuller (ADF) test and the Phillip Perron (PP) test were used in the analysis to determine the unit root level of the research variables. According to the fallouts, all of the variables employed in this study are stationary at level, i.e., I(0), and no variable is stationary at first I(1) or second difference I(2). The Autoregressive Conditional Heteroskedasticity-Lagrange Multiplier (ARCH-LM) test was used in the study, with a degree of freedom of 20. The results showed that the research factors had a strong ARCH impact. Also Figure (1) designated that big shocks in returns are followed by high volatility, and the volatility clustering effect in present for all markets. Substantial trends and increasing volatility are found from 2007 to 2009, coinciding to the subprime crisis. Prices in the US stock markets and OIL, in particular, fell sharply during this time period. GOLD prices were similarly low during the subprime crisis, followed by a quick rebound in later periods. This might be attributed to a rise in GOLD demand like a safe haven asset. It means that VAR-DCC-MEGARCH model is perfect for this analysis. The outcomes of the Ljung-Box test denoted these series have significant serial correlation at 20 degrees of freedom.

Table 2. Unit root tests for the sampled variables

	ADF		PP				Ljung-Box(20)	ARCH-LM
	I(0)	I(1)	I(0)	I(1)				
BOR	-27,517***	-14,543***	-27,518***	-351,051***			65.1***	301.66***
CACR	-26,4703***	-13,926***	-26,475***	-243,252***			44.938***	166.47***
CSR	-28,703***	-15,077***	-29,501***	-254,707***			20.904	59.671***
DAXR	-25,0781***	-14,29***	-25,107***	233,93***			28.801*	256.25***
GR	-24,846***	-15,59***	-24,838***	-283,317***			56.304***	144.28***
HSR	-27,6778***	-18,844***	-27,708***	-267,769***			62.423***	212.27***
NKR	-27,3175***	-15,562***	-27,534***	-256,867***			23.16***	204.67***
SPR	-30,042***	-14,864***	-29,934***	-365,522***			43.94***	163.55***
WTIR	-27,4191***	-27,388***	-27,388***	-459,072***			41.908***	193.57***

Note: The Table 2 represent the result of unit root test by using ADF and PP with the intercept. the Ljung–Box (20)statistic for serial correlation in the squared returns. ARCH-LM is the test for conditional heteroskedasticity. ***Null hypothesis is rejected at 1% confidence level.

The Box-Ljung test (1978) is a diagnostic tool used to test the lack of fit of a time series model, the Ljung-Box test a statistical test of whether any of a group of autocorrelation of a time series is different from zero. Instead of testing randomness at each distinct lag, it tests the "overall" randomness based on a number of lags, and is therefore a portmanteau test.

The Ljung Box test defined as:

H_0: the data are independently distributed

H_a: The data are not independently distributed: they exhibit serial correlation

$$Q = n(n+2)\sum_{k=1}^{h} \frac{\widehat{\varrho_k^2}}{n-k}$$

N: the sample size, ϱ_k^2: the sample autocorrelation at lag k, h: the number of lags being tested.

Under H_0 the statistic Q asymptotically follows a ${}^2(h)$. For significance level "a" the critical region for rejection of the hypothesis of randomness is Q > $\chi^2_{1-a,h}$

3.2 Econometric Analysis

The research employed the following method to calculate the daily stock price returns. (Bhuyan et al. 2016; Shehzad, Liu, and Tiwari 2020),

$$Rt = (\ln (R_{it} / R_{it-1}))\times 100 \qquad (1)$$

Where Rt is the daily returns, and R_{it} denominates the closing prices of stock at time t and t-1.

3.3 Mean and Volatility Spillovers Model

This study utilised the bivariate Vector Autoregressive (VAR), Dynamic Conditional Correlation (DCC), and Multivariate Exponential Generalized Autoregressive Conditional Heteroskedasticity (MEGARCH) models, in accordance with the methodology of Engle (2002), to determine the mean and shock spillover patterns between numerous financial markets and commodity markets. The suggested DCC GARCH model by Engle (2002, 2002) can calculate the time-varying correlation of several matrices (Bauwens, Laurent, and Rombouts 2006). Additionally, the EGARCH model effectively measures the impact of asymmetry (Sikhosana and Aye, 2018). The examination calls for the following bivariate model:

$$\mathbf{Y}_{i,t} = \Pi_{i,0} + \sum_{i=1}^{n} \Pi_{i,j} \mathbf{Y}_{j,t-1} + \zeta_{i,t}, \text{ For } i = 1\ldots,n, \tag{2}$$

$Y_{i,t}$: Stock return series i,

$\pi_{i,0}$= constant term

If i≠j $\pi_{i,j}$: estimate the mean return transmission from j to i

If i= j $\pi_{i,j}$: present the lagged returns effect for the upcoming period of its own return series.

ζi,t: the random error term of series I at time t

Where, mean Equation (Equation 2) includes the VAR model with one lag period, and $Y_{i,t}$ nominates the stock return series i and $\pi_{i,0}$ is the constant term. However, if i≠j then $\pi_{i,j}$ estimate the mean return transmission from j to i and when i=j then it measures the lagged returns effect for the upcoming period of its own return series. Whereas, ζ symbolizes the random error term of series i at time t.

On the other hand, $\lambda^2_{i,t}$ in Equation 3 determines the conditional volatility of series i at time t in our bivariate model, and ω_i the intercept coefficient of variance series i. Likewise, if the case is i=j, ki,j denominate the coefficient, which calculates the volatility spillovers from variance series j to i. On the other hand, when i=j, ki,j shows the Autoregressive Conditional Heteroskedasticity (ARCH) effect of series i. Additionally, $\Psi_i$the coefficient that talks about the impact of its own volatility on next day volatility i.e. GARCH effect, and Φ_j the parameter that assesses the asymmetric effect of variance series j. Here n=2 for both equations.

$$\lambda^2_{i,t} = \exp\left\{ \omega_i + \sum\nolimits_{i=0}^{n} k_{i,j} \left(\frac{|\zeta_{j,t-1}|}{\sqrt{\lambda^2_{j,t-1}}} + \Phi_j \frac{\zeta_{j,t-1}}{\sqrt{\lambda^2_{j,t-1}}} \right) + \Psi_i \ln(\lambda^2_{i,t-1}) \right.$$

For i= 1.......n (3)

$\lambda^2_{i,t}$: Conditional Volatility of series i at time t
ω_i: The intercept coefficient of variance series i
$k_{i,j}$: if i ≠ j the volatility spillovers from variance series j to i
If i = j shows the ARCH effect of series i
Ψ_i= The impact of its own volatility on next day volatility I,e GARCH effect
Φ_j: The parameter that assesses the asymmetry effect of variance series j
N=2;

3.4 Dynamic Conditional Correlation DCC

Engle (2002) concludes that: the bivariate version of this model provides a very good approximation of a variety of time-varying correlation processes. According to Engle (2002), the comparison of the DCC with the simple multivariate GARCH and several other estimators shows that the DCC is often the most accurate.

This study followed (Engle 2002) and set the DCC model as follows,

$$H_t = \Xi_t R_t \Xi_t \tag{4}$$

In Equation 4, **Ht** nominates the covariance, and conditional matrix of n×n size and **Rt** determines the positive conditional correlation, whereas Ξ_t is the matrix of time-varying residuals.

H_t: Covariance n*n, **Ξ_t:** matrix of time varying residuals ; **R_t**: Positive conditional correlation

Where

$$\Xi_t = \text{diag}\left(\sigma_{1,t}, \ldots, \sigma_{n,t}\right) \tag{5}$$

And

$$R_t = diag\left(\frac{1}{\sqrt{\varphi_{1,1,t}}}, \ldots, \frac{1}{\sqrt{\varphi_{n,n,t}}}\right)\beta_t\, diag\left(\frac{1}{\sqrt{\varphi_{1,1,t}}}, \ldots, \frac{1}{\sqrt{\varphi_{n,n,t}}}\right) \tag{6}$$

Where ω_t denotes symmetric positive definite matrix,

$$\beta = \begin{pmatrix} \varphi_{1,1,t} & \cdots & \varphi_{1,n,t} \\ \vdots & \ddots & \vdots \\ \varphi_{1,n,t} & \cdots & \varphi_{n,n,t} \end{pmatrix} \tag{7}$$

$$\beta_t = (1 - \Gamma - \varpi)\bar{\beta} + d\,\Phi_{t-1}\Phi_{t-1} + q\beta_{t-1} \tag{8}$$

3Γ, ϖ represent the DCC coefficient,$\bar{\boldsymbol{\beta}}$:inconditional correlation of standard residual,

$\boldsymbol{\Phi}_{t-1}$: Matrix of standardized residuals,

In addition, $\bar{\beta}$ is the unconditional correlation matrix of standardized residuals, and Φ_t is the n×1 matrix of standardized residuals. Γ, ϖ are the DCC coefficients, and their sum is supposed to be between 0 and 1. Thus, this is our multivariate VAR-DCC-MEGARCH model based on the normal distribution. Time-varying correlation between series I and j can be obtained as follows;

$$\Omega_{ij,t} = \frac{\varphi_{i,j,t}}{\sqrt{\varphi_{i,j,t}\varphi_{j,j,t}}} \tag{9}$$

This is our VAR-DCC-MEGARCH model, which is newly extended based on Koutmos (1996)-type constant conditional correlation (CCC-MEGARCH). However, Koutmos (1996) used a CCC model with normal distribution errors and the model was not a DCC model. Hence the model VAR-DCC-MEGARCH with normal distribution is a extension of the Koutmos (1996) type model. We note that the mean equations of our model employ VAR (1) implying that we can examine the causal effects between index market of the sample.

Therefore, our model will be very useful and highly novel because return transmission and asymmetric volatility spillovers are analyzed in one model.

3.4.1 Evaluation of Optimal Portfolios and Hedging

This study follows the methodology of kroner and sultan (1993) to measure the optimal hedge between the indexes. the research hedges the long position of asset i with the short position asset j as follows,

$$\wedge_{i,j,t} = \frac{\Phi_{i,j,t}}{\Phi^2_{j,t}} \tag{10}$$

Here $\boldsymbol{\Phi}_{i,j,t}$ nominates the time-varying covariance between asset j and i; while, $\boldsymbol{\Phi}^2_{j,t}$ indicates the conditional variance of asset j at time t.

In addition, the study considered optimal portfolio weights as outlined below (Kroner and Ng, 1998),

$$K_{i,j,t} = \Phi^2_{j,t} - \frac{\Phi_{i,j,t}}{\Phi^2_{j,t}} - 2\Phi_{i,j,t} + \Phi^2_{i,t} \tag{11}$$

$$\kappa_{i,j,t} = \begin{cases} 0, if\,\kappa_{i,j,t} < 0 \\ \kappa_{i,j,t}, if 0 \leq \kappa_{i,j,t} \leq 1 \\ 1, if\,\kappa_{i,j,t} > 1 \end{cases} \tag{12}$$

$\kappa_{i,j,t}$ Indicates the time varying optimal weights of asset i at time t. Hence, the optimal weights for asset j at time t can be ascertained as $1\text{-}\kappa_{i,j,t}$.

4.0 RESULTS AND DISCUSSION

In this study, we analyzed the VAR-DCC-MEGARCH model for GFC era in two parts due to the multicollinearity, strong correlation, and sparse data on stock markets. Where panel 1 includes the market indices Canadian CSR, Nikkei 225, S&P 500, CAC40, and commodity indexes such Gold, Brent crude oil, and West Texas crude oil. Panel 2 includes the Hong Sang index markets, and the German DAX30 index.

4.1 Return Transmission

Starting with the VAR results for the returns in our mean equations in the table 3 and table 4, one of the clearest results is that one lag period. The returns of the CACR index are strongly positively correlated with the returns of BOR and NKR at time t-1, suggesting that an increase in the returns of these two at time t-1 will also raise the returns of CACR. A negative return on gold will aggravate the situation since gold returns at time t-1 have had a substantial negative influence during the global financial crisis. In addition, the statistics of the propagation of WTIR and BOR return at t-1 to the Chinese index NKR are positively significant, meaning that NKR performance improves as a result of a rise in WTIR and BOR return at t-1. The recovery of the CSR, SPR, and BOR indexes at t-1 has a favorable effect on the commodities index, which benefits gold. The constant term of WTIR is significantly which implies the average value is different from zero, so the returns of NKR and BOR indices at t-1 are positively related to the return of WTIR at time t. The return of the gold index is immaterially negative to the SPR index. The spillover of WTIR returns at t-1 is negative on the SPR index where during the GFC an increase in WTIR returns will aggravate the situation of SPR at time t. On the other hand, the BOR is positively significant, meaning that a rise in BOR returns at time t-1 will have a positive impact on the returns of SPR at time t. The effects of return spillover revealed that the BOR index's current-day returns are significantly and negatively impacted by the BOR's historical returns (Brent oil). BOR's constant term is therefore significantly positive.

The returns of the BOR index at time t-1 and the CACR index are inversely correlated, meaning that when BOR raises, CACR's performance at time t will also decline. The spillover returns from BOR to DAXR at time t-1 are negatively significant, and the spillover returns parameters from the day before demonstrated that the returns from GR and WTIR to DAXR at time t-1 are not significant. The HSR index at time t is significantly impacted positively by the Gold index's return spillover at time t-1. In addition, the HSR at time t is negatively influenced by the HSR's return at time t-1. The outcomes of the VAR model during the GFC era demonstrated that growing returns spillover of GR at the previous day returns significantly reducing the return.

Table 3. VAR results for Panel 1

Variable	Coefficient	T-STAT	P-Value
CSR			
Π_{CST}	0,0392	0,8834	0,3770
Π_{CSR}	-0,0376	-0,8624	0,3885
Π_{GR}	0,1959	1,2924	0,1962
Π_{NKR}	0,0179	1,8666	0,0620
Π_{WTIR}	0,0235	0,8373	0,4024
Π_{SPR}	-0,0868	1,1861	0,2356
Π_{CACR}	-0,0731	-0,3821	0,7024
Π_{BOR}	0,0962	-2,3283	0,0199
GR			
Π_{CST}	0,0214	0,4643	0,6424
Π_{CSR}	0,0421	4,3252	0,0000
Π_{GR}	0,0520	1,5378	0,1241
Π_{NKR}	-0,0917	-0,3974	0,6910
Π_{WTIR}	0,0726	-0,0637	0,9492
Π_{SPR}	0,0003	-2,4751	0,0133
Π_{CACR}	0,0053	0,0791	0,9370
Π_{BOR}	0,0306	-2,4730	0,0134
NKR			
Π_{CST}	-0,0173	-0,3596	0,7191
Π_{CSR}	0,0435	0,3799	0,7040

continued on following page

Table 3. Continued

Variable	Coefficient	T-STAT	P-Value
Π_{GR}	-0,0096	-2,6032	0,0092
Π_{NKR}	-0,2002	-7,9334	0,0000
Π_{WTIR}	0,0879	3,3876	0,0007
Π_{SPR}	0,0176	9,9404	0,0000
Π_{CACR}	-0,0026	6,7779	0,0000
Π_{BOR}	0,0564	-1,7053	0,0881
WTIR			
Π_{CST}	0,1649	2,0605	0,0394
Π_{CSR}	0,0233	0,2990	0,7650
Π_{GR}	-0,0018	1,2350	0,2168
Π_{NKR}	0,1019	2,0878	0,0368
Π_{WTIR}	0,0503	1,0038	0,3155
Π_{SPR}	-0,0546	-0,0508	0,9595
Π_{CACR}	0,0455	0,4398	0,6601
Π_{BOR}	0,0398	-4,0284	0,0001
SPR			
Π_{CST}	-0,0117	-0,2521	0,8009
Π_{CSR}	0,0470	-1,8946	0,0581
Π_{GR}	-0,1018	0,0084	0,9933
Π_{NKR}	0,4260	0,7185	0,4724
Π_{WTIR}	-0,0036	-1,8712	0,0613
Π_{SPR}	-0,0668	-1,6049	0,1085
Π_{CACR}	0,4189	-0,6002	0,5484
Π_{BOR}	0,0346	1,7433	0,0813
CACR			
Π_{CST}	0,0102	0,2070	0,8360
Π_{CSR}	-0,0129	-1,5075	0,1317
Π_{GR}	0,0028	0,1478	0,8825
Π_{NKR}	0,2478	-0,0993	0,9209
Π_{WTIR}	0,0268	1,4743	0,1404
Π_{SPR}	-0,0213	9,5219	0,0000
Π_{CACR}	-0,2719	-7,2444	0,0000
Π_{BOR}	-0,0212	-2,1397	0,0324
BOR			

continued on following page

Table 3. Continued

Variable	Coefficient	T-STAT	P-Value
Π_{CST}	0,1829	2,4557	0,0141
Π_{CSR}	-0,0782	1,3139	0,1889
Π_{GR}	-0,0862	0,5593	0,5760
Π_{NKR}	-0,0620	1,4412	0,1495
Π_{WTIR}	-0,2440	0,8522	0,3941
Π_{SPR}	0,0615	0,5208	0,6025
Π_{CACR}	-0,0798	-0,3740	0,7084
Π_{BOR}	-0,2024	-3,5918	0,0003

Table 4. VAR results for Panel 2

Variable	Coefficient	T-STAT	P-Value
DAXR			
Π_{CST}	0,0468	0,9333	0,3507
Π_{DAXR}	-0,0052	-0,1553	0,8765
Π_{GR}	-0,0067	-0,1127	0,9103
Π_{WTIR}	-0,0257	1,0162	0,3095
Π_{BOR}	-0,0025	-1,6460	0,0998
Π_{HSR}	0,4018	1,2418	0,2143
GR			
Π_{CST}	0,0100	0,2175	0,8278
Π_{DAXR}	-0,0041	-0,2216	0,8246
Π_{GR}	0,0642	1,9465	0,0516
Π_{WTIR}	0,0812	0,6536	0,5134
Π_{BOR}	0,0512	-1,4844	0,1377
Π_{HSR}	0,1872	0,5875	0,5569
WTIR			
Π_{CST}	0,1452	1,7603	0,0784
Π_{DAXR}	0,0321	-0,4697	0,6385
Π_{GR}	0,0189	1,3675	0,1715
Π_{WTIR}	0,1003	1,9320	0,0534
Π_{BOR}	0,0922	-5,0568	0,0000
Π_{HSR}	0,0486	2,9109	0,0036

continued on following page

Table 4. Continued

Variable	Coefficient	T-STAT	P-Value
BOR			
Π_{CST}	0,1595	2,0814	0,0374
Π_{DAXR}	-0,0612	-0,0484	0,9614
Π_{GR}	-0,0505	0,9294	0,3527
Π_{WTIR}	-0,3093	1,9117	0,0559
Π_{BOR}	-0,2609	-4,5915	0,0000
Π_{HSR}	-0,0757	2,5801	0,0099
HSR			
Π_{CST}	0,0702	1,0200	0,3077
Π_{DAXR}	0,0323	8,7878	0,0000
Π_{GR}	0,0139	3,7784	0,0002
Π_{WTIR}	0,1243	1,1204	0,2626
Π_{BOR}	0,1024	-1,4820	0,1383
Π_{HSR}	-0,1662	-4,6632	0,0000

Note: This table reports the VAR model results as in Eq. 2

4.2 Volatility Spillovers

Our results in tables 5 and 6 proved that only the volatility propagation parameter of CACR to WTIR is statistically negative at the 10 percent level and all volatility propagation parameters of CSR GR NKR WTIR SPR and BOR to WTIR are statistically insignificant The second finding is that the volatility parameters of CACR and CSR are negative and significant at the 5 percent level, which means that a disturbance in the latter two can disrupt the SPR market during the GFC period. At the same time, the volatility propagation parameter from WTIR to SPR is positively significant at the 10 percent level.

Conversely, the impact of WTIR volatility on the CACR is positively significant, meaning that the performance of the WTIR market can stabilize or destabilize the French market. The other indices in Panel A have no impact on the variance of the CACR because they are all statistically insignificant. During the GFC period, the volatility spillover parameters from the CACR to the BOR are negative and significant at the 10 percent level, implying that shocks that occurred in these markets affect the variance of the other during the GFC period. The shock that occurred in the variance of Brent oil (BOR) at time t imperatively affects its own returns at time t+1, which means that the BOR index has a significant ARCH effect, also the volatility spillover parameter of WTIR on BOR is positive and significant during the GFC period.

We can identify the volatility spillover effect of all market indices on NKR and CSR are not significant. The volatility spillover effect of the CSR index variance on GR is negatively significant at 5 percent, i.e., a negative shock to the Canadian market will automatically impact the gold market. On the other hand, the volatility spillover from the Gold index has no effect on the CSR.

Table 5. Outcomes of DCC-MEGARCH model (Panel 1)

Parameters	Coef	Std. Error	t value	Pr(>|t|)
ω_{CSR}	-0,0066	0,0414	-0,1593	0,8735
ω_{GR}	0,0406	0,0560	0,7261	0,4678
ω_{NKR}	-0,0809	0,0451	-1,7925	0,0731
ω_{WTIR}	-0,0358	0,0320	-1,1170	0,2640
ω_{SPR}	0,0165	0,0341	0,4848	0,6278
ω_{CACR}	-0,0361	0,0546	-0,6612	0,5085
ω_{BOR}	0,0064	0,0288	0,2206	0,8254
Ψ_{CSR}	0,9778	0,0029	334,7654	0,0000
Ψ_{GR}	0,9916	0,0001	14618,0980	0,0000
Ψ_{NKR}	0,9724	0,0723	13,4462	0,0000
Ψ_{WTIR}	0,9856	0,0000	30435,6798	0,0000
Ψ_{SPR}	0,9839	0,0003	3107,2744	0,0000
Ψ_{CACR}	0,9801	0,0002	4183,9426	0,0000
Ψ_{BOR}	0,9834	0,0000	42822,4260	0,0000
φ_{CSR}	0,1400	0,0426	3,2838	0,0010
φ_{GR}	0,0629	0,0108	5,7971	0,0000
φ_{NKR}	0,2276	0,0837	2,7195	0,0065
φ_{WTIR}	0,0701	0,0068	10,3391	0,0000
φ_{SPR}	0,0900	0,0076	11,8402	0,0000
φ_{CACR}	0,0559	0,0085	6,5747	0,0000
φ_{BOR}	0,0731	0,0052	13,9505	0,0000
Γ	0,0187	0,0032	5,8498	0,0000
Π	0,9567	0,0085	112,5799	0,0000

Note: Note: ω_n: Constant term of index Ψ_n: the impact of its own volatility on next day volatility I,e GARCH effect φ_n: parameter that assesses the asymmetry effect of variance series j Gamma factor (Γ, Π): the DCC parameters. We have divided the whole data into two Panels due to less observations and access of variables. (Only VAR and DCC-MEGARCH results should be defined separately; however, we can define correlation, hedging, and other things without dividing into Panels).

The results of equation (3) during the period of the global financial crisis indicated that the constant term of the indices in panel 1 is not significant, only for the NKR index is negatively significant at the 10 perce1nt level. The survey specified that an increase in the volatility of all market indexes in Panel 1 significantly amplified their own volatility, inferring that these indexes have a strong GARCH effect. The gamma factors of the indices in the sample are positively significant, indicating that positive news falling on the market has a more significant impact on these indices than negative news. The DCC (ɼ, Π) parameters of the DCC MEGARCH model for panel 1 indicated positive and significant values. The sum of these coefficients is less than unity, confirming that this model is mean-reverting (see table 7) .

Table 6. Regression indices VAR-DCC-MEGARCH (PANEL 1)

	Estimate	Std. Error	t value	Pr(>|t|)
CSR				
CSR	-0,0613	0,0401	-1,5291	0,1262
GR	0,0108	0,0200	0,5421	0,5877
NKR	0,0199	0,0187	1,0683	0,2854
WTIR	0,0163	0,0251	0,6493	0,5161
SPR	-0,0281	0,0405	-0,6935	0,4880
CACR	-0,0396	0,0365	-1,0846	0,2781
BOR	-0,0083	0,0264	-0,3156	0,7523
GR				
CSR	-0,0779	0,0313	-2,4885	0,0128
GR	-0,0371	0,0358	-1,0368	0,2999
NKR	-0,0095	0,0161	-0,5865	0,5575
WTIR	-0,0040	0,0183	-0,2205	0,8255
SPR	0,0061	0,0335	0,1824	0,8553
CACR	0,0091	0,0299	0,3052	0,7602
BOR	0,0162	0,0213	0,7594	0,4476
NKR				
CSR	0,0291	0,0914	0,3185	0,7501
GR	0,0029	0,0475	0,0620	0,9506
NKR	-0,0423	0,0419	-1,0090	0,3130
WTIR	0,0034	0,0266	0,1292	0,8972
SPR	0,0245	0,0755	0,3239	0,7460
CACR	-0,0524	0,0544	-0,9642	0,3350

continued on following page

Table 6. Continued

	Estimate	Std. Error	t value	Pr(>|t|)
BOR	-0,0156	0,0885	-0,1758	0,8605
WTIR				
CSR	-0,0469	0,0289	-1,6249	0,1042
GR	0,0325	0,0200	1,6245	0,1043
NKR	0,0212	0,0162	1,3072	0,1911
WTIR	0,0227	0,0192	1,1836	0,2366
SPR	0,0339	0,0300	1,1296	0,2587
CACR	-0,0528	0,0279	-1,8901	0,0587
BOR	-0,0257	0,0222	-1,1564	0,2475
SPR				
CSR	-0,0720	0,0285	-2,5262	0,0115
GR	-0,0084	0,0175	-0,4777	0,6329
NKR	-0,0124	0,0172	-0,7227	0,4699
WTIR	0,0382	0,0206	1,8561	0,0634
SPR	0,0146	0,0335	0,4376	0,6617
CACR	-0,0647	0,0317	-2,0374	0,0416
BOR	-0,0150	0,0241	-0,6209	0,5347
CACR				
CSR	-0,0287	0,0347	-0,8257	0,4090
GR	-0,0239	0,0181	-1,3200	0,1868
NKR	-0,0102	0,0162	-0,6292	0,5292
WTIR	0,0420	0,0194	2,1646	0,0304
SPR	0,0366	0,0405	0,9045	0,3657
CACR	-0,0598	0,0440	-1,3604	0,1737
BOR	-0,0331	0,0222	-1,4938	0,1352
BOR				
CSR	-0,0315	0,0284	-1,1109	0,2666
GR	0,0205	0,0176	1,1602	0,2460
NKR	0,0236	0,0168	1,4029	0,1607
WTIR	0,0464	0,0194	2,3928	0,0167
SPR	0,0261	0,0287	0,9117	0,3619
CACR	-0,0524	0,0269	-1,9451	0,0518
BOR	-0,0611	0,0263	-2,3232	0,0202

Note: The information Criteria; Akaike: 22.929; Bayes: 24.060; Shibata: 22.833; Hannan-Quinn: 23.368

Table 7. Outcomes of DCC-MEGARCH model PANEL 2

Parameters	Coef	Std. Error	t value	Pr(>|t|)
ω_{DAXR}	0,0073	0,0367	0,1977	0,8433
ω_{GR}	0,0125	0,0605	0,2073	0,8358
ω_{WTIR}	-0,0165	0,0418	-0,3952	0,6927
ω_{BOR}	-0,5009	0,2532	-1,9783	0,0479
ω_{HSR}	0,0116	0,1537	0,0756	0,9397
Ψ_{DAXR}	0,9809	0,0004	2540,8441	0,0000
Ψ_{GR}	0,9796	0,0051	190,4058	0,0000
Ψ_{WTIR}	0,9847	0,0001	12005,1054	0,0000
Ψ_{BOR}	0,3780	0,1152	3,2816	0,0010
Ψ_{HSR}	0,9597	0,0013	762,7672	0,0000
φ_{DAXR}	0,0688	0,0092	7,4993	0,0000
φ_{GR}	0,0736	0,0502	1,4666	0,1425
φ_{WTIR}	0,0511	0,0107	4,7748	0,0000
φ_{BOR}	0,9024	0,2692	3,3525	0,0008
φ_{HSR}	0,6079	0,0605	10,0402	0,0000
Γ	0,0044	0,0015	3,0389	0,0024
Π	0,9743	0,0105	92,5703	0,0000

Note: ω_n: Constant term of index Ψ_n: the impact of its own volatility on next day volatility I.e. GARCH effect φ_n: parameter that assesses the asymmetry effect of variance series j Gamma factor (Γ, Π): the DCC parameters.
Source: Author's calculation.

Table 8. Regression index VAR-DCC-MEGARCH (PANEL 2)

Parameters	Estimate	Std. Error	t value	Pr(>|t|)
DAXR				
DAXR	-0,0782	0,0298	-2,6205	0,0088
GR	-0,0158	0,0197	-0,8010	0,4231
WTIR	0,0158	0,0196	0,8066	0,4199
BOR	-0,0022	0,0233	-0,0947	0,9246
HSR	-0,0261	0,0144	-1,8124	0,0699
GR				
DAXR	-0,0463	0,0285	-1,6225	0,1047
GR	-0,0267	0,0423	-0,6317	0,5276
WTIR	-0,0097	0,0233	-0,4182	0,6758

continued on following page

Table 8. Continued

Parameters	Estimate	Std. Error	t value	Pr(>ltl)
BOR	0,0170	0,0296	0,5740	0,5660
HSR	-0,0201	0,0166	-1,2098	0,2263
WTIR				
DAXR	-0,0714	0,0276	-2,5842	0,0098
GR	0,0214	0,0192	1,1171	0,2640
WTIR	0,0051	0,0247	0,2077	0,8354
BOR	-0,0185	0,0243	-0,7606	0,4469
HSR	-0,0031	0,0134	-0,2306	0,8176
BOR				
DAXR	-0,1132	0,0732	-1,5464	0,1220
GR	0,0570	0,0641	0,8885	0,3743
WTIR	0,0624	0,0491	1,2723	0,2033
BOR	-0,1249	0,0665	-1,8775	0,0604
HSR	0,0162	0,0357	0,4528	0,6507
HSR				
DAXR	0,0092	0,0443	0,2087	0,8347
GR	0,0329	0,0268	1,2254	0,2204
WTIR	0,0220	0,0310	0,7094	0,4781
BOR	-0,0569	0,0376	-1,5147	0,1299
HSR	-0,0547	0,0332	-1,6437	0,1002

Note: The information Criteria ; Akaike: 23.891 ; Bayes: 25.170; Shibata: 23.623; Hannan-Quinn: 22.818

For panel 2presented in table 8, we have as market indices the DAXR, and the HSR with the commodity indices (GOLD Return, Brent Oil Return, and WTI Return). The change in the variance of the DAXR, and HSR at time t evocatively affects their own variance at time t+1, which suggests that the German index market and the HONG SONG index market show a significant GARCH effect. The results of equation (3) during the GFC period indicate that the constant term of Brent oil (WBOR) for Panel 2 is negatively significant, but the other indices denote a non-significant constant term.

In addition, the volatility propagation statistics indicate that the volatility of DAXR strongly increased the volatility of the WTIR index, while the volatility propagation from WTIR to DAXR was not significant during the GFC period. The investigation showed that the shocks evaluated on the standardized residuals of the DAXR index imperceptibly affect its own return series. This indicates that the DAXR index has a significant ARCH effect. Although the shocks estimated by the standardized residuals of Brent OIL (BOR) at time t impact its own returns at time t+1, which means that the BOR index has a significant ARCH effect. The survey specified that an increase in the volatility of the panel 2 indices strongly amplified their own volatility, inferring that the indices exhibit a GARCH effect. The gamma factor of the GR index (φ_{GR}) contains a positive and significant value, indicating that positive news that occurs in the market has a more significant impact on the GR than negative news. On the other hand, the gamma parameter for the WTIR index and the BOR index ($\varphi_{WTIR}\varphi_{BOR}$) contains positive and insignificant leverage for these markets. The same results for the other indices in Panel 2 during the GFC period. The DCC parameters (ɼ, Π) of the DCC-MEGARCH model for Panel 2 are positive and significant. Moreover, the sum of these factors does not cross the limit of unity, which indicates that the DCC-MEGARCH model is mean-reverting.

4.3.1 Time-Varying Correlation

Table 9. Last day correlation (Panel 1)

	CSR	GR	NKR	WTIR	SPR	CACR	BOR
CSR	1						
GR	0.3965884	1					
NKR	0.1040221	0.02646456	1				
WTIR	0.3874364	0.40421429	0.18239032	1			
SPR	0.7295922	0.15865949	0.17546469	0.2463959	1		
CACR	0.5769674	0.11334363	0.25119689	0.2691329	0.6642010	1	
BOR	0.3696815	0.44306733	0.17029986	0.8939951	0.2228845	0.2934602	1

Note: This table reports the last day correlation matrix for Panel 1 during GFC.

Table 10. Last day correlation (Panel 2)

	DAXR	GR	WTIR	BOR	HSR
DAXR	1				
GR	0.1292053	1			
WTIR	0.2664528	0.3988176	1		
BOR	0.2838818	0.3448385	0.8140115	1	
HSR	0.2975810	0.1428700	0.2288849	0.2814320	1

Note: This table reports the last day correlation matrix for Panel 2 during GFC. Source: Author's calculation.

The tables 9 and 10 of last day correlation presented the correlation between market indices and commodity indices on the [4]last day of the panel sampling period. The results showed that the Canadian CSR Index is highly correlated with commodity indices (GR, WTIR, and BOR,) during the global financial crisis. The correlation between the French CACR, and BOR, index is the highest compared to the correlations with the other commodity indices (WTIR, and GR), is 29% during the global financial crisis. In addition, we can notice that the correlation between the commodity indices is important.

The last day correlation table showed that the American index SPR, and the Chinese index NKR, have a higher correlation with the oil indices than the GOLD index. The last day correlation of global financial crisis shows that German index DAXR, and Japanese index HSR, are less correlated with Gold (0.12, 0.14, respectively) than oil indexes (WTIR, BOR,). The results confirmed that these markets have a correlation with the commodity markets, and are strongly correlated with the oil indices than Gold.

The correlation between the GOLD index and the international indices is low. What we can notice from the two tables of last day correlation is that the correlation between the selected commodity indices and the international indices is low. On the other hand, there is a strong correlation between the GOLD, Brent Oil and the WTIR, index. This means that if a shock hits one of these markets the contagion effect and shock propagation will be faster during the Global financial crisis.

4.3.2 Optimal Portfolios and Hedging

The optimal hedge ratios (i.e. time-varying betas) are estimated from Eq. (4) using a VAR-DCC-MEGARCH (1,1) model.

Table 11 and table 12 represent the summary of the optimal time-varying hedge ratio between index markets and commodity indices for the GFC period. The results revealed that the average hedge ratio of the CACR/GR index is 0.086, which implies that the long position of the CACR index can be hedged by a short position of GR of 8.6 percent.

Similarly, the Chinese NKR/GR index is 0.0085, which implies that the long position of NKR can be covered by a GR short position of 0.85 cents. For a crisis period, the hedge ratio of NKR/GR is very close to zero, so Gold represents a safe haven asset for the Chinese NKR index. On the other hand, the lowest hedge value for the Canadian CSR index is with WTIR, where CSR/WTIR is equal to 0.2, which implies that the $1 long position can be hedged for 20 cents. Similarly, and in the same table, we determined the hedge ratios of the commodity indices. The results showed that for GR, WTIR and BOR, should be hedged with the Chinese NKR index during the global financial crisis as they represent the lowest ratios

Table 11. Summary of time-varying hedging during GFC (Panel 1).

Colonne1	BOR/ CACR	BOR/CSR	BOR/NKR	BOR/SPR	CACR/BOR	CACR/GR	CACR/ WTIR	CSR/BOR
Min	-0,1319	0,2599	-0,1826	-0,1604	-0,0531	-0,3861	-0,0872	0,1337
Median	0,4140	0,6506	0,2354	0,2838	0,1773	0,1149	0,1500	0,2242
Mean	0,4241	0,6762	0,2530	0,3295	0,1697	0,0861	0,1418	0,2450
Max	1,0007	1,3828	0,8219	0,9411	0,3330	0,3255	0,3115	0,5685
	CSR/GR	CSR/ WTIR	GR/CACR	GR/CSR	GR/NKR	GR/SPR	NKR/BOR	NKR/GR
Min	-0,0758	0,1133	-0,3254	-0,0361	-0,1605	-0,2669	-0,0677	-0,2031
Median	0,2508	0,1918	0,1029	0,2807	0,0019	0,0584	0,0880	0,0017
Mean	0,2576	0,2140	0,0657	0,2663	0,0032	0,0426	0,0967	0,0085
Max	0,5412	0,5155	0,3133	0,5387	0,1485	0,3055	0,3283	0,2717
	NKR/ WTIR	SPR/BOR	SPR/GR	SPR/ WTIR	WTIR/ CACR	WTIR/ CSR	WTIR/NKR	WTIR/ SPR
Min	-0,0565	-0,0685	-0,4245	-0,0699	-0,2847	0,2825	-0,1374	-0,1988
Median	0,0729	0,1235	0,0689	0,1005	0,4333	0,7087	0,2576	0,3232
Mean	0,0833	0,1231	0,0389	0,1045	0,4551	0,7468	0,2827	0,3658
Max	0,3016	0,3689	0,2557	0,3381	1,0998	1,3972	0,9669	1,0379

Note:This table reports the optimal hedge ratios (HR) for panel 1 from Eq. (10),

Table 12. Summary of time-varying hedging during GFC (Panel 2).

Colonne1	BOR/DAXR	BOR/HSR	DAXR/BOR	HSR/BOR
MIN	0,2974	0,0636	0,0237	0,0495
MEDIAN	1,4309	0,3688	0,0481	0,1948
MEAN	1,3907	0,391	0,0559	0,2178
MAX	2,852	2,3085	0,2158	1,1642
	GR/DAXR	GR/HSR	DAXR/GR	HSR/GR
MIN	-0,0304	0,0061	-0,0404	0,1455
MEDIAN	0,0961	0,0244	0,1107	0,3546
MEAN	0,088	0,0241	0,1051	0,4124
MAX	0,1656	0,0757	0,2033	1,1131
	WTIR/DAXR	WTIR/HSR	DAXR/WTIR	HSR/WTIR
MIN	0,1993	0,0345	0,0638	0,1501

continued on following page

Table 12. Continued

Colonne1	BOR/DAXR	BOR/HSR	DAXR/BOR	HSR/BOR
MEDIAN	0,4091	0,0961	0,1395	0,4501
MEAN	0,4286	0,1048	0,1387	0,4819
MAX	0,9074	0,3244	0,2298	1,1323

Note: This table reports the optimal hedge ratios (HR) for panel 2 from Eq. (10),

Table 13 summarizes the optimal portfolio allocations to Gold, Brent, and WTI oil, with the financial assets of America, Europe and Asia during the global financial crisis. The findings suggest that, for risk minimization given the expected return, the optimal weights are generally above 50% for Gold for all sample market indices, with the exception of the HSR index, in which investors should hold 4% of their wealth in Gold while the remainder should be invested in the Hong Song stock index also In this time of crisis, Hong Song (HSR) should have invested 20% of its investment in WTI crude oil, according to the ideal portfolio weight. In this vein, Arouri et al. (2015) state that the emergence of successive financial turbulence and crises has forced investors to consider alternative investment instruments by including Gold in their portfolio as a safe haven asset.

Table 13. Summary of optimal weights during GFC

	MIN	MEDIAN	MEAN	MAX
CACR/BOR	-331,269	1,398	2,839	177,714
CACR/GR	0,217	0,509	0,517	1,164
CACR/WTIR	-1324,284	1,718	13,334	5375,881
CSR/BOR	-2426,757	1,829	0,800	693,236
CSR/GR	0,135	0,536	0,591	1,854
CSR/WTIR	-452,392	2,378	3,171	325,089
NKR/BOR	0,291	1,307	1,608	7,912
NKR/GR	0,141	0,558	0,565	1,377
NKR/WTIR	0,438	1,477	2,027	11,094
SPR/BOR	0,317	1,253	1,717	11,102
SPR/GR	0,204	0,501	0,527	0,962
DAXR/BOR	-2489,542	11,522	16,871	3423,398
DAXR/GR	0,248	0,511	0,522	0,987
DAXR/WTIR	0,742	1,715	2,314	12,424
HSR/BOR	-430,951	2,857	4,109	201,436

continued on following page

Table 13. Continued

	MIN	MEDIAN	MEAN	MAX
HSR/GR	-0,001	0,037	0,046	0,349
HSR/WTIR	-0,004	0,125	0,204	1,856

Note: This table reports the optimal portfolio weights as in Eq. (11).

4.4 Results of Diagnostic Models

In order to evaluate the serial correlation in the standardized residuals and its square, the study has applied the test of Breusch and Pagan (2006) at 20 degrees of freedom. The verdicts of this test, given in Table 14, stated that there is no evidence of serial correlation in the standardized residuals and square of standardized residuals of both Panels. Consequently, the VAR-DCC-MEGARCH model is correctly fitted on these markets.

Table 14. Diagnostics Test of VAR-DCC-MEGARCH

Variables	Q(20)	P-value	Q2(20)	P-values
Panel 1				
CSR	24,98	0,2046	24,086	0,2387
GR	16,22	0,7029	21,529	0,3666
NKR	20,337	0,437	13,041	0,8756
WTIR	16,835	0,6636	37,267	0,01087
SPR	24,532	0,2199	23,38	0,2705
CACR	30,014	0,06963	35,793	0,01626
BOR	10,309	0,9622	17,057	0,6497
Panel 2				
DAXR	33,839	0,02724	21,171	0,3872
GR	12,427	0,9007	19,465	0,4918
WTIR	23,666	0,2573	18,725	0,5398
BOR	58,805	1,09E-05	96,636	5,01E-12
HSR	24,963	0,2029	14,46	0,8064

Note: This table reports the diagnostic tests for model misspecification: Ljung–Box Q2(10) and Q2(20), and the ARCH test on the residuals of the estimated VAR-DCC model. p-values associated with the statistical tests are reported in brackets. Lower p-values cast doubt on the correct specification of the model.

5.0 CONCLUSION

Following the subprime crisis (2007–2009), global financial markets were severely disrupted, undermining both financial and economic stability. This study analyzed the non-linear behavior of ten prominent stock markets globally, including the S&P500, Canadian stock market index (GSPTSE), DAX30, CAC40, Nikkei 225, and Hang Seng index (HSR). Additionally, three critical commodities—Brent oil, WTI crude oil, and Gold—were examined, given their global trading significance. The study utilized the VAR-DCC-MEGARCH model to capture the dynamic asymmetric relationships between these major indices and commodity markets during the subprime crisis.

The empirical results reveal that correlations between the markets varied significantly over time, with a marked decline during the Global Financial Crisis (GFC). Gold proved to be an effective hedge, reducing downside risks for indices in Europe, America, and Asia during market downturns. The findings also demonstrated that incorporating Gold into portfolios of the French market, S&P500, and Nikkei 225 improved risk-adjusted performance during the subprime crisis, while Brent oil proved beneficial for the Japanese HSR and German DAXR markets. Moreover, WTI Crude Oil acted as a safe haven for the Canadian market in 2009. These insights suggest that investors should prioritize Gold over crude oil to mitigate risks and diversify portfolios more effectively during periods of financial turbulence.

In the context of financial sustainability, these findings underscore the importance of resilient and diversified portfolios that are capable of withstanding systemic shocks. Gold's role as a hedge during crises highlights its relevance for long-term financial stability, particularly in the face of economic uncertainties. This aligns with Environmental, Social, and Governance (ESG) principles, which emphasize responsible risk management, transparency, and long-term value creation in financial decision-making. Additionally, the use of commodities like Gold as a hedging tool is in line with Sustainable Development Goal (SDG) 8 (Decent Work and Economic Growth), as it supports the creation of robust financial systems that protect economic stability during periods of crisis. Furthermore, by promoting efficient risk management and portfolio diversification, this study also touches upon SDG 12 (Responsible Consumption and Production), as effective market risk mitigation contributes to more responsible and sustainable financial practices.

The novel contribution of this chapter lies in its application of the VAR-DCC-MEGARCH model, which provides a nuanced understanding of the evolving risk dynamics between stock markets and commodity markets during a financial crisis. This analysis is particularly relevant for policymakers and investors aiming to build resilient financial systems. The findings highlight the importance of including commodities like Gold in sustainable investment strategies, which are essential for maintaining financial sustainability during periods of extreme market volatility.

5.1 Future Research Directions

The findings and methodology of this chapter open several promising avenues for future scholarly inquiry:

- **Incorporating ESG Factors:** Future research could integrate Environmental, Social, and Governance (ESG) scores into the volatility and correlation analysis. A critical question is whether high-ESG assets demonstrate different spillover dynamics or hedging properties during crises, potentially acting as a new class of sustainable safe havens.
- **Analysis of Post-Crisis Regulatory Regimes:** Investigating how the implementation of macroprudential regulations (e.g., Dodd-Frank Act, Basel III) has altered the fundamental nature of cross-market spillovers would provide valuable insights for policymakers.
- **Expansion to Cryptocurrencies and Digital Assets:** The burgeoning asset class of cryptocurrencies presents a new frontier. Research could explore their spillover effects with traditional commodities and equities, examining whether they act as a hedge, a safe haven, or a source of contagion.
- **High-Frequency Data Analysis:** Employing intraday data could uncover spillover mechanisms that operate at a much finer timescale, enhancing the understanding of how news and shocks are instantaneously digested by interconnected markets.
- **Network Analysis of Spillovers:** Combining the DCC-MEGARCH framework with network theory could visually and quantitatively map the topology of financial contagion, identifying systemically important "transmitter" and "receiver" markets in a global network.

7.0 CHAPTER SUMMARY

- The chapter employs a sophisticated VAR-DCC-MEGARCH model to analyze return transmissions, volatility spillovers, and dynamic correlations between seven major global stock indices and three key commodities (Gold, Brent Oil, WTI Oil) during the 2007-2009 Global Financial Crisis.
- Empirical results confirm significant time-varying correlations and asymmetric volatility spillovers between the markets, with these interlinkages intensifying during the crisis period.

- Gold is identified as a effective hedge and safe haven for most major equity markets (including the S&P 500, CAC40, and Nikkei 225) during the GFC, consistently demonstrating low hedge ratios and improving portfolio risk-adjusted performance.
- Crude oil indices (Brent and WTI) showed higher and more volatile correlations with equities, offering less reliable hedging benefits, though WTI was found to be a safe haven for the Canadian market.
- The study provides actionable insights for sustainable portfolio management, demonstrating that dynamic hedging strategies based on time-varying correlations are superior to static approaches, especially in crisis conditions.
- The findings underscore the importance of commodity diversification, particularly into gold, for building financially sustainable and resilient investment portfolios that can endure systemic shocks, thereby contributing to the stability goals embedded within broader ESG and sustainability frameworks.

CHAPTER QUESTIONS

This section provides a series of questions designed to test comprehension, stimulate critical thinking, and inspire further research.

True or False Questions

1. During the Global Financial Crisis (GFC), the average returns for all major stock indices in the study were negative, while the average returns for the commodity indices (Gold, Brent, WTI) were positive.
2. The VAR-DCC-MEGARCH model assumes that correlations between financial assets remain constant over time, especially during periods of market stress.
3. The empirical results of the chapter indicate that Gold demonstrated strong safe-haven properties for most major equity markets during the crisis period.
4. The "leverage effect" in financial econometrics refers to the phenomenon where positive news has a greater impact on volatility than negative news of the same magnitude.
5. The diagnostic tests, including the Ljung-Box Q-statistic, confirmed the presence of significant serial correlation in the standardized residuals, suggesting the VAR-DCC-MEGARCH model was misspecified.
6. The optimal hedge ratio calculated in the chapter suggests that to hedge a long position in the S&P 500, an investor would need to take a substantially larger short position in Gold compared to a short position in WTI oil.

7. The chapter's findings suggest that the dynamic correlations between Brent oil and WTI oil were lower than the correlations between these oil indices and the various international stock markets.
8. A key theoretical evolution discussed is the progression from the Constant Conditional Correlation (CCC) model to the Dynamic Conditional Correlation (DCC) model to better capture time-varying market inter-dependencies.
9. The study found that volatility spillovers were unidirectional, primarily flowing from equity markets to commodity markets, with no significant feedback effects.
10. The application of the VAR-DCC-MEGARCH model in this context is considered novel because it integrates the analysis of return transmission and asymmetric volatility spillovers within a single, unified framework.

Multiple Choice Questions

11. The primary econometric methodology employed in this chapter to analyze time-varying correlations and volatility spillovers is:
    A) A simple Ordinary Least Squares (OLS) regression.
    B) A univariate GARCH model.
    C) A Vector Autoregressive Dynamic Conditional Correlation Multivariate Exponential GARCH (VAR-DCC-MEGARCH) model.
    D) A Cointegration and Error Correction Model (ECM).
    E) A standard Capital Asset Pricing Model (CAPM).
12. According to the chapter's descriptive statistics, which of the following assets exhibited the highest unconditional volatility during the GFC?
    A) Gold (GR)
    B) The S&P 500 Index (SPR)
    C) The CAC 40 Index (CACR)
    D) The Hang Seng Index (HSR)
    E) West Texas Intermediate Crude Oil (WTIR)
13. The chapter identifies Gold as a effective safe-haven asset because:
    A) Its price always increased when stock markets fell.
    B) It had consistently high and positive correlation with all equity indices.
    C) It demonstrated low hedge ratios and improved risk-adjusted performance in portfolios during the crisis.
    D) It completely insulated portfolios from any losses during the financial crisis.
    E) It was the best-performing asset in absolute terms during the sample period.
14. The theoretical advancement of the EGARCH model over the standard GARCH model is its ability to:
    A) Model the mean returns of a time series.

B) Capture the asymmetric impact of positive and negative news on volatility (the leverage effect).
C) Assume a constant long-run variance.
D) Eliminate the need for diagnostic testing.
E) Model correlations between more than two assets simultaneously.

15. A key finding regarding the optimal portfolio weights was that:
    A) Investors should allocate 100% of their wealth to WTI oil during a crisis.
    B) For most market indices, the optimal weight for Gold was generally above 50% for risk minimization.
    C) The Hong Seng Index (HSR) required a majority allocation to Brent oil.
    D) Diversification between stocks and commodities was found to be ineffective during the GFC.
    E) The optimal weights remained static throughout the crisis period.
16. The DCC parameters (ɼ and Π) in the model must satisfy which of the following conditions for the model to be mean-reverting?
    A) Their product must be greater than 1.
    B) Their sum must be greater than 1.
    C) Their sum must be less than 1.
    D) They must both be equal to zero.
    E) They must both be negative.
17. The chapter's literature review cites the work of Baur and McDermott (2010) primarily for their contribution to understanding:
    A) Volatility spillovers between oil and equity sectors.
    B) The role of Gold as a safe haven and hedge in developed stock markets.
    C) The impact of macroeconomic news on exchange rates.
    D) The technical trading rules for commodity futures.
    E) The structural breaks in market correlations due to monetary integration.
18. The Jarque-Bera test results for the return series in the chapter led to the rejection of the null hypothesis, indicating that the returns:
    A) Were stationary at the first difference, I(1).
    B) Followed a normal distribution.
    C) Deviated significantly from a normal distribution and were leptokurtic.
    D) Had no unit roots.
    E) Showed no evidence of ARCH effects.
19. In the context of this chapter, a "volatility spillover" is best defined as:
    A) The transmission of mean returns from one market to another.
    B) The long-term equilibrium relationship between commodity prices.
    C) The phenomenon where a shock to volatility in one market influences the volatility in another market.
    D) The constant correlation between two assets in a portfolio.

E) The daily calculation of log-differenced price returns.

20. The chapter links its findings to Sustainable Development Goal (SDG) 8: Decent Work and Economic Growth, by arguing that:
    A) Commodity trading creates the most jobs in a modern economy.
    B) Robust financial systems and effective risk management contribute to economic stability.
    C) All investments should be directed towards green energy projects.
    D) Gold mining is a primary source of decent work in developing nations.
    E) Financial speculation should be heavily regulated to protect workers.

Short Answer Questions

21. Briefly explain what the "leverage effect" signifies in the context of the EGARCH model and its implication for modeling financial volatility.
22. State one key difference between the Constant Conditional Correlation (CCC) and Dynamic Conditional Correlation (DCC) multivariate GARCH models.
23. Based on the chapter's results, what was the general relationship between the dynamic correlations of equity indices with Gold compared to their correlations with crude oil indices during the GFC?
24. How does the VAR component of the VAR-DCC-MEGARCH model contribute to the overall analysis?
25. What is the practical interpretation of an optimal hedge ratio of 0.20 for a pair of assets, say CSR/WTIR?
26. Identify two diagnostic tests used in the chapter to validate the specification of the econometric model and state what they test for.
27. Why was the study period (2007-2009) particularly suited for an analysis of volatility spillovers and safe-haven assets?
28. In one sentence, summarize the chapter's core finding regarding the role of Gold for an international investor during the 2007-2009 financial crisis.

Essay Questions

29. Elaborate on the theoretical evolution from univariate ARCH to multivariate DCC-GARCH models. How does the VAR-DCC-MEGARCH model used in this chapter represent a synthesis of these advancements?
30. Discuss the empirical findings related to return transmission and volatility spillovers between the commodity markets (Gold, Oil) and the equity markets as presented in the chapter. What were the key directional patterns and their implications?

31. Explain the concepts of "optimal hedge ratio" and "optimal portfolio weight" as operationalized in the chapter. How do these two measures assist an investor in achieving different financial objectives?
32. Critically assess the methodology employed in the chapter. What are the strengths of using a VAR-DCC-MEGARCH model for this research question, and what potential limitations might this approach have?
33. The chapter situates its findings within the context of financial sustainability and ESG principles. Analyze how effective risk management and portfolio diversification, as demonstrated in the chapter, contribute to these broader goals.
34. Compare and contrast the safe-haven properties of Gold versus crude oil (Brent/WTI) as revealed by the chapter's analysis. Support your answer with specific evidence from the results, such as correlation and hedging metrics.

Graduate Level Research Questions

35. **Propose a research design** to investigate whether the safe-haven properties of Gold identified during the 2007-2009 GFC held during a subsequent crisis, such as the COVID-19 market crash of 2020. What new variables or methodological adjustments would you consider?
36. **Critically evaluate** the potential impact of including ESG-focused equity indices (e.g., S&P 500 ESG Index) in the analysis. Formulate a hypothesis on how their volatility spillover patterns with commodities might differ from conventional indices.
37. **How might the rise of cryptocurrency assets (e.g., Bitcoin)** alter the traditional dynamics between equities and commodities? Design a study to analyze whether Bitcoin acts as a safe haven, a hedge, or a source of contagion in a modern portfolio context.
38. **The chapter uses daily data.** Discuss the theoretical and practical implications of using high-frequency (e.g., hourly or tick) data to study volatility spillovers. What new insights and challenges would this present?
39. **Explore the policy implications** of the chapter's findings. Based on the evidence of cross-market contagion, what specific macroprudential policy tools could a financial regulator employ to enhance systemic resilience?

Doctoral Level Research Questions

40. **The VAR-DCC-MEGARCH model, while flexible, assumes a elliptical conditional distribution.** Develop a methodological critique and propose an alternative modeling framework (e.g., a copula-based approach or a regime-switching model) that could more effectively capture extreme tail dependence

and non-linearities in spillover mechanisms during crisis regimes. Justify your choice.

41. **The concept of *"pure contagion"* versus *"interdependence"* is a central debate in financial crises literature.** Using the Forbes and Rigobon (2002) test or a more recent methodology, design a research project to rigorously test for the presence of pure contagion from the U.S. equity market to the commodity markets in this chapter's dataset, controlling for fundamental interdependence.
42. **Network theory offers a powerful lens for understanding systemic risk.** Conceptualize a study that transforms the time-varying variance-covariance matrices from the DCC-MEGARCH model into a dynamic, directed network of volatility spillovers. How would you identify systemically important *"transmitter"* and *"receiver"* markets, and how would the topology of this network evolve through the phases of the GFC?

Post-Doctoral Research Direction Questions

43. **The findings on Gold's stability present a paradox within the resource extraction literature, which highlights its significant environmental and social costs.** Forge a novel research agenda that integrates financial econometrics with environmental economics to develop a "sustainability-adjusted" safe-haven metric. How can the ESG performance of Gold mining be quantified and incorporated into its perceived risk-diversification benefits for truly sustainable portfolios?
44. **Current risk models, including the one in this chapter, are largely backward-looking and may fail in the face of structural breaks caused by climate change.** Propose a frontier research program to develop a forward-looking, climate-integrated financial risk model. How can physical climate risk scenarios and transition risk pathways be embedded within a dynamic spillover framework to stress-test the stability of the entire commodity-equity-financial system?
45. **The proliferation of algorithmic and high-frequency trading (HFT) has fundamentally altered market microstructure.** Design a theoretical and empirical research plan to investigate the hypothesis that HFT acts as an amplifier of volatility spillovers during stress periods by creating "machine-led contagion." What unique data and identification strategies would be required to disentangle human-driven interdependence from machine-driven contagion channels?

REFERENCES

Ahmed, S. M. (2009). Volatility spillovers from the US to Southeast Asian stock markets. *Journal of Asia-Pacific Business*, *10*(2), 132–152.

Aldasoro, I., Borio, C., & Drehmann, M. (2022). Early warning indicators of banking crises: Expanding the toolkit. *Journal of Financial Stability*, *60*, 100992.

Arouri, M. E., Lahiani, A., & Nguyen, D. K. (2015). World Gold Prices and Stock Returns in China: Insights for Hedging and Diversification Strategies. *Economic Modelling*, *44*, 273–282. DOI: 10.1016/j.econmod.2014.10.030

Arouri, M. E. H., Jouini, J., & Nguyen, D. K. (2011a). Volatility spillovers between oil prices and stock sector returns: Implications for portfolio management. *Journal of International Money and Finance*, *30*(7), 1387–1405. DOI: 10.1016/j.jimonfin.2011.07.008

Arouri, M. E. H., Jouini, J., & Nguyen, D. K. (2012). On the impacts of oil price fluctuations on European equity markets: Volatility spillover and hedging effectiveness. *Energy Economics*, *34*(2), 611–617. DOI: 10.1016/j.eneco.2011.08.009

Arouri, M. E. H., Lahiani, A., & Nguyen, D. K. (2011b). Return and volatility transmission between world oil prices and stock markets of the GCC countries. *Economic Modelling*, *28*(4), 1815–1825. DOI: 10.1016/j.econmod.2011.03.012

Batten, J. A., Ciner, C., & Lucey, B. M. (2010). The macroeconomic determinants of volatility in precious metals markets. *Resources Policy*, *35*(2), 65–71. DOI: 10.1016/j.resourpol.2009.12.002

Baur, D. G., & McDermott, T. K. (2010). Is gold a safe haven? International evidence. *Journal of Banking & Finance*, *34*(8), 1886–1898. DOI: 10.1016/j.jbankfin.2009.12.008

Bauwens, L., Laurent, S., & Rombouts, J. V. (2006). Multivariate GARCH models: A survey. *Journal of Applied Econometrics*, *21*(1), 79–109. DOI: 10.1002/jae.842

Bhunia, A. (2013). Cointegration and causal relationship among crude price, domestic gold price and financial variables: an evidence of BSE and NSE. *Journal of contemporary issues in business research*, *2*(1), 1-10.

Bhuyan, R., Robbani, M. G., Talukdar, B., & Jain, A. (2016). Information transmission and dynamics of stock price movements: An empirical analysis of BRICS and US stock markets. *International Review of Economics & Finance*, *46*, 180–195. DOI: 10.1016/j.iref.2016.09.004

Bollerslev, T. (1986). Generalized autoregressive conditional heteroskedasticity. *Journal of Econometrics, 31*(3), 307–327. DOI: 10.1016/0304-4076(86)90063-1

Bollerslev, T. (1990). Modelling the coherence in short-run nominal exchange rates: A multivariate generalized ARCH model. *The Review of Economics and Statistics, 72*(3), 498–505. DOI: 10.2307/2109358

Breusch, T. S., & Pagan, A. R. (2006). The Lagrange Multiplier Test and Its Applications to Model Specification in Econometrics. *The Review of Economic Studies*. Advance online publication. DOI: 10.2307/2297111

Chang, C. L., McAleer, M., & Tansuchat, R. (2013). Conditional correlations and volatility spillovers between crude oil and stock index returns. *The North American Journal of Economics and Finance, 25*, 116–138. DOI: 10.1016/j.najef.2012.06.002

Chen, G., Firth, M., & Rui, O. M. (2002). Stock market linkages: Evidence from Latin America. *Journal of Banking & Finance, 26*(6), 1113–1141. DOI: 10.1016/S0378-4266(01)00160-1

Chi, J., Li, K., & Young, M. (2006). Financial integration in East Asian equity markets. *Pacific Economic Review, 11*(4), 513–526. DOI: 10.1111/j.1468-0106.2006.00332.x

Coudert, V., Couharde, C., & Mignon, V. (2015). On the impact of volatility on the real exchange rate–terms of trade nexus: Revisiting commodity currencies. *Journal of International Money and Finance, 58*, 110–127. DOI: 10.1016/j.jimonfin.2015.08.007

Demirer, R., Diebold, F. X., Liu, L., & Yilmaz, K. (2020). Estimating global bank network connectedness. *Journal of Applied Econometrics, 35*(1), 1–23. DOI: 10.1002/jae.2585

Dimpfl, T., & Jung, R. C. (2012). Financial market spillovers around the globe. *Applied Financial Economics, 22*(1), 45–57. DOI: 10.1080/09603107.2011.597721

Du, X., Cindy, L. Y., & Hayes, D. J. (2011). Speculation and volatility spillover in the crude oil and agricultural commodity markets: A Bayesian analysis. *Energy Economics, 33*(3), 497–503. DOI: 10.1016/j.eneco.2010.12.015

Ebrahim, Z., Inderwildi, O. R., & King, D. A. (2014). Macroeconomic impacts of oil price volatility: Mitigation and resilience. *Frontiers in Energy, 8*(1), 9–24. DOI: 10.1007/s11708-014-0303-0

Engle, R. (2002). Dynamic conditional correlation: A simple class of multivariate generalized autoregressive conditional heteroskedasticity models. *Journal of Business & Economic Statistics, 20*(3), 339–350. DOI: 10.1198/073500102288618487

Engle, R. F. (1982). Autoregressive conditional heteroscedasticity with estimates of the variance of United Kingdom inflation. *Econometrica*, *50*(4), 987–1007. DOI: 10.2307/1912773

Ewing, B. T., & Malik, F. (2016). Volatility spillovers between oil prices and the stock market under structural breaks. *Global Finance Journal*, *29*, 12–23. DOI: 10.1016/j.gfj.2015.04.008

Forbes, K. (2000). The Asian flu and Russian virus: firm-level evidence on how crises are transmitted internationally.

Forbes, K. J., & Rigobon, R. (2002). No contagion, only interdependence: Measuring stock market comovements. *The Journal of Finance*, *57*(5), 2223–2261. DOI: 10.1111/0022-1082.00494

Fornari, F., Monticelli, C., Pericoli, M., & Tivegna, M. (2002). The impact of news on the exchange rate of the lira and long-term interest rates. *Economic Modelling*, *19*(4), 611–639. DOI: 10.1016/S0264-9993(00)00073-0

Hassan, S. A., & Malik, F. (2007). Multivariate GARCH modeling of sector volatility transmission. *The Quarterly Review of Economics and Finance*, *47*(3), 470–480. DOI: 10.1016/j.qref.2006.05.006

He, L. (2001). Volatility spillovers and the role of leading financial centres. *Quarterly Review. Indexes - Banca Nazionale del Lavoro*, *54*(217), 137–164.

He, L. J., & Chen, S. P. (2011). Aggregate and individual commodity futures markets volatility spillovers. *Journal of Futures Markets*, *31*(8), 739–764.

Hemche, O., Jawadi, F., Maliki, S. B., & Cheffou, A. I. (2016). On the study of contagion in the context of the subprime crisis: A dynamic conditional correlation–multivariate GARCH approach. *Economic Modelling*, *52*, 292–299. DOI: 10.1016/j.econmod.2014.09.004

Jang, H., & Sul, W. (2002). The Asian financial crisis and the co-movement of Asian stock markets. *Journal of Asian Economics*, *13*(1), 94–104. DOI: 10.1016/S1049-0078(01)00115-4

Kearney, C., & Potì, V. (2006). Correlation dynamics in European equity markets. *Research in International Business and Finance*, *20*(3), 305–321. DOI: 10.1016/j.ribaf.2005.05.006

Kenourgios, D., & Dimitriou, D. (2015). Contagion of the Global Financial Crisis and the real economy: A regional analysis. *Economic Modelling*, *44*, 283–293. DOI: 10.1016/j.econmod.2014.10.048

Koutmos, G. (1996). Modeling the dynamic interdependence of major European stock markets. *Journal of Business Finance & Accounting, 23*(7), 975–988. DOI: 10.1111/j.1468-5957.1996.tb01035.x

Kroner, K. F., & Ng, V. K. (1998). Modeling asymmetric comovements of asset returns. *Review of Financial Studies, 11*(4), 817–844. DOI: 10.1093/rfs/11.4.817

Kroner, K. F., & Sultan, J. (1993). Time-varying distributions and dynamic hedging with foreign currency futures. *Journal of Financial and Quantitative Analysis, 28*(4), 535–551. DOI: 10.2307/2331164

Kumar, S., Inani, S. K., & Rawat, V. (2012). Volatility spillovers between oil and stock market returns. *International Journal of Energy Sector Management, 6*(2), 205–219.

Li, Y., & Giles, D. E. (2015). Modelling volatility spillover effects between developed stock markets and Asian emerging stock markets. *International Journal of Finance & Economics, 20*(2), 155–177. DOI: 10.1002/ijfe.1506

Lien, D., & Yang, L. (2008). Asymmetric effect of basis on dynamic futures hedging: Empirical evidence from commodity markets. *Journal of Banking & Finance, 32*(2), 187–198. DOI: 10.1016/j.jbankfin.2007.01.026

Ljung, G. M., & Box, G. E. P. (1978). On a measure of lack of fit in time series models. *Biometrika, 65*(2), 297–303. DOI: 10.1093/biomet/65.2.297

Malik, F., & Ewing, B. T. (2009). Volatility transmission between oil prices and equity

Martin, V., Dunis, C., & von Mettenheim, H. J. (2002). A test for volatility spillovers. *Economics Letters, 76*(1), 77–84. DOI: 10.1016/S0165-1765(02)00027-7

Mensi, W., Beljid, M., Boubaker, A., & Managi, S. (2013). Correlations and volatility spillovers across commodity and stock markets: Linking energies, food, and gold. *Economic Modelling, 32*, 15–22. DOI: 10.1016/j.econmod.2013.01.023

Miralles-Marcelo, J. L., Miralles-Quirós, J. L., & del Mar Miralles-Quirós, M. (2013). Multivariate GARCH models and risk minimizing portfolios: The importance of medium and small firms. *The Spanish Review of Financial Economics, 11*(1), 29–38. DOI: 10.1016/j.srfe.2013.03.001

Monroe-White, T., Kerlin, J. A., & Zook, S. (2015). A quantitative critique of Kerlin's macro-institutional social enterprise framework. *Social Enterprise Journal, 11*(2), 178–201. DOI: 10.1108/SEJ-03-2015-0008

Morvan, J. (2009). *Marchés et instruments financiers*. Dunod.

Nelson, D. B. (1991). Conditional heteroskedasticity in asset returns: A new approach. *Econometrica, 59*(2), 347–370. DOI: 10.2307/2938260

(Note: Cited as 2020 in text — likely a preprint or submission year; published in 2021)

Öztek, M. F., & Öcal, N. (2017). Financial crises and the nature of correlation between commodity and stock markets. *International Review of Economics & Finance, 48*, 56–68. DOI: 10.1016/j.iref.2016.11.008

Pindyck, R. S. (2004). Volatility in natural gas and oil markets. *The Journal of Energy and Development, 30*(1), 1–19.

Reboredo, J. C., & Ugolini, A. (2020). The impact of ESG ratings on the systemic risk of European blue-chip firms. *Journal of Financial Stability, 53*, 100833.

Sadorsky, P. (2012). Correlations and volatility spillovers between oil prices and the stock prices of clean energy and technology companies. *Energy Economics, 34*(1), 248–255. DOI: 10.1016/j.eneco.2011.03.006

Saeed, T., Bouri, E., & Alsulami, H. (2021). Extreme return connectedness and its determinants between clean/green and dirty energy investments. *Energy Economics, 96*, 105017. DOI: 10.1016/j.eneco.2020.105017

Saleem, K. (2009). International linkage of the Russian market and the Russian financial crisis: A multivariate GARCH analysis. *Research in International Business and Finance, 23*(3), 243–256. DOI: 10.1016/j.ribaf.2008.09.003

Shehzad, K., Liu, X., Tiwari, A., Arif, M., & Rauf, A. (2021). Analysing time difference and volatility linkages between China and the United States during financial crises and stable period using VARX-DCC-MEGARCH model. *International Journal of Finance & Economics, 26*(1), 814–833. DOI: 10.1002/ijfe.1822

Shehzad, K., Liu, X., Tiwari, A., Arif, M., & Rauf, A. (2021). Analysing time difference and volatility linkages between China and the United States during financial crises and stable period using VARX-DCC-MEGARCH model. *International Journal of Finance & Economics, 26*(1), 814–833. DOI: 10.1002/ijfe.1822

Sikhosana, A., & Aye, G. C. (2018). Asymmetric volatility transmission between the real exchange rate and stock returns in South Africa. *Economic Analysis and Policy, 60*, 1–8. DOI: 10.1016/j.eap.2018.08.002

Singh, P., Kumar, B., & Pandey, A. (2010). Price and volatility spillovers across North American, European and Asian stock markets. *International Review of Financial Analysis, 19*(1), 55–64. DOI: 10.1016/j.irfa.2009.11.001

Syllignakis, M. N., & Kouretas, G. P. (2011). Dynamic correlation analysis of financial contagion: Evidence from the Central and Eastern European markets. *International Review of Economics & Finance*, *20*(4), 717–732. DOI: 10.1016/j.iref.2011.01.006

Tiwari, A. K., Aye, G. C., Gupta, R., & Gkillas, K. (2020). Gold-oil dependence dynamics and the role of geopolitical risks: Evidence from a Markov-switching time-varying copula model. *Energy Economics*, *88*, 104748. DOI: 10.1016/j.eneco.2020.104748

Tsay, R. S. (2005). *Analysis of financial time series*. John wiley & sons. DOI: 10.1002/0471746193

Tsuji, C. (2018). Return transmission and asymmetric volatility spillovers between oil futures and oil equities: New DCC-MEGARCH analyses. *Economic Modelling*, *74*, 167–185. DOI: 10.1016/j.econmod.2018.05.007

Vivian, A., & Wohar, M. E. (2012). Commodity volatility breaks. *Journal of International Financial Markets, Institutions and Money*, *22*(2), 395–422. DOI: 10.1016/j.intfin.2011.12.003

Wang, S. L., & McPhail, L. (2014). Impacts of energy shocks on US agricultural productivity growth and commodity prices—A structural VAR analysis. *Energy Economics*, *46*, 435–444. DOI: 10.1016/j.eneco.2014.05.006

Wang, S. S., Rui, O. M., & Firth, M. (2002). Return and volatility behavior of dually-traded stocks: The case of Hong Kong. *Journal of International Money and Finance*, *21*(2), 265–293. DOI: 10.1016/S0261-5606(01)00039-0

World Bank. (2023). *Global Economic Prospects*. The World Bank Group.

Yang, J., Kolari, J. W., & Min, I. (2003). Stock market integration and financial crises: The case of Asia. *Applied Financial Economics*, *13*(7), 477–486. DOI: 10.1080/09603100210161965

Yilmaz, K. (2010). Return and volatility spillovers among the East Asian equity markets. *Journal of Asian Economics*, *21*(3), 304–313. DOI: 10.1016/j.asieco.2009.09.001

Yu, L., Wang, S., & Lai, K. K. (2008). Forecasting crude oil price with an EMD-based neural network ensemble learning paradigm. *Energy Economics*, *30*(5), 2623–2635. DOI: 10.1016/j.eneco.2008.05.003

Zhang, Y. J., & Wei, Y. M. (2010). The crude oil market and the gold market: Evidence for cointegration, causality and price discovery. *Resources Policy*, *35*(3), 168–177. DOI: 10.1016/j.resourpol.2010.05.003

Zouch, M. A., Abbes, M. B., & Boujelbene, Y. (2011). Subprime crisis and volatility spillover. *International Journal of Monetary Economics and Finance*, *4*(1), 1. DOI: 10.1504/IJMEF.2011.038266

KEY TERMS AND DEFINITIONS

Dynamic Conditional Correlation (DCC): An econometric technique that estimates how the correlation between two or more asset returns changes over time, providing a more realistic picture of interdependencies than constant correlation models.

Financial Contagion: A scenario where a financial shock in one country, market, or institution spreads to others, often characterized by a significant increase in cross-market correlations after the shock.

Hedge Ratio: The proportion of an asset that should be sold short to hedge against the price risk of a long position in another asset. An optimal hedge ratio minimizes the variance of the portfolio's returns.

Leverage Effect: The observed empirical phenomenon where negative asset returns lead to a greater increase in future volatility than positive returns of the same magnitude, often attributed to the effect of increased financial leverage on a company's risk profile.

Safe-Haven Asset: An asset that is uncorrelated or negatively correlated with another asset or portfolio during periods of market stress or turmoil. Its value is expected to be stable or increase when mainstream markets decline.

VAR-DCC-MEGARCH Model: A comprehensive multivariate econometric model that combines: a Vector Autoregression (VAR) to model mean return spillovers, a Multivariate Exponential GARCH (MEGARCH) to capture asymmetric volatility spillovers, and a Dynamic Conditional Correlation (DCC) estimator to model time-varying correlations.

Volatility Spillover: The transmission of volatility shocks from one financial market to another. It signifies how uncertainty or turbulence originating in one asset class can infect other, seemingly unrelated, markets.

ENDNOTES

1 The S&P 500 Index (SPR), established by Standard & Poor's in 1962, is the most representative of the US economy of the three major indexes, accounting for nearly 80% of the US stock market by market value.

2 WTI crude oil and Brent crude oil are priced by two different markets, i.e., Europe and America and it reveals how different regions prices can affect stocks of the same and other regions.

3 Where $\bar{\beta}$ is the 2*2 unconditional correlation matrixes of the standardized residuals. $\varphi_{i,t}$, Φ_t is the 2*1 matrix of the standardized residuals. The parameters r, ϖ are nonnegative with a sum of less than unity, and the time varying correlation coefficients between series 1 and 2

TEACHING NOTE

This teaching note is designed to assist instructors in facilitating an under-graduate and graduate-level seminar on the intricate relationships between global financial markets, commodities, and risk management during a period of systemic crisis. The chapter serves as a sophisticated case study in applied financial econometrics, with profound implications for sustainable finance and resilient portfolio construction.

Concise Summary for the Teacher

This chapter presents an advanced empirical investigation into the volatility spillovers and dynamic correlations between seven major global equity markets (S&P 500, DAX 30, CAC 40, Nikkei 225, Hang Seng, etc.) and three key commodity assets (Gold, Brent Crude, WTI Crude) during the Global Financial Crisis (GFC) of 2007-2009. Utilizing a sophisticated VAR-DCC-MEGARCH model, the research captures the time-varying and asymmetric nature of these interlinkages.

The core findings reveal that:

- Gold consistently acted as a effective safe-haven asset and hedge for most major equity markets (e.g., S&P 500, CAC 40, Nikkei 225), demonstrating low hedge ratios and improving portfolio risk-adjusted performance during the turmoil.
- Crude oil indices (Brent & WTI) exhibited higher, more volatile correlations with equities, offering less reliable hedging benefits, though WTI served as a safe-haven for the Canadian market.
- Dynamic correlations between all assets intensified during the crisis, underscoring the phenomenon of financial contagion.
- The study provides actionable insights for dynamic hedging strategies and optimal portfolio weights, arguing that such risk management is crucial for financial sustainability and aligns with the long-term stability goals embedded in ESG principles and SDG 8 (Decent Work and Economic Growth).

Chapter Synopsis

The chapter begins by contextualizing the increased volatility and integration of global markets, setting the stage for an analysis of the GFC as a stress test for international portfolios. The literature review establishes the chapter's niche by focusing on the commodity-equity nexus during crisis, building upon foundational work in volatility spillovers and safe-haven assets. Methodologically, it details the application of the VAR-DCC-MEGARCH model, explaining its superiority over constant-correlation models in capturing the evolving transmission of returns, volatility, and correlation. The empirical results are presented in two panels, detailing significant return and volatility spillovers, time-varying correlations, and calculated optimal hedge ratios and portfolio weights. The conclusion powerfully links these technical findings to the broader themes of financial sustainability, advocating for the inclusion of commodities like gold in resilient, sustainable investment strategies.

Key Learning Objectives

Upon engaging in this chapter, students should be able to:

1. Remember the key characteristics of the VAR, DCC, and EGARCH components of the econometric model used.
2. Understand the concepts of volatility spillovers, dynamic conditional correlation, and the "leverage effect" in financial time series.
3. Apply the concepts of optimal hedge ratios and portfolio weights to a hypothetical two-asset portfolio.
4. Analyze the empirical results to differentiate the safe-haven properties of gold from those of crude oil during a crisis.
5. Evaluate the strengths and limitations of the VAR-DCC-MEGARCH methodology for analyzing financial market interdependencies.
6. Create a sustainable investment strategy proposal that incorporates the chapter's findings on dynamic hedging and portfolio diversification to enhance financial resilience.

Core Themes/Theses for Discussion

1. **The Asymmetric Nature of Risk:** Financial volatility is not symmetric; negative news (the "leverage effect") and cross-market spillovers intensify during crises, demanding sophisticated, time-varying models for accurate assessment.
2. **Gold as a Sustainable Safe Haven:** In times of systemic equity market failure, gold transcends its role as a mere commodity to become a critical instrument for financial stability and portfolio sustainability.
3. **Dynamic vs. Static Risk Management:** The failure of constant-correlation assumptions during the GFC makes a compelling case for dynamic hedging strategies as a core component of modern, sustainable finance.
4. **Financial Sustainability as a Precursor to Broader Sustainability:** Resilient financial systems, capable of withstanding shocks through effective diversification, are a foundational prerequisite for achieving long-term economic growth (SDG 8) and responsible economic practices (SDG 12).

5. **Methodological Rigor in Sustainable Finance:** The chapter implicitly argues that robust, quantitative empirical analysis is essential for moving sustainable finance from a conceptual framework to a discipline grounded in evidence-based strategy.

Suggested Teaching Pathway (90-Minute Seminar)

- **Introduction (10 mins):** Frame the session around a central question: "How can investors build portfolios that are not only profitable but also resilient and sustainable in the face of systemic shocks?"
- **Context & Theory (15 mins):** Briefly review the stylized facts of financial time series (volatility clustering, fat tails) and the evolution from ARCH to DCC models. Use the chapter's "Theoretic Evolution" section.
- **Methodology Deep Dive (20 mins):** Facilitate a guided walk-through of the VAR-DCC-MEGARCH model. Use a whiteboard to illustrate how the VAR captures return spillovers, the MEGARCH captures asymmetric volatility, and the DCC captures evolving correlations.
- **Findings & Implications (25 mins):** Lead a discussion on the key results. Use Tables 9, 10, 11, and 13 to visually compare correlations and hedging effectiveness. Focus the discussion on the stark contrast between gold and oil.
- **Synthesis & Critique (15 mins):** Connect the findings back to sustainability (ESG, SDGs). Then, open the floor for a critical evaluation of the model's assumptions (e.g., normality, linearity) and the practical challenges of implementing such dynamic strategies.
- **Conclusion (5 mins):** Summarize the key takeaway: Sustainable investing requires an understanding of complex, non-linear market dynamics, especially during crises.

Pedagogical Tools & Resources

- **Whiteboard/Visualizer:** Essential for diagramming the VAR-DCC-MEGARCH model structure.
- **Data Projection:** Display key tables (3, 5, 9, 11, 13) to anchor the discussion in empirical evidence.
- **Case Study:** A short vignette of a pension fund manager in 2008 deciding whether to increase allocation to gold or energy equities.
- **Pre-Reading:** Assign the chapter's Introduction, Literature Review, and Conclusion sections as mandatory pre-reading. The detailed results can be covered in class.

Note on Sensitivity

The 2007-2009 financial crisis caused significant real-world economic hardship, including widespread job losses and home foreclosures. While this chapter focuses on quantitative market dynamics, instructors should be mindful of this context. The discussion can be framed not as an abstract exercise, but as a crucial learning endeavor to build more stable financial systems that protect societies from future crises. Emphasize that the goal of such research is to mitigate human and economic suffering by improving systemic resilience.

Key Questions for Class Discussion

1. **The chapter finds gold to be a superior safe-haven to oil. What fundamental economic or behavioral reasons might explain this phenomenon beyond the statistical evidence?**
    - o *Direction:* Discuss gold's historical role as a store of value, its non-industrial uses versus oil's tie to economic growth, and investor psychology during *"flight-to-safety"* episodes.
2. **The VAR-DCC-MEGARCH model is complex. What are the practical trade-offs for a portfolio manager between implementing such a dynamic strategy and relying on simpler, constant correlation models?**
    - o *Direction:* Debate cost, computational resources, model risk, client communication, and whether the benefits of dynamic hedging outweigh the complexities during *"normal"* market periods.
3. **The study period is a defined crisis. How transferable are these findings to periods of normal market volatility or to different types of crises (e.g., the COVID-19 crash)?**
    - o *Direction:* Encourage students to hypothesize how correlations might behave in a demand-side (COVID) vs. a financial-system-side (GFC) shock. Discuss the concept of *"regime change"* in markets.
4. **The chapter links its findings to SDG 8. How exactly does effective portfolio risk management for wealthy investors contribute to "decent work and economic growth" for the broader society?**
    - o *Direction:* Explore the concept of financial stability as a public good. Stable capital markets facilitate investment, business growth, and job creation, preventing credit crunches and deep recessions that destroy jobs.
5. **Critique the division of the analysis into two panels. Does this methodological choice potentially miss important spillover effects between the indices separated into different panels?**

- *Direction:* This is a critical thinking question about research design. Students should identify the limitations and propose how a single, larger model (if computationally feasible) might yield different insights.

6. **The *"leverage effect"* is a key reason for using an EGARCH specification. In your own words, why might a negative return on a stock index lead to a larger increase in future volatility than a positive return?**
   - *Direction:* Guide students to think about corporate balance sheets (increased financial leverage as equity falls) and behavioral finance (investor fear and uncertainty magnifying selling pressure).
7. **If you were to integrate an ESG equity index into this analysis, what is your hypothesis for how its volatility spillovers with commodities would compare to a conventional index like the S&P 500?**
   - *Direction:* Prompt students to consider if high-ESG firms are less cyclical, have different risk profiles, or might be more/less correlated with commodity prices due to their business models.
8. **Looking at the optimal portfolio weights (Table 13), the allocation to gold is often over 50%. Does such a heavy allocation to a non-income-producing asset seem like a sustainable long-term strategy?**
   - *Direction:* Differentiate between a tactical, crisis-era allocation and a strategic, long-term one. Discuss the opportunity cost of holding gold and the balance between crisis resilience and long-term growth.
9. **The diagnostic tests (Table 14) show some significant Q2 statistics. What does this imply, and how might it affect our confidence in the model's conclusions?**
   - *Direction:* Explain that significant Q2 statistics indicate remaining volatility clustering not captured by the model, a common issue in financial econometrics. Discuss this as a limitation but not necessarily a fatal flaw.
10. **Based on this chapter, what single piece of advice would you give to a regulator concerned with systemic-risk about the role of commodity markets?**
    - *Direction:* Answers could include monitoring commodity-equity correlations as a crisis warning indicator, understanding that commodities are not a monolithic asset class for risk purposes, or considering the systemic implications of large-scale flows into "safe-haven" commodities.

Chapter 9

Investors Views on Sustainability Assurance and Its Impact on Investment Decisions

Andrew William Mortimore
Bureau Veritas Australia and New Zealand, Australia

Junaid M. Shaikh
Universiti Teknologi Brunei, Brunei

Mohamed Mihilar Shamil
https://orcid.org/0000-0002-5533-5129
Hong Kong Metropolitan University, Hong Kong

ABSTRACT

This study explores the importance of independent assurance of sustainability reports to investors and its impact on their investment decisions. A survey was conducted targeting professional investors from large investment firms in developed countries. The findings reveal that the majority of investors consider ESG information and independent assurance of sustainability reports when making investment decisions. Investors employ different approaches to assess ESG information and agree that public listed firms should annually publish ESG information that is subjected to independent assurance. Investors identified several benefits of independent assurance, including increased trust and credibility, reduced risk, better engagement from the board and CEO, strengthened internal reporting systems, and improved

DOI: 10.4018/979-8-3693-9714-5.ch009

communication with stakeholders. The study contributes to the existing literature by verifying the importance of independent assurance of sustainability reports from an investor's perspective and provides implications for practitioners and future research.

1.0 INTRODUCTION

Environmental, Social and Governance (ESG) has emerged as one of the fastest growing phenomena in the business-government-society domain (Kim & Yoon, 2023) and has been drawn into the field of investments. Sustainability or ESG disclosures are increasingly being considered by investors when they evaluate a company's strategy, risk profile and ultimately, its long-term value as an investment (Strott et al., 2016). Although research on sustainability and ESG reporting has grown significantly in recent years, there has been limited empirical evidence to date whether independent assurance of sustainability or ESG reports, which are otherwise not verified by a third party, is something that investors consider in their investment decisions. Verifying the accuracy of sustainability or ESG reports and ensuring their compliance with relevant standards is a crucial function of independent assurance. Whilst the independent assurance of financial reports and disclosures has long been a mandatory practice for publicly listed firms, the same process for ESG disclosures and sustainability reports remains largely voluntary across most jurisdictions. Nevertheless, the number of firms choosing to seek independent assurance for sustainability reports is growing according to the Global Reporting Initiative (GRI) database and KPMG's Sustainability Reporting Survey (2022).

Apart from sustainability reports, ESG rating providers are becoming increasingly important for investors to assess and compare non-financial performance of entities over time (Sridharan, 2018). ESG raters are now possibly impacting the returns on an ever-expanding pool of investments, as well as strategic decisions of companies. Currently, there are a few firms providing sustainability ratings on organizations and the collective influence of these external rating agencies is only set to grow in the future as ESG disclosures become mainstream. Some of the leading companies that provide ESG information and ratings include Bloomberg, MSCI, Sustainalytics, CDP, RepRisk and Trucost.

An investment with a social element or purpose is generally described as a responsible investment (Hill, 2020). Expanding on the above notion, considering ESG criteria to assess investment strategies and decisions can be regarded as sustainable or ESG related investment. The total assets of sustainable funds almost reached US $3 trillion in 2023 from a meagre US $329 billion in 2014 and the number of sustainable funds has risen from 1,714 in 2014 to 7,485 in 2023 (UNCTAD, 2024). Similarly, from 2022, the signatories of United Nations backed Principles for Responsible Investment (PRI) have exceeded 5,000 with assets valued at US $ 128.4 trillion (PRI, 2024). Furthermore, the Global Sustainable investment was US $ 30.3 trillion in 2022 (GSIA, 2022).

Despite the growth in responsible investment, there is no unified framework for sustainability or integrated reporting that makes like-for-like comparisons within and across industries difficult. EY's Fifth Global Institutional Investor Survey (2020) found that investors strongly desire a standardised framework for measuring and communicating intangible value, and a robust link between mainstream financial and ESG reporting. Furthermore, the survey also reported that to improve the evaluation of ESG performance, investors need more consistent and thorough nonfinancial data from organizations to bolster their approach (EY, 2020). It can be stated that investors are likely to somewhat dissatisfied with the ESG information they receive from organisations.

From an organisational standpoint, several frameworks and standards have emerged that advocates presentation of ESG information. Organisations often disclose ESG information in accordance with various combinations of reporting frameworks, including the Global Reporting Initiative (GRI), the Sustainability Accounting Standards Board (SASB), International Integrated Reporting Council (IIRC) and the Task Force on Climate-Related Financial Disclosures (TCFD) (Silk et al., 2020). Additional notable reporting mechanisms include those established by the UN Global Compact and the Sustainable Development Goals (SDGs), the CDP (Carbon Disclosure Project) and the Climate Disclosure Standards Board. The lack of a unified agreeable framework for sustainability or integrated reporting is compounded by the growing number of entities sharing this information with stakeholders. Annual non-financial or integrated reports remain a popular form of disclosure for organisations to showcase their ESG performance to stakeholders. Globally, the number of annually published sustainability reports continues to increase year on year. According to UNCTAD's World Investment Report 2024, TCFD, PRI, ISSB, GRI, and SASB are the top five sustainability standards or frameworks used by sustainable funds (2024).

Thus, there appears to be a pressing need and opportunity to examine the importance investors place on independent assurance of sustainability reports and its influence on their investment decisions. Accordingly, the chapter aims to explore the degree to which institutional investors value independent assurance of sustainability reports and seeks to determine whether independent assurance impacts investment strategies. Understanding the value of independent assurance from the eyes of investors will assist organisations in formulating their sustainability or integrated reporting strategy and in deciding on whether independent assurance should be considered or not.

1.1 Overview

This chapter presents a seminal empirical investigation into the value that institutional investors place on the independent assurance of corporate sustainability reports. The research addresses a critical gap in the literature by quantitatively assessing whether this form of verification influences investment strategies and decision-making processes. Through a meticulously designed global survey of 100 investment professionals from leading firms in developed markets, the study provides robust evidence that independent assurance is not merely a peripheral compliance exercise but a significant factor that enhances the credibility and utility of Environmental, Social, and Governance (ESG) information for capital allocation.

1.2 Background

The ascendancy of ESG factors in investment paradigms represents a fundamental shift in modern finance. As noted by Kim and Yoon (2023), ESG has become a dominant phenomenon, with sustainable investment assets experiencing exponential growth, reaching nearly US$3 trillion in 2023 (UNCTAD, 2024). This surge is underpinned by investor recognition that ESG performance is intrinsically linked to a company's long-term risk profile and value-creation potential (Strott et al., 2016). However, this evolution has outpaced the development of a unified reporting and verification infrastructure. Unlike financial statements, sustainability reports largely remain subject to voluntary and fragmented reporting frameworks (GRI, SASB, TCFD) and, crucially, their independent assurance is not universally mandated. This creates an information asymmetry and a credibility deficit, prompting the central research question: do investors value and act upon independently assured sustainability data?

1.3 Benefits of the Research

The research offers substantial benefits by delivering much-needed empirical validation in the ESG domain. It moves beyond theoretical postulations to provide statistical evidence from the ultimate users of ESG reports: investors. The findings demonstrate that assurance is a key mechanism for mitigating investment risk. For instance, the study reveals that a primary reason investors value assurance is that it *"increases trust and credibility"* and leads to *"reduced risk and increased value."* This aligns with Ballou et al. (2018), who argued that the absence of assurance negatively impacts the perceived quality of information. By quantifying investor sentiment (for example, 94-100% of respondents across regions agree that some level of assurance is necessary), the research provides corporate managers and regulators with a compelling, data-driven case for enhancing assurance practices, thereby fostering more efficient and transparent capital markets.

2.0 LITERATURE REVIEW

The chapter is situated within a growing but still maturing body of literature on sustainability assurance. It builds upon the foundational work of scholars like O'Dwyer (2011), who posited that sustainability reports cannot be deemed reliable without independent verification. The chapter also engages with the discourse on the proliferation of ESG rating providers (Sridharan, 2018) and the challenges of comparability due to a lack of a unified reporting framework, a concern echoed in EY's (2020) investor survey. The research directly responds to calls from organizations like the Global Sustainable Investment Alliance (GSIA, 2022) and the UN Principles for Responsible Investment (PRI, 2024) for more rigorous and trustworthy ESG data to support the burgeoning responsible investment ecosystem.

2.1 Theoretic Background

The theoretical underpinnings of this research are implicitly rooted in legitimacy theory and signaling theory. Legitimacy theory suggests that organizations voluntarily disclose and assure non-financial information to align with societal values and maintain their *"license to operate."* By obtaining independent assurance, a company signals its commitment to transparency and ethical governance, thereby enhancing its legitimacy in the eyes of stakeholders. Signaling theory further elucidates this dynamic; in a market flooded with ESG claims, assurance acts as a credible signal that distinguishes high-quality, sustainable firms from those engaged in *"greenwashing."* This costly and verifiable signal reduces information asymmetry and helps investors make more informed decisions.

2.2 Theory Evolution

The evolution of theoretical applications in this space reflects the mainstreaming of ESG. Initially, legitimacy theory was often applied to explain why companies began sustainability reporting at all. As the practice became more common, signaling theory gained prominence to explain why firms would go a step further to have these reports assured. This chapter's findings signify a further evolution: these theories are now being validated from the *investor's perspective*. The data confirms that investors do, in fact, decode these signals and use them to confer legitimacy, thereby influencing capital flows. This bridges a critical gap between organizational motives and stakeholder response.

2.3 In-depth Literature Synthesis

The chapter provides a solid foundation on the demand for sustainability assurance. To further enrich the discourse, this synthesis integrates pivotal literature from leading journals and regulatory bodies that illuminate the evolving landscape of non-financial verification.

A critical stream of research delves into the qualitative aspects of assurance that influence its perceived value. Cohen and Simnett (2015) established that the *level* of assurance (reasonable vs. limited) and the *type* of assurer (accountant vs. sustainability consultant) significantly affect the credibility of reports in the eyes of users. Their work suggests that while the chapter finds strong demand for assurance, the market is likely to become increasingly discerning, differentiating between basic checks and high-quality, rigorous assurance engagements. This is echoed by the International Auditing and Assurance Standards Board (IAASB, 2022), which, in its exposure draft for a global sustainability assurance standard (ISSA 5000), emphasizes the need for robust methodologies, proper evidence, and assurer competence to prevent "assurance-washing" and ensure that practice meets investor expectations.

Furthermore, the strategic rationale for assurance is powerfully articulated by Eccles, Ioannou, and Serafeim (2014) in their seminal research. They found that firms adopting robust sustainability practices and reporting—which increasingly includes assurance—demonstrate superior stock market and accounting performance over the long term. This provides a compelling, performance-based argument that complements the risk-mitigation rationale presented in the chapter. Assurance is not merely a defensive tool but a proactive signal of high-quality management and long-term orientation.

From a regulatory perspective, the landscape is shifting from voluntary to mandatory. The European Commission's (2021) proposal for the Corporate Sustainability Reporting Directive (CSRD) represents a tectonic shift, requiring limited assurance and laying the groundwork for reasonable assurance for a vast number of EU and non-EU companies. This regulatory momentum, also seen in the International Sustainability Standards Board's (ISSB, 2023) IFRS S1 and S2, which explicitly encourage assurance, validates the chapter's findings that investor demand is being met with concrete policy action. As noted by the World Business Council for Sustainable Development (WBCSD, 2023), this convergence of market demand and regulatory mandate is creating a *"new era of corporate accountability,"* where comprehensive and assured sustainability disclosure becomes as table-stakes as financial reporting.

Finally, the perspective of industry bodies like the International Chamber of Commerce (ICC, 2022) adds a crucial pragmatic dimension. The ICC emphasizes that for assurance to be scalable and effective, especially for small and medium-sized enterprises within global supply chains, a proportionate, risk-based approach is essential. This highlights a future challenge: balancing the demand for high-quality assurance with the practicalities and costs of implementation across diverse corporate landscapes.

3.0 METHODOLOGY

The population for the survey comprised professional investors in large investment firms established in countries with developed capital and financial markets. The rationale for selecting investors from a limited number of investment firms established in developed countries is that responsible investing is more prevalent in these countries, investment firms have more capital invested in these countries, and independent assurance of sustainability reports and ESG disclosures is an established practice in these countries. Further, a broader study involving smaller investment firms in developing countries was avoided to control for differences in macro environment and business climate. Next, it was imperative to select a pool of appropriate and knowledgeable key informants who were engaged in investment decisions by verifying their details (Skarmeas et al., 2016). Accordingly, it was deemed that professional investors holding the positions of portfolio and fund manager, trader or investor, or financial analyst can be regarded as key informants because they are directly involved in investment decisions or conduct quantitative analysis supporting investment decisions. Identifying and inviting key informants to participate in a survey increases the reliability of the gathered data. Moreover, inviting multiple participants from the same firm helps reduce the source of common method variance (Eden et al., 2020).

The sample frame for this study was developed from the CFA Institute (CFA Institute, 2018) which is a membership organisation representing both finance and investment management professionals primarily involved in activities related to the investment decision-making process as well as investment management firms primarily engaged in asset management and investment. This is an entrusted membership-based institute where registration is based on verification of qualifications and competency as an investment and finance professional. However, CFA membership includes many finance professionals and not just investment professionals. The survey specifically targeted individuals working in portfolio and fund management, investors, and financial analysis, resulting in a pool of 3,253 potential participants. Next, a list of large investment firms was gathered by identifying the top 20 firms globally and then adding the top six firms from Australia and New Zealand (Pacific Region). This method yielded 1,098 potential respondents. Every subgroup category of investment professionals from each of the large investment firms was reviewed, and three subgroups of respondents were encountered (portfolio and fund managers, investors, and financial analysts). Accordingly, stratified random sampling was employed. Stratified sampling involves extracting proportionate representation of multiple groups of participants considered in a study (Muneer et al., 2017). This method also offers an opportunity to reduce sampling error, increase the level of confidence (Iacobucci & Churchill, 2018), and ensure a wider representation of the subgroups, which may accurately reflect the population (Johnson & Christiansen, 2019).

A self-administered online survey approach was deemed the most appropriate, as potential respondents were globally scattered (Malhotra, 2019; Zikmund et al., 2019). The main strengths of this method are respondent anonymity and confidentiality, no restrictions on expressions, and a fair temporal response (Johnson & Christiansen, 2019). This also facilitates record keeping and generates uniform data from different respondents. Another important advantage of this method is its minimal cost compared with other methods. However, it cannot be safely said that among all the data collection methods, one is the best, and the selected method is not without limitations. Considering all these factors, an online survey was conducted for this study because of its ability to collect data economically in a short period of time from internationally scattered participants. However, the survey method suffers from a low response rate for various reasons, including survey fatigue of a typical email survey. Keeping this in mind, measures were taken to increase the response rate to reduce response bias and increase the validity of statistical inference (Iacobucci & Churchill, 2018). The identified 1,098 potential participants were contacted by email to solicit participation in the survey. The email with the survey was sent from the university email address to add credibility to the request and request participation in the survey. It was stressed that the study was conducted only for academic purposes and that participation in this study was completely voluntary, anonymous, and confidential. Access to the supplied information is limited to researchers. It was envisaged that this process would maximise the usable responses.

Several questionnaire items were developed to align with the scope of the survey. Some question items required the respondents to respond to predetermined categories, and some question items required the respondents to rate their perceptions on a five-point Likert scale ranging from 1 *"strongly disagree"* to 5 *"strongly agree"*. The survey yielded 100 responses from invited participants. Considering the variation in respondents both geographically and by sub-groups, 100 responses were deemed as a representative sample. The overall response rate was 9.11%. A review of the collected data also revealed that some respondents had not submitted responses pertaining to demographic and firm-employment characteristics. Further, to minimise the threat of non-response bias, early (78) and late (22) responses were compared using t-tests. Early and late responses were categorised based on whether the responses were received within two weeks from the sending date of the online survey, and responses were received two weeks after the sending date of the online survey. The t-test results revealed that there was no significant difference between early and late responses.

The initial data analysis proceeded with the examination of data collected and handling of missing data. This step is relevant to gain insights into the data characteristics and analysis (Hair et al., 2015). it was observed that there were no missing data related to the question items, however some demographic characteristics of respondents were absent. Quantitative Analysis using frequency distribution was used to present the results in tabular form.

3.1 Methodology Justification

The methodology is robust and prudently justified. The focus on large investment firms in developed countries control macroeconomic variables and ensures the sample is drawn from markets where ESG investing and assurance are most advanced. Employing stratified random sampling from the CFA Institute directory ensures a representative cross-section of key informants—portfolio managers, investors, and financial analysts—directly involved in investment decisions, thereby enhancing the validity and reliability of the data (Skarmeas et al., 2016). The self-administered online survey, despite its inherent limitation of a modest response rate (9.11%), was the most feasible method for a globally dispersed population. The authors further bolstered the methodology's rigor by testing non-response bias, finding no significant difference between early and late respondents.

4.0 RESULTS AND FINDINGS

The results paint a coherent and compelling picture of global investor sentiment:

- **Widespread ESG Integration:** Most investors, particularly in Europe and Australasia, consistently consider ESG criteria.
- **Demand for Standardization and Assurance:** Overwhelming majorities believe public companies should be required to report annually on ESG metrics and that these reports should undergo independent assurance.

- **Preferred Assurance Providers:** Investors show a strong preference for assurance from independent professional firms, either specialized ESG services or accounting/audit firms with relevant expertise.
- **Impact on Investment Decisions:** A significant majority (63% to 94%) either already consider or plan to consider assurance in their decisions.
- **Primary Motivations:** The key drivers for valuing assurance are enhanced trust/credibility, risk reduction, and improved internal governance.
- **Barriers:** For the minority who do not value assurance, the primary reasons are a perceived lack of risk reduction and credibility, highlighting a need for further education on assurance quality.

4.1 Descriptive statistics

Table 1 shows that the sample comprised mostly of male respondents (72%) as opposed to female respondents (28%). Table 4 also shows that respondents varied widely in terms of their age groups. The highest representation of the respondents (54.26%) was from the age group of 35 to 44, followed by the age group of 45 to 54 years (21.28%), and a relatively younger generation of age group below 35 years (20.21%). In terms of respondents' job positions, around three-fifths of the key informants in the survey held key decision-making positions, either as direct investors or managers of the investment firm (57.89%). Additionally, 24.21% of key informants held occupational positions as investment analysts and ESG advisors. The key informants' overall position within the firm signifies high-profile participation in the survey, which contributes to the quality of the data collected. Regarding the respondents' place of work, majority (59%) were from institutional investment firms. Institutional investment firms are those that typically buy, sell, and manage stocks, bonds, and securities on behalf of their clients. There are generally six types of institutional investment firms: endowment funds, commercial banks, mutual funds, pension funds, and insurance companies. Asset management firms make up the next largest group of respondents (25%). Asset management firms are considered those that invest pooled funds from clients, putting the capital to work through different investments including stocks, bonds, real estate and more. Asset management firms manage hedge funds and pension plans and create pooled structures such as mutual funds and index funds. Private investment firms make up 5% of the respondents' place of work. Private investment firms are considered those firms that are not publicly listed or traded. While institutional investors target investments in publicly traded companies, private investment firms often target non-public companies as well as publicly traded companies as investment targets. Private investment firms include individuals, venture capital companies and groups of individuals or families. 11% of the respondents classified their place of work as other.

Regarding the distribution of participants by geographical regions, the North America comprising Canada and the United States of America, accounts for the largest proportion of respondents at 36%. Europe make up the next largest group of respondents (31%). Respondents from this region comes from the United Kingdom, Germany, France, Spain, Switzerland, Netherlands, Ireland and Luxembourg. The Pacific region of Australia and New Zealand make up the next largest group of respondents at 25%. Finally, Asia makes up the smallest category of respondents with 8%. Respondents in Asia were from Singapore and Hong Kong. The regional distribution of respondents appears relatively balanced, given the rationale for choosing Developed Countries as the research context and selecting the largest investment firms that controls most of the investments.

Table 1. Respondents' Characteristics

Demographic Characteristics		**Frequency**	**Percent**
Gender	Male	68	72.34
	Female	26	27.66
	Total	94	100
Age	Up to 34 years	19	20.21
	35 – 44	51	54.26
	45 – 54	20	21.28
	over 55 years	4	4.25
	Total	94	100
Designation	Investment Analyst	18	18.95
	ESG Advisor	5	5.26
	Investor	20	21.05
	Manager	35	36.84
	Other	17	17.9
	Total	95	100
Firm Type	Institutional Investment Firm	58	58.59
	Private Investment Firm	5	5.05
	Asset Management Firm	25	25.25
	Other	11	11.11
	Total	99	100

continued on following page

Table 1. Continued

Demographic Characteristics		Frequency	Percent
Region	Europe	31	31
	North America	36	36
	Asia-Pacific	33	8
	Total	100	100

Figure 1 shows that an overwhelming majority of investors except in North America, do currently consider ESG criteria in their investment decisions. Only a minor percentage of investors in only three regions indicated that they rarely or never consider ESG criteria when making an investment decision. Investors in Europe, Australia and New Zealand are more likely to apply ESG criteria into their investment strategy than their counterparts in North America and Asia. Strott et al. (2016) has suggested that investors consider ESG information when they evaluate a company's strategy, risk profile, and its long-term value as an investment.

Figure 1. Consideration of ESG Factors in Investment Decisions

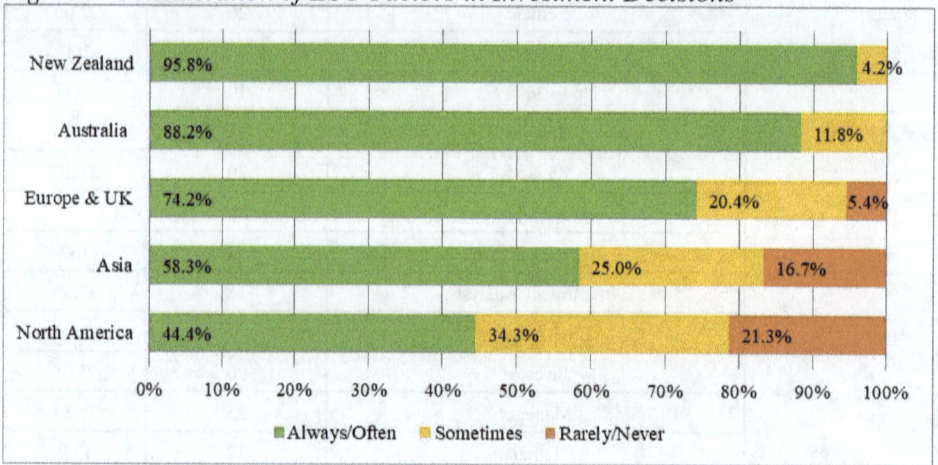

Figure 2 presents the responses for how investors access ESG information of entities. The popularity of approaches applied to access ESG information varies across regions and top three approaches to access ESG information are third party research; public information; and annual reports and company statements. Investors from Australia and New Zealand are more likely to directly engage with companies to access ESG information compared to investors from Europe, North America and Asia. Investors from North America, in comparison to investors from other regions, seem to prefer third-party research to other means of accessing ESG information. Only a small percentage of the respondents stated that they relied on regulatory filings and other external sources of ESG information. Regional differences in ESG information access methods highlight the need for companies to tailor their ESG disclosure strategies to meet the diverse preferences of their global investor base.

Figure 2. How Investors Access ESG Information

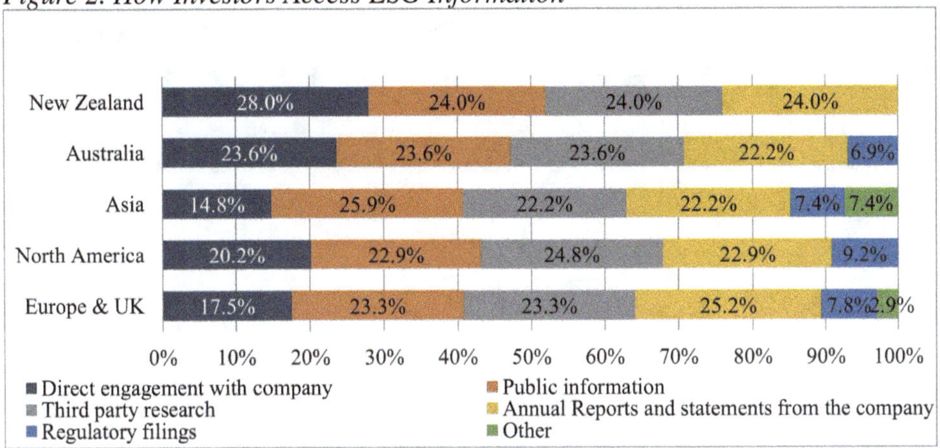

The views of investors on whether public quoted companies should be required to report annually on a set of ESG indicators in accordance with a relevant reporting framework is presented in Figure 3. An overwhelming majority of investors agrees that quoted entities should be annually obligated to provide a range of ESG metrics, in accordance with an appropriate reporting framework. Similarly, an overwhelming majority of investors indicated that sustainability reports produced by companies should be subjected some level of independent assurance (see Figure 4 for more details). O'Dwyer (2011) states that sustainability reports can't be deemed reliable or complete if independent assurance are not undertaken for such reports. Accordingly, it can be asserted that investors value independent assurance of sustainability reports as it enhances credibility and supports responsible investments.

Figure 3. Should Public Companies Annually Required to Report on a Set of ESG Indicators

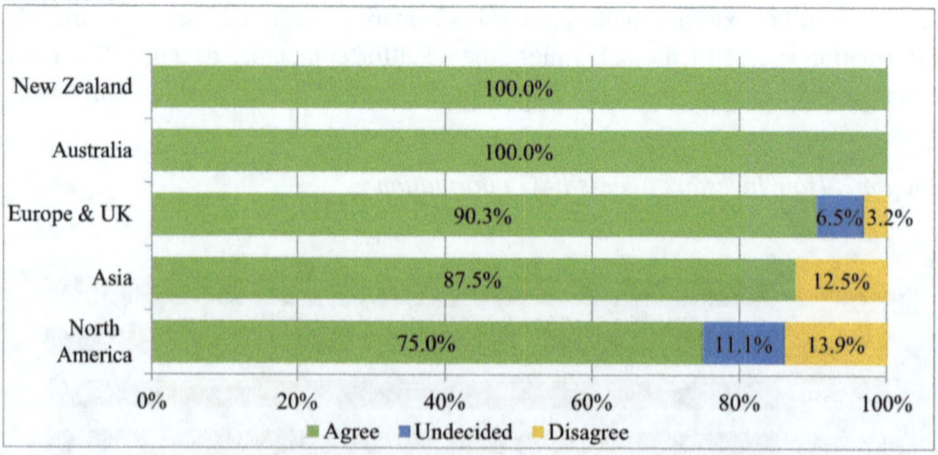

Figure 4. Should a Company's Sustainability Report Subjected to Some Level of Assurance

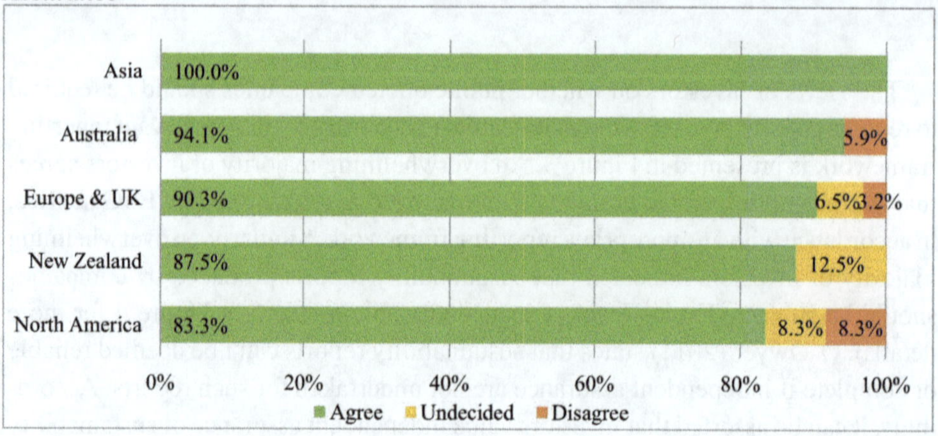

Figure 5 illustrates regional variations in investor views on who they feel are better position to undertake independent assurance for sustainability reports produced by entities. The analysis indicates that a significant majority of investors across all regions (between 74% and 88%) agree that independent assurance should be undertaken by at least one of the two types of independent assurance providers, being either; independent professional services firms with accreditation for sustainability assurance or independent professional accounting or auditing firms with expertise on sustainability assurance. This suggests that external assurance of sustainability reports is more valued than self-disclosures made by companies. In contrast to Australian investors, those from other regions show a preference for independent professional firms specialising in ESG matters over independent professional accounting firms when it comes to conducting sustainability assurance. The high percentage indicates a growing recognition of the importance of third-party verification in enhancing the credibility and reliability of sustainability information and a global shift towards valuing independently assured sustainability reports.

Figure 5. Who is Best Positioned to Provide Sustainability Report Assurance

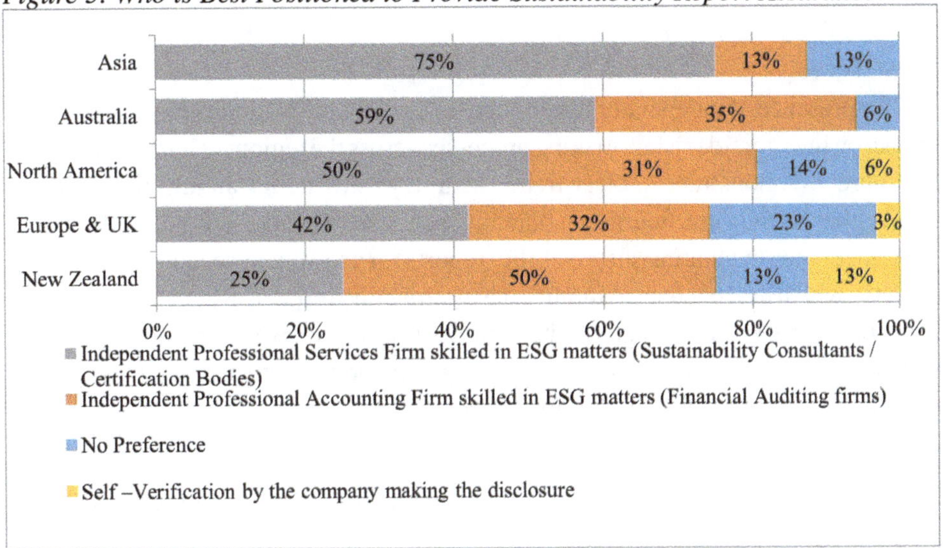

Figure 6 shows the investors views on the level of independent assurance of sustainability reports is necessary. Investors from all regions (from 94% to 100%) agree that sustainability report should be subjected to some level of independent assurance, whether that be either; reasonable (sufficient appropriate evidence is reviewed to conclude that disclosures conform in all material respects) or limited (sufficient appropriate evidence is reviewed to conclude that disclosures are plausible). This again conforms that investors do value independent assurance of sustainability reports.

Figure 6. Level of Independent Assurance of Sustainability Reports

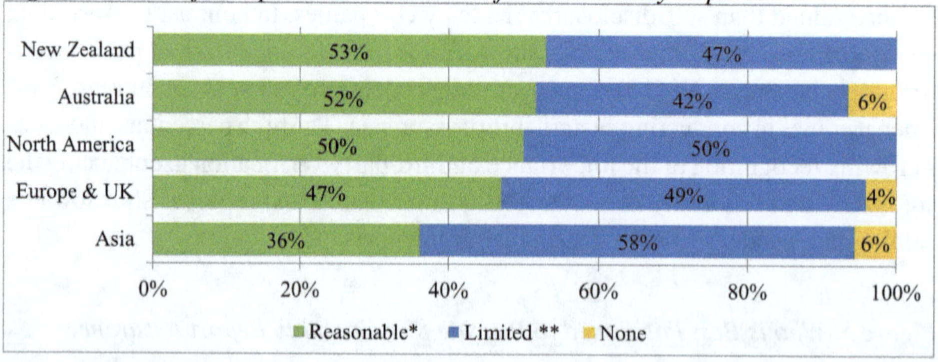

The presence of independent assurance for sustainability reports has a substantial impact on investors' decision-making processes across the regions. The data presented in Figure 7 demonstrates a clear trend, with most investors (ranging from 63% to 94%) either already considering or planning to consider the presence of independent assurance when evaluating sustainability reports for investment decisions. Whilst the extent to which independent assurance of sustainability reports influences investment decisions differs among regions, its significance and relevance to investors can't be disregarded as it underscores the growing demand for transparent and verifiable sustainability information in the investment community.

Figure 7. Do Investors Consider Independent Assurance of Sustainability Reports for Investment Decisions

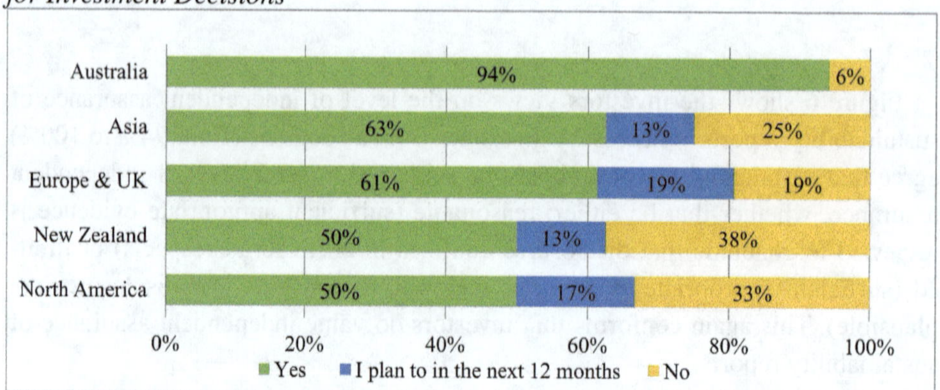

Figure 8 presents the views of investors on why they consider independent assurance of sustainability reports in their investment decisions across different regions. The analysis indicates five reasons why independent assurance of sustainability reports are important for investors. The primary reason for seeking independent assurance of sustainability reports is that it increases the trust and credibility of ESG information. The other motivations for considering independent assurance of sustainability reports are reduced risk and increased value; improved board and CEO level engagement; strengthens internal reporting and management systems; and demonstrates improved stakeholder communications.

Figure 8. Reasons for Considering Independent Assurance of Sustainability Reports by Investors

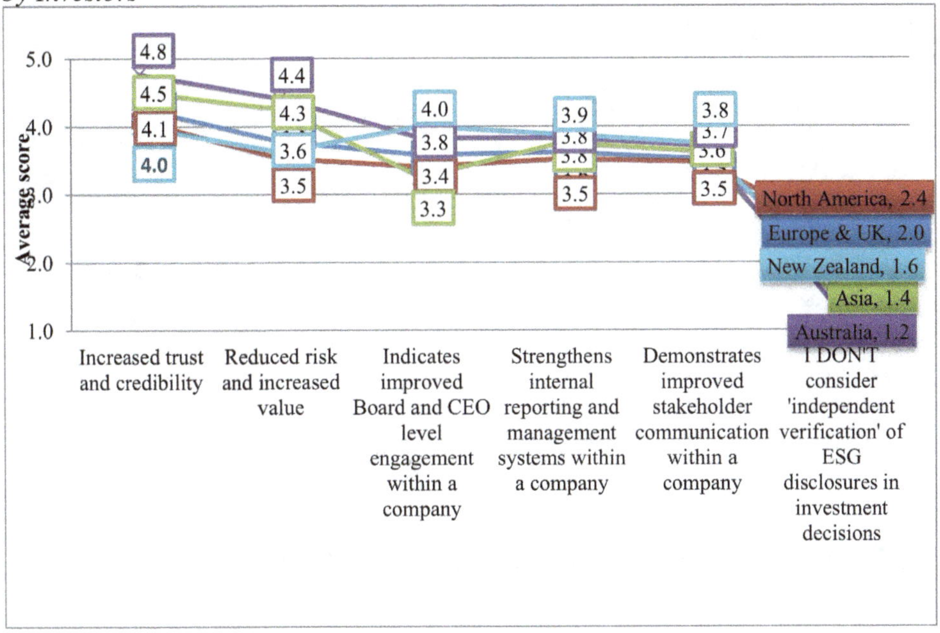

Figure 9 explores why some investors may not consider independent assurance of sustainability reports for investment decisions. It is evident that some investors do not consider the independent assurance of sustainability reports because they do not reduce risk or increase value and do not increase trust and credibility. Although some of these findings average scores are comparatively lower than values in the Figure 8, they contrast with what is being mentioned in favour of considering the independent assurance of sustainability reports in Figure 13. Other reasons that fail to capture the value of independent assurance of sustainability reports for investors include lack of demand from clients, insufficient knowledge, it is expensive, and inability to integrate ESG information in the quantitative models. Thus, a need arises to create more awareness on sustainability by external agencies among investors, provide opportunities for investors to sharpen their skills on sustainability dimension, and improve existing quantitative focused investment models to include sustainability-related information.

Figure 9. Reasons for Not Considering Independent Assurance of Sustainability Reports by Investors

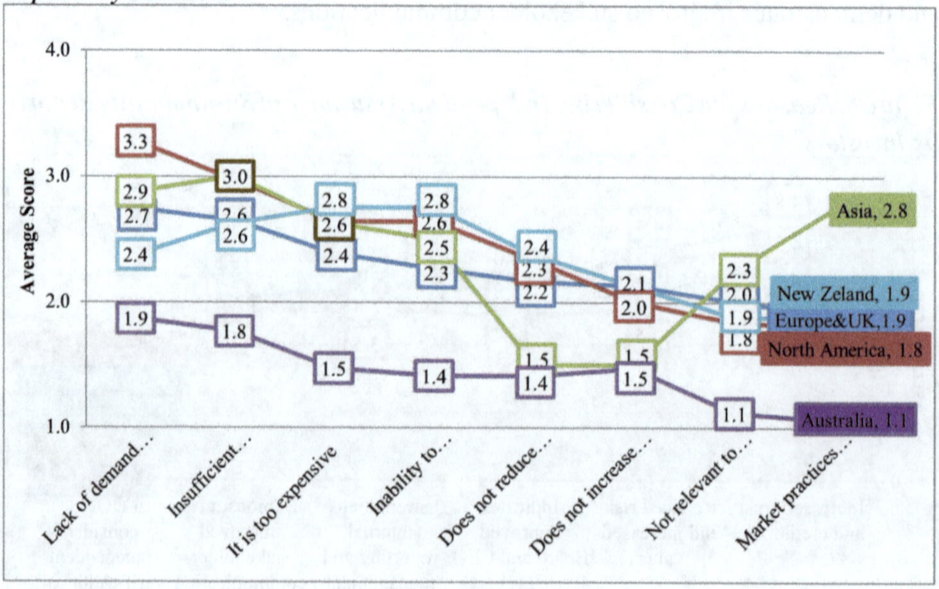

4.2 Analysis of Results in Retrospect of Theories and Literature

The results strongly corroborate the theoretical frameworks and existing literature. The high demand for assurance validates the tenets of signaling theory; investors are actively seeking and valuing these credible signals to cut through ESG noise. The regional variations (e.g., North American investors' greater reliance on third-party research) reflect the differing stages of ESG market maturity and institutional contexts, adding nuance to the global narrative. The findings directly support O'Dwyer's (2011) assertion on the necessity of assurance for reliability and align with Ballou et al. (2018) on the link between assurance and information quality. Furthermore, the identified benefits—such as improved board engagement and strengthened internal systems—extend beyond external reporting to underscore how assurance can drive internal value creation, a point increasingly emphasized by practitioners (KPMG, 2022).

5.0 CONCLUSION

Sustainability or ESG disclosures are being used by investors to assess the ESG performance of organizations to make informed investment decisions that contributes to responsible investment. Accordingly, investors rely on the quality of ESG information to make responsible investment decisions. Independent assurance of sustainability or ESG reports is one such way that the quality of such reports is ensured. Ballou et al. (2018) suggested that like any reported information by an organization, a lack of independent assurance of ESG information impacts its perception of quality. However, the ever-expanding list of frameworks and standards for sustainability reporting and the discrepancy between mandatory-voluntary sustainability reporting in different jurisdictions adds complexity in determining the quality of such information. As responsible investment continues to evolve as mainstream investment practice, it is important for sustainability reporting standards and tools to be harmonized so an organization's ESG impact can be disclosed and assessed with greater clarity and cohesion and to allow like-for-like comparisons between organizations and industries (Ng, 2017). In this study, we aimed to explore how investors assess the importance of independent assurance of sustainability reports for investment decisions. For this purpose, a survey targeting investors employed investment firms operating in developed economies was conducted. The survey yielded valuable insights on investors preferences for independent assurance of sustainability reports and how it may impact investment decisions.

Results of the survey reveals that many of the investors across different geographical regions consider ESG information and independent assurance of sustainability reports when making investment decisions. Findings also revealed that investors: employs different approaches to assess ESG information; agrees that public listed firms should be annually publishing ESG information; and agrees that sustainability reports should be subjected to independent assurance. Investors have also identified that independent assurance of sustainability reports: increased trust and creditability; reduced risk and increased value; improved board and CEO level engagement; strengthens internal reporting and management systems; and improves communication between stakeholder and the firm. Recognizing the importance of sustainability reporting assurance by the respondents of our survey validates the argument of Murphy (2018) that higher quality information is seen as more trustworthy and, ultimately, more useful for firms and their stakeholders, including investors. Supporting this notion, GRI (2021) suggest that the foundation of sustainability reporting is to enhance transparency of organisational impact on economy, environment and people.

Our study contributes to the literature by exploring the views of investors on the importance of independent assurance of sustainability reports for investment decisions. It verifies that such assurance is not only considered important but is often already a factor in investment analysis and decision-making, although the level of consideration varies across investment firms and regions. Several implications emerge from the findings of this study. As investors are calling for more ESG information and independent assurance of sustainability reports, boards and the executives are expected to take a more proactive approach to sustainability governance, practice and reporting to access capital, build a stronger corporate brand and promote sustainable long-term growth benefitting customers and investors. Ignoring such calls may come at the expense of organizational legitimacy and reputation. As the sustainability reporting landscape continues to evolve, it is crucial for organizations to stay informed about disclosure trends and adapt their non-financial reporting mechanisms accordingly. This will not only help them meet investor expectations but also position them favourably in an increasingly ESG-conscious markets.

5.1 Stakeholders Recommendations

For Regulators (e.g., SEC, ESMA, ISSB): Accelerate the move towards a mandatory, principles-based assurance requirement for sustainability reports, building upon the baseline established by the European Corporate Sustainability Reporting Directive (CSRD). This will create a level playing field and enhance global comparability.

For Standard-Setters (e.g., IAASB, IFAC): Develop and harmonize global assurance standards for sustainability information (e.g., ISSA 5000) to ensure consistency and rigor in assurance engagements, regardless of the provider type.

For Corporate Boards: Proactively integrate high-quality sustainability assurance into their governance and reporting cycles. View it not as a cost, but as a strategic investment to access lower-cost capital, enhance corporate reputation, and improve risk management.

For Assurance Providers: Invest in building specialized ESG competency across both accounting and niche consulting firms to meet the sophisticated and growing investor demand for high-quality verification.

5.2 Implications for Stakeholders

For Companies: Ignoring the investor demand for assured ESG data poses a material reputational and financial risk, potentially leading to a higher cost of capital and diminished investor interest.

For Investors: The research empowers investors to formally incorporate the presence (and quality) of sustainability assurance into their due diligence and valuation models, leading to more robust and resilient portfolios.

For Assurance Profession: It signals a significant growth market, necessitating an expansion of services, training, and methodologies to serve both corporate clients and the ultimate end-users of the reports—the investment community.

5.3 Future Research Directions

Future research can build upon these findings to further generalize the value and importance of independent assurance from an investor's context. Practitioners may gain additional insights into responsible investment from an investor's perspective and the challenges faced by both organizations and investors when making like-for-like comparisons between companies and sectors. More specific research directions may be pursued through these potentially promising research strands:

Qualitative Deep-Dive: Conduct in-depth interviews with investors to explore the nuanced decision-making processes behind their views on assurance, including how they assess the quality of different assurance providers.

Emerging Markets Context: Replicate this study in major developing economies to understand how ESG assurance is valued in different institutional and regulatory contexts.

Impact on Financial Performance: A longitudinal study to empirically test the correlation between the adoption of sustainability assurance and subsequent corporate financial performance or stock market valuation.

Assurance Quality Metrics: Research aimed at developing a framework for investors to evaluate the *quality* of an assurance statement (e.g., scope, materiality process, level of assurance) beyond its mere presence.

CHAPTER QUESTIONS

True and False Questions (Knowledge & Comprehension)

1. The independent assurance of sustainability reports is a mandatory practice for publicly listed firms across most global jurisdictions, mirroring the requirements for financial reports.
2. According to the chapter, the primary reason institutional investors value the independent assurance of sustainability reports is that it demonstrates improved stakeholder communications.
3. Signaling theory suggests that independent assurance acts as a credible mechanism for high-quality firms to distinguish themselves from those engaged in "greenwashing."

4. The methodological approach for this study involved a series of in-depth, qualitative interviews with retail investors from emerging markets.
5. The survey results indicated that a majority of investors in North America access ESG information primarily through direct engagement with companies, unlike their counterparts in other regions.
6. The International Sustainability Standards Board (ISSB) has developed standards that explicitly discourage the assurance of sustainability-related financial disclosures.
7. A key finding was that investors show a strong preference for sustainability assurance to be provided by the company's internal audit department rather than independent external firms.
8. The concept of "limited assurance" in a sustainability context provides a higher level of verification confidence than "reasonable assurance."
9. The study found no statistically significant difference between early and late survey responses, which helped to mitigate concerns regarding non-response bias.
10. Legitimacy theory, as cited in the chapter, posits that organizations seek independent assurance primarily to reduce their operational costs.

Multiple Choice Questions (Comprehension & Application)

11. According to the global survey data presented, what is the most frequently cited reason investors value the independent assurance of sustainability reports?
    A) It demonstrates improved stakeholder communications.
    B) It strengthens internal reporting and management systems.
    C) It increases trust and credibility of ESG information.
    D) It improves board and CEO level engagement.
    E) It is a mandatory requirement in their home jurisdiction.
12. The theoretical framework of this chapter is most explicitly grounded in which two theories?
    A) Stakeholder Theory and Institutional Theory
    B) Legitimacy Theory and Signaling Theory
    C) Agency Theory and Stewardship Theory
    D) Contingency Theory and Resource-Based View
    E) Transaction Cost Economics and Upper Echelons Theory
13. The sampling strategy for the survey deliberately excluded smaller investment firms in developing countries primarily to:
    A) Reduce the overall cost and complexity of the research.
    B) Focus on markets where retail investor influence is highest.
    C) Control for differences in macro environment and business climate.

D) Ensure a higher survey response rate.
E) Align with the research preferences of the CFA Institute.

14. Which of the following regulatory developments is highlighted in the chapter as representing a "tectonic shift" towards mandatory sustainability assurance?
    A) The Sustainability Accounting Standards Board (SASB) standards.
    B) The Global Reporting Initiative (GRI) guidelines.
    C) The European Commission's Corporate Sustainability Reporting Directive (CSRD).
    D) The Principles for Responsible Investment (PRI).
    E) The Carbon Disclosure Project (CDP).
15. The study identified a regional variation in the preferred *provider* of sustainability assurance. Which region demonstrated a distinct preference for independent professional firms specializing in ESG matters over accounting firms?
    A) Australia and New Zealand
    B) North America
    C) Europe
    D) Asia
    E) All regions showed a uniform preference for accounting firms.
16. What was the stated overall response rate for the global survey of investment professionals?
    A) 5.25%
    B) 9.11%
    C) 15.70%
    D) 22.30%
    E) 31.00%
17. According to the literature synthesis, the work of Cohen and Simnett (2015) suggests that the future market for assurance will likely become more discerning based on:
    A) The cost of the assurance engagement.
    B) The political affiliations of the assurance provider.
    C) The level (reasonable vs. limited) and type of assurer.
    D) The length of the final assurance statement.
    E) The use of proprietary versus public reporting frameworks.
18. Which of the following is NOT listed in the chapter as a key implication of the research findings for corporate boards?
    A) View sustainability assurance as a strategic investment.
    B) Proactively integrate high-quality assurance into governance cycles.
    C) Use assurance primarily as a tool for marketing and public relations.
    D) Enhance corporate reputation and improve risk management.
    E) Access lower-cost capital by meeting investor expectations.

19. The chapter suggests that the lack of a unified sustainability reporting framework primarily leads to:
   A) A decrease in the overall volume of sustainability reports published.
   B) Difficulties in making like-for-like comparisons between companies.
   C) Increased mandatory assurance requirements from governments.
   D) A reduction in investor interest in ESG factors altogether.
   E) The irrelevance of ESG rating providers like MSCI and Sustainalytics.
20. What methodological step did the authors take to address the potential for non-response bias in their survey?
   A) They increased the sample size by 50%.
   B) They compared early and late responses using t-tests.
   C) They offered financial incentives for participation.
   D) They conducted follow-up interviews with non-respondents.
   E) They used a different questionnaire for late respondents.

Short Answer Questions (Application & Analysis)

21. Briefly define *"Limited Assurance"* in the context of sustainability reporting and contrast it with *"Reasonable Assurance."*
22. Identify two distinct barriers, as revealed by the survey, that explain why a minority of investors do not value the independent assurance of sustainability reports.
23. How does the chapter utilize the concept of *"Signaling Theory"* to explain the strategic value for a company in obtaining independent assurance for its sustainability report?
24. Summarize the key demographic characteristic of the survey respondents in terms of their primary role or designation within their investment firms.
25. Based on the findings, describe the regional variation in how investors from Australia and New Zealand differ from those in North America regarding their primary method of accessing ESG information.
26. What is the significance of the International Auditing and Assurance Standards Board's (IAASB) development of ISSA 5000, as discussed in the chapter?
27. Explain, using one example from the chapter, how the demand for independent assurance is evolving from a voluntary practice to a more regulated one.
28. According to the study, what are the two most preferred types of providers for conducting independent assurance on sustainability reports?

Essay Questions (Analysis & Evaluation)

29. Critically analyze how the chapter's findings regarding investor preferences for assurance providers (specialist ESG firms vs. accounting/audit firms) could create both opportunities and challenges for the assurance profession.
30. Evaluate the robustness of the study's methodology. Justify your evaluation by discussing two strengths of the sampling strategy and one inherent limitation of the survey method used.
31. Synthesize the evidence from the chapter to construct a persuasive argument a corporate board could justify the additional expense of obtaining a *"reasonable"* level of assurance versus a *"limited"* level.
32. The chapter positions independent assurance as a solution to information asymmetry. Analyze how the proliferation of different ESG reporting frameworks (e.g., GRI, SASB, TCFD) exacerbates this asymmetry and discuss how assurance can mitigate this issue.
33. Drawing from the theoretical background and the empirical results, evaluate the statement: *"Independent sustainability assurance is transitioning from a legitimacy-seeking exercise for companies to a value-creating signal for investors."*
34. The research identifies *"reduced risk and increased value"* as a key motivation for investors. Analyze the mechanisms through which the assurance of a non-financial report could lead to a perception of reduced investment risk.

In-depth Questions for Master's Students (Synthesis & Evaluation)

35. **Comparative Analysis:** Design a research proposal that compares the valuation of sustainability assurance between institutional investors in a developed market (e.g., the UK) and an emerging market (e.g., Brazil). What key institutional, regulatory, and cultural variables would your research need to control for?
36. **Policy Design:** Based on the chapter's findings and the current regulatory trajectory (e.g., CSRD, ISSB), synthesize a set of three core principles that a national regulator should include in a policy mandating sustainability assurance. Justify each principle with evidence from the chapter.
37. **Theoretical Extension:** The chapter applies signaling and legitimacy theory. Propose how a third theoretical lens, such as *institutional theory*, could provide an alternative or complementary explanation for the global convergence in investor demand for assurance, particularly in the context of differing regional practices.

38. **Methodological Critique and Proposal:** The study relies on survey data capturing investor *perceptions*. Propose a complementary quantitative research design using archival data (e.g., stock prices, corporate bond yields) to test whether the *presence* of sustainability assurance has a measurable impact on a company's cost of capital.
39. **Future Scenarios:** Synthesizing the trends in the chapter, project the landscape of the sustainability assurance profession a decade from now. Consider the potential for market consolidation among providers, the role of technology and AI in the assurance process, and the likely minimum standard for assurance (limited vs. reasonable).

In-depth Questions for PhD Scholars (Synthesis & Creation)

40. **Causal Complexity:** The chapter establishes a correlation between investor demand and assurance. Design a longitudinal, mixed-methods study to investigate the *causal mechanisms* through which assurance actually influences investment decisions. How would you isolate the effect of assurance from other firm-specific and market-wide factors? Consider using both quantitative data on portfolio allocations and qualitative protocol analysis with investors.
41. **Theoretical Problematization:** Critically deconstruct the application of legitimacy theory in this context. Does investor demand for assurance truly reflect a quest for broader societal legitimacy, or does it signify the emergence of a new, financially-material *epistemic regime* where non-financial data is simply becoming a new form of financial data? Develop a theoretical argument supported by literature from economic sociology and critical accounting.
42. **Construct Validation:** The research treats "independent assurance" as a somewhat homogeneous construct. However, the quality and rigor of assurance engagements can vary significantly. Propose a framework for deconstructing and measuring the *quality* of an assurance statement itself (e.g., scope, materiality process, assurer competence, recommendations). How could such a framework be empirically validated and what would be the challenges in its operationalization?

In-depth Questions for Post-Doctoral Researchers (Creation & Direction)

43. **Paradigm-Shifting Inquiry:** Current research, including this chapter, focuses on how assurance reduces information asymmetry. Propose a research program that investigates a more radical premise: that high-quality sustainability assurance fundamentally alters the nature of the corporate-investor relationship by fostering *relational contracting* based on shared long-term value creation. What

novel theoretical constructs and methodological approaches (e.g., ethnographic studies of investor-company dialogues) would this require?

44. **Systemic Impact Research:** Move beyond the firm and investor dyad. Design a large-scale, multi-country study to investigate the macro-level consequences of widespread sustainability assurance adoption. How does it influence systemic financial stability, the allocation of capital towards sustainable activities at a societal level, and the potential for creating new, unintended forms of market exclusion for firms that cannot afford high-quality assurance?
45. **Epistemological and Ethical Inquiry:** The assurance process involves translating complex, often qualitative, social and environmental phenomena into auditable metrics. Frame a critical research agenda that investigates the *politics and power dynamics* inherent in this process. Who defines what is *"material"* and *"assurable"?* What are the risks of *"assurance-washing"* and the marginalization of non-quantifiable impacts? This inquiry should draw from science and technology studies (STS) and political economy.

KEY TERMS AND DEFINITIONS

REFERENCES

Ballou, B., Chen, P.-C., Grenier, J. H., & Heitger, D. L. (2018). Corporate social responsibility assurance and reporting quality. *Journal of Accounting and Public Policy*, *37*(2), 167–188. DOI: 10.1016/j.jaccpubpol.2018.02.001

CFA Institute. (2018). *CFA Institute: Global Association for Investment Management Professionals*. https://www.cfainstitute.org/en/membership/directory

Cohen, J. R., & Simnett, R. (2015). CSR and assurance services: A research agenda. *Auditing*, *34*(1), 59–74. DOI: 10.2308/ajpt-50876

Eccles, R. G., Ioannou, I., & Serafeim, G. (2014). The impact of corporate sustainability on organizational processes and performance. *Management Science*, *60*(11), 2835–2857. DOI: 10.1287/mnsc.2014.1984

Eden, L., Nielsen, B., & Verbeke, A. (2020). *Research Methods in International Business*. Palgrave Macmillan. DOI: 10.1007/978-3-030-22113-3

European Commission. (2021). Proposal for a directive of the European Parliament and of the Council amending Regulation (EU) No 537/2014, Directive 2004/109/EC, Directive 2006/43/EC and Directive 2013/34/EU, as regards corporate sustainability reporting. COM(2021) 189 final.

EY. (2020). *Fifth Global Institutional Investor Survey*. EY Global.

Global Sustainable Investment Alliance (GSIA). (2022). *Global Sustainable Investment Review 2022*. http://www.gsi-alliance.org

GRI. (2021). *A short introduction to the GRI standards*. GRI, Netherlands. https://www.globalreporting.org/media/wtaf14tw/a-short-introduction-to-the-gri-standards.pdf

GSIA. (2022). *Global Sustainable Investment Review 2022*. GSIA. https://www.gsi-alliance.org/members-resources/gsir2022/

Hair, J. F., Celsi, M. W., Money, A. H., Samouel, P., & Page, M. J. (2015). *Essentials of Business Research Methods* (2nd ed.). Routledge. DOI: 10.4324/9781315704562

Hill, J. (2020). *Environmental, Social, and Governance (ESG) Investing: A Balanced Analysis of the Theory and Practice of a Sustainable Portfolio*. Academic Press.

Iacobucci, D., & Churchill, G. (2018). *Marketing Research: Methodological Foundations* (12th ed.). Create Space Independent Publishing Platform.

International Auditing and Assurance Standards Board (IAASB). (2022). *International Standard on Sustainability Assurance (ISSA) 5000, General Requirements for Sustainability Assurance Engagements* [Exposure Draft]. International Federation of Accountants. https://www.ifac.org/iaasb/publications/international-standard-sustainability-assurance-issa-5000-general-requirements-sustainability-assurance

International Chamber of Commerce (ICC). (2022). *ICC guidance on responsible sourcing*. ICC.

International Sustainability Standards Board (ISSB). (2023). IFRS S1 General Requirements for Disclosure of Sustainability-related Financial Information. IFRS Foundation. https://www.ifrs.org/issued-standards/ifrs-sustainability-standards-navigator/ifrs-s1-general-requirements/

Johnson, R. B., & Christensen, L. (2019). *Educational Research: Quantitative, Qualitative, and Mixed Approaches* (7th ed.). SAGE Publications.

Kim, S., & Yoon, A. (2023). Analyzing Active Fund Managers' Commitment to ESG: Evidence from the United Nations Principles for Responsible Investment. *Management Science*, *69*(2), 741–758. DOI: 10.1287/mnsc.2022.4394

Kotsantonis, S., & Serafeim, G. (2019). Four things no one will tell you about ESG data. *The Bank of America Journal of Applied Corporate Finance*, *31*(2), 50–58. DOI: 10.1111/jacf.12346

KPMG. (2022). *Survey of Sustainability Reporting 2022: Big Shifts, Small Steps*. KPMG International.

Malhotra, N. K. (2019). *Marketing Research: An Applied Orientation* (7th ed.). Pearson Publishing.

Muneer, S., Shabbir, J., & Khalil, A. (2017. Estimation of finite population mean in simple random sampling and stratified random sampling using two auxiliary variables. *Journal of Communications in Statistics - Theory and Methods,* 46(5), 2181 – 2192.

Murphy, W. J. (2018). *Independent Assurance: Providing assurance to organizations across a wide range of sectors and variety of assurance scopes*. KPMG Sustainability Services, www.kpmg.com/ca/en/home/services/audit/sustainability-services/independent-assurance

Ng, J. (2017). *Responsible Investment: How It Can Become Mainstream Practice*. Market Mogul.

O'Dwyer, B. (2011). The Case of Sustainability Assurance: Constructing a New Assurance Service. *Contemporary Accounting Research*, *28*(4), 1230–1266. DOI: 10.1111/j.1911-3846.2011.01108.x

PRI. (2024). *Annual report 2024*. Retrieved October 15, 2024, from https://www.unpri.org/about-us/about-the-pri/annual-report#storytext-end

Principles for Responsible Investment (PRI). (2024). *Annual report 2024*. Retrieved from https://www.unpri.org/annual-report-2024

Skarmeas, D., Zeriti, A., & Baltas, G. (2016). Relationship Value: Drivers and Outcomes in International Marketing Channels. *Journal of International Marketing*, 24(1), page(s): 22-40.

Sridharan, V. (2018). *Bridging the Disclosure Gap: Investor Perspectives on Environmental, Social, & Governance (ESG)*. Disclosures.

Sridharan, V. (2018). *Bridging the disclosure gap: Investor perspectives on environmental, social, & governance (ESG) disclosures*. SASB.

Strott, E., Carey, C., & Wilson, S. (2016). *Investors, corporates, and ESG: Bridging the gap*. PwC's Governance Insights Center.

UNCTAD. (2024). *World Investment Report 2024: Investment facilitation and digital government*. United Nations Publications.

United Nations Conference on Trade and Development (UNCTAD). (2024). *World Investment Report 2024: Investment facilitation and digital government*. United Nations Publications.

World Business Council for Sustainable Development (WBCSD). (2023). *Assurance of sustainability reporting: A guide to the evolving landscape*. WBCSD. https://www.wbcsd.org/

ADDITIONAL READING

Eccles, R. G., Ioannou, I., & Serafeim, G. (2014). The impact of corporate sustainability on organizational processes and performance. *Management Science*, *60*(11), 2835–2857. DOI: 10.1287/mnsc.2014.1984

International Auditing and Assurance Standards Board (IAASB). (2022). *International Standard on Sustainability Assurance (ISSA) 5000, General Requirements for Sustainability Assurance Engagements* [Exposure Draft]. International Federation of Accountants.

International Sustainability Standards Board (ISSB). (2023). *IFRS S1 General Requirements for Disclosure of Sustainability-related Financial Information and IFRS S2 Climate-related Disclosures*. IFRS Foundation.

Kotsantonis, S., & Serafeim, G. (2019). Four things no one will tell you about ESG data. *The Bank of America Journal of Applied Corporate Finance*, *31*(2), 50–58. DOI: 10.1111/jacf.12346

Environmental, Social, and Governance (ESG): A structured framework used to evaluate a company's strategic management of risks and opportunities related to environmental stewardship, social responsibility, and ethical governance. This evaluation is increasingly integral to assessing a firm's long-term value and risk profile.

Independent Assurance (in a sustainability context): A systematic, evidence-based verification process conducted by a qualified third party not employed by the organization. Its objective is to provide an opinion on reliability, credibility, and adherence to predefined criteria of the information presented in a sustainability or ESG report.

Limited Assurance: A lower, but still meaningful, level of assurance where the practitioner concludes whether anything has come to their attention that causes them to believe the subject matter is materially misstated. It provides a negative form of expression (e.g., "Based on our work, nothing has come to our attention...").

Reasonable Assurance: The highest level of assurance, analogous to a financial audit, where the practitioner concludes that the subject matter is free from material misstatement. It provides a positive form of expression (e.g., "In our opinion, the report is presented fairly...").

Signaling Theory: An economic concept suggesting that in markets with information asymmetry, parties with high-quality attributes (e.g., strong ESG performance) will undertake costly, verifiable actions (e.g., independent assurance) to credibly "*signal*" their quality to the market, thereby distinguishing themselves from lower-quality counterparts.

Sustainability/ESG Reporting Frameworks: Rulesets and principles that guide organizations in disclosing their ESG performance. Prominent examples include the Global Reporting Initiative (GRI) for comprehensive reporting and the Sustainability Accounting Standards Board (SASB) standards for industry-specific, financially material disclosures.

TEACHING NOTE

Concise Summary for the Teacher

This chapter presents a seminal, empirically driven investigation into a critical nexus in modern finance: the value institutional investors assign to the independent assurance of corporate sustainability reports. Moving beyond theoretical postulations, the research employs a robust global survey of 100 investment professionals to provide compelling evidence that assurance is a significant factor in investment decision-making. The findings demonstrate an overwhelming investor consensus on the necessity of assurance, primarily for enhancing the credibility of ESG data and mitigating investment risk. The chapter effectively bridges theoretical frameworks (Signaling and Legitimacy Theory) with practical investor behaviour, offering profound implications for corporate boards, assurance providers, and regulators. It serves as an ideal platform for discussing the evolving nature of corporate accountability, the mechanics of non-financial markets, and the future of sustainable finance.

Chapter Synopsis

The chapter begins by establishing the meteoric rise of ESG factors in investment paradigms, juxtaposed against a backdrop of voluntary, fragmented reporting and a lack of unified verification standards. This context creates a pressing information asymmetry, framing the central research question: Do investors value and act upon independently assured sustainability data? The study's methodology—a stratified random sample of investment professionals from large firms in developed markets—is meticulously detailed and justified. The results are unequivocal: a strong majority of investors globally demand assurance, view it as a tool for risk reduction and value creation, and are increasingly factoring it into capital allocation decisions. The discussion elegantly weaves these findings back to core theories, showing how assurance acts as a credible signal and legitimacy-conferring mechanism. The chapter concludes with actionable stakeholder recommendations and a forward-looking research agenda.

Key Learning Objectives

Upon engaging in this chapter, students should be able to:

1. **Remember** the key distinctions between voluntary sustainability assurance and mandatory financial audit requirements.

2. **Understand** the core principles of signaling and legitimacy theory as they apply to ESG disclosure and assurance.
3. **Apply** the chapter's empirical findings to predict how different corporate assurance strategies might be perceived by the investment community.
4. **Analyze** the regional variations in investor preferences to critique a one-size-fits-all approach to corporate ESG disclosure.
5. **Evaluate** the robustness of the research methodology, identifying its strengths in sampling and its limitations in generalizability.
6. **Create** a preliminary strategy for a company or assurance provider to navigate the evolving landscape of sustainability verification.

Core Themes/Theses for Discussion

1. **From Voluntary to Vital:** Independent sustainability assurance is transitioning from a niche, voluntary practice to a mainstream expectation that materially influences investment capital flows.
2. **The Credibility Dividend:** The primary value of assurance lies not in the data itself, but in the enhanced trust and credibility it confers, which investors translate into perceptions of reduced risk.
3. **Theoretical Validation in Practice:** Signaling and Legitimacy theories are not merely academic constructs; they are actively validated by the decision-making calculus of sophisticated market actors.
4. **The Nuance of Global Consensus:** While a global demand for assurance exists, regional differences in its implementation (preferred providers, data sources) demand nuanced corporate strategies.
5. **The Assurer's Dilemma:** The investor preference for both accounting firms and specialist consultancies creates a dynamic competitive landscape with implications for service quality, standards, and professional expertise.

Suggested Teaching Pathway (90-Minute Session)

Introduction (10 mins): Begin with a provocative question: "If a company's sustainability report isn't independently verified, can you trust it?" Use this to introduce the core problem of credibility in ESG data.

Context & Theory (15 mins): Lecturette covering the growth of ESG investing, the problem of fragmented reporting, and an overview of Signaling and Legitimacy Theory. Use analogies (e.g., a quality seal on a product) to make theories accessible.

Methodology Deep Dive (10 mins): Facilitate a brief discussion on the research design. Ask: "What are the trade-offs in focusing only on large firms in developed markets?" This reinforces research literacy.

Findings & Analysis (25 mins): Walk through the key findings (Figs 1-9). Use think-pair-share for questions like: "Why might 'increased trust' be more important to investors than 'improved stakeholder communications'?"

Implications & Synthesis (20 mins): Divide students into three groups representing Corporate Boards, Assurance Providers, and Regulators. Task each group with developing 2-3 key takeaways or action items from the chapter's findings.

Conclusion & Look Ahead (10 mins): Recap the core argument and introduce one of the future research questions to leave students contemplating the evolving nature of the field.

Pedagogical Tools & Resources

Case Study: Pair this chapter with a brief case study on a company that faced "greenwashing" allegations, highlighting the potential value of robust assurance (e.g., a voluntary early adopter of reasonable assurance).

In-Class Polling: Use live polls to survey student opinions on key questions before revealing the chapter's data, creating a personal connection to the material.

Assurance Statement Analysis: Provide students with real (anonymized) examples of a *"limited"* and a *"reasonable"* assurance statement. Have them compare and contrast the language and conclusions.

Regulatory Update: Provide a one-page handout summarizing the latest status of the CSRD, ISSB, and ISSA 5000 to ground the discussion in current events.

Note on Sensitivity

- The chapter and subsequent discussion may reveal tensions between the Global North and South regarding the imposition of sustainability standards. Acknowledge that the study's focus on developed markets is a limitation and that the cost and applicability of assurance in emerging economies is a critical, unresolved issue.
- The demographic data (72% male respondents) can be used to discuss the lack of diversity within the investment industry itself and how this might shape the perception and prioritization of ESG issues.
- Be prepared to address sceptical views on ESG investing itself. Guide the discussion towards the chapter's empirical evidence of investor behaviour, rather than debating the moral imperative of ESG.

Key Questions for Class Discussion

1. **Beyond Trust:** The board of a company argues that their sustainability report is "inherently credible." Using signaling theory, what counter-arguments, based on this chapter, would you present to convince them to seek assurance?
    - o *Direction:* Push students to articulate how assurance is a *costly and verifiable* action that competitors cannot easily replicate, thus making it a credible signal.
2. **The Regional Strategy:** The findings show European investors prefer specialist ESG assurers, while Australians show more trust in accounting firms. If you were the Head of IR for a multinational corporation, how would you tailor your assurance and communication strategy?
    - o *Direction:* Encourage discussion on whether to use multiple assurers, how to highlight the assurer's credentials in different regions, and the importance of a globally recognized standard like ISSA 5000.
3. **The *"Why Not":*** A significant minority of investors do not value assurance, citing a lack of risk reduction. Is this a failure of the assurance product, or a failure of communication from the assurance providers?
    - o *Direction:* Guide students to consider the difference between limited and reasonable assurance, the quality of assurance engagement, and the need for investors to be educated on how to "read" an assurance statement.
4. **The Cost-Benefit Analysis:** The chapter frames assurance as a *"strategic investment."* What tangible financial metrics could a CFO use to measure the return on this investment, based on the motivation's investors listed?
    - o *Direction:* Steer the discussion towards lower cost of capital (reduced risk), higher valuations (increased value), and improved access to a specific pool of ESG-focused capital.
5. **The Limitation Lens:** The study's sample is exclusively from developed markets. How might the results differ if replicated in a major emerging market like India or Brazil? What new variables would come into play?
    - o *Direction:* Elicit factors such as regulatory pressure, investor sophistication, family-owned business structures, and different material ESG issues (e.g., water stress, community relations).
6. **The Future of the Profession:** Given the investor openness to both accounting and consulting firms, what unique advantages does each type of provider bring to an assurance engagement, and what are their potential weaknesses?
    - o *Direction:* Accounting firms bring brand reputation for rigor and audit methodology; consultants bring deep topical expertise. The challenge is balancing methodological rigor with subject matter depth.

7. **The Regulatory Impetus:** The CSRD is described as a *"tectonic shift."* Does this regulatory move risk making assurance a mere 'compliance checkbox,' thereby undermining its value as a strategic signal?
    - o *Direction:* Discuss the difference between a *"compliance mindset"* and a *"strategic mindset."* Will mandating the minimum (limited assurance) simply create a floor, or will it stifle innovation?
8. **The Internal Value:** One of the investor-identified benefits is that assurance *"strengthens internal reporting and management systems."* How might the process of being audited on ESG metrics actually improve a company's internal operations?
    - o *Direction:* Connect this to better data collection processes, improved internal controls, and more informed strategic decision-making at the board level regarding ESG risks and opportunities.
9. **The Next Frontier:** The chapter calls for research on *"Assurance Quality Metrics."* What two or three specific elements would you include in a scorecard to evaluate the quality of an assurance statement?
    - o *Direction:* Potential elements: the scope of work (how many KPIs?), the description of the materiality process, the specific qualifications and independence of the assurer, and the nature of the recommendations provided.
10. **A Paradigm Shift?:** The Post-Doctoral question suggests assurance could foster *"relational contracting."* Is this realistic, or is the investor-company relationship inherently transactional? Can verified ESG data build deeper trust?
    - o *Direction:* This is a speculative but crucial question. Encourage students to think about long-term horizons, collaborative engagements on sustainability goals, and move beyond quarterly earnings pressure.

Compilation of References

Aaker, D. A., & Joachimsthaler, E. (2000). *Brand Leadership*. The Free Press.

Adams, C. A. (2020). *The Sustainable Development Goals, integrated thinking and the integrated report*. IFRS Foundation. https://integratedreporting.ifrs.org/wp-content/uploads/2017/09/SDGs-and-the-integrated-report_full17.pdf

Adams, C. A., Alhamood, A. M., & He, X. (2022). The development and implementation of GRI standards: practice and policy issues. In *Handbook of accounting and sustainability* (pp. 26–43). Edward Elgar Publishing. DOI: 10.4337/9781800373518.00009

Adams, C. A., Alhamood, A., He, X., Tian, J., Wang, L., & Wang, Y. (2021). *The double-materiality concept: Application and issues*. Global Reporting Initiative.

Adams, C., & Narayanan, V. (2010). The 'standardization' of sustainability reporting. In *Sustainability accounting and accountability* (pp. 89–104). Routledge.

Afzal, A., Rasoulinezhad, E., & Malik, Z. (2022). Green finance and sustainable development in Europe. *Ekonomska Istrazivanja*, *35*(1), 5150–5163. DOI: 10.1080/1331677X.2021.2024081

Agle, B. R., & Kelley, P. C. (2001). Ensuring validity in the measurement of corporate social performance: Lessons from corporate United Way and PAC campaigns. *Journal of Business Ethics*, *31*(3), 271–284. DOI: 10.1023/A:1010797011622

Agrawal, R., Agrawal, S., Samadhiya, A., Kumar, A., Luthra, S., & Jain, V. (2024). Adoption of green finance and green innovation for achieving circularity: An exploratory review and future directions. *Geoscience Frontiers*, *15*(4), 101669. DOI: 10.1016/j.gsf.2023.101669

Ahmed, H., Mohieldin, M., Verbeek, J., & Aboulmagd, F. (2015). On the sustainable development goals and the role of Islamic finance. *World Bank Policy Research Working Paper*, (7266).

Ahmed, S. M. (2009). Volatility spillovers from the US to Southeast Asian stock markets. *Journal of Asia-Pacific Business, 10*(2), 132 ??152.

Ahrholdt, D. C., Gudergan, S. P., & Ringle, C. M. (2017). Enhancing service loyalty. *Journal of Travel Research, 56*(4), 436–450. DOI: 10.1177/0047287516649058

Alazzani, A., & Wan-Hussin, W. N. (2013). Global Reporting Initiative's environmental reporting: A study of oil and gas companies. *Ecological Indicators, 32*, 19–24. DOI: 10.1016/j.ecolind.2013.02.019

Aldasoro, I., Borio, C., & Drehmann, M. (2022). Early warning indicators of banking crises: Expanding the toolkit. *Journal of Financial Stability, 60*, 100992.

Allman, E., & Won, J. (2021). The Effect of ESG Disclosure on Corporate Investment Efficiency. SSRN Electronic Journal. DOI: 10.2139/ssrn.3816592

Al-Roubaie, A., & Sarea, A. M. (2019). Green investment and sustainable development: The case of Islamic finance. *Journal of Islamic Business and Management, 9*(1). Advance online publication. DOI: 10.26501/jibm/2019.0901-002

Amezaga, A. (2019). Cultural field and literature in minority languages: Basque under Francoism. *Poetics, 77*, 101398. DOI: 10.1016/j.poetic.2019.101398

An Overview of SDGs | NITI Aayog. (n.d.). Www.niti.gov.in. https://www.niti.gov.in/overview-sustainable-development-goals

Andrew, J., & Cortese, C. L. (2011). Carbon disclosures: Comparability, the carbon disclosure project and the greenhouse gas protocol. Australasian Accounting. *Business and Finance Journal, 5*(4), 5–18.

Apaza-Panca, C. M., Flores Quevedo, L. A., & Reyes, L. M. C. (2024). Green marketing to promote the natural protected area. *Sustainable Technology and Entrepreneurship, 3*(3), 100067. DOI: 10.1016/j.stae.2023.100067

Arouri, M. E. H., Jouini, J., & Nguyen, D. K. (2011a). Volatility spillovers between oil prices and stock sector returns: Implications for portfolio management. *Journal of International Money and Finance, 30*(7), 1387 ??1405. DOI: 10.1016/j.jimonfin.2011.07.008

Arouri, M. E. H., Jouini, J., & Nguyen, D. K. (2012). On the impacts of oil price fluctuations on European equity markets: Volatility spillover and hedging effectiveness. *Energy Economics, 34*(2), 611 ??617. DOI: 10.1016/j.eneco.2011.08.009

Arouri, M. E. H., Lahiani, A., & Nguyen, D. K. (2011b). Return and volatility transmission between world oil prices and stock markets of the GCC countries. *Economic Modelling, 28*(4), 1815 ??1825. DOI: 10.1016/j.econmod.2011.03.012

Arouri, M. E., Lahiani, A., & Nguyen, D. K. (2015). World Gold Prices and Stock Returns in China: Insights for Hedging and Diversification Strategies. *Economic Modelling*, *44*, 273 ??282. DOI: 10.1016/j.econmod.2014.10.030

Athanasoglou, P. P., Brissimis, S. N., & Delis, M. D. (2008). Bank specific, industry-specific and macroeconomic determinants of bank profitability. *Journal of International Financial Markets, Institutions and Money*, *18*(2), 121–136. DOI: 10.1016/j.intfin.2006.07.001

Atteridge, A., Shrivastava, M., Pahuja, N., & Upadhyay, H. (2012). Climate policy in india: What shapes international, national and state policy? *Ambio*, *41*(S1), 68–77. DOI: 10.1007/s13280-011-0242-5

Aydoğmuş, M., Gülay, G., & Ergun, K.AYDOĞMUŞ. (2022). Impact Of Esg Performance On Firm Value And Profitability. *Borsa Istanbul Review*, *22*(2), S119–S127. DOI: 10.1016/j.bir.2022.11.006

Azad, M. A. K., Islam, M. A., Sobhani, F. A., Hassan, M. S., & Masukujjaman, M. (2022). Revisiting the Current Status of Green Finance and Sustainable Finance Disbursement: A Policy Insights. *Sustainability (Basel)*, *14*(14), 8911. DOI: 10.3390/su14148911

Azam, M., Boubaker, S., & Hunjra, A. I. (2023). Dynamic Institutions as Pillars for Sustainable Development. *In Governance in the Developing World: Transnational Insights on Economic Development* (pp. 1–22). Singapore: Springer. *Nature in Singapore*. Advance online publication. DOI: 10.1007/978-981-99-2493-6_1

Baird, P. L., Geylani, P. C., & Roberts, J. A. (2011, December 9). Corporate Social and Financial Performance Re-Examined: Industry Effects in a Linear Mixed Model Analysis. Springer Science+Business Media, 109(3), 367-388. 10.1007/s10551-011-1135-z

Bajaj, P., & Youdon, C. (2021). Towards a Comprehensive Climate Adaptation Framework for India's Port Infrastructure and Operations: Lessons from Global Best Practices. *Environmental Science & Sustainable Development*, *6*(2), 48–59. DOI: 10.21625/essd.v6i2.837

Balaji, K. (2023). Exploring the Drivers and Effects on Supply Chain Resilience and Performance in an Emerging Market Using Artificial Intelligence. 2023 3rd International Conference on Smart Generation Computing, Communication and Networking (SMART GENCON), 1–6. DOI: 10.1109/SMARTGENCON60755.2023.10442071

Balaji, K. (2025a). AI as a Game Changer: How Digital Entrepreneurs Are Redefining Business Practices. In Tunio, M. (Ed.), *Improving Entrepreneurial Processes Through Advanced AI* (pp. 21–48). IGI Global Scientific Publishing., DOI: 10.4018/979-8-3693-1495-1.ch002

Balaji, K. (2025b). E-Government and E-Governance: Driving Digital Transformation in Public Administration. In Wongmahesak, K., Ahmad, J., & Mustanir, A. (Eds.), *Public Governance Practices in the Age of AI* (pp. 23–44). IGI Global Scientific Publishing., DOI: 10.4018/979-8-3693-9286-7.ch002

Balaji, K. (2025c). Harnessing AI and Blockchain in Sustainability Assurance: Trends Shaping the Future of Verification. In Khatib, S., & Abbas, A. (Eds.), *Navigating Trust in Sustainability Reporting and Assurance* (pp. 215–242). IGI Global Scientific Publishing., DOI: 10.4018/979-8-3373-0117-4.ch007

Balboni, P., & Kate Elizabeth Francis. (2024). Data Ethics and Digital Sustainability: Bridging Legal Data Protection Compliance and ESG for a Responsible Data-Driven Future. DOI: 10.2139/ssrn.4884478

Ballou, B., Chen, P.-C., Grenier, J. H., & Heitger, D. L. (2018). Corporate social responsibility assurance and reporting quality. *Journal of Accounting and Public Policy*, *37*(2), 167–188. DOI: 10.1016/j.jaccpubpol.2018.02.001

Bande, M. H. (2022, November – December). Corporate Social Responsibility and Financial Performance of Deposit Money Banks in Nigeria. *International Journal of Management Studies and Social Science Research*, *4*(6). Advance online publication. DOI: 10.56293/IJMSSSR.2022.4534

Bank for International Settlements (BIS). (2022). *Green Islamic finance: Opportunities and challenges*. BIS Papers, No. 128. Retrieved from https://www.bis.org/publ/bppdf/bispap128.htm

Barney, J. (1991). Firm resources and sustained competitive advantage. *Journal of Management*, *17*(1), 99–120. DOI: 10.1177/014920639101700108

Barykin, S., Strimovskaya, A., Sergeev, S., Borisoglebskaya, L., Dedyukhina, N., Sklyarov, I., Sklyarova, J., & Saychenko, L. (2023). Smart City Logistics on the Basis of Digital Tools for ESG Goals Achievement. *Sustainability (Basel)*, *15*(6), 5507–5507. DOI: 10.3390/su15065507

Batten, J. A., Ciner, C., & Lucey, B. M. (2010). The macroeconomic determinants of volatility in precious metals markets. *Resources Policy*, *35*(2), 65 ??71. DOI: 10.1016/j.resourpol.2009.12.002

Baur, D. G., & McDermott, T. K. (2010). Is gold a safe haven? International evidence. *Journal of Banking & Finance*, *34*(8), 1886 ??1898. DOI: 10.1016/j.jbankfin.2009.12.008

Bauwens, L., Laurent, S., & Rombouts, J. V. (2006). Multivariate GARCH models: A survey. *Journal of Applied Econometrics*, *21*(1), 79 ??109. DOI: 10.1002/jae.842

Becchetti, L., Ciciretti, R., Hasan, I., & Kobeissi, N. (2012, November 1). Corporate social responsibility and shareholder's value. Elsevier BV, 65(11), 1628-1635. 10.1016/j.jbusres.2011.10.022

Becerra, E. P., & Korgaonkar, P. K. (2011). Effects of trust beliefs on consumers' online intentions. *European Journal of Marketing*, *45*(6), 936–962. DOI: 10.1108/03090561111119921

Belkaoui, A. (1976). The impact of the disclosure of the environmental effects of organizational behavior on the market. *Financial Management*, *5*(4), 26–31. DOI: 10.2307/3665454

Ben Brik, A., Rettab, B., & Mellahi, K. (2011). Market orientation, corporate social responsibility, and business performance. *Journal of Business Ethics*, *99*(3), 307–324. DOI: 10.1007/s10551-010-0658-z

Berg, F., Kölbel, J. F., & Rigobon, R. (2022). Aggregate Confusion: The Divergence of ESG Ratings. *Review of Finance*, *26*(6), 1315–1344. DOI: 10.1093/rof/rfac033

Bergquist, A. (2017). Business and Sustainability: New Business History Perspectives. Social Science Research Network. DOI: 10.2139/ssrn.3055587

Berkes, F. (2017). *Sacred ecology*. Routledge. DOI: 10.4324/9781315114644

Bhattacharyya, U. (2023, April 19). Understanding the regulatory framework for sustainable finance in India. NLS Business Law Review. https://www.nlsblr.com/post/understanding-the-regulatory-framework-for-sustainable-finance-in-india

Bhunia, A. (2013). Cointegration and causal relationship among crude price, domestic gold price and financial variables: an evidence of BSE and NSE. *Journal of contemporary issues in business research, 2*(1), 1-10.

Bhuyan, R., Robbani, M. G., Talukdar, B., & Jain, A. (2016). Information transmission and dynamics of stock price movements: An empirical analysis of BRICS and US stock markets. *International Review of Economics & Finance*, *46*, 180 ??195. DOI: 10.1016/j.iref.2016.09.004

Bigné, J. E., Moliner, M. A., & Callarisa, L. J. (2000). El valor y la fidelización de clientes: Una propuesta de modelo dinámico de comportamiento. *Revista Europea de Dirección y Economía de La Empresa*, *9*(3), 65–78.

Bist, S. (2022, February 14). Why businesses need to bridge ESG goals with digital transformation. Times of India Blog. https://timesofindia.indiatimes.com/blogs/voices/why-businesses-need-to-bridge-esg-goals-with-digital-transformation/

BNP PARIBAS. (2021). *THE PATH TO ESG: NO TURNING BACK FOR ASSET OWNERS AND MANAGERS*. https://securities.cib.bnpparibas/app/uploads/sites/3/2021/09/the-esg-global-survey-2021.pdf

Bollerslev, T. (1986). Generalized autoregressive conditional heteroskedasticity. *Journal of Econometrics*, *31*(3), 307 ??327. DOI: 10.1016/0304-4076(86)90063-1

Bollerslev, T. (1990). Modelling the coherence in short-run nominal exchange rates: A multivariate generalized ARCH model. *The Review of Economics and Statistics*, *72*(3), 498 ??505. DOI: 10.2307/2109358

Bowen, H. R. (2013). *Social responsibilities of the businessman*. University of Iowa Press. DOI: 10.2307/j.ctt20q1w8f

Brakus, J. J., Schmitt, B. H., & Zarantonello, L. (2009). Brand experience: What is it? How is it measured? Does it affect loyalty? *Journal of Marketing*, *73*(3), 52–68. DOI: 10.1509/jmkg.73.3.052

Breusch, T. S., & Pagan, A. R. (2006). The Lagrange Multiplier Test and Its Applications to Model Specification in Econometrics. *The Review of Economic Studies*. Advance online publication. DOI: 10.2307/2297111

Bukhari, S. A. A., Hashim, F., & Amran, A. (2023). Green banking: A strategy for attainment of UN-Sustainable Development Goals 2030. *International Journal of Environment and Sustainable Development*, *22*(1), 13–31. DOI: 10.1504/IJESD.2023.127419

Busco, C., Consolandi, C., Eccles, R. G., & Sofra, E. (2020). A preliminary analysis of SASB reporting: Disclosure topics, financial relevance, and the financial intensity of ESG materiality. *The Bank of America Journal of Applied Corporate Finance*, *32*(2), 117–125. DOI: 10.1111/jacf.12411

Cajias, M., Fuerst, F., & Bienert, S. (2014). Can investing in corporate social responsibility lower a company's cost of capital? *Studies in Economics and Finance*, *31*(2), 202–222. DOI: 10.1108/SEF-05-2013-0067

Canada Revenue Agency (CRA). (2024). *International Financial Reporting Standards (IFRS)*. Government of Canada. https://www.canada.ca/en/revenue-agency/services/tax/businesses/topics/international-financial-reporting-standards-ifrs.html

Carroll, A. B. (2016). Carroll's pyramid of CSR: taking another look. *International journal of corporate social responsibility*, 1, 1-8.

Carroll, A. B. (1979). A three-dimensional conceptual model of corporate performance. *Academy of Management Review*, *4*(4), 497–505. DOI: 10.2307/257850

Carroll, A. B. (1999). Corporate Social Responsibility - Evolution of a Definitional Construct. *Business & Society*, *38*(3), 268–295. DOI: 10.1177/000765039903800303

CDP. (2022). *CDP Media factsheet*. https://cdn.cdp.net/cdp-production/comfy/cms/files/files/000/003/419/original/CDP-Media-Factsheet.pdf

CDP. (2023a). *CDP Climate Change 2023 Questionnaire*. https://guidance.cdp.net/en/guidance?cid=46&ctype=theme&idtype=ThemeID&incchild=1&microsite=0&otype=Questionnaire&tags=TAG-13071%2CTAG-605%2CTAG-599

CDP. (2023b). *CDP Forests 2023 Questionnaire*. https://guidance.cdp.net/en/guidance?cid=47&ctype=theme&idtype=ThemeID&incchild=1&microsite=0&otype=Questionnaire&tags=TAG-646%2CTAG-609%2CTAG-599

CDP. (2024a). *Who we are*. https://www.cdp.net/en/info/about-us

CDP. (2024b). *CDP and the Sustainable Development Goals (SDGs)*. https://www.cdp.net/en/policy/program-areas/sustainable-development-goals

Çeliktopuz, E. (2024). Unveiling climate change impacts on agricultural sustainability: insights from the United States. Bio Web of Conferences, 85, 01015. https://doi.org/DOI: 10.1051/bioconf/20248501015

Cellier, A., & Chollet, P. (2012). Corporate Social Responsibility Rating Information: Relevance and Impacts on Financial Markets. In Boubaker, S., & Nguyen, D. K. (Eds.), *Board Directors and Corporate Social Responsibility* (pp. 179–201)., DOI: 10.1057/9780230389304_10

CFA Institute. (2018). *CFA Institute: Global Association for Investment Management Professionals*. https://www.cfainstitute.org/en/membership/directory

Chand, R., & Kour, M. (2025). Sustainable Finance and ESG Investing: Pathways to Long-Term Business Success. In Building Business Knowledge for Complex Modern Business Environments (pp. 121-148). IGI Global. DOI: DOI: 10.4018/979-8-3693-6447-5.ch005

Chang, C. L., McAleer, M., & Tansuchat, R. (2013). Conditional correlations and volatility spillovers between crude oil and stock index returns. *The North American Journal of Economics and Finance*, *25*, 116 ??138. DOI: 10.1016/j.najef.2012.06.002

Chaturvedi, A., Chandran, K., & Surendran, U. (2018). Revisiting climate change adaptation through proactive policy designing and institutional mechanism. *Tropical Plant Research*, *5*(1), 14–18. DOI: 10.22271/tpr.2018.v5.i1.003

Chen, G., Firth, M., & Rui, O. M. (2002). Stock market linkages: Evidence from Latin America. *Journal of Banking & Finance*, *26*(6), 1113 ??1141. DOI: 10.1016/S0378-4266(01)00160-1

Chen, J., Siddik, A. B., Zheng, G. W., Masukujjaman, M., & Bekhzod, S. (2022). The effect of green banking practices on banks' environmental performance and green financing: An empirical study. *Energies*, *15*(4), 1292. DOI: 10.3390/en15041292

Chen, L., Mao, C., & Gao, Y. (2023). Executive compensation stickiness and ESG performance: The role of digital transformation. *Frontiers in Environmental Science*, *11*, 1166080. Advance online publication. DOI: 10.3389/fenvs.2023.1166080

Chen, S. (2024). The Influence of Artificial Intelligence and Digital Technology on ESG Reporting Quality. *International Journal of Global Economics and Management*, *3*(1), 301–310. DOI: 10.62051/IJGEM.v3n1.36

Chen, W., Xie, Y., & He, K. (2024). Environmental, social, and governance performance and corporate innovation novelty. *International Journal of Innovation Studies*, *8*(2), 109–131. DOI: 10.1016/j.ijis.2024.01.003

Chen, Y.-C., Wu, J.-H., Peng, L., & Yeh, R. C. (2015). Consumer benefit creation in online group buying: The social capital and platform synergy effect and the mediating role of participation. *Electronic Commerce Research and Applications*, *14*(6), 499–513. DOI: 10.1016/j.elerap.2015.07.003

Chih, H., Chih, H., & Chen, T. (2009, September 29). On the Determinants of Corporate Social Responsibility: International Evidence on the Financial Industry. Springer Science+Business Media, 93(1), 115-135. 10.1007/s10551-009-0186-x

Chi, J., Li, K., & Young, M. (2006). Financial integration in East Asian equity markets. *Pacific Economic Review*, *11*(4), 513 ??526. DOI: 10.1111/j.1468-0106.2006.00332.x

Chin, M. Y., Ong, S. L., Ooi, D. B. Y., & Puah, C. H. (2022). The impact of green finance on environmental degradation in BRI region. *Environment, Development and Sustainability*, *26*(1), 303–318. DOI: 10.1007/s10668-022-02709-5 PMID: 36277420

Chiu, I. H., Lin, L., & Rouch, D. (2022). Law and regulation for sustainable finance. *European Business Organization Law Review*, *23*(1), 1–7. DOI: 10.1007/s40804-021-00230-2

Chowdhury, A., & Nehal, M N. (2020, January 1). Effect of Corporate Social Responsibility Expenditures on Financial Performance in Banking Sector of Bangladesh. DOI: 10.18178/joebm.2020.8.1.610

Christensen, H. B., Hail, L., & Leuz, C. (n.d., 2017). Mandatory CSR and Sustainability Reporting: Economic Analysis and Literature Review.

Chronopoulos, D. K., Liu, H., McMillan, F. J., & Wilson, J. O. S. (2015). The dynamics of US bank profitability. *European Journal of Finance*, *21*(5), 426–443. DOI: 10.1080/1351847X.2013.838184

Chungyalpa, W. (2021). Understanding Business Sustainability: The What, the Why, and the How of Sustainable Business Practices. *Indian Journal of Sustainable Development*, *5*(1 & 2), 24–37. https://www.researchgate.net/publication/352837459_Understanding_Business_Sustainability_The_What_the_Why_and_the_How_of_Sustainable_Business_Practices

Claessens, S., Djankov, S., Fan, J. P. H., & Lang, L. H. P. (2002). Disentangling the Incentive and Entrenchment Effects of Large Shareholdings. *The Journal of Finance*, *57*(6), 2741–2771. DOI: 10.1111/1540-6261.00511

Climate Change Knowledge Portal. (2017). *Homepage | World Bank Climate Change Knowledge Portal*. Worldbank.org. https://climateknowledgeportal.worldbank.org/

Cocosila, M., & Igonor, A. (2015). How important is the "social" in social networking? A perceived value empirical investigation. *Information Technology & People*, *28*(2), 366–382. DOI: 10.1108/ITP-03-2014-0055

Cohen, J. R., & Simnett, R. (2015). CSR and assurance services: A research agenda. *Auditing*, *34*(1), 59–74. DOI: 10.2308/ajpt-50876

Cornett, M. M., Erhemjamts, O., & Tehranian, H. (2016, September 1). Greed or good deeds: An examination of the relation between corporate social responsibility and the financial performance of U.S. commercial banks around the financial crisis. Elsevier BV, 70, 137-159. doi.org/10.1016/j.jbankfin.2016.04.024

Coudert, V., Couharde, C., & Mignon, V. (2015). On the impact of volatility on the real exchange rate ??terms of trade nexus: Revisiting commodity currencies. *Journal of International Money and Finance*, *58*, 110 ??127. DOI: 10.1016/j.jimonfin.2015.08.007

Country Climate and Development Reports (CCDRs). (n.d.). World Bank. https://www.worldbank.org/en/publication/country-climate-development-reports

Cricelli, L., & Strazzullo, S. (2021). The Economic Aspect of Digital Sustainability: A Systematic review. *Sustainability (Basel)*, *13*(15), 8241. DOI: 10.3390/su13158241

Cruz, C. A., & Matos, F. (2023). ESG Maturity: A Software Framework for the Challenges of ESG Data in Investment. *Sustainability (Basel)*, *15*(3), 2610. DOI: 10.3390/su15032610

David, O. (2012, January 1). An assessment of the impact of corporate social responsibility on Nigerian society: The examples of banking and communication industries. http://www.universalresearchjournals.org/ujmbr/Pdf/2012/May/Olanrewaju.pdf

De Freitas Netto, S. V., Falcão Sobral, M. F., Ribeiro, A. R. B., & Soares, G. R. (2020). Concepts and forms of greenwashing: A systematic review. *Environmental Sciences Europe*, *32*(1), 19. DOI: 10.1186/s12302-020-0300-3

Delgado-Ballester, E., Luis, J. Á., & Án, M.-A. (2001). Brand trust in the context of consumer loyalty. *European Journal of Marketing*, *35*(11/12), 35. DOI: 10.1108/EUM0000000006475

Deloitte. (2023). The future of ESG data: How digital transformation is driving decision-making. Deloitte Insights. https://www2.deloitte.com/us/en/insights/topics/digital-transformation/digital-esg-data-transformation.html

Deloitte. *Business responsibility and sustainability report:* (2024, January 3). Deloitte India. https://www2.deloitte.com/in/en/pages/finance/articles/business-responsibility-and-sustainability-report.html

Demirer, R., Diebold, F. X., Liu, L., & Yilmaz, K. (2020). Estimating global bank network connectedness. *Journal of Applied Econometrics*, *35*(1), 1 ??23. DOI: 10.1002/jae.2585

Demirguc-Kunt, A., & Huizinga, H. (2000). Financial structure and bank profitability. Policy Research Working Paper Series 2430.The World Bank.

Dimpfl, T., & Jung, R. C. (2012). Financial market spillovers around the globe. *Applied Financial Economics*, *22*(1), 45 ??57. DOI: 10.1080/09603107.2011.597721

Dimson, E., Marsh, P., & Staunton, M. (2020). Divergent ESG Ratings. *Journal of Portfolio Management*, *47*(1), 75–87. DOI: 10.3905/jpm.2020.1.175

Dubash, N. (2016). Safeguarding development and limiting vulnerability: India's stakes in the paris agreement. *Wiley Interdisciplinary Reviews: Climate Change*, *8*(2), e444. Advance online publication. DOI: 10.1002/wcc.444

Ducros, A., & Kelly, L. (2024). How ambitious are nature assessment tools for the private sector?.

Du, X., Cindy, L. Y., & Hayes, D. J. (2011). Speculation and volatility spillover in the crude oil and agricultural commodity markets: A Bayesian analysis. *Energy Economics, 33*(3), 497 ??503. DOI: 10.1016/j.eneco.2010.12.015

Dyck, A., Lins, K. V., Roth, L., & Wagner, H. F. (2019). Do institutional investors drive corporate social responsibility? International evidence. *Journal of Financial Economics, 131*(3), 693–714. DOI: 10.1016/j.jfineco.2018.08.013

Ebrahim, Z., Inderwildi, O. R., & King, D. A. (2014). Macroeconomic impacts of oil price volatility: Mitigation and resilience. *Frontiers in Energy, 8*(1), 9 ??24. DOI: 10.1007/s11708-014-0303-0

Eccles, R. G., Ioannou, I., & Serafeim, G. (2014). The impact of corporate sustainability on organizational processes and performance. *Management Science, 60*(11), 2835–2857. DOI: 10.1287/mnsc.2014.1984

Eccles, R. G., & Klimenko, S. (2019). The investor revolution: Shareholders are getting serious about sustainability. *Harvard Business Review, 97*(3), 106–116.

Eccles, R. G., & Serafeim, G. (2013). The performance frontier: Innovating for a sustainable strategy. *Harvard Business Review, 91*(5), 50–60. PMID: 23898735

Eccles, R. G., Serafeim, G., Seth, D., & Ming, C. C. Y. (2013). The Performance Frontier: Innovating for a Sustainable Strategy: Interaction. *Harvard Business Review, 91*(7), 17–18.

Eden, L., Nielsen, B., & Verbeke, A. (2020). *Research Methods in International Business*. Palgrave Macmillan. DOI: 10.1007/978-3-030-22113-3

Elif, & Halil, H. (2017). Corporate Social Responsibility and Firm Performance: Evidence from an Emerging Market. Accounting and Finance Research, 6(4), 42. DOI: 10.5430/afr.v6n4p42

Ellili, N. O. D., & Nobanee, H. (2023). Impact of economic, environmental, and corporate social responsibility reporting on financial performance of UAE banks. *Environment, Development and Sustainability, 25*(5), 3967–3983. DOI: 10.1007/s10668-022-02225-6 PMID: 35280966

Engle, R. (2002). Dynamic conditional correlation: A simple class of multivariate generalized autoregressive conditional heteroskedasticity models. *Journal of Business & Economic Statistics, 20*(3), 339 ??350. DOI: 10.1198/073500102288618487

Engle, R. F. (1982). Autoregressive conditional heteroscedasticity with estimates of the variance of United Kingdom inflation. *Econometrica*, *50*(4), 987 ??1007. DOI: 10.2307/1912773

Erdem, T., & Swait, J. (2004). Brand credibility, Brand consideration, and choice. *The Journal of Consumer Research*, *31*(1), 191–198. DOI: 10.1086/383434

Esteban-Sánchez, P., González, M. D. L. C., & Paredes-Gázquez, J. D. (2017, September 1). Corporate social performance and its relation with corporate financial performance: International evidence in the banking industry. *Journal of Cleaner Production*, *162*, 1102–1110. DOI: 10.1016/j.jclepro.2017.06.127

European Commission. (2021). Proposal for a directive of the European Parliament and of the Council amending Regulation (EU) No 537/2014, Directive 2004/109/EC, Directive 2006/43/EC and Directive 2013/34/EU, as regards corporate sustainability reporting. COM(2021) 189 final.

European Commission. (2022). Corporate Sustainability Reporting Directive (CSRD). Directive (EU) 2022/2464 of the European Parliament and of the Council.

European Commission. (2022). Corporate Sustainability Reporting Directive (CSRD). Directive (EU) 2022/2464 of the European Parliament and of the Council. https://eur-lex.europa.eu/legal-content/EN/TXT/?uri=CELEX:32022L2464

Ewing, B. T., & Malik, F. (2016). Volatility spillovers between oil prices and the stock market under structural breaks. *Global Finance Journal*, *29*, 12 ??23. DOI: 10.1016/j.gfj.2015.04.008

EY ESG Compass - Innovation to transform sustainability journey. (2024). Ey.com. https://www.ey.com/en_in/services/climate-change-sustainability-services/esg-compass

EY. (2020). *Fifth Global Institutional Investor Survey*. EY Global.

Faccia, A., Manni, F., & Capitanio, F. (2021). Mandatory ESG Reporting and XBRL Taxonomies Combination: ESG Ratings and Income Statement, a Sustainable Value-Added Disclosure. *Sustainability (Basel)*, *13*(16), 8876. DOI: 10.3390/su13168876

Feder, B. J. (1989). Who will subscribe to the Valdez Principles? *The New York Times*, 10, F6.

Financial Reporting and Assurance Standards (FRAS) Canada. (2023). *Independent Review Committee on Standard Setting issues Final Recommendations*. https://www.frascanada.ca/en/about/ircss-final-recommendations#:~:text=The%20Independent%20Review%20Committee%20of,the%20future%20%E2%80%93%20including%20sustainability%20standards

Financial Reporting and Assurance Standards (FRAS) Canada. (2024). *Media Release – Canadian Sustainability Standards Board Releases Feedback Statement on Proposed Sustainability Disclosure Standards*. https://www.frascanada.ca/en/cssb/news-listings/2024-feedback-statement-media-release

Fishbein, M. A., & Ajzen, I. (1975). *Belief, attitude, intention, and behavior: An introduction to theory and research*. Addison-Wesley.

Forbes, K. (2000). The Asian flu and Russian virus: firm-level evidence on how crises are transmitted internationally.

Forbes, K. J., & Rigobon, R. (2002). No contagion, only interdependence: Measuring stock market comovements. *The Journal of Finance*, *57*(5), 2223 ??2261. DOI: 10.1111/0022-1082.00494

Fornari, F., Monticelli, C., Pericoli, M., & Tivegna, M. (2002). The impact of news on the exchange rate of the lira and long-term interest rates. *Economic Modelling*, *19*(4), 611 ??639. DOI: 10.1016/S0264-9993(00)00073-0

Frederick, W. C. (2006). *Corporation, be good!: the story of corporate social responsibility*. Dog Ear Publishing.

Freeman, R. E. (1984). *Strategic management: A stakeholder approach*. Pitman.

Freeman, R. E., Dmytriyev, S. D., & Phillips, R. A. (2021). Stakeholder theory and the resource-based view of the firm. *Journal of Management*, *47*(7), 1757–1770. DOI: 10.1177/0149206321993576

Freeman, R. E., & Reed, D. L. (1983, April 1). Stockholders and Stakeholders: A New Perspective on Corporate Governance. *California Management Review*, *25*(3), 88–106. DOI: 10.2307/41165018

Friess, D. A., Aung, T. T., Huxham, M., Lovelock, C., Mukherjee, N., & Sasmito, S. (2019). SDG 14: Life below Water – Impacts on Mangroves. In Katila, P., Pierce Colfer, C. J., de Jong, W., Galloway, G., Pacheco, P., & Winkel, G. (Eds.), *Sustainable Development Goals: Their Impacts on Forests and People* (pp. 445–481). Cambridge University Press. DOI: 10.1017/9781108765015.016

Friess, D. A., Rogers, K., Lovelock, C. E., Krauss, K. W., Hamilton, S. E., Lee, S. Y., Lucas, R., Primavera, J., Rajkaran, A., & Shi, S. (2019). The state of the world's mangrove forests: Past, present, and future. *Annual Review of Environment and Resources*, *44*(1), 89–115. DOI: 10.1146/annurev-environ-101718-033302

Fry, F. L., & Hock, R. J. (1976). Who Claims Corporate Responsibility? The Biggest and the Worst. *Business & Society Review* (00453609), (18).

Fujjiwara, N., Georgiev, A., & Alessi, M. (2010, May 27). The Merit of Sectoral Approaches in Transitioning Towards a Global Carbon Market. *Ssrn*.com. https://papers.ssrn.com/sol3/papers.cfm ?abstract_id=2863987

George, G., Merrill, R. K., & Schillebeeckx, S. J. D. (2021). Digital sustainability and entrepreneurship: How digital innovations are driving the entrepreneurial pursuit of sustainable development. *Business Strategy and the Environment*, *30*(5), 2382–2399. DOI: 10.1002/bse.2744

Ghoniyah, N., & Hartono, S. (2020). How Islamic and conventional bank in Indonesia contributing sustainable development goals achievement. *Cogent Economics & Finance, 8*(1), 1856458. https://doi.org/. 2020.1856458DOI: 10.1080/23322039

Giechaskiel, B., Clairotte, M., Valverde-Morales, V., Bonnel, P., Kregar, Z., Franco, V., & Dilara, P. (2018). Framework for the assessment of PEMS (Portable Emissions Measurement Systems) uncertainty. *Environmental Research, 166*, 251–260. DOI: 10.1016/j.envres.2018.06.012 PMID: 29908456

Gilbert, S. (2002, November). The transparency evolution. []. THE ENVIRONMENTAL LAW INSTITUTE.]. *The Environmental Forum (Washington, D.C.), 19*(6), 18–27.

Global Reporting Initiative (GRI), & CDP. (2017). *Linking GRI and CDP: How are the GRI Sustainability Reporting Standards and CDP's 2017 climate change questions aligned?* Global Reporting. https://www.globalreporting.org/media/zrtnajcx/gri-standards-and-cdp-2017-climate-change-linkage-document.pdf

Global Reporting Initiative (GRI). (2016). *GRI 411: Rights of Indigenous Peoples 2016.* GSSB. https://transparencylab.org/Documentation/Advocacy,%20Monitoring,%20Sustainable%20-%20Responsible%20Initiatives/Global%20Reporting%20Initiative/GRI%20411%20Rights%20of%20Indigenous%20Peoples_2016.pdf

Global Reporting Initiative (GRI). (2021a). *A Short Introduction to the GRI Standards.* https://www.globalreporting.org/media/wtaf14tw/a-short-introduction-to-the-gri-standards.pdf

Global Reporting Initiative (GRI). (2021b). *GRI 11: Oil and Gas Sector 2021.* https://www.accountabilitycounsel.org/wp-content/uploads/2021/10/gri-11-oil-and-gas-sector-2021.pdf

Global Reporting Initiative (GRI). (2022a). *GRI 12: Coal Sector 2022.* https://www.globalreporting.org/media/zr3bcrc0/coal_onepager-leaflet.pdf

Global Reporting Initiative (GRI). (2022b). *GRI 13: Agriculture Aquaculture and Fishing Sectors 2022.* https://freshproduce.org.uk/files/GRI-13_-Agriculture-Aquaculture-and-Fishing-Sectors-2022.pdf

Global Reporting Initiative (GRI). (2024a). *About GRI.* https://www.globalreporting.org/about-gri/#:~:text=GRI%20(Global%20Reporting%20Initiative)%20is,language%20to%20communicate%20those%20impacts

Global Reporting Initiative (GRI). (2024b). *Our mission and history.* https://www.globalreporting.org/about-gri/mission-history/

Global Reporting Initiative (GRI). (2024c). *SDG Initiatives.* https://www.globalreporting.org/public-policy/sustainable-development/sdg-initiatives/

Global Reporting Initiative (GRI). (2024d). *Linking GRI reporting to other requirements.* https://www.globalreporting.org/how-to-use-the-gri-standards/global-alignment/

Global Reporting Initiative (GRI). (2024e). *GRI 14: Mining Sector 2024.* https://incp.org.co/wp-content/uploads/2024/02/GRI-14-Sector-minero-2024.pdf

Global Sustainable Investment Alliance (GSIA). (2022). *Global Sustainable Investment Review 2022.* http://www.gsi-alliance.org

Gololo, I A. (2019, July 1). Corporate Social Responsibility Disclosure and Financial Performance of Quoted Nigerian Cement Companies. DOI: 10.15294/ibarj.v3i2.60

Gray, R., Kouhy, R., & Lavers, S. (1995, May 1). Corporate social and environmental reporting. Emerald Publishing Limited, 8(2), 47-77. 10.1108/09513579510146996

GRI. (2021). *A short introduction to the GRI standards.* GRI, Netherlands. https://www.globalreporting.org/media/wtaf14tw/a-short-introduction-to-the-gri-standards.pdf

GSIA. (2022). *Global Sustainable Investment Review 2022.* GSIA. https://www.gsi-alliance.org/members-resources/gsir2022/

Guillot, J. (2020). *What Is the Connection Between SASB and the SDGs?* SASB. https://sasb.ifrs.org/blog/what-is-the-connection-between-sasb-and-the-sdgs/

Guillot, J., & Hales, J. (2021). *Materiality: The Word that Launched a Thousand Debates*. SASB. https://sasb.ifrs.org/blog/materiality-the-word-that-launched-a-thousand-debates/#:~:text=SASB%20introduced%20the%20term%20%E2%80%9Centerprise,value%20relative%20to%20its%20potential

Gupta, J. (2001). India and climate change policy: Between diplomatic defensiveness and industrial transformation. *Energy & Environment, 12*(2-3), 217–236. DOI: 10.1260/0958305011500715

Hafez, H. (2015). Corporate social responsibility and financial performance: An empirical study on Egyptian banks. *Corporate Ownership and Control, 12*(2), 107–127. DOI: 10.22495/cocv12i2p9

Hair, J. F., Celsi, M. W., Money, A. H., Samouel, P., & Page, M. J. (2015). *Essentials of Business Research Methods* (2nd ed.). Routledge. DOI: 10.4324/9781315704562

Hales, J. (2021). Sustainability accounting standards board (SASB). In *World Scientific Encyclopedia of Climate Change: Case Studies of Climate Risk, Action, and Opportunity Volume 3* (pp. 37-41).

Harahap, B., Risfandy, T., & Futri, I. N. (2023). Islamic Law, Islamic Finance, and Sustainable Development Goals: A Systematic Literature Review. *Sustainability (Basel), 15*(8), 6626. DOI: 10.3390/su15086626

Hareda. (2024). "NATIONAL GREEN HYDROGEN MISSION | New & Renewable Energy Department | India." *Hareda.gov.in*, hareda.gov.in/national-green-hydrogen-mission/

Hartley, N., Kunz, W., & Tarbit, J. (2024). The corporate digital responsibility (CDR) calculus: How and why organizations reconcile digital and ethical trade-offs for growth. *Organizational Dynamics, 53*(2), 101056–101056. DOI: 10.1016/j.orgdyn.2024.101056

Hassani, H., Huang, X., & Silva, E. (2019). Big Data and Climate Change. *Big Data and Cognitive Computing, 3*(1), 12. DOI: 10.3390/bdcc3010012

Hassan, S. A., & Malik, F. (2007). Multivariate GARCH modeling of sector volatility transmission. *The Quarterly Review of Economics and Finance, 47*(3), 470 ??480. DOI: 10.1016/j.qref.2006.05.006

Hatayama, H. (2022). The metals industry and the Sustainable Development Goals: The relationship explored based on SDG reporting. *Resources, Conservation and Recycling, 178*, 106081. DOI: 10.1016/j.resconrec.2021.106081

Hazelhurst, T., Footer, J., & Norris, D. (2024). Dollars and Sense; Reviewing Industry Implementation of the Climate-Related Disclosures Mandate in New Zealand. *European Journal of Sustainable Development, 13*(3), 1–1. DOI: 10.14207/ejsd.2024.v13n3p1

He, L. (2001). Volatility spillovers and the role of leading financial centres. *Quarterly Review. Indexes - Banca Nazionale del Lavoro, 54*(217), 137 ??164.

He, L. J., & Chen, S. P. (2011). Aggregate and individual commodity futures markets volatility spillovers. *Journal of Futures Markets, 31*(8), 739 ??764.

Hemche, O., Jawadi, F., Maliki, S. B., & Cheffou, A. I. (2016). On the study of contagion in the context of the subprime crisis: A dynamic conditional correlation ??multivariate GARCH approach. *Economic Modelling, 52*, 292 ??299. DOI: 10.1016/j.econmod.2014.09.004

Henri, D. A., Provencher, J. F., Bowles, E., Taylor, J. J., Steel, J., Chelick, C., Popp, J. N., Cooke, S. J., Rytwinski, T., McGregor, D., Ford, A. T., & Alexander, S. M. (2021). Weaving Indigenous knowledge systems and Western sciences in terrestrial research, monitoring and management in Canada: A protocol for a systematic map. *Ecological Solutions and Evidence, 2*(2), e12057. DOI: 10.1002/2688-8319.12057

Henseler, J., Ringle, C. M., & Sarstedt, M. (2015). A new criterion for assessing discriminant validity in variance-based structural equation modeling. *Journal of the Academy of Marketing Science, 43*(1), 115–135. DOI: 10.1007/s11747-014-0403-8

Hernandez, M. S., Sentosa, I., Gaudreault, F., Davison, I., & Sharin, F. H. (2023, May 1). The Emergence of The Metaverse in The Digital Blockchain Economy: Applying the ESG Framework for A Sustainable Future. IEEE Xplore. DOI: 10.1109/ICACITE57410.2023.10182839

Hernandez-Fernandez, A., & Lewis, M. C. (2019). Brand authenticity leads to perceived value and brand trust. *European Journal of Management and Business Economics, 28*(3), 222–238. DOI: 10.1108/EJMBE-10-2017-0027

Hill, J. (2020). *Environmental, Social, and Governance (ESG) Investing: A Balanced Analysis of the Theory and Practice of a Sustainable Portfolio*. Academic Press.

Horváth, D., & Szabó, R. Z. (2019). Driving forces and barriers of Industry 4.0: Do multinational and small and medium-sized companies have equal opportunities? *Technological Forecasting and Social Change, 146*, 119–132. DOI: 10.1016/j.techfore.2019.05.021

Huang, Q., Fang, J., Xue, X., & Gao, H. (2023). Does Digital Innovation Produce Better ESG Performance? An Empirical Test of Shenzhen A-Listed Firms in China. DOI: 10.2139/ssrn.4390649

Huang, T. K., Wang, Y. T., & Lin, K. Y. (2022). Enhancing brand loyalty through online brand communities: The role of community benefits. *Journal of Product and Brand Management*, *31*(5), 823–838. DOI: 10.1108/JPBM-08-2020-3027

Hughes, A., Urban, M. A., & Wójcik, D. (2021). Alternative ESG Ratings: How Technological Innovation Is Reshaping Sustainable Investment. *Sustainability (Basel)*, *13*(6), 3551. DOI: 10.3390/su13063551

Hunjra, A. I., Azam, M., Bruna, M. G., Verhoeven, P., & Al-Faryan, M. A. S. (2022). Sustainable development: The impact of political risk, macroeconomic policy uncertainty and ethnic conflict. *International Review of Financial Analysis*, *84*, 102370. DOI: 10.1016/j.irfa.2022.102370

Hussain, M., Yang, S., Zahid, R. M. A., & Maqsood, U. S. (2023). ESG in the Digital Age: Unravelling the impact of Strategic Digital orientation. Social Science Research Network. DOI: 10.2139/ ssrn.4543836

Hussain, S., Hussain, E., Saxena, P., Sharma, A., Thathola, P., & Sonwani, S. (2024). Navigating the impact of climate change in india: A perspective on climate action (sdg13) and sustainable cities and communities (sdg11). *Frontiers in Sustainable Cities*, *5*, 1308684. Advance online publication. DOI: 10.3389/frsc.2023.1308684

Iacobucci, D., & Churchill, G. (2018). *Marketing Research: Methodological Foundations* (12th ed.). Create Space Independent Publishing Platform.

Ibrahim, S. S., Daud, D., Hidayah, K., Shaharuddin, A., & Al-Amin, A. A. M. (2023). Waqf integrated income generating model (WIIGM) for enhancing sustainable development goals (SDGS) in Malaysia: An evaluation of behavioural intention. *International Journal of Ethics and Systems*, *39*(4), 841–858. DOI: 10.1108/IJOES-02-2022-0030

IFRS Foundation. (2018). *Who we are and what we do*. https://www.ifrs.org/content/dam/ifrs/about-us/who-we-are/who-we-are-english-2018-final.pdf

IFRS Foundation. (2022). *ISSB describes the concept of sustainability and its articulation with financial value creation, and announces plans to advance work on natural ecosystems and just transition*. https://www.ifrs.org/news-and-events/news/2022/12/issb-describes-the-concept-of-sustainability/

IFRS Foundation. (2023). *IFRS S1 General Requirements for Disclosure of Sustainability-related Financial Information and IFRS S2 Climate-related Disclosures.* International Sustainability Standards Board.

IFRS Foundation. (2023). *IFRS S1 General Requirements for Disclosure of Sustainability-related Financial Information.* International Sustainability Standards Board.

IFRS Foundation. (2023a). *ISSB issues inaugural global sustainability disclosure standards.* https://www.ifrs.org/news-and-events/news/2023/06/issb-issues-ifrs-s1-ifrs-s2/

IFRS Foundation. (2023d). *IFRS Foundation welcomes culmination of TCFD work and transfer of TCFD monitoring responsibilities to ISSB from 2024.* https://www.ifrs.org/news-and-events/news/2023/07/foundation-welcomes-tcfd-responsibilities-from-2024/

IFRS Foundation. (2023e). *Coal Operations Sustainability Accounting Standard.* SASB. https://d3flraxduht3gu.cloudfront.net/latest_standards/coal-operations-standard_en-gb.pdf

IFRS Foundation. (2023f). *Metals & Mining Sustainability Accounting Standard.* SASB. https://d3flraxduht3gu.cloudfront.net/latest_standards/metals-and-mining-standard_en-gb.pdf

IFRS Foundation. (2023g). *Oil & Gas – Exploration & Production Sustainability Accounting Standard.* SASB. https://d3flraxduht3gu.cloudfront.net/latest_standards/oil-and-gas-exploration-and-production-standard_en-gb.pdf

IFRS Foundation. (2023h). *IFRS S1: General Requirements for Disclosure of Sustainability-related Financial Information.* https://www.ifrs.org/content/dam/ifrs/publications/pdf-standards-issb/english/2023/issued/part-a/issb-2023-a-ifrs-s2-climate-related-disclosures.pdf?bypass=on

IFRS Foundation. (2023i). *IFRS S2: Climate-related Disclosures.* https://www.ifrs.org/content/dam/ifrs/publications/pdf-standards-issb/english/2023/issued/part-a/issb-2023-a-ifrs-s2-climate-related-disclosures.pdf?bypass=on

IFRS Foundation. (2024a). *SASB Standards and other ESG frameworks.* SASB. https://sasb.ifrs.org/about/sasb-and-other-esg-frameworks/#:~:text=Frameworks%20provide%20principles%2Dbased%20guidance,for%20each%20topic%2C%20including%20metrics

IFRS Foundation. (2024b). *Governance archive.* SASB. https://sasb.ifrs.org/about/governance-archive/

IFRS Foundation. (2024c). *Find your industry*. SASB. https://sasb.ifrs.org/find-your-industry/

IFRS Foundation. (2024d). *About the International Sustainability Standards Board*. https://www.ifrs.org/groups/international-sustainability-standards-board/

IFRS Foundation. (2024e). *IFRS Foundation Monitoring Board (Monitoring Board)*. https://www.ifrs.org/groups/monitoring-board/

Independent Review Committee on Standard Setting in Canada (IRCSSC). (2021). *What an International Sustainability Standards Board means for Canada*. Cision Canada. https://www.newswire.ca/news-releases/what-an-international-sustainability-standards-board-means-for-canada-863993456.html

Independent Review Committee on Standard Setting in Canada (IRCSSC). (2023a). *Final Report*. https://pcacsitecorewebcontent.blob.core.windows.net/sitecorewebcontent/ircss/IRCSS-final-recommendations-report.pdf

India incorporates green bonds into its climate finance strategy. (2023, June 12). World Bank Blogs. https://blogs.worldbank.org/en/climatechange/india-incorporates-green-bonds-its-climate-finance-strategy

India, E. "Maharashtra's Solar Surge: Powering RE Growth with Solar Energy - Asia Pacific | Energetica India Magazine." *Energetica India Magazine, India Energy News, Renewable Energy News, Conventional Power Generation, Companies Guide...*, 5 Sept. 2024, www.energetica-india.net/news/maharashtras-solar-surge-powering-re-growth-with-solar-energy. Accessed 23 Nov. 2024.

India's debut in the sovereign green bond market: First deal landed a greenium! (2023, March 7). Climate Bonds Initiative. https://www.climatebonds.net/2023/03/india%E2%80%99s-debut-sovereign-green-bond-market-first-deal-landed-greenium

Indian capital market regulator's updated green debt guidelines: Unlocking the potential of sustainable finance. (n.d.). IEEFA | Institute for Energy Economics and Financial Analysis. https://ieefa.org/resources/indian-capital-market-regulators-updated-green-debt-guidelines-unlocking-potential

Indian Express. (2023, October 4). *Every state, UT saw extreme weather event on at least 1 day in 2023: Report*. The Indian Express. https://indianexpress.com/article/india/every-state-ut-saw-extreme-weather-event-on-at-least-1-day-in-2023-report-9186013/

Infosys Limited. (2022). Infosys ESG Report 2022-23 HIGHLIGHTS: Carbon-neutral organization for 4 consecutive years and empowering 8.5 million lives with digital skilling. Infosys.com. https://www.infosys.com/newsroom/features/2023/infosys-esg-report-2022 23.html#:~:text=Features-

Ingram, R. W., & Frazier, K. B. (1980). Environmental performance and corporate disclosure. *Journal of Accounting Research, 18*(2), 614–622. DOI: 10.2307/2490597

Institute and Faculty of Actuaries. (2024). *The Paris Agreement and the Task Force on Climate-related Financial Disclosures.* https://actuaries.org.uk/learn/lifelong-learning/sustainability-and-lifelong-learning/climate-change-curated-library/the-paris-agreement-and-the-task-force-on-climate-related-financial-disclosures/

International Auditing and Assurance Standards Board (IAASB). (2022). *International Standard on Sustainability Assurance (ISSA) 5000, General Requirements for Sustainability Assurance Engagements* [Exposure Draft]. International Federation of Accountants. https://www.ifac.org/iaasb/publications/international-standard-sustainability-assurance-issa-5000-general-requirements-sustainability-assurance

International Chamber of Commerce (ICC). (2022). *ICC guidance on responsible sourcing*. ICC.

International Sustainability Standards Board (ISSB). (2023). IFRS S1 General Requirements for Disclosure of Sustainability-related Financial Information. IFRS Foundation. https://www.ifrs.org/issued-standards/ifrs-sustainability-standards-navigator/ifrs-s1-general-requirements/

Irfan, M. (2021, January). Do Shariah Indices converge? Evidence from Gulf Cooperation Council countries. *International Journal of Business Excellence, 23*(2), 251–269. DOI: 10.1504/IJBEX.2021.113448

Irfan, M., Elhoseny, M., Kassim, S., & Metawa, N. (2023). *Advanced Machine Learning Algorithms for Complex Financial Applications.* IGI Global., DOI: 10.4018/978-1-6684-4483-2

Irfan, M., Elmogy, M., Gupta, S., Khalifa, F., & Dias, R. (2024). *AI-Driven Decentralized Finance and the Future of Finance*. IGI Global., DOI: 10.4018/979-8-3693-6321-8

Irfan, M., Elmogy, M., Majid, M. S., & El-Sappagh, S. (2023). *The Impact of AI Innovation on Financial Sectors in the Era of Industry 5.0.* IGI Global., DOI: 10.4018/979-8-3693-0082-4

Irfan, M., Hussainey, K., Chan Bukhari, S. A., & Nam, Y. (Eds.). (2024). *Issues of Sustainability in AI and New-Age Thematic Investing*. IGI Global Publisher., DOI: 10.4018/979-8-3693-3282-5

Irfan, M., Kadry, S., Sharif, M., & Ullah Khan, H. (2023). *Fintech Applications in Islamic Finance: AI, Machine Learning, and Blockchain Techniques*. IGI Global., DOI: 10.4018/979-8-3693-1038-0

Islamic Financial Services Board (IFSB). (2022). *Islamic Financial Services Industry Stability Report 2022*. IFSB.

ISP. (2024, May 21). Sovereign green bonds: Fueling India's sustainability Indian School of Public Policy -. https://www.ispp.org.in/sovereign-green-bonds-fuelling-indias-sustainability-revolution/

Itotenaan, H O., Samy, M., & Bampton, R. (2014, May 6). A phenomenological study of CSR policy making and implementation in developed countries. DOI: 10.1108/JGR-03-2014-0008

Jan, A. A., Lai, F. W., Asif, M., Akhtar, S., & Ullah, S. (2023a). Embedding sustainability into bank strategy: Implications for sustainable development goals reporting. *International Journal of Sustainable Development & World Ecology, 30*(3), 229–243. https://doi.org/. 2134230DOI: 10.1080/13504509.2022

Jan, A., Rahman, H. U., Zahid, M., Salameh, A. A., Khan, P. A., Al-Faryan, M. A. S., & Ali, H. E. (2023b). Islamic corporate sustainability practices index aligned with SDGs towards better financial performance: Evidence from the Malaysian and Indonesian Islamic banking industry. *Journal of Cleaner Production, 405*, 136860. DOI: 10.1016/j.jclepro.2023.136860

Jang, H., & Sul, W. (2002). The Asian financial crisis and the co-movement of Asian stock markets. *Journal of Asian Economics, 13*(1), 94 ??104. DOI: 10.1016/S1049-0078(01)00115-4

Janicka, M., & Sajnóg, A. (2022). The ESG Reporting of EU Public Companies—Does the Company's Capitalisation Matter? *Sustainability (Basel), 14*(7), 4279. DOI: 10.3390/su14074279

Javed, M., Rashid, M. A., & Hussain, G. (2016). When does it pay to be good – A contingency perspective on corporate social and financial performance: Would it work? *Journal of Cleaner Production, 133*, 1062–1073. DOI: 10.1016/j.jclepro.2016.05.163

Jeon, H. J. (2022). Does the relationship between brand attitude, brand attachment and purchase intention vary based on the type of prosocial expression-based brand emoji? *Journal of Product and Brand Management, 31*(8), 1180–1195. Advance online publication. DOI: 10.1108/JPBM-09-2021-3660

Jiakui, C., Abbas, J., Najam, H., Liu, J., & Abbas, J. (2023). Green technological innovation, green finance, and financial development and their role in green total factor productivity: Empirical insights from China. *Journal of Cleaner Production, 382*, 135131. Johan, S. (2022). Complementary or Substitute: Sharia Financing Green Financing and Sustainable Development Goals? *International Journal of Sustainable Development & Planning, 17* (2), 487–495.DOI: 10.1016/j.jclepro.2022.135131

Jingyong, W., Song, Z., & Li-Da, X. (2023). Digital Technology For Good: Path and Influence—Based on the Study of ESG performance of listed companies in China. *Applied Sciences (Basel, Switzerland), 13*(5), 2862. DOI: 10.3390/app13052862

Johnson, R. B., & Christensen, L. (2019). *Educational Research: Quantitative, Qualitative, and Mixed Approaches* (7th ed.). SAGE Publications.

Jonsdottir, B., Sigurjónsson, Þ. O., Jóhannsdóttir, L., & Wendt, S. (2022). Barriers to using ESG data for investment decisions. *Sustainability (Basel), 14*(9), 5157. DOI: 10.3390/su14095157

Julia, L., Natale, D., & Cordella, A. (n.d.). ESGTech: Guiding ESG Regulation and Digital Governance. Retrieved September 10, 2024, from https://scholarspace.manoa.hawaii.edu/server /api/core/bitstreams/ee378dba-64a0-4404-8e32-e1635cabe44c/content

Kang, J., & Hustvedt, G. (2014). Building trust between consumers and corporations: The role of consumer perceptions of transparency and social responsibility. *Journal of Business Ethics, 125*(2), 253–265. DOI: 10.1007/s10551-013-1916-7

Karim, R., Ghazali, F., & Ansari, A. (2020). Renewable energy regulations in indonesia and india: A comparative study on legal framework. *Journal of Indonesian Legal Studies, 5*(2), 361–390. DOI: 10.15294/jils.v5i2.41986

Kearney, C., & Pot? , V. (2006). Correlation dynamics in European equity markets. *Research in International Business and Finance, 20*(3), 305 ??321. DOI: 10.1016/j.ribaf.2005.05.006

Keller, K. L., & Lehmann, D. R. (2006). Brands and branding: Research findings and future priorities. *Marketing Science, 25*(6), 740–759. DOI: 10.1287/mksc.1050.0153

Kemfert, C., & Schmalz, S. (2019). Sustainable finance: Political challenges of development and implementation of framework conditions. *Green Finance, 1*(3), 237–248. DOI: 10.3934/GF.2019.3.237

Kenourgios, D., & Dimitriou, D. (2015). Contagion of the Global Financial Crisis and the real economy: A regional analysis. *Economic Modelling, 44*, 283 ??293. DOI: 10.1016/j.econmod.2014.10.048

Kılıç, M., Kuzey, C., & Uyar, A. (2015, June 1). The impact of ownership and board structure on Corporate Social Responsibility (CSR) reporting in the Turkish banking industry. Emerald Publishing Limited, 15(3), 357-374. 10.1108/cg-02-2014-0022

Kim, J., Morris, J. D., & Swait, J. (2008). Antecedents of true brand loyalty. *Journal of Advertising, 37*(2), 99–117. DOI: 10.2753/JOA0091-3367370208

Kim, S., & Yoon, A. (2023). Analyzing Active Fund Managers' Commitment to ESG: Evidence from the United Nations Principles for Responsible Investment. *Management Science, 69*(2), 741–758. DOI: 10.1287/mnsc.2022.4394

Kopnina, H. (2015). Sustainability: New strategic thinking for business. *Environment, Development and Sustainability, 19*(1), 27–43. DOI: 10.1007/s10668-015-9723-1

Kotsantonis, S., & Serafeim, G. (2019). Four Things No One Will Tell You About ESG Data. *The Bank of America Journal of Applied Corporate Finance, 31*(2), 50–58. DOI: 10.1111/jacf.12346

Koutmos, G. (1996). Modeling the dynamic interdependence of major European stock markets. *Journal of Business Finance & Accounting, 23*(7), 975 ??988. DOI: 10.1111/j.1468-5957.1996.tb01035.x

KPMG International. (2013). *GRI's G4 Guidelines: the impact on reporting*. KPMG International. https://assets.kpmg.com/content/dam/kpmg/pdf/2013/06/g4-the-impact-on-reporting-v2.pdf

KPMG. (2022). *Survey of Sustainability Reporting 2022: Big Shifts, Small Steps*. KPMG International.

Kraus, S., Durst, S., Ferreira, J. J., Veiga, P. M., Kailer, N., & Weinmann, A. (2022). Digital transformation in business and management research: An overview of the current status quo. International Journal of Information Management, 63, 102466. fomgt.2021. 102466DOI: 10.1016/j.ijin

Kreft, C., Angst, M., Huber, R., & Finger, R. (2023). Farmers' social networks and regional spillover effects in agricultural climate change mitigation. *Climatic Change, 176*(2), 8. Advance online publication. DOI: 10.1007/s10584-023-03484-6

Kressmann, F., Sirgy, M. J., Herrmann, A., Huber, F., Huber, S., & Lee, D. J. (2006). Direct and indirect effects of self-image congruence on brand loyalty. *Journal of Business Research, 59*(9), 955–964. DOI: 10.1016/j.jbusres.2006.06.001

Krippendorff, K. (1984, March 1). Content Analysis: An Introduction to its Methodology.. Beverly Hills, CA: Sage, 238

Kroner, K. F., & Ng, V. K. (1998). Modeling asymmetric comovements of asset returns. *Review of Financial Studies, 11*(4), 817 ??844. DOI: 10.1093/rfs/11.4.817

Kroner, K. F., & Sultan, J. (1993). Time-varying distributions and dynamic hedging with foreign currency futures. *Journal of Financial and Quantitative Analysis, 28*(4), 535 ??551. DOI: 10.2307/2331164

Krüger, P. (2015). Corporate goodness and shareholder wealth. *Journal of Financial Economics, 115*(2), 304–329. DOI: 10.1016/j.jfineco.2014.09.008

Kuikka, A., & Laukkanen, T. (2012). Brand loyalty and the role of hedonic value. *Journal of Product and Brand Management, 21*(7), 529–537. DOI: 10.1108/10610421211276277

Kumar, S., Inani, S. K., & Rawat, V. (2012). Volatility spillovers between oil and stock market returns. *International Journal of Energy Sector Management, 6*(2), 205 ??219.

Kwilinski, A., Lyulyov, O., & Pimonenko, T. (2023). Unlocking Sustainable Value through Digital Transformation: An Examination of ESG Performance. *Information (Basel), 14*(8), 444–444. DOI: 10.3390/info14080444

Kwilinski, A., Lyulyov, O., & Pimonenko, T. (2024). The role of country's green brand and digitalization in enhancing environmental, social, and governance performance. Ekonomia I Środowisko, 87(4), 1–22. DOI: 10.34659/eis.2023.87.4.613

Lam, S. K., Ahearne, M., Mullins, R., Hayati, B., & Schillewaert, N. (2013). Exploring the dynamics of antecedents to consumer–brand identification with a new brand. *Journal of the Academy of Marketing Science, 41*(2), 234–252. DOI: 10.1007/s11747-012-0301-x

Lam, S. Y., & Shankar, V. (2014). Asymmetries in the effects of drivers of brand loyalty between early and late adopters and across technology generations. *Journal of Interactive Marketing, 28*(1), 26–42. DOI: 10.1016/j.intmar.2013.06.004

Larcker, D. F., Pomorski, L., Tayan, B., & Watts, E. M. (2022, August 2). ESG Ratings: A Compass without Direction. Papers.*ssrn*.com. https://papers.ssrn.com/sol3/papers.cfm?abstract_id=4179647

Lau, H. C., & Tsai, S. C. (2023). Global Decarbonization: Current Status and What It Will Take to Achieve Net Zero by 2050. *Energies, 16*(23), 7800. DOI: 10.3390/en16237800

Lee, J. W. (2020). Green finance and sustainable development goals: The case of China. *The Journal of Asian Finance, Economics and Business*, *7*(7), 577–586. DOI: 10.13106/jafeb.2020.vol7.no7.577

Lee, O., Joo, H., Choi, H., & Cheon, M. (2022). Proposing an Integrated Approach to Analyzing ESG Data via Machine Learning and Deep Learning Algorithms. *Sustainability (Basel), 14*(14), 8745. DOI: 10.3390/su14148745

Lerner, L. D., & Fryxell, G. E. (1988). An empirical study of the predictors of corporate social performance: A multi-dimensional analysis. *Journal of Business Ethics*, •••, 951–959.

Lien, D., & Yang, L. (2008). Asymmetric effect of basis on dynamic futures hedging: Empirical evidence from commodity markets. *Journal of Banking & Finance*, *32*(2), 187 ??198. DOI: 10.1016/j.jbankfin.2007.01.026

Lifestyle for Environment - LiFE. (2022, October 11). MyGov.in. https://www.mygov.in/life/

Lindgreen, A., & Swaen, V. (2010). Corporate social responsibility. *International Journal of Management Reviews*, *12*(1), 1–7. DOI: 10.1111/j.1468-2370.2009.00277.x

Lindgreen, A., Swaen, V., & Johnston, W. J. (2009). Corporate social responsibility: An empirical investigation of US organizations. *Journal of Business Ethics*, *85*(S2), 303–323. DOI: 10.1007/s10551-008-9738-8

Li, T., Wang, K., Sueyoshi, T., & Wang, D. D. (2021). ESG: Research Progress and Future Prospects. *Sustainability (Basel), 13*(21), 11663. DOI: 10.3390/su132111663

Liu, X., & Anbumozhi, V. (2009). Determinant factors of corporate environmental information disclosure: An empirical study of Chinese listed companies. *Journal of Cleaner Production*, *17*(6), 593–600. DOI: 10.1016/j.jclepro.2008.10.001

Li, Y., & Giles, D. E. (2015). Modelling volatility spillover effects between developed stock markets and Asian emerging stock markets. *International Journal of Finance & Economics*, *20*(2), 155 ??177. DOI: 10.1002/ijfe.1506

Ljung, G. M., & Box, G. E. P. (1978). On a measure of lack of fit in time series models. *Biometrika*, *65*(2), 297 ??303. DOI: 10.1093/biomet/65.2.297

Lubowiecki-Vikuk, A., Dąbrowska, A., & Machnik, A. (2021). Responsible consumer and lifestyle: Sustainability insights. *Sustainable Production and Consumption*, *25*, 91–101. DOI: 10.1016/j.spc.2020.08.007 PMID: 32864405

Macpherson, M., Gasperini, A., & Bosco, M. (2021). Implications for artificial intelligence and ESG data. Social Science Research Network. DOI: 10.2139/ssrn.3863599

Mahindra Sustainability Report I Low Carbon Business I Mahindra. (n.d.). Www.mahindra.com. https://www.mahindra.com/sustainability

Majeed, N., Sharif, R., Sheeraz, M. N., Sajjad, S., Maqsood, H., Imran, M., Jamshaid, M. U., Arif, M., & Hussain, M. B. (2023). Impact of climate change on agriculture & vice versa: A review. *JQAAS*, *3*(01), 1–15. DOI: 10.38211/jqaas.2023.3.31

Makni, R., Francoeur, C., & Bellavance, F. (2009). Causality between Corporate Social Performance and Financial Performance: Evidence from Canadian Firms. *Journal of Business Ethics*, *89*(3), 409–422. DOI: 10.1007/s10551-008-0007-7

Malhotra, N. K. (2019). *Marketing Research: An Applied Orientation* (7th ed.). Pearson Publishing.

Malik, F., & Ewing, B. T. (2009). Volatility transmission between oil prices and equity

Mandloi, S., Bangre, J., Aher, S. B., Sharma, O. P., Prajapati, S., & Singh, S. (2023). Conservation agriculture as a climate change mitigation strategy: A review. *International Journal of Environment and Climate Change*, *13*(11), 3230–3242. DOI: 10.9734/ijecc/2023/v13i113495

Margolis, J. D., & Walsh, J. P. (2003). Misery loves companies: Rethinking social initiatives by business. *Administrative Science Quarterly*, *48*(2), 268–305. DOI: 10.2307/3556659

Marquis, C., & Toffel, M. W. (2012). The Globalization of Corporate Social Responsibility: A Study of the Adoption of the Global Reporting Initiative. Harvard Business School Working Paper.

Martín, L., & Sánchez-Ortiz, N. (2023). To be digital or not to be, that is the ESG question. *Boletín de Estudios Económicos*, *77*(233), 109–124. DOI: 10.18543/bee.2638

Martin, V., Dunis, C., & von Mettenheim, H. J. (2002). A test for volatility spillovers. *Economics Letters*, *76*(1), 77 ??84. DOI: 10.1016/S0165-1765(02)00027-7

Matuszak, Ł., & Różańska, E. (2017). An examination of the relationship between CSR disclosure and financial performance: The case of Polish banks. DOI: 10.24818/jamis.2017.04005

Mayer, R. C., Davis, J. H., & Schoorman, F. D. (1995). An integrative model of organizational trust. *Academy of Management Review*, *20*(3), 709. DOI: 10.2307/258792

McKnight, D. H., Choudhury, V., & Kacmar, C. (2002). Developing and validating trust measures for e-commerce: An integrative typology. *Information Systems Research*, *13*(3), 334–359. DOI: 10.1287/isre.13.3.334.81

Mensi, W., Beljid, M., Boubaker, A., & Managi, S. (2013). Correlations and volatility spillovers across commodity and stock markets: Linking energies, food, and gold. *Economic Modelling*, *32*, 15 ??22. DOI: 10.1016/j.econmod.2013.01.023

Migliorelli, M. (2021). What Do We Mean by Sustainable Finance? Assessing Existing Frameworks and Policy Risks. *Sustainability (Basel)*, *13*(2), 975. DOI: 10.3390/su13020975

Ministry New and Renewable Energy. https://mnre.gov.in/solar-overview/

Ministry of Environment. Forest and Climate Change, Green India Missionhttps://moef.gov.in/moef/division/forest-divisions-2/green-india-mission-gim/

Ministry of Jal Shakti. Department of Water Resources, https://nwm.gov.in/objective-national-water-mission

Ministry of Power. https://powermin.gov.in/en/content/energy-efficiency

Miquel-Segarra, S., Rangel Pérez, C., & Monfort, A. (2023). Análisis del uso de Twitter como plataforma estratégica de diálogo: Las empresas del IBEX35 y la difusión de mensajes sobre COVID. *Revista de Comunicación*, *22*(1). Advance online publication. DOI: 10.26441/RC22.1-2023-2989

Miralles-Marcelo, J. L., Miralles-Quir??s, J. L., & del Mar Miralles-Quir??s, M. (2013). Multivariate GARCH models and risk minimizing portfolios: The importance of medium and small firms. *The Spanish Review of Financial Economics*, *11*(1), 29 ??38. DOI: 10.1016/j.srfe.2013.03.001

MoEFCC. (2021). India: Third Biennial Update Report to the United Nations Framework Convention on Climate Change. Ministry of Environment, Forest and Climate Change, Government of India. https://unfccc.int/documents/268470

Mohr, L. A., Webb, D. J., & Harris, K. E. (2001). Do consumers expect companies to be socially responsible? The impact of corporate social responsibility on buying behavior. *The Journal of Consumer Affairs*, *35*(1), 45–72. DOI: 10.1111/j.1745-6606.2001.tb00102.x

Molinillo, S., Ekinci, Y., & Japutra, A. (2019). A consumer-based brand performance model for assessing brand success. *International Journal of Market Research, 61*(1), 93–110. DOI: 10.1177/1470785318762990

Monfort, A., Sebastián, A., & López, B. (2015). Corporate identity in the brand co-creation era. *Communication Papers, 4*(08), 31. DOI: 10.33115/udg_bib/cp.v4i08.22065

Monfort, A., & Villagra, N. (2016). Corporate social responsibility and corporate foundations in building responsible brands. *El Profesional de la Información, 25*(5), 767–777. DOI: 10.3145/epi.2016.sep.07

Monroe-White, T., Kerlin, J. A., & Zook, S. (2015). A quantitative critique of Kerlin ??s macro-institutional social enterprise framework. *Social Enterprise Journal, 11*(2), 178 ??201. DOI: 10.1108/SEJ-03-2015-0008

Morvan, J. (2009). *March??s et instruments financiers.* Dunod.

Mulligan, C., Morsfield, S., & Cheikosman, E. (2023). Blockchain for sustainability: A systematic literature review for policy impact. *Telecommunications Policy, 48*(2), 102676. DOI: 10.1016/j.telpol.2023.102676

Muneer, S., Shabbir, J., & Khalil, A. (2017. Estimation of finite population mean in simple random sampling and stratified random sampling using two auxiliary variables. *Journal of Communications in Statistics - Theory and Methods,* 46(5), 2181 – 2192.

Murphy, W. J. (2018). *Independent Assurance: Providing assurance to organizations across a wide range of sectors and variety of assurance scopes.* KPMG Sustainability Services, www.kpmg.com/ca/en/home/services/audit/sustainability-services/independent-assurance

National Mission for a Green India, https://mpforest.gov.in/img/files/GIM_Implementation_Guidelines.pdf

National Mission for Sustainable Agriculture. (n.d.). Nmsa.dac.gov.in. https://nmsa.dac.gov.in/

National Mission for Sustaining the Himalayan Ecosystem https://nihroorkee.gov.in/major-projects/national-mission-sustaining-himalayan-ecosystem-nmshe

National Mission on Himalayan Studies https://nmhs.org.in/pdf/National%20Mission%20on%20Himalayan%20Studies.pdf

National Mission on Sustainable Habitat. Ministry of Housing and Urban Affairs, GoI https://mohua.gov.in/upload/uploadfiles/files/NMSH-2021.pdf

Nelson, D. B. (1991). Conditional heteroskedasticity in asset returns: A new approach. *Econometrica, 59*(2), 347 ??370. DOI: 10.2307/2938260

Ng, J. (2017). *Responsible Investment: How It Can Become Mainstream Practice*. Market Mogul.

Nguyen, A. H., Do, M. H. T., Hoang, T. G., & Nguyen, L. Q. T. (2023). Green financing for sustainable development: Insights from multiple cases of Vietnamese commercial banks. *Business Strategy and the Environment, 32*(1), 321–335. DOI: 10.1002/bse.3132

Nguyen, B. N. (2018). The effect of corporate social responsibility disclosure on financial performance: Evidence from credit institutions in Vietnam. *Asian Social Science, 14*(4), 109–122. DOI: 10.5539/ass.v14n4p109

Nguyen, V. T., & Hang, T. T. (2022, December 31). Bui & Chi H.D (2022). The impacts of corporate social responsibility to corporate financial performance: A case study of Vietnamese commercial banks. *Cogent Economics & Finance, 10*(1), 2132642. Advance online publication. DOI: 10.1080/23322039.2022.2132642

Niresh, J A., & Silva, W H E. (2018, January 31). The Nexus between Corporate Social Responsibility Disclosure and Financial Performance: Evidence from the Listed Banks, Finance and Insurance Companies in Sri Lanka. DOI: 10.5430/afr.v7n2p65

Nollet, J., Filis, G., & Mitrokostas, E. (2016). Corporate social responsibility and financial performance: A non-linear and disaggregated approach. *Economic Modelling, 52*, 400–407. DOI: 10.1016/j.econmod.2015.09.019

Nugroho, L., Badawi, A., & Hidayah, N. (2019). Discourses of sustainable finance implementation in Islamic bank (Cases studies in bank Mandiri Syariah 2018). *International Journal of Financial Research, 10*(6), 108. DOI: 10.5430/ijfr.v10n6p108

O'Dwyer, B. (2011). The Case of Sustainability Assurance: Constructing a New Assurance Service. *Contemporary Accounting Research, 28*(4), 1230–1266. DOI: 10.1111/j.1911-3846.2011.01108.x

O'Dwyer, B., Humphrey, C., & Rowbottom, N. (2024). From institutional integration to institutional demise: The disintegration of the International Integrated Reporting Council (IIRC). *Critical Perspectives on Accounting, 99*, 102699. DOI: 10.1016/j.cpa.2023.102699

O'Dwyer, B., & Unerman, J. (2020). Shifting the focus of sustainability accounting from impacts to risks and dependencies: Researching the transformative potential of TCFD reporting. *Accounting, Auditing & Accountability Journal, 33*(5), 1113–1141. DOI: 10.1108/AAAJ-02-2020-4445

Ozili, P. K. (2022, February 1). Sustainability and sustainable development research around the world. https://papers.ssrn.com/sol3/papers.cfm?abstract_id=4024990

Pahuja, N., Pruthi, A., & Raj, A.. (2020). *Mainstreaming Sustainable Development and Enhancing Climate Resilience: New Opportunities for States in India*. TERI.

Papazian, A. V. (2023). Sustainability in Finance: Frameworks, Standards, and Scores. In *Hardwiring Sustainability into Financial Mathematics: Implications for Money Mechanics* (pp. 29–67). Springer Nature Switzerland. DOI: 10.1007/978-3-031-45689-3_3

Papista, E., & Dimitriadis, S. (2019). Consumer – green brand relationships: Revisiting benefits, relationship quality and outcomes. *Journal of Product and Brand Management*, *28*(2), 166–187. DOI: 10.1108/JPBM-09-2016-1316

Parris, D. L., & Guzmán, F. (2022). Evolving brand boundaries and expectations: Looking back on brand equity, brand loyalty, and brand image research to move forward. *Journal of Product and Brand Management*. Advance online publication. DOI: 10.1108/JPBM-06-2021-3528

Partner, (2023). Tech in ESG: role of data analytics and benchmarking in ESG. Ey.com. https://www.ey.com/en_in/media/podcasts/tech-in-esg/2023/01/tech-in-esg-role-of-data-analytics-and-benchmarking-in-esg

Patowary, M. M. I. (2019). Incorporating Sustainability in Business Model: A literature review. Social Science Research Network. DOI: 10.2139/ssrn.3643604

Peng, Y., Chen, H., & Li, T. (2023). The Impact of Digital Transformation on ESG: A Case Study of Chinese-Listed Companies. *Sustainability (Basel)*, *15*(20), 15072. DOI: 10.3390/su152015072

Pindyck, R. S. (2004). Volatility in natural gas and oil markets. *The Journal of Energy and Development*, *30*(1), 1 ??19.

Platonova, E., Asutay, M., Dixon, R., & Mohammad, S. (2016, July 1). The Impact of Corporate Social Responsibility Disclosure on Financial Performance: Evidence from the GCC Islamic Banking Sector. DOI: 10.1007/s10551-016-3229-0

Porter, P., & Kramer, M. R. (2007). Strategy and society: The link between competitive advantage and corporate social responsibility. *Strategic Direction*, *23*(5). Advance online publication. DOI: 10.1108/sd.2007.05623ead.006

PRI. (2024). *Annual report 2024*. Retrieved October 15, 2024, from https://www.unpri.org/about-us/about-the-pri/annual-report#storytext-end

Principles for Responsible Investment (PRI). (2024). *Annual report 2024*. Retrieved from https://www.unpri.org/annual-report-2024

Priyadarshan, P., & Parulekar, A. (2023, August 15). *SEBI's expansion of ESG mutual funds schemes: Demystifying its implications*. IRCCL. https://www.irccl.in/post/sebi-s-expansion-of-esg-mutual-funds-schemes-demystifying-its-implications

Puriwat, W., & Tripopsakul, S. (2022). From ESG to DESG: The Impact of DESG (Digital Environmental, Social, and Governance) on Customer Attitudes and Brand Equity. *Sustainability (Basel)*, *14*(17), 10480. DOI: 10.3390/su141710480

Ramzan, M., Amin, M., & Abbas, M. (2021, January 1). How does corporate social responsibility affect financial performance, financial stability, and financial inclusion in the banking sector? Evidence from Pakistan. DOI: 10.1016/j.ribaf.2020.101314

Rao, N. D., & Baer, P. (2012). "Decent Living" Emissions: A Conceptual Framework. *Sustainability (Basel)*, *4*(4), 656–681. DOI: 10.3390/su4040656

Razak, L A., Ismail, I., Ishak, I., Yamin, M., & Syah, A L N. (2019, February 20). Factors affecting the corporate social responsibility disclosure (Case study at PT. Semen Tonasa). DOI: 10.1088/1755-1315/235/1/012074

Rebello, A. (2024, July 4). *BRSR reporting in India: Full form, applicability, format, guidelines, benefits*. cleartax. https://cleartax.in/s/brsr-reporting

Reboredo, J. C., & Ugolini, A. (2020). The impact of ESG ratings on the systemic risk of European blue-chip firms. *Journal of Financial Stability*, *53*, 100833.

Rehman, S. U., Kraus, S., Shah, S. A., Khanin, D., & Mahto, R. V. (2021). Analyzing the relationship between green innovation and environmental performance in large manufacturing firms. Technological Forecasting and Social Change, 163, 120481. . 2020.120481DOI: 10. 1016/j.techfore

Rodríguez Diez, J., Tomé-Torquemada, S., Vicente, A., Reyes, J., & Orcajo, G. A. (2023). Decarbonization Pathways, Strategies, and Use Cases to Achieve Net-Zero CO2 Emissions in the Steelmaking Industry. *Energies*, *16*(21), 7360. DOI: 10.3390/en16217360

Rodriguez, A., Cotran, H., & Stewart, L. S. (2017). Evaluating the effectiveness of sustainability disclosure: Findings from a recent SASB study. *The Bank of America Journal of Applied Corporate Finance*, *29*(2), 100–108. DOI: 10.1111/jacf.12237

Ronaldo, R., & Suryanto, T. (2022). Green finance and sustainability development goals in Indonesian Fund Village. *Resources Policy*, *78*, 102839. DOI: 10.1016/j.resourpol.2022.102839

Rossato, C., & Castellani, P. (2020). The contribution of digitalisation to business longevity from a competitiveness perspective. *The TQM Journal*, *32*(4), 617–645. DOI: 10.1108/TQM-02-2020-0032

Roy, S., Debnath, P., Vulević, A., & Mitra, S. (2023). Incorporating climate change resilience in india's railway infrastructure: Challenges and potential. *Mechatronics and Intelligent Transportation Systems*, *2*(2). Advance online publication. DOI: 10.56578/mits020205

Ruan, L., & Liu, H. (2021). Environmental, Social, Governance Activities and Firm Performance: Evidence from China. *Sustainability (Basel)*, *13*(2), 767. DOI: 10.3390/su13020767

Ruiz, B., Esteban, Á., & Gutiérrez, S. (2014). Determinants of reputation of leading Spanish financial institutions among their customers in a context of economic crisis. *Business Research Quarterly*, *17*(4), 259–278. DOI: 10.1016/j.brq.2014.04.002

Ruiz, B., García, J. A., & Revilla, A. (2016). Antecedents and consequences of bank reputation: A comparison of the United Kingdom and Spain. *International Marketing Review*, *33*(6), 781–805. DOI: 10.1108/IMR-06-2015-0147

Rupley, K. H., Brown, D., & Marshall, S. (2017). Evolution of corporate reporting: From stand-alone corporate social responsibility reporting to integrated reporting. *Research in Accounting Regulation*, *29*(2), 172–176. DOI: 10.1016/j.racreg.2017.09.010

Saba, I., Khan, A., & Jawed, H. (2021). Islamic Finance and SDGs: Connecting Dots. Islamic Finance and Sustainable Development: A Sustainable Economic Framework for Muslim and Non-Muslim Countries, 55-76.DOI: 10.1007/978-3-030-76016-8_4

Sadorsky, P. (2012). Correlations and volatility spillovers between oil prices and the stock prices of clean energy and technology companies. *Energy Economics*, *34*(1), 248 ??255. DOI: 10.1016/j.eneco.2011.03.006

Saeed, M., & Kersten, W. (2019). Drivers of Sustainable Supply Chain Management: Identification and Classification. *Sustainability (Basel)*, *11*(4), 1137. DOI: 10.3390/su11041137

Saeed, T., Bouri, E., & Alsulami, H. (2021). Extreme return connectedness and its determinants between clean/green and dirty energy investments. *Energy Economics*, *96*, 105017. DOI: 10.1016/j.eneco.2020.105017

Sætra, H. S. (2021). A Framework for Evaluating and Disclosing the ESG Related Impacts of AI with the SDGs. *Sustainability (Basel)*, *13*(15), 8503. DOI: 10.3390/su13158503

Sætra, H. S. (2022). The AI ESG protocol: Evaluating and disclosing the environment, social, and governance implications of artificial intelligence capabilities, assets, and activities. *Sustainable Development (Bradford), 31*(2), 1027–1037. DOI: 10.1002/sd.2438

Saki, F. (2020, October 1). Corporate Social Responsibility on Financial Performance: A Study of the Bangladeshi DSE Listed Private Commercial Banks. DOI: 10.52962/ipjaf.2020.4.4.110

Saleem, K. (2009). International linkage of the Russian market and the Russian financial crisis: A multivariate GARCH analysis. *Research in International Business and Finance, 23*(3), 243 ??256. DOI: 10.1016/j.ribaf.2008.09.003

Sánchez-Flores, R. B., Cruz-Sotelo, S. E., Ojeda-Benitez, S., & Ramírez-Barreto, Ma. E. (2020). Sustainable Supply Chain Management—A Literature Review on Emerging Economies. Sustainability, 12(17), 6972. MDPI. DOI: 10.3390/su12176972

Sang, Y., Loganathan, K., & Lin, L. (2024). Digital Transformation and Firm ESG Performance: The Mediating Role of Corporate Risk-Taking and the Moderating Role of Top Management Team. *Sustainability (Basel), 16*(14), 5907–5907. DOI: 10.3390/su16145907

Sarpong, F. A., Sappor, P., Nyantakyi, G., Ahakwa, I., Esther Agyeiwaa, O., & Blandful Cobbinah, B. (2023). From traditional roots to digital bytes: Can digitalizing ESG improves Ghanaian rural banks' brand equity through stakeholder engagement, and customer loyalty? *Cogent Business & Management, 10*(2), 2232159.

Saxena, A., Singh, R., Gehlot, A., Akram, S. V., Twala, B., Singh, A., Montero, E. C., & Priyadarshi, N. (2022). Technologies Empowered Environmental, Social, and Governance (ESG): An Industry 4.0 landscape. *Sustainability (Basel), 15*(1), 309. DOI: 10.3390/su15010309

Sebastián-Morillas, A., Monfort, A., & López-Vázquez, B. (2024). Effects of perceived value and customer service on brand satisfaction. *Journal of Promotion Management, 30*(2), 187–203. DOI: 10.1080/10496491.2023.2253231

Sebi puts in place regulatory framework for value chain ESG disclosures for listed entities. (2023, July 12). Moneycontrol. https://www.moneycontrol.com/news/business/sebi-puts-in-place-regulatory-framework-for-value-chain-esg-disclosures-for-listed-entities-10948501.html

SEBI's vision for ESG in India: A strategic roadmap for sustainability and transparency. (2024, November 19). Oren - The Enterprise Sustainability Platform. https://www.orennow.com/blog/sebis-vision-for-esg-in-india-a-strategic-roadmap-for-sustainability-and-transparency

Sekhon, A. K., & Kathuria, L. M. (2019). Analyzing the impact of corporate social responsibility on corporate financial performance: Evidence from top Indian firms. *Corporate Governance (Bradford), 20*(1), 143–157. DOI: 10.1108/CG-04-2019-0135

Senyigit, Y. B., & Shuaibu, M. A. (2017). The effect of corporate social responsibility on financial perfor mance: Evidence from the banking industry in emerging economies. *Journal of Business Studies Quarterly, 9*(1), 22–31. https://www.proquest.com/ openview/12bac8dfbde31d2aa9fd277b769dd16e/1?pq-origsite=gscholar&cbl=1056382

Setyowati, A. B. (2020). Governing sustainable finance: Insights from Indonesia. *Climate Policy*. Advance online publication. DOI: 10.1080/14693062.2020.1858741

Shahid, M., Sulub, Y. A., Mohtesham, M. M. J., & Abdullah, M. (2023). Analyzing the commonalities between Islamic social finance and sustainable development goals. *International Journal of Ethics and Systems*. DOI: 10.1108/IJOES-04-2022-0082

Sharma, D., & Singh, S. (2016). Instituting environmental sustainability and climate resilience into the governance process: Exploring the potential of new urban development schemes in india. *International Area Studies Review, 19*(1), 90–103. DOI: 10.1177/2233865916632942

Sharma, R., & Jain, V. (2019). CSR, Trust, brand loyalty and brand equity: Empirical evidences from sportswear industry in the NCR region of India. Metamorphosis. *Journal of Management Research, 18*(1), 57–67.

Shehzad, K., Liu, X., Tiwari, A., Arif, M., & Rauf, A. (2021). Analysing time difference and volatility linkages between China and the United States during financial crises and stable period using VARX ??DCC ??MEGARCH model. *International Journal of Finance & Economics, 26*(1), 814 ??833. DOI: 10.1002/ijfe.1822

Shome, S., Hassan, M. K., Verma, S., & Panigrahi, T. R. (2023). Impact investment for sustainable development: A bibliometric analysis. *International Review of Economics & Finance, 84*, 770–800. https://doi.org/. iref.2022.12.001DOI: 10.1016/j

Sichtmann, C. (2007). An analysis of antecedents and consequences of trust in a corporate brand. *European Journal of Marketing, 41*(9/10), 999–1015. DOI: 10.1108/03090560710773318

Siew, R. Y. (2015). A review of corporate sustainability reporting tools (SRTs). *Journal of Environmental Management, 164*, 180–195. DOI: 10.1016/j.jenvman.2015.09.010 PMID: 26379255

Sikhosana, A., & Aye, G. C. (2018). Asymmetric volatility transmission between the real exchange rate and stock returns in South Africa. *Economic Analysis and Policy, 60*, 1 ??8. DOI: 10.1016/j.eap.2018.08.002

Simpson, W. G., & Kohers, T. (2002). The link between corporate social and financial performance: Evidence from the banking industry. *Journal of Business Ethics, 35*(2), 97–109. DOI: 10.1023/A:1013082525900

Singh, P., Kumar, B., & Pandey, A. (2010). Price and volatility spillovers across North American, European and Asian stock markets. *International Review of Financial Analysis, 19*(1), 55 ??64. DOI: 10.1016/j.irfa.2009.11.001

Siueia, T T., Wang, J., & Deladem, T G. (2019, July 1). Corporate Social Responsibility and financial performance: A comparative study in the Sub-Saharan Africa banking sector. DOI: 10.1016/j.jclepro.2019.04.027

Skarmeas, D., Zeriti, A., & Baltas, G. (2016). Relationship Value: Drivers and Outcomes in International Marketing Channels. *Journal of International Marketing*, 24(1), page(s): 22-40.

Smith, J. A.III. (1995). The CERES principles: Model for public environmental accountability. *Review of European Community & International Environmental Law*, *4*(2), 116–122. DOI: 10.1111/j.1467-9388.1995.tb00209.x

Soana, M. G. (2011, May 28). The Relationship Between Corporate Social Performance and Corporate Financial Performance in the Banking Sector. Springer Science+Business Media, 104(1), 133-148. 10.1007/s10551-011-0894-x

Sridharan, V. (2018). *Bridging the disclosure gap: Investor perspectives on environmental, social, & governance (ESG) disclosures*. SASB.

Sridharan, V. (2018). *Bridging the Disclosure Gap: Investor Perspectives on Environmental, Social, & Governance (ESG)*. Disclosures.

Srivastava, S., & Trivedi, S. (2023). *Indian capital market regulator's updated green debt guidelines: Unlocking the potential of sustainable finance*. Institute for Energy Economics and Financial Analysis.

Stefanopoulou, A. (2023). Improve time and energy efficiency in multi-uav coverage swarms by optimizing thetake-off/landing positions. DOI: 10.21203/rs.3.rs-3671974/v1

Strott, E., Carey, C., & Wilson, S. (2016). *Investors, corporates, and ESG: Bridging the gap*. PwC's Governance Insights Center.

Stuermer, M., Abu-Tayeh, G., & Myrach, T. (2016). Digital sustainability: Basic conditions for sustainable digital artifacts and their ecosystems. *Sustainability Science, 12*(2), 247–262. DOI: 10.1007/s11625-016-0412-2 PMID: 30174752

Sung, Y., & Kim, J. (2010). Effects of brand personality on brand trust and brand affect. *Psychology and Marketing, 27*(7), 639–661. DOI: 10.1002/mar.20349

Su, X., Wang, S., & Li, F. (2023). The Impact of Digital Transformation on ESG Performance Based on the Mediating Effect of Dynamic Capabilities. *Sustainability (Basel), 15*(18), 13506. DOI: 10.3390/su151813506

Sweeney, J. C., & Soutar, G. N. (2001). Consumer perceived value: The development of a multiple item scale. *Journal of Retailing, 77*(2), 203–220. DOI: 10.1016/S0022-4359(01)00041-0

Syllignakis, M. N., & Kouretas, G. P. (2011). Dynamic correlation analysis of financial contagion: Evidence from the Central and Eastern European markets. *International Review of Economics & Finance, 20*(4), 717 ??732. DOI: 10.1016/j.iref.2011.01.006

Synergy Solutions for a World in Crisis: Tackling Climate and SDG Action Together | Department of Economic and Social Affairs. (2023). Sdgs.un.org. https://sdgs.un.org/synergy-solutions-world-crisis-tackling-climate-and-sdg-action-together

Szegedi, K., Khan, Y., & Lentner, C. (2020). Corporate social responsibility and financial performance: Evidence from Pakistani listed banks. *Sustainability (Basel), 12*(10), 4080. DOI: 10.3390/su12104080

Tafti, S F., Hosseini, S F., & Emami, S A. (2012, October 1). Assessment the Corporate Social Responsibility According to Islamic Values (Case Study: Sarmayeh Bank). DOI: 10.1016/j.sbspro.2012.09.1095

Taherdoost, H. (2022). Machine Learning Algorithms: Features and Applications. In Wang, J. (Ed.), *Encyclopedia of Data Science and Machine Learning* (pp. 938–960). IGI Global., DOI: 10.4018/978-1-7998-9220-5.ch054

Task Force on Climate-related Financial Disclosures (TCFD). (2017). *Recommendations of the Task Force on Climate-related Financial Disclosures*. https://assets.bbhub.io/company/sites/60/2021/10/FINAL-2017-TCFD-Report.pdf

Task Force on Climate-related Financial Disclosures (TCFD). (2021). Final Report: Recommendations of the Task Force on Climate-related Financial Disclosures. Financial Stability Board.

Task Force on Climate-related Financial Disclosures (TCFD). (2024a). *Task Force on Climate-related Financial Disclosures*. https://www.fsb-tcfd.org/#:~:text=The%20Financial%20Stability%20Board%20

Task Force on Climate-related Financial Disclosures (TCFD). (2024b). *About*. https://www.fsb-tcfd.org/about/

Taskforce on Nature-related Financial Disclosures (TNFD). (2023b). *Recommendations of the Taskforce on Nature-related Financial Disclosures*. https://tnfd.global/wp-content/uploads/2023/08/Recommendations_of_the_Taskforce_on_Nature-related_Financial_Disclosures_September_2023.pdf

Taskforce on Nature-related Financial Disclosures (TNFD). (2023c). *Guidance on engagement with Indigenous Peoples, Local Communities and affected stakeholders*. https://tnfd.global/wp-content/uploads/2023/08/Guidance_on_engagement_with_Indigenous_Peoples_Local_Communities_and_affected_stakeholders_v1.pdf?v=1695138220

Taskforce on Nature-related Financial Disclosures (TNFD). (2024a). *Our history*. https://tnfd.global/about/history/

Taşkın, D. (2015, October 29). The Relationship between CSR and Banks' Financial Performance: Evidence from Turkey., 10(39), 21-21. 10.19168/jyu.97694

Taşkın, D. (2015). The relationship between CSR and banks' financial performance: Evidence from Turkey. *Journal of Yaşar University, 10*(39), 21–30. DOI: 10.19168/jyu.97694

Taskin, D., Azam, M., Hunjra, A. I., & Al-Faryan, M. A. S. (2023). Role of ethnic conflicts, regularization and natural resource abundance in sustainable development. *Resources Policy, 85*, 103936. DOI: 10.1016/j.resourpol.2023.103936

Tiwari, A. K., Aye, G. C., Gupta, R., & Gkillas, K. (2020). Gold-oil dependence dynamics and the role of geopolitical risks: Evidence from a Markov-switching time-varying copula model. *Energy Economics, 88*, 104748. DOI: 10.1016/j.eneco.2020.104748

Tran, Q. T., Vo, T. D., & Le, X. T. (2021). Relationship between profitability and corporate social responsibility disclosure: Evidence from Vietnamese listed banks. *The Journal of Asian Finance, Economics and Business, 8*(3), 875–883. DOI: 10.13106/jafeb.2021.vol8.no3.0875

Trevino, R., & Treviño, E. (2021). Análisis entre imagen de la tienda y satisfacción del cliente en tiendas minoristas transnacionales en el sector autoservicio. Estudios Gerenciales, 556–565. DOI: 10.18046/j.estger.2021.161.4293

Tripathi, M., & Bhattacharya, N. (2023). Environmentally sound technologies for climate change mitigation in brics countries: A comparative policy and legal perspective. *Environmental Policy and Law*, *53*(2-3), 181–196. DOI: 10.3233/EPL-220067

Tsay, R. S. (2005). *Analysis of financial time series*. John wiley & sons. DOI: 10.1002/0471746193

Tsuji, C. (2018). Return transmission and asymmetric volatility spillovers between oil futures and oil equities: New DCC-MEGARCH analyses. *Economic Modelling*, *74*, 167 ??185. DOI: 10.1016/j.econmod.2018.05.007

Ullman, A. (1985). A Critical Examination of the Relationship Among Social Performance, Social Disclosure, and Economic Performance. *Academy of Management Review*, *10*(3), 540–577. DOI: 10.2307/258135

UNCTAD. (2024). *World Investment Report 2024: Investment facilitation and digital government*. United Nations Publications.

Unerman, J., Bebbington, J., & O'dwyer, B. (2018). Corporate reporting and accounting for externalities. *Accounting and Business Research*, *48*(5), 497–522. DOI: 10.1080/00014788.2018.1470155

UNICEF. Climate Change and environmental sustainability. (2021). https://www.unicef.org/india/what-we-do/climate-change

United Nations (UN). (2024a). *Transforming our world: the 2030 Agenda for Sustainable Development*. https://sdgs.un.org/2030agenda

United Nations (UN). (2024b). *Global indicator framework for the Sustainable Development Goals and targets of the 2030 Agenda for Sustainable Development*. https://unstats.un.org/sdgs/indicators/Global-Indicator-Framework-after-2024-refinement-English.pdf

United Nations Conference on Trade and Development (UNCTAD). (2024). *World Investment Report 2024: Investment facilitation and digital government*. United Nations Publications.

United Nations Environment Programme (UNEP). (2011). Towards a green economy: Pathways to sustainable development and poverty eradication - A synthesis for policy makers. UNEP. Retrieved from https://www.unep.org/greeneconomy

United Nations Environment Programme (UNEP). (2021). *The UN & TNFD: Stewarding Systems Change*. https://www.unepfi.org/themes/ecosystems/the-un-and-tnfd/

United Nations Environment Programme (UNEP). (2023). *The Taskforce on Nature-related Financial Disclosures (TNFD) launches its final recommendations*. https://www.unepfi.org/themes/ecosystems/tnfd-final-recommendations/

United Nations. (2023). *The Sustainable Development Goals Report 2023: Special Edition*. Unstats.un.org

United Nations. (2024). *The 17 Sustainable Development Goals*. United Nations. https://sdgs.un.org/goals

Varma, N., Kelkar, U., Bhardwaj, S., Singh, P., & Mishra, A. (2014, December). Climate Change, Disasters and Development: Testing the Waters for Adaptive Governance in India. *Vision: The Journal of Business Perspective*, *18*(4), 327–338. DOI: 10.1177/0972262914551664

Vihma, A. (2011). India and the global climate governance: Between principles and pragmatism. *Journal of Environment & Development*, *20*(1), 69–94. DOI: 10.1177/1070496510394325

Vinuesa, R., Azizpour, H., Leite, I., Balaam, M., Dignum, V., Domisch, S., Felländer, A., Langhans, S. D., Tegmark, M., & Nerini, F. F. (2020). The role of artificial intelligence in achieving the Sustainable Development Goals. *Nature Communications*, *11*(1), 233. Advance online publication. DOI: 10.1038/s41467-019-14108-y PMID: 31932590

Vivian, A., & Wohar, M. E. (2012). Commodity volatility breaks. *Journal of International Financial Markets, Institutions and Money*, *22*(2), 395 ??422. DOI: 10.1016/j.intfin.2011.12.003

Waddock, S. (2003). Stakeholder performance implications of corporate responsibility. *International Journal of Business Performance Management*, *5*(2-3), 114–124. DOI: 10.1504/IJBPM.2003.003262

Waddock, S. A., & Graves, S. B. (1997). The corporate social performance—Financial performance link. *Strategic Management Journal*, *18*(4), 303–319. DOI: 10.1002/(SICI)1097-0266(199704)18:4<303::AID-SMJ869>3.0.CO;2-G

Wahab, N. A., Yusof, R. M., Zainuddin, Z., Shamsuddin, J. N., & Mohamad, S. F. N. (2023). Charting future growth for Islamic finance talents in Malaysia: A bibliometric analysis on the Islamic finance domains and future research gaps. *Journal of Islamic Accounting and Business Research*, *14*(5), 812–837. DOI: 10.1108/JIABR-02-2022-0045

Walker, N. L., Styles, D., Coughlan, P., & Williams, A. P. (2022). Cross-sector sustainability benchmarking of major utilities in the United Kingdom. *Utilities Policy*, *78*, 101417. DOI: 10.1016/j.jup.2022.101417

Wang, K. H., Zhao, Y. X., Jiang, C. F., & Li, Z. Z. (2022). Does green finance inspire sustainable development? Evidence from a global perspective. *Economic Analysis and Policy, 75*, 412–426. https://doi.org/. 2022.06.002DOI: 10.1016/j.eap

Wang, J., Hong, Z., & Long, H. (2023). Digital Transformation Empowers ESG Performance in the Manufacturing Industry: From ESG to DESG. *SAGE Open*, *13*(4), 21582440231204158. Advance online publication. DOI: 10.1177/21582440231204158

Wang, L., & Tuttle, B. (2014). Using corporate social responsibility performance to evaluate financial disclosure credibility. *Accounting and Business Research*, *44*(5), 523–544. DOI: 10.1080/00014788.2014.922408

Wang, Q., Dou, J., & Jia, S. (2016). A meta-analytic review of corporate social responsibility and corporate financial performance: The moderating effect of contextual factors. *Business & Society*, *55*(8), 1083–1121. DOI: 10.1177/0007650315584317

Wang, S. L., & McPhail, L. (2014). Impacts of energy shocks on US agricultural productivity growth and commodity prices ??A structural VAR analysis. *Energy Economics*, *46*, 435 ??444. DOI: 10.1016/j.eneco.2014.05.006

Wang, S. S., Rui, O. M., & Firth, M. (2002). Return and volatility behavior of dually-traded stocks: The case of Hong Kong. *Journal of International Money and Finance*, *21*(2), 265 ??293. DOI: 10.1016/S0261-5606(01)00039-0

WBCSD. (2023). ESG-Integrated Value Creation: A practical guide for boards and C-suite. World Business Council for Sustainable Development. https://www.wbcsd.org/

Weber, P R. (1990, January 31). Basic content analysis (2nd ed.). . SAGE Publications, Inc., 2, 12

Weshah, S R., & Ahmad, A D., & R., A A M. (2012, September 29). The Impact of Adopting Corporate Social Responsibility on Corporate Financial Performance: Evidence from Jordanian Banks. *Interdisciplinary Journal of Contemporary Research in Business*, *4*(5), 11.

Wood, D. J. (1991). Social issues in management: Theory and research in corporate social performance. *Journal of Management*, *17*(2), 383–406. DOI: 10.1177/014920639101700206

Wood, D. J. (2010). Measuring corporate social performance: A review. *International Journal of Management Reviews, 12*(1), 50–84. DOI: 10.1111/j.1468-2370.2009.00274.x

World Bank Group & Islamic Development Bank (IsDB). (2021). *Global Report on Islamic Finance: Building Resilience through Sustainable Finance*. World Bank. https://doi.org/DOI: 10.1596/978-1-4648-1738-7

World Bank. (2021). *Mobilizing Finance for a Green and Inclusive Recovery in the Middle East and North Africa*. World Bank Group.

World Bank. (2023). *Global Economic Prospects*. The World Bank Group.

World Business Council for Sustainable Development (WBCSD). (2023). *Assurance of sustainability reporting: A guide to the evolving landscape*. WBCSD. https://www.wbcsd.org/

World Economic Forum (WEF). (2020). Measuring Stakeholder Capitalism: Towards Common Metrics and Consistent Reporting of Sustainable Value Creation. World Economic Forum.

World Economic Forum. (2022). Bridging Digital and Environmental Goals: A Framework for Sectoral Action. https://www.weforum.org/publications/bridging-digital-and-environmental-goals-a-framework-for-sectoral-action/

Wu, M., & Shen, C. (2013, September 1). Corporate social responsibility in the banking industry: Motives and financial performance. Elsevier BV, 37(9), 3529-3547. doi.org/10.1016/j.jbankfin.2013.04.023

Wu, S., & Liu, Y. (2023). A study on the Impact of Digital Transformation on Corporate ESG Performance: The Mediating Role of Green Innovation. *Sustainability (Basel), 15*(8), 6568. DOI: 10.3390/su15086568

Wut, T. M., Lee, D., Ip, W. M., & Lee, S. W. (2021). Digital Sustainability in the Organization: Scale development and validation. *Sustainability (Basel), 13*(6), 3530. DOI: 10.3390/su13063530

Yang, J., Kolari, J. W., & Min, I. (2003). Stock market integration and financial crises: The case of Asia. *Applied Financial Economics, 13*(7), 477 ??486. DOI: 10.1080/09603100210161965

Yilmaz, K. (2010). Return and volatility spillovers among the East Asian equity markets. *Journal of Asian Economics, 21*(3), 304 ??313. DOI: 10.1016/j.asieco.2009.09.001

Yu, L., Wang, S., & Lai, K. K. (2008). Forecasting crude oil price with an EMD-based neural network ensemble learning paradigm. *Energy Economics*, *30*(5), 2623 ??2635. DOI: 10.1016/j.eneco.2008.05.003

Yu, M., Liu, F., & Lee, J. A. (2019). Consumers' responses to negative publicity: The influence of culture on information search and negative word-of-mouth. *Journal of Brand Management*, *26*(2), 141–156. DOI: 10.1057/s41262-018-0123-3

Zeithaml, V. A. (1988). Consumer perceptions of price, quality, and value: A means-end model and synthesis of evidence. *Journal of Marketing*, *52*(3), 2–22. DOI: 10.1177/002224298805200302

Zhang, C., & Jin, S. (2022). What drives sustainable development of enterprises? Focusing on ESG management and green technology innovation. *Sustainability (Basel)*, *14*(18), 11695. DOI: 10.3390/su141811695

Zhang, Y. J., & Wei, Y. M. (2010). The crude oil market and the gold market: Evidence for cointegration, causality and price discovery. *Resources Policy*, *35*(3), 168 ??177. DOI: 10.1016/j.resourpol.2010.05.003

Zhong, Y., Zhao, H., & Yin, T. (2023). Resource Bundling: How Does Enterprise Digital Transformation Affect Enterprise ESG Development? *Sustainability (Basel)*, *15*(2), 1319. DOI: 10.3390/su15021319

Zhou, G., Liu, L., & Luo, S. (2022). Sustainable development, ESG performance and company market value: Mediating effect of financial performance. *Business Strategy and the Environment*, *31*(7), 3371–3387. DOI: 10.1002/bse.3089

Zhou, M., & Li, X. (2022). Influence of green finance and renewable energy resources over the sustainable development goal of clean energy in China. *Resources Policy*, *78*, 102816. DOI: 10.1016/j.resourpol.2022.102816

Zouch, M. A., Abbes, M. B., & Boujelbene, Y. (2011). Subprime crisis and volatility spillover. *International Journal of Monetary Economics and Finance*, *4*(1), 1. DOI: 10.1504/IJMEF.2011.038266

About the Contributors

Muhammad Qureshi Ph.D. Universiti Utara Malaysia (Accredited by AMBA and AACSB) Postdoc Universiti Malaysia Perlis (UniMap) International Research Fellow Universiti Malaysia Perlis (UniMap). He earned his Ph.D. degree in Human Resource Management from University Utara Malaysia which is AMBA and AACSB accredited, Postdoctoral & International Research Fellow at University Malaysia Perlis. Dr. Qureshi has a wide international exposure and almost 14 years of work experience in teaching, research, and Industry level. He has published in A* Journal, International journal of hospitality management Impact factor 10.427 and earned Emerald Literati Awards from The TQM Journal. He has several Impact Factor publications to his credit in Scopus Q1, ABDC, ABS SSCI, SCI, ESCI and other top-notch research journals. He is a reviewer of several high-ranking research journals. He has been invited as Session Chair and Keynote Speaker in a number of International Conferences. Dr. Qureshi has deep knowledge of quantitative and qualitative research and has presented in universities such as Oxford, United Kingdom. Harvard and MIT, USA. He nurtures and spearheads many research programs at his university and is a key protagonist of an inspirational research leadership. He has supervised more than 10 MS and PhD Thesis. He is well respected in the international research community and has a number of research publications in the area of Human Resource Management, CSR, Fintech, and Quantitative & Qualitative Research.

Farhan Mahboob An ideal profession for broad-spectrum multidisciplinary corporate & academic teaching/training, curriculum designing, research, applications, consultancy, creative solutions, strategic planning, business analytics, organizational scrutiny, strategic planning, and executive grooming. Granted Phd in Business Administration (specializing in Finance), after being awarded the degree of MBA, from Heriot-Watt University (UK, 2022 QS Rank 270), with emphasis in International Trade & Finance. Had completed the degree of

Bachelor of Science in Business Administration, from the University Of Arizona (USA, AACSB, 2022 QS Rank 268) double majoring in Management Information Systems & Operations Management. Have taught a variety of Management Science (Business Administration) and IT/MIS courses at the graduate and undergraduate levels, in addition to supervising MBA and BBA thesis (proposal & defense), while pursuing multi-disciplinary (corporate governance, fintech, finance, economics, econometrics, ethics, management, SCM) research (published in double-blind peer-reviewed Scopus indexed journals), as well as presenting at International Research Conferences (Awarded Best Conference Paper-AIMC-2021), such as Academy of Management. Organized, result-oriented (certified) professional with over 10 years' experience in research, academia, IT & corporate executive grooming. Have IT certifications from Cisco, Microsoft, Sun Microsystems (now Oracle) and Symantec (now acquired by Broadcom). Have attend numerous profession trainings of networking, network security, routing, and switching by Avaya, Cisco, Network Associates, Nortel Networks, Oracle, Symantec and Microsoft.

***

K. Balaji is an Assistant Professor in Business and Management, Christ University, Bengaluru, India. He did Ph.D. from KLU Business School, KL University,Vijayawada. He is having 12 years of teaching experience. He has to his credit 23 Research Articles published in reputed National and International Journals. He has participated and presented more than 12 papers in both National and International Seminars/Conferences and also attended more than 50 workshops/ FDPS organized by various reputed organizations. He has also participated in more than 50 seminars / webinars organized by various reputed organizations. He has also attended in 6 Short Term Training programs.He has successfully conducted 3 webinars, one 5 day FDP and one International Conference on Reimaging marketing in New Normal. He is a ratified as Assistant Professor by both JNTUH, JNTU Anantapur and Sri Venkateswara University,Tirupati. His specialized areas include, Accounting and Financial management, Marketing Management, Retailing Management, Consumer Behavior studies, Entrepreneurship and Business Laws.

Puja Chopra, Ph.D., MBA, is an accomplished academician and Assistant Professor at Christ University, with over 15 years of teaching experience in renowned private and government universities. She holds a Ph.D. in Applied Economics, along with double M.A. degrees in Economics and English, showcasing her strong interdisciplinary foundation. Dr. Chopra specializes in the intersection of Economics and Finance and has an impressive record of publications in prestigious journals, including those indexed in Scopus, ABDC, and UGC CARE. Her passion for academic excellence and innovative teaching has shaped countless future leaders, and she remains committed to fostering intellectual growth in higher education.

Amr ElAlfy is a leading scholar in sustainability disclosure and ESG (Environmental, Social, and Governance) issues, with a particular focus on non-financial reporting practices. His research explores the significance of sustainability risks and opportunities through a double materiality lens, connecting financial and non-financial metrics to aid decision-makers in promoting sustainable growth and responsible investment strategies. Dr. ElAlfy is a Co-investigator for the municipal net-zero action research partnership (N-ZAP) project, reflecting his commitment to advancing sustainability at the local level. Additionally, he serves as the Associate Director of the Waterloo Institute for Sustainable Aeronautics (WISA), where he focuses on enhancing the ESG performance within the aeronautics sector. Dr. ElAlfy brings extensive experience from his tenure in business development roles within multinational conglomerates such as Nestlé and 3M. During his time in the Middle East and Africa (MEA) region, he led marketing and Corporate Social Responsibility (CSR) initiatives, showcasing his ability to drive responsible business practices in diverse and complex markets. Furthermore, Dr. ElAlfy has been instrumental in the development and translation of the Global Reporting Initiative (GRI) Sustainability Universal and Sector Standards, reinforcing his status as a key contributor to the field of sustainability disclosure.

Mohammad Irfan is a Professor at the School of Business and Commerce, Chandigarh University, Lucknow (Unnao), India. He earned his Ph.D. from the Central University of Haryana and holds an MBA in Finance, an M.Com in Accounts and Law, and an MA in Economics. A UGC-JRF/SRF/NET qualifier in Management and Commerce, he also holds certifications from NSE (NCFM) and BSE. With more than sixteen years of teaching and research experience, Dr. Irfan's expertise includes Security Analysis and Portfolio Management (SAPM), Artificial Intelligence, Machine Learning, Blockchain, Cryptocurrency, Financial Engineering, FinTech, Green Finance, and Alternative Finance. He has authored over 109 Scopus-indexed research papers in reputed journals such as The Journal of Economic Cooperation and Development (Q2), International Journal of Business Excellence, Montenegrin Journal of Economics (Q2), Cogent Business & Management (Q2), and Journal of Islamic Monetary Economics and Finance. His work has received 700+ citations with an H-index of 15. He has also published 12 books with Springer and IGI Global and is listed among the World's Top 2% Scientists.

Hayfa Kazouz is a Doctor in Economics at the Faculty of Economic Sciences and Management, University of Sousse, Tunisia. She is a member of the LAREMFIQ

Laboratory (Laboratory of Research in Economics, Management, and Quantitative Finance). Her research focuses on financial economics, with particular interest in energy markets, risk transmission, and the intersection of sustainability and finance. ORCID authenticated by owner ORCID iD: 0000-0002-1874-9744

Shelley Khosla is an accomplished academician and researcher, currently serving as an Associate Professor at the University School of Business Studies, Rayat Bahra Professional University, Hoshiarpur. She holds a doctorate in Business Administration-Management, with a specialization in Human Resource Management (HRM), and qualified the prestigious UGC-NET in 2011. With over sixteen years of rich academic experience, Dr. Khosla has earned recognition as a respected faculty in the domains of Human Resource Management, Organizational Behavior, Training & Development, and Leadership Development. She is widely appreciated for her innovative, student-centric teaching methodology, seamlessly blending case studies, simulations, and real-world business applications to create immersive learning experiences. Being a passionate mentor, she has successfully guided numerous postgraduate students in their research pursuits. Beyond teaching, Dr. Khosla plays an active role in research and development, contributing significantly to UGC-listed, peer-reviewed, and Scopus-indexed journals. Also contributed her writings in IGI Global, Wiley and Bentham Science. She has presented her work at various national and international conferences and seminars, showcasing her commitment to advancing knowledge in her field. Her contributions extend further to research projects, published patents, and presented papers under IEEE conferences, reflecting her versatility as both an educator and researcher. Driven by academic excellence and innovation, Dr. Khosla continues to inspire students and peers alike, making a meaningful impact on both academia and the professional world.

Manjit Kour is working as Professor at University Business School at Chandigarh University. She holds a PhD in Business Management from IK Gujral Punjab Technical University, India. She has a good research record with several research papers published in reputed journals. She is an editorial board member and reviewer of many reputed journals including Scopus and ABDC-indexed journals. Her areas of interest include sustainability, green practices, Fintech, online marketing trends and business ethics.

Momin Farhan has accumulated many years of experience in the fields of Artificial Intelligence, Machine Learning, Business Intelligence, and Analytics. Throughout his career, he has gained extensive expertise in the fintech and retail industries, driving the implementation of data-driven solutions and advanced technologies. Currently, Momin is contributing to a Fortune 500 company, applying his knowledge and skills to address complex business challenges and deliver impactful outcomes.

Asim Mehboob is serving as a Senior Lecturer at Mohammad Ali Jinnah University. Mr. Asim has almost 22 years of experience which includes corporate and teaching experience at leading academic institutions at various levels in Pakistan and abroad. He holds Eight Masters degrees in different domains; M.Phil. in Finance, Master of Law, M.Phil. in Social Sciences, MBA, MA Economics and M. Com, MA International Relations and MA Political Science. He is an active member of Chartered Professional Accountants (CPA Canada), Certified General Accountant (CGA Canada) and Association of Chartered Certified Accountants (ACCA U.K), also worked as Head of commerce department and Program coordinator in different Institutes and Colleges.

Muhammad Zahid (Ph.D.) is currently working as a Professor and Dean of Faculty of Transport and Logistics at Muscat University (Oman) before which he also served as Dean (and Prof) of Management Sciences at Bahria Business School, Bahria University, Pakistan. He obtained his postdoctoral fellowship from Universiti Malaysia Kelantan and his Ph.D. in Management from Universiti Teknologi PETRONAS Malaysia. He received his MS in Management and Master of Commerce degrees from Pakistan earlier. After completing a master's degree, he served the banking industry for 8 years as a branch and customer services manager. His area of concentration is corporate sustainability and financial performance. He has published two books in the area of sustainability and numerous research papers in indexed journals. For his outstanding research work, he has been awarded "The Award for Excellence—2016 Outstanding Journal Papers from Emerald Group Publishing" and the Best Paper Award (2014) in the International Symposium on Research in Innovation and Sustainability 2014 (ISoRIS' 14) 15-16 October 2014, Malacca, Malaysia. Moreover, he holds experience in editorship and is an invited reviewer of well-reputed journals in management, corporate sustainability, corporate governance and finance, gender in management, financial performance, sustainable development goals, and education for sustainable development. He has supervised more than 30 research students and worked on several research grants in the aforementioned areas with the academic institutes of Malaysia, Saudi Arabia, and Pakistan. He also has expertise in working with regulatory bodies such as the Pakistan Stock Exchange (PSX) in designing sustainability guidelines and reports in the business and academic domains (Impact Ranking). He can be contacted at mianmz11@gmail.com.

Index

S

T

V

www.ingramcontent.com/pod-product-compliance
Lightning Source LLC
LaVergne TN
LVHW062328300926
849161LV00007B/1613